17746

D1429356

Gower Handbook
of Programme
Management

GOWER HANDBOOK OF PROGRAMME MANAGEMENT

Geoff Reiss
Malcolm Anthony
John Chapman
Geoff Leigh
Adrian Pyne
Paul Rayner

GOWER

Published by
Gower Publishing Limited
Gower House
Croft Road
Aldershot
Hampshire GU11 3HR
England

Gower Publishing Company
Suite 420
101 Cherry Street
Burlington
VT 05401-4405
USA

Geoff Reiss, Malcom Anthony, John Chapman, Geof Leigh, Adrian Pyne and Paul Rayner have asserted their right under the Copyright, Designs and Patents Act, 1988 to be identified as Authors of this work.

British Library Cataloguing in Publication Data
Gower handbook of programme management
  1. Organizational change 2. Project management
  I. Reiss, Geoff, 1945– II. Handbook of programme management
  658.4'06

  ISBN 0 566 08603 4

Library of Congress Control Number: 2006933684

Typeset in Century Old Style by IML Typographers, Birkenhead and printed in Great Britain by TJ International Ltd, Padstow, Cornwall.

Contents

List of tables

List of figures

Notes on contributors

Geoff Reiss has concentrated, throughout his 40-year career, on project and programme management. He is a Fellow of the APM and Chairman of ProgM, the Association for Project Management (APM)/British Computer Society Specific Interest Group in Programme Management. He founded and is today Senior Architect at the Program Management Group plc, where he leads a team developing the new and innovative products in the programme management arena that make up the Hydra Suite.

After 12 years as a project planner for Bovis in UK, the Middle and Far East, Geoff co-authored the Apple Project Manager, Pertmaster and Pertmaster Advance project management software systems. He was a founder and Features Editor of *Project Manager Today* magazine, where he often wrote the 'Project of the Month'.

His first books, *Project Management Demystified: Today's Tools and Techniques* (1995, Spon Press) and *Programme Management Demystified* (1996, Chapman & Hall) have become two of the UK's best-selling books in their topics. His third book, *One Project Too Many*, was published in August 2004 by Project Manager Today publications and his fourth is the *Gower Handbook of Programme Management*.

Geoff has a master's degree in project management and sat on the review panels for both the first and second version of the UK government's publication on this topic: *Managing Successful Programmes: Delivering Business Change in Multi-project Environments* (2003, The Stationery Office). He is a Subject Matter Expert in the Project Management Institute's Program & Portfolio Management Standards Project initiative. He is a Programme Board member for the new Programme Management qualifications due in Q2 2007.

Geoff chaired the Editorial Board of the ProgM initiative in Project Selection and Benefit Management and was a member of the UK National Computing Centre's programme management initiative. He has presented papers on project and programme management topics at a very wide range of conferences and seminars throughout the world. He continues to be formative in the development of programme management philosophy and best practice.

Malcolm Anthony is a Chartered Management Accountant who undertook a number of financial management roles, including Financial Director for the UK subsidiary of a US aerospace engineering company, before joining Coopers & Lybrand Management Consulting Services (C&L MCS), later to become PricewaterhouseCoopers (PwC) in 1988. At C&L, Malcolm initially worked on large financial management and performance improvement projects, designed to improve the cost competitiveness of the organizations undertaking them. As a result of working on these large; complex and challenging client engagements, Malcolm developed a strong interest in and capability for managing projects and programmes. This in turn led, in 1997, to him being appointed as an author of PwC's PPM, Project and Programme Management method. The resulting method, which is still in use within the firm today, was the first common standard for project and programme management to be introduced within the firm. In 1998, Malcolm was appointed as Programme Manager responsible for the post-merger integration of PwC's Management Consulting businesses around the world, a role he undertook for the full 12 months' duration of the programme.

Malcolm left PwC in 1999 to set up his own consulting business focused exclusively on project and programme management. ProjectProject Limited has worked with many large, blue chip companies during the past 6 years and has developed strong relationships with many thought leaders in the field of project and programme management.

Malcolm is, in addition to his accounting qualification, an accredited PRINCE2 practitioner, an accredited MSP practitioner and an MBA.

The Gower Handbook of Programme Management is the first book to bear Malcolm's name on the cover; however, he has contributed magazine articles on the topic of project and programme management as well as making a contribution to a book on financial management while with PwC.

John Chapman is Programme Director for Touchstone, a leading IT Services Group (www.touchstone.co.uk). He has been Implementing Financial Accounting and Enterprise Solutions for more than 15 years. In addition, he has managed the delivery of e-procurement solutions, document management systems, and led programmes of business change.

John is an experienced Programme Manager, Project Manager, Project and Programme Director. He is a certified PRINCE2 practitioner. He is Treasurer of ProgM.

John holds a Bsc (Hons) degree in Computing Science and is an acknowledged contributor to the first edition of *Managing Successful Programmes: Delivering Business Change in Multi-project Environments* (1999, CCTA), the standard work upon which formal certification of programme management practitioners is based. He is author of *Project and Programme Accounting*, published by Project Manager Today publications.

John's charitable work includes being on the Board of Trustees of YMCA Training (www.ymcatraining.org.uk). This is a national charity with an annual income of over £18 million. Operating from over 35 centres, it is dedicated to providing education and training for 16 to 19 year olds, and employment-related services for adults. As part of his commitment to supporting YMCA Training, he sits on the Finance Committee.

John's professional qualifications include being a full Member of the Institute of Directors and a Fellow of the Institute of Sales and Marketing Management.

Geof Leigh is an experienced programme manager who has been involved in project and programme management for the last 30 years. In the mid 1970s, he pioneered the use of computers in UK local government for multi-project scheduling. He has supported a number of organizations with difficult projects, improving the capability of many project and programme managers via training, or mentoring. He has run many workshops on programme and project management in the private sector, public sector and to postgraduates at university.

Originally he qualified as a Fellow of the Institute of Management Services (FMS). He is an accredited PRINCE2 practitioner, accredited Managing Successful Programmes (MSP) practitioner, approved MSP trainer and a certified business process engineer (Six Sigma Black Belt).

When helping organizations improve their change management capabilities, whether via training, coaching or mentoring, Geof can build rapport quickly and enjoys facilitating the learning process. As he is still active in programme and project management, he brings current real-world experience to help others learn. Geof has developed and delivered a good range of bespoke and generic programme management courses. He gets satisfaction when he sees that he has delivered successfully.

Geof's career has included :

- management of a large portfolio of capital building projects for UK local government, where he developed methods very similar to the basis now used in programme management;

- working within the private sector as Managing Director of a small software house, developing and delivering software packages and bespoke solutions for insurance, sales and marketing;
- Development Manager within the Sun Alliance Group, including a successful period at the Sun Alliance subsidiary, the Ra Group;
- Head of the Group Programmme Office at the Press Association;
- IT Strategy and Planning Manager at GE Capital Bank (GCF), where Geof and his team introduced new processes and produced the company's first systems strategy and the programme to realize the benefits. He was a significant contributor to the global processes GE Capital introduced for the Corporate Programme Management Office.

Geof is now a freelance consultant working with many blue chip private sector companies and public sector organizations, helping them to improve their performance through effective programme and project management. He is co-author with Geoff Reiss of the business novel about programme and project management, *One Project Too Many* (2004, Project Management Today publications).

Adrian Pyne is a professional manager who has for more than 15 years made his home in programme management, gaining experience in a variety of industries including telecommunications, finance, government, aviation and e-commerce. For 10 years, Adrian has been secretary of ProgM. With ProgM, Adrian has gained a reputation as a leader in programme management evolution, writing, and presenting and leading numerous seminars. The UK Office of Government Commerce (OGC) invited Adrian to join the review panel for MSP. He is also a long-term active member of the APM and more recently a member of the Institute of Directors (IoD).

Beginning his journey with British Telecom, Adrian progressed from IT development and design to IT project management, before moving to project and programme management in their engineering division. In 1995, Adrian became an independent consultant and until 2004 led major change programmes, some international, with values in excess of £200 million. As a consultant, Adrian has designed, built and operated programme management approaches and corporate programme offices, leading to the effective delivery of major business benefits.

Adrian's portfolio includes:

- a £45 million international technology programme to develop and roll out a state-of-the-art interactive in-flight entertainment system for a major world airline;

- leading the programme management of a major transformation programme for a UK retail bank; Programme Manager for an international investment finance company, where he successfully delivered a new business-to-customer investment finance e-business which is still growing;
- being invited by the then COO of the Department of Work and Pensions to join a team of programme management specialists, where he helped bring a major change programme back on track, developed a multi-supplier contracting and delivery model, and helped to develop and implement Centres of Excellence to OGC standards.

In 2004, Adrian joined Cable & Wireless as Programme Director in charge of customer programmes and project management. Here he managed the portfolio of customer programmes and projects from pre-sale to delivery. Adrian also re-built the customer project delivery capability including new standards and templates, both central and customer programme offices, tools, assurance processes and bid support. He has recently left Cable & Wireless and is once again a consultant.

Paul Rayner joined IBM as a junior systems analyst after leaving university in the UK. Here, he helped to spread the benefits of information technology (IT) to Australasia and Southern Africa. On returning to the UK he founded a software business to develop a range of application packages for personal computers. With several thousand of these supplied to users in all continents, client support issues made Paul realize that however clever the computer systems in theory, in practice they were only as good as the people who installed and used them. This led to a life-long interest in the ways that IT and other technologies can be used to make the world a better place, and the many and varied ways in which people fail to realize the potential that these technologies could provide.

At this point, Paul sold his software interests and established himself as an independent management consultant. Appreciating that effective use can only be made of systems that really meet users' needs, he developed a practical approach to ensuring software quality and helped many commercial IT organizations to introduce the concept of quality assurance, frequently assisting them to gain recognition under the TickIT scheme of ISO9000 certification.

In recent years, Paul has worked with LogicaCMG, a large, British-based IT organization that operates around the world and specializes in supplying and implementing large and sophisticated IT systems to enable clients to improve their efficiency and effectiveness. A key element in such improvement is usually a programme of organizational change management. As a Managing Consultant within the company's Public Sector Division, Paul has played key roles in many such programmes, including establishing and managing complex, multi-million pound programmes of business change. He has also continued to advise clients on how they may improve their own management of vital change programmes.

Paul has always been keen to place technology-enabled change programmes within the wider business context. This has been helped by his role as a non-executive director of an NHS Trust, as a member of the Rail Users Consultative Committee and as a Chair of school governors. Paul is also the Vice-Chairman of ProgM, the programme management special interest group, where he led the development of the Programme Management Maturity Model, a new approach to measuring, benchmarking and improving programme management.

Paul holds an MBA, is a Fellow of the Institute of Management Consultants and is a registered practitioner of the PRINCE2 project management and ITIL® (the IT Infrastructure Library) service management methodologies. He is the author of many articles and papers on programme management and related management issues.

Acknowledgements

Many people have helped to create this work, but the following have made a specially valuable contribution by reviewing early drafts of parts of this book:

Michel Thiery
Allen Ruddick
Peter Brosnon
Tim Craven
Kathy Hudson
Phillip Reeds
Damian Edwards

We are indebted to the team at Gower Publishing for their invaluable help in creating this book and especially Guy Loft, Nikki Dines, Sarah Price, Fiona Martin and the ever-patient Jonathan Norman.

Part I

An Introduction to Programme Management

1 Introduction

1.1 WELCOME

Welcome to the *Gower Handbook of Programme Management*! The team of authors hope that you will enjoy reading this book and gain a great deal from it.

In this first chapter, you will discover some fundamentals about programme management and its relationship with both portfolio and project management. You will learn that the terms have yet to settle down and that they may have different meanings to different people in different situations.

While you may decide to read the book from start to finish, most people at some time will occasionally wish to dip into it to find guidance on specific topics. The information you seek will reflect your position, the organization in which you work and the issue you are facing. You will discover in this introduction how the author team has prepared this book to suit these differing interests and how to find the parts most valuable to you at any one time.

There is much you and your organization may take from this book in terms of knowledge, templates, concepts, systems and approaches. We hope that the programme management process outlined in Chapter 2 and the programme management improvement process in Chapter 16 will be exceptionally useful. These components, we hope, will support your desire to improve your organization's maturity in programme management.

In the 1980s, the UK led the world in the emerging techniques for project management. In the first decade of the second millennium, the UK leads the world in programme management thinking. While the USA has developed thinking in project portfolio management through the Project Portfolio Management Standard initiative, the majority of the rest of the world has yet to generally adopt these ideas. We hope this book will help to spread the message and benefits of programme management throughout the world.

1.2 WHY YOU SHOULD READ THIS BOOK

This is a large book containing some lengthy chapters. The author team expects that readers will wish to dip into the content to find specific text, advice, guidance and value on a topic.

If you are working in an organization that runs a number of projects, and especially if those projects are designed to deliver change to your own organization, you will find this book very valuable.

If you are to play a role in the projects, or in the programme that bring the projects into a cohesive whole, or if you wish there were some way of thinking about your organization's projects holistically, you will find this book essential reading.

If you are researching programme management, you will find that this book gives a great deal of knowledge as well as guidance to other sources of information.

We have attempted to show how organizations can deliver change in an efficient, organized and well-managed way so that the maximum benefit can be derived from its investments.

While we plan later editions of this book, we will not be able to maintain the pace of change in the emerging world of programme management. For this and other reasons, this book is supported by a website at www.gowerpub.com, where you will find updated information and connections to other websites focusing on programme management.

In the view of the authors, programme management surrounds and supports project management. Programme management techniques aim to help organizations select portfolios of projects, establish organizational structures to support those projects and to extract maximum benefit from them. Project management, working within a programme management environment, delivers the specific products of those projects.

You should not expect this book to help you run individual projects. It will help you to select and define the best projects to undertake; to organize them in a holistic manner; to establish an environment within which projects may be consistently managed and to maximize the benefits your organization gains from them.

There are many other books that will help you to understand how to take a project from definition to delivery. The *Gower Handbook of Project Management* (Turner and Simister, 2000) is one of them.

This book is divided into four parts:

I   **Introduction to programme management:** Starts by introducing the topic, the terminology and basic concepts. It then proposes a complete lifecycle for delivering maximum benefit from investment in organizational change.

II **A supporting infrastructure:** Describes the techniques and support infrastructure that will be required to deliver efficient organizational change.

III **Programme management maturity:** Describes ways of measuring and improving an organization's ability to deliver effective change.
    Appendices: Practical and usable references to other sources of information.

While a team of six authors worked on this book, it is not simply a collection of essays. The author team worked together to design and create the content and to agree on a general layout and style. The team members took responsibility for sections where their specialist knowledge was most relevant. The book therefore is the result of a number of projects, each run by a project manager, all working within a single programme managed by a programme manager. The book is not, however, written in 'one voice' but does to some degree reflect the style of the author or authors of each section. The author team therefore will use the term 'we' to refer to the authors collectively.

We hope this book meets your needs.

1.3 AN OVERVIEW OF PROGRAMME MANAGEMENT

To understand programme management it is best to understand the history of project management, so let us begin with a short trip back into recent history.

The early days of project management by computer were mostly spent on wet and windy construction sites. Among the world's first construction projects to use personal computers and critical path planning techniques were the Clarendon Wing at Leeds General Infirmary, UK and Hope Hospital in Manchester, UK in the early 1980s. Heavy engineering and the space race drove the need to understand how massive dams, roads, missiles, satellites and hospitals would be assembled. However, engineering project managers did not consider the reason for building the particular building or plant – they simply built them for someone else.

5

In the 1990s, project management techniques spread out from the wet and windy site offices of heavy engineering and the laboratories of the space industries into the cosy warm offices of high-technology industries such as information technology (IT) and telecommunications.

As project management moved into the last decade of the millennium, a much larger number of relatively small projects were being planned using project management tools. A wide range of technology-led industries had adopted both the tools and philosophies that worked so well on large physical projects.

But these technology-led projects shared resources with many other projects and with the normal business-as-usual workload, so the approaches we now group under the title of programme management emerged to address these differences. While the single project model failed to address many issues, programme management offered a way to deal with the total project workload holistically.

Around the time that the Y2K bug brought a gleam to the eye of many IT people, we saw the early days of programme management and the widest ever use of project management and planning. No longer was this exclusive to construction; in fact the technology-led industries were moving away from, and considerably outnumbered, construction users.

As the new millennium dawned, a world of resource-centric programme management started to emerge where there is much greater involvement for the team members than for the resources of the engineering worksite. Personal plans and timesheets started to form a key component of most planning systems and the Internet provided web-based tools enabling international project teams to cooperate without geographical barriers.

Governance had by this time become a popular theme as the number of projects created a need to ensure that they all follow some key processes consistently. As an example of a simple process: all projects should have a properly approved project initiation document (PID) that lays out what that project aims to achieve. PRINCE2 provided a framework for good governance.

Industry and Government began to 'do their projects right' but wondered if they were doing the right projects.

As the first decade of the third millennium advanced, the most significant developments lay in the emerging brand of tools and techniques that help organizations select the best projects to undertake. While some organizations still suffer from interminable delays, many organizations have improved their ability to deliver on time. But there is very little confidence among Chief Executive Offices (CEOs) and Chief Financial Officers (CFOs) that the best possible investments are being selected.

The reason for this is that the majority of today's projects are those designed to change the host organization and to deliver benefits – what we today call change programmes. The scarcity of resource will always limit the organization's ability to deliver change and this makes it vital for every organization to spend a little time selecting those programmes of work that will deliver the greatest benefit. That might imply selecting the development of new products or services, the relocation of facilities or rationalization of processes to improve service levels.

IT departments felt a cold wind of change and quickly perceived the need to be seen to be delivering value, so we saw a number of IT-led change programmes. From IT, both people and ideas moved into the business arena so that today we see a plethora of organization-led change programmes.

The Project Selection and Benefit Management initiative led by ProgM – the programme management specific interest group of the Association for Project Management (see Appendix B for contact details) – is a part of the drive to a new era where programme managers in both the public and private sectors will model and monitor projects in terms their benefits.

This attitude received wide support from industrial leaders and senior members of government alike. Here is a quotation from the 'Improving Programme and Project Delivery (IPPD)' report from the UK Government's Office of Public Service Reform (OPSR):

> That's why the implementation of this report is so important. I am pleased that one of its key recommendations – establishing Programme and Project Management 'centres of excellence' within departments – has already been endorsed by the Cabinet.
>
> Achieving this requires clear leadership from the top and better delivery on the ground. Better programme and project management (PPM) in the Civil Service has a key role to play. Of course these new centres must recruit the right people, develop programme management skills, and promote the delivery culture. I welcome the commitment to training for change and development opportunities on offer to civil servants to fulfil these requirements. (Tony Blair, UK Prime Minister, OPSR, 2003, Foreword)

Another quote comes from the same report:

> Delivery is top of the Government's agenda and better programme and project management (PPM) will improve the Civil Service capability and capacity to deliver. Research conducted by the Office of Public Services Reform (OPSR) and CMPS [now the National School of Government] shows that increasingly PPM techniques are successfully being applied to policy development and delivery, as well as traditional procurement tasks. (OPSR, 2003, Foreword)

References to these reports and other websites are included in Part IV of this book.

The government has encapsulated the relationships between change, programme and project management into a single diagram (see Figure 1.1).

7

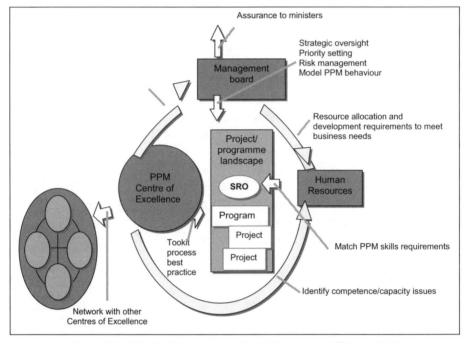

Figure 1.1 The role of programme and project management Encapsulated

To learn more about the UK government initiative 'Improving Programme and Project Delivery by Creating Departmental 'Centres of Excellence', visit the website from which the Figure 1.1 has been taken: www.pm.gov.uk/files/word/Centre%20of%20Excellence%20ToR.doc

1.3.1 DEFINITIONS

Here are two definitions of programme management.

● Programme management is the orchestration of organizational change.
● Programme management is the coordinated management of a portfolio of projects that change organizations to achieve benefits that are of strategic importance.

The first is succinct. The second is only slightly longer and is the UK government definition, contained within *Managing Successful Programmes*, a publication from the Office of Government Commerce (OCG; OCG, 2003).

Organizations trying to change and improve themselves need a new concept to provide a link between:

- investment in organizational change
- projects delivering the capacity to change
- the adoption of those changes
- harvesting the benefits of those organizational changes.

Typically, a change involves contributions from many parts of the organization. There is often a significant IT component, but there are nearly always organizational issues, training and processes that must change as well.

For example, a new product launch will involve projects in manufacturing, sales, marketing, support and transport before it can deliver its benefit of increased income.

Often there are many-to-many relationships between projects and benefits. Some projects work in synergy to deliver benefit, some provide technology platforms on which other projects deliver benefits. It is rare that a single project delivers a benefit on its own. For example, it is only when the quality control procedures, monitoring software and training projects have ended that a manufacturing organization can expect to see the expected reductions in returned goods. Only after the hospital ward has been built, the equipment installed and commissioned and the staff recruited and trained will the waiting lists be shorter.

The concepts of 'programme' and 'programme management' provide an umbrella that sits over and above projects and shows the often complex links between many projects and many benefits (see Figure 1.2).

Programme management involves in selecting the best projects in which to invest, initiating and defining those projects and deriving the maximum benefit from the change. A programme is therefore the glue that brings together projects and benefits.

1.3.2 THE PROGRAMME MANAGEMENT CYCLE

A programme management cycle should follow certain stages. This is not a one-off process but a regular review of the organization, its objectives, its current workload and expectations. The primary steps are:

1. **Define the organization's strategy:** The objectives set by the senior management are laid out in terms of strategy and, wherever possible, in numerical terms. Examples include 5 per cent increase in turnover, 10 per cent decrease in wastage, 7 per cent less accidents or 6 per cent reduction in staff turnover. While financial objectives are relatively easy to define, the balanced score card and key performance indicators (KPIs) provide mechanisms to set out non-financial objectives in measurable terms.

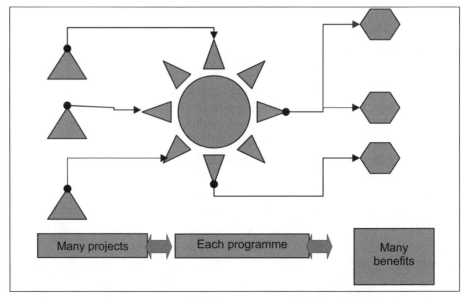

Figure 1.2 Relating projects, programmes and benefits

2. **Collect and evaluate candidate programmes:** The organization is encouraged to come up with ideas for change and each idea joins the list of candidates. Each candidate programme will vie with others to prove itself worthy of investment.
3. **Select and prioritize candidate programmes:** Each serious candidate programme is evaluated in terms of the financial and resource investments required to deliver the change; the financial and non-financial benefits expected from the change; the risk profile and timescales and especially their alignment with the delivery of the organizations stated objectives.

All existing and potential programmes are then modelled and considered in order to make a rational choice of the most desirable programmes and yet stay within the organization's ability to deliver the changes.

This approach is so much better than the usual highly political and emotional battles over project selection.

1. **Initiate selected programmes:** New programmes of work are added to current programmes and initiated in a simple but formal manner.
2. **Define projects to deliver programmes:** Once the programmes have been initiated, it is relatively easy to define and initiate the projects that will deliver the capacity for change. This is a programme management role.
3. **Initiate projects:** The projects are initiated and passed to the selected project

managers. They understand how each project fits into and contributes to the organization's wider aims.

4. **Manage programmes and projects:** Projects are managed by the project managers and each programme by a programme manager. All should obey appropriate and workable processes such as those laid out in PRINCE2 and *Managing Successful Programmes* (OGC, 2003). Ideally few, if any projects, run outside of the adopted framework.

5. **Close projects:** Each project ends with a deliverable to the programme manager. A new IT system, a new production facility, a trained workforce and a safety video are examples of project deliverables.

6. **Close programmes:** A programme creates a new capability by combining the deliverables of a number of projects. The programme manager hands this capability to a manager within the organization. The organization then utilizes the new capability and harvests the benefits it makes possible. For example, the organization utilizes a new warehouse and benefits through reduced transportation costs.

7. **Derive and monitor benefits:** The programme management team will be involved in measuring the benefits and feeding this data back into the organization, providing the basis for the next round of projects.

This is not a one-off process, but a rolling cycle. In some organizations, the cycle time is slow – up to 5 years; in many it is as short as once a quarter.

1.3.3 THE VALUE PATH

The value path (see Figure 1.3) shows how projects create deliverables that, when combined into a programme, deliver the capability to change. Only when this capability is used by the organization is a benefit actually realized. The value path supports the programme management cycle by demonstrating the objectives at each level of a programme and project management community.

Some examples follow.

● In a specialist organization developing tools and services for programme management, the Program Management Group plc, there are a number of overlapping programmes. Numerous software development projects are conceived to provide new tools aimed at the programme management marketplace. Each of these projects will fail to deliver benefits without the testing, technical support and training workshop projects that combine into a development programme. There are further programmes aimed at improving service levels, opening new markets and reducing running costs.

● The Standard Chartered Bank installed a telephone network across Africa. This

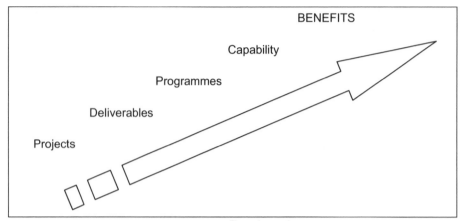

Figure 1.3 The value path

delivered no direct benefit, but on that backbone a number of projects delivered reduced running costs and improved service levels to bank account holders, money dealers and exchangers and other parts of the banking business.

- Syrris, a small company specializing in drug discovery, is overrun with numbers of speculative new product development programmes, each aimed at launching a diagnostic tool to the pharmaceutical market. Each new product idea is tested in terms of the required investment, expected return and risk before joining the active workload on a 'survival of the fittest' basis.

- Transport for London has a portfolio of programmes, each of which creates a component of the London transport infrastructure. These programmes combine construction, ticketing, marketing and integration projects to deliver improvements to Londoners.

1.3.4 PORTFOLIO MANAGEMENT

One of the major barriers to successful change programmes is the intense personal and political emotion that is involved in programme selection. Rarely is there any degree of logic; normally selection and prioritization is the result of a highly personal battle.

Portfolio management techniques tend to reduce the intense emotional and political heat by providing a more logical programme selection process. One element of portfolio management is benefit mapping. There is often a complex many-to-many relationship between programmes and benefits and benefit mapping helps to show these relationships. This technique provides a simple mechanism of graphically showing the inter-connections between projects, programmes and benefits.

A simple diagram or table showing on one side projects and on the other benefits, with programmes in the centre, will provide a clearer view of the:

- route to benefits
- dependencies (between projects, deliverables, facilities and benefits)
- distribution of budget
- distribution of responsibility.

The diagram will provide a basis for:

- risk management
- programme monitoring
- budgetary control.

A diagram is included in the worked example in Appendix C.

1.3.5 INTERNAL VS. EXTERNAL PROGRAMMES

Some programme management teams think in terms of internal vs. external programmes.

Internal programmes involve:

- a controlled environment
- internal change, for example, change related to a new internal process, reorganization, IT systems
- relatively low risk.

External programmes involve:

- a less controlled environment
- a change subject to impact from environmental effects, for example, new product launch or a marketing initiative
- relatively high risk.

It is clear that external programmes will benefit from constant monitoring of the external marketplace or environment, as this may undermine or reinforce the case for a specific programme. A health scare may terminate a new food product programme but, equally, may reinforce the case for a drug launch programme.

To enable a rational programme selection process some key areas of definition are required for every contender programme.

To enable portfolio management decision making every programme should have, long before it is accepted into the workload, certain requisites:

- mandate – a written statement of the purpose
- an owner and/or sponsor

- a list of benefits
  - for financial benefits:
    - ○ 'no change' cost or income levels over time
    - ○ 'post change' cost or income levels over time
  - · for non-financial benefits:
    - ○ measures of strategic alignment through KPIs
    - ○ risk estimates (schedule risk, cost risk, benefit delivery risk)
    - ○ financial investment required
    - ○ resource requirement.

Financial benefits can easily be derived by considering the no change/post change levels. In the case of a cost reduction exercise, it is possible to model how the cost of an operation is expected to rise over time if no change is delivered. However, the costs may be stabilized or even reduced following a change programme. An example would be the running costs of a call centre when considering a programme to outsource the service offshore. A typical graph is shown in Figure 1.4. In the example, the running costs of a certain operation are expected to grow rapidly over the next four quarters. However, a change programme is expected to deliver efficiency savings such that the running costs will reduce slightly over the same time period.

In another example, the income derived from a product can be expected to reduce over time, but programmes to market or enhance the product can help to stabilize or even increase income levels.

Comparing 'no change' and 'post change' income or expenditure levels for each programme helps provide financial comparisons of programmes.

1.3.6 A BENEFIT MANAGEMENT CYCLE

Figure 1.5 summarizes the cycle described below.

Starting at the highest point on the cycle we see the strategic plans that the organization has set as its targets. There are normally simple high-level statements of the organization's objectives. In the two stages that follow, the strategy is broken down into detailed numeric data probably using both financial and KPIs for non-financial objectives. Examples of KPIs include levels of customer retention or levels of staff turnover.

Contender programmes are then examined in terms of their impact on these KPIs and financial contribution. A group of the programmes that collectively are within the organization's ability to deliver and accept change is selected. Once each programme is initiated, the programme management teams can identify and initiate the projects that will deliver the required outcomes. The projects then create deliverables. These deliverables are combined by the programme to create

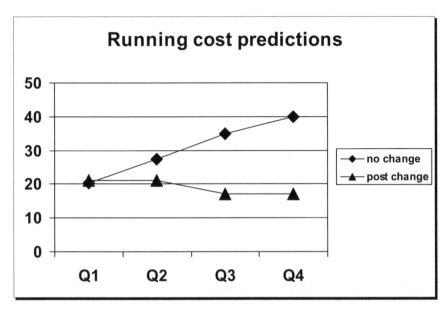

Figure 1.4 A typical cost of comparison graph

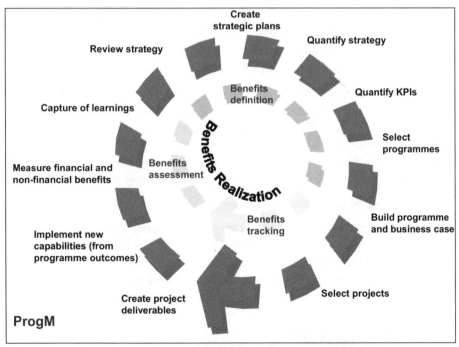

Figure 1.5 High Level Benefits Management Process Model – V2
Source: ProgM; developed as part of the initiative on Programme Management

15

a capability within the organization. The business uses the new capabilities (for example, the new warehouse, quality control system or training) and therefore delivers the associated benefits.

Benefits are measured and where expected benefits are no longer expected or reduced, for any reason, the programme management team reports the issue.

As benefits are actually achieved the organization changes. Measurement of these improvements leads the organization to a revised strategy and the continuation of the cycle.

The inner cycle shows how the programme management team starts with benefit definition, moves on to tracking the benefits as the team move towards benefit delivery and ends each cycle assessing the benefits actually delivered.

The report supporting this is available on the programme management website at www.e-programme.com/projectselection.htm.

1.4 DEFINITIONS OF PROGRAMME MANAGEMENT AND RELATED TERMS

The OGC is a part of the UK government and has published an important publication called *Managing Successful Programmes* (OGC, 2003).

The publication contains this definition of programme management:

> Programme management is the coordinated management of a portfolio of projects that change organizations to achieve benefits that are of strategic importance.

This definition of programme management is concerned with the delivery of organizational change. An organization that follows this definition should have established goals at an organizational level and be running one or more programmes with the intent of striving towards those objectives. Such programmes are driven by the benefits they are expected to deliver.

Another simple definition of programme management is:

> The orchestration of organizational change.

There are other meanings for the term programme management, some of which do not imply organizational change, and these are discussed in Section 1.5 below.

For comparison and positioning purposes, we offer definitions of four related topics in a programme management environment: project management, change management, benefit management and project portfolio management.

1.4.1 PROJECT MANAGEMENT

Project management is the delivery of pre-defined products.

It is the purpose of project management to take a project from the definition stage to delivery of previously defined products. It is the purpose of programme management to define projects and to take the products of those projects, combine them to provide the opportunity for organizational change, integrate them into the organization and deliver benefit through change. Much of this book is concerned with the delivery of beneficial change.

1.4.2 CHANGE MANAGEMENT

Change management is the management of change.

At the micro level, change management involves a set of techniques used to implant new technology and processes. These might include training, roll-out processes and the human aspects known as 'hearts & minds' to maximize the acceptance of changes to routine.

At the macro level, change management contains ideas about what interventions to make, making them and then reviewing how these are working.

Programme management teams can regard change management as a set of techniques that are used to support project and programme work. Change management professionals can regard programme management as a technique that is essential to the delivery side of change (see Figure 1.6).

1.4.3 BENEFIT MANAGEMENT

Benefit management is a process for the optimization or maximization of benefits from organization change programmes.

There are differing views of the role programme management plays in delivering or harvesting benefits. We regard benefit management as an important part of the programme management process.

A programme should deliver to the organization the ability to change through new systems, processes and, perhaps, physical resources such as warehouses, transport or IT. For example, a programme might deliver a warehouse and a stock control system that will reduce cost and improve customer service for a distribution company

Before benefit may be gained, these new systems and other resources must be put to use through adoption into the day-to-day management of the organization. The distribution manager must adopt the new technology, make required changes to the department's structure and deliver the benefit by running the more efficient department.

The general term for the distribution manager in the example above, that is, the person with the role responsible for taking the new functionality and delivering the benefits, would be 'business user'.

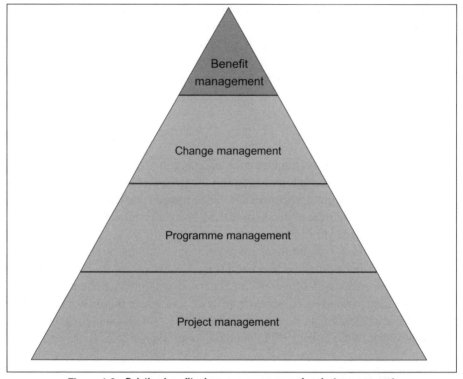

Figure 1.6   Relating benefit, change, programme and project management

The issue is to understand the relationship between the programme management and business user. The programme management process delivers the capability for change while the business user must utilize this capability to deliver the benefit.

The business user shares responsibility with the programme management team for adoption of these new capabilities and the delivery of benefits.

In the view of the OGC, the programme team's responsibility ends when the new functionality is handed over and accepted by the business user.

1.4.4 PROJECT PORTFOLIO MANAGEMENT

In the USA, Australasia and some parts of northern Europe, the term 'project portfolio management', sometimes known simply as 'portfolio management', has emerged. In addition, Americans tend to use the spelling *program* as opposed to *programme*, which is UK-English usage.

There is a very considerable overlap between programme management and project portfolio management. Project portfolio management seems generally in the USA to focus on change through the development and launch of new products in the business marketplace. Project portfolio management often refers to the process of selecting and prioritizing projects of work and where that is the case, the term program management is used to refer to the execution of those projects.

In the author team's view, new product development and launch is one type of programme management. Other equally important areas are the improvement in service levels of commercial organizations (banks and other services industries); non-commercial organizations (government operations including taxation and health) and other public services.

We propose Figure 1.7 to understand the differences between the US English and UK English use of these terms.

In US terminology, the term project portfolio management refers to the whole process of delivering change from project and program(me) selection through to benefit delivery. Once program(me)s and projects have been selected, the term program management is used to describe the process of delivering the required changes.

In UK terminology, and specifically in the UK government publications in this area, the term programme management refers to the whole process of delivering change from project and programme selection through to benefit delivery.

Please refer to the glossary in Appendix A for more definitions and terms.

US English		Activity	UK English
Project portfolio management		Selecting which program(me)s to invest in	Programme management
	Program management	Managing a number of program(me)s	
		Managing a number of projects	
		Managing benefits	

Figure 1.7   The relationship between US and UK terminology

19

1.5 TYPES OF PROGRAMMES

This section discusses the variety of organizations and situations described as programme management to enable readers to understand their own situations in relation to other programme management environments of which they may have little or no experience.

1.5.1 FUNDAMENTAL TYPES OF PROGRAMME

Programme management has been defined in many different ways. This is to be expected, as it means different things to different organizations.

There is one common theme to all the definitions, which we propose is the starting point.

> Programme management is the management of a portfolio of projects that have something in common.

The 'something in common' is where all the variations come from. There are some typical common threads, which are listed below. What is important for your organization is to work out how and why you choose to group projects together. You may decide that your organization has more than one of these reasons for grouping projects into portfolios or programmes.

1.5.1.1 The strategically driven programme organization

The OGC definition of programme management is:

> Programme management is the co-ordinated management of a portfolio of projects that change organizations to achieve benefits that are of strategic importance.

The OGC's guide, *Managing Successful Programmes* (OGC, 2003) talks about defining the long-term objectives of the organization. Once these long-term objectives are established, the organization should identify portfolios of projects that help attain these objectives and think carefully about the benefits these projects are designed to bring about.

It advises the organization to set up structures to manage the programme and keep the strategic objectives in mind. These kinds of projects are likely to change the organization itself. Examples of such programmes include relocation and expansion programmes as well as rationalization and reorganization programmes.

In this scenario, programme management must focus on delivering the benefits the organization expects, as defined in its strategy.

1.5.1.2 The multi-project income-driven programme organization

For organizations in this group, programme management is directing a portfolio of projects that benefit from a consolidated approach by maximizing the output from the resources utilized on income generating work.

Jobbing engineering companies, software houses contracting for work, architectural practices and many other types of organization run many simultaneous projects, each of which results in the delivery of a product or service to a customer. They may not contribute towards the strategic corporate goals of the host organization.

Typically, the result of such a project is an output delivered to a client for payment. The common elements of the projects are that they run simultaneously, or at least overlap with each other, they share resources and are each expected to generate some income. One project's cancellation does not necessarily change the organization's general direction.

The primary aim here is to manage the programme of projects to generate the maximum income for every person in the pool. Such organizations are not attempting to change themselves but may be attempting to change their clients. For example, a consultancy may deliver change to their customers by improving the client's processes.

1.5.1.3 The customer-centric programme organization

The management of a portfolio of projects within an organization for the same customer.

Consider a company performing work for many customers and with a close relationship with some of those customers. The supplier organization might have a number of projects in hand for one particular customer and appoint a programme manager to coordinate the total workload for that customer. Such a programme manager will have a team of project managers, each of which is working on one or more projects for the specific customer.

Such projects need not be linked logically, but almost certainly share the same resources. They may be carried out by different teams within the contracting organization, but probably share the same functional departments. Ideas and techniques from one group may be carried over to the other groups. Specialist resources work part time on many projects.

The focus here is similar to the first scenario but programme management will concentrate on the customer's goals, not those of the contracting organization.

1.5.1.4 Common method

A coordinated approach that applies a common method, lifecycle and set of standards to improve the capability of the project management community.

The projects in this programme may have very little in common, other than they are all in the same organization.

In this situation, programme management might want to regard this as the first improvement step, but expecting to eventually get to one of the other more mature states.

1.5.1.5 Very large programmes

And finally some organizations use the term programme management to refer to very large projects. This is especially true in USA where, for example, the Moon Landing Program included a very large number of projects, all of which aimed at the same single objective, an objective eloquently expressed by J.F. Kennedy: 'We aim to put a man on the surface of the moon and bring him safely back to Earth before the end of the decade'. A wide range of projects, including launchers, assembly buildings, tracking equipment, the moon lander and orbiter, plus recovery and health screening systems made up a single programme aimed at this single objective.

1.5.2 SOME DIFFERENCES BETWEEN PROGRAMME AND PROJECT MANAGEMENT

Table 1.1 aims to highlight some significant differences between project and programme management in an attempt to clarify the value and purpose of each set of techniques.

1.5.3 SOME DIFFERENCES BETWEEN PROGRAMME AND PROJECT PLANNING

The need for planning and control is common to all programmes and projects and some differences have been observed when comparing project and programme planning. These are included to emphasize the required changes in thinking in both the planning and management of projects and programmes and to set the scene for those moving from project to programme management.

In these terms, we have compared the techniques of project planning as found on major, physical projects with programme planning as found on a portfolio of generally smaller and less physical projects.

Table 1.1   Differences between programme and project management

Programmes	Projects
Less well-defined end date, some go on forever, or until a defined organization state has been achieved	Defined start and finish dates
Focus is on delivering benefits (which may be both financial and non-financial), requires involvement after projects have ended. Every programme must directly benefit the organization in some way	Focus is on delivering products. These products will be used by the operational part of the organization, but not all of them will directly produce benefits
More complex; interface with the strategy, contain many projects, drive operational change	Simpler; only have to focus on delivering defined products
Exist in a world that is constantly changing. These changes need to be constantly monitored and their impact on the programme and its projects controlled and managed	Projects are 'ring fenced'. Change control is a more structured and easier to control activity
Macro view; have to consider the combined effect of a portfolio of projects, which should produce synergistic benefits, but sometimes conflict with each other. A balanced view is needed, which sometimes is detrimental to a few projects in the portfolio	Micro view; only concerned with delivering what has been defined, on time, in budget and to acceptable quality. Project managers are only concerned with other projects if their project is dependent on them. They will fight against any other project that threatens the success of their own project

1.5.3.1 Planning timescales

The classic use of project planning is in heavy engineering. Bridges, power stations and construction projects provided the early project management tools. Their interest is predicting the demand for resources, typically, over the next few months. Project planners calculate the number of resources that they expect to be required and a separate department hires the crews.

On heavy engineering projects, foremen and charge hands direct the individual workers on a short-term basis and this work is generally not planned by project management methods. While projects may have a shorter overall duration, programmes tend to be very long. The programme planner's role is concerned with the long-term capacity of the organization as well as the specific plans for the next few weeks or months.

1.5.3.2 Complexity

Classic engineering projects are nearly always a new challenge. Each major project presents new challenges and tools and techniques are required to help the team understand the process that would be followed to assemble the deliverable. For example, critical path analysis or the critical path method is a process of modelling a project in terms of the tasks that are required and the dependencies between those tasks. Much of critical path thinking stems from a need in the 1960s for the Polaris project team to understand the logical process of construction and assembly that would lead to a working missile.

Projects within programmes generally follow a defined and distinct pattern. Many projects are run under a methodology that precisely spells out the process in great detail. The problem in programme management is rarely one of understanding the process, but of scheduling the resources against time, other projects and non-project workloads.

1.5.3.3 Multiple projects

Large engineering projects tend to be isolated. The planning problem is to maximize the efficiency of the teams of workers on the one single project. The complexities of multi-projects are not considered, as they do not exist. There is no need to think about cross-project conflicts, multi-project resource optimization or a whole host of elements that have come to the fore as project management has spread into a world where many projects progress within the same organization against a background of non-project work.

Typically, on a single project, the timescale and objectives are set contractually. The team need to know what resources will be required to achieve these goals. In the multi-project environment, the resource pool is much more stable and the team need to prioritize the work load to keep the resource fully occupied and to finish projects as early as possible.

1.5.3.4 Resources

Engineering project management focuses on classes of resources. Planners tend to deal with numbers of welders, bricklayers and labourers. The histogram is a tool to demonstrate how many of a type of resource will be required and to help reduce the peak demands for each class of resource in the interests of economy.

Within programmes, planners tend to deal with individuals. There are individuals with many skills that may be used to meet the needs of the many projects. In programme management, histograms are less useful, as the requirement is to show how many hours per day a person needs to work on each project or programme.

1.5.3.5 The working day

Labourers, bricklayers and welders normally work full time on the one project in which they are involved at any one time. In programmes of projects, it is very rare that anyone works full time on any one project. Many projects vie for each resource's time with the non-project workload and other administrative jobs.

1.5.3.6 Physical projects

Engineering projects allow for a simple way of achievement monitoring through simply counting the bricks or pipe-lengths; the physical achievements on the project. There is often a physical measure of progress. A relationship between what has been achieved and what remains to be achieved can often be calculated in quantitative terms. Most projects within programmes work towards non-physical deliverables. Where there are physical deliverables, measures of progress tend to be qualitative rather than quantitative. It is difficult to accurately measure progress towards a software product, a reorganization or marketing project except by an artificial measure such as metrics. Measures of achievement at the task level are rarely of any value in helping to understand the remaining work. Hence the need for timesheet recording systems that aim to measure time spent and estimates to complete.

There are exceptions to this general principle. For example, consider a training project that is a part of implementation programme, It will be possible to monitor the number of people trained and the number remaining to be trained. Quantitative measures should be used to monitor progress where they are appropriate. However, they will be normally significant parts of a programme where only qualitative measures are available.

1.5.3.7 Conclusion

There is a widening gap between the management, planning and control of large engineering projects and change programmes. There is clearly a need to plan each project regardless of its nature. However, the need for planning each project in a programme is subordinate to the need to plan in light of all projects within the programme. This is especially true where projects share resources and this is normally the case in programme management.

Therefore we propose a separation of the terms project and programme planning as follows:

- Project planning is mostly relevant to large engineering projects where physical projects are executed and where resources are only rarely shared with other projects.

● Programme planning is mostly concerned with the planning of multiple, high-technology, non-physical projects sharing, predominately, human resources.

1.6 CHANGE PROGRAMMES: THE FOCUS OF THIS BOOK

The focus of this book is on benefit-driven change programmes – the author team's meaning of programme management. This includes issues that may be superfluous to those readers managing a portfolio of projects for purposes other than change, but this approach ensures that most readers will be able to find what they need.

1.7 BENEFITS OF PROGRAMME MANAGEMENT

We have observed huge benefits on organizations that have adopted programme management thinking and methods. These benefits of programme management can be grouped into two broad headings. These are not mutually exclusive and many organizations have gained through both approaches.

1.7.1 TOP-DOWN APPROACH

Many organizations using programme management techniques define organizational objectives and then define programmes of projects to deliver the changes – the full meaning of programme management. Such organizations benefit by:

● choosing the projects that will deliver maximum or optimal benefit and yet are collectively within the organizations capability to deliver;
● prioritizing those projects that deliver the greatest benefit and that most closely align with strategy;
● eliminating the projects that will not deliver a benefit or that do not align with the organization's strategy.

Such organizations will have Programme Boards charged with delivering specific changes to the organization and will carefully select the best projects by comparing the required investment with the expected benefits.

Such organizations will have visibility across a wide portfolio of projects and programmes and will have confidence that all initiatives are being developed in a broadly similar way with similar processes and check points.

1.7.2 BOTTOM-UP APPROACH

Here, the organization is running a portfolio of projects and feels a need to coordinate them. The organization wishes to ensure that projects are managed in a consistent manner using shared processes and procedures. Such organizations will have a Programme and Project Support Office that maintains standard forms and processes that every project should follow. There will be processes for starting and closing projects and for requesting and releasing resources for the project teams. There will be a standardized approach to reporting on the progress of each project.

Such organizations will see the benefit of programme management in the following ways:

● there will be a consistent approach to projects that will tend to support improved delivery;
● there will be fewer failed projects;
● resources will be allocated to work in a rational manner such that prioritized projects meet least resource bottlenecks;
● it will be possible to monitor all projects in a similar manner so that the programme and senior management teams will be able to take tactical decisions based on accurate data.

1.8 HOW TO USE THIS BOOK

This book is not a cook book, but a set of guidelines or a 'toolbox'.

Pragmatism needs to be exercised in its use, and a solution right for one place, one situation or one organization may not necessarily fit elsewhere. We cannot therefore fail to remind you to 'bring your brain along'. Attempts to blindly apply these techniques can be 'foolish consistency'. To quote Ralph Waldo Emerson: 'foolish consistency is the hobgoblin of little minds!'

This book aims to cover a wide range of the key topics of programme management and recognizes that:

● different organizations have different needs;
● different organizations have different levels of programme management maturity;
● there are a wide range of roles that the reader may play.

Therefore the following paragraphs lay out the content of the book so that a reader may easily locate specific content.

1.8.1 PART I: INTRODUCTION TO PROGRAMME MANAGEMENT

- Chapter 1 – Introduction: The chapter you are now reading.
- Chapter 2 – The programme management process: Chapter 2 proposes an overall process for defining, communicating and delivering change – most relevant to those in a change-orientated programme management environment. It is a comprehensive and detailed examination of the programme management lifecycle from initial consideration to closure. It explains how some organizations will find it appropriate to select components of this process. Chapter 2 examines the major steps of the programme management process as follows:

  1. **Start-up:** Where the opportunities and approaches for change are evaluated to decide whether or not to undertake the work required to define a programme.
  2. **Define programme:** Where the programme is defined, documented and evaluated to create a programme definition document (PDD) and a programme business case. When the PDD and business case are approved the programme moves to step 3.
  3. **Establish programme:** Where the resources, infrastructure and control processes required to achieve the programme's objectives are acquired and implemented. Also where programme team members and stakeholders are trained and informed of their roles and responsibilities.
  4. **Manage programme:** Where the projects comprising the programme are undertaken and outputs delivered to business users.
  5. **Closure:** Where, once all the programme (and its projects) deliverables have been completed and responsibility for operational control of the improved capability has been handed over to line management, and sufficient benefits measure has been completed to judge success, the programme is terminated.

  Chapter 2 is designed to help an organization to establish practical processes and is therefore different to most other sections. It is brief and specific to the point of terseness.

1.8.2 PART II: A SUPPORTING INFRASTRUCTURE

To support a practical programme management lifecycle, the organization will need to set in place a number of supporting structures. The size, style and precise role of these supporting structures will vary as will the level of maturity at any specific point in time. Part II therefore explains the organizational issues and topic areas that support the process of programme management. It lists these supporting structures and explains where they relate to benefit-driven programmes and to portfolios of projects. Part II comprises the following chapters:

- Chapter 3 – Programme organization and governance
- Chapter 4 – Programme planning and control
- Chapter 5 – Benefits management
- Chapter 6 – Stakeholder management
- Chapter 7 – Management of risks and issues
- Chapter 8 – Programme assurance and quality
- Chapter 9 – Configuration management
- Chapter 10 – Internal communications
- Chapter 11 – Programme accounting and financial control
- Chapter 12 – Management of scope and change
- Chapter 13 – The programme office
- Chapter 14 – Programme knowledge management.

Part II is intended to outline the need for, style of, and alternative ways of providing the possible range of support.

1.8.3 PART III: PROGRAMME MANAGEMENT MATURITY

Part III recognizes that every organization has achieved its own level of maturity in the key programme management functions. It recognizes that each organization has its own ambitions and requirements to improve on its maturity in these key areas.

This part explains the concept of the Programme Management Maturity Model (PMMM) in Chapter 15 and the Programme Management Improvement Process (PMIP), a process by which an organization can define its own maturity, consider and select requirements for improvement in maturity and set about delivering those improvements in Chapter 16.

The PMMM provides a widely used benchmarking process that an organization can use to evaluate its own strengths and weaknesses in 10 key areas of programme management in comparison with a wide range of other organizations that have used the same benchmarking process.

The PMIP assumes that an organization has been evaluated by use of the PMMM and wishes to improve its programme management maturity. The PMIP lays out the processes and structures that an organization should establish to achieve one of five levels in each of the ten key areas of programme management.

Therefore the PMIP allows an organization to plan the most beneficial programme management improvements it can make and a sequence of improvements over time to deliver improving programme management maturity.

1.8.4 APPENDICES

The appendices contain a glossary of terms, references to other sources of information and a worked example of a programme definition document.

1.9 CONCLUSION

We, the team of authors, sincerely hope that you will benefit from this book and be able to deliver benefit to your own organization.

You might use elements in Chapter 2 to help establish or improve the programme management process within your organization. You may find in Part II advice that will help you to support your organization's efforts to provide an environment within which project and programmes can proceed effectively. You might use Part III to identify and plan improvements to your organization and Part IV will lead you towards other sources of help and advice.

You may use this book to develop your own skills and therefore your own effectiveness.

We, the authors, have gained a great deal from writing this book and hope you gain as much or more from reading it.

REFERENCES

OGC (2003) *Managing Successful Programmes: Delivering Business Change in Multi-project Environments*. Second edition. London: The Stationery Office.

OPSR (2003) 'Improving Programme and Project Delivery', available from: www.ogc.gov.uk/index.asp?id=1000546/.

Turner, J. Rodney and Simister, Stephen J. (2002) *Gower Handbook of Project Management*. Aldershot: Gower.

2 The programme management process

2.1 INTRODUCTION

This book follows a structure that covers both the process to be followed and the supporting infrastructure required to successfully complete a programme of change. In this chapter, we will describe the programme process, also referred to as the programme lifecycle, to provide the steps a programme will follow and the checkpoints that can be used to ensure success.

2.1.1 THE CONCEPT OF THE PROGRAMME LIFECYCLE

A programme, just like a project, has a beginning, middle and an end. Once the programme is complete, a new cycle of change begins. For this reason we refer to the stages of a programme as the programme lifecycle. Figure 2.1 shows the programme lifecycle, which comprises five stages:

1. **Start-up:** Where opportunities and approaches for change are evaluated to decide whether or not to define a programme.
2. **Define programme:** Where the programme is defined, documented and evaluated to create a PDD and a programme business case. When the PDD and business case are approved, the programme moves to step 3.
3. **Establish programme:** Where the resources, infrastructure and control processes required to achieve the programme's objectives are acquired and implemented. Also where programme team members and stakeholders are informed of, and trained in, their roles and responsibilities.
3. **Manage programme:** Where the projects comprising the programme are undertaken and outputs delivered to business users.
4. **Closure:** Where, once all the programme (and its projects') deliverables have been completed, responsibility for operational control of the improved

capability has been handed over to line management, and sufficient benefits measures have been completed to judge success, the programme is terminated. If during the programme it becomes clear that it cannot complete successfully, it may be terminated early.

Each stage of the lifecycle is described more fully later in this chapter.

It is always important to start well. Experience from many walks of life tells us that it is better to get things right first time than fix them later. So it is with programmes of change. If the programme is properly established in the early preparation phase, life during the Programme Execution stage is made considerably easier. The lifecycle is designed to help programme managers establish their programmes correctly. It achieves this in two ways:

- by providing a route-map, particularly useful for teams new to programme management, that aids understanding of the requirements and challenges that will be placed upon the programme during its lifetime; and
- by specifying that relatively small amounts of work are commissioned and undertaken in the early stages of a programme, building up the workload as more information and certainty are achieved. In this manner, commitments of cost and effort are balanced against the levels of risk in the programme.

It is the objective of the Start-up stage to be certain there is sufficient information available to undertake the Define stage, during which a programme definition and business case will be fully developed. Only once these are complete is the programme allocated the funds and resources to proceed to the Establish stage, and only once successfully established are the full resources made available for programme execution.

Having started well, that is with a well-defined and supported programme, it is important to maintain the momentum. Programme execution provides guidance on how to ensure that early gains are not squandered.

Finishing well ensures that experiences and lessons learned are captured and made available for all future programmes. The Closure stage is where a programme is terminated in an orderly manner, benefits documented and all learning points captured and disseminated.

2.1.2 THE USE OF A PROCESS-BASED MODEL OF PROGRAMME MANAGEMENT

The description of the lifecycle adopted in this book uses a process-based approach. That is to say programme management is represented as a single process, comprising a number of stages. Each stage is described using the convention of:

Programme management process

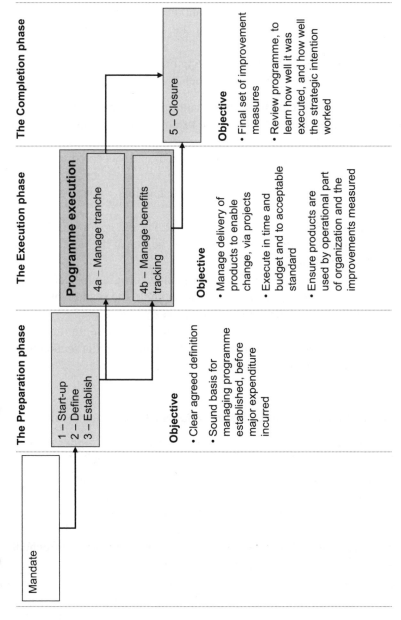

The Preparation phase	The Execution phase	The Completion phase

Mandate

1 – Start-up
2 – Define
3 – Establish

Programme execution

4a – Manage tranche

4b – Manage benefits tracking

5 – Closure

Objective
• Clear agreed definition
• Sound basis for managing programme established, before major expenditure incurred

Objective
• Manage delivery of products to enable change, via projects
• Execute in time and budget and to acceptable standard
• Ensure products are used by operational part of organization and the improvements measured

Objective
• Final set of improvement measures
• Review programme, to learn how well it was executed, and how well the strategic intention worked

Figure 2.1   The overall programme management process

33

- Inputs – elements taken into the stage to be converted into outputs.
- Outputs – products of the stage created from inputs by the completion of actions.
- Actions – work completed to convert inputs into outputs.
- Controls – procedures to ensure that the stage is managed and controlled. Controls often take the form of checklists and approval gates that ensure all work has been completed before moving on to the next step.
- Resources – people, equipment and tools required to complete the stage.

Understanding these elements at each stage of the lifecycle provides a detailed checklist that a programme manager can use to ensure that all is in place for the programme to succeed.

This approach provides a well-recognized and accepted convention for describing a process such as the programme lifecycle. A high-level representation of the programme lifecycle using this convention is shown at Figure 2.2.

Inputs on the left of each diagram are used via the actions in the middle to produce the outputs on the right, using the resources at the bottom and assured by the controls at the top.

The lifecycle has been designed to help manage programmes of change more effectively. Understanding the lifecycle will also help the reader navigate around this book and find the sections that are of interest.

Appendix C of this book provides a worked example of programme documentation. Extracts from this are included in parts of this section to help the reader more fully understand the process.

2.1.3 USING THE LIFECYCLE TO MANAGE PROGRAMMES

In an ideal world, programmes of change are derived from higher-level strategic decisions or processes. The host organization will have identified that a gap exists between its desired performance and that which it is likely to achieve. In order to close this gap a programme, or indeed a number of programmes of change may be proposed. The proposal for a programme to be undertaken is called a programme mandate. The programme mandate describes the objectives for the programme together with an indication of the type and scale of benefits it is expected to deliver. The programme mandate, together with the corporate strategy are the two fundamental starting points for a programme of change, the former provides the definition, the latter the context against which it is evaluated.

Programmes are always started by something. In a well-run organization, this will be the strategy (see Figure 2.3).

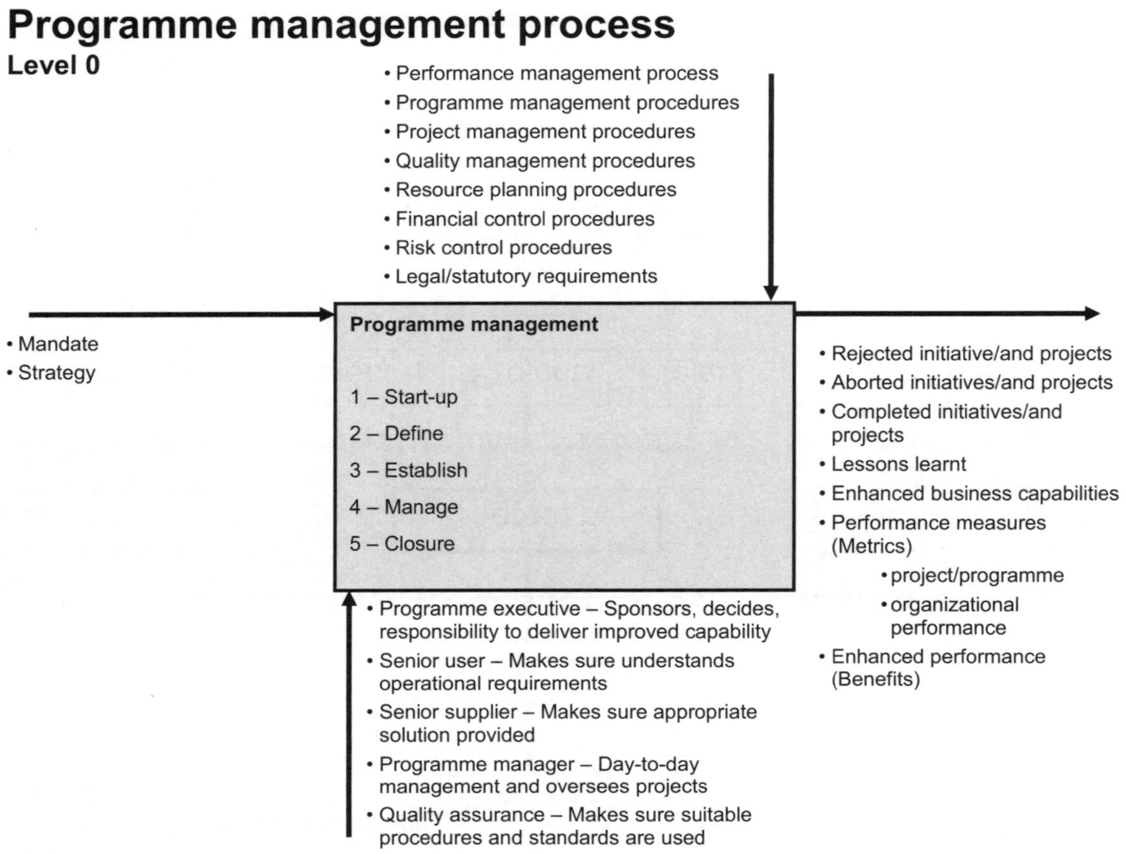

Programme management process
Level 0

- Performance management process
- Programme management procedures
- Project management procedures
- Quality management procedures
- Resource planning procedures
- Financial control procedures
- Risk control procedures
- Legal/statutory requirements

- Mandate
- Strategy

Programme management

1 – Start-up
2 – Define
3 – Establish
4 – Manage
5 – Closure

- Programme executive – Sponsors, decides, responsibility to deliver improved capability
- Senior user – Makes sure understands operational requirements
- Senior supplier – Makes sure appropriate solution provided
- Programme manager – Day-to-day management and oversees projects
- Quality assurance – Makes sure suitable procedures and standards are used

- Rejected initiative/and projects
- Aborted initiatives/and projects
- Completed initiatives/and projects
- Lessons learnt
- Enhanced business capabilities
- Performance measures (Metrics)
  - project/programme
  - organizational performance
- Enhanced performance (Benefits)

Figure 2.2   The programme lifecycle using process-based conventions

35

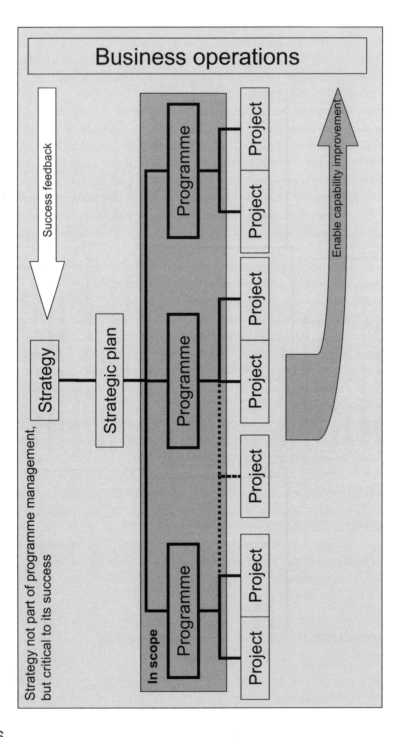

Figure 2.3   The context of programme management

This is undeniably how change programmes should be initiated; however, the reality is often considerably less structured and rational. Often programmes are initiated without a formal evaluation and assessment of their relationship with corporate strategy. In other cases, the strategy is insufficiently well defined to provide the necessary direction.

The programme management lifecycle advocated in this handbook highlights the need for a clear programme mandate and corporate strategy as the basis for a successful programme of change. However, the authors are acutely aware that these documents and the guidance that they should contain are often missing when programme managers are given their remits. In these less than perfect situations, the programme mandate checklist set out in this book can provide a framework to confirm a common understanding of objectives among senior stakeholders and achieve agreement about what the programme is expected to deliver.

Upon successful completion of each stage in the lifecycle, the organization will be in possession of sufficient information and understanding to proceed to the next stage, abandon or revise the programme. These end-of-stage points are referred to as *control gates* and provide senior management with a mechanism to control the release of resources to the programme. Only once the questions posed during a stage are answered and the risks and benefits become better understood, are resources required to undertake the next stage made available. In this way, the commercial risks of the programme to the organization can be managed and contained.

Many programme managers reading this book will find themselves in the situation of having a programme in progress, probably in the Programme Execution stage where some, even many, of the required steps in earlier stages have not been completed. Where this is the case, the programme is likely to be experiencing difficulties resulting from the work not completed. The programme lifecycle provides a checklist that a programme manager in this situation can use to ensure that all of the inputs required for the current stage are in place. If they are not, or their quality is poor, this is likely to be the source of the programme's difficulties. Having used the checklist to identify any such shortcomings, steps can be taken to provide the missing information/decisions and enable the programme to be brought back under control.

2.1.4 THE PROGRAMME LIFECYCLE IS NOT A LINEAR PROCESS

Programmes of change vary in size enormously, from mergers of major international companies to organizational changes in a small enterprise. While scale can vary, guiding principles remain the same. Very large programmes are often structured so that the execution of the individual projects within the programme is undertaken in waves or *tranches*. This is done either because projects in later tranches are dependent upon earlier ones or to reduce the levels of complexity and change at any one time. Figure 2.4 illustrates how tranches may overlap to support the phased achievement of programme benefits. A major reason programmes are ultimately adjudged to have failed is because external or internal circumstances have changed. Hence the need for opportunities to re-evaluate at the end of each tranche and come to a decision as to whether to continue, change or stop the programme. The programme lifecycle accommodates multiple tranche programmes by allowing programmes to cycle back to a previous stage from any point. For example, if a programme completes a tranche of implementation projects and finds that the environment has changed significantly, it may be required to return to the Define stage to confirm its business case and acquire new approvals, before being allowed to continue. If alternatively no significant change in the environment had occurred, the programme would return to the Establish stage to set up the next tranche of implementation projects under the approvals already in place. Where there is considerable uncertainty about the successful outcome of a programme, an early tranche can be designated as a 'proof of concept' or pilot. This tests assumptions and clarifies the degree of uncertainty. Senior management can then make decisions about the major investment that follows with a better understanding of the risk and likelihood of success. This approach is often used when launching new products.

2.1.5 WAYS TO USE THE LIFECYCLE

The lifecycle supports two modes of use, depending upon programme status:

- for the programme manager who has been handed a programme mandate and asked to initiate a new programme, it provides a route-map of the complete journey to programme success;
- for the programme manager of an established programme it provides a diagnostic tool to help understand what, if anything, is going wrong and why.

How each reader uses this book and the programme lifecycle will depend upon which of the two situations they find themselves in, that is:

- Readers in the first category are recommended to start at the beginning of the lifecycle and read through in sequence. They should focus on the early stages, that is, Start-Up and Define, while acquiring an overview of future stages. This will ensure a focus on current requirements while also understanding how these fit into future stages.

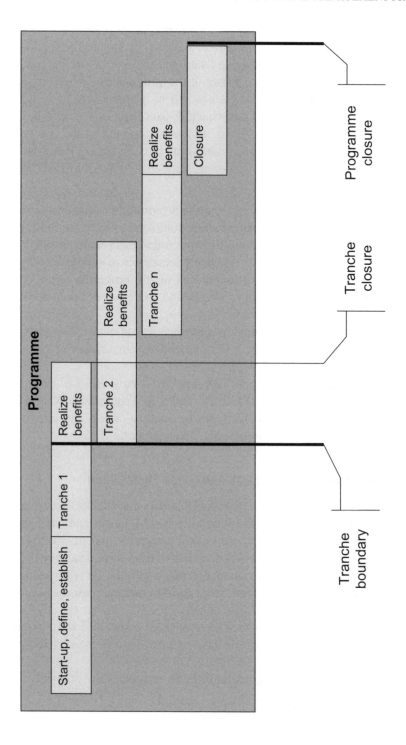

Figure 2.4 Programme conventions

- For the programme manager of an established programme we recommend beginning with the current programme stage. They should focus initially on the inputs and check that all those listed as required for the current stage have been provided by earlier stages of the programme. Where inputs are missing or substandard, tasks will need to be planned and undertaken to make up the shortfall. Once any shortfall from previous stages has been addressed, the book can be used, from that point forward, as for new programmes. It may be the case, in extreme circumstances, that missing or substandard inputs are so significant, that abandoning or restarting the programme will need to be considered.

Part II of this handbook explains in detail the programme management support environment that is required to successfully complete a programme of change. Each of these support elements uses the programme lifecycle to establish when during the life of the programme a particular intervention or support process step is required. In this way, the two dimensions of the programme lifecycle are linked, that is, the time sequence of events and the elements that need to be managed.

Figure 2.5 illustrates the relationship between the programme lifecycle and the elements of the support environment, emphasizing the importance of the support environment throughout the whole lifecycle.

Part III of the handbook provides two mechanisms, the Programme Management Maturity Model (PMMM) and the Programme Management Improvement Process (PMIP), which can be used to assess and improve the effectiveness of each aspect of programme management.

2.1.6 THE PROGRAMME LIFECYCLE AS A DECISION FRAMEWORK

Prospective programmes of change inevitably contain uncertainty. How much will it cost? What will be the benefit? How long will it take? Estimates and assessments will be made at the outset; however, these will inevitably become more reliable and accurate as the programme proceeds. It is vital therefore to balance the value of resources committed to a programme of change with the certainty of success. Put simply, it is inadvisable to commit large sums of money when the outcome is uncertain.

A lower-risk approach is to balance the resources committed with the degree of certainty available. The programme lifecycle provides a framework to manage this commitment of resource.

As previously stated, the programme lifecycle comprises five stages:

1. **Start-up:** Develop an agreed programme brief.

Programme management process

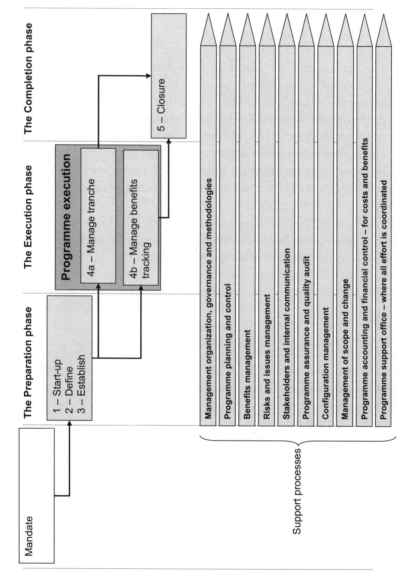

Figure 2.5   The programme management process in more detail

2. **Define programme:** Develop an agreed programme definition.
3. **Establish programme:** Set up programme infrastructure and processes.
4. **Manage programme:** Execute the programme plan.
5. **Closure:** Close down and hand over to 'business as usual' (BAU).

Each stage requires greater resource than its predecessor, and delivers greater certainty of outcome. Therefore at the completion of each stage there needs to be a control gate through which the programme must pass. This is a go/no go decision for the programme based on up-to-date information derived from the recently completed stage. Where a programme receives a 'go' decision, it will be the trigger to release funds and resources to complete the next stage (or tranche if the programme has been subdivided into tranches). Overall programme budget and resource commitment should also be updated at the end of each stage; however, only resources required for the next stage (or tranche) will be released. Using this process, an organization maintains full control of all resources until a programme fully demonstrates how they will be used and the benefits that will be delivered.

The programme lifecycle stages are summarized in Table 2.1. Each stage is described in more detail below. Additionally, at the end of each section there is a 'quick reference' table that summarizes the stage.

2.2 START-UP (STEP 1)

The objective of the Start-up stage is to evaluate if the proposed programme of change is worth pursuing and if so does it justify an initial investment to develop an approach and plan (that is, proceed to Define stage). Upon completion of the Start-up stage, the organization must decide if resources, time and money are to be committed to a full evaluation of the costs and benefits of the programme. As a result, Start-Up should be relatively short and focus on developing a brief for the proposed programme, together with detailed estimates of the work required to complete stage 2 – Define programme. Start-up should answer the question: 'Is this programme worth an investment of resources to define it, or should it be discarded now?' Only the effort required to answer this question, and estimate the work required in the Define stage should be expended during Start-up.

In an ideal environment, one where change programmes are identified and defined as part of business planning (strategy identification), Start-up would be undertaken during this process. Where, however, business planning does not fulfil this role, it is important that an organization quickly assesses potential costs and benefits before committing resources to the programme.

Table 2.1   Stages of the programme lifecycle

Stage	Key output	Control gate test	Funds released	Programme budget
From strategy process	Programme mandate organization strategy	**These are the key inputs to the programme management lifecycle from other business processes, i.e. strategy development and business planning**		
1. Start-up	Approved brief Approval to start and budget for Define stage Risk register	Is the common understanding and shared belief that the programme is worth doing and sufficiently robust to invest resources in defining the programme?	To undertake Define stage	Define stage budget approved
2. Define programme	PDD	Does the programme as set out in the PDD support the investment required?	To undertake Establish stage	Initial programme budget approved and baselined
3. Establish programme	Infrastructure Procedures Programme plan	Does the programme now have an adequate infrastructure to ensure good governance?	To undertake Manage Programme stage	Programme budget established and placed under formal change control
4. Manage programme	Completed projects, deliverables handed over, enables enhanced capabilities to start	Are all projects complete? Have their deliverables been accepted and embedded into operational use? Have benefit measurements started? Are there no unacceptable risks and issues understanding?	To undertake Closure stage	Budgets closed
5. Closure	Terminated programme Lessons learned, Remaining resources released	Has the programme been closed in an orderly manner? Have all lessons learned been captured? Have sufficient benefit measures been captured to judge success?	None	Closing financial report prepared

2.2.1 OVERVIEW

Start-up is designed to expand on an original requirement to initiate a programme of change and produce a clear programme brief, including a risk assessment of the programme plus budgeted costs and resources to undertake a fuller evaluation during the Define stage.

Work to develop a programme brief will usually be undertaken by a relatively small team, often just the appointed programme manager with assistance from 'business as usual' colleagues and completed in a short period of time. Developing a programme brief will normally be subject to the requirements of an organization's internal control procedures including programme management methods and financial planning and reporting requirements.

Figure 2.6 illustrates the inputs, outputs and steps required to undertake the Start-up stage of the programme.

2.2.1.1 Inputs required

The key inputs required to undertake the Start-up stage of a change programme are:

- programme mandate and documentation describing the organization's strategy and objectives;
- appointment of a Programme Executive (that is, a programme director or senior responsible owner (SRO));
- appointment of a programme manager.

The programme executive is normally drawn from the senior management team that originated and approved the programme mandate. The appointment will include a description of their role, similar to a job description. The programme executive is empowered to make decisions on behalf of the programme. At first, the authority granted will normally be described in broad, descriptive terms. Later when more detailed plans and estimates have been prepared, the authority granted can be related directly to these. The programme executive will then appoint the programme manager, or at least approve their appointment and provide them with their role description.

A programme mandate is a short definition of the proposed programme's objectives, together with any specific guidance on how these should be achieved. The more complete a programme mandate, the easier it is to complete the Start-up stage. Where a mandate comprises something as limited as 'we need to replace all the accounting systems' (not an example of a well-developed mandate), the work required to agree objectives, scope and approach and so on during Start-up will be more significant. A well-developed programme mandate, setting out

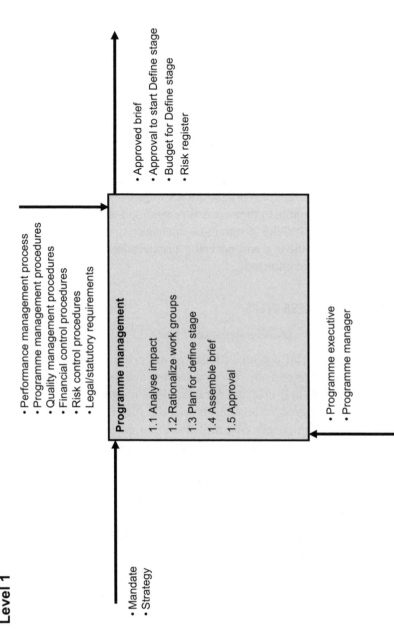

1 Start-up
Level 1

- Mandate
- Strategy

- Performance management process
- Programme management procedures
- Quality management procedures
- Financial control procedures
- Risk control procedures
- Legal/statutory requirements

Programme management

1.1 Analyse impact
1.2 Rationalize work groups
1.3 Plan for define stage
1.4 Assemble brief
1.5 Approval

- Approved brief
- Approval to start Define stage
- Budget for Define stage
- Risk register

- Programme executive
- Programme manager

Figure 2.6 The Start-up process

clearly what the organization wishes to achieve and any known difficulties that may be encountered, will enable the Start-up stage to be undertaken more quickly and effectively.

Information and documentation of an organization's strategy often varies significantly in content and style. In many cases it does not exist as a formal document. An organization's strategy should define the context in which the potential programme's value and benefits will be assessed. The key question is 'how will this programme help the organization achieve its strategy?' If there is no explicit strategy, this question will be very difficult to answer. In the absence of a documented strategy, or where it provides insufficient information, the appointed programme executive and programme manager will need to confirm the organization's objectives with senior management as part of the Start-up stage. This is usually undertaken by conducting interviews and discussions with senior executives that crystallize the organization's objectives and how the proposed programme will contribute to them. It is very common when establishing a major change programme for the programme manager to undertake a significant amount of work identifying and agreeing organizational objectives before the Start-up stage can be completed.

2.2.2 DETAILED PROCESS STEPS

Start-up comprises five process steps; see Figure 2.7.

1. Analyse impact: The potential impact of the programme in support of the organization's goals and objectives is assessed and quantified together with an early estimate of likely cost and duration of the programme.
2. Rationalize work groups: Identification of the major elements of work to be undertaken by the programme organized into groups of activities to assist planning and evaluation. For example, all potential systems-related changes or all initiatives in one geographic location may be grouped together.
3. Plan for Define stage: To provide a full assessment of the time and costs required if the next (Define) stage is undertaken.
4. Assemble brief: Produce a document setting out the results of the impact analysis, work group definition and Define stage plan for review by senior management
5. Approval: Senior management representatives evaluate and approve/reject programme's continuation to the Define stage.

Detailed instructions for each step are set out below.

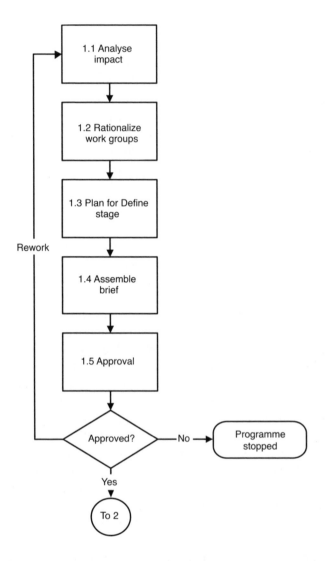

Figure 2.7   The Start-up process steps

Controls

Most organizations have their own processes and procedures for evaluating financial and business impacts of proposed change initiatives. These procedures must be adhered to when evaluating any programme of change as for any other investment or resource commitment decision. Failure to do so is likely to result in significant rework and programme decisions being delayed.

Scaling

All steps in the Start-up stage should be completed irrespective of the size and complexity of the programme under consideration. While the scale of programme will impact the level of detail required in the deliverables from each step, each step should be completed. As stated above, the initial step (analyse impact) may be undertaken as part of a wider business planning process that has identified change requirements. If this is the case, step 1.1. can be considered to be complete, as long as the information provided is still relevant. If an organization has not completed this analysis the programme must undertake it as part of Start-up.

Critical success factors

A clear understanding of the organization's objectives and strategy is essential if an effective programme is to be developed. Even at this early stage of development, it is important that this input finds its way into the programme definition. It is impossible to assess the value of any prospective programme without the context provided by the organization's strategy and aspirations.

The strategy and objectives need to be corroborated with and by the major programme stakeholders. Without this shared understanding, valuable time and effort will be wasted. It is particularly important that all stakeholder views are aligned at this early stage while changes to programme scope and objectives can still be made without incurring significant costs and delays.

It is essential to involve a wide range of subject matter experts in analysing the impact of the programme on the organization, identifying the changes required and how they may best be achieved. These may be technical experts (for example, IT, legal experts), key stakeholder groups (for example, unions or works councils) or business leaders (for example, senior managers). Involvement of a broad range of stakeholders at this early stage will ensure a complete and well-thought-through evaluation can be undertaken in a relatively short period of time.

It is vital not to attempt to define every detail of the programme at this early stage. Start-up is intended to identify if the proposed programme is worth a further investment to develop a complete definition (Define stage) and evaluation, not to provide that fuller evaluation.

2.2.2.1 Analyse impact (step 1.1)

Part 1: Define current state

Objective

To identify and quantify the current, that is, baseline, situation from which proposed programme improvements will be assessed and measured.

Inputs

A programme manager should be able to assemble the following information, prior to commencing to define the current state:

- **programme mandate** – description of programme scope and objectives
- **business strategy documents** – common view of organization's goals
- **business imperatives** – critical success factors, to achieving agreed strategy
- **business processes** – currently undertaken
- **stakeholder groups** – within and outside the organization
- **capability groups** – who possesses what skills?
- **business locations** – where does the organization operate?
- **products and services** – what does the organization provide to its customers/users?
- **channels to market** – how are products/services distributed?

Instructions

If the programme mandate does not clearly set out business requirements, the following actions will be required:

- **Identify and confirm organization strategy:** List all documents that describe the organization strategy, identify owners and obtain copies of the documents. If these documents are complete and well organized, the outputs of this step may already be contained within them. If not, activities will need to be undertaken to obtain this information. This is often done in interviews and meetings with the senior managers and/or directors.
- **Determine the business imperatives:** that is, define what the organization must do to achieve success. These should be definitive statements such as, 'we must be able to offer every customer a customized service to meet their needs'. Imperatives may also be defined or imposed by legislation or a regulatory body.

- **Identify and describe current and future business processes:** Define how processes operate currently and how it is intended they will change in the future, using the following dimensions:
  - What does the process do?
  - Which products/services and distribution channels does it interact with?
  - Is it limited to certain geography?
  - What volumes of transactions pass through the process, especially peak volumes?
  - Which stakeholders are affected?
  - What technology, including IT systems, supports the process?
  - What capabilities (skills) are required for successful operation; that is, how does each process fit into each capability group?
- **Identify and describe the current and future stakeholders:** Identify key stakeholders and how their situation will be different from today, describing the stakeholders in the following terms:
  - How do they relate to the organization, are they customer, suppliers, investors, and so on?
  - Do they only relate via certain products/services and distribution channels?
  - Are they only concerned with certain geographic regions?
  - How many are there, now and predicted? Predicted can be an estimate of natural growth or the estimated/desired change from the impact of the programme.
- **Identify and describe current and future capability (that is, skill) groups:** Capability groups are the combination of people plus their skills and experience, the processes used, and the tools/information they require. This section defines how these capabilities will be different from today, using the following terms:
  - What are the key skills?
  - Which processes, products and channels are relevant to each group?
  - Is the group limited to certain geographic regions?
  - How many people in the organization are in each group today, and how many need to be in the future?
  - Is there any notable weakness in a group; skills, experience, process, tools or information?
- **Identify and describe the current and future business locations:** Define how these locations will be different from today. You should consider describing the locations in the following terms:
  - Where are they?
  - What are their key functions?
  - What facilities will they need?

- What is their capacity, people, product throughput, and so on?
- Are there any major change constraints, leases, limited room for expansion, and so on?
- **Identify and describe the current and future products/services:** Define how these products/services will be different from today, describing them in the following terms:
  - What are they?
  - Through which distribution channels do they operate?
  - Are they limited to certain geographic regions?
  - What is the volumes throughput, especially peak volume?
  - On which processes are they dependent?
- **Identify and describe the current and future (distribution) channels to market:** Define how channels will be different from today, describing them in the following terms:
  - Which customers does it serve?
  - Which products/services does it support?
  - Is it limited to certain geographic regions?
  - What are the volumes throughput, especially peak volumes?
  - Which stakeholders are affected?
- **Collate benefits:** Analyse the information collected above into the benefits summary table, describing how the organization will benefit, including:
  - The target (if available) as a quantified number (for example increase revenue to £10 million) or text.
  - When the benefits are required, usually to an accuracy of the nearest quarter year.
  - What changes, as identified in the steps above, will produce this benefit?
  - What other initiatives or current programmes might adversely affect or be affected by this programme?

The outputs from this step should be collated into a business architecture blueprint; see the worked example in Appendix C of this book.

Part 2: Identify the change required

- **Make a list of the current business systems:** If the organization has a separate technical strategy and there is a definition of the future target business systems, describe these as well. Consider describing the systems by identifying the following aspects:
  - What is their purpose?
  - Which processes do they support?

- – Are they limited to certain geographic regions?
- – What are the volumes throughputs, especially peak volumes?
- – Which capability groups are they dependent on for proper functioning?
- – Are there any external technologies or other drivers that might influence changes in the future?
- – Are there any internal drivers that may influence future changes? These could include depreciation policy, cost of maintenance, quality of output, and so on.

- **Make a list of the current information systems:** If the organization has a separate technical strategy and there is a definition of the future target information systems, describe these as well. Consider describing each system by identifying:
  - – What is their purpose?
  - – Through which channels do they operate?
  - – Are they limited to certain geographic regions?
  - – What are the volumes throughputs, especially peak volumes?
  - – Which processes do they support?
  - – Which capability groups are they dependent on for proper functioning?
  - – Are there any external technologies or other drivers that might influence changes in the future?
  - – Are there any internal drivers that may influence future changes? These could include depreciation, cost of maintenance, quality of the output, and so on.

Verify changes identified in Part 2 above against the organization strategy. As a final step you will need to assess which changes are due directly to the programme change and which are due to other drivers. For example, an IT system change may be required to support a business process change. It is the business process change that is driven by the strategy and included in the objectives of the programme, whereas the IT change is an enabling change. A simple and effective technique for undertaking this analysis is to link business process changes to the strategy, then relate all other changes and potential initiatives to theses changes in business processes. Any other changes not related to business process changes should be verified by mapping them directly back to the strategy.

Results should be reviewed with all stakeholders critical to the success of the programme.

Part 3: Check programme and project management maturity

Part III of this book sets out PMMM. The PMMM is a framework for assessing an organization's capability to implement a programme of change. Even at this early stage it is recommended that you assess your organization's programme management maturity, as this will provide important insights into the work that will need to be undertaken if the programme is to be set up to succeed. Details of how to undertake a PMMM assessment can be found in Part III of this book.

It is important not to propose programmes that promise changes beyond their capability to deliver. If senior management are asking for unrealistic change and improvements, PMMM can be used to demonstrate why their desires cannot currently be achieved. The PMIP is a series of structured activities, designed to be used in conjunction with the PMMM, that can be used to overcome any shortcomings identified by a PMMM assessment. Where risks are identified due to a lack of programme management capability, PMIP activities can be incorporated into plans for Define and Establish stages to rectify these shortcomings. In this manner, deficiencies in programme management capability can be overcome in a positive and constructive manner.

There are two outputs from the analyse impact step, of Start-up:

- a business architecture blueprint – see example below
- a PMMM assessment.

Business architecture blueprint

These are sample extracts; see Appendix C for an example of the full document.

Business processes: Personal communications directorate – personal development initiative

Process name	Description of future process	How will it differ from today
Define personal development needs	Assess, define, and agree each individual's personal development needs	More structured approach, via agreed process, will ensure each individual's needs are based on an objective assessment and there is agreement between that person and their manager. This will provide input to 'Create Personal Development Plan'

Operation and functions (capability groups)

Here we have considered those functions/capabilities that are relevant to this programme. Capabilities will sometimes be delivered (at least in part) by information or manufacturing systems.

Future targets should include performance and cost information where applicable.

HR – Training

Function/capability	Current	Future target
Deliver training	Internal ability to deliver training is very limited. This is assumed to be one important factor that inhibits the effectiveness of training. 90% of training is delivered by external organizations; 15 days per year per head per annum	90% internal, only highly specialized training, infrequently required, to be delivered by external organizations. Training cost per head to reduce by 25%; 20 days per year per head per annum

Operations outputs – products and services

Describes any existing products and services that will be affected by the programme and any new products and services that will be required.

Product or service	Description of current products	Future products
Training workshops	Buy 90% of them in from external training organizations	Will develop training workshops for 90% of our needs and sell extra capacity to other divisions

Operations delivery logistics – channels to market

Describes any existing channels that will be affected by the programme and any new channels that will be required. If you make available a product or a service to another organization, even if it is free, you must have at least one channel to promote and 'sell'.

Channels to market	Description of current channels	Description and targets for future channels
Professional publications	None	This is one option for a new way to sell extra training capacity, at least one of these channels will need to be set up

Stakeholder groups

Internal and external stakeholders who are dependent on the future success of the organization and who will be affected by the changes to its architecture. This is your prediction of the changes to stakeholders' roles and numbers.

Stakeholder groups	Role	How much will it grow/shrink
HR*	To help individuals to monitor their own needs and to identify areas of weakness at both a personal and organizational level	+1 in first year. Staff to manage improved personal development and training processes
Third-party training provider	These will be replaced in all but the most specialist areas	–90%
Training Staff*	A training team will be built to provide the training requirements	+6
Catering Staff*	The catering team will expand to provide catering in the training facility	+2

2.2.2.2 Rationalize work groups (step 1.2)

Work groups are packages of linked activities that will be managed via projects within the wider programme. It is important at this point to define prospective work groups. Simply creating a list of all activities required to achieve the programme's goals runs the risk of either gaps or duplication. The objective of this step therefore is to produce a coherent set of linked Work Groups (that is, potential projects) that will achieve the programme objectives with as little overlap or omission as possible.

Inputs

From the original definition of the programme:

- programme mandate
- business strategy.

From the previous steps:

- blueprint.

From the programme office:

- current programmes and projects.

Instructions

- Collect the outputs from the previous process steps (analyse impact).
- List all changes that are required for the proposed programme to be successful.

- Identify the status of projects in all current programmes that impact on common areas of the organization, using the dimensions as previously:
  - business processes
  - stakeholder groups
  - capability groups
  - business locations
  - products and services
  - channels to market
  - business systems
  - information systems.
- Highlight scope overlaps between the proposed and current programmes.
- Convene a workshop attended by key stakeholders and experts in the areas likely to change, to identify potential work groups. These are activities that provide 'solutions' that enable the organization to change and improve as desired. They are *not* yet projects; that thinking comes later and requires consideration beyond just the 'solutions' themselves.
- Using an 'affinity' technique (see the appendix at the end of this chapter), or other suitable approach, group like changes into work groups. The changes are the 'gaps' identified in the business architecture blueprint, as the difference between the current position and the target state required at a point in the future.
- Document workshop output using the work group template.

Typical outputs from the Rationalize Work Groups Step are:

- **Identified work groups:** That is, logical groupings of activities capable of being planned and executed as projects within the overall programme, such as:
  - infrastructure project(s) – for example, to establish the network, hardware and software that all systems developed for the programme will access;
  - business process improvement project(s) – for example, to reduce mistakes, improve productivity and enable an increase in throughput.

Note: A single work group will not always become a single project. Work groups may be too small and be combined with others to make a sensibly sized project. Alternatively, work groups may be too large and need to be split into separate projects to make them manageable. Figure 2.8 shows an example of a work group template.

Work group name / Relationship with	New training centre	Processes to offer and deliver workshops	Process to manage facilities	Training workshops	Booking system	Training equipment	Catering facilities
Process name and description	Enables 'Offer workshops' Needs new manage facilities process	New processes	Changes needed to include new training centre	Offered and delivered by new processes	Needs new process	Enables 'Deliver workshops'	Supports 'Deliver workshops'
Stakeholder groups	Managed by HR Used by trainers, catering and staff	Managed by HR training Delivered to staff	Managed by HR Supported by Facilities	Delivered by trainers to staff	Managed by HR training for operations managers and staff	Supervised by trainers Used by staff	Operated by catering for staff being trained
Capability groups	Deliver training carried out here	Defined by new processes		New – Deliver training	New – part of Manage Training	New – part of 'Manage training'	New – part of 'Deliver training'
Business locations	Requires land or existing building	New training centre	New training centre	New training centre	New training centre	New training centre	New training centre
Products and services	Training workshops delivered here	Training workshop are the output		New product			
Channels to market	Details of centre included in promotional material	Details of how to book included in promotional material		Details of workshops included in promotional material		Details of equipment included in promotional material	Details of facilities included in promotional material
Information systems	Located here	Support processes	Support processes	Details of workshops included in information systems	Located in new training centre		
Manufacturing systems							

Figure 2.8   Example of a work group template

2.2.2.3 Plan for Define stage (step 1.3)

Why do this?

Planning for the Define stage demonstrates to the programme executive, and then to the programme board, that via the Define stage the programme will be adequately defined and planned. One of the objectives of the Start-up stage is to assure senior management that the programme has the capability to deliver the required benefits. At the end of this stage, management will be asked to approve expenditure, based on the programme brief, to undertake detailed planning, that is, the Define stage. To approve this, management needs to know the programme's cost and duration.

Inputs

From the original inputs to the programme:

- programme mandate
- business strategy.

From the previous step:

- business architecture blueprint
- work groups.

Instructions

- Obtain copies of the following:
    - programme mandate
    - business strategy
    - business architecture blueprint
    - work groups.
- Identify the Define stage objectives and deliverables.
- Identify all Define stage stakeholders and define a project governance structure for the stage, to ensure that the work is adequately controlled and all stakeholders are fully engaged.
- Develop milestone and activity plans to achieve Define stage objectives.
- Estimate resources required and costs to be incurred to complete the Define stage.
- Identify and evaluate potential risks to achieving Define stage plan.
- Document the plan for the Define stage.

Outputs

Outputs are:

- work plan for Define stage
- cost and resource requirements for Define stage.

2.2.2.4 Assemble programme brief (step 1.4)

Why do this?

The programme brief is the key deliverable from this stage. Based on this document, the programme executive and then the programme board must be able to decide whether to:

1. discontinue the programme;
2. authorize the programme to move to the Define stage; or
3. request additional information to be collected and presented to enable (1) or (2) to be decided.

Inputs

From the original definition of the programme:

- programme mandate
- business strategy.

From the previous steps:

- business architecture blueprint
- work groups
- current initiatives that overlap the programme, and may need to be stopped, amended or integrated
- work plan for Define stage
- cost and resource requirements for Define stage.

Instructions

- Develop a benefits summary from the outputs above.
- Develop a programme vision statement. See the appendix at the end of this chapter.
- Copy the vision statement into the programme brief document .
- Produce initial benefits profiles and include them in the programme brief document. See the appendix at the end of this chapter. Note that these profiles will be refined further in the Define stage.

- Collect the outputs from the previous process step 'rationalize work groups'.
- Collect a list of initiatives that overlap the programme. Add narrative if needed to explain the nature and extent of the overlap.
- Carry out a risk analysis and log any new risks or issues.
- Align the work groups to the business imperatives or strategic objective, to categorize them into priority groups.
- In the Programme Plan section, state any interim milestones that the programme must plan to meet. These constraints may be provided in the mandate or may have been discovered in the previous steps.
- Assemble the brief.

Outputs

The output is the programme brief; see the example in Figure 2.9.

Programme brief

PURPOSE OF DOCUMENT
'Identifying a Programme' organizes the requirements of the organization, so it is clearly understood what activity and investment is needed to make the change necessary to achieve the expected benefits. The purpose of this document is to provide an informed basis for the programme executive to decide whether they want to continue with the Programme, and to start the definition of the programme.

VISION STATEMENT
The overall objective of the organization is to be the most successful worldwide telecommunications group through the provision of world-call telecommunication products and services. In particular, the organization has made a clear statement on customer commitment based on value for money and excellent performance backed by guarantee.

To make a contribution to these objectives the Business Processes Re-organization Programme (BPR) will have to find ways to increase performance in many individual processes within the business. The programme will also provide a measurement and coordination system to demonstrate the improvements delivered.

Now that the BPR programme is underway it has become clear that Telekom BV does not have adequate means to develop its staff, so they will be able to effectively operate the new and improved processes, that will be the outcome from this programme. A separate initiative (this programme) will address this problem. The strategy group have compared Telekom BV with other telcos who have their own purpose built training facilities. If we develop a similar purpose-built training centre and supporting facilities, we can expect our training cost per head to reduce by 25 per cent, and to be able to increase the opportunities for training from 15 days per year per head per annum to 20 days.

Many other organizations in the region also lack adequate training facilities. A preliminary survey by the strategy group indicates they will be willing to use our facilities. This is expected to contribute 25 per cent to its operating costs.

BENEFITS PROFILES

WORK GROUP DEFINITIONS

PROCESSES

Name and description
Change required
Impact on
      –   Stakeholder Groups
      –   Capability Groups
      –   Business Locations
      –   Products and Services
      –   Channels to Market
      –   Information Systems
      –   Manufacturing Systems

CROSS-REFERENCE TO BUSINESS IMPERATIVES

RISKS AND ISSUES

PROGRAMME PLAN

As key milestones, targets and or constraints

PLAN FOR DEFINE STAGE

Figure 2.9   Example structure for a programme brief, with one section ('Vision statement') completed

2.2.2.5 Approve programme brief (step 1.5)

Why do this?

A change programme is a major commitment for any organization. At the conclusion of the Start-up stage sufficient information must be presented to the programme executive and then to the programme board, to allow them to reach one of three decisions:

1. discontinue the programme;
2. authorize the programme to move to the Define stage; or
3. request additional information to be collected and presented to enable (1) or (2) to be decided.

Ultimately only decisions (1) or (2) are allowable.

Moving a programme to the next stage, that is, Define, will incur significant cost on behalf of the organization. The programme executive and programme board must make this commitment in full knowledge of these costs and associated benefits and communicate these to the whole organization. It is essential, as a programme completes each stage of its lifecycle, that a decision to stop or continue is made by senior management and fully documented. Without this clear commitment to proceed, the programme will continually struggle for support and sponsorship.

Inputs

From the original definition of the programme:

● programme mandate
● business strategy.

From the previous step:

● programme brief.

Instructions

● Distribute the brief to the programme executive, senior managers, and all critical stakeholder representatives.
● Explain the process for reviewing the documents, for providing comments, and how the brief will be approved.
● Update the brief from comments received. Consider a workshop if there are many conflicting comments that need to be resolved.
● Distribute the final brief.
● Convene, or obtain a time allocation at, a meeting of the body responsible for approving programme expenditure within the organization.
● Present the programme brief to this body and, ultimately, obtain approval to proceed to the next stage, Define.

Note: It may be necessary to undertake additional work before the programme brief can be approved, or indeed the programme may be rejected as not in the organization's best interest.

Outputs

The output is a go/no go decision about whether to proceed to the Define stage.

2.2.3 QUICK REFERENCE

This section summarizes the Start-up stage of a programme in a quick reference form.

	Inputs	How	Who	Output	Quality	Techniques
1.1 Analyse impact	Programme mandate business strategy	Identify changes to be delivered by the programme Assess impact on organization	Strategy team Senior managers Programme executive Programme manager Subject experts	Business architecture blueprint	Does the Impact assessment provide a clear understanding of the change and help decide if the programme is worth pursuing?	Business analysis Strategic review Financial modelling Business architecture
1.2 Rationalize work groups	Programme mandate Business strategy Business architecture Blueprint Current programmes and projects	List changes from blueprint Organize changes into work groups	Strategy team Senior Managers Programme manager	Work groups Relationship to current programmes and projects	Does each work group/ programme form a coherent package of work?	Affinity grouping
1.3 Plan for Define stage	Programme mandate Business strategy Business architecture Blueprint work groups	Identify team required for Define stage Assess workload Prepare work plan for Define stage	Programme manager Strategy team	Work plan for Define stage Cost and resource requirements for Define stage	Have the skills, resources, costs and time required to define the programme(s) been adequately assessed?	Estimating and planning

	Inputs	How	Who	Output	Quality	Techniques
1.4 Assemble brief	Programme mandate Business strategy Impact assessment Set of programmes and work groups Work plan for Define stage Cost and resource requirements for Define stage	Define business need and Vision Define benefits Identify key stakeholders Define costs Assess risks Map work groups to strategic objectives Produce programme brief	Strategy team Senior managers Programme manager	Programme brief	Does the programme brief contain sufficient information such that a decision to proceed, or abort, can be made by senior management?	Defining benefits Risk analysis
1.5 Approval	Programme mandate Business strategy Programme brief	Senior management review	Senior management	Go/no go decision, whether to proceed to Define stage	Has a clear decision been made?	Review and decision making

2.3 DEFINE PROGRAMME

2.3.1 OVERVIEW

2.3.1.1 Purpose and objectives

For the programme to have reached the Define stage the programme executive will have considered the programme brief prepared during the Start-up stage and decided to:

● proceed with the programme, at least to this next stage; and
● provide funding and resources.

The purpose and objective of the Define stage is to produce a detailed approach and plan for the programme. This approach and plan must contain sufficient detail and analysis to enable the programme board and programme executive to decide whether or not to launch the programme. The decision gateway at the end of the Define stage provides the last opportunity to discontinue the programme prior to significant expenditures being committed. At the conclusion of the Define stage only a relatively small proportion of the eventual programme cost should have been spent or committed. The Define stage must produce a sufficiently robust approach and plan to enable the programme executive to commit the vast majority of cost and resource required to undertake the programme. It must also demonstrate an acceptable return on the investment required.

2.3.1.2 Scaling

The scale of programmes is almost limitless. Changing the IT systems and working procedures for a family owned engineering company would benefit enormously from the application of the principles set out in this handbook. Equally a programme can involve the merger of two global companies or the hosting of an Olympic Games. What then should a programme manager consider in order to achieve an appropriate scale of approach?

Consider the following when defining a programme of change:

- The size and number of projects and initiatives to be coordinated within the programme is a key consideration. Individuals have limited 'bandwidth' (that is, ability to manage complexity, information, decisions, and so on). Therefore it is necessary, as the scope and scale of the programme grows, to introduce more levels of management and reporting. With this comes complexity and cost. Regrettably there is no escaping this dilemma.
- The maturity of the organization in managing programmes and projects at all levels. Programme and project management and indeed the management of change generally are not as intuitive as many managers would suggest. If an organization has a history of mis-steps and poor project/programme execution, the current programme will carry a much higher risk of failure. Lessons learned and reviews with staff involved in previous projects and programmes will assist the programme manager in identifying where additional resources and process will be required. Additionally the PMMM and PMIP described in Part III of this handbook can assist in identifying and rectifying shortcomings in this area.
- Geographic location of the programme can have a significant impact. Despite huge advances in communications, video conferencing, web-meetings, e-mail, and so on, the greater the geographical dispersion of the programme, the greater the need for formal processes and procedures.
- Organizational pressures – for example, levels of cooperation between operating groups and stakeholders.

- As the programme grows in size and complexity, so the need for more layers of management increases, as does the need for formal processes and procedures. The lower the levels of project and programme management maturity in the organization, the greater the need for formal processes and procedures. The more the programme teams are dispersed, the greater the need for formal processes and procedures.

The worst case scenario therefore is a global, highly complex programme being undertaken by an organization with no track record of successful programme completion. If your programme looks like this, you will probably need much more than this handbook to be successful.

2.3.1.3 Critical success factors

- Do not plan in too much detail; more detailed plans will be prepared later as each tranche and project are prepared.
- Concentrate on establishing the priorities, identifying quick wins that can realize early benefits, dependencies between projects, and ensuring that project deliverables are clearly mapped to the benefits expected.
- The best overall approach for the programme will be a blend of the approach required to deliver each work group, the relationships between work groups and organization functions, together with the organization's capability to manage change.
- For organizations with limited experience of managing change, the approach should be kept as simple as possible. Divide the programme so there is a strong bond between work groups and functions (those functions will try harder) and support each function by using experienced project and programme managers.
- Use relatively simple, well-understood, financial modelling techniques unless you have the services of experienced investment appraisal specialists.
- If your organization has limited programme management capability and experience, you *must* build time into your plans to allow for development and learning.
- It is essential to establish an adequate infrastructure and put in place support tools, processes and procedures to manage the programme. These must be able to function within the current programme and project management capabilities of the organization. A good infrastructure will not guarantee success for the programme, but a bad one will almost certainly guarantee failure.
- Make sure you understand the attitude of all of the stakeholders in the programme. For those whose stance is not where it needs to be (those who

could jeopardize the Programme's success) you must develop a strategy to influence them and thus positively change their attitude. Seek assistance in this from the programme executive if necessary.

2.3.1.4 Inputs

- business strategy
- programme brief, containing:
  - high-level assessment of programme impact
  - business architecture blueprint
- work groups
- organization strategy
- lessons learned (from other programmes).

The programme brief, approved at the conclusion of the previous stage, is the key input to the Define stage. It should contain, at a summary level, everything that is, and needs to be, known about the programme at this stage. In addition, the most up-to-date version of the organization's business strategy and plans are important to ensure that the context within which the programme is planned is current and correctly understood. Lessons learned from previous projects and programmes within the organization will provide insights into what works well and what does not.

Figures 2.10 and 2.11 illustrate the inputs, outputs and steps required to undertake the Define programme stage.

2.3.2 DETAILED PROCESS STEPS

2.3.2.1 Develop the programme approach (step 2.1)

Why do this?

Programme planning is essentially a cascade process, initially an overall approach must be defined, for example, to consolidate common and shared services for all European countries of operations into a single European shared service centre, retaining only sales and customer service activities in each country.

This represents the broad approach; the individual work groups and projects can then flesh out and define how this will be implemented. The approach will guide and direct those members of the programme team preparing more detailed plans. Another factor to consider is which parts of the organization should undertake development and delivery of the various changes required via the programme's constituent projects. The outline approach will define the relationships and capabilities of those functions as they relate to changes the

2 Define programme
Level 1

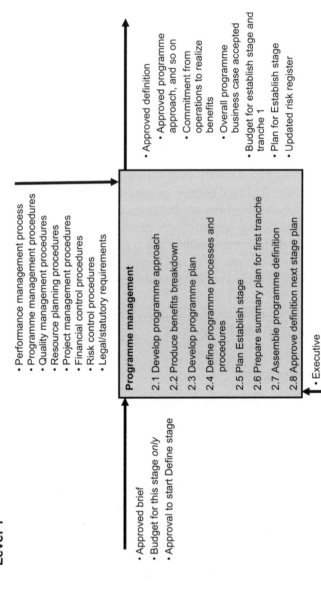

- Approved brief
- Budget for this stage *only*
- Approval to start Define stage

- Performance management process
- Programme management procedures
- Quality management procedures
- Resource planning procedures
- Project management procedures
- Financial control procedures
- Risk control procedures
- Legal/statutory requirements

Programme management

2.1 Develop programme approach

2.2 Produce benefits breakdown

2.3 Develop programme plan

2.4 Define programme processes and procedures

2.5 Plan Establish stage

2.6 Prepare summary plan for first tranche

2.7 Assemble programme definition

2.8 Approve definition next stage plan

- Executive
- Senior user
- Senior supplier
- Programme manager
- Quality assurance

- Approved definition
- Approved programme approach, and so on
- Commitment from operations to realize benefits
- Overall programme business case accepted
- Budget for establish stage and tranche 1
- Plan for Establish stage
- Updated risk register

Figure 2.10   The Define process

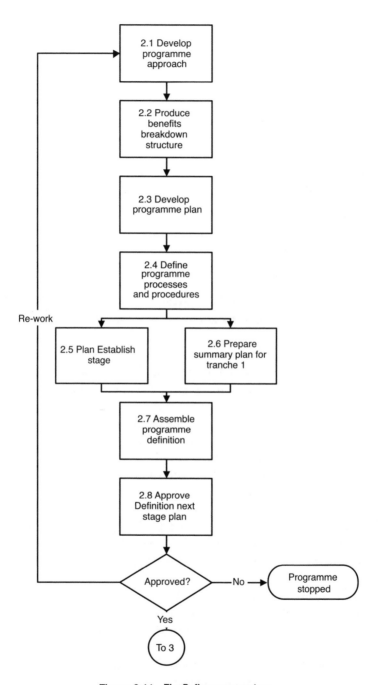

Figure 2.11   The Define process steps

programme needs to deliver and suggest where each element of the programme should be undertaken.

Inputs

The inputs are:

- high-level assessment of programme impact
- business architecture blueprint
- work groups
- programme brief
- strategy
- lessons learned (from other programmes)
- project management maturity assessment.

Instructions

- Obtain outputs from the previous process step (Start-up) – PMMM – and identify weaknesses requiring attention. See examples in Figures 2.12 and 2.13 .
- Obtain outputs from the previous process step (Start-up) – success and shortfalls from lessons learned. Extract and list any successes and shortfalls that are relevant to managing this programme. See examples in Figures 2.12 and 2.13.
- Obtain programme brief approved in the previous step (Start-up).
- Analyse factors, particularly external ones that may impact the programme and how they might change over its life.
- Analyse potential programme organization structures, considering the current change management capability of the organization.
- Assess whether the programme(s) should be aligned to the operational structure of the organization (aligned to functions) or whether a 'cross-functional' change management structure would be more appropriate.
- Decide how to overcome or support any gaps or deficiencies in required capabilities.
- Review and revise as required the work groups identified during the previous stage (Start-up) and link these into the chosen structure.
- For each work group consider alternative approaches: develop in-house, outsource/sub-contract, buy a package solution, and so on. Eliminate any non-starters, prioritize the remainder; choose the highest priorities to model in the next step. Evaluate the potential impact of external impacts, risks and issues:
  - Enlist the help of 'experts' who understand how external events, risks and

issues could affect your programme, for example from finance, legal, marketing.

- Brief experts on the scope of the programme, the nature of the change it is aiming to make and the expected timescale.
- Brainstorm and assess possible external events (for example, new legislation), risks and issues, showing how and when these events could affect different parts of the programme.
- Plot the results into a table similar to that shown in Figure 2.12 for detrimental impacts, and into a similar table for positive impacts.
- Identify actions to avoid or minimize the impact of detrimental impacts.
- Identify actions to exploit and optimize positive impacts.
- Later, when arranging work groups into projects and developing the Programme plan, this analysis will be used to develop a more formal risk analysis.

- Evaluate Programme and Change Management Capability, using an analysis matrix such as that illustrated in Figure 2.13.

- In the top right box, plot work groups where you have limited experience of managing this type of change and previous attempts have produced little success.

- In the top left box, plot work groups where you have limited experience of this type of change, but there has been reasonable success from previous attempts.

- In the bottom right box plot work groups where you have a broader experience of this type of change, but have still only achieved limited success.

- In the bottom left box, plot work groups where you have a broader experience of this type of change and have achieved acceptable success.

- Structure the programme using the decision diagram (Figure 2.14). Avoid mixed structures unless you are very experienced and successful at managing large complex programmes of change.

  Organize work groups, into either :
  - projects, using the relationship between work groups and benefits; or
  - operational functions.

- The two matrices shown in Figures 2.15 and 2.16 are designed to assist this process and should be completed as follows:
  - Work group and function (see Figure 2.15)
    - ○ Enter titles of functions in the column headings.
    - ○ Enter work group names in the row headings.
    - ○ For each work group in each column plot the relationship between the function and work group. Strong relationships are where a function has a lot of experience in the composition of the work group and/or expects to obtain a lot of benefit from the desired changes.

71

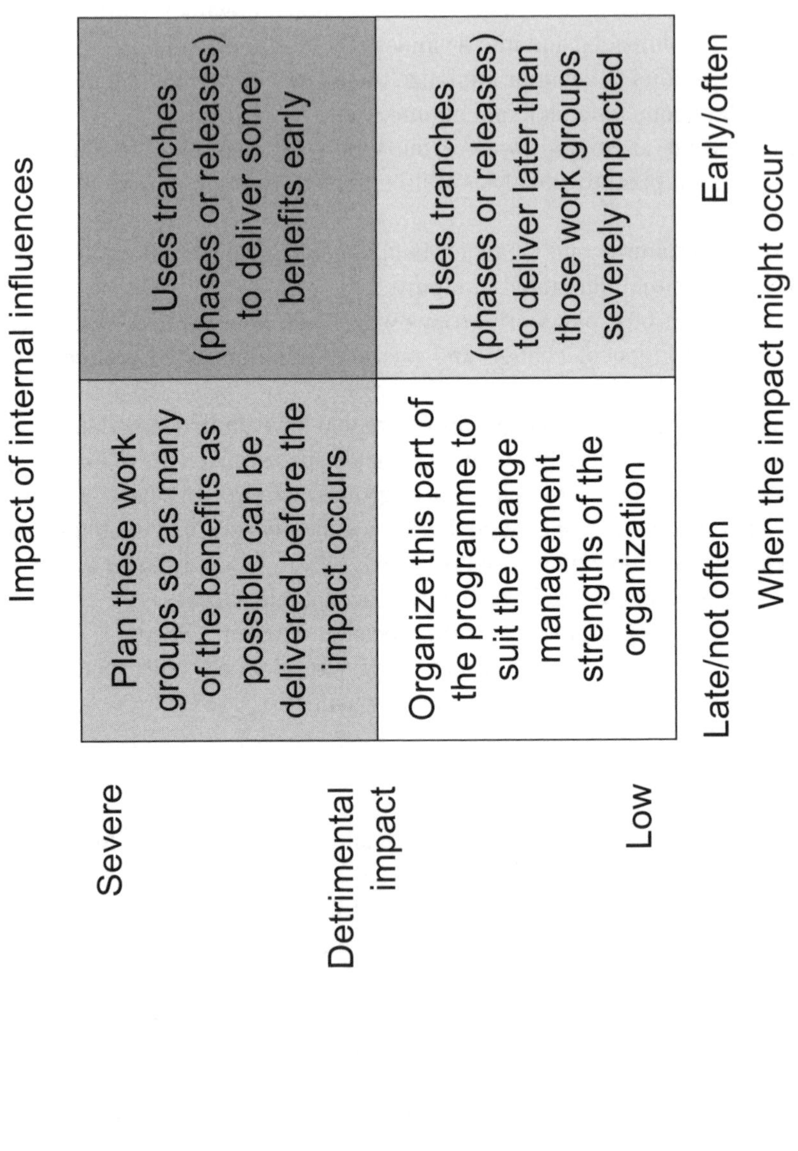

Impact of internal influences

	Early/often
Uses tranches (phases or releases) to deliver some benefits early	Uses tranches (phases or releases) to deliver later than those work groups severely impacted
Plan these work groups so as many of the benefits as possible can be delivered before the impact occurs	Organize this part of the programme to suit the change management strengths of the organization

Severe — Detrimental impact — Low

Late/not often — Early/often

When the impact might occur

Figure 2.12   Evaluating external influences (a similar diagram can be produced for positive impacts)

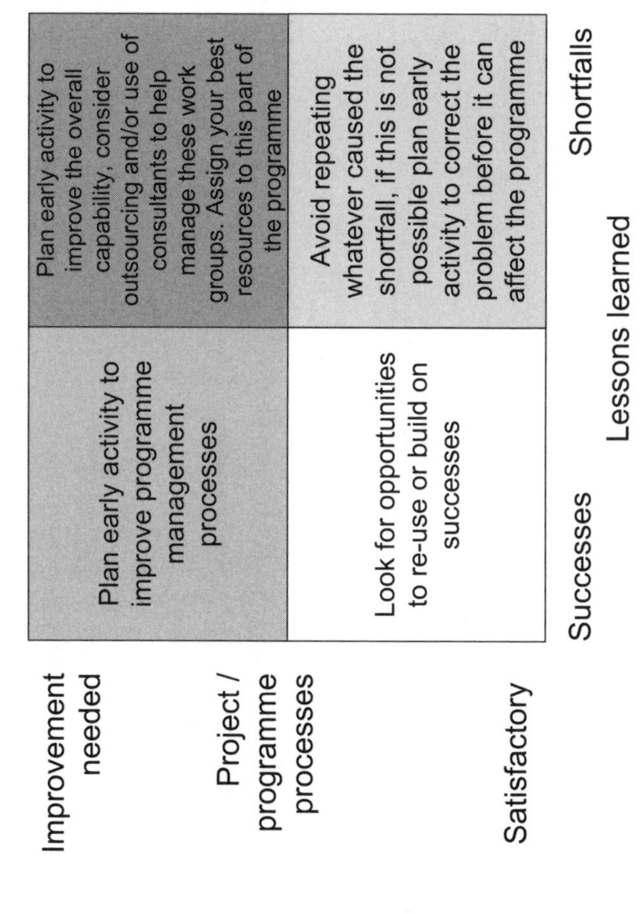

	Successes	Shortfalls
Improvement needed	Plan early activity to improve programme management processes	Plan early activity to improve the overall capability, consider outsourcing and/or use of consultants to help manage these work groups. Assign your best resources to this part of the programme
Satisfactory	Look for opportunities to re-use or build on successes	Avoid repeating whatever caused the shortfall, if this is not possible plan early activity to correct the problem before it can affect the programme

Project / programme processes (row axis) — *Lessons learned* (column axis)

Figure 2.13   Evaluating change management capabilities

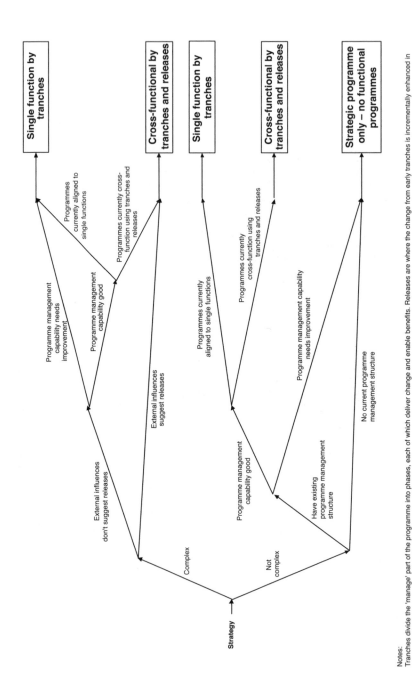

Figure 2.14 Structuring the programme decision tree

Notes:
Tranches divide the 'manage' part of the programme into phases, each of which deliver change and enable benefits. Releases are where the change from early tranches is incrementally enhanced in later tranches. The decision made in here indicates the preferred structure of the programme. Other programmes within the same organization may be organized using a different structure. Mixed structures in an organization are acceptable, indeed commom. However, this may make the programmes more difficult to manage and therefore more risky.

- ○ If there are several functions with strong relationships, you may want to consider splitting the work group, or sharing responsibility across functions, or assigning one function as the lead.
  - Work group and benefit
    - ○ Enter names for each benefit as column headings. It is also useful to include the provision of enabling infrastructures and capabilities, such as IT infrastructure or key competences, as (intermediate) benefit columns.
    - ○ Enter work group names in the row headings.
    - ○ For each work group in each column plot the correlation between the benefit and work group using a scale such as High, Medium, Low and None. High correlation is when a work group is expected to deliver a high proportion of the required benefit.
- Having completed these analyses review the resulting tables for:
  - work groups that cluster around functions within the organization, for example, several work groups predominantly impacting upon Finance;
  - work groups that combine to deliver specific benefits or enabling infrastructures, for example, several work groups that combined together provide improved customer experience.
- In many organizations, projects are often aligned to technical speciality. Performance improvements might require processes to be re-engineered, and the new working practices to be supported by better IT systems. This is often delivered through two separate projects, which don't communication and collaborate with each other properly. In such circumstances you might wish to consider managing such change as one project.

Using these groupings and other knowledge of the organization, it should now be practical to define a series of implementation projects which, taken together, will deliver the programme objectives. To achieve this take the following steps:

- Combine work groups into projects based on Functional and benefits linkages.
- Where work groups do not fit any particular combination, consider establishing them as individual projects.
- Identify the function most closely associated with each resulting project and assign a senior manager from that function as project executive or senior user.
- Document each resulting project using the following criteria:
  - project title and description
  - project executive
  - work groups included
  - project deliverables (products)

Name of function Work goups	Operations management	Operations engineers	HR management	HR training	Catering	Facilities management	IT
New training centre	Weak	Weak	Strong	Strong	Medium	Strong	Medium
Processes to offer and deliver workshops	Weak	Weak	Strong	Strong	Weak	Weak	Strong
Process to manage facilities	Weak	Weak	Medium	Medium	Medium	Strong	Weak
Training workshops	Medium	Medium	Strong	Strong	Weak	Weak	Medium
Booking system	Medium	Weak	Strong	Strong	Medium	Weak	Strong
Training equipment	Medium	Medium	Strong	Strong	Weak	Medium	Medium
Catering facilities	Medium	Medium	Strong	Strong	Strong	Strong	Weak

Figure 2.15 Example of a work group template used to show the relationship between the changes required and organizational functions

Name of Benefit Work groups	Reduced training cost	Income from training
New training centre	High	High
Processes to offer and deliver workshops	High	High
Process to manage facilities	Low	*Medium*
Training workshops	High	High
Booking system	High	High
Training equipment	*Medium*	*Medium*
Catering facilities	Low	*Medium*

Figure 2.16   Example of a work group template used to show the relationship between the changes required and benefits

- benefits to be delivered and/or supported
- approach to be taken, for example, for an information systems project, the proposed approach may include, in-house development, package purchase, outsourced provider, and so on.

Collate and summarize these project definitions for inclusion into the Approach section of the programme definition.

- These are only initial project definitions. They will be extended later, once the programme plan has been developed.

2.3.2.2 Produce benefits breakdown structure (step 2.2)

Why do this?

The ultimate success of a programme is measured in terms of whether or not it delivers the planned benefits. The purpose of this step is to model the relationships between:

- planned benefits
- capabilities required to enable benefits to be realized
- project deliverables (products) that create or improve these capabilities.

Capabilities are skills, facilities, resources, and so on, without which a benefit cannot be realized. For example, in order to provide the required benefits of

77

reduced cost and improved customer service, a telephone call centre is required to enhance three capabilities:

- improved interaction with other functions within the host organization, delivered through business process re-design
- enhanced telephone skills and techniques, delivered through training
- upgraded IT and telephone systems, delivered through a technology deployment.

Only when all three capabilities are in place can the benefits of reduced cost and improved customer service be delivered. Typically project deliverables (products or outputs) enable new or improved capabilities, which are combined by the organization to achieve benefits.

A benefits breakdown structure (BBS) document should set out the linkages between project deliverables (products or outputs), capabilities and benefits, providing a clear link between projects within the programme and ultimate benefits.

Developing a BBS also provides a framework that should become part of programme reporting and benefits management, linking programme activity and planned outcomes.

Inputs

Inputs are:

- high-level assessment of programme impact as set out in the business architecture blueprint
- business architecture blueprint
- programme objectives
- programme deliverables
- programme approach options.

Instructions

- Create a BBS for each prospective approach under consideration for the programme. Techniques to complete this are set out in Figures 2.17 and 2.18.
- Use modelling tools as appropriate to assess alternative approaches identified.
- Choose the preferred approach for each work group.
- Produce the final BBS for the chosen approaches.

Outputs

Outputs are:

78

- programme capabilities
- programme benefits
- benefit owners
- benefit breakdown structure and flow
- assessment of external influences
- preferred programme approach options.

Figures 2.17 and 2.18 give an example of a BBS and flow diagram.

Instructions

- Create the BBS:
  - Plot all the benefits on level 1 in the benefits structure (you may wish to use separate pages for each benefit, or group of benefits, for clarity).
  - Identify the enablers. These are the 'things' that will change in the organization, which in turn are expected to lead to the benefits desired. These 'things' are defined in the work groups identified earlier. List the changes by work group.
  - Identify the events that allow the enablers to be activated. These are usually outputs delivered by projects, that when put into operation (the event) enable something to work better (and thus realize the benefit). Note that there may be more than one event required to realize the benefits required.
  Create the benefits flow diagram:
  - Copy each of the event boxes from the structure sheet to the flow sheet.
  - Arrange each box so the right edge is where you plan to deliver the change that will enable the benefits to start. Try to keep all the events in a work group together in the same programme.
  - If one event is dependent on another, arrange them to follow on or draw a connecting arrow between them.
  - To the right of the event boxes that enable the benefits to start, enter the expected benefit values.
  - At the bottom of the chart enter the required benefit values.
  - Hold workshops/interviews, and so on, to find ways to improve the benefits flow. Some ways to do this are:
    - ○ arrange events that create high benefit values earlier in the programme;
    - ○ break an event into more smaller events, so some of them can deliver benefits earlier.
  - Look for natural breakpoints and mark these as the ends of tranches. Breakpoints occur when there is a step change in the capability of the organization and benefits can start to be realized.

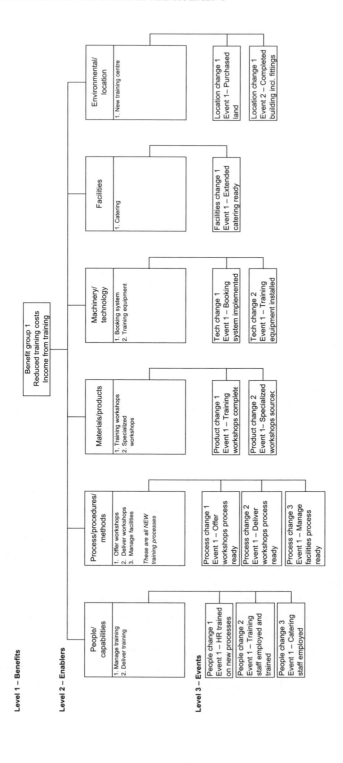

Figure 2.17   Benefits breakdown structure

Notes:

- When you first create the BBS, it will be at a summary level. The events will be based on work groups identified. Later, you will refine this and the events will become based on projects in programmes. At that point you can refine costs and benefit estimates.
- These cost and benefit estimates will need to be re-assessed throughout the programme lifecycle. This should be done at least at the end of each tranche, and approval to continue obtained from the programme board and programme executive.

2.3.2.3 Develop programme plan (step 2.3)

Why do this?

The programme plan is the critical control document. It is important, when developing the programme plan, to focus on interdependencies between the projects and initiatives that comprise the programme.

Inputs

Inputs are:

- programme objectives
- programme deliverables
- programme work groups
- (high-level) programme plan as targets and or constraints
- programme capabilities
- programme benefits
- BBS and flow
- preferred programme approach options
- programme and change management capability gaps
- assessment of external influences.

Instructions

- At this stage, the programme plan will only be at a summary level, as it will be based on the work groups identified and the approach chosen. Use the matrices output from the previous steps to help you work out how to arrange the work groups into a portfolio of projects.
- As discussed above (see the bullet 'Organize work groups' in the Instructions section to 2.3.2.2), work groups may be organized around functions or benefits. It is important to bear in mind decisions made while structuring the

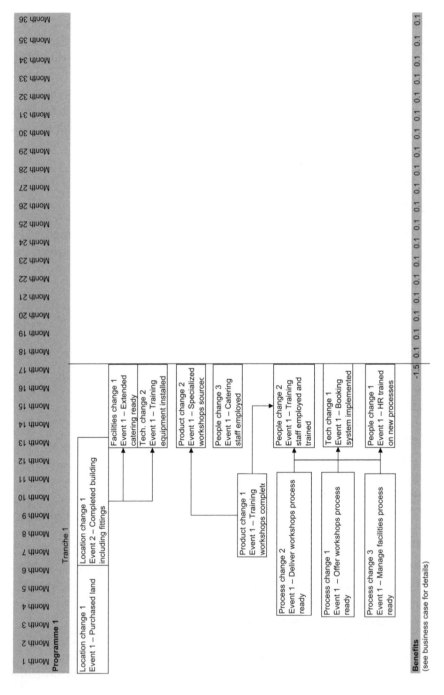

Figure 2.18 Benefits flow diagram (note that the boxes are *not* yet projects)

programme(s). For example, be wary of arranging the work groups into cross-functional projects if your organization does not have a positive track record of working in this manner.

- Remember that the 'programme and change management capability gaps' need to be assigned to one or more projects, and that the improved capability needs to be in place early in the programme lifecycle to reduce the risk of failure.
- Use the outputs from the previous process steps – the business architecture blueprint, work groups and the benefit flows – to define the scope and content of each project.
- Create a plan for the programme that matches the scope and flow of events as depicted in the BBS. Where there are interfaces and dependencies between projects, make sure you annotate each plan accordingly (see the example in Figure 2.19).
- Use the priority list for work groups to help you produce a priority list for this programme. This is an ordered list of tranches and projects within each tranche, with highest priorities at the top.
- Define dependent projects and the nature of each dependency, and indicate which will deliver which changes. Projects produce and hand over their outputs to operational parts of the organization. Their use and the consequential changes are the outcome, which if successful will realize benefits. Often the outputs from several projects need to be delivered, as the operational functions can only change when a complete set are in place. For example, for a new training facility, the building, new processes to manage training, training workshops, IT, catering, and so on, are all required, but might have been delivered by separate projects. The programme must design the project portfolio with this in mind; it must ensure that documents are clear about dependencies and combinations, first to brief new projects as they start, and second to provide a baseline against which progress can be assessed.
- Develop high-level work, resource and cost estimates. Use this and the information from the benefits profiles to develop the initial programme business case.

Outputs

Outputs are:

- programme plan (route-map)
- programme resource (capability) requirements
- programme risk assessment and mitigations
- initial programme business case (see Figure 2.20).

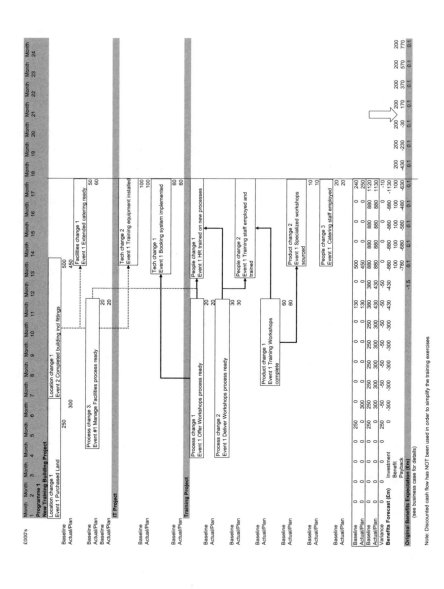

Figure 2.19 A simple programme plan (the workgroups from the benefits flow diagram above have no been arranged into three projects)

2.3.2.4 Define programme processes and procedures (step 2.4)

Why do this?

A programme is a major undertaking involving many vital decisions and large volumes of complex information. Before commencing a programme infrastructure and procedures need to be in place to process and analyse information and ensure that decisions are taken in a timely and ordered manner. This step ensures that people, processes, tools and infrastructure are available and working satisfactorily from programme commencement.

As discussed earlier (See Section 2.3.1.3, 'Critical success factors'), the larger, more complex or geographically diverse a programme becomes, the greater is the need for reliable and robust procedures and processes. Likewise, the less experienced and capable the organization is at managing programmes, the greater the need for reliable and robust procedures and processes. All programmes require formal processes and procedures, how formal will depend upon the factors listed above.

Inputs

Inputs are:

- programme brief
- preferred programme approach options
- best practice programme processes and procedures
- current state of programme processes, comprising:
  - management, organization, governance and method
  - programme planning and control
  - benefits management
  - management of stakeholders
  - issue and risk management
  - quality
  - configuration management
  - communication
  - programme accounting
  - management of scope and change.

Instructions

- Identify and summarize current programme/project management processes, tools, infrastructure and the people who support it.
- Obtain outputs from the previous process steps – programme management capability assessment.

BUSINESS CASE

PURPOSE OF DOCUMENT

To document the justification for the undertaking of a programme project based on the estimated cost of development and the anticipated business benefits to be gained.
The business case is used to say why the forecast effort and time will be worth the expenditure. The ongoing viability of the project will be monitored by the project board against the business case.

- Reasons
- Benefits
- Benefits Realization
- Cost and Timescale
- Investment Appraisal

Figure 2.20 Example template for a business case

- Define the processes, tools and infrastructure that will be required for this programme, making best use of existing proven facilities and identifying improvements indicated by the PMIP set out in Part III of this handbook. Detailed requirements for each process can be found in the relevant chapters in Part II of this handbook.

Outputs

Outputs are:

- programme processes and procedures required
- actions, as indicated by the PMIP, required to establish programme processes and procedures.

2.3.2.5 Plan Establish stage (step 2.5)

Why do this?

Upon successful completion of the Define stage, a programme will typically move swiftly into the Establish stage. Establish involves constructing the physical infrastructure, team, processes and procedures required to execute the programme. To await approval of the Define stage before developing a project plan for the Establish stage would introduce an unnecessary and potentially expensive delay into the overall Programme timetable.

Inputs

Inputs are:

- programme mandate
- business strategy
- programme plan (route-map)
- programme capabilities
- programme benefits
- agreed programme processes and procedures
- requirements for project procedures.

Instructions

Planning an Establish stage is a classic project management exercise, where the objective of the project is to 'establish the programme'. The steps comprise:

1. Confirm the goals and objectives for the project, that is, to establish the programme environment, team, and so on.
2. Define project governance arrangements, roles and responsibilities.
3. Identify all stakeholders and develop engagement and communication plans.
4. Identify project risks and define mitigation actions.
5. Define project milestones, tasks, deliverables and timetable.
6. Estimate resource requirements and costs.
7. Document all outcomes in the form of a project initiation document and plan.

Outputs

Outputs are:

- project initiation document and plan for Establish stage
- cost and resource requirements for Establish stage.

2.3.2.6 Prepare summary plan for tranche 1 (step 2.6)

Why do this?

Larger programmes are often undertaken in 'tranches' or 'phases' or some similar term, meaning that the work is broken down into smaller more manageable sections. Where the programme will be executed in a single 'tranche', for example, a post-merger integration programme, where everything must be achieved concurrently, this step will cover the whole programme. For programmes executed in tranches, this step should focus on the initial work to be undertaken. Later tranches will then be planned as they become due.

The detailed planning of individual projects will be undertaken in the next stage, the Establish stage. The tranche 1 plan at this stage should provide the programme executive with a clear indication of what will be achieved by the initial

87

tranche of projects completed, the timescale for completion and the cost. It is good practice to arrange tranches of activity so that they enable a step change in the organization's capability. For example, in an international roll-out of a new IT system, tranches of work undertaken may reflect geographic regions. Each tranche's completion extends system coverage to another geographic region. A common tranche structure comprises an initial 'pilot' exercise followed by a series of 'roll-outs'.

Inputs

Inputs are:

- programme plan (route-map)
- programme objectives
- programme deliverables
- BBS and flow
- programme benefits.

Instructions

- Confirm the operational change and organization capability improvement that this tranche will deliver. Determine which group of projects in the programme will enable this organizational change to be implemented and show how a flow of benefits will start as a result of that change (derived from the BBS created earlier).
- Identify all the projects that the tranche must manage and the products that are the end outcome from these projects.
- State the tranche objectives by showing which parts of the programme's business architecture blueprint the tranche will deliver.
- Provide a statement of how and when the tranche objectives are to be achieved, by showing when the projects will deliver the major products, how operational change will be enabled, when the consequential benefits will start to flow and the resources required for the projects and benefits tracking.
- Assess and log any new risks that have been identified.
- Identify the tranche controls, reporting points and frequencies.
- Update the programme's business case.
- Propose the tranche tolerances.
- Specify the quality controls for the tranche and identify the resources needed for them.
- Assemble the tranche plan report for inclusion in the PDD.

Outputs

Outputs are:

- summary programme plan for tranche 1
- tranche 1 project outlines.

2.3.2.7 Assemble programme definition (step 2.7)

Why do this?

A programme is a major undertaking and inevitably requires significant investment. It is clearly vital that those who will approve the programme and the investment, that is, the programme executive, are convinced of a sound basis for proceeding. The programme definition must demonstrate a sound basis by:

- tracing its origins back to the strategy and the programme mandate, that is, the organization's original instruction;
- articulating a clear vision of how the programme will achieve its objectives;
- providing the who, what, why, how and when of the programme, upon which senior management can exercise their judgement objectively;
- demonstrating that programme teams will receive clear and explicit direction from the outset, thereby increasing the likelihood of success.

Following a decision to proceed to the Establish stage, a programme will begin to incur significantly higher levels of resource and costs. It is therefore vital that this decision is based on as thorough an assessment as possible.

Inputs

Inputs are:

- programme mandate
- business strategy
- programme plan (route-map)
- BBS
- programme benefits
- programme resource requirements
- summary programme plan for tranche 1
- tranche 1 project outlines.

Instructions

- The products of the various planning and analysis activities need to be drawn together into a document that can be reviewed by the programme executive

89

and enable them to decide whether or not to proceed with the programme as defined.

- The precise format of the document is likely to be decided by organizational norms and preferences, however the contents should include all of the outputs listed below.

Outputs

Output is a programme definition report (document) containing:

- programme objective – what the programme seeks to achieve
- benefits to be realized – by the programme
- scope (including phase/tranche 1) – what is included, what is not
- sponsors – who, among senior management, are committed to and charged with the success of this programme
- stakeholders – who is impacted by or impacts upon the programme
- programme team and resources – what the programme team will comprise; includes suppliers and sub-contractors (an example of a programme team structure is shown in Figure 2.21)
- milestone plan – the critical steps through the programme
- deliverables and quality plan – what will be delivered and how its quality will be assured
- governance, roles and responsibilities – how programme decisions will be made
- risks, issues and mitigation – what challenges, known and unknown, face the programme and how they will be addressed.

Figure 2.22 gives an example of the structure of a programme definition document. See the worked example in Appendix C, which contains the complete programme definition for the example case study.

Programme business case

The justification for undertaking a programme is significantly based on estimated cost versus anticipated business benefits. A business case quantifies these costs and benefits and provides a yardstick against which the ongoing viability of the programme will be monitored. At this stage of programme development, it is unlikely that detailed costs will be available for all planned work and activity. Early stages/tranches will typically be costed in some detail while later stages will often be represented by broader estimates. These later stage estimates will need to be updated as the programme proceeds and potentially additional funding approved if early estimates prove inadequate.

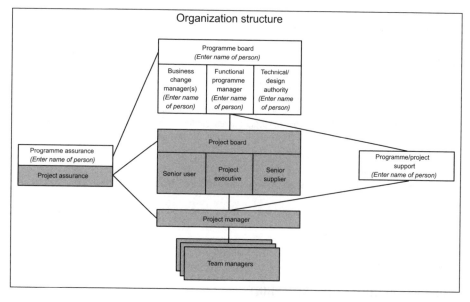

Figure 2.21   Programme organization structure

A programme business case should include sections covering:

- cost of work to be undertaken
- timing of expenditures
- benefits to be realized
- timing of benefits realization
- profit and loss and cash flow implications of the programme
- investment appraisal, for example, return on investment (ROI).

Further details of the cost components of a programme business case can be found in Chapter 11, 'Programme accounting and financial control', while benefits realization is more fully explored in Chapter 5, 'Benefits management'.

2.3.2.8 Approve (programme) definition and Establish stage plan (step 2.8)

Why do this?

A change programme is a major commitment for any organization. At the conclusion of the Define stage sufficient information must be presented to the programme board to allow them to reach one of three decisions:

1. discontinue the programme;
2. authorize the programme to move to the Establish stage; or
3. request additional information to enable (1) or (2) to be decided.

PROGRAMME DEFINITION

PURPOSE OF DOCUMENT

The programme executive decided to continue with the programme, based on the programme brief and to stat the definition of the programme. The definition work has produced more detail and a better insight into the programme proposed. A programme is a major undertaking and often requires significant investment. It is important that those who will approve the programmes and the investment can be convinced that there is a sound basis for proceeding. This document will demonstrate that sound basis because it:

1. allows the reader to trace its origins back to the strategy, which was effectively the organization's original instruction;
2. provides a breakdown of the who, what, why, how and when, against which senior managment can use their judgement objectively;
3. demonstrated that the programme teams will be given explicit and clear direction from the outset, thus increasing the likelihood of success.

VISION STATEMENT

BUSINESS ARCHITECTURE BLUEPRINT

WORK GROUP DEFINITIONS

BENEFITS BREAKDOWN STRUCTURE

BENEFITS PROFILES

Including benefits measurement processes

PROGRAMME PLAN

To include:

- Management Control Points (tollgates) at least for Start, Closure, end of each tranche
- The schedule for producing highlight reports
- Tolerances for cost and time
- A list of projects with their planned start and finish dates

ORGANIZATION STRUCTURE

STAKEHOLDER ANALYSIS

COMMUNICATIONS STRATEGY AND PLAN

QUALITY MANAGEMENT STRATEGY

RISKS AND ISSUES

Risk and issues management strategy

Risk and issues log (summary)

BUSINESS CASE

Figure 2.22   Example of the structure of a programme definition

Ultimately only decisions (1) or (2) are allowable.

Moving to the Establish stage represents a commitment to significant cost by an organization. It is vital, as the programme completes each stage of its lifecycle, that a decision to stop or continue is made by senior management and fully documented It is essential that those members of senior management making the decision do so in full knowledge of the commitment and cost that their decision represents. Without this clear commitment to proceed, the programme will continually struggle for support, sponsorship and funds.

Inputs

The input is the PDD.

Instructions

- Distribute the PDD to the programme executive and board, for review.
- Explain the process for reviewing the documents, for providing comments, and how the PDD will be approved.
- Update the PDD from comments received. Consider a workshop if there are many conflicting comments that need to be resolved.
- Distribute the final PDD.
- Convene a programme board meeting to approve the PDD and thereby authorize the programme to continue to the next stage.

Outputs

The output is a go/no go decision about whether to proceed to Establish stage.

2.3.3 QUICK REFERENCE

This section summarizes the Define stage of a programme in a quick reference form.

	Inputs	How	Who	Output	Quality	Techniques
2.1 Develop programme approach(s)	High-level assessment of programme impact Business architecture blueprint Work groups Programme brief strategy Lessons learned (from other programmes)	Confirm/ develop programme objectives Identify programme deliverables Develop alternate approaches and assess	Programme manager Programme team Subject specialists	Programme objectives Programme deliverables Programme approach options	Will the defined approach achieve the programme objective(s)? Do the programme work-streams organize the work in a logical manner? Is the (high-level) programme plan achievable?	Programme planning Programme approach design
2.2 Produce benefits breakdown	High-level assessment of programme impact Business architecture blueprint Programme objectives Programme deliverables Programme approach options	Identify/agree benefits required Identify/agree capabilities required Baseline current performance Link benefits to capabilities Link capabilities to programme deliverables Identify benefit owners Define benefits breakdown and flow Evaluate and select preferred programme approach options	Programme manager Programme team Senior management Subject specialists	Programme capabilities Programme benefits Benefit owners BBS and flow Preferred programme approach options	Can the programme deliver the capabilities required? Will the capabilities deliver the benefits required? Are the benefit owners capable of delivering the benefits?	Benefits mapping Cost/benefit analysis Financial analysis

	Inputs	How	Who	Output	Quality	Techniques
2.3 Develop programme plan	Programme objectives Programme deliverables Programme work-streams (High-level) programme plan Programme capabilities Programme benefits BBS and flow Preferred programme approach options	Identify projects to comprise the programme Derive project mile-stone plans Develop overall programme plan (route-map) Define programme Resource (capability) requirements and availability Undertake risk assessment Initial business case	Programme manager Programme team	Programme plan (route-map) Programme resource (capability) requirements Programme risk assessment and mitigations	Does the programme plan (route-map) adequately describe/ define the programme for it to be commenced? Is the risk acceptable? Is the plan achievable? Does it cover all the changes required?	Project planning Programme planning Business case
2.4 Define programme processes and procedures	Programme brief Preferred programme approach options Best practice programme processes and procedures	Confirm programme objectives and scope Identify programme stakeholders and their issues Review best practice programme processes and procedures Review and amend procedures as required Agree with sponsors	Programme manager Programme team	Agreed programme processes and procedures Requirements for project procedures	Are the defined/ agreed programme processes and procedures appropriate/ capable of controlling the programme	Programme processes and procedures development

	Inputs	How	Who	Output	Quality	Techniques
2.5 Plan Establish stage	Programme plan (route-map) Programme management capabilities/ improvements Agreed programme processes and procedures Requirements for project procedures	Identify team required for Establish stage Assess workload Prepare work-plan for Establish stage	Programme manager Programme team	Work plan for Establish stage Cost and resource requirements for Establish stage	Have the skills, resources, costs and time required to establish the Programme(s) been adequately assessed?	Project assessment and planning
2.6 Prepare summary plan for tranche 1	Programme plan (route-map) Programme objectives Programme deliverables BBS and flow Programme benefits	Prioritize/ select objectives to be achieved in tranche 1 Develop/ expand programme plan for tranche 1 Define and plan all projects in tranche 1	Programme manager Programme team	Summary programme plan for tranche 1 Tranche 1 project outlines	Are definitions and plans sufficiently well prepared and complete to commence tranche 1?	Project planning Programme planning
2.7 Assemble programme definition	Programme mandate Business strategy Programme plan (route-map) Programme benefits Programme resource requirements Summary programme plan for tranche 1 Tranche 1 project outlines	Document all information into PDD	Programme Manager Programme team	PDD	Does the PDD fully describe the programme and its objectives	PDD development

	Inputs	How	Who	Output	Quality	Techniques
2.8 Approve definition and Establish stage plan	PDD	Senior management review	Programme board (senior management)	Go/no-go decision about whether to proceed to Establish stage	Has a clear decision been made?	Review and decision making

2.4 ESTABLISH PROGRAMME

2.4.1 OVERVIEW

2.4.1.1 Purpose and objectives

This stage's primary objective is to take the programme approach, as defined in the PDD, and establish the infrastructure and processes to enable work on the programme to be undertaken. At the commencement of this stage, management of the host organization should be clear and in agreement concerning what needs to be achieved. At the conclusion of the stage all the necessary elements required to undertake the first 'tranche' of programme activity should be on the 'starting grid' and ready to go.

2.4.1.2 Inputs

The key input to the Establish stage is the PDD, which contains a full definition of the programme to be completed as authorized by the programme board (senior management of the organization). The PDD is the equivalent of an architect's plans and drawings, detailing what the programme needs to achieve and the methods to be employed. In 2.3.2.5 ('Plan Establish stage'), we recommended you treat establishing the programme as a project. The project definition and plans for this work, output from 2.3.2.5 are also important inputs.

2.4.1.3 How

The Establish stage addresses and completes six tasks (see Figures 2.23 and 2.24):

- Set up the physical infrastructure required to undertake the programme, for example, programme office accommodation, IT systems, and communications.
- Set up the processes and procedures required to undertake the programme, for example, planning, change control, acceptance.

- Preparation of detailed plans for each project, or initiative, to be undertaken during the first tranche of programme activity. If all projects and initiatives included in the programme are to be undertaken together, clearly, tranche 1 planning will encompass the whole programme.

   Note: The concept of programme tranches has been used throughout this approach to programme management to emphasize that, especially on very large programmes, it is impractical and frankly unwise to attempt to undertake the whole programme as a single exercise. Breaking a large programme into tranches provides an effective way of managing execution risk.

- Establish a communication plan for the tranche and the programme.
- Develop and confirm project briefs for each project within the tranche. This document forms the 'contract' between the programme and the project that guides all interactions from this point forward.
- Confirm that senior management agrees to the programme undertaking the projects included in the initial tranche, or indeed the whole programme.

2.4.2 DETAILED PROCESS STEPS

2.4.2.1 Set up physical infrastructure to support programme (step 3.1)

Why do this?

Any programme of significant scale will require some form of physical infrastructure to support it. Best practice indicates that a programme management office (PMO) should be established to control and coordinate the programme. The PMO and its staff will require, among other things:

- accommodation
- office equipment and supplies, for example, copying machines, furniture
- communications, for example, telephones, fax machines, Internet access, e-mail
- IT systems, for example, web-meeting, project planning, document management
- PMO team, for example, programme managers, planners.

In addition, the infrastructure requirements of each of the projects and initiatives included within the programme will need to be considered. It is unlikely that the PMO will plan for and provide all the requirements for every constituent project; however coordination of elements such as communications and planning tools is essential. Setting up the Physical Infrastructure and PMO team is a project in

3 Establish programme
Level 1

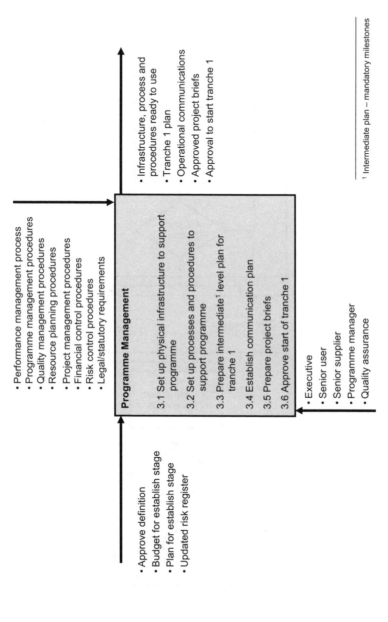

- Approve definition
- Budget for establish stage
- Plan for establish stage
- Updated risk register

- Performance management process
- Programme management procedures
- Quality management procedures
- Resource planning procedures
- Project management procedures
- Financial control procedures
- Risk control procedures
- Legal/statutory requirements

Programme Management

3.1 Set up physical infrastructure to support programme

3.2 Set up processes and procedures to support programme

3.3 Prepare intermediate[1] level plan for tranche 1

3.4 Establish communication plan

3.5 Prepare project briefs

3.6 Approve start of tranche 1

- Infrastructure, process and procedures ready to use
- Tranche 1 plan
- Operational communications
- Approved project briefs
- Approval to start tranche 1

- Executive
- Senior user
- Senior supplier
- Programme manager
- Quality assurance

[1] Intermediate plan – mandatory milestones

Figure 2.23   The Establish process

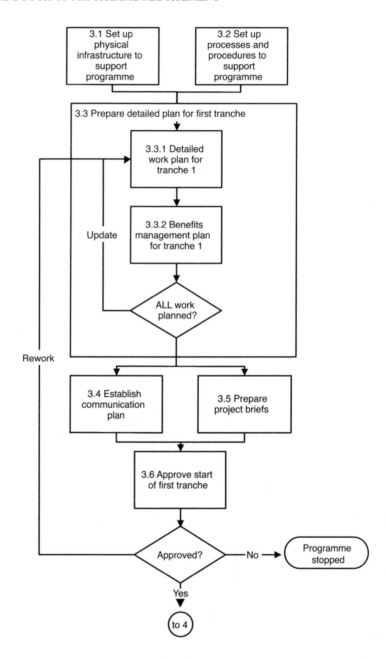

Figure 2.24 The Establish process steps

itself and should be planned and executed with the same level of attention to detail as any other project in the programme.

See Chapter 13, 'The programme office', for more information.

Inputs

Inputs are:

- the approved PDD
- defined programme processes and procedures from Section 2.3 above.

Instructions

- Develop a full listing of all infrastructure requirements with members of the PMO and other programme stakeholders.
- Discuss requirements with providers of infrastructure and services. These may be within the organization (for example, IT) or suppliers, to identify how each can best be fulfilled.
- Define and document a proposed approach to provide all required facilities and obtain programme executive approval.
- Develop a project plan, with participation from all stakeholders, to implement the approved infrastructure.
- Implement the project plan, including, design, install, test and acceptance phases.

Outputs

Outputs are:

- the required infrastructure in place, configured and operating
- the PMO team in place.

2.4.2.2 Set-up processes and procedures to support programme (step 3.2)

Why do this?

A programme is a major undertaking where large volumes of information will be processed and analysed over a long period of time. In addition, many decisions will be required, the precise nature of which is impossible to predict at the commencement of a large programme. The only way this degree of uncertainty can be effectively managed is through well-defined and documented procedures that allow every stakeholder to fully understand what is required of them, when and by whom.

Inputs

Inputs are:

- the approved PDD
- defined programme processes and procedures from Section 2.3 above.

Instructions

All programmes require the establishment of processes and procedures to control and manage information flow, reporting and, critically, decision making. Part II of this handbook contains extensive guidance on how to establish and maintain these processes and procedures. The processes and procedures required are:

- **Organization and governance:** how roles and responsibilities are to be assigned and amended.
- **Planning and control:** how planning is to be undertaken and control exercised over the programme.
- **Benefits:** How benefits are to be defined, planned, measured, managed and assured.
- **Stakeholders and communications:** How the programme will communicate with all interested parties.
- **Risk and issues:** How risks and issues will be identified, mitigated and managed.
- **Assurance and quality:** How the programme will ensure that all deliverables meet their defined standards.
- **Configuration:** How all deliverables will be defined, measured and accepted.
- **Communication** How stakeholders will be informed of programme progress and developments.
- **Accounting and financial control:** How the financial implications of the programme will be evaluated and reported.
- **Scope and change:** How variations from the original plan will be evaluated, approved and monitored.
- **Knowledge management:** How information and knowledge critical to the programme will be acquired, collated, distributed and utilized.

Each of these processes and procedures needs to be defined and documented (see Section 2.3). When all programme processes and procedures have been implemented, the PMO should provide training to team members and other stakeholders to ensure that they fully understand the procedures they will be required to follow, throughout the programme. This will almost certainly require different training to be provided to different groups of stakeholders to reflect how they will each interact with the programme.

Outputs

Outputs are:

- the processes and procedures as defined are in place, configured and fully operative;
- programme stakeholders and team members have been briefed (and trained if needed) and are now able to adequately operate the processes and procedures using the tools provided by the previous step.

2.4.2.3 Prepare detailed plan for tranche 1 (step 3.3/3.3.1)

Why do this?

The programme is now taking shape, the overall approach and plan has been agreed, the physical and procedural infrastructures are being established and the PMO team is being recruited, trained and installed. It is now time to focus on what will be achieved in the first (potentially only) tranche of projects. While the overall objectives, approach and timeline have been established as part of the PDD, this activity will further define these elements to a level that will enable the required work to be undertaken.

Inputs

If this is the first or only tranche, outputs are:

- PDD
- business architecture blueprint
- business case
- BBS
- programme plan
- summary tranche plan from Define stage.

If this is the second or later tranche, outputs are all of the above, plus:

- end tranche report for the tranche most recently completed
- latest highlight report for the programme
- updated business case
- current benefit profiles.

Instructions

The following steps refine the summary tranche plan prepared during the Define stage:

103

- Define the products (deliverables) that are the end outcome from these projects.
- State the tranche objectives by showing which parts of the programme's business architecture blueprint and benefits the tranche will deliver.
- Review and update the statement of how and when a tranches's objectives are to be achieved; by showing:
  - when the projects will deliver the products;
  - how operational change will be enabled;
  - when consequential benefits will start to flow;
  - resources required.
- Review and amend, if required, tranche controls and reporting.
- Update programme's business case.
- Review (and if necessary amend) the tranche's tolerances.
- Review the quality controls and confirm the resources needed for them will be available.
- Review, update and extend the tranche plan and forward to the programme executive for approval. Note: Do not start the tranche until this approval is granted.

Outputs

The output is the tranche plan for approval by the programme executive (see Figure 2.25).

2.4.2.4 Benefits management plan for tranche 1 (step 3.3/3.3.2)

Why do this?

To ensure that benefits have been identified, quantified and agreed with appropriate stakeholders. If benefits are to be effectively delivered, it is essential that stakeholders in the organization take full responsibility for their delivery. If this is not accomplished, the programme may well deliver the promised capability to the organization, however, no benefits will actually be realized, because operational managers (stakeholders) do not apply the programme's outputs.

Inputs

The inputs are:

- draft detailed tranche 1 programme plan
- draft updated tranche 1 project outlines
- draft programme/project resource requirements

TRANCHE PLAN

PURPOSE OF DOCUMENT

- used as the basis for programme management control throughout the tranche;
- demonstrates how a group of projects in the programme will enable organizational change to be implemented and shows how a flow of benefits will start as a result of that change;
- identifies all the projects that the tranche must manage and the products that are the end outcome from these projects;
- states the tranche's objectives showing which parts of the programme's business architecture blueprint the tranche will deliver;
- provides a statement of how and when a tranches's objectives are to be achieved, by showing the projects, operational change and resources required;
- identifies the tranche's control and reporting points and frequencies;
- provides a baseline against which tranche progress will be measured;
- records the tranche tolerances;
- specifies the quality controls for the tranche and identifies the resources needed for them.

PLAN DESCRIPTION

PLAN COVERAGE

BUSINESS ARCHITECTURE BLUEPRINT

Show which parts of the programme's blueprint this tranche will deliver

List of projects	Start	Finish	Products output	Cross-ref to blueprint

PLANNED APPROACH

QUALITY PLAN

Quality control methods to be used
Quality test or check resources

PLAN PREREQUISITES

EXTERNAL DEPENDENCIES

TOLERANCES

Time
Budget

PLAN MONITORING AND CONTROLS

REPORTING

PLANNING ASSUMPTIONS

GRAPHICAL TRANCHE PLANS:

Resources, activities, dates
Benefits breakdown structure
Benefits flow diagram
Benefits profiles
Schedule (to include)
   Activity network
   Financial budget

TABLE OF RESOURCE REQUIREMENTS

RISK ASSESSMENT

PRODUCT DESCRIPTIONS FOR MAJOR PRODUCTS

These are output from the projects in the programme that will be handed over to operational management. Show how these relate to the benefits measurement processes operational management will use to track and measure the benefits.

UPDATED BUSINESS CASE

Figure 2.25   Example template for a tranche plan

- definition of deliverables
- programme benefits
- benefit owners
- BBS.

Instructions

- Obtain benefits profiles.
- Obtain BBS.
- Obtain programme plans.
- Obtain business architecture blueprint.

- List the 'entities' that will change in order for the benefits to be realized.
- For each entity confirm the owner.
- Agree the benefits measurement definition with owner.
- Agree when the baseline measurement will take place, who will do it and who will approve it.
- Identify any gaps in the programme plan.
- Update the tranche plan to fill any gaps and to ensure the benefits management activities are fully integrated with other work.
- Update each benefit profile.

Entities are real world things that support the business, including:

- business processes
- stakeholder groups
- capability groups
- business locations
- products and services
- channels to market
- information systems
- manufacturing systems.

Outputs

The outputs are:

- updated benefits profiles approved by organization's management (see Figure 2.26)
- management commitment to deploy programme-delivered capability and measure resulting benefits
- updated tranche plan.

2.4.2.5 Establish communication plan (step 3.4)

Why do this?

Stakeholders are vital to the success of any programme. They provide critical inputs, make key decisions and receive outputs from the programme. It is therefore essential that they are well informed about the programme's objectives, approach, progress and problems.

Some stakeholders may be perceived as barriers to success, others may be less supportive than is required, while yet others will be highly supportive and provide a continuous source of energy and encouragement. Each of these stakeholders will need to be influenced (see Chapter 6, 'Stakeholder

107

BENEFIT PROFILE

PURPOSE

A definition, to understand what must be done to realize the benefit, how it will be measured, what will produce the step change in the capability of the organization so the benefit can start to be realized, any risks and issues.

DESCRIPTION OF THE BENEFIT

What is the benefit?

OBSERVABLE DIFFERENCES POST-PROGRAMME

WHICH PART OF THE ORGANIZATION WILL BENEFIT?

HOW IT WILL BE MEASURED OR TESTED

List the entities that will change in order to deliver a capability change in the organization that, in turn, will deliver the benefit required. For each entity defined, how it can be measured at the start of the programme (current) and when the changes are complete and operationalized (achieved versus target).

Current measures

To be stated when the programme starts

Target measures

To be stated when the programme is defined as the benefit required from the strategy. The achievement to be measured and compared to the target

REQUIRED CHANGES TO CURRENT BUSINESS PROCESSES

DEPENDENCIES ON OTHER BENEFITS

DEPENDENCIES ON PROGRAMMES/PROJECTS

Financial profile

	Year 1			Year 2			Year 3		
	Q1	Q2	Q3	Q4	Q1	Q2	Q3	Q4	Q1
Cost £000s									
Benefits £000s									

Notes:

1. Modify the table for the overall timescale required.
2. Because the relationship between project and benefits is often complex, the cost here might only be the direct benefits cost of activities such as measuring the benefits, with all other costs assessed in the overall business case.

Entities are real world things that support the business, including:
- Business processes
- Stakeholder groups
- Capability groups
- Business locations
- Products and services
- Channels to market
- Information systems
- Manufacturing systems

Figure 2.26   Example template for a benefit profile

management') to maximize their positive, or minimize their negative, impact upon the programme. Appropriate and timely communication with all stakeholders is one very important way to positively influence their behaviour, while poor or non-existent communication is a much quoted reason why many programmes and projects fail.

Inputs

The inputs are:

- PDD
- procedures and infrastructure.

Instructions

- Review the communications strategy contained in the PDD.
- Review physical infrastructure, processes and procedures required to support the programme.
- Review local standards for programme reporting.
- List programme stakeholders.
- List communication channels.
- Complete a stakeholder communication matrix setting out which stakeholders will receive which message, via which communications channel.
- Identify and plan activities required to deliver messages set out in communication matrix.
- Inform stakeholders of proposed communication plan.

Outputs

The outputs are:

- a stakeholder map (see Figure 2.27)
- a communications strategy and plan (see Figure 2.28).

Some of this is derived from the stakeholder analysis above and some is to support the good management of the programme.

2.4.2.6 Prepare project briefs (step 3.5)

Why do this?

The key purpose of a programme structure and plan is to ensure that all activities undertaken are directed towards a common set of goals and objectives. This is the time to ensure that all constituent projects are aligned with these objectives and initiated as per the agreed programme and tranche plans.

Preparing project briefs assists in guiding detailed project planning undertaken during the Manage stage, and helps to ensure alignment and consistency.

Inputs

Inputs are:

- approved programme definition
- proposed tranche 1 plan.

Instructions

- Review programme plan and identify when projects included in tranche 1 are scheduled to commence.
- Produce project briefs for projects in tranche 1. Forward these to the programme executive for review and comment.
- Update the briefs based on comments received.
- Obtain programme executive approval for project briefs and authorization to commence initial projects, based on approved project briefs.

Outputs

The outputs are approved project briefs for tranche 1.

Names	Interests (+)/Concerns (∇)							
	Own development and training	New job	Development of their/all staff	Managing the changes	Personal impact of the changes	Could act as sales channel	Loss of income	Learn new processes
Manage-ment	+		+	∇				
All staff	+				∇			
HR	+		+	∇				
Training staff		+						∇
Third-party training providers						+	∇	
Catering staff		+						∇

Figure 2.27   Example of a stakeholder map

What	Who	How	To	When	Why
Programme definition	Programme manager	Team briefing workshops	Programme team Project teams as appointed	When approved	Explain what the programme is about
Programme overview	SRO and manager	Presentation	All managers and staff affected	At start and as each change is due to be implemented	Explain what it is all about and why How it affects them How they will be supported
Highlight reports	Programme manager	E-mail, discuss at monthly meeting	SRO	Monthly	Report progress
End tranche and end programme reports	Programme manager	E-mail, present and discuss at review meetings	SRO	As they occur	Report achievements, get approval to continue

Progress bulletins	Programme manager	Intranet and notice boards	All	Milestones to announce good news	Keep staff informed and motivated
Exception reporting	Programme manager	Direct contact with SRO, e-mail report, then meeting to discuss	SRO	IMMEDIATELY, if programme has or is predicted to go out of tolerance	Now, don't expect to deliver agreed benefits, need to reconsider if programme is still viable/desirable

Figure 2.28 Example of a communications strategy and plan

2.4.2.7 Approve start of tranche 1 (step 3.6)

Why do this?

The programme board need to be satisfied that:

- all projects to be undertaken in tranche 1 have been correctly defined, that is, project brief approved;
- no significant changes have occurred to the approved programme definition document;
- all projects in tranche 1 will be properly initiated.

Moving into the Manage Programme stage represents the single largest increase in level of commitment throughout the lifecycle. Senior management should only approve continuation to this next stage once fully satisfied that as detailed as possible plans and estimates have been prepared and presented.

Inputs

Inputs are:

- approved programme definition
- proposed tranche 1 plan
- project briefs.

Instructions

- Provide copies of project briefs, the proposed tranche 1 plan and the approved programme definition document to the programme board or alternate approving body.
- Convene a programme board meeting and obtain approval.

112

Outputs

Outputs are:

- approved tranche 1 plan
- approved project briefs for tranche 1.

2.4.3 QUICK REFERENCE

This section summarizes the Establish stage of a programme in a quick reference form.

	Inputs	How	Who	Output	Quality	Techniques
3.1 Set up physical infracture to support programme	PDD	Identify infrastructure requirements Acquire infrastructure requirements Establish PMO	Programme manager Programme team	Infrastructure requirements PMO	Will the programme infrastructure support the programme?	Planning and procurement PMO
3.2 Set up processes and procedures to support programme	PDD	Establish (extended) programme team Define and implement programme processes and procedures	Programme manager Programme team PMO	Programme processes and procedures	Will the programme processes and procedures support the programme?	Programme processes and procedures
3.3 Prepare detailed plan for tranche 1		The two detailed steps below may be iterative				

	Inputs	How	Who	Output	Quality	Techniques
3.3.1 Detailed work plan for tranche 1	PDD Summary programme plan for tranche 1 Tranche 1 project outlines	Review existing plans Revise/update plans and PDDs as required Define deliverables that will enable capability improvement that will allow benefits to be realized	Programme manager Programme team PMO Project managers Project teams	Draft detailed (tranche 1) programme plan Draft updated tranche 1 project outlines Draft programme/ project resource requirements Definition of deliverables that will enable capability improvement that will allow benefits to be realized	Is it clear how project deliverables will enable operational improvements that will produce defined benefits? Does the work plan include all the activity needed to apply the programmes processes and procedures?	Programme planning Project planning
3.3.2 Benefits management plan for tranche 1	Draft detailed (tranche 1) programme plan Draft updated tranche 1 project outlines Draft programme/ project resource requirements Definition of deliverables that will enable capability improvement	Verify operation commits to be ready to use deliverables to improve its capability Verify benefits measurement processes are planned to be in place and operational manager commits to measure Identify any gaps in the	Programme manager Programme team Operational manager Project managers	Detailed (tranche 1) programme plan Operational management commitment to take deliverables, use them and measure improvements benefits	Does the operational manager understand what they have to do and resources they have to provide to realize and measure the benefits? Are operational managers committed to delivering the benefits? Are the programme	Benefits measurement Operational readiness planning

	that will allow benefits to be realized Programme benefits Benefit owners BBS	draft plan with regard to operation readiness work and benefits measurement work Integrate benefits			and project plans sufficiently complete to commence tranche 1? Are resource requirements consistent with the programme business case	
3.4 Establish communication plan	PDD	Identify and agree stakeholders Identify stakeholder concerns and required messages Establish communication channels Map stakeholders, channel and messages Develop communication plan	Programme manager Programme team Change manager	Programme communication plan	Does the programme communication plan establish how all stakeholders will be kept informed of all aspects of the programme?	Change management communications planning
3.5 Prepare project briefs	Programme PDD Detailed (tranche 1) programme plan Updated tranche 1 project outlines	Specify project objectives and deliverables Identify project stakeholders, risks, benefits and approach Assemble project brief	Project managers Project teams Programme manager Programme team PMO	Tranche 1 project briefs	Are the project briefs of sufficient quality to allow the initiation of all proposed projects	Project planning and definition

	Inputs	How	Who	Output	Quality	Techniques
3.6 Approve start of tranche 1	PDD Detailed (tranche 1) programme plan Operational management commitment Programme processes and procedures Tranche 1 project briefs Programme/ project resource requirements	Senior programme management review	Programme board (senior management)	Go/no-go decision, whether to proceed to tranche 1	Has a clear decision been made? Have all the necessary commitments been obtained from all the stakeholders for this tranche?	Review and decision making

2.5 MANAGE PROGRAMME

2.5.1 OVERVIEW

2.5.1.1 Purpose and objectives

The Manage programme stage is the business end of the programme. While this is represented as one stage of five in the whole programme management lifecycle, this stage is likely to comprise at least 80 per cent of the elapsed time of the programme. All earlier stages have been preparation for this one.

If all preceding stages have been completed effectively, the programme will have a clear set of objectives, a plan every stakeholder understands and approves, plus the infrastructure, team and procedures to carry it through.

The Manage programme stage builds upon these sound foundations to deliver the benefits that the organization requires.

2.5.1.2 Inputs

Inputs to the Manage programme stage are the materials and decisions produced during the earlier stages, including:

- infrastructure requirements
- programme processes and procedures

- detailed (tranche 1) programme plan
- tranche 1 project briefs
- programme/project resource requirements
- programme communication plan

In other words, everything the PMO and programme team will require to undertake the programme.

2.5.1.3 Scaling

Scaling is more relevant during this stage than at any other point in the lifecycle. Tasks required to establish a small programme are much the same as for a large one. There will be more stakeholders, locations, individual projects, and so on, in a larger programme, but the steps are still essentially the same. The steps are also the same for the Manage programme stage; however, here scale can have a significant impact, with numbers of stakeholders, locations, individual projects, and so on, influencing the size of the programme team and how it is organized. The PMO similarly will vary in its configuration and size, depending on the scale of the programme. Each individual project within the programme is likely to have its own project team and infrastructure, the most significant impact of scale therefore is on coordinating resources, infrastructure and procedures. An example of this is programme IT systems. For very large programmes, it may be economically efficient to implement programme-wide systems that improve the efficiency of data collection and reporting, for smaller programmes this may be unviable.

Additionally, in a large programme, there are a significantly greater number of interactions: between organizations, between people in the organizations and between projects. These interactions all have to be managed to avoid confusion and chaos. As stated above, while the process is essentially the same for a small programme as a large one, in a larger programme more rigour and formality is required if increased risk of failure is to be avoided. This requirement reflects the fact that as more elements, that is, projects, organization units, stakeholders, become involved in a programme, the complexity increases exponentially, in line with the possible number of interactions. This level of complexity rapidly swamps even the most experienced and talented programme manager's ability to manage and therefore requires more formal procedures to prevent errors and omissions.

2.5.1.4 Critical success factors

Despite the careful planning and preparation that will have been undertaken up to this point, it is inevitable that as soon as the first projects get under way things

117

will begin to go wrong. Field Marshal Helmuth Karl Bernhard von Moltke (1800–1891) famously said about military plans that 'no plan ever survives first contact with the enemy'. From the moment the first project commences, plans come under pressure. It is at this point that another famous military quotation comes in to play: 'Plans are worthless, but planning is everything' (Dwight D. Eisenhower in a speech to the National Defense Executive Reserve Conference in Washington, DC, 14 November 1957). The key point is that thorough planning is essential if all stakeholders are to be fully prepared for the challenges of the programme and respond flexibly to unexpected events. To remain rigidly fixed to a given plan will inevitably end in disaster. The most important contribution a programme manager can make to the success of a programme is to remain focused, at all times, on the benefits required by the organization and to continuously update the key stakeholders on what needs to be done to achieve them. This may require that the original plan, or at least elements of it, be adapted or even significantly rethought as events unfold. Flexibility, while focused on the programme's objectives, is the key to success. Adapting original plans to accommodate changes in knowledge and/or circumstances is vitally important; however, so too is a disciplined process of change control, if the programme is not to descend into anarchy. There is a vast difference between a flexible plan properly managed and no plan at all.

The key activities to be undertaken during this stage are set out in Figures 2.29 and 2.30.

2.5.2 DETAILED PROCESS STEPS

2.5.2.1 START-UP TRANCHE (STEP 4.1)

Why do this?

A programme seeks to ensure that the benefits required by the organization are realized, by managing a portfolio of projects. It is organizational changes, that is, enhanced capabilities, enabled by products delivered by projects that deliver these benefits. This step initiates approved projects with clear instructions (project brief) in order to produce a PDD (also known as PID) and plan consistent with and complementary to all other projects in the programme.

Inputs

Inputs are:

- business architecture blueprint
- programme plan

118

4 Manage programme
Level 1

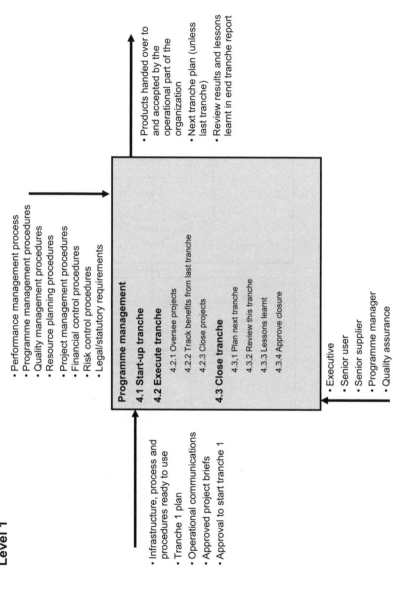

- Performance management process
- Programme management procedures
- Quality management procedures
- Resource planning procedures
- Project management procedures
- Financial control procedures
- Risk control procedures
- Legal/statutory requirements

Programme management

4.1 Start-up tranche

4.2 Execute tranche

4.2.1 Oversee projects

4.2.2 Track benefits from last tranche

4.2.3 Close projects

4.3 Close tranche

4.3,1 Plan next tranche

4.3.2 Review this tranche

4.3.3 Lessons learnt

4.3.4 Approve closure

- Infrastructure, process and procedures ready to use
- Tranche 1 plan
- Operational communications
- Approved project briefs
- Approval to start tranche 1

- Products handed over to and accepted by the operational part of the organization
- Next tranche plan (unless last tranche)
- Review results and lessons learnt in end tranche report

- Executive
- Senior user
- Senior supplier
- Programme manager
- Quality assurance

Figure 2.29   The Manage process

119

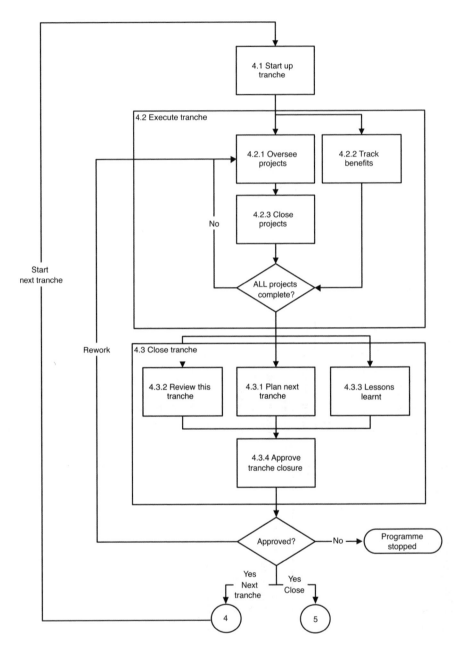

Figure 2.30 The Manage process steps

- BBS
- infrastructure requirements
- programme processes and procedures
- detailed (tranche 1) programme plan
- updated tranche 1project outlines
- programme/project resource requirements
- programme communication plan
- project briefs approved at the end of the previous stage or tranche.

Instructions

- Appoint the project executive and project manager. utilize the project briefs to explain what each project is required to achieve and use the PDD (and any other appropriate material) to explain the programme objectives and how their project will be required to contribute.
- Instruct the project manager to produce a PDD, for approval by the programme board. The project will need to go through the following steps to produce this document:
  1. Design and appoint project team.
  2. Define project approach.
  3. Identify and evaluate impact of project stakeholders.
  4. Define and plan project deliverables and quality criteria.
  5. Map project deliverables (products) to benefits.
  6. Plan project milestones, activities and timetable.
  7. Estimate and plan project resources.
  8. Define project risks and mitigation approach.
  9. Refine business case.
  10. Set-up project controls (in line with the programme infrastructure, processes and procedures set up in 3.1 and 3.2).
  11. Assemble PDD.
  12. Obtain approval of PDD from programme executive.
- Once the PDD has been approved the project executive will need to be informed.

Outputs

Outputs are:

- project briefs
- PDDs.

Note: Not all projects start at the beginning of a tranche. For those that start later in the tranche repeat the above steps when required.

121

2.5.2.2 Execute tranche (step 4.2)

Why do this?

The primary role of the programme manager and the PMO is to ensure that planned benefits are realized. To this end, they must oversee individual projects, monitoring their progress against plan and achievement of the objectives assigned in the PDD.

As stated previously, not everything will proceed as planned and it is therefore important to identify and respond to variances quickly and effectively.

Inputs

Inputs from the programme are:

- current programme plan and business case
- project initiation timetable (plan)
- a rolled-up view of all project plans plus the cumulative impact of recommended changes
- updated business architecture blueprint, showing how the organization is changing as the projects deliver
- benefits variances for programme – expressed as the sum of actual benefits plus current plan expected benefits versus baseline expected benefits.

Inputs from each project, via the PMO are:

- periodic project highlight reports, that is, regular progress and expectation information
- end of stage reports, stage plans and any other decision gateway approvals
- deliverables and acceptance progress and expectations
- project exception reports and plans
- risk and issues logs
- current project plans
- time variances – for the next stage in each project, as planned date compared to baseline date
- deliverables variances – actual and expected
- cost variances for each project, as actual compared to baseline expected cost to date, and estimated cost to complete compared to baseline plan.

Instructions

Oversee projects (step 4.2.1) and track benefits (step 4.2.2.):

- At the frequency agreed in each PDD(communications plan) obtain a copy of the project's highlight report.

- At each project decision gateway, obtain the relevant report from the project manager:
  - end of initiation: PDD and next stage plan
  - end of each project stage: end stage report and next stage plan
  - end of the project lessons learned report and end project report.
- At the project lifecycle decision gateways (additional to the above), obtain decision gateway reports, as specified in local standards.
- Obtain reports on the actual benefits realized from those appointed to measure them.
- Prior to reporting to the programme board (see below), undertake the following analysis, health check assessment and overall rating:
  - Assess the programme's objectives and scope:
    - Update the business architecture blueprint to show changes achieved so far.
    - From project briefs approved in the last period, indicate which projects are now actively delivering what changes.
    - From the end project reports for projects closed in the last period, indicate the changes that have now been achieved.
    - From the projects' requests for change approvals in the last period, update the blueprint to reflect the change of scope in the projects.
    - Determine if there are now gaps in the change requirements depicted in the blueprint by unallocated items.
    - For these gaps determine what new projects are needed or which current projects need to have their scope increased.
    - Estimate the cost of these changes, estimate the impact on benefit flows, include these figures in the roll-up below.
  - Analyse the status of the programme:
    - Produce a rolled up summary for the whole programme. Derive variances against the baseline programme plan, for costs, time and benefits.
    - Determine whether rolled-up costs and time are within the tolerance agreed by the programme executive.
    - Compare the rolled up estimate of benefits with the baselined benefit profile, determine whether the variance is outside agreed tolerance limits.
    - From the risks and issues for each project assess whether there is an adverse impact on the programme such that it has or is likely to exceed its tolerances.
    - From the risks and issues logs for the programme, if there are actions assigned to the outstanding risks and issues that have not progressed

to plan, assess whether there is an adverse impact on the programme such that it has or is likely to exceed its tolerances.

- Make sure all the projects are following the prescribed process and are being effectively managed.

- For each project, if it has passed a stage boundary, check whether the project board has approved continuing the project.

- Obtain a summary of operational changes in the organization, implemented since the last report. These will be as a result of the products delivered by projects. This must be accompanied by evidence that these products were all delivered to an acceptable quality standard. There must also be evidence that the operational part of the business has accepted the products, is using them and is monitoring the improvements so actual benefits realized can be assessed.

- Ensure that all project risks and issues are all being recorded and actively managed. Also make sure that the expected future impact of risks and issues (including contingency) is fully included in current project plans.

- Look for evidence that the projects have adequate and properly executed management control points. Process management dashboards, that is, regular summary reports containing key project performance metrics, can help with this.

- Examine the impact of any changes in the projects that have a knock on effect via dependencies:
  - Review projects upon which other projects are dependent, or where several projects combine deliverables. Analyse the effect of any delay in these projects that affects the planned completion of dependent project deliverables. Where receiving projects are at risk of slippage, this should be managed as an issue.
  - Review projects that rely upon deliverables (products) from another programme. Identify all risks due to non or late delivery and manage as an issue.
  - Identify changes in scope to any of the products a project will deliver to another project. Check that the new product definition meets the requirements of the receiving projects. If not, log and manage this as an issue.
  - Identify changes in requirements for any products a project will receive from another programme. Check that the new product meets the requirements of the receiving projects. If not, log and manage this as an issue.

- Identify external and other influences that may affect the future outcome of the programme and the strategy.

- Liaise with programme sponsor and other senior managers, as required, for advice on external trends in your organization's external environment that might impact the programme. Where these are detected, recommend any changes that will be required in the programme.
- Examine the issues log for formal requests for change (change of scope, change of priorities, and so on, for any project in the programme or for the whole programme).
- Assess the cumulative impact of potential changes and add to the values already calculated.
- Assess the effect of the above on current priorities:
  - where potential changes to the programme will now exclude projects, because higher priority projects are going to consume the resources available;
  - where potential changes to the programme will now free up some resources, so that lower priority projects could be included;
  - where external influences change the factors that will mean some parts of the programme now have a different priority ranking.
- Rate the overall state of the programme using the guidelines below and the findings from step 2.4. above:
  - green (if all of the following apply):
    - ○ programme is within tolerance using the rolled up values from all projects;
    - ○ projects have demonstrated without qualification that risks and issues are being properly managed;
    - ○ projects have demonstrated without qualification that the project management process and management control points are being properly executed.
  - amber (if any of the following applies):
    - ○ programme is within tolerance using the rolled-up values from all the programme's projects, but one or more projects are out of tolerance;
    - ○ some risks or issues are not being adequately recorded, are not being adequately managed, or the impact/corrective action/preventative measures are not included in current project plans; whilst this is not necessarily cause for immediate concern project management attention is required to address this;
    - ○ there are some minor breaches of the project management process; while not necessarily cause for immediate concern project management attention is required to address this;
  - red – a cause for immediate concern that must be addressed and corrected before the programme continues (if any of the following apply):

- ○ programme is outside (or predicted to go outside) the tolerance agreed using the rolled-up values from all the programme's projects;
- ○ risks or issues are not being adequately recorded, are not being adequately managed, or the impact/corrective action/preventative measures are not included in current project plans; there is cause for immediate concern as project management attention is not addressing the problem;
- ○ there are significant or frequent breaches of the project management process; there is cause for immediate concern as project management attention is not addressing the problem;
- ○ if the programme is not green but you have some doubts about the precise state of the programme/project, request a health check or audit (see Chapter 3, 'Programme organization and governance').
- – Update estimates to complete the rest of the programme, for costs, time and benefits.
- – Obtain a copy of the current business case for the programme, update it using the actual data collected above, and the estimates to complete the programme.
- – Using the above inputs, report to the programme executive as follows:
  - ○ Highlight reports, to the schedule agreed in the communications plan (a section of the PDD), with recommendations to start projects by attaching their project mandates (see Section 2.5.2.6, 'Approve tranche closure');
  - ○ programme exception report and plan; do this immediately if the status is red.
- – Document the decisions made by the programme executive while directing the programme, including actions.
- – Distribute these documented decisions to the programme executive and any other stakeholder as stated in the communication plan.
- – Distribute the actions to those to whom they are assigned.
- – Update the programme plan to reflect the decisions made and actions agreed.
- – Send all outputs to the PMO for storing in the programme's filing system, and to maintain version logs
- – Track benefits: costs attributable to each benefit and measures of benefits realized so far. Update the benefit profiles. See also Chapter 5, 'Benefits Management'.

Close projects:

- • The programme manager will receive notification that a project is complete from the project manager together with an end of project report.

- If completion is approved by the project board, the project will be decommissioned and a project evaluation carried out. It is important that this evaluation is assessed against the objectives of the whole programme. In particular, this is to determine whether there are any follow on actions from the project that are critical to the success of the programme and the realization of the benefits planned.
- The projects produce and hand over their outputs to operational functions within the organization. Their use and the consequential changes are the outcome, which if successful realizes benefits. Often the outputs from several projects need to be delivered together, as operational functions can only change when they have a full set. For example; for a new training facility, the building, new processes to manage training, IT, catering, and so on, are all required, but might have been delivered by separate projects.
- The programme designed the project portfolio during the Define stage. It must now ensure that projects hand over complete sets of deliverables (products) as required, and that the operational functions are ready and able to use them.

Outputs

The output is a highlight report (see Figure 2.31).

2.5.2.3 Close tranche (Manage tranche boundary)

Planning subsequent tranches cannot be fully completed until preceding ones have completed. However, it will always be necessary to commence planning a tranche before completion of earlier ones. Therefore, while steps within 'Manage programme' are presented sequentially, they will inevitably be undertaken concurrently.

Why do this?

The purpose of this step is to prepare a plan to deliver the next tranche of projects and therefore programme benefits. The tranche approach is intended to enable organizations to take on a manageable level of programme activity and at the same time allows learning from early tranches to be used to plan and execute later ones. A classic example would be an initial tranche comprising of one or more pilot projects that will deliver benefits in their own right but will also develop improved organization capability to be deployed later in the programme. The pilots might confirm both that the programme's approach produces the required deliverables and that these work well in operational use. Benefits of this approach include early wins for a part of the organization and a reduction in the risk of failure for the rest of the programme.

HIGHLIGHT REPORT

PURPOSE OF DOCUMENT

To provide the programme executive with a summary of the programme status at intervals defined by them.

DATE OF REPORT

PERIOD COVERED

OVERALL STATUS

Programme and projects	Red/amber/green
This programme	
{Project 1}	
{Project 2}	
{Project 3}	

BUDGET STATUS

Cost variances for the programme, as actual cost to date compared to baselined expected cost to date, and estimated total cost compared to baselined total cost.

Cost variances for each project, as actual cost to date compared to baselined expected cost to date, and estimated total cost compared to baselined total cost.

SCHEDULE STATUS

Time variances for the next tollgate in this programme, as planned date compared to baseline date.

Time variances for the next tollgate in each project, as planned date compared to baseline date.

BENEFITS STATUS

Benefits variances for this programme, as (actual benefits plus current plan expected benefits) compared to baselined expected benefits.

PROGRAMME TRANCHES COMPLETED (TOLLGATE APPROVALS) DURING THE PERIOD

Tranche/tollgate	Date approved

PROJECT STAGES COMPLETED DURING THE PERIOD

Project stage	Date approved

TRANCHES/TOLLGATE DUE FOR COMPLETION IN THE NEXT PERIOD

Tranche/tollgate	Date planned

PROJECT STAGES DUE FOR COMPLETION IN THE NEXT PERIOD

Project stage	Date planned

PROBLEMS

Actual

New risks and issues from this programme and its projects, where the impact cannot be kept within the agreed tolerances for the whole programme.

Potential

New risks and issues from this programme and its projects, where they could impact the whole programme, but the projects can currently contain the impact within their agreed tolerance.

PROGRAMME ISSUE STATUS

IMPACT OF CHANGES

Budget
Schedule
Benefit

Figure 2.31 Example template for a programme highlight report

129

When planning, programme managers and their teams should look to extract all 'lessons learned' from earlier tranches, and indeed previous projects and programmes.

Inputs

Inputs are:

- programme definition
- business architecture blueprint
- BBS
- current programme plan
- end tranche report for the tranche just ending
- latest highlight report for the programme
- current business case
- current benefit profiles.

Instructions

- Identify the operational change and organization capability improvement that this next tranche will deliver.
- Determine which group of projects in the programme will enable this organizational change to be implemented and show benefits that will result from the change
- State the tranche's objectives by showing which parts of the programme's business architecture blueprint the tranche will deliver.
- Review and update the statement of how and when a tranches's objectives are to be achieved, showing when the projects will deliver the major products, how operational change will be enabled, when the consequential benefits will start to flow and resources required for project and benefit tracking.
- Review and update the tranche's control and reporting points and frequencies, based on controls and reporting in previous tranches.
- Update the programme's business case (when the data is available from the tranche just ending).
- Review and, if necessary, propose a change to the tranche's tolerances, based on experience from previous tranches.
- Review the quality controls for the tranche and confirm the resources needed for them will be available.

Outputs

Outputs are:

- tranche plan for approval by the programme executive
- tranche plan.

2.5.2.4 Prepare detailed plan for next tranche (step 4.3.1)

Why do this?

The end of each tranche is a control point; approval for the next tranche must be sought. The programme must demonstrate that what has been achieved so far is working well enough to warrant continuing. Lessons learned from the tranche now ending and any earlier tranches must be studied carefully and the programme refined where necessary, ideally to the improve chance of success and increase the benefits.

Inputs

Inputs are:

- PDD
- business architecture blueprint
- business case
- BBS
- programme plan
- summary tranche plan from Define stage.
- end tranche report for the tranche most recently completed
- Latest highlight report for the programme
- updated business case
- current benefit profiles.

Instructions

The following steps refine the summary tranche plan prepared during the Define stage:

- Define the products (deliverables) that are the end outcome from these projects.
- State the tranche objectives by showing which parts of the programme's business architecture blueprint and benefits the tranche will deliver.
- Review and update the statement of how and when a tranches's objectives are to be achieved, by showing:

  - when the Projects will deliver the products;
  - how operational change will be enabled;

- when consequential benefits will start to flow;
- resources required.
- Review and amend, if required, tranche controls and reporting.
- Update programme's business case.
- Review (and if necessary amend) the tranche's tolerances.
- Review the quality controls and confirm the resources needed for them will be available.
- Review, update and extend the tranche plan and forward to the programme executive for approval. Note: *Do not start the tranche until this approval is granted.*

Outputs

The output is a tranche plan for approval by the programme executive.

2.5.2.5 Review this tranche (step 4.3.2)

Why do this?

The purpose of this step is to demonstrate to the programme board that:

- the programme is on target to deliver the benefits required;
- a current valid business case exists;
- the programme should continue.

If any of the preceding points are not the case, the programme should be restructured or terminated. As previously stated, the tranche approach allows an organization to tackle the programme in manageable sections and derive learning from each tranche before continuing. 'Review this tranche' provides an important checkpoint for both the progress and process of the programme. Outcomes from this step provide an up-to-date status and understanding, which should assist the controlled start and monitoring of later tranches. Clearly if this is the last or only tranche of the programme, these activities are subsumed into stage 5 of the programme lifecycle, that is, the Closure stage.

Inputs

From each project, via the PMO, the inputs are:

- highlight reports
- end of stage reports, stage plans and any other decision gateway approvals
- project exception reports and plans
- risk and issues logs
- current project plans.

For the programme, the inputs are:

- current business case
- risk and issues logs
- current programme plan, including actual data to date for time, costs and benefits.

A programme summary, to highlight:

- time variances for the next stage in each project, as planned date compared to baseline date
- cost variances for each project, as actual cost to date compared to baselined expected cost to date, and estimated total cost compared to baselined total cost.
- benefits variances for this programme, as actual benefits plus current plan expected benefits compared to baselined expected benefits.

Instructions

Having identified that the current tranche is ending:

- Organize a programme board meeting to consider the reports that this process step will produce.
- Obtain a copy of the last programme highlight report.
- For any project decision gateway that has occurred since the last programme highlight report, obtain the following relevant reports from the project manager:
  - end of initiation: PDD and next stage plan
  - end of each project stage: end stage report and next stage plan
  - end of the project: lessons learned report and end project report.
- At the project lifecycle decision gateways (additional to the above), obtain decision gateway reports, as specified in local standards.
- Obtain reports on the actual benefits realized from the those appointed to measure benefits.
- Analyse the status of the programme.
- Produce a rolled up summary for the whole programme. Derive summary variances against the baseline programme plan, for costs, time and benefits.
- Determine whether rolled-up costs and time are within the tolerance agreed by the programme board.
- Compare the rolled up estimate of benefits with the baseline profile, determine whether the variance is outside agreed tolerance limits.

- From the risks and issues for each project, assess whether there is an adverse impact on the programme such that it has or is likely to exceed its tolerances.
- From the risks and issues logs for the programme, if there are actions assigned to the outstanding risks and issues that have not progressed to plan, assess whether there is an adverse impact on the programme such that it has or is likely to exceed its tolerances.
- Make sure all projects are following the prescribed process and are being effectively managed.
- Ensure the relevant project board has approved each project stage gateway.
- Obtain a summary of operational changes implemented since the last report. These will be as a result of the products delivered by the programme's projects. This must be accompanied by evidence that products were delivered to an acceptable quality standard. There must also be evidence that operational functions within the business have accepted the products, are using them and are monitoring the improvements so that actual benefits can be assessed.
- Ensure that all risks and issues are being recorded and actively managed. Also make sure that the expected future impact of risks and issues (including contingency) is fully included in current project plans.
- Ensure that projects have adequate and properly executed management control points. Process management dashboards can help with this.
- Examine the impact of any changes in the projects that have a knock on effect via dependencies.
- Look at projects that deliver something to other projects, or where several projects have to combine their deliverables before handing over to the organization. If there has been any delay in these projects that affects the planned completion of these deliverables, analyse the effect on the receiving projects. If this puts the receiving projects out of tolerance, log and manage this as an issue.
- Examine the impact of any changes in the projects that have a knock on effect via dependencies:
  - Review projects upon which other projects are dependent, or where several projects combine deliverables. Analyse the effect of any delay in these projects that affects the planned completion of dependent project deliverables. Where receiving projects are at risk of slippage, this should be managed as an issue.
  - Review projects that rely upon deliverables (products) from another programme. Identify all risks due to non or late delivery and manage as an issue.
- Identify external and other influences that may affect the future outcome of the programme and the strategy.

- Liaise with programme sponsor and other senior managers, as required, for advice on external trends in your organization's external environment that might impact the programme. Where these are detected recommend any changes that will be required in the programme.
- Examine the issues log for formal requests for change (change of scope, change of priorities, and so on, for any project in the programme or for the whole programme). See Chapter 7, 'Management of risks and issues'.
- Assess the cumulative impact of potential changes and add to the values already calculated.
- Assess the effect of the above on current priorities:
  - where potential changes to the programme will now exclude projects, because higher priority projects are going to consume the resources available;
  - where potential changes to the programme will now free up some resources, so that lower priority could be included;
  - where external influences change the factors that will mean some parts of the programme now have a different priority ranking.
- Rate the overall state of the programme using the guidelines below and the findings from section 2.4. above.
  - green (if all of the following apply):
    - ○ programme is within tolerance using the rolled-up values from all projects;
    - ○ projects have demonstrated without qualification that risks and issues are being properly managed;
    - ○ projects have demonstrated without qualification that the project management process and management control points are being properly executed.
  - amber (if any of the following applies):
    - ○ programme is within tolerance using the rolled up values from all the programme's projects, but one or more projects are out of tolerance;
    - ○ some risks or issues are not being adequately recorded, are not being adequately managed, or the impact/corrective action/preventative measures are not included in current project plans; whilst this is not necessarily cause for immediate concern, project management attention is required to address this;
    - ○ there are some minor breaches of the project management process; whilst not necessarily cause for immediate concern project management attention is required to address this.
  - red – a cause for immediate concern that must be addressed and corrected before the programme should continue (if any of the following apply):

- ○ programme is outside (or predicted to go outside) the tolerance agreed using the rolled-up values from all the programme's projects;
- ○ risks or issues are not being adequately recorded, are not being adequately managed, or the impact/corrective action/preventative measures are not included in current project plans; there is cause for immediate concern as project management attention is not addressing the problem;
- ○ there are significant or frequent breaches of the project management process; there is cause for immediate concern as project management attention is not addressing the problem;
- ○ if the programme is not green, but you have some doubts about the precise state of the programme/project, request a health check or audit (see Chapter 3, 'Programme organization and governance').
- Obtain a summary of outstanding programme risks. Reassess the programme's risk from now to completion.
- Update estimates to complete the rest of the programme, for costs, time and benefits.
- Obtain a copy of the current business case for the programme, update it using the actual data collected above and the estimates to complete the programme.
- Using the above inputs, prepare the report(s) below for the programme board's approval:
  - end of tranche report (decision gateway approvals)
  - programme exception report and plan; do this immediately if the status is red.

Outputs

Outputs to the programme board are:

- end of tranche report (see Figure 2.32)
- exception report and plan (Note: Attach the latest copy of the programme highlight report).

2.5.2.6 Lessons learned (step 4.3.3)

Why do this?

It is inevitable that the programme as undertaken will be different, to some degree, from the one planned. A structured review of lessons learned provides an opportunity to ensure that any problems, and opportunities, encountered during the current tranche can be addressed and hopefully avoided or exploited in the future. One of the problems with this type of review is that it can often be seen as

END OF TRANCHE REPORT

PURPOSE OF DOCUMENT

The purpose of the end tranche report is to give a summary of progress to date, the overall programme situation and sufficient information to ask for a programme executive decision on what to do next with the programme.

CURRENT TRANCHE PLAN, INCLUDING:

- actuals for time and cost
- actual benefits realized
- variances for time, cost and benefits against the baselined plan and benefits profile.

STATUS OF THE PROGRAMME:

Red, amber or green

PROGRAMME PLAN OUTLOOK

- estimates for time and cost to complete the programme
- estimate for benefits still to be realized as an updated benefits profile
- variances for estimated time, cost and benefits (for the whole programme) against the baselined plan and benefits profile.

BUSINESS CASE REVIEW

RISK REVIEW

PROGRAMME ISSUES

QUALITY STATISTICS

PROGRAMME MANAGER'S RECOMMENDATION

Figure 2.32   Example template for an end of tranche report

'fighting the last battle', that is, making sure the same problems don't arise again, rather than focusing on broader learning. This is a danger that must be guarded against; however, there is great value in understanding:

- what worked well, so that it can be retained and encouraged;
- what worked less well, so that it can be planned for and avoided.

The most productive outcome from this step is typically a relatively small number of lessons that can be effectively applied to provide real improvements for future activities.

Inputs

Inputs are:

- project lessons learned; from individual project completion
- programme lessons learned; cumulative from all projects, tranches, and so on.

Instructions

Collate information from lessons learned reports into a summary for the tranche currently closing. If required, convene a workshop attended by members of programme and project teams to provide additional input and evaluation of important lessons to be learned.

Outputs

Ouptus are:

- Successes – what worked well
- Shortfalls – what worked less well.

2.5.2.7 Approve tranche closure (step 4.3.4)

Why do this?

Each tranche has been approved by the programme board, who authorize resources to enhance one or more of the organization's capabilities and thereby derive the planned benefits. Now that all projects in the current tranche have been completed, it is important to ensure that an enhanced capability has been created and that benefits are being both delivered and measured. Where there are further tranches to a programme, ensuring benefits are being delivered, as planned, is normally a prerequisite to obtaining approval for the next tranche.

Inputs

Inputs are:

- end of tranche report
- exception report and plan
- programme highlight report.

Instructions

- Provide copies of end of tranche report, exception report and programme highlight report to the programme board.
- Convene a programme board meeting and obtain approval for tranche completion.
- Forward a minute of the approval to the PMO for baselining and version control.
- If this is the end of the programme, go to Stage 5, Closure.
- Otherwise review and conclude 'Plan next tranche'.

Outputs

Outputs from the programme board are:

- decision gateway decisions; update the end of tranche report
- decisions on recommendations for dealing with issues, including request for change decisions, update the risk and issues logs
- decisions on recommendations for managing risks, update the risk and issues logs
- decisions on exception reports and plans, update the strategic programme plan
- other ad hoc decisions and requests
- actions agreed as a consequence of the decisions, updated programme plan and risk and issues logs
- updated individual project plan, risk and issues
- approved project mandates for next tranche project start-ups.

2.5.3 QUICK REFERENCE

This section summarizes the Manage programme stage of a programme in a quick reference form.

	Inputs	How	Who	Output	Quality	Techniques
4.1 Start up tranche	Infrastructure requirements Programe processes and procedures Detailed (tranche) programme plan Updated tranche project outlines Programme/ project resource requirements Programme communi- cation plan Project briefs	Issue project briefs to project teams Define project governance and reporting requirements Define project processes and procedures to be adopted Projects produce PDDs (PIDs), programme reviews for compliance with programme objectives and plans Approve project plans and procedures Approve project resource	Programme manager Programme team PMO Project managers Project teams Programme sponsors	Approved PDDs (PIDs) Projects commenced	Are the project plans sufficiently robust to commence the projects in this tranche? Are resources available/ affordable to commence the projects in this tranche? Do the project procedures comply with the requirements established for the programme? Are all projects under way? Are projects within project tolerance, is the programme without tolerance?	Project planning

	Inputs	How	Who	Output	Quality	Techniques
4.2 Execute tranche						
4.2.1 Oversee projects	Programme capabilities Project briefs Approved project plans Approved project resources Approved project procedures Projects commenced	Monitor progress and achievement Evaluate project progress on the programme's issues, risks, business case and benefits Ensure projects maintain procedures Report variations to progress and achievement, reforecast benefits Initiate corrective actions Review and amend plan as required Manage dependencies	Programme manager Programme team PMO Project managers Project teams Programme sponsors All other stakeholders	Completed projects Project deliverables	Are the projects, and therefore the programme, achieving their objectives? Are there any situations developing that could cause the programme to miss its objectives? Is senior management being kept fully appraised of the programme's progress and likely outcome?	Project management Programme management
4.2.2 Track benefits	Programme benefits Benefit owners BBS	Confirm capabilities delivered, signed off and in use Confirm benefits being measured Confirm benefits expected against	Programme manager Programme team PMO Project managers Project teams Operational managers	Deliverables/ capabilities handed over to the organization Benefits measurements Benefits achievement forecast	Have deliverables/ capabilities, necessary for benefits to be achieved been handed over to operational management? Has operational	Approval and acceptance management Financial and business reporting Financial and business planning

	Inputs	How	Who	Output	Quality	Techniques
		target (as actual benefits to date plus reforecast)	Programme sponsors		management deployed the deliverables/ capabilities? Has operational management implemented measurement procedures for the benefit? Is benefits achievement information being provided to the programme?	
4.2.3 Close projects	Completed projects Project deliverables Deliverables/ capabilities handed over to the organization Benefits measurements Benefits achievement forecast	Confirm project delivered all its products Re-affirm commitment to use/ measure receive lessons learned and project review reports Confirm project de-commissioned	Programme manager Programme team PMO Project managers Project teams Operational managers Programme sponsors All other stakeholders	Closed projects Project lessons learned Project closure sign-off (programme board)	Has the project handed over all deliverables? Has the project mitigated/ closed all residual risks? Has the project fulfilled/ transferred all programme dependencies?	Post project review Review and documentation

	Inputs	How	Who	Output	Quality	Techniques
4.3 Close tranche						
4.3.1 Plan next tranche	PDD Summary programme plan for tranche just ending Tranche just ending project outlines	Review existing plans Revise/update plans and PDDs as required Define deliverables that will enable capability improvement that will allow benefits to be realized	Programme manager Programme team PMO Project managers Project teams	Draft detailed (next tranche) programme plan Draft updated next tranche project outlines Draft programme/project resource requirements Definition of deliverables that will enable capability improvement that will allow benefits to be realized	Is it clear how project deliverables will enable operational improvements that will produce defined benefits? Does the work plan include all the activity needed to apply the programme's processes and procedures?	Programme planning Project planning
4.3.2 Review this tranche	Closed projects Project lessons learned Project closure sign-off (programme board)	Confirm all projects are closed Confirm all benefits measured as agreed	Programme manager Programme team PMO Programme board	Tranche closure documentation	Has the tranche handed over all deliverables? Has the tranche mitigated/closed all residual risks? Has the tranche fulfilled/transferred all programme dependencies?	Review and documentation

	Inputs	How	Who	Output	Quality	Techniques
4.3.3 Lessons learned	Project lessons learned Programme lessons learned	Assemble all project and programme lessons learned Recommend any follow on actions	Programme manager Programme team PMO Programme board Project managers	Tranche lessons learned	Have all lessons from this tranche been identified, analysed, documented and made available to future tranches/ programmes?	Post-tranche review
4.3.4 Approve tranche closure	Tranche closure documentation Tranche lessons learned	Programme board review to confirm tranche closure and approve start of next tranche (if any)	Programme manager Programme board	Tranche closure sign-off Next tranche approved (if any)	Is the operation now in a steady state with the new capabilities? Do we have enough benefit measures to confirm the business case?	Review meeting

2.6 CLOSURE

2.6.1 OVERVIEW

2.6.1.1 Purpose and objectives

Closure is, as the name implies, the end of the programme. Closure often does not happen at all and many programmes do not so much end as fade away. As the programme nears completion, key team members are re-assigned to 'more important' activities and the importance of finishing the programme as well as it began is often sacrificed to false expediency. There are a number of specific tasks that should be achieved during this stage if the good work of earlier stages is not to be undermined. These tasks include:

● Undertake decommissioning of the programme team, PMO and the physical infrastructure used to support the programme as a properly managed project in its own right. Failing to do this will lead to equipment being lost and team members becoming frustrated and demoralized as, possibly, years of hard work are devalued by a poor ending.

- Hand over records and data to the organization. Many programmes produce initial positive results only for the long-term benefits to be squandered because knowledge and information is not handed over to the organization in an effective manner.
- Extract the final lessons learned from the programme team before it disbands and the knowledge is potentially lost. This will be particularly true if, as is often the case, a high proportion of the team are contractors or consultants.
- Ensure that all arrangements for benefits realization are in place and responsibility has passed to the organization's operational management.

2.6.1.2 Inputs

Inputs are:

- all tranche closure sign-offs
- all tranche lessons learned
- benefits realized to date
- benefits achievement forecast, including commitment of BAU management.

2.6.1.3 Scaling

The time and effort required to complete programme closure does vary with the size of the programme, but many of the tasks are the same irrespective of scale. The decommissioning of the physical infrastructure will depend on programme size and the type of tools used. However, the lessons learned exercise will probably involve more participants for a large programme, but the nature of the activity is likely to be very similar. If the programme has been well organized and managed, closure will require minimal effort. For example, if lessons learned are recorded and collated throughout the programme, this part of closure then requires very little effort.

2.6.1.4 Critical success factors

Most important is treating the final, often unrecognized, stage of the programme as a project in its own right. The programme executive and the programme team should be incentivized to complete the programme in an orderly manner. Successful sign off of the Closure stage should be a component of any incentives, financial and otherwise.

2.6.1.5 How

Figure 2.33 lists the key activities that need to be carried out during the Closure stage.

5 Closure
Level 1

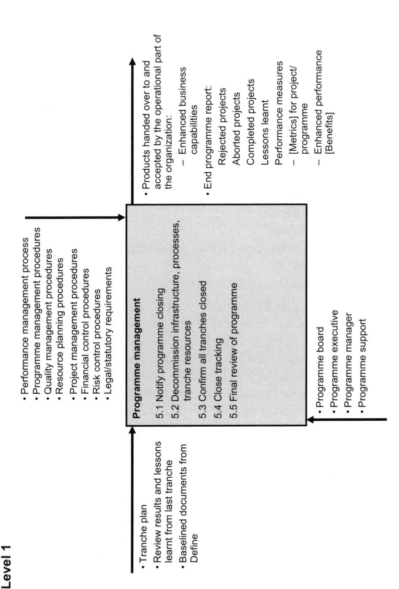

- Tranche plan
- Review results and lessons learnt from last tranche
- Baselined documents from Define

- Performance management process
- Programme management procedures
- Quality management procedures
- Resource planning procedures
- Project management procedures
- Financial control procedures
- Risk control procedures
- Legal/statutory requirements

Programme management

5.1 Notify programme closing
5.2 Decommission infrastructure, processes, tranche resources
5.3 Confirm all tranches closed
5.4 Close tracking
5.5 Final review of programme

- Programme board
- Programme executive
- Programme manager
- Programme support

- Products handed over to and accepted by the operational part of the organization:
  – Enhanced business capabilities
- End programme report:
  Rejected projects
  Aborted projects
  Completed projects
  Lessons learnt
  Performance measures
  – [Metrics] for project/ programme
  – Enhanced performance [Benefits]

Figure 2.33   The Closure process

2.6.2 DETAILED PROCESS STEPS

Figure 2.34 lists the Closure stage process steps.

2.6.2.1 NOTIFY PROGRAMME ABOUT TO CLOSE (STEP 5.1)

Why do this?

Closure comprises the final assessment of the programme and the decommissioning of its resource and infrastructure. These tasks cannot be undertaken until the changes the programme was created to bring about have been delivered.

Inputs

The inputs are programme and tranche plans.

Instructions

- When the final tranche is ready to close, notify the programme team, stakeholders and PMO that the programme is about to prepare to close. At this time, produce the draft end programme report. This will contain a summary of the instructions for the programme review, a timetable and will be formatted to include the results of the review.
- Notify the following that the programme is closing and information from all its projects will need to be prepared for input to the programme board as part of the end programme report:
    - those responsible for the benefits measurement processes as stated in the programme definition, and confirmed at project closure
    - all project managers for projects in the programme
    - PMO.

Outputs

The output is a draft end programme report, including instructions and timetable for the review.

2.6.2.2 DECOMMISSION PROGRAMME (STEP 5.2)

Why do this?

Every programme should come to an orderly close. The customers of the programme (that is, stakeholders) and the programme board should have agreed

147

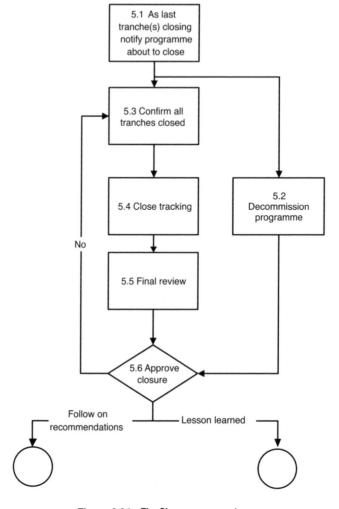

Figure 2.34 The Closure process steps

that everything expected has been delivered, or that any outstanding matters are included in agreed follow-on actions.

Those involved in the programme, and those who wish to use the programme resources about to be released, need to be informed so that resources can be allocated to new activities as soon as possible.

Programme records need to be retained to assist with future audits, or to help others understand the lessons learned.

When the organization is reviewing and updating its strategy, input from all programmes is critical. This will inform the organization about how previous

148

strategic plans delivered the benefits required, and how well these plans were executed.

Inputs

Inputs are:

- programme infrastructure
- programme team.

Instructions

- Complete all outstanding documents and pass to the PMO for filing.
- Prepare the project closure notification and identify who needs to receive it.
- Prepare to release any resources still allocated to the programme. Inform the PMO to update the resource plan to indicate the resources that are due to be released shortly.
- Prepare instructions to decommission any infrastructure set up to manage the programme. This excludes any infrastructure that will be needed to store archives after closure of the programme and any shared with other programmes.

Outputs

Ouputs are:

- programme resource released
- programme infrastructure decommissioned.

2.6.2.3 Confirm all tranches closed (step 5.3)

Why do this?

To assess the outcomes from all tranches against the original definition and business case. This review is a final check that all work planned for the programme has been completed and programme objectives have been achieved.

Inputs

Inputs are:

- end tranche report for all tranches
- lessons learned reports for all tranches.

Instructions

Make sure that all the tranches have been formally closed and that the end tranche reports and lessons learned reports have been signed off.

Outputs

Ouputs are:

- draft end programme report
- end programme review timetable and arrangements
- end tranche reports
- lessons learned reports.

2.6.2.4 Close tracking (step 5.4)

Why do this?

When planning the programme, judgements were made about how long benefits should be tracked and measured. This is a balance between collecting enough data to conclude success or failure and the cost of the tracking and measuring effort. This activity must now be transferred from a Programme responsibility; the Programme will no longer exist to carry this work out, to BAU (business as usual) responsibility. To facilitate this hand over of responsibility, benefits achieved to date should be collated and documented to form the basis of the work to be transferred. Ideally responsibility for continuing achievement of benefits initiated by the programme will have been transferred to BAU management as part of the programme's activity.

Inputs

Inputs are:

- results from benefits tracking and measuring activity undertaken as part of the programme
- arrangements for benefits measurement to be handed over to BAU management.

Instructions

- Collect, collate and report benefits achievement data and conclusions.
- Confirm with BAU management arrangements for continuation of benefits tracking and reporting.
- Confirm with organizational senior management arrangements and responsibilities for ongoing benefits delivery.

Outputs

Outputs are:

- results of benefits measures
- confirmed benefits delivery and realization responsibilities.

2.6.2.5 Final review of the programme (step 5.5)

Why do this?

When the organization is reviewing and updating its strategy, input from change programmes is vitally important, as it will inform the organization about how effectively previous strategic initiatives delivered the benefits required. This process step comprises preparing a report setting out how the programme has contributed to the organization's strategy, how successful it has been and, where there have been shortfalls, how these could be addressed by future initiatives.

During the Define stage of the Programme the organization agreed to make substantial investments in changes that it believed would produce a worthwhile return. The actual outcomes of the programme, the consequential benefits together with the cost of achieving this should now be compared with the approved and baselined plans and business case, to judge whether the programme was indeed a success.

Inputs

Inputs are:

- business imperatives
- issue log
- risk log
- baselined benefits profile
- baselined BBS
- baselined functional programme business architecture blueprint
- functional programme plan
- baseline business case
- current business case
- programme definition
- programme exception reports
- end project reports
- end tranche reports
- benefit measures

- current benefits forecast
- lessons learned reports from the programme's projects.

Instructions

- Assess the achievement of the programme's objectives.
- Summarize the organization changes completed compared with the original targets as set out in the business architecture blueprint.
- Compare actual achievements against the baselined business architecture blueprint:
  - business processes – ways of working and procedures
  - stakeholder groups – configuration and capabilities
  - business locations – locations added, disposed of and reconfigured
  - products and services – developed, discontinued and reconfigured
  - channels to market – developed, discontinued and reconfigured.
- Assess how the functional programme has met the business imperatives originally specified in the PDD.
- Cross-reference the above achievements to show which contributed to the business imperatives. Add a rating to indicate whether the contribution was significant or not.
- Assess performance against planned targets.
- Compare benefits achievement to date and expected future benefits achievement to original benefits plan. Analyse and explain reasons for variances and recommend corrective actions to be undertaken by BAU management.
- Update the programme business case with final actual cost data and compare to the original baselined business case included in the PDD.
- Summarize the approved programme changes, showing:
  - effects on original project plan
  - effects on business case
  - impact on benefits.
- Provide quality statistics and show how the quality plan was met/not met.
- Analyse lessons learned, summarizing lessons learned reports from the programme and its constituent projects and recommending any follow-on actions.
- List recommendations for the organization's strategy group or senior management to include in future change programmes.
- Make any post-programme review recommendations, for one or more of the following reasons:
  - because business change is not yet stabilized;

- because there are non-critical risks and issues that can be adequately managed by operations or another programme;
- because there are more opportunities for improvements and benefits, but better managed by another programme.
- Update the end programme report.

Outputs

The output is the end programme report.

2.6.2.6 Approve closure (step 5.6)

Why do this?

This step ensures that the closure of the programme is fully approved by the programme board, who are responsible for ensuring that the programme achieves the benefits required. It also provides final confirmation that the programme is complete and provides for the dissolution of the programme board.

Inputs

The input is the end programme report.

Instructions

- Present the end programme report to the programme board.
- Notify the following that the programme has completed its work and has closed:
  - strategic programme manager
  - functional programme team
  - the programme's project teams
  - stakeholders.

Release the resources still assigned to the programme, notify each individual and the PMO.

Outputs

The output is the approved end programme report (see Figure 2.35).

END PROGRAMME REPORT

PURPOSE OF DOCUMENT

The report is the programme manager's report to the programme executive, which will be passed on to the organization's strategy group via the strategic programme manager. It shows how well the programme has performed against its brief, including the original estimated cost, schedule, benefits profiles and tolerances, the revised business case and final version of the programme plan.

ACHIEVEMENT OF THE PROGRAMME'S OBJECTIVES

Summarize the organization changes completed compared with the original targets (the grey boxes) set out in the business architectural blueprint.

BUSINESS PROCESSES

Process name	Description of future process	How will it differ from today?	Changes actually achieved

STAKEHOLDER GROUPS

Stakeholder groups	Role	How much will it grow/shrink?	How much it actually grew or shrank

CAPABILITY GROUPS

Capability	Current	Future target	Actual capability achieved

BUSINESS LOCATIONS

Locations	Description of current locations	Future locations required	New locations delivered

PRODUCTS AND SERVICES

Product or service	Description of current products	Future products	New products delivered

CHANNELS TO MARKET

Channels to market	Description of current channels	Description and targets for future channels	Channels delivered and volumes achieved

ASSESS HOW THE PROGRAMME MET THE BUSINESS IMPERATIVES

Business imperatives	Contributors	Rating

- Contributors is a cross-reference to the changes made in the organization, derived from the business architecture blueprint tables above.
- Rating is the programme manager's assessment as to how well the contributors met the need.

PERFORMANCE AGAINST PLANNED TARGETS

Benefits

Copy the baselined BBS. Update it from actuals. Compare the two benefits curves to show how the programme under/over performed. Show how performance of the programme against time targets affected the benefits realized, using the benefits flow chart.

Business case

Update the business case with actuals, compare to the baselined business case.

APPROVED PROGRAMME CHANGES

List the approved changes and show:

- effects on original project plan
- effects on business case
- impact on benefits.

155

QUALITY STATISTICS

Show how the approved quality plan was met/not met.

LESSONS LEARNED

Summarize from the lessons learned reports from the programme and its projects.

Project/programme	Description of success	Evidence/any other supporting information

Project/programme	Description of shortfalls	Evidence/any other supporting information

FOLLOW ON ACTIONS

A list of any recommendations for the strategy group to include in the next strategy and strategic programme.

POST-PROGRAMME REVIEW

If a further review is needed, because business change is not yet stabilized.
  Review date:
  Review plan:

Figure 2.35   Example template for an end programme report

2.6.3 QUICK REFERENCE

	Inputs	How	Who	Output	Quality	Techniques
5.1 Notify programme about to close	Programme and tranche plans	Notify the programme team, stakeholders and programme support that the programme is about to prepare to close	Programme manager PMO	Notify that programme preparing to close Draft end progrmame report Review timetable	Is the review timetable realistic? Have all those who need to be informed been notified?	Planning stakeholder communications

	Inputs	How	Who	Output	Quality	Techniques
		Produce the draft end programme report; this will contain a summary of the instructions for the review and a timetable				
5.2 Decommission programme	Notify that programme preparing to close Benefits achievement forecast	Confirm all tranches closed Decommission infrastructure, processes, tranche resources	Programme manager Programme team PMO	Infrastructure decommiss-ioned Resources released	Have all resources been re-assigned?	Resource management
5.3 Confirm all tranches closed	Tranche closure sign-off Tranche lessons learned	Programme support from current plans	PMO	Confirmation all tranches closed	Has all learning been captured and retained for future use?	
5.4 Close tracking	Notify that programme preparing to close	Close tracking and collect results Hand over all benefits tracking to operational management, if needed	Programme manager Benefits owners	Results of benefits measures	Have all benefits owners confirmed tracking stopped or responsibility handed over to operational managers? Have all benefits measurement results been collected?	Benefits tracking

	Inputs	How	Who	Output	Quality	Techniques
5.5 Final review	Business imperatives Issue log Risk log Baselined benefits profile Baselined BBS Baselined functional programme Business architecture blueprint Functional programme plan Baseline business case Current business case Programme definition Programme exception reports End project reports End tranche reports Benefit measures Current benefits forecast Lessons learned Reports from the programme's projects	Final review of programme including overall lessons learned Document programme achievements	Programme executive Programme manager PMO Stakeholders Benefits owners	Programme closure sign-off documentation Programme lessons learned Programme achievement report	Has the programme achieved its objectives? Do the benefits achieved and planned to be achieved meet the organization's requirements for change?	Post-programme review

	Inputs	How	Who	Output	Quality	Techniques
5.6 Approve programme closed	Programme closure sign-off Documentation Programme Lessons learned Programme achievement report	Sign off closure Decide on any follow-on recommend-ations	Programme board	Programme closure sign-off	Is the programme closed? Has all activity on the programme and its project stopped?	Review meeting

2.7 APPENDIX

2.7.1 ORGANIZING STRATEGIC REQUIREMENTS INTO WORK GROUPS USING AN AFFINITY DIAGRAM

An affinity diagram can help you organize requirements into work groups as a first step towards determining the projects in a programme (see Figures 2.36, 2.37 and 2.38).

2.7.2 HOW TO USE THE AFFINITY DIAGRAM

1. Take the requirements identified as the 'gaps' between the current position and the target future state, derived from the business architecture blueprint, and phrase the item in a full sentence and place on a card or Post-it® note.
2. Use at least the first 20 cards.
3. Sort the cards simultaneously into related groups.
4. For each grouping, create summary header cards.
5. Draw the final affinity diagram connecting all finalized header cards with their groupings.
6. Each of these groupings is a work group.

2.7.3 EXAMPLE DIAGRAMS

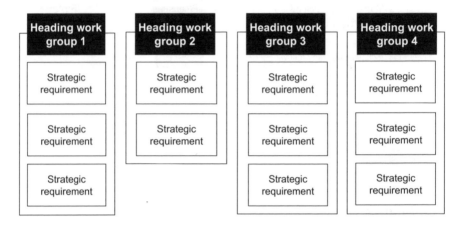

Figure 2.36 Format for arranging requirements into work groups

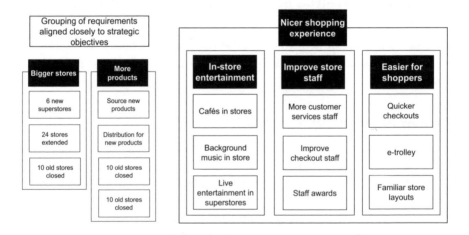

Figure 2.37 Example of requirements aligned to strategic objectives

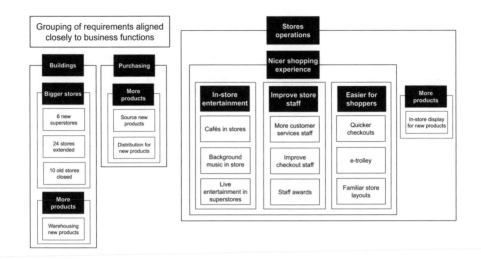

Figure 2.38   Example of requirements aligned to business functions

Part II
A Supporting Infrastructure

3 Programme organization and governance

3.1 INTRODUCTION

Like any management undertaking, programmes require organization and structure if they are to be successful. This must operate at three clearly distinct levels:

- Within the programme, there must be appropriate organizations and structures for the component projects to ensure that all contribute fully to the achievement of the programme's objectives. The design and maintenance of these is an essential programme function. Activities and functions performed with the component projects are referred to as operating at the 'project level'.
- At the level of the programme itself, there must be appropriate organization and structure to ensure that all the necessary 'programme level' processes are correctly undertaken.
- Furthermore, the programme must interface with the rest of the organization, with its strategies and corporate plans, and with other programmes and major initiatives. Part of this interfacing is concerned with ensuring that the programme operates efficiently and effectively in accordance with the overall interests of the parent organization. This aspect of programme management is termed governance and is discussed in greater detail in from Section 3.6 onwards.

These three levels of organization and structure, and the general relationships between them, are shown in diagrammatic form in Figure 3.1.

The senior management of the organization has the obligation to ensure effective corporate governance. Some of this obligation is delegated to programmes. The programmes will, in turn, delegate some of their obligations down to their component projects.

Each level must have agreed arrangements to report up to its parent level,

165

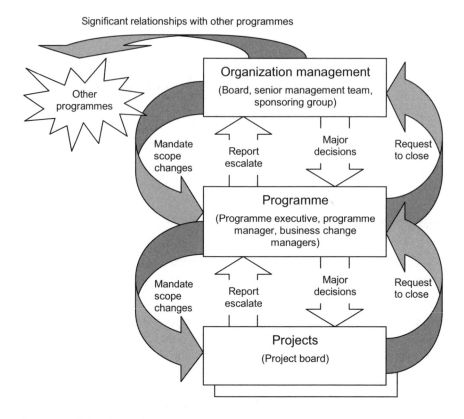

Figure 3.1 Various levels of organization and structure required for effective programme management

especially for decisions beyond their authority. For example, circumstance inside or outside the organization might change unexpectedly causing the senior management to change the programme (scope change). This is turn often means the programme must change some of its projects. (These external changes are discussed further in Section 3.7.3 'Reacting to external environment changes'.)

Of course, the structure shown in Figure 3.1. may need to be adjusted to fit in with that of the organization as a whole. In reality, there may be more layers, especially in larger organizations. Figure 3.2 shows a variant used within a large financial organization. The key point is that there must be a clear understanding of and demarcation between the roles and responsibilities of each of the different levels.

Since the component projects are the means by through which programmes implement changes, it is essential that they be run properly – by appropriately skilled and experienced project managers working with properly trained and

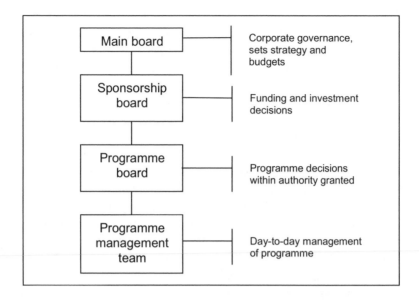

Figure 3.2   Alternative example of organization levels above a programme team

resourced project teams. It is assumed throughout this handbook that a consistent approach is adopted to the management of projects, such as that provided by the PRINCE2 methodology.[1]

3.2 PROGRAMME STRUCTURE

Although every programme is unique and will thus have a unique organization and structure, all have to cope with the same vagaries of human nature and thus have to deal with similar problems and difficulties. Experience shows that giving the programme a clear-cut structure with well-understood organization of roles and responsibilities contributes greatly to success.

A key element of the structure is to ensure a clear distinction between project-, programme- and corporate-level activities and functions, with appropriate responsibilities allocated to specific posts. For example, in a programme where specialist external contractors working on a fixed-price basis are responsible for component projects, each is likely to have their own procedures for procurement, testing, and so on, with the programme having little responsibility for this

---

1   PRINCE2 is a widely used methodology, sponsored by the UK Government's Office of Government Commerce (OGC). PRINCE® is a registered trade mark of OGC.

167

function. Moreover, each contractor is likely to have their own, discrete processes for financial control with the programme responsible only for managing the finances of programme-level activities and for accumulating the costs of the overall programme. Thus procurement and financial control could be deemed to be primarily 'project-level' functions. By contrast, within an internally managed programme of organizational change, all procurement might be handled through the corporate procurement function and all accounting provided by the corporate accounts department – that is, they might be deemed primarily 'corporate-level' functions.

However, even in these two extreme cases, the programme will have a responsibility for ensuring consistency. In the first example, the programme is likely to specify levels of 'goods inward' testing that might need to apply. In the second example, the programme and or the component projects will be responsible for identifying what needs to be procured and defining specifications. In both examples, the programme will need to accumulate costs and ensure that they are consistent with agreed budgets.[2]

For some processes there must be activities at all levels. For example, in accordance with good practice, each component project will operate risk identification and management processes to ensure that it can deliver the appropriate products with the agreed time and cost parameters. However, if a project identifies a risk that is outside its span of control, such as a critical dependency upon another project within the programme, there must be arrangements whereby the risk can be escalated to the programme level for resolution. If the dependency were upon a project within another programme, then the risk might need to be escalated to senior management for resolution, that is, to the 'corporate level'. Thus the risk management process will need to function at all levels in order to ensure all categories of risk are dealt with effectively.

Defining the structure of the programme and ensuring that responsibilities are clearly allocated, understood and agreed at all levels is a key responsibility of the programme manager. Typically they will be defined in the programme delivery plan.

Figure 3.3 shows an example of a programme structure diagram taken from a programme delivery plan. In this programme, a consortium of contractors (the partners) is being led by a prime contractor (Wizz Co) to undertake a programme of work for ABC Ltd. The diagram shows the main groups at each level with interfaces between them.

---

2   The programme office typically has a major responsibility with respect to such 'programme-level' functions – see Section 3.4.6 'Programme support'.

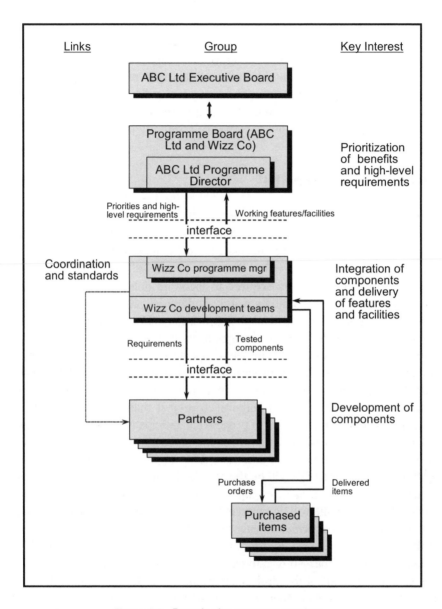

Figure 3.3   Example of a programme structure

The programme delivery plan should also identify which groups are responsible for which functions and activities and how they interface with each other. In the example shown in Figure 3.3, each contractor had their own contract, which specified in detail their roles and responsibilities. While all conformed in general to the structure shown in the diagram, each had variations in detail resulting from their separately negotiated contracts and these had also to be reflected within the delivery plan.

3.3 PROJECT ENVIRONMENT

A key role of the programme is to set the environment within which the component projects will operate. Research shows that a supportive environment contributes significantly to the success of individual projects (Gray, 2001). There is a strong positive correlation between a stable environment, in which component project managers are free to focus on delivery, and the success of those projects in terms of on-time, within-budget delivery. Thus an essential role of the programme director is to insulate the projects from the turmoil of corporate politics and to carefully manage changes to project scope.

An essential contributor to a project-supportive environment is the leadership and direction provided by the programme's management team, but the research quoted above suggests that this leadership must be supportive: too much focus on the penalties of failure will demoralize project managers and lead them to 'protect their backs' rather than to proactively anticipate and solve problems.

The personal leadership of the programme manager needs to be supported by the specific 'programme-level' functions that support the component projects. Another contributor to this will be the standards and guidelines provided by the programme, such as those developed by the programme assurance function. Finally, the programme will be responsible for establishing appropriate reporting and communication activities to ensure that not only is a global picture built up for the programme as a whole, but also that information on progress, trends and mutual assistance is passed own to each project and the teams within it.

A specific element of the project environment is the tolerance within which component projects can operate. Tolerance is the extent to which project managers are allowed to deviate from agreed time and cost plans before they need to escalate and seek formal approval. No project ever goes 100% according to plan and an agreed level of tolerance provides the manager of a component project with the freedom to handle the unexpected. Setting such tolerances is usually the responsibility of the programme manager and is normally a counter-part of the budget setting and risk management processes, whereby risks are identified and assessed and a contingency established to cope with them (see Chapter 7, 'Management of risks and issues' for further guidance on the handling of risks and issues). This contingency may be expressed in terms of time or money (or both). By setting a tolerance within which a project can operate, the programme manager is effectively delegating the control of part of this contingency to the project manager.

Different projects may have different levels of tolerance. Inherently difficult and risky projects are likely to need greater contingency, and hence more tolerance, than simple and straightforward ones. Furthermore, different levels of tolerance may be specified for time and cost. For example, it may be inappropriate to give tolerance on time to a critically important project on which the rest of the programme depends, yet it may be perfectly appropriate to give a large tolerance on money.

Of course, the use of tolerance must be carefully constrained, in accordance with agreed rules, otherwise it will tend to become a 'project manager's slush fund'. Furthermore, tolerance should be related to the particular tranches to which a risk is related and, if not required by the end of the tranche, should be reclaimed by the programme (see Section 2.4, 'Establish programme', for more detail on programme tranches). Thus a contingency set aside to cover the cost of the project team in the event of difficulties in getting a client to sign of the specifications may be reclaimed if there turn out to be no difficulties and the specifications are speedily agreed and signed. Such reclaimed amounts may then, at the programme manager's discretion, be used by another project that is having greater than expected difficulty.

3.4 PROGRAMME ORGANIZATION

A vital part of organizing a programme is identifying who should do what. This is normally achieved through a 'Roles and Responsibilities' section within the programme delivery plan. Figure 3.4 shows a typical programme organization chart, identifying the key positions.

For each of the posts identified in the chart, there should be guidance to the specific roles and responsibilities, examples of which are given below.

3.4.1 PROGRAMME DIRECTOR (OTHERWISE KNOWN AS PROGRAMME EXECUTIVE OR SENIOR RESPONSIBLE OWNER)

For each programme there should be a senior executive allocated to direct the initiative in line with corporate strategy and to provide high-level sponsorship.

171

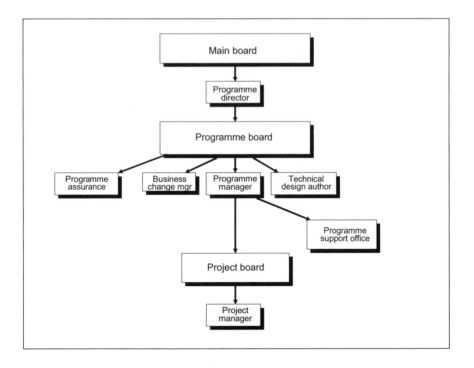

Figure 3.4 Typical programme organization chart

This sponsorship includes ensuring adequate resources are made available; usually this means money but it could include the time of users to specify requirements, try out prototypes or acceptance test final deliverables. This executive also has a vital role in maintaining the stability of the programme by protecting it from senior managers who may wish the programme's resources to be diverted to their own 'pet' programmes and projects.

Typically, the executive is referred to as the programme director, reflecting the fact that they would typically be a member of the main board of directors, delegated to ensure that the wishes of that board are achieved within the programme. Sometimes they may instead be referred to as 'the sponsor', reflecting the vital sponsorship role. In other programmes the term 'programme executive' is used. Within the UK public sector, this person is usually referred to as the Senior Responsible Owner (SRO), that is, 'the single individual with overall responsibility for ensuring that the programme meets its objectives and delivers the projected benefits' (see Cabinet Office, 2000).

The programme director is normally responsible for reporting back to the main board about the programme's progress and helping that board to appreciate any additional opportunities or major risks revealed by the programme. They also have a major role to play in ensuring effective governance within the programme, which is discussed more fully from Section 3.6 onwards.

The programme director is usually a part-time post, as most of the day-to-day management of the programme will be provided by the programme manager, but specific responsibilities would typically include:

- Appoint the programme manager and the other members of the programme board.
- On behalf of the main board, approve overall budgets and targets for the programme.
- On behalf of the main board ensure that an adequate business case exists for the programme, with responsibilities for benefit delivery clearly identified (where appropriately, to fellow directors and to line managers).
- Ensure the aims of the programme continue to be in line with the strategic goals, and in particular focused on the benefits to be realized.
- Secure resources for the programme; mainly budgets and people.
- Set agendas and chair programme board meetings.
- Escalate corporate-level risks and issues to fellow directors or to the main board and facilitate their resolution.
- Provide assistance and guidance, as required, to the programme manager.

3.4.2 PROGRAMME MANAGER

The programme manager carries out day-to-day management of the programme and supervises the component projects. To this end, they must ensure that the management and support environment for each project is adequate. They need to understand the whole programme and how the component projects and their deliverables interrelate.

The programme manager should keep up to date on the current status of every project and of the programme as a whole in terms of cost, time, resource, delivery, risks, issues, changes, variances and exceptions. In this, they will be greatly assisted by the programme support office.

It is particularly important that they take early control of any problems that may impact on the success of the programme. They must also provide oversight of the project managers and ensure that they are effectively managing their individual projects.

The programme manager will normally be a member of the programme board and will work closely with the programme director, particularly with respect to stakeholder management, financial and progress reporting and benefit delivery.

Specific responsibilities of the programme manager typically include:

- Appoint, manage and motivate the project managers.
- Determine and agree the overall approach, direction and integrity of the programme (with the help of others such as the programme director and programme assurance manager).
- Ensure appropriate plans, standards and guidance are available for the whole programme and its component projects. (Where necessary, organize their review and approval by the programme board. Some aspects of this may be provided by the programme assurance function).
- Establish effective systems and procedures throughout the programme to ensure the correct flow of information, including that relating to costs, deliverables, timescales, and so on. Ensure that these interface, where necessary, with 'corporate-level' procedures and systems.
- Allocate responsibilities and resources to each project, approve the plans of individual projects and monitor their usage of resources and achievement of results.
- Set project tolerances and monitor their usage. Where appropriate, reallocate contingency funds between projects.
- Ensure that dependencies between the component projects within the programme and dependencies with other programmes are identified. Resolve conflicts between component projects and liaise with other programme managers to ensure changes in this programme's projects or other related projects do not produce an unacceptable impact.
- Take responsibility for overall progress and appropriate use of resource, take corrective action where necessary. If corrective action cannot keep the programme on course to success, report this to the programme director
- Report to the programme director at an agreed frequency (for example, in highlight reports). Where necessary, provide exception reports and answer ad-hoc questions from the main board.
- Upon programme completion, ensure the programme is closed in a controlled manner, and that the lessons learned and any recommended follow-on actions are reported to the programme director.

3.4.3 TECHNICAL DESIGN AUTHORITY

Where the component projects involve an element of technical design, it is essential to have a common approach, not only to ensure that the various technical products will interface correctly with each other, but also to ensure that they do not compromise the existing technical infrastructure. For example, if the programme is going to involve the creation of new IT facilities, these will have to interface with the existing networks, servers, databases and applications. In these circumstances, it is usual to have a technical design authority to ensure a consistent approach throughout the programme.

The technical design authority is responsible for ensuring that the programme and its component projects complies with the organization's standards and policies and any legislation or regulations set by relevant outside bodies. The role must ensure that the components of the programmes and projects are consistent in accordance with standards and policies in force. These may be legal, regulatory, technical, contractual or corporate directives. To achieve this, the technical design authority must ensure that the interfaces (communications) between programmes, projects and the guardians of the organization's standards and policies, are adequate.

Specific responsibilities typically include:

- Review programmes and projects to ensure compliance with relevant standards and policies.
- Review risks and issues to determine if they might cause a violation of standards and policies.
- Review quality plans and logs to ensure there is adequate quality assurance in respect of the standards and policies.
- Take a proactive role in any programme or project where a serious breach has happened or is likely, and the programme/project manager does not have it under control.
- Advise the programme director on any changes to standards and policies that will be needed to support the programme.
- Advise the programme director on any changes to standards and policies that will be needed due to external influences (for example, changes in legislation).
- Liaise with the programme office to ensure that such changes are adequately delegated to a programme or project.

3.4.4 BUSINESS CHANGE MANAGER

At the present time, around a quarter of all programmes are primarily focused on organizational change and nearly half are focussed on implementing major IT systems, with substantial associated change activities.[3] Because these activities are dependent upon the unpredictable responses of human beings, and because these human beings are usually required to maintain 'business as usual' (BAU)

---

3 These statistics are based upon information within the databaes of the Programme Management Maturity Model, described in Chapter 15.

activities and thus are likely only to be available for a limited amount of time to support business change, a very different approach is needed to managing as compared to more traditional activities such as IT development or building construction. Because of this difference, it is usual in such programmes to appoint a business change manager with specific responsibility for managing those functions and activities that lead to change in culture, organizational structure or processes.

In some programmes, the business change manager also works to ensure that the organization is able to realize the expected business benefits from the use of new capabilities. Since overall responsibility for the eventual realization of these benefits lies with the programme director, it is logical for the business change manager to report to the programme director, alongside the programme manager. The business change manager is normally a member of the programme board.

Typical responsibilities of the business change manager include:

- Ensure the interests of the sponsoring group are met by the programme.
- Obtain assurance for the sponsoring group that the delivery of new capability is compatible with realization of the benefits.
- Work with the programme manager to ensure that the work of the programme, including the scoping of each project, covers the necessary aspects required to deliver the products or services that will lead to operational benefits.
- Work with the programme manager to identify projects that will contribute to realizing benefits and achieving outcomes.
- Identify, define and track the benefits and outcomes required of the programme.
- Identify and implement the maximum improvements in business operations (both existing and newly created) as groups of projects deliver their products or services into operational use.
- Manage the realization of benefits and ensure that continued accrual of benefits can be achieved and measured after the programme has been completed.
- Establish and implement the mechanisms by which benefits can be realized and measured.
- Take the lead on transition management; ensure that BAU is maintained during the transition and the changes are effectively integrated into the business.
- Prepare the affected business areas for the transition to new ways of working; potentially implement new business processes.
- Optimize the timing of the release of project deliverables into business operations.

Further guidance on benefit management, including the business change manager's role, can be found in Chapter 5 'Benefits management'.

3.4.5 PROGRAMME BOARD

The programme board is the group or committee responsible for the direction setting and leadership of a programme. This board usually includes representatives of key stakeholder groups, partners or investors. The programme director would typically chair such a board.

Typical responsibilities of a programme board include:

- Make go/no go decisions at key points[4] in a programme, where such authority has been delegated by the main board (or equivalent).
- Make go/no go decisions when an exception occurs and the programme must change.
- Create an environment in which the programme can thrive.
- Endorse, advise and support the programme director.
- Provide continued commitment and endorsement in support of the programme director at programme milestones.
- Approve the progress of the programme against the strategic objectives.
- Provide visible leadership and commitment to the programme at communication events.
- Confirm successful delivery and sign-off at the closure of the programme.

Note that in some organizations, the programme board may be referred to as a sponsoring group. In some very large organizations, the sponsoring group may provide an additional level of governance over and above that provided by the programme board, as shown in Figure 3.2.

3.4.6 PROGRAMME SUPPORT

All programmes require a degree of administration and it will often not be appropriate for the programme manager to fill this role. For this reason, if a permanent programme office does not exist, it is normal to create a programme office for the programme, under the supervision of a programme office manager. This office will provide the central services that the programme and projects require. These might include the maintenance of consolidated project plans, the

---

4 Key points are typically, end of Start-up stage, approve the brief; end of Define stage, approve the programme definition and permission to start first tranche; end of each tranche, permission to close that tranche and start next tranche; Closure stage, permission to close programme, see Chapter 2 'The programme management process' for more details.

maintenance of programme (and project) accounts, the consolidation of progress reports (highlight reports) and other information to produce consolidated progress reports, and so on.

Typical responsibilities of the programme office include:

- Track and report: track measurements, report on progress.
- Information management: hold master copies of all programme information, generate all necessary quality management documentation, maintain, control and update programme documentation, establish and maintain the index to an electronic library of programme information.
- Financial accounting: assist the programme manager with budget control for the programme, maintaining status reports on all projects in the programme.
- Track risks and issues.
- Analyse interfaces and critical dependencies between projects and recommend appropriate actions to the programme manager.
- Maintain the list of stakeholders and their interests.
- Quality control: establish consistent practices and standards adhering to the programme governance arrangements, including project planning, reporting, change control, analysing risks and maintaining and updating the risk log for the programme.
- Change control: register changes for subsequent investigation and resolution, monitor items identified as requiring action, prompt timely actions, report on whether required actions have been carried out.
- The programme office may provide additional expertise across the programme, for example:
  - provide a strategic overview of all programmes and interdependencies, and report upward to senior management;
  - provide consultancy-style support to project delivery teams at initiation and throughout the lifecycle of the programme; ensure a common approach is adopted and share good practice;
  - carry out health checks and advise on solutions during the lifetime of the programme and individual projects; for example, facilitate workshops involving project teams, stakeholders and members of the programme team.

See also Chapter 13, 'The programme office', which has further detail on programme support.

3.4.7 PROGRAMME ASSURANCE

The programme director, and programme board members if any, are usually not allocated full time to the programme. They rely heavily on information provided by the programme. While they may get comfort from the receipt of regular reports and communications, they need to have independent assurance that everything is going as the programme manager describes. This is the role of the programme assurance function.

Programme assurance responsibilities belong to the programme board but they can, and almost invariably do, delegate all or part of the role. This role must be independent of the programme manager and their direct reports.

Further guidance on the roles and responsibilities of this function can be found in Chapter 8 'Programme assurance and quality'.

3.5 PROGRAMME LEADERSHIP

Successful programmes require good leadership and clear direction setting at all levels. Programmes pursue strategic objectives by translating them into clear briefs for their projects and establishing a sound framework for benefits management. Leading, directing and managing a programme provides the 'bridge' between strategic objectives and projects.

Each of the component projects within the programme will tend to have its own priorities and objectives (especially where each is being managed by a separate subcontractor), yet for the programme to be successful, all must work together for the greater good. This will require the programme manager to build the project managers into a coherent and well-focused team. This often means leading by example: not breaking their own rules, not reneging on their own values, not overriding strategy for their own pet initiatives and so on.

3.5.1 TEAM BUILDING

The key principles for effective team building within a programme environment are:

- empowered decision making, giving individuals the authority to fulfil their roles effectively;
- motivation, reward and appraisal systems, which are vital for fostering the attitudes and energy to drive the programme;
- visible commitment and authority, with enough seniority to:
  - ensure the correct resources are available to the programme;
  - influence and engage with stakeholders;
  - balance the programme's priorities with those of the ongoing business operations;

179

- focus on benefits realization;
- relevant skills and experience to provide active management of:
  - the cultural and people issues involved in change;
  - the programme's finances and the inevitable conflicting demands on resources;
  - the coordination of the programme's projects to the transition to new operational services while maintaining business as usual.

Assembling the resources to work together does not automatically make a successful team. More is usually needed:

- The team needs to be set clear goals.
- Each member of the team needs a defined role.
- To enable each member of the team to perform well, they need good instruction, tasks, targets, standards, and so on.
- The team needs to be defined so it has sufficient skills, and team members need to know where else they can go if supplementary skills are required.
- The team members must know how they will accomplish their tasks and roles. Some of this will come as instruction via programme documents, some of it will come from the abilities and experience of each team member.
- Assembling a group of people to work together does not always make a successful team. They may therefore need ongoing support, encouragement, control and other similar assistance to make sure they quickly start to function effectively. This assistance will be needed throughout the programme, especially as members of the team come and go. The programme director must provide this assistance personally and may need to enlist others to help with team building. Examples of the type of support and assistance are as follows:
  - Direct the team to keep them focused on the benefits, and obsessed with quality and control.
  - Ensure they have adequate freedom to work making best use of their talents and experience, however.
  - Regularly check they have unity of purpose, look for evidence of rivalries, barriers, distrust and anything else that might destroy the team's effectiveness.
  - It is very rare in any programme that the team members will have all the knowledge, skills and expertise that will be required. They must have time allowed for continuous education, learning from other programmes, and so on. The time, cost and risk associated with this must of course be assessed and must be an acceptable part of the business case.

3.5.2 PROGRAMME RESOURCING

An important responsibility of the programme manager is ensuring that adequate resources are available to the programme and to its component projects. It cannot be assumed that somehow the right people (or other resources) will automatically be available when the time comes. Failure to address resourcing issues is one the main contributors to programme failure.

Of course, the programme manager may not have the authority or internal influence to obtain resources in competition with the needs of other programmes or of the organization's BAU activities. In these circumstances, they are likely to need the help of the programme director or the programme board.

3.5.2.1 Forecasting requirements

The programme manager must produce reliable forecasts of the resources that will be required compared to the expected availability at the time they will be needed. In a large organization with complex change programmes, this may be assigned to a resource manager role.

3.5.2.2 Managing the supply pool

The programme manager must make sure that adequate arrangements are in place, via information flows from HR, facilities management, and so on to understand the capacity and nature of resource availability over time. The programme team must understand the organization's policies for the recruitment or procurement of permanent resource.

There must be effective frameworks in place to manage resources and in particular to quickly resolve issues where there are conflicting priorities between programmes and operational business as usual.

See also Chapter 4 'Programme planning and control' for further guidance on programme resource methods.

3.6 PROGRAMME GOVERNANCE

The money and other resources that the programme spends are not the property of the programme. They belong to the organization as a whole and those responsible for the stewardship of the organization, such as the board of directors, must ensure that the programme spending is subjected to the same control as all other activities of the organization. The processes and activities that provide these controls are generally referred to as programme governance.

Sustaining the current business and growing into new business models are generally stakeholder expectations and can be achieved only with adequate governance of the programmes that deliver organizational change. Programme governance, like other governance subjects, is the responsibility of the main board of directors. It is not an isolated discipline or activity, but rather is integral to the governance of the organization as a whole.

On the basis of the above, programme governance can be described as

> the responsibility of the main board of directors (or their equivalent on the public sector) and the organization's senior executive management. It is an integral part of the governance of the whole organization and consists of the leadership and organizational structures and processes to ensure that the programme sustains and extends the organization's strategies and objectives.

Programme governance thus provides the overarching control mechanism of the programme and provides the 'backdrop' for all activities of managing the programme and achieving the programme's outcomes.

On this basis, we can extend the concept of programme governance to function at several levels:

- The main board of directors (as the most senior management team) will usually delegate aspects of its authority to a subgroup that can find the necessary time to provide effective scrutiny and guidance. This is usually referred to as the programme board, although sometimes it is referred to as 'the sponsoring group'.
- The programme board is responsible for ensuring that proper controls are in place within the programme and thus provides the foundation for governance within the programme. The chair of the programme board will be the usually be the programme director, with defined authority and responsibility, as outlined in Section 3.1 'Programme director'.
- Programme assurance is a responsibility of the programme board. Usually, however, such work needs to be carried out by specialists, so the board will delegate the work to the programme assurance manager and their team. As described in Chapter 8 'Programme assurance and quality', the programme assurance function thus reports not to the programme manager or the programme director, but to the programme board.
- The technical design authority may perform a specialized form of programme assurance by ensuring that the programme and its deliverables conform to agreed technical architectures and standards.

Large organizations with many programmes sometimes establish a strategic programme board to assist with the overall coordination and decision making for all programmes of strategic importance. Where this exists, the main board of directors may also delegate some governance authority to this group.

Table 3.1 compares the similarities and differences between corporate and programme governance, in the private sector.

Table 3.1   Programme governance vs. corporate governance

Issue	Corporate governance	Programme governance
Structure of the board Management of the board	The role of chairman and chief executive should be divided. There should be: a. regular board meetings; b. a clear division of responsibility between members, with no single director being allowed unfettered discretion to make decisions; c. a formal written schedule of matters for approval by the board.	The programme board should have a balanced structure including representation from the key divisions/stakeholders being affected: a. programme board meetings are regularly held; b. there is a clear delineation of responsibilities on the programme board; c. the programme board has a regular agenda of items to review including the projects in the programme.
Board competence	Directors should initially receive instruction on their responsibilities following their appointment and instruction and training from time to time.	Programme directors and other members of the programme board who have no programme or project experience should be trained before taking up their role.
Board membership	Boards should establish nomination committees.	The make-up of the programme board should provide a balanced view of key stakeholders.
Remuneration	A remuneration committee is required and its members are required to have no business or other relationship with the company which could affect the independence of their judgement.	Where the programme director or programme manager has a personal interest, or their company has an interest, in one or more of the projects, then this must be declared. The programme director or programme manager should withdraw from any discussion on the project.
Financial controls	The board has a duty to present an assessment of the company's financial position	The programme board should ensure the production of up-to-date financial and management accounts.
Other internal controls	Directors of listed companies must: a. conduct a review at least once a year and report to shareholders on the effectiveness of the company's system of internal control; or b. where there is no formal internal	The programme management arrangements should include Internal controls for: a. financial approval and management b. benefit management c. risk management d. planning and tracking

control system, annually review the situation and report to the shareholders why the board does not consider such a system necessary and outline other procedures in place to provide information to the board.	e. change control f. documentation management g. reporting h. programme assurance, including checkpoints and audits.

3.6.1 GOVERNANCE ACTIVITIES

3.6.1.1 Strategic-level activities

Organizations exercise some their corporate governance obligations through strategy or policy setting in order to set objectives for continuous performance improvement. These high-level objectives will be achieved through organizational changes, which need to be planned and managed. The scale of such changes is often too great to be contained in one programme. Strategic planning and management is outside the scope of this book, but the link between strategy and each programme is so critical to the success of both that it is included as a brief overview.

The organization's main board of directors (as the senior management team) must ensure that there is a mechanism so that all of its strategy is effectively implemented:

- All programmes (of strategic importance), and their projects, must collectively be aiming to deliver improvements and benefits that equate to the total improvements and benefits stated in the strategy.
- Their total funding and resource requirements must not exceed the abilities of the organization. For financial funds expenditure must be planned and managed within the budgetary limits set, for resources planned work must be within the capacity and capability limits of those resources that can be made available for programme and project work.
- Where programme demands exceed the funds and/or resource available, the organization must have a mechanism to prioritize and choose those programmes that will make the greatest contribution to the strategy.
- Given that programmes will progress at a rate different from that planned, a person or body must have the responsibility to oversee all programmes. If the sum of these programmes will consume more funds than available, over stretch resources, leave gaps in the strategy, or if the programmes are pursuing work not of strategic importance, this body must report back the senior management.

Governance can have broad responsibilities – corporate governance for the entire organization, governance for a strategic programme that oversees many other

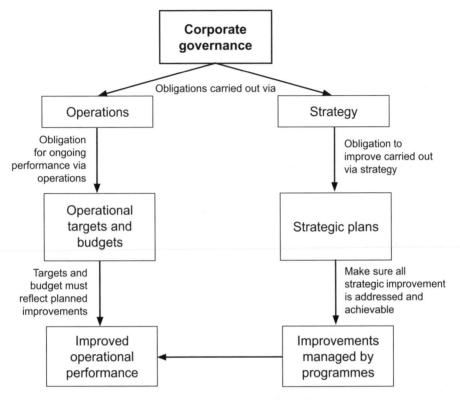

Figure 3.5 **Governance takes place at many levels**

programmes – or, with a narrower focus, governance can be for just one programme. All of these interact with each other so operational and programme organization structures must be designed to cope with this (see Figure 3.5).

3.6.1.2 Sponsoring the programme

Programme sponsorship means making the investment decision and providing top-level endorsement of the rationale and objectives for the programme. Sponsorship also means continuing senior management commitment to promoting and supporting the changes introduced by the programme and championing the implementation of the new capabilities delivered by the programme to ensure that the expected benefits are realized and the desired outcomes achieved.

KEY GOVERNANCE DOCUMENTS

Listed below are examples of documents that are usually deemed important to the governance of programmes. Further guidance on the purpose and origin of these can be found in Chapter 2 'The programme management process'.

STRATEGY DOCUMENTS

The main board of directors will usually have a set of documents outlining the overall corporate strategy and the policies that support it, such as:

- Business strategy and policies – explains the overall future direction of the organization, assumption and conclusions about how to get to the desired improved state, and will set out corporate objectives. Programmes of strategic importance should always map back to the relevant aspects of these.
- Business plans and budgets – all organizations will have operational plans and budgets. These may provide guidance and constraints that the programme will need to work within.
- Business architecture blueprints – some organizations will use 'blueprints' at a strategic level to describe the future structure and state of the organization and its interfaces with the external world, its customers and its suppliers. Where such documents exist, the programme should map across to those parts that it is expected to deliver.

PROGRAMME BRIEF

The purpose of this document is to provide an informed basis for the programme board to decide whether they want to go ahead with the programme and to start the definition process. This document will not usually contain the full business case or programme justification, which will normally be developed during the programme definition process.

BUSINESS CASE

The business case formally documents the justification for the programme in terms of the estimated cost of development and the anticipated business benefits to be gained. The case should explain why the forecast effort and time will be worthwhile and that the programme can be implemented within acceptable levels of risk. The programme board should review the ongoing viability of the programme at intervals against this business case.

HIGHLIGHT REPORTS

These provide the programme director and the programme board with a summary of the programme status at predefined intervals.

EXCEPTION REPORTS

Exception reports should be produced whenever costs, timescales or benefits projections for a programme tranche are forecast to be outside the agreed tolerance levels set. They should be prepared by the programme manager in order to advise the programme director and the programme board of the situation. After consideration of such reports, the director or the board may require an exception plan to be developed to allow the programme to recover from the situation.

RISK REGISTER

This should be kept up to date by the programme manager to enable the programme director and the programme board to see that adequate progress is being made on preventing, mitigating or planning for risk and that the overall level of risk within the programme is acceptable.

The programme's sponsors are usually drawn from senior management, such as members of the main board of directors, and are responsible for the investment decision, defining the direction of the business and establishing frameworks to achieve the desired objectives. They must take the lead in establishing the values and behaviours required by the change effort, often 'leading by example'. Without the commitment and direct involvement of senior management, a transformational change is unlikely to progress successfully.

The life of a programme, and the period of transition in particular, is a time of uncertainty. Many normal procedures, reporting relationships and responsibilities may no longer apply. All of the sponsors must take the lead in establishing a style of leadership appropriate to the organization and the nature of the change. In most change situations, there will need to be increased emphasis on motivation of staff, promotion of team-working, empowerment at appropriate levels, encouragement of initiatives, and recognition of appropriate risk-taking.

Programme sponsorship is normally exercised through the programme board, as described in section 3.4.5 'Programme board'. The sponsors will delegate to and empower the programme board so that programme-level governance, management and control on a day-by-day basis, is practical. This must be done with defined limits of authority and clear rules for reporting back to the sponsors, especially when key decisions need to be made.

It is vital for effective sponsorship and governance that those involved have the necessary information. The box above gives examples of the sort of information that would typically be provided.

3.7 REASONS WHY PROGRAMMES FAIL

Given that some programmes are based on 'strategic bets', it is inevitable that some will fail. It is important to get to the point where the success or failure of such strategic bets can be judged, with minimum expenditure. An example of a strategic bet is where a new product is to be launched and the organization assumes this will gain a favourable share of its market. Nevertheless, in spite of the vast amounts of money spent on them, many programmes fail in that they do not deliver the business improvements that were expected. An example of a failed programme can be found in Case Study 3.1.

CASE STUDY 3.1: ZUIDERZEEWERKEN PROGRAMME

INTRODUCTION

The Dutch Zuiderzeewerken programme is an example of strategic programme leading to the physical creation of a whole new province across a period of three-quarters of a century.

The Dutch have been reclaiming land from the sea and creating polders ever since the thirteenth century. By the end of the nineteenth century, they were confident enough to contemplate their largest reclamation yet – the conversion into farmland of the stormy and unpredictable gulf of the North Sea known to the Dutch as the Zuider Zee. In 1913, Cornelis Lely, a prominent hydraulic engineer, became Minister of Public Works and in 1916 disastrous floods combined with restrictions on food imports associated with World War I threatened a food shortage. This was the spur to turn the engineers' dreams into hard reality.

PROGRAMME INITIATION

The Dutch Parliament initiated the programme in 1918 with the aim of damming the mouth of the gulf and then reclaiming five polders of new agricultural land, together with shipping locks, sluices and pumping stations. The expected benefits were to:

- protect the central Netherlands from flooding following tidal surges in the North Sea;

- increase the Dutch food supply with new agricultural land;

- improve water management by creating a fresh water lake out of the former uncontrolled salt water inlet.

To manage the day-to-day affairs of the programme a whole government department was created – the Dienst der Zuiderzeewerken – and the Minister of Public Works took responsibility for programme sponsorship.

COMPONENT PROJECTS

The programme started with the small, 1.5 mile-long Amsteldiep Dyke to link the island of Wieringen to the mainland. This took from 1920 to 1924 to complete but tested the construction methods to be used for the main dykes.

At this point, doubts were raised over the financial value of the programme, but a review concluded that not only was the programme worthwhile but that work should

189

be accelerated. As a result, work started on the 19-mile-long main dam across the mouth of the gulf, the Afsluit Dyke. This was finally completed in 1933 after an army of 5000 men had moved over 36 million cubic yards of sand and clay.

Over the next 30 years, four great polders were created within or next to the *Ijsselmeer*, the fresh water lake impounded behind the dam. Each was a massive programme in its own right, involving projects to raise an encircling dyke, dig drainage canals and construct massive pumping stations. Once the water had been pumped out, a sequence of crops was planted over several years to dry out the clay of the former sea bed. New villages and towns were then constructed and settlers moved in to farm the new land. The overall timetable for the major dyke building and polder drainage projects within the programme is shown in Table 3.2.

Table 3.2   Key dates in the Zuiderzeewerken programme

Project	Length (km)	Start	Closure	Drained
Amsteldiep Dyke	2.5	June 1920	July 1924	–
Afsluit Dyke	32	January 1927	May 1932	–
Wieringermeer	18	1927	July 1929	August 1930
Noordoostpolder	55	1936	December 1940	September 1942
Eastern Flevoland	90	Early 1950	September 1956	June 1957
Southern Flevoland	70	Early 1959	October 1967	May 29 1968
Houtrib Dyke	28	1963	September 1975	–

World War II slowed the process and in 1945 retreating German troops blew up the dykes of the Wieringermeer polder, destroying the work of two decades. Nevertheless, by 1970, 640 sq miles (1650 sq km) of new land had been created, providing homes and employment for over 100 000 people and work had started on the fifth polder, to be known as Markerwaard.

The overall layout of the various polders and dykes created by the programme is shown in the sketch map included as Figure 3.6.

CHANGING PRIORITIES

By this time, however, Dutch attitudes were changing and the programme had to change accordingly.

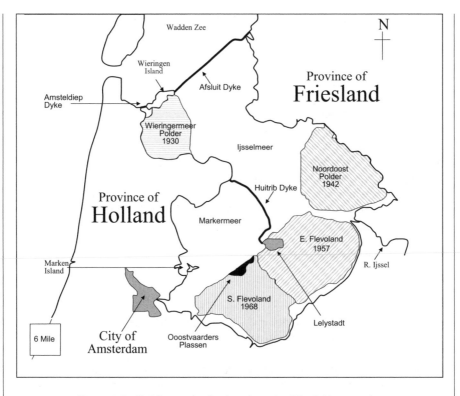

Figure 3.6 Sketch map showing key elements of the Zuiderzeewerken

As a member of the European Community, the Netherlands no longer needed to be self-sufficient in food. Indeed, only 3 years later, the Dutch Parliament passed an act requiring 10 per cent of all agricultural land to be set aside to curb overproduction of subsidized agricultural produce. On the other hand, the Dutch were much more conscious of general environmental issues and of the importance of space for leisure and recreation for the populations of their expanding cities. This had already affected planning of new polders. For example, in the first two polders (Wieringermeer and Noordoost), over 85 per cent of the land was devoted to agriculture, whereas in the most recent (South Flevoland) only 50 per cent was allocated to this use. Changing agricultural needs and increased motorized mobility meant that many of the agricultural villages originally planned were no longer necessary. In one case, building had been about to start when further work on it was cancelled. A significant area of the South Flevoland polder, the Oostvaarders Plassen, had originally been left for subsequent development as a heavy industry zone. Instead, after only a couple of years this landscape of shallow pools, islets and swamps became a popular resting and foraging area for many species of waterfowl, to the extent

191

that it rapidly turned into a nature reserve of national significance. As a result, the area was rezoned to become one of the most important nature reserves in the Netherlands.

Work on the enclosing dyke for the Markerwaard polder had started in 1941, only to be interrupted by World War II. A new start was made in 1963 and the 17-mile-long Houtrib Dyke was completed in 1975. However, strong opposition from environmentalists and leisure seekers had broken the consensus that had supported the Zuiderzeewerken programme since its inception. The balance of advantage had changed. The Huitrib Dyke already provided protection from flooding and there was no longer a pressing need for new agricultural land. Indeed, intensive agriculture was now seen as a threat to water supplies. It was also now realized that draining the polder would upset the water levels in the surrounding dry-land areas, causing the peat to dry out and land levels to sink. When compared against the costs of restoring the water balance, the value of the extra agricultural output seemed less attractive.

PROGRAMME TERMINATION

Political opposition grew so that in 1986 the government decided to indefinitely postpone the completion of the polder.

In 1996, the programme was reorganized as a normal state administration in charge of maintaining the sluices, locks, bridges and dykes in the region.

Over 78 years, the programme had successfully transformed the once capricious heart of the Netherlands into fertile agricultural land with many new communities combined with an extensive fresh water supply and, although not originally envisioned, a collection of valuable ecological and recreational areas. The three main polders were officially designated as Flevoland, the 12th province of the Netherlands and now provides homes to more than 350 000 people. The capital is Lelystadt, named after the engineer who initiated the whole programme. The completed Houtrib Dyke now forms a highway linking the Flevoland polders with North Holland and the enclosed fresh water lake is now called the Markermeer.

The causes of programme failure are varied and often complex. However, they generally fall into three groups:

- the initiative was a bad idea in the first place;
- there was poor implementation of the change;
- the external environment changed during the life of the programme.

3.7.1 A BAD IDEA IN THE FIRST PLACE

Following the process steps outlined in Chapter 2, 'The programme management process', will greatly improve the chances of weeding out bad ideas at an early stage. While not perfect, following a formal process is much better than guessing or relying on some indeterminate 'management experience'.

If it is unclear whether or not a programme will work, consider an early 'Proof of Concept' tranche, as outlined in Figure 3.7.

3.7.2 POOR IMPLEMENTATION OF THE CHANGE

Governance arrangements must ensure that the programme teams effectively plan and manage the activities that enable the organization to change and improve. This is important in its own right, but also if the programme fails, it will be necessary to be able to differentiate between poor implementation and a badly implemented programme. Otherwise the organization risks making the same mistakes over and over again.

As explained in Section 3.1, effective programmes have to be built on competence in the various skills on which the component projects are based. For this reason, it is vital for a programme to ensure adequate resources.

Guidance on resourcing can be found in Section 3.5.2 'Programme resourcing'.

3.7.3 REACTING TO EXTERNAL ENVIRONMENT CHANGES

The external environment often influences why a programme should be started in the first place. This could, for example, be competitor activity, legislation, social behaviour. This external environment never stands still and must be monitored carefully, first to spot changes and then to understand the impact on programmes.

Many programmes set out to solve problems or exploit opportunities that are driven by the events in the world outside the organization. This external world constantly changes. The size and nature of the problem or opportunity may alter rendering the programme more or less desirable. Governance must ensure that programmes are able to regularly monitor this external world, recognize the changes and assess the impact. They then may need to change to minimize the

Consider a company that thinks is has spotted a gap in the market for a new product.

At this point it doesn't know if it can make the product for an affordable price or to a standard acceptable to the customer. It also doesn't know if any of its competitors are aiming at the same market gap. If it uses the first tranche of the programme as a proof of concept, with small-scale production, it can test these uncertainties in the marketplace.

If the response is positive, the company will have established a market presence ahead of its competitors and production, marketing and distribution can safely be scaled up. If the proof of concept response is negative, the company can back out with minimal costs.

Figure 3.7   Example of use of proof of concept tranche

loss of benefits or conversely exploit the new opportunity. In some cases, the programme may need to be abandoned.

Examples of how environmental change requires adjustment of the programme can be found in the introduction to Chapter 12 'Management of scope and change'.

Programme governance, as exercised through the programme board, has a critical responsibility to help ensure programme success. If necessary, the board must decide to radically reform or even scrap the programme. The earlier this is done, the cheaper it will be to fix the problem. Unfortunately many organizations still try to fix programmes that are too far gone to succeed.

Case Study 3.2 illustrates the types of problem encountered in programmes of business change and lists remedial actions.

CASE STUDY SUMMARY 3.2: AN EXAMPLE OF A PROGRAMME THAT FAILED

This case study is based on a report by the National Audit Office.

The UK's National Audit Office scrutinizes the spending of central government departments and agencies to ensure economy, efficiency and effectiveness. It reports directly to Parliament and is independent of the UK government. It frequently reviews major public sector programmes and its reports are available from its web site at www.nao.org.uk

This case study is a summary of one such report. Names have been changed to make it anonymous, but it identifies the sort of problems that have afflicted many large programmes of business change in both the public and the private sectors. It also lists the actions that can be taken to rectify the problems that were identified.

INTRODUCTION

1. In 1993, the Departmental Information Systems Strategy (DISS) was established to achieve a common high-quality information technology infrastructure across all of the department's offices and semi-autonomous branches through which its services are provided to the citizens of England and Wales. The initial national programme was for the provision of a nation-wide computer infrastructure (comprising personal computers, operating software and a communications network supported by common servers) and a Work Recording and Management System (WORAMS). The implementation programme was managed by the Department's Production Unit. IXZ Information Systems Limited (IXZ), the main contractor, operates under an enabling agreement, signed in December 1994, to install the infrastructure and WORAMS, and provide a managed service. The agreement with IXZ was due to end in December 2001. The cost of implementing the strategy over 10 years was projected to be £97 million. Roll-out of the DISS infrastructure began in 1995 and was scheduled to be completed by March 1999.

2. The Department's Internal Inspection Unit carried out a thematic inspection of the Department's use of information, including the progress made in the implementation of the DISS strategy. The Unit's report – 'Using Information and Technology to Improve Efficiency' – was published in October 2000. The Unit

identified weaknesses in the information available to operational staff and in the IT systems and concluded that the Department needed to make very significant improvements to give operational staff the IT systems and support they needed.

3. The National Audit Office collaborated with the Department's Internal Inspection Unit in its work. This report presents the results of the National Audit Office's further examination of what lessons could be learned from the Department's management of the DISS and WORAMS programme.

KEY FINDINGS

THE CURRENT SITUATION

4. By the end of March 2001, the DISS computer network covered 49 out of the 54 branches and offices. From 1 April 2001, there will be a reorganized structure with 42 local areas of which 38 have access to the DISS network. Given that the network was introduced into autonomous and locally managed branches, this was a notable achievement. The infrastructure has led to improved communication within and between branches and offices.

5. Links with Head Office and the systems of other related agencies have yet to be made. The WORAMS work management system was introduced in 39 out of the 54 branches, and is used substantially by 16 of these, representing only 20 per cent of the Department's budget. WORAMS has proved difficult to use, and its development, overseen by the Head Office, did not keep pace in all respects with changing business requirements. As a result of the limitations with WORAMS, the Department has suspended its further development except for essential maintenance of the software.

6. The full economic cost of the DISS infrastructure, support and the development and maintenance of WORAMS is expected to be at least £118 million by the end of 2001, which would be 70 per cent at constant prices above the expenditure forecast in the Department's original business case for the same time period. The enabling agreement with IXZ is largely open ended, with additional expenditure commitments being made as and when required. Poor specification of expected outputs, weaknesses in service monitoring and inadequate control by the Department over the issue of purchase orders contributed to the higher than expected cost of the programme. Since early 2000, the Department has held back its pursuit of IT development work because of concerns as to whether new purchase orders under its enabling agreement with IXZ would meet European public procurement requirements.

7. The introduction of a national infrastructure and work management system was always likely to present a significant management challenge. However, the Department's programme management team suffered from a lack of continuity in its leadership and was not fully resourced to deal with the scale of the issues facing it. In its first seven years, for example, the programme team had seven Programme Directors. In terms of day-to-day programme and project management, we found that responsibilities were not always clear, and that communication between the Department's Head Office and the branches was not always effective. The Department has already recognized some of these issues and the Information and Technology Group for the new national structure is planned to have a complement of around 50 staff compared to the previous effective complement of 12.5.

ON INSTALLING DISS

8. By the end of 2000 the DISS network extended across 47 out of 54 branches, covering 87 per cent of the premises within the networked areas; and it was rolled out to a further two branches by the end of March 2001. The Department told us that it remained committed to extending DISS across all areas but, as at February 2001, had yet to make the necessary arrangements.

9. Forty two of the 47 branches on DISS by the end of 2000 reported to us that DISS had brought improvements in communications within their areas. DISS has not yet delivered the planned new links with other related Government information systems. This was partly because WORAMS had not been adopted by all branches and partly because of delays in the development of information systems by other related Government agencies. DISS has not provided the expected Internet access and external e-mail services. The progress of these and other developments has been affected by the Department's decision not to allow new purchase orders under the enabling agreement with IXZ because of concerns as to whether this would be in compliance with European public procurement requirements.

10. The Department promoted but did not actively monitor other benefits from the DISS programme, including business change within the operation of the branches. As a result, it is not possible to quantify the business benefits derived from the introduction of these systems. Costs and achievements have not been monitored against projections in the original business case.

ON THE PROBLEMS WITH WORAMS

11. Users have found WORAMS difficult to operate. Consultants commissioned by the board overseeing the programme reported that the user interface contained

defects that compromised the ability of users to perform their work. The Department did not ensure that the development of WORAMS kept pace in all respects with changing business needs, for instance it does not provide local branches with direct access to operational data held by other areas in order to help in the transfer of case information, nor does it provide a national database to support new local procedures to improve the management of high-risk cases. Generally branches were having to rely on paper files, card indexes and registers to retain and access information on cases presenting a risk of harm to the public.

12. The development of WORAMS was based on software already operating in one branch. The Department underestimated the technical risks associated with transferring an existing system onto the DISS network. The poor user interface of WORAMS was evident from an early stage, along with the other technical problems and faults which had not been resolved by initial testing. In July 1996, a review commissioned by the Department from an IT consultant from the Central Computer and Telecommunications Agency noted several risks. In the consultant's view, acceptance and pilot testing of WORAMS suffered from a lack of clear direction, criteria to measure success, and coordination. Even if formally accepted, the consultant thought that the system's acceptability and usability were unknown. The Department team sought to address these problems but did not prevent the roll out of poor quality software.

13. The requirement for WORAMS to produce reports for management purposes was not adequately specified at the start of the development cycle, nor was a subsequent requirement from the Department for IXZ to develop standard reports using specialist software, known as GQL, which extracts data from databases. The Inspection Unit found that branches had to invest their own unbudgeted resources to make the GQL software work satisfactorily. GQL had been installed in 46 branches by early 2000.

14. The Department initially expected that WORAMS would cost some £4 million but it now estimates it will have cost almost £11 million at constant prices by December 2001, including the costs of work to ensure year 2000 compliance and the costs of the additional reporting tool. During the course of the DISS programme, branches on the DISS network spent nearly £1.2 million on the purchase and development of supplementary software to record and manage cases. The five branches still not on DISS have spent additional resources developing their alternative work management system. They estimate they have spent some £350 000 on development work and a further £30 000 a year supporting it. In total some 27 branches are developing or using alternative computerized systems for recording or managing case details. This position has resulted in case records being held in a number of different formats, creating

problems for the transfer of cases between branches. A major challenge for any new national work management system will be the need to manage the migration of information from existing systems.

ON THE CONTRACT WITH IXZ

15. The Department's contract with IXZ was drawn up in the form of an enabling agreement. It provides for the Department and its branches to take out purchase orders from a specified range of products and services at prices set out in schedules to the agreement. The performance of IXZ was not managed effectively. Monitoring of service levels against the enabling agreement was sporadic; and performance against the service level agreement, not agreed until 1998, was not monitored systematically.

16. The Department raised a total of 69 purchase orders between December 1994 and March 2000 and consultants commissioned by the Department concluded in 1998 that there were unnecessary orders, duplication and overlap, and a risk of overpayment. To rationalize the situation the Department negotiated with IXZ a consolidated purchase order for support and maintenance at a cost of £5.4 million a year with effect from 1 April 2000. The Department's Audit and Assurance Unit concluded that there had been significant inadequacies in the negotiation of the consolidated purchase order. The purchase order specifies the resources IXZ is to use to support DISS rather than deliverables, leaving value for money at risk. In recognition of this the Department has introduced tighter service delivery management procedures.

17. Since November 1999 the Department has had concerns about whether letting new purchase orders under its enabling agreement with IXZ would comply with the competition requirements under European Public Procurement Directives. Legal advice received by the Department suggests that any new purchase orders raised under the enabling agreement are unlawful. The Department has now concluded that over the remaining period of the IXZ agreement, up to December 2001, any IT development work which is needed, and which cannot be delivered by IXZ within the terms of the consolidated support and maintenance agreement, would have to be procured through separate legal agreements.

18. Failure by the Department to prioritize the necessary preparatory work has contributed to delay in establishing a new strategic partnership to follow the end of the enabling agreement with IXZ in December 2001. As a result the Department is likely to have to bear additional costs from a proposed separate interim contract after the expiry of the current enabling agreement. The work to manage this interim contract is known as the first phase procurement project. On

the other hand, the Department considers that this delay has brought the advantage of allowing the new national business strategy and change programme to be specified more definitively before key decisions are taken on the strategic contract.

ON THE SKILLS AND RESOURCES OF THE MANAGEMENT TEAM:

19. Over the course of the programme, from 1993 to the end of 2000 there have been seven Programme Directors in charge of the DISS programme, of whom only two had significant experience of managing major IT-based business change programmes. The programme management team also suffered frequent changes of staff. Technical experts and specialists within the team tended to be consultants working on short-term assignments.

20. From 1996 the programme's management controls and reporting arrangements were based on the PRINCE2 project management methodology. But the management structure did not include a programme assurance function. Furthermore, formal project management methods were not embedded firmly in working practices and they fell into disuse.

21. In January 2000 consultants reported to the Department that its Information Services capability was badly under-resourced with misaligned skills, and that this was exposing the Department and its operations to significant business risk.

RECOMMENDATIONS FOR THE FUTURE

22. At the end of 1999 the Department started reviewing its IT strategy and in July 2000 it drew up a recovery programme to address challenges thrown up by the DISS programme. The new Information Systems Programme Board, which is now responsible for defining the IT requirements of the reorganized Department and overseeing their implementation, is taking this work forward. The new IT strategy work makes a commitment to develop further the national systems and to achieve links with other related agencies. We recommend that:

- the Department ensures that the national network is completed and extended to the national directorate to provide a backbone for the operation and accountability of the new structure;
- the Production Unit ensures that its new information strategy is firmly linked with the Department's business strategy and that performance on IT is reviewed at least annually, in full consultation with the branches; and Production Unit takes every opportunity, on future IT development, to re-

engineer existing administrative systems to enable the full business benefits of IT to be achieved.

23. Current plans propose a modular approach to addressing the needs for work management software, utilizing systems developed by local branches and introducing a new national case index. We recommend that the Department:

- develops proper user specifications for work management systems to succeed WORAMS, building on current experience and reflecting clear statements of the business objectives and requirements for the new national service – in particular, it should address their usability and their ability to produce management information;
- ensures that proposals for any new national case management system, or any other major technical developments, are subject to a full evaluation of the likely technical risks before going ahead;
- ensures that the organizational implications of any future IT developments are properly evaluated and that there is full user involvement, with effective management arrangements to ensure that issues arising at local level can be fed back quickly to appropriate contacts within both the Department and the supplier;
- ensures that there are effective arrangements for keeping the branches informed of progress against targets in the strategy;
- explores the best contractual options for developing software to succeed WORAMS and, in adopting a modular approach, to ensure that a strong overall design is developed so that the modules fit together well; and
- ensures that test plans, with clear objectives and criteria for determining success, are formally agreed with suppliers prior to starting the design and development of new software.

24. The plan being taken forward by the Information Systems Programme Board stresses the importance of tighter supplier management and sets expectations for the procurement of the first phase and subsequent strategic contracts to follow on from the enabling agreement with IXZ. We recommend that the Department:

- agrees with IXZ specific deliverables for the remainder of the contract to ensure that it gets value from the support and maintenance agreement;
- ensures that its future IT contracts are not open ended and crucial elements not left to post-contract negotiations – they should be based on a clear specification of the expected outputs and quality of service and should ensure that appropriate contract risks are borne by the contractor; and

- ensures that it effectively manages its suppliers, involving systematic and strategic monitoring of contract performance.

25. The Department has recruited a new Head of IT for the Production Unit. His management team will comprise a Head of IT Strategy, Head of Service Management and a Head of Programme Management and he will have a complement of some 50 staff. The Department has agreed that programme assurance will be a priority, and has appointed an experienced consultant to provide quality assurance for the first phase procurement project. We recommend that the Department:

    - pays full regard to recent recommendations made by the Committee of Public Accounts and the Cabinet Office relating to the management of IT projects;
    - undertakes a full risk assessment of its new Information Systems Strategy and introduces proper risk management procedures;
    - provides for greater continuity of leadership for its IT programme and adequate staffing; and
    - ensures that the programme's management team reflects an appropriate balance between the advantages gained from using secondees and the need for project experience and continuity. Timely and appropriate training should be provided to project management staff when necessary.

REFERENCES

Cabinet Office (2000) *Successful IT: Modernising Government in Action*. London: The Stationery Office.

Gray, R.J. (2001), 'Organisational Climate and Project Success', *International Journal of Project Management*, 19(2): 103–09.

4 Programme planning and control

4.1 INTRODUCTION

This chapter covers the techniques for planning and controlling a number of programmes, each comprising a number of projects. It does not cover techniques for the planning and control of individual projects such as network planning, critical path analysis, work breakdown structures and resource assignments.

This chapter therefore deals with:

- The differences between programme planning and project planning including the planning of programmes and portfolios and single projects;
- progress measurement in the non-physical workload of most programmes;
- the responsibility for planning when resources are shared by functional and project teams;
- the case for standardization and the role of the programme office;
- the need for planning for the delivery of benefits;
- mechanisms for programme and portfolio planning and control;
- barriers to successful programme planning;
- the need for communicating the plans;
- statistical analysis of historic data across many projects.

4.2 A DEFINITION

A definition of programme planning is:

> The cooperative planning and monitoring of multiple resources across multiple workloads.

It is assumed that each project is planned using techniques such as critical path, precedence networks and work breakdown structures. It is assumed that the organization has a number of people who share their working time across:

- a range of projects
- a 'business as usual' (BAU) workload
- 'non-work' activities such as holidays, training and illness.

This chapter considers the differences between the planning and control of a single project and a portfolio or programme of projects and then considers some approaches to the latter environment.

4.3 DIFFERENCES BETWEEN PROGRAMME PLANNING AND PROJECT PLANNING

This section outlines why planning and control of projects and programmes are very different.

4.3.1 PROGRAMMES VERSUS PORTFOLIOS

We have discussed why organizations choose to run projects. They may be projects designed to change the organization through the delivery of benefits, they may be projects designed to deliver a product to a customer. They may be part of a very large single objective and are sometimes referred to as *delivery programmes*. In other chapters of this handbook, the reasons for selecting programmes of projects where the projects are intended to deliver change to the host organization is discussed. These are sometimes known as *change programmes*.

Programme planning and control applies in all cases (see Figure 4.1). The purpose of each programme and project has little influence over the need to plan and monitor the work. However, the parts of the lifecycle that are normally planned does vary when considering different types of programmes (see Section 1.6, 'Types of programmes') In the case of planning within a supplier organization working on programmes, planning and control is normally concerned with the period of time between the award of a contract by a customer to a supplier through to delivery by the supplier to the customer.

In the case of change programmes run by an organization intending to achieve internal change, planning and control often forms part of the project selection process and continues into the period when benefits are delivered.

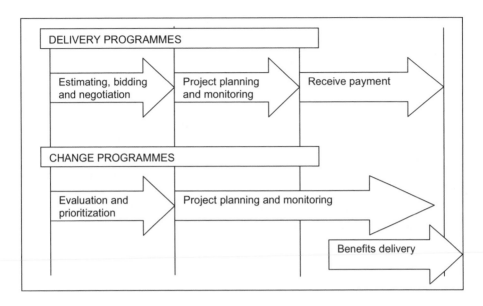

Figure 4.1 Planning in delivery and change programmes

4.3.2 SINGLE PROJECT VERSUS MULTIPLE PROJECTS

The techniques of programme and project planning have become polarized with the large, single, physical engineering project at one end of the scale and the portfolio of relatively small, technological and/or change programmes at the other.

Typically, on the engineering worksite, the construction team is not concerned with the rationale for the project as they begin with a design of a deliverable and their mission is to create that deliverable. There is often a model or drawings of the deliverable. The decision to proceed with the overall project is taken by a group separate from the engineering team. The value of the deliverable is experienced by a group long after the engineering team have departed.

For example, a hotel chain may investigate and evaluate the commercial potential for a hotel in a specific area. In the early stages, they will purchase land and instruct a design team to create a design. Engineering construction organizations will receive invitations to negotiate or bid for the construction work and one will erect the hotel. Once the engineering construction team have completed the work, the hotel chain will carry out marketing, personnel recruitment and other projects to make the hotel function and they will enjoy the benefit of the income it generates.

From the perspective of the engineering construction team, there is only one

205

project. A single management structure contains all the people who are devoted to the construction of the hotel. A number of contractors and subcontractors may be working towards the one single objective. In this environment, planning will typically be represented by a single hierarchy of plans with one overall plan supported by more detailed plans for elements of the construction project (see Figure 4.2).

In many organizations, there will be a wide range of programmes in progress at any one time. These programmes will be designed to deliver improvements to the host organization and many people will be working on a range of programmes simultaneously as well as maintaining the smooth operation of the business – BAU.

A complex management structure will include functional departments, programmes and projects where interests and motivations will vary very significantly.

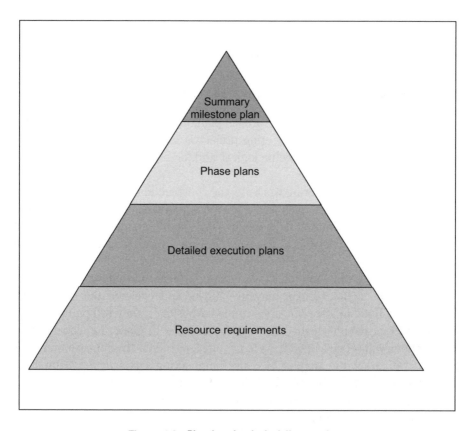

Figure 4.2   Planning of a single delivery project

In this environment, there will be many programme and project plans interacting with each other and the BAU workload (see Figure 4.3).

It is especially important in these environments to ensure that there is a clear understanding of the allocation of responsibility for planning and control and especially over the allocation of resources.

4.3.3 FOCUS ON CHANGE OR DELIVERY

The focus in the world of change programme management is on the delivery of change. The benefit derived from a programme could be an improved way of working, a new product or service or reduced running costs of an operation within the organization.

Very frequently, the benefits are derived from utilizing the combined outputs of many projects. Commonly, a programme delivers benefits that rely on a whole range of projects. Projects are often distributed throughout the organization and to outside agencies and contractors following their specialisms. For example, a hospital ward might comprise the following projects:

- **Design:** Executed by a retained architectural practice.
- **Construction:** Executed by a retained building contractor.
- **Equipment:** Executed by an internal department specialist in supplying medical equipment.
- **Commission:** Staff training and protocols executed by the hospital staff.

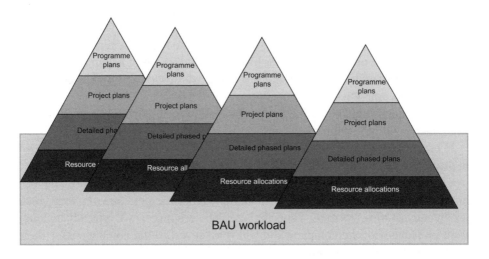

Figure 4.3 Planning of multiple change projects

Programme planning and control must span all of these activities and the inter-relationships between the projects including the delivery of benefits.

Changes in the environment may change the case for or the purpose of a programme and therefore change budget or timescale or scope. For example, a programme to launch a new product or service may be fundamentally altered by a change in the marketplace such as a competitor launching a similar product.

Therefore, planning and control covers the whole change delivery process from the investigation stage, where the viability is scrutinized, through the execution stage and into the benefit delivery stage when the changes are delivered and the benefits realized.

In comparison, planning for the single project normally focuses on delivering the deliverable – typically for a reward, so time and cost often outweigh other factors. For example, a construction company might build a hotel but would have no involvement with the hiring of staff, establishing the booking systems, purchase of consumables and the ongoing management of the business operations of the hotel.

4.3.4 CLASSES OF RESOURCES VERSUS TEAM MEMBERS

Single civil engineering projects typically focus on the use of classes of resource. Planning will be task centric and use resources such as welders, labourers and painters. The requirement faced by the planner is to develop a plan that fits the timescale and to predict the requirement for such resources. A resource histogram is a suitable tool to show the predicted requirement for each trade and the project management team will use histograms to plan the recruitment the required resources. Such resources will normally be available in relatively short timescales, in the order of a week or less, and will be able to become productive in a similar timescale. Typically, the resources will leave the organization when their work is complete.

The planner is unlikely to have any relationship with individual resources and will typically not know their names.

Programmes of projects normally involve specific individuals and the purpose of planning is to maximize the utilization or output of those individuals.

The resources available to perform the tasks on the projects are normally well known as individuals. Very often, certain individuals are members of a very small group capable of performing a specific task. The resources will typically be long-term employees of the company and will remain within the company after their work on each project is complete.

In the extreme case, only one person can perform a task. Any other person would require extensive training. Simple tasks can be undertaken by contractors sourced to help with specific activities whose employment will be temporary.

Recruitment on many specialized types of work is long term. A time span of 6 months or more between the decision to recruit additional people and the point where they become fully productive is not unusual.

These resources may be involved in many projects and will very often have a BAU workload plus a range of personal related activities, including personal development and holidays.

The programme planner's role therefore is to understand that the workload is made up of many projects combined into many programmes, each of which has a priority, an alignment with the organization's objective and a number of expected benefits. The planner's prime role therefore is to help the management team to maximize the benefit the organization can deliver from the individuals employed by the business. A second role will be to recommend areas where long-term recruitment will be appropriate.

4.3.5 PROGRESS MEASUREMENT

This section compares the problems of monitoring progress across single tasks in physical and non-physical projects and suggests some appropriate techniques.

There are four areas in which there are major differences between single, physical projects and programmes of high-technology projects with predominantly non-physical deliverables, described below.

4.3.5.1 Regularity of progress

Many single projects deliver physical projects and therefore allow physical measurement of achievement. It is possible to 'count the bricks laid'; 'metres of pipe fitted' or 'steelwork painted'. In this environment, production rates are relatively constant across the life of a task. A task laying 1000 bricks can be generally regarded as 50 per cent complete when 500 bricks are laid (see Figure 4.4). Even where the relationship is not quite this simple, a relationship can usually be found.

Programmes typically contain non-physical deliverables – software, documentation, testing and systems developed. Arguably there is no measurable progress until, for example, the software is seen to actually work. The programmer may have a view of how much work has been done and how much remains to be done, but there are no physical elements to count (see Figure 4.5).

Attempts have been made to transfer the concept of counting individual components by, for example, counting lines of code. This has proved inadequate

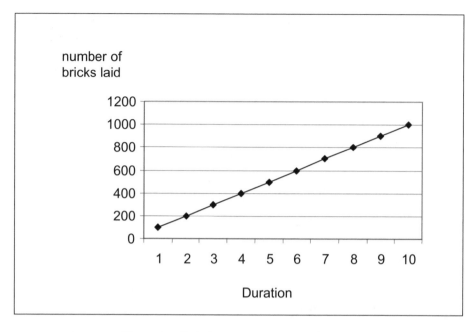

Figure 4.4   Typical progress on physical deliverable

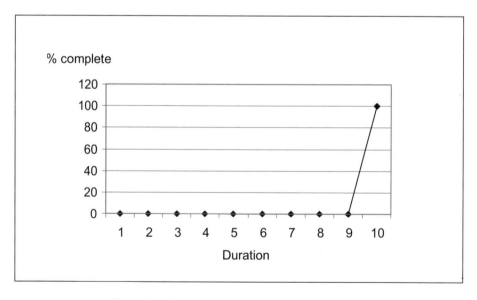

Figure 4.5   Typical progress on non-physical deliverable

as it is only the completed set of lines of code that provides the product. There is no accurate way of estimating the number of lines of code and gaps may not be apparent.

There is no reliable way of measuring the percentage completion of a task with a non-physical deliverable. There is no equivalent of a regular production rate.

4.3.5.2 Early warning signs

There is another issue when monitoring work. If the estimated duration for a task representing the laying of 1000 bricks is inaccurate, this will show up after the first few progress monitor checks. The planner will observe that the actual laying of bricks is happening at a rate inconsistent with the predicted rate. The planner will investigate the cause for this through discussion with the relevant manager to discover if the rate is likely to continue at the currently observed rate, increase or decrease. Simple mathematics allow the planner to change the rate and predict a new end date for the task and the effect this will have on other work.

As it is often difficult or impossible to measure progress in any rational way in programmes of high-technology, non-physical work, this approach is inadequate to meet the needs of the programme planner.

4.3.5.3 The individual role

Finally, human resources such as bricklayers and painters are not normally involved in the progress monitoring process. There is generally a manager who is involved in planning and monitoring the work under their direct control. The project planner or project planning team therefore discusses progress with a number of managers.

In the programme management world, the individual human resource will be sufficiently involved in the workload to understand the planning and control aspects of their individual contribution. A timesheet system closely integrated with a planning and control system will provide valuable information about the distribution of time across the projects and non-project workload. This may include both estimates of planned work and records of actual work. Each individual human resource should play a role in estimating their own work and recording actual work done through such a system. The individual team members are in the best position to understand their own work and the time it has taken and will take to complete.

For these reasons, programme planners wishing to monitor progress successfully should find a way ask the individual human resources for their estimates of remaining time or effort. These estimates should be checked or approved by their managers to avoid the dangers associated with misunderstandings and poor time management.

All team members should understand the comparative priorities of the programmes, projects and BAU work they are involved in and their role within those initiatives. They should manage their time or have their time managed accordingly.

4.3.5.4 Estimates to complete

Programme planners focus on the remaining work to be done or the remaining time to be spent and schedule accordingly.

Asking for an estimate of remaining work to be done or the remaining time to be spent on a task makes no assumptions about production rates nor about the accuracy of the original estimate for the task. It is immediately helpful to the planning process. Team members will be aware of barriers to progress and can raise issues or in another way communicate reasons why they believe work will proceed as they predict. It is not associated with a 'blame' culture, but is associated with a realistic and open culture.

Individual team members should be asked to:

- provide estimates of remaining effort or time on current activities;
- raise issues that might prevent work from proceeding;
- estimate when the work should be progressed and completed.

This means they are included in the planning process and regard the programme, project and team plans with a sense of ownership. They feel part of the management and planning processes and generally react well to this. This has been found to be a highly motivating factor.

4.3.6 SHARED RESOURCES AND THE FUNCTIONAL TEAM ROLE

In the single project environment, almost everyone on the project works towards the completion of the project and very often this is on a full-time basis. In the programme management environment, this is no longer the case. Most people are involved in many projects, often at the same time and may have an ongoing BAU workload as well.

Individual human resources are often grouped into specialist, functional teams or departments headed by a team leader or manager. The term *functional team* serves to indicate how these teams provide a specialist function to the organization.

These specialist teams might include:

- Software Team
- Hardware Team

- Communications Team
- Documentation Group
- Installation Services
- Testing Centre.

A management structure will show many-to-many relationships between the projects and these functional teams and it is vital that every organization makes the relationships clear. An organizational structure supported by role definitions held within a methodology such as *Managing Successful Programmes* (OGC, 2003) will help to clarify the roles and relationships between individuals working on a programme or group of programmes.

Many project managers have the responsibility to deliver particular projects, but have no authority over the human resources who are vital to that delivery. Project managers are expected, through their own powers of persuasion and personal contacts within the organization, to divert a number of team members from their current work to gain their contribution to the specific projects. Often these team members will face a confused set of priorities from a number of project managers and their own head of department. In the worst case, their contribution to each project damages their own ability to meet their other personal success criteria.

A great many projects fail to achieve their objectives due to a lack of clarity in this area. It is a common cause of dissatisfaction within the organization and can be very demoralizing.

This section lays out the general rule for a more formal understanding of the relationships between project managers and human resources and the impact this has on programme planning and control.

This assumes that the human resources report to and are grouped into functional teams and that projects require input from these people to move towards completion (see Figure 4.6). The functional team contains the resources that specialize in a specific area of the organization and include groups such as IT, Software, Java Programmers or Documentation. These teams work on a variety of programmes as well as having a BAU workload. Many project managers compete for input from these specialist groups and to deliver a specific project usually involves gaining input from some or all of these functional groups.

A resource pool is a special form of a functional team in that it has no BAU workload.

This environment is sometimes referred to as *matrix management* to represent the idea that the requirements of the projects are at right angles to the requirements of the specialist or functional teams.

In matrix management terminology, a work package is the work a specific functional team are required to perform on a specific project (see Figure 4.7).

213

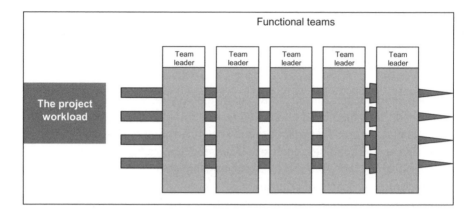

Figure 4.6   Functional teams

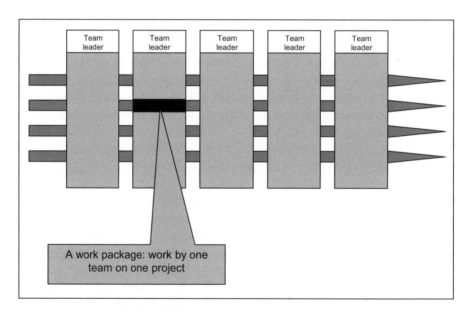

Figure 4.7   Functional teams, projects and work packages

There are only two workable relationships between project managers and team members in a specialist group, two ways of managing work packages: the *delegation* method and the *loan* or *secondment* method. The requirement and responsibility for planning and control is different according to the chosen form. It is important to note that many organizations use both of these models depending on the nature of the functional teams and the nature of the projects being undertaken.

4.4 THE DELEGATION METHOD

In the delegation method, a project manager asks a team leader to perform a work package. A work package is the work one functional team performs on one project. The request should always go to the team leader – never directly to a team member.

The request defines the work to be done, when it is required, the inputs that will be available and deliverables expected. There may be a budget.

The functional team leader decides which individual or individuals should work on the project and when they should contribute. The functional team leader will understand the many projects that require the team's input, the team's holidays and other commitments, the skills within the functional team that this work package requires and the need to challenge them with new work.

The project manager need not know the person or people working on the work package and in some cases may never even meet them. The project manager should not in this case issue instructions to the team member. The relationship is very much like that between an architect and a building contractor in that negotiations and instructions go through the foreman or team leader to the individual workers.

A disadvantage is that there is no 'project team' and many people find project teams exciting and motivating.

Delegation may take place at many levels: programme manager to project manager, project manager to phase manager, project or phase manager to functional manager.

In the delegation method, the responsibility for detailed planning and the assignment of people to tasks rests with the functional team leader. Typically, the project manager will have a plan showing the overall project timescale and the timescale for each work package agreed with the functional team leaders.

The project plan in Figure 4.8 shows only work at the work package level.

The functional team leader will tend to have a much more detailed plan showing each individual team member's workload over the forthcoming period. In the functional team leader's plan, each work package may be broken down into a number of tasks and these tasks will be assigned to individual team members.

Figure 4.9 shows a functional team leader's plan at the assignment level with details of the team and their workload.

This is not a project plan, but a plan for a team covering a specific period. It will include the team's contribution to many projects and may also detail non-project work as well. Some organizations refer to these as *work plans.*

The team members will update the functional team leader through a timesheet and the functional team leader will bring the team plan up to date in light of these timesheets.

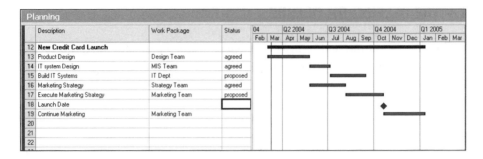

Figure 4.8   Project plan at the work package level

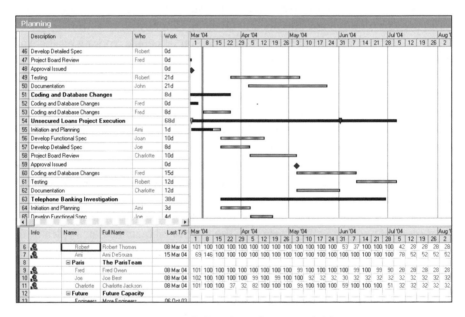

Figure 4.9   Project plan at the resource level

The functional team leader will update the project manager by providing latest scheduled dates for each work package being undertaken by the functional team for that project manager.

The project manager's plans will be kept up to date by reference to update information from the functional team leaders. The individual's timesheets will not be relevant to the project manager, as the timesheets will update the department plan with totals of recorded actual work done, cash spent, work to be done, cash to be spent and timing. This summarized information is then passed to the project manager by the team leader on a regular basis.

4.5 THE LOAN OR SECONDMENT METHOD

Here a person is loaned full time or part time from a functional team to a project team.

The project manager requests from the functional team leader the loan of a resource. The project manager asks for a person by name or describes the skills the required person should have. The project manager defines the time period of the proposed loan and the part of the person's time required. After a negotiation an individual is seconded from the functional team to the project team. The project team is made up of people loaned to the project team from a variety of functional teams.

The project team is therefore formed from full-time and part-time loaned members. Members of the team will tend to come and go during the life of the project, but there is a sense of team. It is a key advantage that a project team exists under this method.

The project manager directly instructs the project team members about their duties and receives updates from them about their progress, achievements and problems.

The project manager may use these seconded people in any suitable way as long as the start and finish date and the part of their time allocated to the project team are respected. If there is a need to go beyond these limits, the project manager should negotiate with the functional team leader once more.

In such cases, the team members will often still refer to their functional manager for personal development and other personnel issues such as holidays and training.

These loaned people have two or more direct reporting lines. They may have their time divided between two or more managers and therefore should report progress to more than one person.

Here the project manager has a responsibility to plan the work at the assignment level. Project plans tend to be in greater detail when work is executed through the secondment model than with the delegation model. The functional manager's plans tend to show when the team members are scheduled to be on loan away from the department. The project manager's plan shows the tasks required and the availability of the resources on loan to the project. The project manager assigns the project team members to specific tasks. Each project team member updates the project manager, probably through a timesheet, and this information is used to update the project plan. The functional team leader's plan is less granular, showing only the work being carried out within the group and the loans of team members to a number of project teams.

Frequently, individual's timesheets are submitted in part to both one or more

217

project managers and the relevant functional manager so that an individual's timesheet may update more than one plan.

When a combination of delegations and loans are used, both project and functional managers maintain detailed plans for the work they are themselves managing at an individual assignment level.

Table 4.1 compares, in summary, the delegation and loan methods.

A resource pool is a special case of the secondment model. A resource pool manager maintains a pool of resources with the sole intention of loaning them out to project managers. The resource manager will be 100 per cent effective if all of the resources are loaned and are scheduled to be loaned out to projects. The prime difference in these terms between a functional team and a resource pool is that a resource pool has no background business as usual work load.

4.6 PLANNING FOR THE DELIVERY OF BENEFITS

In project planning, the planner is concerned only with the delivery of the project. In programme planning, the planner should maintain a plan through to the delivery of benefits. As change projects are drawn to completion, their deliverables or outputs are normally drawn together to create a new capability for the organization. This new capability will be handed over to a business user who will then change the way in which that part of the business is run and deliver the

Table 4.1   Comparison of delegation and loan models

Delegation	Loan
Defined work package	A person with a skill
Timescale for the work	Start and end dates of the loan
Inputs to enable to work to proceed	Percentage of the team member's time
Outputs or deliverables expected	
Budget	
Project manager plans at work package level, functional manager plans at the assignment level	Functional manager plans loans and other work at the assignment level. Project manager plans at the assignment level
Team leader requests and receives updates from team members	Project manager requests and receives updates from team members

benefit. For example, consider the outsourcing of a support operation. This might include a number of projects such as:

● searching for suitable contractors;
● specifying and agreeing a service level agreement;
● customer awareness training;
● staff reduction or redeployment;
● disposal or reuse of existing premises;
● communications and wide area network (WAN) installation;
● establishing monitoring processes.

Once most these projects are completed, the programme manager can hand over the newly operating outsourced system to the appropriate business user who will be involved in some final implementation and handover work and who will manage the new contractor and deliver the reduction in running costs to the organization.

The programme planner should ensure that plans cover the whole process and should monitor those plans until the delivery of benefits is well underway. There should be a clear understanding of the point at which programme planning ceases.

4.7 MECHANISMS FOR PROGRAMME AND PORTFOLIO PLANNING AND CONTROL

There are two models for planning and control of a portfolio of projects. They are known as:

● consolidation model
● delegation model.

Each of these models is described below.

4.7.1 THE CONSOLIDATION MODEL

The consolidation model assumes that a number of discrete project and other plans exist and that from time to time these plans are consolidated into a programme plan.

Seven stages in the planning of a portfolio of projects have been identified:

1. **Planning:** The process of planning each project in terms of time and resource requirements. This is similar to the planning of a single project.
2. **Transmission:** The transmission of the individual project plans to a central point.

3. **Consolidation:** The process of combining the many individual project plans into a programme plan.
4. **Evaluation:** Exposure of inter-project conflicts and identification of problems, especially multi-project resource over-demands.
5. **Experimentation and decision making:** The process of experimenting with alternative strategies to find optimal schedules for the future workload.
6. **Dissemination:** The dissemination of decisions taken back to the individual project teams and the modification of individual project plans.
7. **Achievement measurement:** Feedback via timesheet systems either to measure effort or to monitor progress, or both.

These are discussed in greater detail below in Section 4.8, 'The consolidation process' and shown in Figure 4.10 later.

This consolidation process is typically the responsibility of the programme office. It is often necessary to chase the many project managers to increase the number of the up-to-date plans available at the time of consolidation. Typically, every iteration of the process takes between 2 and 4 weeks.

This consolidation process has a number of objectives, described below.

4.7.1.1 Reporting

Once the many project plans have been consolidated into one large plan, reports summarizing all projects may be prepared for management. These reports are typically produced once a month. Modern web-based tools permit more frequent reporting, perhaps on a weekly basis.

4.7.1.2 Logical connections

There are often logical connections between projects. It is common for a task in one project to logically depend on an output from a task in another. For example, the testing of software in a software development project might depend on the availability of hardware or a network being purchased and installed in another project. These are often known as off-project, cross-project or inter-project dependencies.

The programme office will have responsibility to ensure that these logical links are scheduled to happen in the correct order and in accordance with their logic despite the changes to the many project plans likely to occur during the programme.

The programme office may maintain a list of such logical links and check that all cross-project links are recognized and respected in a consolidated plan. Where delays in one project are likely to impact another, it is clearly important that the programme office advises both interested project managers of the impending problem.

4.7.1.3 Resource conflicts

Many projects will make demands on the same resources and each project manager will tend to plan to use these resources with little regard for the work they have to do on other projects, to meet BAU workload and for personal reasons, including training and holidays. Project managers often have no way of knowing the resources that will be available to them in detail. The result is that projects may be planned based on unrealistic assumptions of resource availability.

Once the many project and other plans are consolidated, the programme office can view the total demand for each resource or type of resource across the many plans and against time. It is possible to compare the total resource requirements across all work with the availability of each resource.

The total demand, made by all projects, on all types of resources can be viewed. You can see, for example, one histogram showing all the programmers working on all projects. This will frequently show an over-demand for many of the resources over time. This is valuable information, as it indicates times when the projects will not proceed as planned due to resource shortfalls. Discussions and negotiations between the many stakeholders, project and programme management should follow and, at the end of the ensuing discussions, some projects will be rescheduled, some contractors hired in and other steps taken to arrive at a workable plan. This is a regular, iterative process.

When planned requirements exceed availability and no resolution is obvious, the programme office should report the problem to the programme management team in good time to minimize the impact.

It is very important that resources are identified and named consistently across the many plans. If inconsistent terminology is used, this process cannot work effectively.

4.7.2 THE CONSOLIDATION PROCESS

The consolidation process has seven steps:

1. **Planning:** The process of planning each project in terms of time and resource requirements. This is similar to the planning of a single project.
2. **Transmission:** The transmission of the individual project plans to a central point.
3. **Consolidation:** The process of combining the many individual project plans into a programme plan.

4. **Evaluation:** Exposure of inter-project conflicts and identification of problems, especially multi-project resource over-demands.
5. **Experimentation and decision making:** The process of experimenting with alternative strategies to find optimal schedules for the future workload.
6. **Dissemination:** The dissemination of decisions taken back to the individual project teams and the modification of individual project plans.
7. **Achievement measurement:** Feedback via timesheet systems either to measure effort or to monitor progress or both.

As with project planning, these stages form a cycle that in some cases is followed weekly but more often monthly.

Ad hoc observations indicate that few organizations are able to execute the whole process in a reasonable timeframe. However, the demands on the planning process require that it is done regularly and in a suitable timeframe. Even with the help of a software solution, this is difficult to achieve. The process is described below.

Figure 4.10 shows three linked, circular paths. Following the middle path and starting with the preparation of many individual project plans, the diagram shows the transmission of these plans to a central location where these many individual plans are consolidated into a programme plan.

The consolidated plans, now forming a programme plan, often then follow a process of evaluation and experimentation during which alternate solutions to the programme plan are discussed and considered. This involves programme, project and team managers and may require resolution of conflict by programme boards and executives.

When decisions are reached and an optimized programme is prepared, it is likely that there will be implications for the single project plans and for the immediately forthcoming workload. Therefore, the selected consolidated plan may be disseminated to those responsible for doing the work and those responsible for maintaining the single project plans. The single project plans are updated to maintain conformity with the programme plan.

The updated single project plans permit the issuing of work instructions to those responsible for doing the work. This should lead to some actual achievement, but commonly the issuing of frequently updated and corrected plans leads to confusion. It is easy, for example, for a team member to work to an out-of-date plan where the priorities are very different from those being followed by their peers.

Achievement measurement through timesheets or other means provides a feedback loop to the single project plans or to the consolidated programme plan.

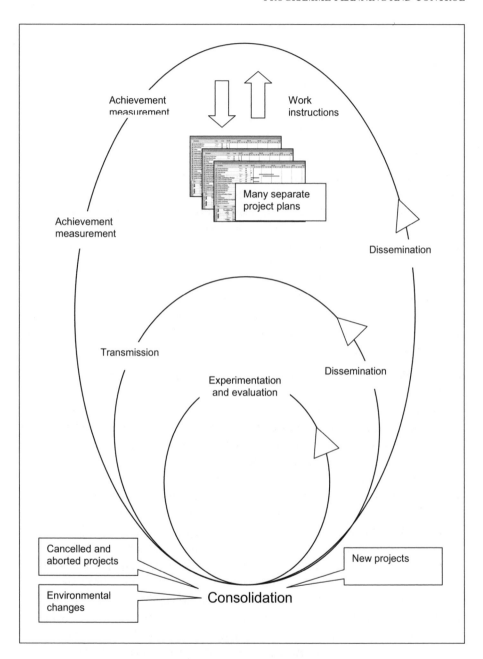

Figure 4.10 The consolidation model

As the single project plans and the achievement measurement feed back to the consolidation process, other factors must receive consideration. Alterations to the project workload – new, cancelled or aborted projects – affect the significance of the single project plans. Environmental changes may alter the priority of individual projects. These factors are considered when the experimentation and decision making stage is undertaken next.

4.7.2.1 Consistency

The consolidated database of plans allows the programme support office to examine multi-project issues by allowing high-level reporting.

It is simple to list all projects in a selected order, perhaps greatest lateness or overspend. The functional or resource managers, for example, the head of the design team, could list all design tasks by getting the multi-project database to search through all projects for design tasks.

But to achieve valuable multi-project reporting across a consolidated plan requires considerable consistency in terminology. The project managers must agree on some conformity to their planning and these must be established from the earliest stages in the programme. For example, consistency needs to be achieved in the following areas:

- **Calendars:** Calendars define when the company, the project and each resource is available to work. Typically, a calendar states that an individual is available 9:00 am to 5:00 pm, with an hour for lunch five days each week. The individual might take all Saturday and Sundays off as well as Bank Holidays. This area is especially important on international programmes where public holidays vary across national borders.
  Consistent calendar formats are required to avoid inaccurate data.
- **Task names:** If users are to successfully search for particular types of tasks, it is important that everyone is using a consistent task naming and numbering form. To a computer database, 'Design nosecone' is completely different from 'Nosecone design', which is also different from 'Nose cone design.'
  This applies to milestones equally and milestone planning is especially important in high-level summaries. Also cross-project links will only effectively operate where the tasks names are recognized by the system.
- **Resource names:** A programmer is totally different if seen through a computer's eyes from 'programmer/analyst'. Ms J. Buchet is another person when read next to Jane Buchet. If different project plans contain different resource names, the software will add them both up into separate groups not realizing that they refer to the same person or trade.
- **Cost centres:** It is common for people to add up the costs associated with

each project and, once again, using consistent category names reduces the risk of getting the cost monitoring wrong.

4.7.3 STRATEGIES FOR IMPLEMENTING THE CONSOLIDATION PROCESS

There are three different strategies using commercially available software tools to implement the process outlined above. These approaches have been observed in a variety of organizations and are designed to make this process work efficiently.

4.7.3.1 Stand-alone

Planners work with their own copy of a popular PC-based project planning system (for example, Microsoft® Project, CA™ Clarity Project Manager) to plan their individual projects. Such systems are popular and easy to use and are well-suited to the planning of single projects.

These plans are transmitted regularly (weekly or fortnightly) via e-mail or perhaps over a Local Area Network (LAN) to a programme office where they are consolidated into a complete plan using the same software. The project office may need special expertise in the intricacy of the software and a powerful, fast PC to manage the large amounts of data.

The project office staff can inspect histograms, summary barcharts and barcharts of similar work, for example, all the design office work.

While achievement measurement is normally carried out by a manual time recording system, there has been an increase in the use of time recording software tools. These are normally used to update single project plans prior to consolidation.

This approach has the advantage of allowing each project team to plan their own work so that they feel ownership of their plans. These popular tools are easy to use. The project or programme office often takes a supporting role advising the management team of conflicts that are generally in terms of resource over-demands.

A high degree of consistency among the many project plans is essential if the many plans are to be consolidated within a reasonable timeframe. There are difficulties in measuring achievement where a resource has been involved in many projects.

Decisions taken in view of the multi-project consolidation are communicated by meetings, printed reports and by other non-electronic means. The individual planners must alter their plans to bring them in line with the programme's requirements. Errors may arise as differences exist between the individual plan and the consolidated plan for each project.

One advantage is the potential for a step-by-step installation of such a system. The consolidation facility can be implemented separately.

4.7.3.2 Integrated

In an integrated environment, the organization normally purchases a site licence of a heavyweight programme planning system. Planners have access to the tool through a local terminal that might be a PC or a terminal on a UNIX or similar system.

Each project is planned locally and the system makes transmission and consolidation completely automatic. Once again, a small team in a project office examine the cross-project demands and report problems.

Decisions taken in light of the cross-project workload can be entered into the system within the project office as well as being communicated verbally and on paper. These systems are expensive and more complex to use. The tendency is for a small number of enthusiasts to enter data on behalf of themselves and other, less computer literate, users.

Any capable planner can add in a new project to the organization-wide programme. This can be done by accessing a library of typical projects or by creating one from scratch. Plans are simple but loaded with resources. Consolidation is immediate and automatic via the network and multi-user software. Each terminal can display a project, summaries of groups of projects and demand for each resource.

Achievement measurement is normally dealt with by a manual system with administrative staff employed to enter details to the multi-project planning system.

Such systems involve a 'big bang' approach and implementation is a significant project in itself. Access to such a system must be controlled so that authority to alter the parts of the model rests with appropriate people. Such systems tend to be complex to use and demand special training. They may not be suitable for the occasional user. They tend to be expensive to install and maintain.

4.7.3.3 Combination

In an attempt to get the best of both worlds, some organizations have created a combination system. Each project team uses a simple stand-alone PC planning system and the project office uses a much more powerful system to integrate the many individual project plans. The individual plans are created and kept up to date using the popular single-project based tools and the files are transferred to a consolidation system. It is likely that such an organization would have a LAN and that the consolidation tool would be manipulated by a project office or programme management team. Consolidation can be achieved by a tool specifically designed for the purpose or by the use of a heavyweight, database-driven, project planning tool. The project office team manipulate the data within the consolidation system and can report on conflicts across the many projects.

Dissemination of information resulting from rescheduling to achieve optimal schedules is not normally possible by software means. Decisions are therefore generally communicated orally from the programme management team to the individual project managers, who modify their plans to bring them into line with the demand of the optimal programme schedule. Inevitably, errors arise as differences exist between the individual plans and the consolidated plan for all projects.

There are problems of data compatibility that must be solved before such a system can work. It is possible for an organization to establish an ethos where projects are individually planned before implementing the consolidation tools and it is even possible to arrange for consolidation of plans created using more than one planning tool.

Achievement measurement tools can be used to feed achievement measurement data into the consolidated plan. This reduces the problems of rationalizing achievement measurement across a range of projects.

These models do not follow the way in which most organizations operate. These models are employed primarily because the existing tools force their users to adopt one of these popular models.

As you normally cannot de-consolidate the big plan back into its many little plans, this new and workable plan needs to be communicated back to those many project managers so that they can bring their plans into line with the master plan.

4.7.4 THE DELEGATION MODEL

The delegation model assumes that plans are maintained for each programme, project and department, and work is delegated from plan to plan. The process of delegating work provides an audit trail of the agreement of managers to do work for each other and also audits changes to the agreement.

Lower-level detailed plans provide automatic update data to higher level, summary plans so that the process of consolidation is made redundant. The lowest plans are at the individual resource level.

Table 4.2 links typical roles to actions in the delegation process.

Most organizations run a large part of their project workload by delegation. Senior programme staff identify projects and delegate them to project managers. These project managers take responsibility for the projects and plan their own workload in appropriate detail. The project managers normally require the efforts

227

Table 4.2   The delegation model

Role	Action
Programme managers Senior project managers Executives	Planning at a strategic level
	Tasks are delegated to project managers
Project managers	Planning individual projects
	Tasks are delegated to departmental managers
Departmental or functional or resource managers	Assigning resources to the tasks
	Publishing the plan informs individual resources electronically
Individual resources	Communicating the workload
	Achievement measurement and updating of plans
Individual resources	The timesheet reports achievement, projects and work plans are updated by the approval of timesheets

of resources within the organization and these may be obtained through the subcontract matrix, the secondment matrix or the resource pool approach.

The senior managers expect to be informed of progress on each project by the appropriate project manager and in appropriate detail. Some form of referee or umpire exists to settle arguments over inter-project prioritization; this is normally a programme management role.

The delegation model follows the way in which organizations work. A multi-user software tool is installed over a LAN and each user is given a 'work plan' within which a project, an individual's or a team's workload can be planned. Connections between work plans are created by the act of 'delegating' work or loaning resources. Upwards reporting follows the connections created by the delegation process. This permits each user to plan at a level that is appropriate to their needs.

For example, a programme manager might plan using a single high-level task per project and delegate, through the software tool, each project to a chosen project manager. The project managers could then break the single tasks down into greater detail within their own work plan, perhaps delegating work to phase, departmental or subproject managers.

Every act of delegation would establish a link between the two 'work plans', which would carry updated information automatically.

In a subcontract matrix organization, work would be delegated to resource or departmental managers who would balance the workload from the many project and subproject managers.

In a secondment matrix, resources would be loaned by the resource managers or departmental managers to the many project and subproject managers on a full time or part time basis.

Individual team members would have their own 'personal work plan'. Once individual resources have been assigned to work, a link between the departmental plan and the personal work plan would be established. Resources would receive work instructions through the system and would report actual achievements.

Achievement measurement data would be transmitted through the assignment link and data describing updated plans would be transmitted up the delegation links.

Each user on the system would see a view of the total workload appropriate to their specific need and would be able to investigate in greater detail by inspection of lower-level plans.

The delegation model works effectively if most of the programme team are using the same or compatible software tools. Such tools generally support good programme management practice and processes.

4.8 BARRIERS TO SUCCESSFUL PROGRAMME PLANNING

This section provides an overview of the barriers that may prevent a successful implementation of a programme planning culture; each of these is discussed below.

4.8.1 RESPONSIBILITY AND AUTHORITY – THE PROGRAMME AND PROJECT MANAGER'S TRAP

Organizations where projects are relatively unusual often do not clearly define the role and the responsibilities of the programme and project manager. This leads to significant dangers. The basic role is reasonably simple and elegant.

The project manager is given the *authority* to do whatever is needed to achieve the project and takes *responsibility* for getting it done.

This is an effective arrangement and one that is entered into by most managers and subordinates regularly. It is the lack of such an understanding that causes the problems.

A project manager may not have authority over:

- the resources required to perform the work
- the purchases necessary in the project
- the way in which the project is run
- the risks that may be taken.

The project manager in this position is unlikely to succeed or at least unlikely to be perceived to have succeeded. It is good practice to ensure that an equitable relationship between authority and responsibility is built into the project manager's role definition.

4.8.2 EXECUTIVE INFORMATION SYSTEMS

In programme management terms, an executive information system (EIS) refers to the idea of looking at many projects in a consistent way, selecting one and drilling down into it for detailed information.

Starting with the total corporate workload, the system creates a list of the projects in a given order, perhaps greatest slippage first, displaying a single bar for each project, including the project with the greatest slippage. The display or report might also show budget and other information.

A typical high-level report might show:

- project name
- planned total cost
- current expected total cost
- planned start and end dates
- current expected start and end dates
- name of project manager.

The senior manager will be able to select a single project and expand it to display the phase level – six or eight bars summarizing the project. It may be that the design phase is well behind so the manager selects the 'design phase' bar and expands it to display the detailed plan.

Such reporting functionality is normally set up by the programme office for the use of the senior management. Very often this is web based and available through an intranet.

There are many benefits of such an EIS system. As everyone uses the same summary bars to give an overview of each project, the senior management can get an overview of the work quickly, without which the task of locating problems would be much harder. Not only can the senior management see overviews of all projects, it is possible to select certain tasks, for example, to see all tasks that fall into a chosen category. For example, it might be useful to see all 'testing' work or all 'design approval work' across all projects.

There can be a huge volume of data. One hundred projects, each with 30 tasks implies 3000 tasks. This is a big plan and it will be hard to gain knowledge from this mass of data.

The ablility to select tasks that pass some certain criteria is important. It will only be possible to select tasks of a like kind if there is some suitable coding system in use. This might imply the use of task numbering, task names or task descriptions to help you locate required groups of tasks. Some software packages provide this feature under the label of a work breakdown structure or a WBS.

This WBS is a structured field where imbedded codes show what kind of work is referred to. Each task contains a space to enter codes for tasks to aid in searching and grouping for example, ENG 95 Design 1020. This might mean this is an ENGineering task taking place in 1995. It involves the Design department and it is part of job number 1020.

A little time invested early on designing a task coding system will deliver significant benefits later on.

There are some techniques to help deal with consistency issues and these have already been discussed in Section 4.7.2 'The consolidation process'.

In some organizations, the programme office has built a model of the typical project undertaken by the organization. The plan will include phases and checks that must be adhered to (for example, main board approval before commencement of manufacturing, creation and approval of the PID) and all the activities that make up the project. The durations of the tasks and the resources that are required to perform them are also estimated. Such a 'template plan' or 'standard plan' is made available for use by all project planners and will comply with the organization's methodology.

When a project planner wishes to create a new plan, rather than starting from a blank sheet, the template is modified to suit the new project.

4.8.2.1 Speed

The earlier discussion about the consolidation model outlined a regular process of consolidating many plans and creating updated summary reports.

The process outlined was:

1. Get the latest data about remaining work.
2. Get the latest update on new projects.
3. Get the latest position of scarce resources.
4. Check upon people's holidays and training courses.
5. Update all the data in the various plans.

6. Process the plan.
7. Distribute the information.

This process is vital, as it supplies senior management with the information on which to make decisions. If your organization does not regularly monitor and update your programme plan, you are simply wasting your time.

To keep up to date with the changing plan of work, you need to set up a system for monitoring what is going on, keeping abreast of changes in priorities, workload and strategies and producing up-to-date plans.

This process can take anything from a few minutes to a few days. You do need to set up a system where the turnaround is fast. Buying software that is very fast clearly helps, but it only helps with step 6 above. Neat and efficient data entry methods shorten step 5 and quick printing shortens step 7. The rest is down to the organization and the way it works and this is where you need to really concentrate.

Speed of feedback is a problem. Many organizations have settled on a monthly update of programme plans as being the best achievable.

4.8.3 TIMESHEETS

If project plans are to maximize their usefulness, they must reflect reality. A plan is an external model of planned work; it is a model of a future.

Due to changing activities and priorities, actual work done will always vary from that planned. This does not imply that the plan was in any way inaccurate but it does imply the need to monitor actual achievement on a regular basis.

The list of actual work done will often bear only a passing resemblance to the work planned for the same period, so it is essential to update plans in light of these actual achievements.

As programme management is generally not in an environment where physical measurement of work done is possible, the most common way of doing this is through a timesheet system.

Timesheets provide a valuable way of finding out what has been achieved at an individual level. Setting up a system for a regular feedback to the project and departmental managers or their planners helps to keep planning central to the management processes, playing a useful and positive role.

A timesheet system should be simple and quick to use. If it is complex or slow it will quickly fall into disuse and gain a bad reputation. It is important to remember that the person who completes a timesheet gains little benefit from doing so. It is a report of work done and that may be valuable to an individual who is senior enough to understand and control their own work pattern. But for an individual whose work is planned by a manager, the timesheet does not provide the preparer with valuable knowledge. Rapid timesheet systems expect the user to simply click on tasks that were planned for the week and enter actual work done. It should be simple to record doing unplanned work by clicking on a list of likely items including sickness.

Timesheet systems that are slow and that do not encourage use require that the timesheet user look up programme, project or task reference numbers on a separate list and enter them. Apart from the laborious nature of this work, it is fraught with error. Before timesheets can be accepted, it may be necessary to correct a significant number of codes that are obviously incorrect. A number of incorrect but valid codes will slip through.

Many organizations have missing timesheet reports that emphasize those people who have not yet completed and submitted their timesheets. In large organizations, this is done by percentage; in smaller organisations, this is done by name. Some systems automatically advise team members and their managers that their timesheets are overdue.

Timesheets are supposed to be a quick, efficient method of collecting data on actual work done. This may be done for a number of reasons. Staff can be paid, people's individual achievements can be monitored, clients (both internal and external) can be invoiced and the timesheet data can be used to update project plans.

A valuable timesheet system will ensure that everyone submits their timesheets quickly and accurately and will help in the preparation of any invoices or cross-charges. The system will prepare data listing the names of people working on named projects and the days on which they worked.

Timesheet data may also be used to gather statistical data on time spent. A valuable timesheet system will produce reports showing where time has been spent over a given period across projects, non-project and non-work items. It will contain the number of days' leave, training and sickness each person has taken. All this information is of great value to the programme management team and general management of the organization.

Therefore, for a wide range of purposes it useful to gather data on the way time has been spent over the last period, generally on a weekly basis.

But for the purposes of project management, the key question that a timesheet should ask for every current task is: How much work or time now remains on this task?

There are a number of systems that require the timesheet user to estimate a percentage complete for each task. There are a number of problems with reliance on percentage complete data.

Asking the team member to estimate the amount of work or time remaining makes no assumptions about the accuracy of the original estimate for the task's duration nor about production rates and interruptions. It makes people think about the work that is left and allows for changes to affect the time that remains on this task: the remaining duration. It is forward looking.

Submitted timesheets should be routed for approval by relevant managers. The risk of errors and misunderstandings make an approval process essential. The approval must be quick and simple and should automatically update the appropriate plan. For example, consider a team member is working on a project and also doing some BAU work for a line manager or perhaps a second project manager. The individual would ideally complete one timesheet showing the work done in the week and their estimates of remaining work on each task.

The timesheet system would split the feedback into two reports, one for the project manager and one for the line manager. These managers would examine the feedback and approve the report. This would have the effect of updating their plans.

An effective and respected timesheet system can be a great help to a programme planning environment. Such a system is 'owned' by all members of the team so that everyone feels that the planning and control system is a shared process. Seen in this light, the timesheet is a part of a collaborative planning and control process and this attitude is likely to lead to a more positive approach to timesheet reporting.

Such a system needs careful management and control. There are a number of PC-based timesheet programs on the market that can be linked into project management software; in such a system lies the basis of a true programme planning system.

4.8.4 DOWN TIME

There is inevitably a background workload plus holidays and training time that has to be dealt with somehow in a programme planning system.

Here are some time-consuming operations that do not relate to specific tasks in the specific projects, but do absorb some of the time available from resources.

- training courses
- internal non-project-related meetings
- holidays
- travelling time
- union meetings
- filling in time sheets
- talking to project planners and managers
- reading books about programme management
- regular background work – user support, filing, backing up computer data.

They all take time. There are a few ways to deal with these demands on your resources' time.

4.8.4.1 Plan on a realistic number of hours per week

You could produce data to help calculate the actual 'project productive' time available each week for each person. Then you use this as a reasonable estimate of the available time each person has. This information is usually a part of the working calendar for the resource.

To avoid confusion, you might use an appropriate term to describe this productive time. Here are some suggestions:

- Available product progress time
- Effective task progress time
- Availability for project work
- Direct project progress time.

These terms do not imply that the rest of the time is wasted, only that it doesn't apply directly to any project.

You might be able to calculate the realistic amount of time you can expect from each resource on a scientific basis.

4.8.4.2 Allow for downtime in productive time

In this strategy, you stick with the standard 40-hour week and plan and monitor against it. When you create tasks and assign people to those tasks, you allow for their downtime in the durations you estimate.

Some organizations use a set of constants that show how long things take to do allowing for the non-project downtime. These constants allow for normal downtime, but are only possible where the organization has a set of historic project-related data to base these estimates upon.

You can therefore always allow for non-productive time in the production rates you use.

4.8.4.3 Add continuous background tasks

These tasks might perhaps absorb the first 10 hours of each resource's time for each week.

Here, you plan on everyone doing their standard week as paid for. They are available for, let's say, 40 hours per week in line with their terms of employment. You then introduce a high-priority, continuous or intermittent tasks absorbing, say, 10 hours of every resource's time. This takes away the time spent on

235

non-project-related work before you can begin allocating the rest of the time to tasks in the various projects.

4.8.4.4 Plan specific downtimes as tasks

This works well in some organizations. It deals with specific and unusual downtime periods rather than the continuous background non-productive or lost time. You create a 'phantom' project called something like 'TRAINING' and create tasks called things like 'Attend programme management training course'. This might have a duration of 3 days and absorb 100 per cent of the time of the people going on it.

You can have another 'phantom project' called HOLIDAYS that contains similar tasks, each of which absorbs 100 per cent of the resource's time and is a very high-priority task. Descriptions might be 'Joe goes on leave', for example.

Tasks in the TRAINING and HOLIDAY groups absorb resources just like any other tasks and, being of a high priority, leave nothing left over for the resources to contribute to other work. You can produce barcharts from these two phantom plans showing everyone's holidays and absences on training courses as part of the planning service provided by the programme office. You can monitor progress against these phantom plans through timesheets and therefore record training, holidays, sickness and other absences for the team.

4.8.5 COMMUNICATING THE PLANS

A major purpose of programme planning is to help the programme management team keep up to date with progress across the portfolio of projects.

To achieve this goal it is vital that understandable and readable reports are produced frequently and quickly.

Reports must meet a number of criteria:

- **Accurate:** They must provide a realistic picture of the work that has been done and, more importantly, the latest expectations of the work that remains to be done.
- **Readable:** They must present the appropriate data in the appropriate level of detail.
- **Timely:** Reports that show the position as it was some weeks ago are going to mislead the management team into taking inappropriate actions.

Reports are increasingly prepared on web pages and displayed over the organization's intranet, as this allows appropriate members of the team quick access to the most up-to-date information and avoids reference to potential out-of-date paper reports.

Reports are often created by the programme office based on plans maintained by the project and other managers. This is done to promote consistency across reporting forms.

The actual content of reports should be defined through collaboration of two parties: the readers and creators of the reports. Readers of reports know the information they require and creators of reports know what can be produced.

To make reporting valuable, a large number of organizations use target or baseline data. This refers to agreed ambitions for programmes and projects. Target timing and budgeting for a project may be agreed within the PID. Reports comparing targets with actual achievement and latest expectations give a clearer, if more complex, picture of project and programme status.

There are times when targets should be modified, for example, when the scope of a project has changed. There should be a process, ideally involving the programme office, for recording and amending targets.

There is a vast list of data that can be reported; below some of the elements that should be included in reports are listed.

4.8.5.1 Summary programme information

This includes:

- ID of each programme
- brief summary of benefits
- target, actual and remaining timing
- target, actual and remaining effort or work
- target, actual and remaining cost
- expected variation of programme end date
- expected budget variation at end of programme
- programme manager's name.

4.8.5.2 Summary project information

This includes:

- ID of each project
- brief summary of deliverables
- target, actual and remaining timing
- target, actual and remaining effort or work
- target, actual and remaining cost
- expected variation to project end date
- expected budget variation at end of project
- project manager's name.

4.8.5.3 Milestone reports

Many organizations give every programme and project a standard set of milestones. These include key stages in the project lifecycle, for example: PID approved; Commence Purchasing phase; Hand over to business user; Project closure. A simple report can list each programme and/or project and show the target or baseline timing against the actual achievements to date and the current expectations for remaining work.

4.8.5.4 Distribution of work

This report shows how an individual, group of individuals, teams and departments have spent, and are planned to spend, their time over a given period.

These are typically pie charts (see Figure 4.11 for an example showing how a group of technicians have spent their time over the preceding three months).

4.8.5.5 Trend charts

These show how an important planned date has changed over time.

In Figure 4.12, on 12/03/03 the predicted end date was 28/06/03. The actual end date was 08/10/03. Such reports show the trend being followed by a predicted date. In this example, the date has been tending towards delay for some months.

4.8.5.6 Risk and issue registers

Every programme and project should have a risk and issue register and these are discussed in Chapter 7 of this handbook.

Where risks and issues are given numeric ratings, it is possible to derive an overall risk rating and issue rating and these can be reported in summary reports. These provide excellent examples of drill-down capabilities, as the report

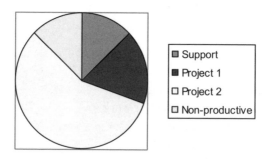

Figure 4.11 Pie chart showing the distribution of work

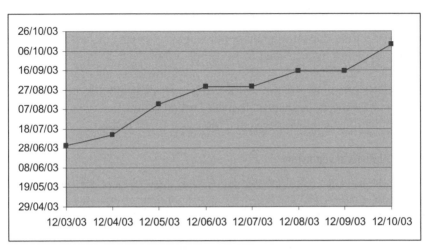

Figure 4.12   Trend chart

reader can drill down from an overall risk rating to inspect the specific risk register in detail.

4.8.5.7 Governance reports

Many organizations have adopted a standard method such as PRINCE2. This method will propose that certain documents be produced and approved during the lifecycle of each project and programme. Reports can show for each programme and project which of these documents have been produced and approved for each project.

4.8.5.8 Exception reports

These show out-of-tolerance incidents and enable the reader to focus on especially contentious issues. Tolerances can be set by the management team and include such items as:

- projects expected to go more than 10 per cent over budget
- programmes expected to be delayed by more than one month
- projects incurring expense without an approved PID
- projects lacking a risk register
- project plans not updated for more than 2 weeks.

4.8.6 STATISTICAL ANALYSIS OF HISTORIC DATA

In an organization that runs a number of similar projects, it is possible is to 'close the loop' by using historic data from completed projects to improve accuracy in future plans. This makes the assumption that knowledge about past projects will enable better planning of future work. Such analysis is likely to be carried out by programme support staff central to a user organization.

A number of possibilities exist and these are listed below.

4.8.6.1 Statistical reporting

It is possible to collect and present data across many projects in a statistical form.

4.8.6.2 Historic task data

It is possible to analyse actual work done and compare it with planned work across a selected range of tasks or projects. It is possible to relate the analysis to task categories and types using a task coding structure and present it in graphical and tabular statistical forms.

Tasks might be classified in various ways, for example:

- **Size:** Small, medium, large, very large or 1,2,3,4,5.
- **Complexity:** Simple, complex, very complex.
- **Familiarity:** Typical, challenging, very challenging.
- **Number of reports:** 1,2,3,4,5.
- **Number of pages:** 0–99,99–199,199–299.
- **Number of functions:** 1,2,3,4,5.

It is also possible to show how predictions of end dates, time and costs vary over time.

The example in Figure 4.13 shows how the predicted end date typically varied over time. On 12/03/03 the predicted end date was 28/06/03. The actual end date was 08/10/03.

Analysis of historic task data could compare targets with intermediary estimates and actual records, therefore comparing actual effort, time and cost against target effort, time and cost for types of projects and work. It is also possible to graphically represent original effort estimates with remaining work as entered on timesheets and actual end dates analysed across many tasks.

Reports should be available linking these reports to individual resources, resource pools, skill used and timescale.

This type of analysis allows the user to understand the levels of accuracy of their historic planning, which should lead to more accurate plans in the future.

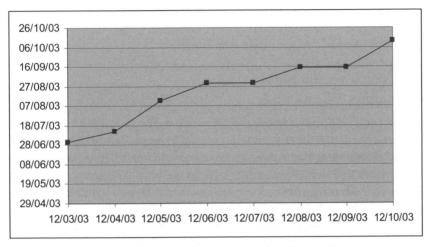

Figure 4.13 Statistically derived trend chart

This output data might generate very useful reports connecting task types to direction, work and budgets analysed over large numbers of tasks.

4.8.6.3 Historic resource data

It is possible to compare for each resource, type of resource, skill types and resource pool variations of planned versus actual effort, how time is spent across project, non-project and non-work categories, as well as trends in sick leave, overtime, excessive working hours.

Valuable reports are available comparing resources and types of resources.

4.8.6.4 Risk register prompt

Through analysis of historic risk registers, it is possible to provide suggested risks that have been raised before on each kind of task or project. This prompts the planner and helps with the creation of new risk registers including historical average impact and likelihood ratings.

If an organization stores standard modules for plans in some form, each associated with skill requirements and based on historic data, these plans will be much more accurate where based on historic analysis of past projects.

4.9 STANDARDIZATION

Where a significant number of plans exist within an organization and where the

241

type of projects is similar there is considerable value of introducing some standardization to programme and project planning. These standards should be 'owned' and maintained by the programme office (see chapter 13 'The programme office').

Some examples of standardization follow:

- **Task identification:** An organization-wide system for task identification will reduce confusion and ease collaboration across the programme management team. A system that identifies the programme, project, work package of every task in a consistent way will ease communication and help to reduce errors. This is sometimes referred to as a work breakdown structure.
- **Resource identification:** A consistent method of identifying resources will similarly reduce errors due to misunderstandings. A system of identifying resources by their group, skill and location in addition to their name written in a consistent way will reduce scope for error and misunderstanding.
- **Standard plans:** Some organizations have libraries of standard plans, each designed to provide an appropriate level of planning and to highlight important issues for specific types of project. Typically such plans include tasks covering governance such as production and approval of programme initiation documents. These help to reduce errors caused by plans that are drawn up at too high a level or in too much detail.

Clearly designed processes for establishing and initiating both programmes and projects will help to ensure that only appropriate work is done and reduce the dangers of duplication.

4.10 SUMMARY

Programme planning provides different challenges from those for single projects. While there is a need for all projects to be planned in appropriate ways, the programme planner has to establish processes and procedures that allow for consistent planning to be carried out across all projects and programmes through to benefit delivery so that the interactions between those project plans can be understood and communicated.

It is common in a programme management environment to find difficulties in progress monitoring due to the absence of physical deliverables, and a mechanism for gaining the involvement and input from the whole community is often advantageous.

Part III of this handbook outlines the Programme Management Improvement Process and, within that, details recommendations for establishing six improving and maturing levels of programme planning and control.

REFERENCES

OGC (2003) *Managing Successful Programmes: Delivering Business in Multi-project Environments.* Second edition. London: The Stationery Office.

5 Benefits management

5.1 WHAT ARE BENEFITS?

No rational person would normally commit to major expenditure of time, effort or money without being clear about what they expect to achieve as a result. This is especially the case with business programmes, where the money being spent actually belongs to others and where the directors and managers who initiated the expenditure may have to account for their actions to the owners. In such circumstances, the expected results of the programme should be expressed in terms of the benefits that will be achieved by the business, such as increased revenue, reduced costs or improved product and service quality.

A common characteristic of many unsuccessful programmes is the vagueness with which the expected benefits are defined. Without clearly defined objectives, it is difficult to maintain focus when subsequent problems occur. The costs of undertaking programmes are real and immediate, while the benefits frequently only occur after the programme is completed and implemented. Furthermore, the people responsible for actually delivering the benefits are often different from those responsible for directing and managing the programme itself. For example, when considering the benefits of investing in IT, the UK's National Health Service advises that:

> Benefits come from the use of IT solutions, not simply from installing them. (NHS, n.d.)

This means that the people responsible for realizing the benefits are normally the users and their line managers, not the programme team that created the capability. As a result, it is only with the expected benefits fully defined, understood and agreed at the start of a programme that an organization can be confident that its investment is likely to be fully successful. Moreover, this understanding must be supported with mechanisms to measure the benefits and with procedures for monitoring, reporting and responding to their achievement or non-achievement.

5.2 PROGRAMMES, PROJECTS AND BENEFITS

The business discipline of defining, agreeing, measuring and reporting on the expected benefits is referred to as *benefit management*. The relationship between projects, programmes and benefit management is frequently quite complex. As shown in Figure 5.1:

- Projects do not deliver benefits, but create deliverables (such as a working IT network, a tested software application, a pool of trained staff, and so on). These must be managed by project managers, who need to be familiar with the methodologies and techniques needed to produce those deliverables. The effectiveness of project managers is determined by the extent to which they provide the required deliverables on time, on budget and on specification.
- Programmes themselves rarely deliver benefits directly, but by combining projects and their deliverables they create the capabilities that will enable the desired benefits to be achieved (for example, the ability for operations staff to work remotely).
- The benefit management processes ensure that the capabilities created by programmes are used to deliver the anticipated business benefits (for example, improved quality, enhanced cost effectiveness, and so on). This use will normally be by the ongoing operations of the organization.

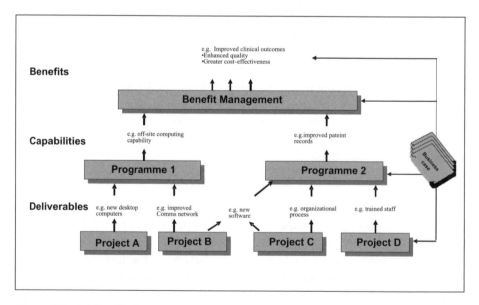

Figure 5.1   Relationships between project deliverables, programme capabilities and business benefits

CASE STUDY 5.1: CONTENT OF A BUSINESS CASE

Many major organizations have their own way of organizing business cases. Below is an outline of what the main board of directors of one major multinational organization expects to see.

Chapter heading	Description
Executive Summary	This is a one- or two-page summary of the key points. Its purpose is to enable busy people to quickly understand the main conclusions and recommendations.
Programme Description	This section explains 'what' is being proposed.
Scope and Business Fit	The scope of the proposed programme, in terms of: ● its physical or organization boundaries, limitations, inclusions and exclusions; ● the relationship between this programme and the organization's overall strategic plans – i.e. what elements of the strategy will be fulfilled by this programme; ● relationships with other programmes; ● any known technical, financial, legal or political constraints; ● benefits to be delivered.
Product or Service Definition	Define the new product(s), service(s) or facilities that are to be developed or procured in sufficient detail to provide the main board (or whoever will give approval) with a clear understanding of the new capability that will be delivered.
Industry and Market Analysis	Explain why it is believed that there is a demand for the new products/services/facilities and what the competition's likely response will be. Use the results of industry or market studies to give the evidence to provide support.
Commercial Policy and Strategy	Identify any policy decisions that will need to be made regarding the new product/service/facility and any commercial relationships that will be necessary at any point – during design, manufacture, implementation, distribution, maintenance and even disposal.

247

Chapter heading	Description
Regulatory and Legal Issues	Any regulatory, legal or similar issues that will need to be addressed.
Objectives and Benefits	Why is the programme being undertaken? What are its objectives? How are these expressed in terms of business benefits? Include a benefit model showing how the features and benefits relate.
Financial Analysis	Describe the financial impact of developing the new product/service/facility. This should cover the whole life. The impact should show the extra revenues or savings on the one hand and the costs on the other, over time. This should present the information in the organization's standard template, so that decision makers can quickly understand what is being shown and make comparisons with the business cases of other programmes.
Programme Plan	A high-level outline of how the programme will be organized, managed and controlled, plus details of the major milestones and deliverables.
Quantitative Analysis	Analyse factors that could affect the estimates of benefits, revenue/savings or costs.
Business Scenario Assumptions	Outline the assumptions that have been made about the marketplace or competition. Show how changes to these might affect the revenues/savings, business benefits or costs.
Critical Success Factors	What will be the major determinants of success – e.g. stable development team, good partnership relationships, piloting of prototypes, and so on.
Risk Analysis	Outline the major risks and show how they might affect the likely revenues/savings, expected benefits and costs.

Note that in some organizations, there is an expectation of an outline business case to be created first, followed by a detailed business case only after further exploration or the completion of a pilot study.

Further guidance on what is expected within the business cases of UK public sector organizations can be found in the 'Successful Delivery Toolkit' section of the website of the Office of Government Commerce (OGC) at http://www.ogc.gov.uk/SDToolkit/reference/deliverylifecycle/bus_case_brief.html.

5.3 THE PROGRAMME BUSINESS CASE

Typically the expected benefits are summarized within the business case, which is one of the key control documents of any programme. In this document, the general objectives of the programme will need to be expressed, as far as possible, in terms of specific benefit expectations or targets.

Examples of some benefit targets can be found in Figure 5.3 below and a summary of the possible content of a business case can be found in Case Study 5.1.

The business case is unlikely to be static throughout the life of the programme; instead it will evolve over time as new understanding and insight is gained into the issues affecting the programme. Because of this, the business case must be regularly reviewed and adjusted in the light of changing circumstances – for example, to reflect changing business priorities. Undertaking such reviews and initiating appropriate amendments to the business case is one of the key responsibilities of the programme board.

5.4 HARD AND SOFT BENEFITS

It is often difficult to convert the pious hopes of programme promoters into specific, detailed and measurable statements of expected benefits. This is particularly so when the expected benefits cannot be expressed in terms of their likely impact on the balance sheet or the profit and loss account. Those that can be so expressed, that is, those which have a tangible financial outcome – such as the likely impact of the programme on pre-tax profits, are usually referred to as 'hard', while those that are intangible and less easy to express and to measure in terms of cash or objective numbers are referred to as 'soft' benefits. Phillips (2003) defines hard benefits as representing the output, quality, cost and time of work-related processes. They are characterized by being objective, relatively easy to measure and easy to convert to money values. By contrast, Phillips characterizes soft benefits as subjective, often difficult to measure, almost always difficult to convert to monetary values, and frequently behaviourally oriented.

Because they are easier to measure and more objective, many organizations seek to justify major investments solely in terms of hard benefits. Indeed, some commercial organizations have defined policies that the only programmes they will allow to proceed are those that generate a specific and measurable ROI, expressed in money terms, that is above a certain minimum level.

There are several drawbacks to focusing solely on hard benefits. Firstly, many of the most valuable benefits are often largely intangible. For example, customer perception of the ethical values of a business can be important in maintaining or enhancing sales over time, yet expressing such perception in meaningful numbers can be exceedingly difficult. Where company policy demands that only hard benefits can be used to justify an investment, one frequently finds complex and meaningless attempts to convert the intangible into financial numbers and while such 'voodoo' figures may look good in a business case, they rarely have any long-term value. Yet by creating spurious precision, they may mislead those planning and directing the programme and result in degraded decision making.

Second, the easy-to-measure and financially oriented benefits are often the long-term results of gaining more immediate soft benefits. For example, as shown in Figure 5.2, a programme of improving the skills of back-office staff within a financial institution might reasonably be expected, eventually, to result in the 'hard' benefit of improved sales. Yet the causal chain by which this will be achieved is long and complex. Moreover, by the time any financial benefits actually accrue, there will probably have been so many changes within the organization and its marketplace that relating the sales improvements back to the original investment in training will be impossible. Yet without that relationship, effective benefit management becomes impossible. A simpler justification, using the soft benefits of staff capability or customer perception, might result in more effective benefit management and thus greater benefits in the long term.

Third, while risks can be managed effectively within a programme (as described in Chapter 7 'Management of risks and issues'), it is much more difficult to factor the impact of risk and uncertainty into long-term financial projection. In the end, however precise the numbers, decision makers have to rely on their own intuition as to which types of risk to allow for and in what combinations. Thus, although considerable effort can be spent in seeking to present a façade of scientific objectivity, decision makers will, in the end, have to rely on their judgement, just as they would with soft benefits.

Finally, many organizations are not driven by financial imperatives, but are concerned with public services or other less easily measured indicators. While non-financial imperatives are valid and may be defined through key performance indicators (KPIs) – see Section 5.5 below – it will often be more difficult to identify hard benefits in such organizations.

Nevertheless, whether relying on hard or soft benefits to justify the might be

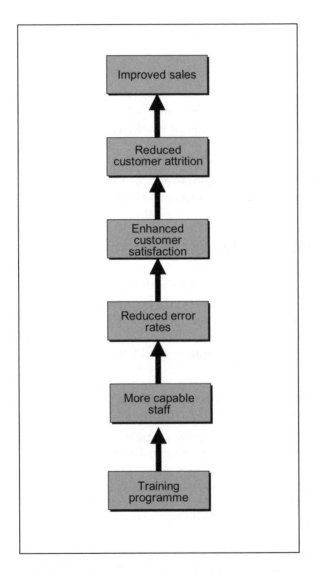

Figure 5.2 Example of a benefit chain showing how 'soft' benefits might be converted into 'hard' benefits

programme, the analysis must be rigorous, comprehensive and agreed by all key decision makers. Furthermore, it should be possible to express all benefits in such a way that their ultimate achievement can be unequivocally established. For example, a measure of the benefits of a programme to improve product quality the award by an independent auditor of a compliance certification against the

251

ISO9001 quality management standard. Thus, whilst the long-term benefits of the programme might all be deemed to be soft and intangible, the award of the certificate would be a very clear milestone on the way to achieving programme success.

Some further examples of expressing general programme objectives in unequivocal fashion can be seen in Figure 5.3.

In practice, successful programmes usually combine a range of hard and soft benefits, with both categories being subject to rigorous analysis. Thus the difference between the two types of benefit becomes less important as hard benefits are tempered with provisos about risk and the vagaries of human nature, and soft benefits are defined in terms of meaningful targets, milestones and measures.

5.5 DELIVERING THE BUSINESS STRATEGY

Few successful organizations operate without some form of business strategy; that is, a set of plans, policies, procedures and visions that helps to plot the course of the organization into the foreseeable future. The execution of this strategy will depend upon combining on-going business as usual (BAU) activities with specific programmes and projects to improve specific aspects of the organization in the

General objective	Specific benefit
Increase revenue	Generate £1 million worth of sales from the website by December 200X
Reduce operating costs	Reduce the costs of printing and postage by the Material Handling Department by 20% during the coming year
Enhance product quality	Reduce average monthly rate of product returns from the current 2% level to below 1% by December 200X
Improve service quality	Reduce the number of penalty payments for sub-standard service by 50% over the next two years.

Figure 5.3   Examples of general programme objectives converted into specific benefit targets

desired manner. Thus the benefits to be delivered by the organization's programmes should collectively deliver the changes and improvements upon which the strategy is based.

A technique frequently used to link individual programmes to corporate strategy is the development of a set of balanced scorecards. This technique, promoted by Kaplan and Norton (1996), is designed to focus all parts of the organization, and all change initiatives, onto achieving long-term corporate goals. The technique involves creating an organizational 'scorecard' identifying a small set of financial and non-financial goals, along the lines shown in Figure 5.4. This is then broken down into lower-level scorecards to show how each division, department, and so on, and each programme contributes towards the achievement of these goals. Benefit management thus provides the mechanism by which the programme and its benefits can be tied in to the achievement of corporate strategy.

In many UK public sector organizations, strategy is established through funding discussions with the Treasury or the sponsoring Ministry and is expressed in the form of KPIs, which show the overall improvements required over time in specific aspects of performance. As in the private sector, it is programmes of business change that make these improvements possible and the changes in KPIs can similarly be broken down in terms of the benefits to be contributed by each programme and project.

Case Study 5.2 describes benefit management as part of the introduction of a document management system.

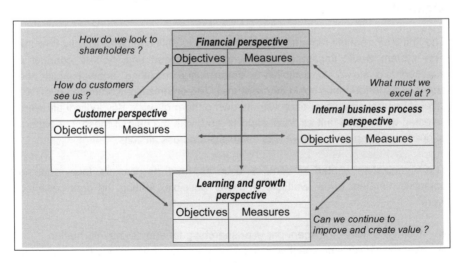

Figure 5.4   Template for a balanced scorecard
Source: Kaplan and Norton, 1996

253

CASE STUDY 5.2: BENEFIT MANAGEMENT IN ERDM PROGRAMME

BACKGROUND

As a result of the growing use of electronic communication, such as e-mails, a large European public-sector organization decided to introduce an Electronic Records and Document Management (EDRM) system for use throughout its operations.

The organization operated approximately 400 different document registries and the principle driver was to reduce the time spent by staff on filing and retrieving documentation. At the same time, the overall growth of the organization's business, both in terms of volume and complexity, was creating difficulties in ensuring 'joined-up working' and it was hoped that the system would reduce the situations where lack of knowledge of what had been agreed in one part resulted in another making contradictory decisions.

At an early stage, the organization decided to treat the initiative as a programme to change the ways that its 5000 professional grade staff worked, rather than as an IT project. It also decided that it would establish a benefit management work stream to track and maximize the business benefits that it actually achieved from its investment. External assistance from the organization's IT partners was sought to plan and manage the change processes, including the management of benefits.

START-UP

The first major benefit management activity was to define in detail exactly how the new system would impact on staff working practices and then to conduct a questionnaire survey to establish a performance 'baseline' against which the changes to performance could be measured. The organization comprised over 100 different operational units, each with its own pattern of work. Key individuals were selected within each unit as 'local experts' and, with the help of these, the pattern of document filing and retrieval was established across all units.

The organization wanted its benefits to be as 'hard' as possible, thus requiring objective numbers to be available wherever possible. Among the data collected were:

- average weekly time spent per user searching for and saving information
- average weekly time spent waiting for information to be retrieved from registries
- volumes of storage space
- postage, copying and printing costs.

As a separate initiative, the organization was also seeking to expand the amount of 'off-site' working, through providing staff with laptop computers. Accordingly, separate sets of statistics on time spent were established for office-based and for off-site staff.

The organization had a clear set of published strategic targets, or KPIs. These, in turn, had been broken down into sub-targets, in a pattern similar to that required when using the balanced scorecard concept. A key responsibility for the ERDM Programme Board was agreeing the relationship between the business case and these KPIs and sub-targets.

Although the new system would provide the potential to significantly reduce the number of staff required within filing repositories, concern about redundancy was such that no staff reductions were included in the business case. Instead, the system had to justify itself on the basis of freeing the time of operational staff for more productive work elsewhere. The results of the initial survey allowed the assumptions within the business case to be tested against 'live' data and to be appropriately revised.

EXECUTION – INITIAL PILOT

Because of the complexity of the organization and the lack of significant experience of similar applications elsewhere, a prototype approach was adopted to the development of the system. A 'standard' software package, which could be customized to meet specific requirements, was chosen to form the basis of the IT system. This was used to create an initial prototype of the system, which was set up in a 'Model Office', where representative groups of staff could try it out using samples of their own work loads.

Following these trials, the new system was rolled out to a small set of work units on a pilot basis. Full training was provided and the units worked as far as possible as if the whole organization had converted. Questionnaires were again used to establish what improvements had resulted. As well as providing guidance on how customization of software, training of staff and communication could be improved, the results of these questionnaires, plus output from feedback workshops, enabled the viability of the whole programme to be re-assessed This assessment provided critical input to the 'Level 4' Gateway Review*, currently required for all major UK government programmes prior to 'go live'.

---

* Gateway Reviews are independent checks of major public-sector programmes organized by the UK's OGC. Such reviews must be conducted at key stages to ensure that the programme still makes good business sense, before it proceeds to the next stage. The 'Level 4' Review veritifies that a programme is ready to 'go live' and that the Business Case still stands up. The subsequent 'Level 5' Review takes place after 'go live', to confirm that all necessary arrangements are in place to maximize the benefits achieved from the programme.

EXECUTION – FULL ROLLOUT

With the information gained during the pilot, a standardized approach to roll-out was developed, which enabled each working unit to be prepared, trained and switched over to the new system in a 4-month period.

With this approach, a rolling programme of roll-out was adopted, enabling the system to be implemented throughout the organization over a period of 1 year, in a controlled fashion, with minimal interruption of normal working.

BENEFIT REALIZATION

With the new system fully rolled out, it was then possible to review its effectiveness. Repeat surveys were undertaken to measure the changes that had been achieved. These were supported by further feedback workshops with representative samples of users. Table 5.1 below, gives examples of some of the measurable or 'hard' benefits achieved by the office-based staff within one work unit.

Table 5.1   Examples of time savings achieved as a result of the EDRM system

Time spent per week	Before EDRM (h/week)	After EDRM (h/week)	Time saved (h/week)	No. of staff affected	Total saving for work unit (h/week)
Searching time	1.5	1	0.5	140	70
Filing time	1.0	0.75	0.25	28	7
Waiting time	1.3	0.75	0.55	140	77

The surveys and workshops also identified that a number of 'soft' benefits had been achieved. For example, many staff reported that they were more likely and better able to share information with colleagues, while others reported that they now had a better understanding of where relevant information was stored. Not every measure was positive. In some work units, some tasks took longer and some activities were felt to be more difficult than before. These disbenefits had to be allowed for when calculating the overall benefits that the organization had achieved from rolling out the system.

The purpose of these new consultations was not just to obtain absolute measures of the benefits so far achieved, but also to provide guidance on what else could be done to maximize the effectiveness of the new system. For example, it was noted that some work units had achieved more from the system than similar units elsewhere in the organization. Using such differences has allowed a form of internal benchmarking to take place, resulting in those units that have achieved less learning from their equivalents who have achieved more.

CLOSURE AND BAU

Use of the system became BAU throughout the organization. However, partly as a result of feedback on the benefits achieved, it was decided to enhance the EDRM system with additional facilities, involving a new cycle of benefit planning, measurement and management.

5.6 THE DIFFICULTIES OF BENEFIT MANAGEMENT

As with many aspects of management, it is not so much the actual definitions of the benefits themselves that create the value, but the understanding and agreement that is generated amongst those involved. Gaining this understanding and agreement is not always easy. As explained above, the relationship between the capability delivered by the programme and the achievement of the desired benefits can be complex. Accordingly, a key stage in the defining and agreeing of benefits will be an analysis of dependencies, leading to the creation of benefit models. These show how various causal chains of benefits interrelate with each other and show the activities or capabilities on which their realization depends. Figure 5.5 shows a model of how aspects of the IT capabilities to be delivered by a programme can lead to a reduction on litigation risk (that is, the risk of being sued for negligence) within a hospital. In this example, the various capabilities are shown at the bottom. The model shows how these are combined and used in different ways to deliver the benefit of 'reduced litigation risk' at the top.

Agreeing the exact relationship between the capabilities delivered by a programme and the benefits that are expected to be achieved can be very difficult, particularly when their delivery depends upon work groups outside the programme team and is expected long after the completion of the programme itself. Yet, only by having a clear understanding of these relationships can roles and responsibilities for the achievement of benefits be agreed. In order to generate this understanding and agreement, many organizations use external consultants to do the necessary analysis and to facilitate the agreement of responsibilities between different work groups.

However desirable the benefit, it is unlikely to be realized if its achievement cannot be effectively measured and progress towards success monitored. Whilst financial benefits may (eventually) show up in the organization's accounts, other benefits may need specific measurement mechanisms to be created or procured.

257

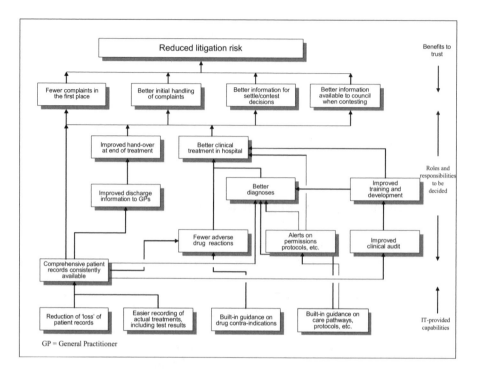

Figure 5.5 Example of a benefit model showing the relationship between IT capabilities and reduction in litigation risk within a hospital

This is frequently a problem with programmes using the Internet to distribute information. Here, special counters may need to be inserted to monitor hits, click-through and actual usage. Figure 5.6 shows the targets that might be set for different categories of use of a new website using such counters.

Even where mechanisms already exist, it can be difficult to agree a baseline against which improvement can be measured and targets against which improvement can be benchmarked. In Figure 5.6, because the site is new, the baseline against which improvement is to be measured is easy to agree – that is, zero. However, it is frequently a major task to agree the current baseline and, if data is not currently available, work should start on this activity before the new capabilities are delivered. It is often impossible to demonstrate the improvements delivered due to a lack of baseline for comparison. Similarly, agreeing on targets and milestones for the future, and therefore potential responsibilities for their achievement, can also involve much difficult and time-consuming negotiation between the various parts of the organization that will be held responsible for their achievement.

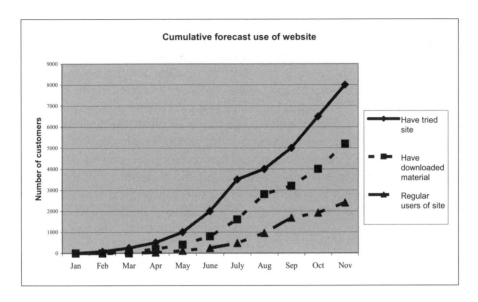

Figure 5.6 Possible benefit profile for accessing a new website to provide product information

A further complication is that many types of soft benefit depend upon perceptions, which change over time. For example, a level of customer service that has been adequate for many years may quickly become unacceptable as a result of innovation by a competitor. As explained by Zeithaml et al. (1990), customer perceptions depend upon expectations and expectations, in their turn, depend upon earlier perceptions.

Agreed roles and responsibilities are usually documented within a benefit realization plan. This document identifies the activities that need to be undertaken to maximize the realization of benefits and shows the responsibilities of the various groups and stakeholders for their achievement.

Good psychology usually requires a programme to deliver some 'early wins' – small improvements delivered early that demonstrate to all involved that the programme is going according to plan and thus that expected long-term benefits will be achieved. Because of this, realization plans can be complex documents involving progressive delivery of benefits over time.

Realization plans are normally accompanied by supporting documentation:

- Benefit profiles describe each benefit – what it is, how it will be realized, who is responsible for it, how it is to be measured, and so on.
- Benefit schedules show benefit realization over time, to give a clear picture of how the benefit stream will build up.

259

In large, complex organizations, the benefit chains can operate in unpredictable ways, so that the achievement of one benefit can have negative consequences on another part of the organization. Because of this, when defining benefits and preparing benefit schedules, it is important to allow for the disbenefits that change often brings. For example, when computer company Hewlett Packard calculated the benefits of acquiring fellow computer maker Compaq in 2002, it had to allow for a fall in combined sales as a result of the uncertainty and demotivation that the acquisition would create among its sales staff.

Once all benefits, targets and baselines have been agreed, and the programme is underway, it becomes necessary to monitor the achievement of the benefits and make adjustments to activities where actual achievement is disappointing (see Figure 5.7). This, of course, may not be because of any failure on the part of the programme team who deliver the capability or of those who use it: it may

Benefits monitoring report for July				
Benefit	Measure	This month target	This month actual	This month status
Website usage	Cumulative number of customers who have accessed site	3500	4216	Green
	Cumulative number who have downloaded material	1600	1579	Amber
	Cumulative number who are regular users (> than 5 downloads)	480	206	Red

Figure 5.7 Example of possible benefit monitoring report, using Red, Amber and Green to indicate benefit realization status

merely be the result over over-optimistic target setting at the start of the programme. Thus, even at this stage, extensive negotiation may be necessary to agree what the results mean and what corrective action, if any, should be taken.

At a conference on benefit management organized by ProgM[1] programme management professionals indicated that they found all aspects of benefit management difficult, but the greatest number reported that their most difficult task was 'identifying and agreeing the business benefits that the initiative is expected to deliver in sufficiently precise and explicit terms', while the second biggest number reported 'gaining effective action from colleagues or management to maximize the business benefits that the investment has made possible' as their most difficult task. These results demonstrate the importance of maintaining a continuous benefit management capability throughout the life of the programme and beyond, since 'agreeing the benefits' is normally undertaken at the start of the benefit management cycle, while 'gaining action to maximise possible benefits' normally takes place towards the end. Further details of this survey can be found in Case Study 5.3.

In summary, the core of benefits management is about explanation, presentation, and negotiation of agreement. The various reports, documents, tools and techniques can help but, in the end, successful benefits management relies on having experienced, business-focused staff, with excellent presentational and inter-personal skills and near-endless patience, to make it all happen.

CASE STUDY 5.3: BENEFIT MANAGEMENT BIGGEST PAIN

At a conference held in central London on the subject of 'Getting Better Value From IT Investments', attendees were asked to complete a questionnaire identifying their 'biggest pain' with respect to benefit management. The questionnaire was based upon one successfully used at a similar conference in the previous year. Fifty-seven questionnaires were completed, mostly by respondents who described themselves as 'Programme Directors', 'Programme Managers' or 'Project Managers working within a programme'. The respondents came from all business sectors and were responsible for a range of different types of programme.

The questionnaire asked respondents to select their 'biggest pain' from the following list:

---

1 'Getting Better Value From IT Investments', organized by ProgM and PROMS-G, 10 April 2003, Inmarsat Conference Centre, London, UK. PROMS-G is the Project Management Special Interest Group of the British Computer Society (BCS) and ProgM is the joint Programme Management Special Interest Group of the BCS and the Association for Project Management

a. identifying and agreeing the business benefits that the initiative is expected to deliver in sufficiently precise and explicit terms;
b. obtaining necessary budgets, resources or management commitment for establishing effective benefit management processes;
c. understanding and agreeing the relationship between different expected business benefits and the costs of their achievement;
d. gaining and maintaining agreement on priorities for business benefit achievement;
e. understanding and agreeing the way in which IT facilities/services actually contribute to the ultimate achievement of business benefits;
f. allocating and agreeing responsibilities for the ultimate delivery of business benefits once the IT facilities/services are implemented and operating;
g. agreeing meaningful mechanisms and metrics for measuring the achievement of expected business benefits;
h. interpreting benefits management data on the actual achievement of benefits and gaining agreement to its meaning and importance;
i. gaining effective action from colleagues or management to maximize the business benefits that the IT investment has made possible.

In spite of the relative complexity of the subject and of the choices offered, the responses were deemed to be good, with only 6 per cent of respondents unable to make a choice and only 6 per cent writing in additional pains. 15 per cent of respondents gave multiple responses.

The general result was as shown in Figure 5.8, which indicates that 'identifying and agreeing expected benefits' (option (a) – 23%) is the biggest pain, with 'gaining effective action' (option (i) – 14%) in second place. Smaller but broadly equal ratings were given for all other choices.

The relatively even spread of ratings suggests that there is no particular aspect of benefit management that is particularly more difficult than others – rather that they are all equally difficult. It should be noted, however, that the choices offered on the questionnaire were essentially in sequence: for example, 'identifying and agreeing expected benefits' (option (a)) is usually one of the first activities in any benefit management work stream, while 'gaining effective action' (option (i)) generally occurs late in such a work stream. Accordingly, the high rating for option (a) may indicate that many respondents were still in the early stages of their benefit management activities.

As in the previous year's survey, there were some interesting differences between the 'biggest pain' of programme managers/directors and of all the others completing the questionnaire. As can be seen in Figure 5.9, programme managers/directors indicated that their biggest pain was getting basic agreement on the benefits to be achieved. All the others recorded that getting budgets/resources or management commitment was the biggest problem, whereas no programme manager/director recorded this. This difference may reflect the greater status and authority that programme managers/directors have, enabling them to more easily obtain budgets, resources and commitment.

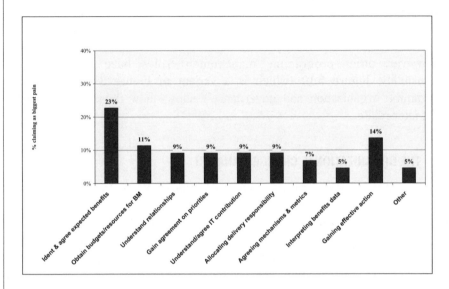

Figure 5.8   Benefit management's biggest pain

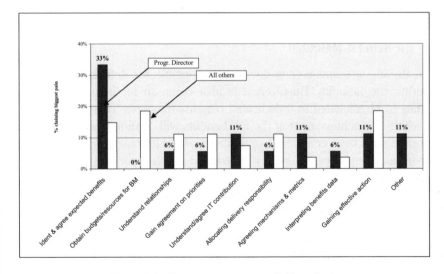

Figure 5.9   Programme management's biggest pain

263

5.7 RESPONSIBILITIES FOR BENEFIT DELIVERY

The programme director has overall responsibility for the successful delivery and realization of the programme and of its anticipated benefits. Thus it is their responsibility to define the overall strategy for maximizing benefits and for ensuring that appropriate staff and resources are allocated to their management and realization

However, other programme management roles have a more direct responsibility. Figure 5.10 (which is a variant of Figure 3.4 in chapter 3, 'Programme organization and governance') shows how these different roles might inter-relate.

5.7.1 THE ORGANIZATIONAL CHANGE MANAGER

It is now common for major programmes of business change to appoint a change manager with specific responsibility for managing those aspects of the programme that involve changing its organizational structure, business processes, ways of working or cultural elements. Where multiple divisions or departments are affected, several organizational change managers may be appointed, with responsibility for organizing change activities within their respective work areas. Organizational change managers will report to the programme director, along with the managers of the various other projects that make up the programme.

5.7.2 THE BENEFIT MANAGER

Often, the change manager is deemed responsible for defining, agreeing and delivering the benefits. However, it is also common for benefit management activities to be allocated to a dedicated benefits manager. This is especially the case where the achievement of the full benefits will continue long after the core programme has been completed, or where the benefit management activities are regarded as so significant that they are treated as a component project within the programme.

The role of the benefit manager is normally to plan and organize all aspects of the benefit management cycle:

- identifying and agreeing the benefits;
- negotiating responsibility for their delivery with line managers and other stakeholders;
- establishing mechanisms for their measurement and reporting;

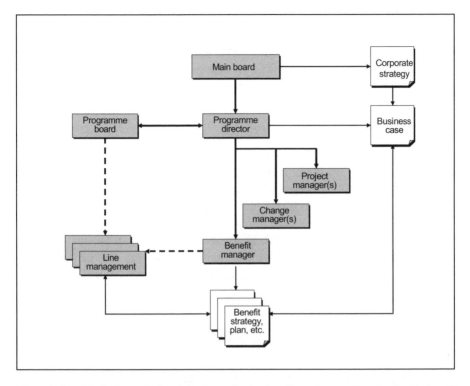

Figure 5.10 A typical organizational structure, showing how the various positions involved in benefit management inter-relate

- monitoring the achievement of benefits; and
- advising the programme director and the change manager on actions that can be taken to maximize the achievement of benefits.

Where the role of benefit manager must continue after the core programme has been completed and the new capabilities implemented, the lines of reporting will need to change, possibly directly to the main board of directors, since the post of programme director is likely to have been abolished upon core programme completion.

5.7.3 THE LINE MANAGERS

Line management normally have a crucial role to play in the actual achievement of benefits. It is their action (or inaction) that will determine the extent to which the new capabilities provided by the programme are used to create the improvements in service, productivity, cost-effectiveness or whatever that form the expected benefits. Frequently, high levels of leadership are required to motivate staff to use the new facilities appropriately, especially where corporate culture and heavy BAU workloads restrict the time available for training and switch over. The delivery of benefits may depend on uncomfortable actions, such as redundancies, and some people are strongly change averse by nature.

5.7.4 THE PROGRAMME BOARD

As explained in chapter 3 'Programme organization and governance', the programme board is normally responsible for assisting the programme director and ensuring that the business case, and thus the benefits that make it up, continue to be appropriate to the organization. This is normally affected through the review at appropriate points of the business case.

Also, because many of the members of this board represent specific groups of line management, or are themselves line managers, they can also play a key role in facilitating the negotiations around who is responsible for actually delivering the benefits.

5.8 PROGRAMME MANAGEMENT AND DELIVERING BENEFITS

5.8.1 OVERVIEW OF DEVELOPING A BENEFIT STRATEGY

The overall process of identifying and delivering a benefit strategy is summarized in Figure 5.11 in the form of a diagram of the level of benefits versus the programme lifecycle stage.

Some points to note about this diagram are:

- At the start of the programme, that is at the Mandate stage, the number and type of benefits known will be limited. Benefits will be rarely identified in measurable terms.
- During the Start-up stage, the process of benefits identification takes place. This could be undertaken through a series of workshops, interviews and reviews of business processes. At this stage the number of type of benefits known and expressed in measurable terms will rise significantly.
- The Programme Execution stage will result in the initiation and completion of a number of component projects. During the running of these projects, further potential benefits may be identified. The benefits identified in the Start-up stage will become inputs to the business case for each project. During project delivery, the business case should be updated to ensure that all the identified benefits are included.

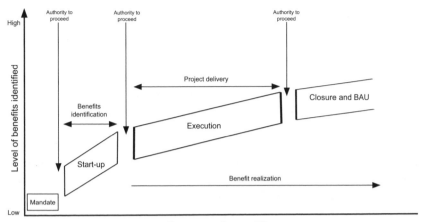

Figure 5.11 Benefit management process, showing changes in level of identified benefit by programme stage

- In the Closure and BAU stage, the users of the new capability should be able to improve their own processes and therefore realize the planned benefits. Note that approval is given to proceed to Programme Closure, and at this point an update on benefits delivery would be required for the whole programme.

The benefit realization process can start as soon as the desired benefits are identified and agreed. Indeed, the achievement of significant benefits early on, often referred to as 'quick wins' can be an important element in maintaining organizational commitment to the programme. Kotter and Cohen (2002) identify six ways in which such wins can help the success of complex programmes:

- **Provide evidence that sacrifices are worth it:** Wins greatly help justify the short-term costs involved.
- **Reward change agents with a pat on the back:** After a lot of hard work, positive feedback builds morale and motivation.
- **Help fine-tune vision and strategies:** Short-term wins give the guiding coalition concrete data on the viability of their ideas.
- **Undermine cynics and self-serving resisters:** Clear improvements in performance make it difficult for people to block needed change.
- **Keep bosses on board:** Provides those higher in the hierarchy with evidence that the transformation on track.
- **Build momentum:** Turns neutrals into supporters, reluctant supporters into active helpers, and so on.

Moreover, during the workshops and other Start-up stage events, problems may be identified in current processing that can be rectified immediately. The very nature of discussing issues improves communication and can assist the organization to focus on its objectives.

Benefit realization will continue through the Project Delivery stage. Project delivery does not mean that benefits have to wait until project closure. Some pre-go live benefits will come through during implementation. Also, some component projects may finish before others.

As explained above, the realization of benefits is likely to continue long after the core programme has been completed. For example, a programme to create a data warehouse (that is, a repository of organizational data, which can subsequently be accessed for any form of 'ad hoc' analysis purpose) may require 6 months to 1 year of operation before a suitable volume of data is stored within the warehouse to give meaningful statistical output. However, it is the management actions that follow from this analysis of the output that will bring actual benefit to the business. This is likely to occur long after the closure of the programme.

5.8.2 PROGRAMME MANDATE ACTIVITIES

There must be an initial reason to even consider undertaking the programme. The mandate provides the authority to start some investigative work. The mandate need not be a formal document: for example, it might be a board meeting minute or even a verbal instruction from a senior member of the organization. Whatever form it takes, the mandate gives the authority to investigate the feasibility of the programme.

5.8.3 PROGRAMME START-UP ACTIVITIES

If a programme is deemed feasible after the preliminary investigation initiated by the mandate, authority may be given to start work on the programme. During this stage, the likely benefits will be identified and agreed. These will then be included within the initial business case.

Furthermore, during this stage, an initial plan will be prepared for the programme. Depending upon the nature of the programme, it may be appropriate to regard the benefit management activities as forming a project in their own right or as a strand of programme management activities. Either way, it will be necessary to identify what needs to be done. This would normally be documented as a benefit strategy.

To complement this strategy, it may be appropriate to schedule the activities in the form of a Gantt chart or time plan.

5.8.4 EXAMPLE BENEFIT MANAGEMENT TIME PLAN

Figure 5.12 is an example of a time plan for the production of a benefit strategy for a large IT programme, as produced by Microsoft Project.

This plan assumes that benefit management will be treated as a distinct work stream in the context of the whole programme. As can be seen, it is divided into stages.

5.8.4.1 Stage 1: Work package initiation

This is the initiation stage of the benefit management project. During this stage, there should be a work package initiation meeting attended by:

- the benefit manager, as manager of the work package
- the programme director, sponsor or senior responsible officer (SRO) responsible for the programme (see Chapter 3, 'Management organization, governance and method', for an explanation of these roles);
- key stakeholders who have an interest in the achievement of benefits or who are likely to be responsible for their delivery. These will normally have been identified during the Programme Mandate stage.

The output from this meeting will be a schedule identifying all that needs to be done. The exact nature of this plan will depend upon the nature of the programme and the culture of the organization. In some organizations, benefits management is seen as a project in its own right and therefore will require a full project initiation document (PID). In others, benefit management is seen as a 'strand' of activities within the programme. When considering the layout and contents of this plan, the benefit manager should identify what would work best within the context of the programme.

5.8.4.2 Stage 2: Education of Stakeholders

In many organizations, the concept of managing benefits in order to ensure their delivery will be new. Accordingly, the various stakeholders will need educating in how benefits are to be identified, modelled and subsequently delivered.

This education process could be as simple as a short presentation explaining what benefits management is. Alternatively, if examples can be called up based on the experience from similar programmes run at other organizations, this will give greater clarity and assist in gaining buy-in.

It would be risky to assume that all the stakeholders will understand the implications of benefits identification and planning. This may apply also to key financial staff, who may deem themselves to be the corporate guardians of all measurement and related activity. At a very minimum, it would be appropriate to have an informal conversation with such staff beforehand to confirm the approach.

269

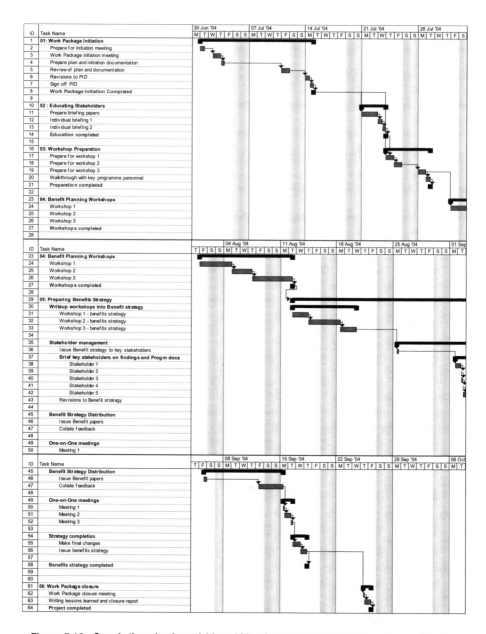

Figure 5.12   Sample time plan for activities within a large programme leading to the creation of a benefit strategy

Finally, discussions with individuals will assist in understanding their perspective on benefit management, for example:

- Will they support the project?
- Will they accept responsibility for delivering certain aspects?

Further guidance on communicating with stakeholders and others to maintain their enthusiasm and 'buy in' can be found in Chapter 6, 'Stakeholder management' and chapter 10, 'Internal communications'.

5.8.4.3 Stage 3: Workshop preparation

Pine and Gilmore (1999) argue that it is necessary to provide an 'experience' to people and that events that are presented in a generic, unexciting way are unlikely to inspire people and therefore unlikely to get them to engage. This will apply particularly to a benefit planning workshop, where the thought of sitting in a room for half a day to talk about system benefits may not inspire excitement on its own.

Case Study 5.4 contains guidance on what to consider when planning a workshop. A key element is to make the workshop interesting and enjoyable for the participants. It may be necessary to run a number of workshops and, in most large organizations, if the first is fun then the organization's informal 'grapevine' will ensure that attendance at the subsequent ones is more forthcoming.

CASE STUDY 5.4: BENEFIT WORKSHOP

This case study contains some practical hints on running benefit workshops.

THE PROCESS

In the project plan detailed earlier, the activities to delivering a benefit strategy were defined. This case study describes one of these activities, the benefit workshop, in greater detail.

Activity	Description
1. Identify a senior person to sponsor this initiative	We want people to turn up, and to take the work seriously. If the request to come to a workshop is not from a senior individual, preferably a main board member, then you might not get people turning up. Furthermore, your initiative might be stopped before it starts.

Activity	Description
2. Identify attendees	Who comes to the workshop is important. You will need to come up with an appropriate mix of individuals, representing different areas of interest.
3. Issue invitations	This needs to be done with suitable notice in place. If you have a central diary system, choose a date when everyone looks free.
4. Telephone in advance/meet in advance	Once the invites have been issued, telephone the attendees in advance. Even better, meet each person in advance. The purpose of this conversation/meeting is to: • understand the difficulties the person faces; • ask them what they would like from the workshop; • get a feel for them as people so the workshop can be run with their own personal style in mind; • get them to collect baseline data on the current system, processes and issues. The visitation order of this is important, especially in highly political companies where job titles, roles and responsibilities, are jealously guarded.
5. Prepare	Once all the individuals have been met, prepare a workshop definition document detailing the logistics for the workshop, for example: • who is attending and their role • the agenda for the day(s) • start and end times • location • pre-requisites • post-workshop activities. The pre-requisites could be to get the attendees to prepare sample documentation, bring example reports they would like to see and so forth. The post-workshop activities are to make it clear what the follow-up will be. This definition should be sent out by e-mail or in the post prior to the workshop.

Activity	Description
6. Run the workshop	See below for some ideas on how to make the workshop an enjoyable experience for the participants.
	It is a good idea for the facilitator to welcome people individually as they arrive, and when they leave, to thank them in person for their attendance.
7. Post-workshop thank-you	Once the workshop is completed, send a courtesy thank you to each of the attendees. Also, it is an idea to send a courtesy thank you to the person's manager for letting them come to the event.

It is not necessary to wait until all of the above is completed before commencing the writing of the benefit strategy. The pre-workshop meetings are likely to throw up possible benefits. It is important that these are captured early.

GETTING PEOPLE TO ATTEND

Imagine the scenario: you have been invited to attend a benefits planning and identification workshop. The subject is 'Improving the paper flow for purchasing, with the programme of business change considering how an e-procurement system could be implemented'. Asleep yet?

Pine and Gilmore argue that 'the problems for business people lie on both sides of the attention equation: on getting and holding the attention of information-flooded employees, ... and on parcelling out their own attention in the face of overwhelming options' (Pine and Gilmore, 1999).

The point is that it is often necessary to gain people's attention, to get them to attend the workshop. One way is to get senior sponsorship so they are encouraged to attend from on high. This should get them to the workshop, but it is also important to get them to listen and to contribute: so try and think of an original way of getting their attention.

MAKING THE WORKSHOP AN EXPERIENCE

Pine and Gilmore (1999) further advocate that it is necessary to 'design memorable events using goods as props and services as the stage ... [to] create experiences that engage customers in an inherently personal way'. Below are two examples of ways in which this advice has been used to engage workshop attendees.

THE FINANCE WORKSHOP

The purpose of the workshop was to look at how the financial procedures and process for the organization could be improved.

A number of the financial controllers were brought together to look at replacing their individual accounting systems with a single combined system. The plan was to create a single new system employing specialist IT technology. The Internet was to be the transport mechanism for connecting in to the system. The workshop was a one-day event, the output from which was a recommendation to proceed with key benefits and issued listed.

To make this more fun, two golf putters were purchased from a nearby UK retailer. These came with plastic golf balls and a plastic circle to put on the floor (representing the hole in the green). The attendees were split into two teams, and set the challenge of scoring the most putts with the least number of hits. Each person in the team had three attempts. The facilitator took a digital camera with him to take photos of the event. The day went down well, and after the event the photos were placed on some HTML pages using a standard software package. This created a record of the event and helped with the team building.

THE PROCUREMENT WORKSHOP

The purpose of this workshop was to identify how an e-Procurement system could be put in to the business. Attendees had travelled from around the country to this one-day event. The attendees were a receptive group who were not scared of coming forward. To get their attention a piece of music was played through the laptop computer with speakers connected. Before the start, attendees were asked 'Who ever can recognize this music in 20 seconds gets £20 pounds. After 5 seconds, the money goes down to £15 pounds, after 10 seconds we are down to £10 and so forth.' This gained everyone's attention immediately!

Short entertaining items which people can copy go down well. Many publishers and book retailers websites, such as Amazon.co.uk website, list books on the subject of 'Pub Games'. There are a number displayed which, for not very much money, will give plenty of ideas about short interludes between workshop discussion items (for example, Zenon, 2003).

Of course, it is not always be necessary to punctuate the workshop's agenda with such items. Indeed, some attendees, particularly senior ones, might regard spending time on such activities as wasteful. The facilitator must always consider the audience and plan the workshop appropriately.

5.8.4.4 Stage 4: Benefit planning workshops

The purpose of the workshops is to bring together different stakeholders in order to gain a clear view of the likely requirements, problems and challenges that will have to be faced, identifying the benefits that the programme can be expected to make possible. The output from these workshops will be the necessary information to prepare a benefit strategy.

Covey (1998) recommends that those who seek success should 'Begin with the end in mind'. For a benefit management work stream, this can be accomplished by means of a vision statement setting out the objectives that the programme is aiming to achieve, along the lines of the examples in Figure 5.3. Once this is defined, the workshops can be used to identify benefits by category, by stakeholder, and so forth. The workshops may also facilitate the collection of baseline data, that is, data on the current levels of benefits against which the improvements generated by the programme can be compared.

5.8.4.5 Stage 5: Preparing benefit strategy

Once the workshops are completed, the benefit strategy can be written. In the early part of this chapter, the different mechanisms for identifying benefits were noted. The strategy needs to be written in a form that enables the data to be modelled based on the basis of different criteria (such as stakeholder, benefit class, date when realized and so forth).

The authors' preference for modelling benefits data is to list it in a spreadsheet and then to use the 'pivot table' functionality to display it in different ways. This data can then be embedded within the formal benefit strategy document. (See Case Study 5.5 for further information on this approach.)

CASE STUDY 5.5: CONTENTS OF A BENEFIT STRATEGY

The benefit strategy document needs to be a confidently written, well thought through piece of work. A possible structure of contents is shown below.

Chapter heading	Description
Management Summary	This is a one-page (two-page at the most) summary of the findings. Ideally this could be extracted and become the basis of the board paper.
Method of Identifying Benefits	This section details how the benefits were identified. Within this section would be subsections as follows:

Chapter heading	Description
	• Explanation of the workshop approach • Attendees at the workshop • Follow-up and who reviewed the document.
Benefit Classification	An explanation of the types of classification used in the document. For example if you are using the Central Computer and Telecommunications Agency (CCTA), (now known as OGC) classes, these need detailing. Benefits will need to be modelled by: • benefit class • when realized • stakeholder or stakeholder group • by solution (project required to deliver the benefit). For those benefits that are quantifiable in financial and non-financial amounts, these should be listed separately. The non-financial amounts would be, for example, number of hours saved through the automation of a process.
Organization Strategy	This should be a summary of the company's strategy. In particular, it should detail the part of the strategy that this programme is proposing to deliver against.
Baseline Data	In improving the performance of the organization, we need something to compare against. This identification of baseline data will be an important comparison in the future.
Benefit List	This is the main section for the document. It should list out the benefits, but modelled according to the types of analysis you have chosen. For example there could be sections: a. by stakeholder group b. by when realized c. by class of benefit d. by project/system e. by degree of explicitness. Presentation order is important, so the most obvious/most important/highest priority need to be at the top of the list. The degree of explicitness is taken from the book, *Delivering Business Value in IT Projects* (Ashurst and Murray, 2002).

Chapter heading	Description
Project list	If it is possible to identify the main projects that are required to deliver the benefits in the programme, these should be listed here. You will note that point (d) above is by project/system. When we move into programme execution, we can link projects to benefits.
	Project information such as costs, timescales and so forth will need confirming; however a summary, if available should be included for completeness.

The following are points to note about the benefit strategy:

● Be careful of putting in generic benefits such as 'The new software is functionally richer'. This can appear superficial and give the naysayer(s) the opportunity to knock your document (see Section 5.4 'Hard and soft benefits' for guidance on how to make benefits specific and measurable).
● Businesses and the business environment change quickly. Companies cannot wait years for benefits to appear. You need to deliver something tangible in months not years (see Section 5.8.1 'Overview of developing a benefit strategy' for a discussion on 'quick wins').
● If the timescales for benefit delivery are identified, link these through to the communication plan. You need to communicate the successes and make it clear that things are happening (see Chapter 6 'Stakeholder management' and Chapter 10 'Internal communications' for more guidance on the management of external and internal communications).
● Do not underestimate the difficulty of collecting baseline data, or the importance of having it. Quantifiable successes are needed to demonstrate effectiveness and to silence the naysayer! (see Case Study 5.2 for guidance on measuring baselines).

Care needs to be taken here. In the excitement of preparing and issuing the benefit strategy, it is easy to forget that ultimate success will depend upon the 'buy-in' of those individuals who will deliver the benefits. For this reason, within the benefits management time plan, a series of one-on-one meetings are scheduled. The strategy document should be circulated to all relevant stakeholders and the benefit manager should go and speak to each key person individually. During these discussions, it may be necessary to negotiate and bargain to gain the necessary commitment, along the lines of: 'OK, I can see that you cannot commit to delivering this benefit as things stand at the moment, but could you do so if facility X was delivered by next Easter?' As a result of such discussions, there may need to be some final changes to the strategy before it can be finalized and issued.

In Case Study 5.5 there is a suggested table of contents for the benefit strategy. See also Case Study 5.6 for an example of a benefit list.

CASE STUDY 5.6: EXAMPLE OF A BENEFIT LIST

Ref	Component project	Description of benefit	How delivered	When realized	Category of benefit	Benefitting stakeholder
1	e-procurement system	Identify amount of money spent with each supplier	All purchases made through raising a formal purchase order, which are all summarized in the same database	9 months from start	Internal Management	Purchasing Dept
2	e-procurement system	Reduced order handling costs	All purchases made through Internet by requisitioner. Requires no additional manual processing by Purchasing Dept.	On live running	Financial	Purchasing Dept
3	New warehouse	Better customer service	New warehouse will allow products to be stored separately in unique bins or pallets, preventing loss or mix up through having to share bins	12 months from start	Customer Service	Sales Department

The table above is a copy from the starting point of a simple benefits strategy. The columns are as follows:

- *Component project* – the project or work stream within the programme that will actually deliver this benefit. (Of course, some benefits cannot be related to individual projects, but are only made possible by the completion of the programme as a whole.)
- *Description of benefit* – self explanatory.
- *How delivered* – this is how we propose to provide a solution which will meet the description of benefit. This is important as we must be able to demonstrate how the benefit is delivered.
- *When realized* – this is so we can identify benefits that are realized prior to go-live, on go-live, after 3 months, after 6 months and so on.
- *Category of benefit* – this allows benefits to be summarized according to their category. In this example, the categories suggested by the CCTA have been used (CCTA, 1999).
- *Benefitting stakeholder* – this is so we can model who will get what in the way of benefits.

CONSIDERATIONS

- You need to identify what types of classifications you want. There could be additional columns such as 'Hard benefits' with a straight yes or no. Remember that the more columns there are, the more that has to be filled in.
- For those entries that are classed as 'productivity improvements', it is worth identifying what hours/days are saved per annum, and if this can be expressed in financial terms then it should be.
- The storing of baseline data is likely to be separate from the above.

5.8.4.6 Stage 6: Work package closure

Work packages, like projects, have a start and a finish. This stage is to terminate the work, agreeing that the objectives have been met. If you are running a programme or project support office, identify the lessons learned and feed them back to this group.

5.8.4.7 The end result

The output from these workshops should include:

- a definition of the benefits that are expected to accrue from the programme as a whole;
- an identification of the projects in the programme;

- the project deliverables in terms of benefits by project;
- baseline data against which the success of the programme can be measured.

Using the Gantt chart in Figure 5.12 as an example, a pivot table[2] can be extracted, as per Figure 5.13. This summarizes the activities in an easy-to-understand tabular form.

Some points to consider in the sample table in Figure 5.13 include the following:

- The benefit management activities started on 1 July. The time plan has some slack in it but not very much. The end date was 26 September, requiring 12 weeks' work.

Sum of Duration_in_Days

Task_Name1	ID	Task_Name2	Task_Name3	Task_Name4	Start_Date	Finish_Date	Total
01: Project Initiation							
	2	Prepare for initiation meeting	(blank)	(blank)	01/Jul	01/Jul	0.50
	3	Project initiation meeting	(blank)	(blank)	02/Jul	03/Jul	1.00
	4	Prepare project plan and initiation documentation	(blank)	(blank)	03/Jul	03/Jul	0.50
	5	Review of plan and documentation	(blank)	(blank)	11/Jul	11/Jul	1.00
	6	Revisions to PID	(blank)	(blank)	14/Jul	14/Jul	0.50
	7	Sign off PID	(blank)	(blank)	14/Jul	14/Jul	0.50
	8	PID Completed	(blank)	(blank)	14/Jul	14/Jul	0.00
01: Project Initiation Total							4.00
02: Educating Stakeholders							
	12	Prepare briefing papers	(blank)	(blank)	21/Jul	22/Jul	2.00
	13	Individual briefing 1	(blank)	(blank)	23/Jul	23/Jul	0.50
	14	Individual briefing 2	(blank)	(blank)	23/Jul	23/Jul	0.50
	15	Education completed	(blank)	(blank)	23/Jul	23/Jul	0.00
02: Educating Stakeholders Total							3.00
03: Workshop Preparation							
	19	Prepare for workshop 1	(blank)	(blank)	24/Jul	24/Jul	1.00
	20	Prepare for workshop 2	(blank)	(blank)	25/Jul	25/Jul	1.00
	21	Prepare for workshop 3	(blank)	(blank)	28/Jul	28/Jul	1.00
	22	Walkthrough with key programme personnel	(blank)	(blank)	29/Jul	29/Jul	0.50
	23	Preparation completed	(blank)	(blank)	29/Jul	29/Jul	0.00
03: Workshop Preparation Total							3.50
04: Benefit Planning Workshops							
	27	Workshop 1	(blank)	(blank)	01/Aug	04/Aug	6.00
	28	Workshop 2	(blank)	(blank)	05/Aug	07/Aug	7.00
	29	Workshop 3	(blank)	(blank)	07/Aug	12/Aug	6.00
	30	Workshops completed	(blank)	(blank)	12/Aug	12/Aug	0.00
04: Benefit Planning Workshops Total							19.00
05: Preparing Benefits Strategy							
	34	Writeup workshops into Benefit strategy	Workshop 1 - benefits strategy	(blank)	12/Aug	14/Aug	2.00
	35	Writeup workshops into Benefit strategy	Workshop 2 - benefits strategy	(blank)	14/Aug	18/Aug	2.00
	36	Writeup workshops into Benefit strategy	Workshop 3 - benefits strategy	(blank)	18/Aug	20/Aug	2.00
	39	Stakeholder management	Issue Benefit strategy to key stakeholders	(blank)	25/Aug	25/Aug	0.50
	41	Stakeholder management	Brief key stakeholders on findings and Progm docs	Stakeholder 1	01/Sep	02/Sep	0.25
	42	Stakeholder management	Brief key stakeholders on findings and Progm docs	Stakeholder 2	02/Sep	02/Sep	0.25
	43	Stakeholder management	Brief key stakeholders on findings and Progm docs	Stakeholder 3	02/Sep	02/Sep	0.25
	44	Stakeholder management	Brief key stakeholders on findings and Progm docs	Stakeholder 4	02/Sep	02/Sep	0.25
	45	Stakeholder management	Brief key stakeholders on findings and Progm docs	Stakeholder 5	02/Sep	03/Sep	0.25
	46	Stakeholder management	Revisions to Benefit strategy	(blank)	05/Sep	05/Sep	0.50
	49	Benefit Strategy Distribution	Issue Benefit papers	(blank)	05/Sep	06/Sep	0.50
	50	Benefit Strategy Distribution	Collate feedback	(blank)	12/Sep	15/Sep	1.00
	53	One-on-One meetings	Meeting 1	(blank)	15/Sep	15/Sep	0.50
	54	One-on-One meetings	Meeting 2	(blank)	15/Sep	16/Sep	0.50
	55	One-on-One meetings	Meeting 3	(blank)	16/Sep	16/Sep	0.50
	58	Strategy completion	Make final changes	(blank)	16/Sep	17/Sep	1.00
	59	Strategy completion	Issue benefits strategy	(blank)	17/Sep	18/Sep	0.50
	61	Benefits strategy completed	(blank)	(blank)	18/Sep	18/Sep	0.00
05: Preparing Benefits Strategy Total							12.76
06: Project closure							
	65	Project closure meeting	(blank)	(blank)	25/Sep	25/Sep	0.50
	66	Writing lessons learned and closure report	(blank)	(blank)	25/Sep	26/Sep	0.50
	67	Project completed	(blank)	(blank)	26/Sep	26/Sep	0.00
06: Project closure Total							1.00
Grand Total							43.26

Project Start	01/Jul	
Project Completion	26/Sep	
End to End Duration	87	(in days)
End to End Duration	12	(in weeks)

Figure 5.13   Pivot table for activities leading to creation of benefit strategy

---

2 This table is created by copying information from the Gantt chart, which has been prepared in the Microsoft Project program, into a Microsoft Excel® spreadsheet. A pivot table is way of quickly sorting large amounts of data. Its rows and columns can be rotated to show different summaries of the data, and it can display the details of areas of interest.

- The individual briefings at WBS 2.2 and 2.3 (ID 13 and 14) then subsequently at 5.2.2.1 through to 5.2.2.5 (ID 41 to 45) inclusive have been shown as taking place one after the other. This is unlikely, as individuals' diaries get booked up, and getting time with senior personnel can be very difficult: so when planning the timescales some additional slack needs to be allowed for.
- The output from these activities (the benefit strategy) should also include an indication of the component projects that require running to deliver the programme.

5.8.5 STRATEGY AGREEMENT

Once prepared, the benefit strategy will need to be agreed by those key stakeholders who will be affected by it and the plan should allow time for this to be achieved. Typically, this will involve the main board of directors or the programme board. In order to gain their agreement, it will be necessary to clarify:

- the date of the board meeting;
- the date when board papers should be issued by;
- whether the benefit strategy will require amending and summarizing to be presented as a board paper. It cannot be assumed that the format which is required for the people working within the programme will be the same as that for the board of directors.

Some other points that need to be considered when working with boards include:

- the board will need to be advised that this is coming on to the agenda – one or two meetings in advance of the time your paper is presented;
- board papers are usually reviewed by the chief executive and/or chairman (or chair depending on your organization) prior to issuing to the full board;
- it would be advisable to meet the chairman, chief executive, finance director, (treasurer if it is a charity or charitable company) and other key board members to give them a full briefing on the proposal, particularly if they are going to do the explaining to their colleagues;
- board papers are issued one or two weeks in advance of the board meeting.

Not presenting to the board on the agreed date will bring doubt into their mind about the ability of the whole programme to deliver; so, if a date has been agreed by when a benefit strategy will be ready, every effort must be made to ensure that it is available on time. So with the delays outlined above in mind, the time plan has been changed in Figure 5.14 with a new stage 06: 'Board Presentation'. Work package closure is now stage 07.

In this revision, more time has been allowed for communication:

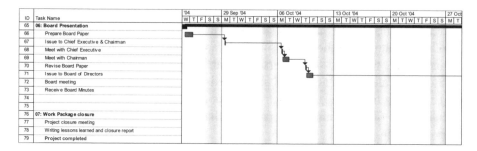

Figure 5.14   Revised time plan to allow for review of benefit strategy by main board of directors

- Stage 6 starts after the completion of the Benefit Strategy.
- It has been assumed that a board paper has to be prepared and is issued to the chief executive and the chairman (the 2 days' slack is to allow for any additional views to be considered prior to issuing).
- The chief executive and the chairman will need time to review the paper, so 5 days' slack is built in.
- There are individual briefings with these two individuals.
- The board paper will probably need to be amended with their comments included.
- This paper is then issued to the board, 3 weeks in advance of the meeting.

From the revised time plan in Figure 5.14, a revised pivot table can be prepared, as shown in Figure 5.15. From this, it can be seen that the timescales for this example now stretch from a July commencement through to the middle of November; some 20 weeks from the start date.

Moreover, in some situations it could take even longer to gain agreement. For example, some boards may require all affected department heads or line managers to agree to a proposal before they will endorse it. In these circumstances, time must be allowed for all the additional consultation, negotiation and agreement that will entail.

5.9 PROGRAMME EXECUTION

During the Start-up stage of a programme, the desired benefits and the component projects that are required to deliver these benefits will be identified. During the Execution stage, these component projects will be undertaken and the benefits will start to be delivered.

As explained in Section 5.2 'Programmes, projects and benefits', projects create the deliverables that are combined into capabilities. It is these capabilities

Sum of Duration_in_Days

Task_Name1	ID	Task_Name2	Task_Name3	Task_Name4	Start_Date	Finish_Date	Total
01: Project Initiation	2	Prepare for initiation meeting	(blank)	(blank)	01/Jul	01/July	0.50
	3	Project initiation meeting	(blank)	(blank)	02/Jul	03/July	1.00
	4	Prepare project plan and initiation documentation	(blank)	(blank)	03/Jul	03/July	0.50
	5	Review of plan and documentation	(blank)	(blank)	11/Jul	11/July	1.00
	6	Revisions to PID	(blank)	(blank)	14/Jul	14/July	0.50
	7	Sign off PID	(blank)	(blank)	14/Jul	14/July	0.50
	8	PID Completed	(blank)	(blank)	14/Jul	14/July	0.00
01: Project Initiation Total							4.00
02 : Educating Stakeholders	12	Prepare briefing papers	(blank)	(blank)	21/Jul	22/July	2.00
	13	Individual briefing 1	(blank)	(blank)	29/Jul	29/July	0.50
	14	Individual briefing 2	(blank)	(blank)	29/Jul	29/July	0.50
	15	Education completed	(blank)	(blank)	29/Jul	29/July	0.00
02 : Educating Stakeholders Total							3.00
03: Workshop Preparation	19	Prepare for workshop 1	(blank)	(blank)	30/Jul	30/July	1.00
	20	Prepare for workshop 2	(blank)	(blank)	31/Jul	31/July	1.00
	21	Prepare for workshop 3	(blank)	(blank)	01/Aug	01/August	1.00
	22	Walkthrough with key programme personnel	(blank)	(blank)	04/Aug	04/August	0.50
	23	Preparation completed	(blank)	(blank)	04/Aug	04/August	0.00
03: Workshop Preparation Total							3.50
04: Benefit Planning Workshops	27	Workshop 1	(blank)	(blank)	07/Aug	08/August	6.00
	28	Workshop 2	(blank)	(blank)	11/Aug	13/August	7.00
	29	Workshop 3	(blank)	(blank)	13/Aug	18/August	6.00
	30	Workshops completed	(blank)	(blank)	18/Aug	18/August	0.00
04: Benefit Planning Workshops Total							19.00
05: Preparing Benefits Strategy	35	Writeup workshops into Benefit strategy	Workshop 1 - benefits strategy	(blank)	18/Aug	20/August	2.00
	36	Writeup workshops into Benefit strategy	Workshop 2 - benefits strategy	(blank)	20/Aug	22/August	2.00
	37	Writeup workshops into Benefit strategy	Workshop 3 - benefits strategy	(blank)	22/Aug	26/August	2.00
	40	Stakeholder management	Issue Benefit strategy to key stakeholders	(blank)	29/Aug	29/August	0.50
	42	Stakeholder management	Brief key stakeholders on findings and Progm docs	Stakeholder 1	05/Sep	06/September	0.25
	43	Stakeholder management	Brief key stakeholders on findings and Progm docs	Stakeholder 2	06/Sep	06/September	0.25
	44	Stakeholder management	Brief key stakeholders on findings and Progm docs	Stakeholder 3	06/Sep	06/September	0.25
	45	Stakeholder management	Brief key stakeholders on findings and Progm docs	Stakeholder 4	06/Sep	06/September	0.25
	46	Stakeholder management	Brief key stakeholders on findings and Progm docs	Stakeholder 5	06/Sep	08/September	0.25
	47	Stakeholder management	Revisions to Benefit strategy	(blank)	10/Sep	10/September	0.50
	50	Benefit Strategy Distribution	Issue Benefit papers	(blank)	10/Sep	11/September	0.50
	51	Benefit Strategy Distribution	Collate feedback	(blank)	18/Sep	19/September	1.00
	54	One-on-One meetings	Meeting 1	(blank)	19/Sep	19/September	0.50
	55	One-on-One meetings	Meeting 2	(blank)	19/Sep	22/September	0.50
	56	One-on-One meetings	Meeting 3	(blank)	22/Sep	22/September	0.50
	59	Strategy completion	Make final changes	(blank)	22/Sep	23/September	1.00
	60	Strategy completion	Issue benefits strategy	(blank)	23/Sep	24/September	0.50
	62	Benefits strategy completed	(blank)	(blank)	24/Sep	24/September	0.00
05: Preparing Benefits Strategy Total							12.76
06: Board Presentation	66	Prepare Board Paper	(blank)	(blank)	24/Sep	25/September	1.00
	67	Issue to Chief Executive & Chairman	(blank)	(blank)	29/Sep	29/September	0.25
	68	Meet with Chief Executive	(blank)	(blank)	06/Oct	06/October	0.50
	69	Meet with Chairman	(blank)	(blank)	06/Oct	07/October	0.50
	70	Revise Board Paper	(blank)	(blank)	09/Oct	09/October	0.50
	71	Issue to Board of Directors	(blank)	(blank)	09/Oct	10/October	0.50
	72	Board meeting	(blank)	(blank)	31/Oct	03/November	1.00
	73	Receive Board Minutes	(blank)	(blank)	10/Nov	10/November	0.25
06: Board Presentation Total							4.50
07: Project closure	77	Project closure meeting	(blank)	(blank)	17/Nov	18/November	0.50
	78	Writing lessons learned and closure report	(blank)	(blank)	18/Nov	18/November	0.50
	79	Project completed	(blank)	(blank)	18/Nov	18/November	0.00
07: Project closure Total							1.00
Grand Total							47.76

Project Start	01-Jul	
Project Completion	18-Nov	
End to End Duration	141	(in days)
End to End Duration	20	(in weeks)

Figure 5.15 Revised pivot table for activities leading to the creation and approval of a benefit strategy

that allow benefits to be achieved. The relationship between projects, capabilities and benefits is often complex, with some features facilitating many benefits and other benefits only achievable when multiple capabilities are in place, as indicated by the benefits model shown in Figure 5.5. What is important here is to understand the relationship between them.

5.9.1 PROGRAMME AND PROJECT DELIVERY

Very often the relationship between projects and programmes is complicated by the integration of a portfolio of discrete projects into a programme. Benefits will often only flow once a number of projects have delivered their outputs and these have been combined to create the capability to deliver benefits.

283

Nevertheless it is valuable to consider the general case of the relationship between each individual project and the benefits with which it is associated. A clear understanding of benefits should be communicated to every project team so that their focus can be on the contribution they are expected to make to those benefits.

Since projects are needed to create the deliverables and capabilities on which benefit achievement is based, the relationship between the benefit strategy and the component projects will be as shown in Figure 5.16.

In Figure 5.16, a single project is considered:

- The benefit strategy, operating throughout the life of the programme, identifies the need for the project and what it is intended to achieve. As the project consists of a number of stages (as would be the case if the project were being managed according to the PRINCE2 methodology (OGC, 2001) it is possible to map those stages in relationship to the associated benefits.
- In the example, during stage 2 of the project, some of the benefits start to be realized. After this there is a continuation of benefits realization through project closure and beyond. For example, the system or other capability being implemented goes live at the end of stage n. Once stage n+1 has been achieved, the capability is live and in use, but any snagging issues or post go-live points are being addressed. Once project closure is completed, the capability is handed over to the business units and responsibility for benefit delivery is passed to the operational managers. Responsibility for benefit measurement still rests with the programme management team.
- The arrows for '6 months later' and '1 year later' are to indicate that very often

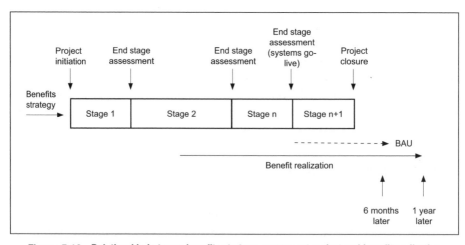

Figure 5.16   Relationship between benefits strategy, component project and benefit realization

benefits will take time before they arrive and will continue for some time. For example, if the objective of the project is to deliver a database of business data that can be analysed, the database will need populating, which may only be possible once the database is in use. Once the database is populated, it can be analysed and this analysis can direct management effort towards improvements. Once in use the benefits of better knowledge about human resource issues will continue for many years.

5.9.2 TRACKING BENEFITS BY PROJECT

Throughout the life of the programme, benefits need to be identified, predicted and tracked at the project level so that project teams are encouraged to maintain a focus on the benefits they are working towards

Project teams should always have a clear understanding of, and a focus on, the:

- reasons for the project
- benefits to be delivered by the project
- benefits realisation – how benefits are to be delivered
- cost and timescales of the project
- investment appraisal of the project
- the interactactions between the projects and other projects within the programme.

The business case is often updated as the project proceeds and the project team must be clear about such changes as changes may affect the direction and prioritization of activities within the project (see Figure 5.17).

Changes to a single project must be fed back into the programme, ideally before the changes have been committed to so that interactions and dependencies on the programme as a whole can be assessed. At the start of the project, the project manager will need to understand that the process of end stage reporting is not simply a matter of reporting back to the project board; anything that might impact the business case needs to be referred back to the programme level through the programme office or directly to the programme manager. The business case for each project will often be updated to include a benefits list showing what has already been achieved, what is expected will be achieved in the future and any benefits that are not longer expected to be delivered. Figure 5.18 shows this process.

It is then the responsibility of the project manager to report back, through the programme office (see Figure 5.18), any changes that have been requested or forced upon the project and that might have an impact on the programme or its benefits.

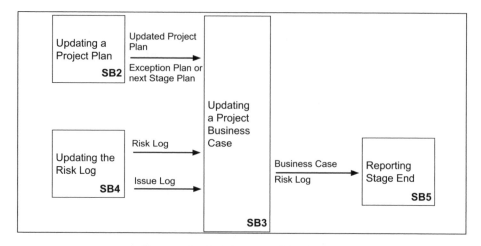

Figure 5.17   Updating project business case
Source: OGC, 2001. Crown copyright material is reproduced wth permission of the controller of HMSO
and the Queen's Printer for Scotland.

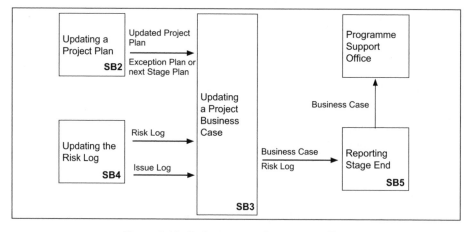

Figure 5.18   Business case and programme office

The process of reporting back to the programme office does not have to be formalized through a written report or separate documentation. Change management or programme management software could be used, as long as it provides functionality that tracks the status of multiple projects. The project manager or a member of the project office will input data into such a system providing updated status on the project, including, for example:

- milestones achieved and scheduled for the future
- costs to date and expected in the future

- benefits realized and anticipated in the future
- benefits delayed or impacted by change.

Status records are most valuable when they are compared with original targets or baselines so that changes and variations can be highlighted and made visible.

5.9.3 TRACKING CROSS-PROJECT BENEFITS

In running a programme of component projects, it is likely that benefits will be realized only when a number of component projects have been completed. Consider, for example, a programme to implement a new enterprise resource planning (ERP) system with an e-procurement system alongside. The former system allows for commitment accounting in the purchase ledger – that is, where a journal is posted to show that a purchase order has been raised and the organization thus has a commitment to subsequently pay for the goods. On its own, this functionality has no use. However, when the e-procurement system is implemented, a transaction will be posted automatically to the ledger whenever a purchase order is raised. The e-procurement system is unable to perform commitment accounting on its own; it is able to generate the transactions but has nowhere, on its own, to post them. Only when the two systems have been implemented does the organization gain any benefit.

As illustrated above, in tracking the delivery of benefits, the relationship between individual benefits and projects is not always clear-cut. In particular, benefits may result from the completion of several projects. In these circumstances, it is especially important that a named individual be assigned responsibility for benefit delivery.

5.10 PROJECT CLOSURE, BENEFIT REALIZATION AND PROGRAMME CLOSURE

As mentioned above, as projects are closed, there may be benefits which are not realized until some time later. It is important that they are passed back into the programme and ensure this delivery is not forgotten. The difficulty comes with the closure of the programme. If the programme is closed without the realization of all benefits, then these need to be passed on to the 'BAU team and the main board will need to monitor.

5.11 BENEFIT MANAGEMENT AND THE COMMUNICATIONS

As discussed in Chapter 6 'Stakeholder management' and Chapter 10 'Internal communications', ensuring that all concerned know what benefits the system will deliver is often vital to programme success. Accordingly, the programme's communication plan should be designed with the a number of objectives including:

● raising awareness among all stakeholders of the benefits and impact of the blueprint;
● keeping all staff in the target business area(s) informed of progress before, during and after implementation or delivery of project outcomes;
● maximizing the benefits obtained from the new business operations.

So the revised diagram in Figure 5.19 shows that, at stage end, progress is reported back to the programme office and the programme office then updates programme communications to reflect these changes.

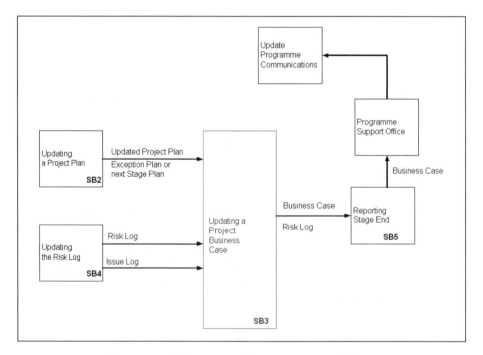

Figure 5.19   Business case and programme communications

CASE STUDY 5.7: EXAMPLE OF A BENEFIT LIST

COLLECTING BASELINE DATA

Baseline data has to be collected early in the programme so that the benefits that will result can be measured. Phillips (2003) suggests a range of possible measures.

- Attitude survey data
- Organizational commitment
- Climate survey data
- Employee complaints
- Grievances
- Discrimination complaints
- Stress reduction
- Employee turnover
- Employee absenteeism
- Employee tardiness
- Employee transfers
- Customer satisfaction survey data
- Customer complaints
- Customer response time
- Teamwork
- Co-operation
- Conflict
- Decisiveness
- Communication

If one of the projects in the programme is to reduce the number of customer complaints, we need to be able to collect:

- baseline data on the current number of complaints – this should be collected over a period of time, and not just a one-day/one-week snapshot;
- data after the completion of the training project to look at the number and type of complaints which are occurring.

Philips talks about *hard* and *soft* data in his (2003) book. Hard data represent the output, quality, cost and time of work-related processes. They are objective, easy to measure and easy to convert to money values. Soft data items are usually subjective, sometimes difficult to measure, almost always difficult to convert to monetary values, and behaviourally oriented.

For your own industry or organization, you will need to identify and define the baseline measures against which your programme and projects will be ultimately measured. The table listed above is expanded out in full at the end of this section. It lists the possible areas of data to collect covering both hard data and soft data. In the planning for the programme, the identification of the data to collect, its subsequent collection and then agreement by all parties that these are the correct measures will be a significant piece of work.

A final consideration, if you are proposing to use questionnaires as a way of gathering information, and you have not been through this process before, get a book like *Using Questionnaires and Surveys to Boost Your Business* by Nick Evans. The time spent reading up on this subject will pay dividends when it comes to preparing the questionnaire, gathering data and analysing the results.

APPENDIX: RETURN ON INVESTMENT

In his book, Phillips (2003) provides two tables of data (pp. 116–17) as examples of hard and soft data.

Examples of Hard Data

Output	Time
Units Produced	Equipment Downtime
Tons Manufactured	Overtime
Items Assembled	On-time shipments
Items Sold	Time to Project Completion
Forms Processed	Processing Time
Loans Approved	Supervisory Time
Inventory Turnover	Training Time
Patients Visited	Meeting Schedules
Applications Processed	Repair Time
Students Graduated	Efficiency
Productivity	Work Stoppages
Work Backlog	Order Rsponse
Shipments	Late Reporting
New Accounts Opened	Lost Time Days

Costs	Quality
Budget Variances	Scrap
Unit Costs	Waste
Cost by Account	Rejects
Variable Costs	Error Rates
Fixed Costs	Rework
Overhead Costs	Shortages
Operating Costs	Product Defects
Number of Cost Reductions	Deviation from Standard
Project Cost Savings	Product Failures
Accident Costs	Inventory Adjustments
Program Costs	Time Card Corrections
Sales Expense	Percent of Tasks Completed Properly
	Number of Accidents

291

Examples of Soft Data

Work Habits	*New Skills*
Absenteeism	Decisions Made
Tardiness	Problems Solved
Visits to the Dispensary	Conflicts Avoided
First Aid Treatments	Grievances Resolved
Violations of Safety Rules	Counselling Success
Number of Communication Breakdowns	Listening
Excessive Breaks	Reading Speed
Follow-up	Intention to use New Skills
	Frequency of Use of New Skills

Work Climate *Development/Advancement*	
Number of Grievances	Number of Promotions
Number of Discrimination Charges	Number of Pay Increases
Employee Complaints	Number of Training Programs Attended
Job Satisfaction	Requests for Transfer
Employee Turnover	Performance Appraisal Ratings
Litigation	Increases in Job Efficiency

Attitudes	*Initiative*
Favourable Reactions	Implementation of New Ideas
Attitude Changes	Successful Completion of Projects
Perceptions of Job responsibilities	Number of Suggestions Implemented
Perceived Changes in Performance	Setting Goals and Objectives
Employee Loyalty	
Increased Confidence	

REFERENCES

Ashurst, A. and Murray, P. (2002) *Delivering Business Value from IT Projects*. London: Financial Times Prentice Hall.

CCTA (1999) *Managing Successful Programmes*. London: The Stationery Office.

Covey, S.R. (1998) *The Seven Habits of Highly Effective People*. New York: Simon & Schuster.

Evans, N. (1995) *Using Questionnaires and Surveys to Boost your Business*. London: Financial Times Prentice Hall.

Kaplan, Robert and Norton, David (1996) *The Balanced Scorecard: Translating Strategy into Action*. Boston, MA: Harvard Business School Press.

Kotter, J.P. and Cohen, D.S. (2002) *The Heart of Change*. Boston, MA: Harvard Business School Press.

NHS (n.d.), 'Guidance for NHS Board Members: Addressing Information Management and Technology in NHS Organisations', National Health Service.

OGC (2001) *Managing Successful Projects with PRINCE2*. London: The Stationery Office.

Phillips, J.J. (2003) *Return on Investment in Training and Performance Improvement Programmes* (2nd edition). Burlington, MA: Butterworth Heinman division of Elsevier Science.

Pine, B.J. and Gilmore, J.J. (1999) *Experience Economy: Work is Theatre and Every Business a Stage*. Cambridge, MA: Harvard Business School Press.

Zeithaml, V., Parasaurimau, A. and Berry, L. (1990) *Delivering Quality Services*. New York: The Free Press, Macmillan.

Zenon, P. (2003) *100 Ways to Win a Tenner*. Singapore: Carlton Books.

293

6 ■ Stakeholder management

6.1 INTRODUCTION

A scrutiny of just about any report on the reasons for the failure of a major programme will reveal that high on the list of causes are misunderstandings, role inconsistencies, lack of leadership or support and sometimes downright stupidity and bloody mindedness. It is clear that a programme can have the best management system possible and a superb delivery management team, but if it does not manage the key individuals on which it depends, it will be seriously impaired or even wrecked completely.

Those people on whom the success of the programme directly or indirectly depends, but who are not under the direct control of the programme manager, are referred to as stakeholders. Stakeholder management is the process of by which those leading and managing a programme organize things so as to manage these people and the inevitable politics that surround the programme. As a management process, it is usually the responsibility of the programme manager. However, since it is so closely linked with the overall direction and leadership of the programme, the sponsor or programme director and the programme board usually have a vital role to play. Thus there is a close interplay between stakeholder management as described in this chapter and programme governance as described in Chapter 3 'Programme organization and governance'.

Many of the techniques used, particularly those relating to communication activities, also relate to the management of the programme's internal staff. These are described in greater detail in Chapter 10 'Internal communications'.

In an ideal world, stakeholder management would be unnecessary, since all would support worthwhile programmes and do what they could to assist. Sadly, the world is far from ideal and managing the politics of programmes is possibly the most important of any of the processes described in this handbook. In a survey, programme directors and managers reported that coping with 'internal obstacles and politics' is their 'biggest pain' and two-thirds reported that coping with the vaguaries of people is their 'biggest pain' – see Case Study 6.1.

The problems of stakeholder management are not new. Five hundred years ago the Italian writer Niccolò Machiavelli wrote:

> And let it be noted that there is no more delicate matter to take in hand, nor more dangerous to conduct, nor more doubtful in its success, than to set up as the leader in the introduction of changes. For he who innovates will have for his enemies all those who are well off under the existing order of things, and only lukewarm supporters in those who might be better off under the new. (Machiavelli, 2003)

Since then, Machiavelli has had 'a bad press'. But as the writer Anthony Jay points out:

> It is a pity that his name has become synonymous with unscrupulous intrigue ....' murderous Machievel' ... his main purpose was simply to analyse what processes had brought political success in the past. And from them, what principles ought to be followed for political success in the present. (Jay, 1967)

Achieving political success with respect to programmes is the essence of stakeholder management.

CASE STUDY 6.1: PROGRAMME MANAGEMENT'S BIGGEST PAIN

INTRODUCTION

At a conference in London on programme management, organized by ProgM* , all attendees were issued a research questionnaire. The objective of the questionnaire was to help build up a profile of the programme management community so that the organizers could better serve that community in the future.

The vast majority of attendees reported that they had an immediate and personal interest in programme management. Seventy-four per cent said that they were, or had recently been, involved with a programme. Among respondents involved with programmes, the principal role was as a programme director or manager: 48 per cent of respondents filled this role. The other major role was as a project manager within a programme, which 24 per cent reported as filling.

BIGGEST PAIN

As shown in Figure 6.1, those who were (or had been recently) involved with a programme found that 'internal obstacles and politics' created the greatest pain (37 per cent). The other major 'pains' included 'balancing the needs of different users/stakeholders' and 'cultural issues'. All these pains have the need to manage the people involved in the programme as a common theme and two thirds of respondents reported one of them as being the causes of their biggest pain. By contrast, only 3 per cent reported that 'complex technology' was their biggest pain.

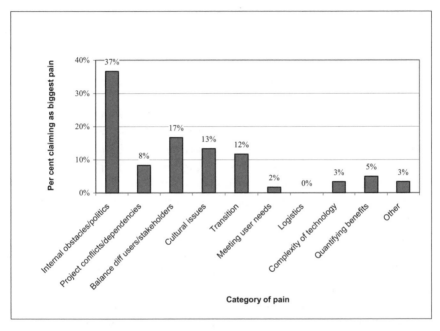

Figure 6.1   Biggest pain in current or most recent programme

These questions in the questionnaire were adapted from those used in a survey of e-commerce programmes conducted amongst 40 senior US and European businessmen by Forrester Research and quoted in *The Economist*, 18 November 2000.

6.2 BENEFITS OF MANAGING STAKEHOLDERS

Apart from reducing active opposition, stakeholder management contributes to the success of a programme in a number of ways, some of which are outlined below.

● **Creating understanding:** People fear what they do not understand. Therefore, promotion of a greater understanding of a programme, its purposes, context, deliverables, delivery structure, and so on can only serve to make stakeholders more comfortable about the programme. Programmes, especially those involving organizational change, contribute to stakeholder fears in a number of ways, for example:

- Operational business managers may fear that their power and influence will be reduced.
- Frequently 'change' is a euphemism for redundancies. Staff may fear that their jobs are to be terminated. Even if no redundancies are threatened, staff may fear that their working practices, job location, work descriptions or even terms of service will be changed unreasonably.
- Customers may be concerned that their products or servicing procedures will be changed.

- **Smoothing the path:** Keeping stakeholders informed, so they feel confident that the programme will not suddenly deliver an unpleasant surprise, will make them feel more comfortable and thus more valued as influencers. Generally, the happier people are that they are being fully informed, the less they are liable to seek to interfere and the more likely they are to actively support the programme. This is smoothing the path or, in other words, oiling the wheels of the programme.

- **Improving the acceptability of programme deliverables:** Active stakeholder management can contribute greatly to the final acceptability and usability of programme outputs. Although there will usually be formal specifications and statements of requirements, these can never be 100 per cent perfect. However, the greater the understanding of the needs and difficulties of key stakeholders, the more likely it is that the final solutions provided will meet those needs.

    Figure 6.2 gives an example of how inadequate stakeholder consultation can significantly harm the programme's prospects of achieving full success.

At least as risky as not using stakeholder management, is doing it badly. Both stakeholder analysis and subsequent communications need to be thoroughly planned and competently executed or the programme will run the risk of its communications being, at best, unfocused and ineffective or, at worst, seriously damaging to the programme.

6.3 PROCESS OVERVIEW

Like most management techniques, stakeholder management can be applied very simply or in increasing levels of complexity. The level chosen will be driven by a

The writer Timothy Lister describes how one day he had to admonish a work team for its failure to gain client approval for the emerging design of a new system.

The team looked suitably embarrassed about their failure to perform something so self-evidently important to the programme's success. Finally, one of the team said, 'We all agree that the client should be seeing this stuff, but our boss has laid down that nothing should be shown to people outside the project without his approval.' She went on to explain that the boss was so swamped that month's of work was piled up in his in box. In the absence of any approval, the team had continued to work as directed, knowing full well that most of what they did would eventually be rejected by the client and have to be reworked. (DeMarco and Lister, 1999)

Figure 6.2   Example of counter-productive approach to controlling team contact with stakeholders

range of factors, including amount of time and resource available to devote to it, and the complexity of the political environment within which the programme must operate. Nevertheless, benefits will be gained from pretty well any investment in stakeholder management and following the relatively simple processes outlined in this chapter will help to overcome any lack of political skills or knowledge on the part of those responsible for the management of the programme.

Essentially, there are three main steps in the stakeholder management process (see Figure 6.3):

1. Identify stakeholders.
2. Analyse stakeholders.
3. Manage stakeholders.

In addition, as with all other programme management processes, the effectiveness of stakeholder management needs to be regularly reviewed and adjustments and improvements made as necessary.

Furthermore, although these steps are presented serially, they are potentially iterative, as shown in Figure 6.3. Each of these steps is described in the subsections that follow.

6.3.1 STAKEHOLDER IDENTIFICATION

The first step is to identify who the programme's stakeholders are. A simple approach is to ask:

● Who 'owns' the programme?
● Who is directly affected by the programme's outcomes?
● Who is involved in the programme?

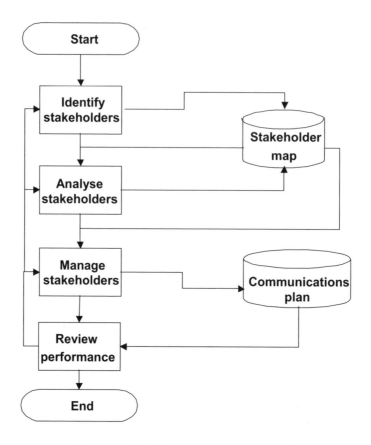

Figure 6.3   Overall stakeholder management process

6.3.1.1 Programme owners

In this context, programme 'ownership' usually means providing the budget, determining the business requirements, or being responsible for delivering the business outcomes and hence the programme's benefits.

Some programmes are burdened with more than one owner. Programmes of organizational change often cut across departmental and divisional boundaries and the programme's benefits may affect multiple business areas. In these circumstances, the organization may require the responsibility for benefits delivery to be shared across multiple executives. For example, an international airline ran a technology refresh programme. Although the programme was directed as a corporate programme, funding and benefits realization reflected the regional structure of the airline. A director from each region was made responsible for the benefits to their region and the programme thus had to operate with multiple programme directors or sponsors.

Coping with multiple owners can be particularly difficult. Frequently they may be internal rivals, competing against each other for promotion to the next senior vacancy or competing for scarce corporate resources to be invested in their departments and not in that of their rivals'. Part of the solution to this lies in ensuring that the programme is well structured and has transparent governance processes so that any self-serving politicking is quickly apparent. The support of effective champions, as outlined below, is also vital, as is the allocation of adequate time and resource to the management of these stakeholders.

The most obvious group of stakeholders will be those executives or senior managers who will provide sign off at key stages. The most important of them will normally be involved in the governance of the programme and thus will be members of the programme board. Guidance on the roles and responsibilities of this board can be found in Chapter 3 and a good board is a critically important tool in the management of other stakeholders. However, no programme manager can assume that all those sitting on the programme board are knowledgeable or effective, so the members of the board must be managed along with all other key stakeholders.

Every successful programme has a champion; a person with influence and political skill who uses these attributes to resolve the internal obstacles and politics that are so challenging to those responsible for the programme's management. Ideally, this person should be appointed as the programme's sponsor or programme director, as described in Section 6.4.1 'Programme director'. In practice, people are not always appointed to programme boards on the basis of their suitability or effectiveness, so it will often be necessary for the programme manager to seek a champion from elsewhere.

6.3.1.2 Directly affected stakeholders

Another important group of stakeholders are those that the programme directly affects. Some examples are:

- those whose working procedures, roles or responsibility are likely to change as a result of revised business processes, structural reorganization, personnel reduction, introduction of new technology, and so on;
- those responsible for selling or marketing new products;
- those responsible for providing customer service or for handling customer queries.

Identifying such people is often more of an art than a science. They may control requirements, budgets, resources or simply influence and should be sought wherever:

- existing business processes will change;
- new business processes will be created;
- resources (including people) will be reduced or increased;
- budgets will be reduced or enlarged;
- workloads or transaction volumes will change;
- responsibilities, or ownership for activities, will change;
- the needs of the programme may conflict with 'business as usual' (BAU) activities, such as where staff will need to be released from their normal work in order to take part in specification, testing, training or implementation activities;
- formal sign-off of documents or deliverables will be required.

It is also wise to look also for those who are not directly involved but will influence others that are. These too are often key stakeholders, although their role may only be to review and advise, rather than authorize. (As explained below in Section 6.4.1 'Categorizing stakeholders', these are sometimes called 'Grand Viziers' in stakeholder management terms and their importance is discussed in greater detail in Section 6.4.2.2 'Assessing power and influence'.)

6.3.1.3 Other involved parties

In many programmes, particularly in the public sector and in large service organizations, the general public are stakeholders and may be involved in many different ways. For example, a programme to reorganize hospital provision in an area is likely to impact on nearly all who live in the area, including:

- existing patients who currently rely on certain facilities for specialist treatments;
- potential patients who want the comfort of knowing that health facilities will be at hand should they ever need them;
- taxpayers who provide the wherewithal;
- local politicians who represent the above or who may wish to gain publicity by supporting or opposing the programme;
- local businesses that supply the hospitals and clinics with goods and services.

Other possible stakeholders could include customers, regulators or opinion formers such as the press/TV/radio, consumer groups, journalists, and so on. In fact, stakeholders can be anyone with a 'stake' in the programme, other sources will relate to the nature of the programme, including trade unions; staff associations and 'industry watchers' such investment analysts.

In many cases, several stakeholders can be deemed to have the same interest and involvement, for example the company's sales force that must sell a new product. In these circumstances, economy of effort means it is sensible to group them into a single entity rather than to treat them as a mass of individuals.

6.3.2 INITIAL STAKEHOLDER MAPPING

As each individual stakeholder or stakeholder group is identified, enter their details on an initial stakeholder map. This is a document that lists the programme's stakeholders and all relevant facts about them and their interests and involvement with the programme. The minimum information that should be collected is:

- Stakeholder name;
- Relationship with programme.

It is also wise to collect the following information that will enable them to be contacted, such as location, e-mail address, phone number, but be aware that collecting information about customers may have implications under the Data Protection Act in the UK or similar legislation elsewhere.

An illustrative example of such a map can be found in Figure 6.4 of Case Study 6.2.

As further information and understanding is gained through the subsequent analysis of stakeholders, the initial map can be turned into a more comprehensive final version as shown in Figure 6.6 of Case Study 6.2.

CASE STUDY 6.2: STAKEHOLDER MAP AND COMMUNICATIONS PLAN

A retail bank was proposing to offshore its contact centre operations from the UK to India. Following a feasibility study, a programme strategy and business case was produced and the programme director was about to start the company's governance process and realized that stakeholder management and a communications plan were key tools in her plan to gain business case approval.

An initial stakeholder map was produced for the programme. Figure 6.4 shows part of it.

Stakeholder	Role	Analysis
Reginal Fryant	Chief Executive	Neutral
Jon Siligo	Chief Information Officer	Ally
Wendy Forlorn	Finance Director	Ally
Franklyn Emphasis	Non-Executive Director	Opponent
Elizabeth Stickmud	Operations Director	Opponent
Patrick Standup	Staff Association representative	Opponent
Rudy Nuisance	Financial journalist	Opponent
Judith Monies	Investment Analyst for major stockholder	Neutral

Figure 6.4   Part of an initial stakeholder map

From this map, an initial communications plan was produced. Figure 6.5 shows part of it.

Objectives	Audiences	Key Messages	Timing
Win support for business case	All stakeholders	Clarify benefits to company	Now
		Risks of not off-shoring	Week before board meeting
	CEO CIO Finance Director Non-Executive Director Investment Analyst for major stockholder	Impact on margins Potential positive impact on share price	
Neutralize opposition	Financial journalist	Programme is enabler for more investment in customer services	Now and week before board meeting
	Director, Customer Operations		Now and weekly
	Director, Customer Operations	New international role	Now
	Staff Association representative	Redeployment opportunities, no enforced rerdundancy and generous voluntary redundancy package	Now and monthly to board meeting.

Figure 6.5   Part of an initial stakeholder communication plan

Note that, following further analysis, the stakeholder map was enlarged along the lines shown in Figure 6.6 and the communications plan was appropriately updated.

Stakeholder	Role	Analysis	Category	Import	Specific interests	Stakeholder management approach	Contact details	Remarks
Reginal Fryant		Neutral	Sultan	High	Keen to maintain reputation of company as reliable investment	Close contact - regular 1-2-1 briefing with Programme Director to keep reminding him of long-term benefits	Reginalf@abcco.com X63785 (Secy = Chris Thomson) M 077-88-99-23-67	Relies heavily on advice of Franklyn Emphasis. Defers on financial matters to Wendy Forlorn
Wendy Forlorn	Finance Director	Ally	Sultan	High	Believes that programme will reduce operating costs and thus enhance profit	Regular engagement by Programme Manager to ensure that Business Case and profile of expected business benefits fully understood and up-to-date	Wendyf@abcco.com X 63782 (PA = Silvia Smith) M 077-88-99-23-45	Programme Sponsor and Chair of Programme Board
Jon Siligo	Chief Information Officer	Ally	Sultan	High	Reliant on programme to upgrade IT network infrastructure	Regular engagement by Technical Architect. Jon to sign off Technical Specification	Jons@abcco.com X 63798 M 077-88-88-12-34	Member of Programme Board Fulfils role of Principal Supplier
Franklyn Emphasis	Non Executive Director	Opponent	Grand Vizier	High	Believes that spend will depress share price in immediate future	Close contact by Programme Director to explain long-term benefits and to show how all likely risks covered by risk mgt strategy and contingencies	f.emphasis@btnet.org Tel 01133-754-239	Represents XYZ Co, a major shareholder. A key influence on Reginal Fryant. Member of Programme Board
Patrick Standup	Staff Association representative	Opponent	Wannabe	Low	Seeking re-election. Wants to demonstrate he is 'tough' with management	Rely on regular meetings that Patrick holds with HR department	Patricks@abcco.com X 55443	
Rudy Nuisance	Financial journalist	Opponent	Prophet	Medium	Thinks big IT programmes are inherently expensive and risky	Programme Manager to brief on plans for programme, including risk arrangements	Rudy@finanince.com Tel 0207-345-6789 M 077-98-76-54-32	A long-time acquaintance of Franklyn Emphasis. They are members of same club and frequently dine together
Maureen Lippy	Coordinator of System User Group	Neutral	Prophet	Medium	Usability of new technology	Gain Maureen's approval of and signature to User Specification. Assist her to convince rest of User Group		Once received, make sure that Franklyn Emphasis knows of Maureen's sign-off of User Specification
Sales staff		Neutral	Followers	Low	Availability and speedy despatch of new product will make sales (and commissions) easier	Keep notified through regular features in staff newsletter		Reginal Fryant has expressed concern that uncertainty my cause best salesmen to leave

Figure 6.6   Example of part of a final stakeholder map

6.3.3 STAKEHOLDER ANALYSIS

Once the stakeholders are identified, they need to be analysed, for without this analysis it will not be possible to effectively manage them. Most basically, stakeholders should be labelled as one of three types: Allies, Neutrals, or Opponents, according to their support or otherwise for the programme. Successful stakeholder management depends on focusing effort efficiently: Allies need to be enlisted; Neutrals need to be converted; and Opponents need to be neutralized. It will subsequently be possible to measure the progress with stakeholder management by recording the progress in moving stakeholders from one category to another, as shown in Figure 6.7.

Stakeholder	Ally	Neutral	Opposer
Stakeholder 1			
Stakeholder 2			
Stakeholder 3			
Stakeholder 4			
Stakeholder 5			
Stakeholder 6			
Stakeholder 7			
Stakeholder 8			
Stakeholder 9			
Stakeholder 10			
Stakeholder 11			
Stakeholder 12			
Stakeholder 13			
Stakeholder 14			
Stakeholder 15			
Stakeholder 16			

Stakeholder	Ally	Neutral	Opposer
Stakeholder 1			
Stakeholder 2			
Stakeholder 3			
Stakeholder 4			
Stakeholder 5			
Stakeholder 6			
Stakeholder 7			
Stakeholder 8			
Stakeholder 9			
Stakeholder 10			
Stakeholder 11			
Stakeholder 12			
Stakeholder 13			
Stakeholder 14			
Stakeholder 15			
Stakeholder 16			

Figure 6.7   Example stakeholder matrices showing change in support over time

It is ironic that a programme established to be of benefit to the whole organization, or even to the whole country, should have opponents, but history is full of examples of highly placed individuals seeking to destroy the initiatives of their colleagues. Case Study 6.1 indicates how significant lateral obstacles and politics can be.

Just as apparently unsuitable people can hold high office in government, they can also hold senior positions in every organization. Stakeholder management is all about recognizing this fact and managing their behaviour so as to ensure the success of the programme. Many of these people will have no compunction about using the programme for their own purposes, so it makes sense for those responsible for the programme to do likewise!

As the true views and interests of each stakeholder are analysed, the details should be recorded on the stakeholder map.

Of course, the devil is in the detail. Stakeholder management can be made as simple or as complex as required. In general, the more detail, the better the resultant understanding of stakeholders' motives and aspirations will be. But the law of diminishing returns also applies – a little effort produces a big benefit, but as more and more time is expended, the additional benefits become smaller and smaller. The art of stakeholder management lies in realizing when an optimum analysis has been reached.

A stakeholder's position with respect to the programme can be determined in a number of ways. The most straightforward is to talk to them, seek an appointment, but prepare first by finding out what you can about them, for example:

- their place in the organization;
- their role with respect to the programme;
- how they may affect the programme;
- how the programme potentially affects them.

It is usually advisable to send an agenda for the meeting beforehand that clearly and simply states the object of the interview. Some examples of possible questions to ask can be found in Figure 6.10 later in this chapter.

If a large number of stakeholders are to be contacted, it may be appropriate to use some form of questionnaire to ensure that all necessary questions are asked and to simplify the comparison of responses. If time or resource is limited, it may be appropriate to replace face-to-face interviews with a questionnaire sent by post or e-mail.

It also makes sense to talk to others who know them, for example, managers in the programme who might work for them and who understand the personalities and the politics.

6.3.4 STAKEHOLDER RESPONSE MATRIX

A simple and effective way of summarizing the programme's stakeholder support is to plot a stakeholder response matrix. Here, each stakeholder is assigned to one of three columns, Ally, Neutral or Opponent. Note the use of RAG (Red, Amber, Green) to denote the attitude of each stakeholder. The RAG notation could be used to show progress and success of your stakeholder management.

Figure 6.7 gives examples of two such matrices, showing clearly how as a result of stakeholder management activities, one former opponent is now an ally and four are now neutrals.

- Regular progress meetings (see Figure 10.2 for a typical reporting sequence);
- Programme board meetings;
- Company intranet;
- Programme-specific intranet;
- Company newsletter – in paper, electronic or CD/video form;
- Programme-specific newsletter;
- Cascade briefings (see Section 10.4 'Communication for motivation' for a description);
- Individual and group e-mails;
- Electronic newsletters;
- Programme plans, strategies and reports;
- Programme repository of documentation;
- Video and teleconferences conferences;
- Issues registers (see Section 7.2 'Issue management' for further details);
- Press releases;
- Articles published in the trade press;
- Face-to-face meetings with key individuals;
- Group meetings and seminars.

Figure 6.8   Examples of communication media usually available within a programme

6.3.5 MANAGING STAKEHOLDERS

With a completed stakeholder map showing who the stakeholders are and their attitudes to your programme, it is possible to consider how each should be managed. The objective of management is to build the necessary support among key stakeholders and to neutralize opposition. In general, there are three possible approaches open to the typical programme manager:

- **Communication:** If the programme has a sound justification, ensuring that key people understand the benefits will often be enough to secure support.
- **Negotiation:** Some stakeholders may have genuine and reasonable objections, but it may be possible to overcome these by negotiating some adjustments to some aspect of the programme.
- **Escalation:** Where objections are unreasonable, it may be appropriate to escalate the problem to the senior managers on the programme board and to let them use their authority and influence.

Guidance on each of these management approaches is provided in the subsections that follow.

In addition, for some, there is a fourth possible approach of 'playing politics' and using deceit and deception of the type immortalized by Machiavelli. Some have a natural affinity for this approach, but most of us do not. For the latter group, this approach is extremely risky. If not played very well it is more likely to gain the player a reputation for dishonesty than it is to gain any effective long-term support.

6.3.5.1 Stakeholder communication

As described in Section 10.4 'Communication for motivation', good communication is just as essential to motivating stakeholders as it is to motivating the programme's own staff. It helps to maintain the enthusiasm of supporters, it can convince neutrals to become supportive, and can sometimes persuade active opponents to leave the programme alone. If well planned, communication with stakeholders can help them to understand:

- the reason for the programme – why the programme is needed and how it will contribute to the objectives of the organization;
- the benefits and rewards from programme success to them or their work group, (such as greater opportunities for promotion, reduced risks, enhanced satisfaction among their set of customers) or consequences of non-success (such as redundancies in their department);
- the ways in which their work will be made easier, for example, through improved information or faster access;
- assurance that particular issues that concern them will be dealt with effectively, for example, through appropriate training and the provision of additional support during transition periods.

Unfortunately, not all communication is 'good' communication. All too frequently communication activities are poorly planned and hastily executed. Prior to any communication activity, it is necessary to consider four things:

- What do we want the communication to achieve?
- Who do we need to communicate with to achieve this?
- What are your key messages to be sent or received?
- When should they be sent or received?

Without these questions being answered, there is a very high risk of communicating the wrong thing to the wrong people and having quite a different impact from that intended. Furthermore, there is rarely a shortage of media available for programme communication. Indeed, there are frequently so many channels that stakeholders can become confused about where to go for the information that they need. A list of typical communication channels and media available to a programme is given in Figure 6.8.

Figure 6.9   Example of pairing arrangements between programme staff and key stakeholders within client organization

The solution is to prepare a communications plan, using the information contained within the stakeholder map. An example of part of an initial communications plan can be found in Case Study 6.2. A study of this example will show the close relationship that stakeholder management and communications planning has to the programme governance process as described in Chapter 3 'Programme organization and governance'.

While the examples of communication activities shown in Figure 6.5 in Case Study 6.2 all feature documentation, communication can take all forms, including attendance at meetings and discussions over lunch or dinner. One approach to handling such discussions that spares the waistline of the programme manager is for various programme staff to 'pair' with specific stakeholders. This is often adopted where an external supplier is working in partnership with a client organization and an example of such pairing, based on that adopted between an IT supplier and a government agency, is shown in Figure 6.9.

A vital tool in communicating with and influencing stakeholders is a detailed understanding of the benefits that the programme will deliver and how they impact on each stakeholder and their interests. Once convinced that the projected benefits are likely to be achieved, many erstwhile opponents will change their views and become neutral if not active allies. Further guidance on the identification of business benefits can be found in Chapter 5 'Benefits management'.

6.3.5.2 Stakeholder Negotiation

Where key stakeholders have valid objections, no amount of communication on its own will fully resolve the problem. It may persuade the stakeholder not to be an obvious opponent on the grounds that everyone else appears to be in favour, but later, when difficulties arise or other stakeholders make objections public, the genuine objections are likely to be raised. Furthermore, opponents may use the late revelation of the problem as a weapon to damage the programme – for example, by claiming that initial planning has been inadequate, otherwise these objections would have been discovered and resolved earlier.

Where genuine objections exist, something positive must be done to remove the objection. Such actions could take any form that is within the control of the programme's management, such as readjust the timetable so that a particular benefit is achieved earlier, or providing additional budgetary support to counter the extra costs that the stakeholder or their department will incur.

However, when proposing such changes, care should be taken to ensure that the stakeholder will become an ally (or at least a neutral) as a result. Wherever possible, such changes should be part of a negotiation whereby, in return for the programme granting some concession to their needs, the programme gains something of value in return.

Critical to a successful negotiation is understanding the other party's position and the relative importance to them of different aspects of the programme. Some techniques for gaining this understanding are described below in Section 6.4 'Refining the stakeholder map'.

With this understanding, it will be possible to work out a possible bargaining position of:

- What is the minimum that the programme needs from the stakeholder?
- What is the maximum that the stakeholder might be prepared to give?
- What is the maximum that the programme could give in return?

With a clear view of how a bargain might be structured, it is then possible to approach the stakeholder with confidence and start negotiating, with the hope of gaining more than the absolute minimum and giving away less than the maximum.

Like most other things, negotiations must be planned and prepared for. The setting should be conducive to calm deliberation and both parties should be in a mood to negotiate. Furthermore, it is vital that those negotiating have the authority to make commitments. It is thus vital to be sure that the stakeholder really is a decision maker – a Sultan or Grand Vizier and not a Wannabe to use the classification described below in Section 6.4.1 'Categorizing stakeholders'.

To initiate meaningful negotiations, it may be necessary for the programme to give an indication of what is possible, along the lines of:

If the programme were able to change aspect XXX, would you, Mr [or Ms] Stakeholder, end your objection to aspect YYY?

Once a deal has been agreed that satisfies the requirements of programme and the stakeholder, it should be confirmed in writing to avoid the possibility of a subsequent dispute about what was agreed and, of course, the programme must adhere to its part of the bargain.

6.3.5.3 Escalation

Sometimes objections are irrational and no amount of communication or negotiation by the programme team will resolve them. Also, some stakeholders are so obsessed by their importance and status that they refuse to negotiate with those they regard as beneath them. In these circumstances, those responsible for the programme can choose to live with the opposition and seek to contain it or mitigate its consequences. Alternatively, if the opposition is too important and critical to ignore, the problem can be escalated upwards for the sponsor or the programme board to resolve.

The resolution of major political issues and the protection of the programme from damage by political infighting is one of the major responsibilities of the sponsor and the programme board.

However, sponsors and programme boards are frequently rather blunt instruments and should generally only be involved as a last resort. For a start, the boards meet only infrequently, resulting in a long delay before the objections can be resolved. Furthermore, members are usually busy people and rarely understand the details of their programme. Accordingly, it is vital that a comprehensive brief is prepared explaining what the problem, is, why it is important for the problem to be resolved and what the most appropriate solution is. Finally, however clear cut the issue, board members are likely to adopt a negotiating stance and trade off some aspect of the programme in return for a concession from the stakeholder – with a result that might not be as advantageous as could have been achieved by the programme's more knowledgeable management team.

Too frequent escalation can also give the programme board the impression that the programme management is not fully up to the job and may encourage interference that can severely restrict the programme manager's scope for manoeuvre and negotiation.

In essence, the involvement of the programme board or sponsor is rather like the possession of nuclear weapons. Having them gives the owner authority and forces others to take the owner seriously and to negotiate sensibly, but nobody really wants to use them since they can only be employed once and the consequences can be awful and unpredictable.

6.4 REFINING THE STAKEHOLDER MAP

Identifying a stakeholder as an Ally, Neutral or Opponent may be enough to start the stakeholder management process. But with limited time and resource, it is vital to focus on those stakeholders who are the most important. Without this focus, much time and effort can be wasted. More seriously, a potential Ally may be alienated because they have been ignored. The trick is to find out which stakeholders deserve the most attention, that is, who are the real stakeholders that are key to the success of the programme. Furthermore, effective communication and negotiation requires a full understanding of the stakeholder's interests and influence.

Several techniques are available for gaining this understanding and are described below.

6.4.1 CATEGORIZING STAKEHOLDERS

One approach to gaining the necessary understanding is to classify stakeholders according to their role within the programme. An exotic but practical classification structure is to identify each as a character in the tale of *The Arabian Nights*, that is, as:

- Sultan;
- Grand Vizier;
- Wannabe;
- Prophet; or
- Follower.

6.4.1.1 Sultans

Sultans are those who are genuinely part of the approvals process, that is, those who have authority over requirements sign off, financial approval or governance. Like oriental Sultans, they have great power and should be treated with care and respect.

There may be several Sultans to be considered, but most will have only a limited

313

range of interests. For example, the IT Director or Chief Information Officer will be greatly concerned about the impact of the programme on their technology, but may have little interest on how the customers or users may respond. By contrast, the Sales Director will be acutely interested in the customer response, but may be indifferent to matters of technology.

It should not be forgotten that a programme will usually require repeat authorizations. Most well-run programmes, and indeed the governance process, will require a number of checkpoints throughout a programme's life cycle. For example, government programmes being undertaken on behalf of the UK government are normally subject to a 'Gateway' review process at key stages to confirm that they are fit to proceed and that funds for the next stage should be released. These key stages are referred to as 'gates'. At each such gate, specific authority is required to proceed. Therefore when identifying stakeholders it is important to identify not only those who will be involved in the initial authorization, but also subsequent authorizations.

6.4.1.2 Grand Viziers

Frequently, the Sultans rely at least in part on the advice of others, usually subordinates. They leave the detail to their equivalent of a Prime Minister – the Grand Vizier. For example, the IT Director is unlikely to have time to keep abreast of the detail of a business case to be set before them and they are likely to delegate the detailed scrutiny to a subordinate. In this case, the subordinate is the Grand Vizier to the IT Director Sultan. Grand Viziers are the 'powers' behind the throne and are also key influencers.

6.4.1.3 Wannabes

While adding the Sultans and Grand Viziers to your stakeholder map, also be on the lookout for the Wannabes. These are the people, usually middle managers, who will claim influence but are not always what they claim. An example of a Wannabe would be a middle manager who claims to have authority at some level over the programme. They may do this for a number of reasons, including the desire to seem more important than they are or a self-delusion that they have such authority. What should be watched for are stakeholders who do not have formal authority but have influence. In these cases, the managers concerned may have influence over stakeholders who do have formal authority.

So the question then is, How to spot these sheep in wolves' clothing? The answer is that you should simply be able to confirm what the authorization process is, and who the signatories are at each stage in the process. Each signatory will be a key stakeholder or Sultan. It is usually easy to spot a potential Wannabe, as they will claim to be in authority and yet not appear on any list of those with authority to sign off programme deliverables.

Note that sometimes an apparent Wannabe is really a Grand Vizier; some who claim influence do, in fact, have it. In general, the more senior the authority, the more likely it is that they will either delegate that authority or rely on the advice of people for work for them. If someone's advice really is listened to, that person is a Grand Vizier.

6.4.1.4 Prophets

A Prophet is a stakeholder who is not only supportive of a change initiative, but will champion it within their work group. This is not quite the same as a programme's champion, who is supportive of the programme as a whole. For example, a change programme that is intended to merge two organizations will ideally require leaders in all parts of the organization to support and drive through the necessary restructure, role changes, process changes, location changes and whatever else is involved. Such active leaders can be termed Prophets.

Prophets can also come from outside the organization. Media figures can be highly influential where a programme will affect a large section of the public, or a large customer base. For example, when a British retail bank announced that it was going to charge for the use of its automated teller machines (ATMs), consumer group representatives mobilized public opinion and persuaded the bank to reverse its policy on charging. This policy changes had a major impact on the programme responsible for developing the technology of the bank's ATM service. By contrast, when British Telecommunications, known as BT set about renumbering the telephone dialling codes throughout Greater London, it took great pains to involve consumer groups and media representatives at an early stage. It supported this with a massive advertising campaign on television and elsewhere employing a popular comedy actress to ensure that everyone affected had a clear idea of what was going in, which contributed greatly to the success of the programme.

6.4.1.5 Followers

Followers are people who are directly impacted by a change programme, but who are not identified as Prophets. This is the mass of stakeholders who usually need to be kept informed of either how they will be affected, or/and how the programme is going. Again, taking the example of two merging companies, the customers of both companies will be impacted by the merger. They may be concerned about levels of service, or that their contact/support points may change. Moreover they are key stakeholders and need to be kept happy, if not, they may decide to take their business elsewhere.

In many programmes, such as those involving major civil engineering undertakings or changes to public services, large numbers of the public may be involved. While individually unimportant, through their elected representatives they can create insurmountable opposition if not correctly handled. Case Study 6.3 gives an example of good practice in the management of such external stakeholders.

CASE STUDY 6.3: EXTERNAL STAKEHOLDER MANAGEMENT ON THE CHANNEL TUNNEL RAIL LINK

The completion of the tunnel under the English Channel between the UK and France removed a historic bottleneck in communication between the two countries. However, it also exposed a new limitation on speedy travel: the inadequacy of rail lines in the UK, within Kent and east London. To overcome this problem, a high-speed rail link was proposed that would allow the Eurostar trains to travel at the same high speed across the south-east corner of England as they already did across Northern France. This required the design of a major high-speed railway line across some of the most beautiful and cherished landscapes in the country.

As the first major new railway in Britain for over a century, it required an Act of Parliament to provide the necessary powers to purchase land, to demolish houses and to divert existing railways, roads, rivers and power lines. This required the railway company to provide detailed plans of its intended route, which provoked intense opposition from those adversely affected. So strong was the opposition, that in spite of the huge expense already incurred, the initial bill was defeated in the House of Commons and the railway company was forced to start all over again.

To avoid a repeated defeat in Parliament, Union Railways, the company created to build the line, made stakeholder management in all its forms one of its highest priorities and recruited an extremely senior programme manager to organize this aspect of the programme. He ensured that the potential impact on the many thousands of stakeholders was given paramount importance throughout all aspects of the route planning.

For example, by using a geographical information system, it was possible to pick potential routes that largely avoided the many obstacles that existed in this crowded part of the UK. These included not only homes and historic churches, but also sites of special scientific interest, colonies of wild animals and even archaeological remains.

Once a short list of technically feasible routes was obtained, an intensive consultation exercise was started with every local authority that was in any way affected. These varied from London boroughs to rural parish councils and all had a different view of what was important. Merely organizing the massive consultation exercise was a larger and more complex than many programmes. For example, each local authority had a different schedule of meetings, some wished to be consulted jointly with their neighbours, some separately, and some changed their minds during the course of the exercise.

Many members of the public expressed concern about the impact of the railway on wildlife and so a comprehensive programme of research was established involving up to 35 ecologists and more than 170 separate studies and surveys. As a result, dormice, badgers and newts have been moved to new homes. In the case of badgers, this required the construction of large underground 'sets', possibly the first time that these creatures have been treated as programme stakeholders.

in December 1996, the UK Parliament passed the Channel Tunnel Rail Link Act and 6 months later the first tenders were issued. The full 68-mile route from Folkestone to the new London terminal at St Pancras is expected to be completed within 9 years.

Source: This case study is based on a presentation given in 2000 in London by Bernard Gambrill, Head of Public Affairs for Union Railways, and on material on the Channel Tunnel Rail Link website www.ctrl.co.uk.

6.4.2 THE NATURE AND DEGREE OF STAKEHOLDER IMPACT

6.4.2.1 Identifying specific interests

Generally, the greater the programme's impact on the stakeholder, or their potential impact upon the programme, the more important the stakeholder. The position of any stakeholder as an ally, and so on, may not be simple. There may only be some programme aspects that they are interested in. In fact this is likely to be true of most internal stakeholders, even many on the programme board. Some questions to ask to help determine what each stakeholder is interested in can be found in Figure 6.10.

Where the impact of the programme on the stakeholder is adverse, opposition should be expected. However, beware of pre-judging the attitude of a stakeholder. For example, the organizational restructuring of a telecommunications company required the loss of a whole area of responsibility from one directorate and considerable opposition was anticipated from the senior management of this unit.

317

- Technical/functional skills, for example:
  - Are there sufficient skilled people to carry through the change (perhaps while still supporting ongoing operational business)?
  - Do I (the stakeholder) have the people and resources needed?
  - Will my (the stakeholder) resource base be reduced?
- Legal/policy control, for example:
  - What are the legal and regulatory impacts of this programme?
- Hierarchical status and authority, for example:
  - What is the organizational impact of this programme on my department, division, etc.?
  - Will my authority be enhanced, reduced, curtailed?
- External influence or credibility, for example:
  - Will the company's/organization's image be enhanced, reduced, damaged by this programme?
- Access to others or control of communications, for example:
  - How will I be able to influence what this programme does?
  - What messages are to be given changes to my organization and how do I ensure they are suitable to me?
- Opinion and leadership, for example:
  - How can I ensure that my views are properly represented?
- Control of resources
  - How will the programme want to use my people?
  - How many of my people will the programme want to use?
  - How do I ensure that supporting the programme will not damage my operational functions?

Figure 6.10   Possible questions to ask stakeholders to ascertain their specific interests

In fact, the change enabled the director to rebalance his resources and create a focus for the directorate that had been diluted by the team that was removed. Thus, once he appreciated the benefits that would accrue to him and his directorate, he became an ally of the programme.

6.4.2.2 Assessing power and influence

The programme will impact on its stakeholders and the stakeholders may also impact on the programme. This is one of the key reasons for stakeholder management: to control the power and influence each stakeholder has to the benefit of the programme.

Power and influence are not the same. Consider the Sultans and Grand Viziers:

the difference between these two types is that one has power (Sultans) and the other has influence (Grand Viziers). Power in this context is exercising direct authority and hence control over some part of the programme's resource. Usually power will mean that person has the authority to release resources, or to withhold them. They may be signatories of business requirements, or for the release of funds. To put it simply, if their signature is needed to make something happen, they have power, whereas, if they are needed to convince someone else to sign something, they have influence.

Those with power may not always reside inside the organization. Where a new financial product is to be developed and launched, a regulatory body is likely be involved and their approval may be required. The regulatory body may be entitled to demand that changes be made or else their approval will be withheld. They clearly wield power in this case.

Influence can also work indirectly. Customers can have influence, either as a group if they make their views known, for example, at product try-outs. Consider the test screening of a new Hollywood blockbuster: audience response can lead to considerable re-editing, and even the re-shooting of scenes. Customers may also influence though a representative group, for example, the Consumer's Association, or a transport users lobby. Such indirect, or even direct influence can potentially alter anything from programme delivery timing, to outcomes or even to the objectives themselves.

6.4.2.3 Incompetent or otherwise destructive stakeholders

Human folly and frailty can also play a part. The most supportive ally can damage a programme, or other event in human affairs. About the Charge of the Light Brigade, Napoleon's Marshall, Pierre Basquet, observed, 'c'est manifique mais c'est ne pas la guerre' (it's magnificent but it is not war), but that magnificent, sad, foolish charge was entirely due to a mis-communication by either Lord Ragbin or the Earl of Lucan. His incompetence caused his death and that of hundreds.

Because of this, another area of possible analysis is to consider whether your allies will behave in ways that will in fact benefit your programme. A key stakeholder may in fact have poor relations with neutral stakeholdeers who you would like to become allies. Beware, then, the well-meaning ally.

Even more dangerous to your programme could be the truly incompetent stakeholder, as the example in Figure 6.11 describes. In this instance, your stakeholder analysis might want to determine whether you can rely on a stakeholder to be able to understand your programme, their role in it, and whether they will, with great enthusiasm, unintentionally wreck your programme.

One example of how politics and patronage have helped inadequate and unsuitable people to achieve high office is provided by the British Lord George Sackville.

In 1759 he had risen to command of the British contingent at the Battle of Minden. During the battle he repeatedly ignored orders from the Commander in Chief to charge the retreating French, allowing them to escape. It was felt that he did this out of personal pique in response to being publicly rebuked by his superior. For this he was court-marshalled, judged to be unfit to hold any military post, and dismissed from the Privy Council.

Ironically, his disgrace endeared him to the next British King, George III. He was so hostile to the actions of his father and the previous government, that Sackville was restored to favour. From 1775 to 1782 this dubious individual was Secretary of State for America and thus responsible for the loss of the 13 colonies that combined to form the United States of America.

Figure 6.11   Example of the power of politics

6.4.3 SELECTING STAKEHOLDERS FOR ACTIVE MANAGEMENT

There are some stakeholders that are ignored at the programme's peril, such as Sultans. Careful consideration should be given before any are excluded. Of course, the degree to which they may be managed might vary. Similarly, any Grand Viziers, while not as important as Sultans, are among the key stakeholders and will usually be included.

Wannabes can often be ignored because they are not as important as they pretend. When assessing their true importance, their true status should be judged; some may in fact be Grand Viziers.

Prophets are often key stakeholders. Usually, there will be only a few true Prophets, often only one.

Once all the stakeholders have been categorized, decisions can be made as to which approach should be adopted to each. The approach will eventually include the amount of contact to be had with a stakeholder, whether as an individual, in a small or large group, and the frequency of contact. The approach will also strongly influence the mode of interaction(s). At this stage it is enough to ascribe to each stakeholder, retained in the stakeholder map, with a single value:

- light touch
- regular engagement
- close contact.

Sultans would normally automatically be rated for close contact, as this is the most influential and powerful group. A refinement concerns those Sultans who will approve key deliverables but are not members of the programme board. These Sultans may only need close contact before and during part of the approvals process, rather than throughout the programme's life. This might of course include any approval checkpoints along the way.

Grand Viziers will usually rate at least regular contact, and some will rate close contact. Again, membership of any approval committee generally indicates a need for close contact. The mechanism for providing this contact is frequently through the preparatory communication, such as the production of committee agendas and the relevant approval documents. This illustrates how stakeholder management and communications planning can be integrated for efficiency with programme governance and with progress reporting processes.

Prophets should be treated as Sultans and rate close contact. Wannabes should be treated as they true status determines.

Followers will usually be managed with at least a light touch, although the exact approach may vary between subgroups. For example, some customers may be more deeply impacted by the programme than others. Therefore the needs of each Follower group should be considered separately.

In each case, it makes sense to classify the stakeholders according to their relative importance, so that programme management time and resource can be used where it will be most effective.

6.4.4 REVIEWING THE STAKEHOLDER MAP

Once completed, it is highly advisable to have the stakeholder map reviewed by the programme's champions and by those who will be involved in the process of managing the stakeholders, such as the programme director, programme manager, programme office manager and communications manager.

However, it should be noted that, as in the example in Figure 6.12, even members of a Programme Board may be neutrals or even opponents of the programme and their involvement in the review process will itself be an exercise in stakeholder management. Furthermore, their discretion can never be relied upon, so anything in the stakeholder map may be fed back to the individual stakeholders. This can lead to difficulties for the programme. Figure 6.13 gives examples where injudicious publication of stakeholder analyses had a negative impact.

In general, the fewer people that have access to the stakeholder map, the better.

Organizational restructuring within the locomotive maintenance facilities of the former British Railways meant that long-standing working practices and job definitions would change. These were enshrined in agreement with the trade unions. These agreements also specified that the trade unions had to be consulted in advance of any plans to change any aspect of these agreements. As a result, it was felt that union agreement should be secured before any management consultants started work on investigating the scope or benefits of such changes.

In due course, a meeting was held with representatives of the three unions involved to explain what was proposed and why it was necessary. No objections were raised and a date was agreed when the consultants could start work.

Unfortunately, when the consultants arrived on site to start work, the local official of one of the unions objected. The agreements stated that the unions should be 'separately consulted' and, because of this, he deemed the previous joint meeting as inadequate.

Separate consultation meetings were then organized with each trade union. Again, no objections were raised and eventually the management consultants were able to start their work.

Although the outcome was successful, the programme was delayed by several weeks and costs increased accordingly through paying insufficient attention to the status of each trade union as a separate and distinct stakeholder.

Figure 6.12   Example of the importance of recognizing stakeholder status

A large IT-based programme within a UK Government department decided to take advantage of an excellent intranet facility. In accordance with common practice, the programme's library of documentation was placed in the shared web space. This included the stakeholder map, containing the analysis of each stakeholder. While the analyses were in no way libellous, some senior managers took great exception to being classed as Opponents and acted extremely negatively as a result.

Similarly, in a large investment bank, where everyone was very conscious of their status and were forever seeking to gain promotion ahead of their peers, showing that someone was of less importance in stakeholder management terms than their rival produced a strong negative reaction and temporarily converted an erstwhile neutral into an active and dangerous opponent. Much time and effort had then to be spent restoring the situation.

Figure 6.13   Examples showing the need for care with opinions held within stakeholder analysis

6.5 STAKEHOLDER MANAGEMENT ROLES AND RESPONSIBILITIES

6.5.1 THE PROGRAMME DIRECTION AND MANAGER TEAM

6.5.1.1 The programme manager

The programme manager is ultimately responsible for the successful management of all aspects of the programme, and this includes stakeholder management. But their time is severely limited and they are likely to need assistance, particularly when dealing with hard-to-contact stakeholders or with the organization's highest levels of management who may be more senior in the hierarchy. As described below, the wise programme manager will work closely with the programme director and other key staff to ensure that all key stakeholders are managed as effectively as time allows. Nevertheless, the programme manager is likely to be the only person who can see the full picture and thus, however much assistance is available, they are responsible for:

- defining the stakeholder management and communications processes;
- producing and owning the stakeholder map.

6.5.1.2 The programme director

The programme director or sponsor has ultimate responsibility for delivery of the programme's benefits to the organization. They should thus have a vested interest ensuring that all involved give the programme effective support. Typical stakeholder management responsibilities of this post included:

- championing the programme to key stakeholders;
- ensuring that the programme board remains committed to the programme;
- providing stakeholder management assistance to the programme manager, where necessary.

One of the most important roles of the programme director is to chair and direct the programme board. This group can itself play a key role in ensuring that other senior stakeholders appreciate the importance of the programme and provide it with sufficient resources and support. Specific stakeholder management responsibilities that fall out from this overall obligation include:

- advising on identifying and interests of key stakeholders for the programme;
- championing the programme within their respective parts of the organization.

323

6.5.2 ELSEWHERE IN THE ORGANIZATION – CORPORATE PR DEPARTMENT

Most organizations have some form of public relations or customer affairs department. These are frequently willing to assist with external public relations. They may also have an internal role such as publishing the company newsletter or managing the organization's internet and intranet sites.

This group can be exploited by a programme in a number of ways:

- It will have expertise in communications and know what works, so can advise on both stakeholder analysis and the communications plan.
- It will have resources on which the programme may be able to call, such as technical authors or graphic designers.
- It will have established channels of communication with critical external stakeholders. For example, the group will have media contacts, especially in specialist media. The group will probably also control the main arteries of internal communications, whether they are in-house magazines or, more likely these days, the intranet. In addition, they can probably have items placed on executive briefings for senior management.

6.5.3 WITHIN THE PROGRAMME

However much assistance is obtained from outside the programme, stakeholder management, including the necessary external and internal communication activities, will remain fundamental to the success of the programme and therefore must remain under the overall control of the programme manager.

6.5.3.1 Communications manager

As discussed in Chapter 10 'Internal communications', the volume of necessary communication activities may be such that it is viable to employ a part-time or full-time communications manager. Typical situations in which such an appointment might be essential include those where the programme:

- is very large or complex;
- involves many parts of the organization;
- is important to a large number of varying stakeholders;
- has considerable external impact, for example, on the customers or the general public, or some sector of it;
- is of significant interest to many external industry or media watchers;
- has complex regulatory aspects;

- is radical in its outcomes or approach;
- has numerous third-party contributors.

The net result of even some of the above is to require extensive communications, and the more work there is to do, the more resource will be needed to carry it out. Indeed, in some circumstances, such as those described in Case Study 6.3, not only is a full time communications manager justified, but also a large and dedicated support staff. In some programmes it may be appropriate for the communications manager to oversee both the programme's internal and external communication, whilst in others it may be more appropriate for separate people to oversee these two aspects.

In any event, the responsibilities of the role usually include:

- production and active management of the communications plan;
- managing the execution of the communications plan, i.e. the production and dissemination of the communications plan deliverables;
- measurement and tracking of the effectiveness of communications.

Further guidance on this role can be found in Section 10.5 'Roles and responsibilities for internal communication'.

6.5.3.2 Programme office manager

As with all aspects of programme management, the programme office should provide the support needed for stakeholder management by the programme manager and others. This might include:

- publishing information, for example on the programme's intranet or portal;
- managing the programme's issue register;
- collating information for management reports;
- maintaining correspondence registers and any programme e-mail box;
- responding to specific requests for information about the programme;
- maintaining diaries and schedules of meetings.

6.5.3.3 Programme staff

Members of the programme's project and work teams, including the management of component projects, can be key players in the management of stakeholders. In their normal interactions with others, such as when discussing requirements, preparing specifications and presenting possible solutions, they are affecting the attitudes and opinions of stakeholders. Ideally, this should all be positive for the programme, but unguarded comments or poorly considered contact can have a negative effect. For example, a technician's comment that something should be 'relatively easy to achieve' might be interpreted -by someone outside the programme as a commitment to deliver, with all sorts of consequences to the programme manager. However, as Figure 6.2 demonstrates, restricting formal contact between team members and stakeholders can be even more counter-productive.

Accordingly, all members of the programme should be briefed on how they deal with stakeholders, what can be communicated freely and what information is restricted, and who to pass to any interesting background information that they acquire to. In general, team members should not be speaking against the programme and should be castigated if they do so. If questioned about the programme by someone from outside, programme staff should either refer to standard communications material provided by the communications manager, or simply refer to the communications manager.

One of the roles of the programme manager is to create the right environment in which the programme, and indeed the programme team, can succeed. Part of this is the team environment, which can include leadership, a good working atmosphere, and perhaps even a breakout area where team members can get away from the hothouse of their desk. it also means that anything that might harm the programme environment should be removed. Figure 6.14 shows how this can be damaging.

Remember that your programme exists within an organization's wider culture and should be integrated with that culture as well as organizational processes.

In his analysis of what creates effective programme teams, the writer Timothy Lister describes many examples of how management approaches work against the success of the programmes that they claim to support. A frequent cause is the insecurity of second- and third-line managers and their desire make an impact that justifies their managerial status. One aspect of this is the imposition of arbitrary rules that militate against work effectiveness.

He recounts how one project team involved in long hours and much evening and weekend work had installed a microwave machine in the office's coffee area. One day, a team member used it to roast some popcorn during normal working hours. Naturally, this left a distinctive smell in the coffee area, which was noticed by a passing manager. His reaction was to issue an e-mail to all staff announcing that 'Popcorn is not professional' and so would henceforth be forbidden. (DeMarco and Lister, 1999)

Figure 6.14   Example of counter-productive managerial behaviour

6.6 CONCLUSION

Stakeholder management cannot be implemented too soon and must be practised throughout the programme's life. However, there are certain stages when it is even more critical than normal:

- during initial start-up (as described in Figure 6.15; stakeholder management is often essential to gaining initial approval, and without such approval the programme would be stillborn);
- at the time of major deliverables and successes;
- at authorization points and review 'gates';
- prior to strategy and budget reviews;
- when crises occur.

However, to be able to effectively manage all key stakeholders at these key stages means that processes and mechanisms must be put in place beforehand to be ready when needed.

Stakeholder management can never start too soon. A key thing to understand is what will interest the different groups of stakeholders. A thousand pages of worthy business case will often be less effective than a single example of illustration.

One of the authors of this handbook once witnessed a presentation to a company's board intended to gain approval for the development of a new compact disk. The Product Manager had to sell his product to the manufacturing company's board.

Of course the board members had the programme's formal business case in front of them. But the key element of the presentation was the way the Product Manager quite literally 'caught the board's eyes' and hence their attention, by reflecting lights from the shiny surface of the prototype compact disk. Needless to say, he got his money for his product development programme and disks are still with us.

Figure 6.15   Example of effective stakeholder management episode

Furthermore, an active programme of stakeholder management will not only prevent the programme from being damaged as a result of internal obstacles and politics, but will actively enhance the quality of deliverables and the business benefits that will be realized as a result. This is because all programmes involve people and inevitably have to make compromises between the desires and objectives of different groups of people. Being proactive about organizing these

327

compromises, through stakeholder management, will mean that the programme is leading rather than being purely reactive.

REFERENCES

DeMarco, T. and Lister, T. (1999) *Peopleware* (2nd edition). New York: Dorset Howe.

Jay, Anthony (1967) *Management and Machieavelli*. London: Hutchinson Business Press.

Machiavelli, N. (2003) *The Prince*. London: Bantam Classics.

7 Management of risks and issues

7.1 INTRODUCTION

The management of uncertainty is a fundamental activity within any programme. These uncertainties take two main forms – risks and issues:

- Risk is some event or set of circumstances that may occur in the future and which, if it does occur, will prevent the programme from achieving its objectives.
- An issue is something that may prevent the programme from achieving its objectives unless some action is taken that is outside the normal cycle of management. Frequently issues are caused by a current lack of knowledge and understanding and therefore the required action is to investigate the matter.

Risks and issues are connected in that some issues, on investigation, may be identified as risks. However, not every issue will be so identified. As the diagram in Figure 7.1 shows, some may be identified as potential changes whilst yet others may turn out to be of no significance and may be ignored.

As can be seen in Figure 7.1, issues may be identified at the programme level, or may be escalated from component projects that make up the programme. One of the responsibilities of the programme management team will be to ensure a common understanding of the circumstances in which such issues should be escalated.

All issues should be recorded and assessed and some may need further investigation before an appropriate action can be agreed. However, not every issue will warrant action: even in the largest programme time and resource is limited and attention must be focused on the most important issues and risks. Accordingly many will be assessed as being not significant.

Some issues may require changes to be initiated. These may not result in formal requests for change, as discussed in Chapter 12 'Management of scope and change', but may merely require adjustment to planned actions that do not

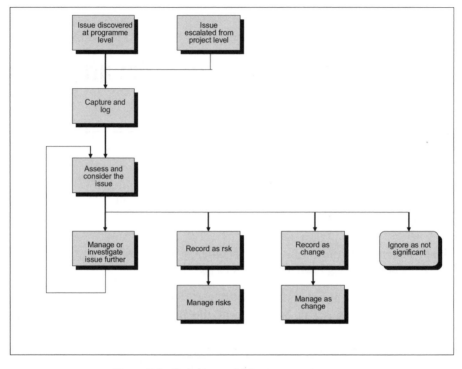

Figure 7.1   Basic issue and risk management process

compromise any of the agreed parameters of the programme. After all, adjusting to circumstances is a key function of management.

Usually only a portion of the issues will actually, upon investigation, turn out to be risks.

7.2 ISSUE MANAGEMENT

Most people seek to overcome the day-to-day uncertainties of their jobs without involving their superiors. However, there will always be circumstances that are outside their knowledge or ability to cope. For example, they may discover that there is a misunderstanding about requirements: what the customer appears to be expecting is different from what the supplier is planning to deliver. Resolving such a situation may be outside their authority, ability, or they may not have the time to handle it. Accordingly, it is an issue that must be resolved and a formal process will be needed to ensure that it is not lost or forgotten.

7.2.1 ESCALATION OF PROJECT LEVEL ISSUES

Within a programme, issues may be identified by those working within component projects (that is at the 'project level') or by members of the programme management team (that is at the 'programme level'). Wherever possible, project-level issues should be resolved within the projects. However, some issues will need to escalated for management at the programme level. These include:

- issues that are so big or complex that the project has insufficient resource or capability to resolve it;
- issues that result from the relationship between component projects and thus need 'programme level' adjudication;
- issues that will affect all projects and would thus benefit from a programme-wide solution;
- issues that relate to the programme as a whole, such as the management of programme objectives; and
- issues that relate to the delivery of benefits after project deliverables have been delivered.

It is the responsibility of the programme management team to provide guidance on when issues should be escalated from projects to programme level.

7.2.2 ISSUE CAPTURE

Various techniques can be used to capture issues. A common approach is to use the regular progress reporting meetings. These meetings include those at which project managers meet with programme management staff, and those where programme management staff meet with key stakeholders.

Some programmes also provide facilities for the programme team to report issues; for example, by means of an Internet-based issue recording system. This latter approach has the advantage of ensuring that all can record problems, but the ability to easily record a problem as an issue may encourage some to pass the work to someone else rather than to resolve it themselves. As a result, this approach requires a greater degree of administration and management control since more issues are likely to be captured and all will need to be assessed and allocated to someone for investigation and/or action. An approach to resolving this problem of potential overload is to require every such issue to be endorsed by a project manager, team leader or phase manager. The manager should consider and then either approve, modify and approve or reject the issue. Acceptance will cause the issue to be added to the issues register.

7.2.3 ISSUES REGISTER

Whatever method is used, all genuine issues should be recorded on an issues register (see Figure 7.2). Typically, this will record:

- Unique identifier or reference number.
- A description of the issue.
- The person raising the issue (and/or their manager).
- An owner: an individual or role that takes responsibility for managing and monitoring the issue.
- The work that may be affected: This will normally be a single task but might refer to a phase of a project, a project, a number of projects, delivery of one or more benefits or a complete programme.
- The estimation of the impact of non-resolution of the issue expressed in a common way.
- Timing, which may include:
  - date of raising the issue
  - expected date for resolution, such as the date by when investigation must be completed.
- Response task: a task given to an individual or team to manage an issue. A wide variety of actions may be taken to deal with issues and if these are significant they may have to be treated as project or programme tasks in their own right, thus requiring a change to programme or project plans.

Related activity	Issue description	Proposed resolution	Owner	Status	Class	Priority	Date raised	Dated resolved	Rating
Mpbs/mpin/spec – telephone banking investigation	Poor statement of requirements	Clarify number of users and screens	Design authority	Closed	Definition	Intermediate	02/03/2004	06/09/2004	50
Mpbs/mpin/spec – telephone banking investigation	Poor statement of requirements	Clarify source range	Design authority	Open	Definition	High	16/03/2004		100
Mpbs/mpin/spec – telephone banking investigation	Budget unclear	Clarify budget definitions	Programme manager	Open	Budget	Showstopper	10/02/2004		1000
NCCL/CCNP/code – coding and database changes	Access rights	Require access rights 24/7	Technical authority	Open	Legal	High	02/03/2004		100
NCCL/CCNP/desg – develop functional spec	Customer requirements	Customers needs to define need	Design authority	Open	Budget	Medium	16/02/2004		10
NCCL/CCNP/desg – develop functional spec	Customer requirements	Require meeting with customers	Design authority	Open	Communications	Medium	16/02/2004		10
NCCL/CCNP/docs – documentation	Translator requirements	We need translation work	Technical authority	Open	Resource mgt	Low	17/02/2004		1
NCCL/CCNP/docs – documentation	Expertise required	We need expert in technology	Programme manager	Open	Resource mgt	Low	22/03/2004		1
NCCL/CCNP/docs – documentation	Artist required	We need artistic input	Programme manager	Open	Resource mgt	High	17/02/2004		100
NCCL/CCNP/docs/2 - documentation	Artist required	We need artistic input	Programme manager	Open	Resource mgt	High	17/02/2004		100
NCCL/CCNP/docs/2 – documentation	Expertise required	We need expert in technology	Programme manager	Open	Resource mgt	Low	17/02/2004		1
NCCL/CCNP/docs/2 – documentation	Translator requirements	We need translation work	Technical authority	Open	Resource mgt	Low	17/02/2004		1

Figure 7.2   Example of an issues register

- Status: this may indicate:
    - 'Live' – a current issue, being investigated or managed.
    - 'Closed' – an issue that has been dealt with. It may now be regarded as a change or a risk; alternatively, it may have been revealed, upon investigation, that it was not, in fact, a problem. If now regarded as a risk, it will be recorded on the risk register and allocated a reference number.
    - 'Dead' – issues that no longer pose a threat.

In this way, the programme issues register will contain all programme-level issues and show the status of each. It will allow the programme management team to consider the status of issues and any planned actions and ensure that all are addressed in a timely manner. This is important since there is often an urgency to ensure that issues are attended to in a timely manner to prevent delays or overspend. It may also be possible to generate statistical data on issues and their states to allow senior management to understand the trends and quantities of issues without being involved in specific cases.

7.3 RISK MANAGEMENT

Because programmes are initiated to create a better future, they must always cope with uncertainty. Nobody knows what the future will bring, but the more astute can usually detect trends and pitfalls, often based upon the experience gained from previous programmes and projects. However, these trends and potential pitfalls are not certainties, merely possibilities. If they were certainties, appropriate actions to cope with them would have been built into programme and project plans. But such actions involve costs and, because risks are only possibilities, it would be wasteful to plan and pay to cope with every one. Accordingly, a considered process is required where the cost incurred is proportionate to the risk.

Furthermore, our worst fears about the future are rarely justified. Whilst some risks actually do occur, many do not. Therefore, an objective of the risk management process is to ensure that appropriate resources are available to cope with the risks that do occur, but a minimum is wasted on coping with those that do not.

Risk management can thus be defined as:

> The task of identifying risks associated with a particular course of actions designed to deliver a particular outcome. Once identified, those risks are managed to limit the potential of adverse results and achieve the desired outcomes.[1]

---

1 A definition provided by the UK's Office of Government Commerce (OGC) in its *Successful Delivery Toolkit* (2005).

7.3.1 OBJECTIVE OF RISK MANAGEMENT

The purpose of risk management is to prevent future events from disrupting the achievement of the programme's anticipated benefits. Since the potential incidents that could occur in the future are virtually unlimited, including war, pestilence and famine, the resources that could be committed to risk management are also potentially unlimited. In practice, the resources are limited by the scale of the benefits that the programme is expected to deliver and thus they must be used where their impact is greatest.

For this reason, it is usual to measure risk and thus permit risk management activities to be focused where they make the greatest contribution to ensuring the certainty of project success.

Some risks are so all embracing that standard procedures and mechanisms will already be in place. For example, the risk that staff will stop work if they are not paid is so great that all organizations put in place payroll systems to ensure regular payment of wages and salaries. Similarly, the risk that quality will be sacrificed in order to save time and money is so great that all programmes will implement comprehensive quality assurance procedures, such as those described in Chapter 8, 'Programme quality management'. Risk management handles specific risks that these generic processes fail to cover adequately.

7.3.2 MEASUREMENT OF RISK

Two factors combine to allow the measurement of the size of each risk:

- Probability: the estimated likelihood of a particular outcome actually happening;
- Impact: the evaluated effect or result of a particular outcome actually happening.

The term exposure refers to the combination of these two estimated factors. The task of risk management is the management of this exposure to an acceptable level, by taking action on either probability, impact or both; it therefore requires identification of the elements to be considered, not all of which may be controllable. It is not necessary or possible to eliminate all risks but it is necessary to recognize and manage risk at all levels.

Within a project, the objective of risk management is primarily aimed at the risks of failure to deliver the expected deliverables in a timely, cost-effective way. Within a programme, by contrast, the objective is to ensure that the required benefits are delivered in a timely and cost-effective way. Therefore the impact of a risk should be expressed in terms of its effect on the programme's objectives. For example, the impact of a delay on a programme that has an objective of making a measurable reduction on an organization's running costs, would be to delay the date at which running costs are reduced. In many programmes, understanding the impact of a risk will involve understanding the complex chains of benefit on which the programme is based, as described in Chapter 5, 'Benefits management'.

7.3.3 QUALITATIVE ASSESSMENT OF RISK

The degree of precision with which exposure needs to be measured will vary from programme to programme and from organization to organization. It may even vary from risk to risk. For example, risks to the trajectory of an inter-planetary space probe may need to be measured extremely accurately since only a fraction of error may cause the vehicle to completely miss its target. By contrast, estimates of the exposure of a business change programme on a particular group of stakeholders cannot be measured precisely and spurious precision in estimating impact could actually be counter-productive.

In practice, most organizations use a fairly rough and ready 'qualitative' approach to estimating exposure, typically based on grading likelihood and impact on the basis of 'high', 'medium' or 'low'. Even this crude approach will result in nine possible gradings of exposure, as demonstrated by Figure 7.3.

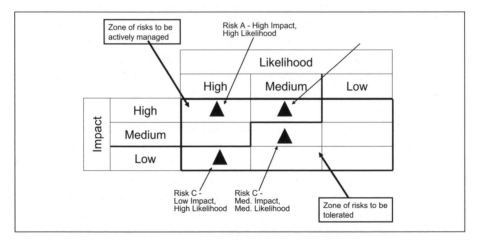

Figure 7.3   Example of a summary risk management profile

Because management time is limited, only the more serious risks (that is, those with the greatest exposure) can be actively managed. The others will merely be recorded and kept under observation to ensure that greater knowledge or changing circumstances does not alter the assessment of impact or likelihood.

Thus, for any programme, and potentially for any particular category of risk, you can draw up a risk management profile, which identifies the level of exposure that will trigger active risk management.

In the example in Figure 7.3, only risks where the impact or likelihood are rated as 'high' and the impact of the other aspect of exposure is 'medium' or 'high' will be so managed. Thus Risk A ('high' impact, 'high' likelihood) and Risk B ('high' impact, 'medium' likelihood) will be managed, whereas: Risk C ('high' likelihood but 'low' impact) and Risk D ('medium' likelihood and 'medium' impact) will be merely kept under observation.

7.3.4 QUANTITATIVE ASSESSMENT OF RISK

In some programmes, differing levels of tolerance will apply to differing types of risk, depending upon the criticality of the objective that they impact. For example, where completion dates are critical, it may be appropriate to use *Monte Carlo* analysis to determine exposure.

This refers to a technique that applies probability to complement traditional critical path analysis in order to estimate likely project durations, so named because it uses randomness in the same way as the casinos at Monte Carlo. From this, the likely delivery dates for various programme benefits may be calculated.

Within a traditional critical path model, planned activities are connected by dependencies that demonstrate how each task depends on the others. Each activity is given an estimated duration and these dependencies are used to provide an analysis of the plan giving a single overall estimated duration of a project and calculation of float. Some activities will be on the critical path and determine the overall project direction. Others will lie off the critical path and may be extended in time without affecting the project completion date.

To permit Monte Carlo analysis, a range of possible durations is added to each task and thus to the likely completion date. For example, it may be estimated that in ideal circumstances a task will take 3 weeks, in normal circumstances 5 weeks and 8 weeks in a worst case. It is also possible to include an estimate of a likelihood for each duration. For example, when servicing an aeroplane, removing an inspection hatch may have a 25 per cent chance of being followed by no work, a 50 per cent chance of being followed by a simple servicing operation, and a 25 per cent chance of being followed by a major replacement.

Once such a model has been built, it may be analysed many times using random selections of activity durations and logical links. The result is a graph relating overall project duration to likelihood and in some situations is very relevant and a vast improvement on a single crude estimate. An example of such a graph is shown in Figure 7.4.

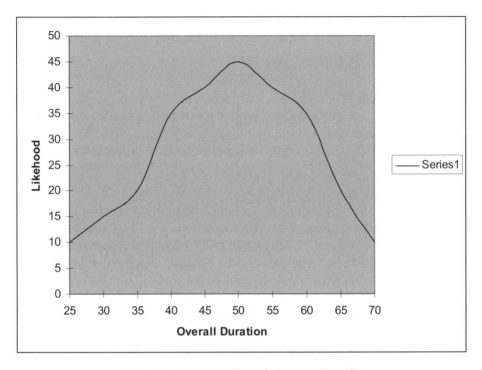

Figure 7.4   Example of a Monte Carlo probability profile

This technique is expensive and time consuming and usually requires specialist computer software, but may be appropriate where unusual challenges are to be faced. It is widely used in the heavy engineering and construction industries, where time overrun will result in serious financial losses to the contractor.[2]

7.4 A RISK MANAGEMENT FRAMEWORK

7.4.1 RISK MANAGEMENT STRATEGY

Some programmes are, by their nature high risk, for example, new product launches in competitive markets. Furthermore, some organizations are very risk averse; they commit to programmes only where risks are small and very manageable. It is important to understand for each programme what level of risk is to be expected and accepted, often referred to as the 'risk appetite'. This would

---

2   For further guidance on this technique see Vase, 1999.

normally be defined in a risk management strategy, which would define how risks are to be managed throughout the programme. Typically, it would identify:

- the overall approach to managing risk
- the techniques for measuring and assessing
- roles and responsibilities
- guidance on escalating risks from project level to programme level
- arrangements for review
- special techniques to be used, including those for handling contingency.

Any such strategy will need to identify the cyclic nature of risk management. As the programme progresses, new risks will be discovered while old risks will cease to be significant. Because of this, risks should be subject to regular review and revision throughout the life of the programme. However, it is vital to have a good grasp of likely risks at the start, since coping with them may consume a significant amount of time and effort and may thus be a major consideration in the initial business case on which the whole decision to proceed with the programme was based.

The risk management strategy will thus need to be built around a lifecycle along the lines shown in Figure 7.5.

The risk management strategy will provide a framework within which risks will be identified, analysed, controlled, monitored and reviewed. The following sections describe the components of this framework in further detail.

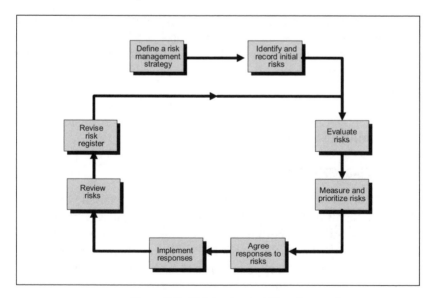

Figure 7.5   Risk management life cycle

7.4.2 IDENTIFY AND RECORD RISKS

There will be areas of risk that are common to many programmes and the identification of common areas of risk will help each programme and project team to locate appropriate risks. It is difficult to consider the right number of risks. While it is tempting to protect oneself from criticism by listing every possible risk no matter how unlikely and minor the impact, this will tend to cloud effective decision making. On the other hand, it is easy to miss important risks and therefore commit to a programme in ignorance of them. To find a balance is a matter for experience and will vary from organization to organization.

An analysis of past programmes will provide expertise to help the risk management of new programmes. This is an especially valuable way in which to use learning lessons from historic work to help in new challenges. An example of such an analysis, summarizing the experience of the IT Department of a multi-national financial organization, can be found in Case Study 7.1.

CASE STUDY 7.1: POSSIBLE RISK AREAS

This checklist summarizes the experience gained from previous programs and will help to identify likely risk areas in new programmes.

- **Customer**: The customer (that is, the business or the user) may not have the technical or commercial expertise to perform adequately their obligations with respect to the project in the manner that you expect. For example, they may be understaffed and thus find it difficult to release people from their normal work for programme activities or there may be no suitable person to act as user representative.

- **Other group companies/divisions**: Other parts of the firm may be involved and they may not have your understanding of what is required or your commitment to achieving success.

- **Development partners and collaborators and other third-parties**: External suppliers of software, hardware and other services may not fully understand their obligations and may not be as careful or as competent as you would wish.

- **Estimating development effort**: The estimates of the work required may not be accurate.

- **Technology**: Some of the proposed work may involve technology that is new or untried or new to the organization. There is thus a risk that problems are underestimated and/or that the technology may under-perform or fail totally.

- **Business critical issues**: It is one thing for implementation of a new, improved method of working to be delayed. It is another thing if the new system damages the company through failing to correctly perform some business critical function.

- **Effect of other programmes or projects**: Other programmes and projects may impact on this by using up resources and management time or because they provide an essential component to this one.

- **Scope of Supply**: The definition of what is required must be sufficiently complete, consistent, stable and understood by all parties to ensure that estimates are based on what is actually wanted and to minimize subsequent 'scope creep'.

- **Hidden and unspecified programme objectives**: There may be unstated requirements assumed by the sponsor that have not been explicitly excluded from the programme – exposing the programme to the risk of argument upon completion.

- **System performance**: The performance requirements may be unclear, or there may be no clear-cut way of measuring whether or not they have been achieved.

- **Timescales**: The timescales insisted upon by the customer may be impractical or may become so if the customer delays giving their acceptance of the proposal.

- **Acceptance**: If the acceptance requirements and procedures are not well defined, the customer may be able to delay acceptance or insist on late changes.

- **Price versus cost**: Pressures to keep the cost within pre-defined budgets may have led to an underestimate of costs and contingencies.

- **Staffing**: It may not be possible to assign the required number of suitable staff, or key staff may be deficient in specific experience.

- **Compliance, evaluation and certification**: the need for legal and statutory compliance may impose uncertainties delays and costs, for example:
  - establishing what is actually required
  - evaluating whether the requirements are met
  - obtaining formal assessment and certification that they have been met.

- **Customer liaison and progress monitoring**: Arrangements for progress review, for sign-off of documents and for handling requests for change need to be clear, agreed and allowed for in time-plan and estimates.

Another common approach is to conduct a brainstorming session. The people involved must be knowledgeable individuals who bring different viewpoints, for example, business manager, commercial manager, QA consultant, project managers, design authority from a similar project and members of the programme team. Where it is not possible to get such a wide range of people together into a single meeting, it may be appropriate to conduct structured interviews.

Once initial risks are identified, they should be recorded in the programme risk register. Similar documents should also exist within each project for recording risks identified at project level.

A typical risk register will record:

- a unique identifier or reference number;
- a description of the risk;
- the benefits or programme objectives that it appears to impact;
- the source – where the risk came from, for example, escalated from a component project;
- the ownership, that is, the person responsible for investigating and assessing and evaluating the risk.

Subsequently, when the risk has been evaluated, further information will be added:

- impact, likelihood and exposure, plus any date dependency;
- agreed responses, including containment mitigation and contingency arrangements;
- person responsible for implementing responses;
- current status of risk; the status may be:
  - Open – being investigated
  - Active – subject to active risk management, with agreed responses to be implemented
  - Non-active – not currently deemed sufficiently important to warrant active management
  - Closed – this risk is deemed no longer likely to affect the programme.

Several software packages are available to record risks. However, many find that a simple database is adequate. Such a database will allow risks to be listed according to responsibility, objective affected, and so on, and these listings can be used to monitor responses at regular progress meetings.

Examples of entries in a risk register can be found in Case Study 7.2. In this example, detailed information on each risk is recorded on an assessment sheet and then summarized in the risk register summary.

CASE STUDY 7.2: SAMPLE RISK REGISTER ENTRIES

Sample Risk Register – Assessment Sheet

Project: New Wages systems software   **Issue** 1

Programme: New Wages System
Date: 2 April

Status: Active

Risk title:

Delay in user acceptance

Description of risk:

There are concerns that the user group may not be able to test and therefore accept the new software in a timely way. There are certain times of the each month and each year when testing and acceptance will not be possible. There are additional concerns that the new system may cause unwelcome changes to the workload of members of the group.

Risk owner:

Programme Manager

Likelihood:

High. The user group have expressed their deep concerns about this aspect of the project.

Impact on schedule/cost/performance/benefits

Very high: If the user group does not accept the software none of the intended benefits will be delivered.

Containment plan:

The management must make suitable users available to carry out testing and acceptance. The work must be planned at an appropriate time to make this possible. The user group must understand more clearly the reason for the new system and the benefits it will deliver.

Contingency:

Refer to task Prg987/Prj004/task654 in the implementation project plan.

Sample Risk Register – Summary Sheet

Project title:	New wages software				**Issue date**	30 April
Programme	New Wages system					

Ref	Risk description	Risk containment plan	Date raised	Date of impact	Risk contingency plan	Likelihood %	Impact (high/ med/ low)
01	Delay in special keyboard supply	Proactive subcontractor plans, early delivery, customer involvement. Penalty clause in supply order			Monthly progress reviews with contractor – consider another supplier	20%	H
02	Overrun software development	Include extra 30% effort in plans for software 1100md	1 March	4 June	Monitor the modelling component very closely – expect effort overrun	30%	M
03	Delay in user acceptance	Advise user group of test philosophy. Include extra review time in plan, and slack of one month prior to ship. No extra effort	2 April	16 June	Allow 2 weeks contingency on Acceptance Test Schedule	50%	H
. . .							

Once completed, the initial risk register will usually be submitted to the appropriate authority (for example the programme board) for endorsement. It will also be subject to review and updating on a regular and planned basis, as described in Section 7.4.10 'Update risk register'.

7.4.3 EVALUATE RISKS

Risks to projects tend to be relatively easy to understand. By contrast, risks to the success of a programme tend to be complex. For example, evaluating a risk within a programme aiming to automate patient records within a hospital may require a thorough assessment of how the risk will impact on each stage of the various benefit chains as described in Chapter 5 'Benefits management'. The sample benefit model shown as Figure 5.4 summarizes the various possible factors that might have a bearing on potential patient litigation that would be impacted by the patient record system.

Many risks can only impact a programme during certain time periods or phases. A classic example of this is provided by the famous 'Year 2000' problem, where many computer programmes were feared not to be able to cope with the change of date from the 20th century (for example, 30–12–99) to the 21st century (for example, 01–01–00). The majority of such risks would occur, if they occurred at all, during the first few days of the year 2000 and, if they had not materialized during that period, they could be ignored. Thus a risk which would have been classed as 'Active' during the final days of 1999, would have been flagged as 'Closed' once the year-end transition had been completed.

7.4.4 MEASURE AND EVALUATE

Once the risk has been evaluated, its exposure can be calculated, in the manner discussed above in Section 7.3.2 'Measurement of risk'.

Those that have a high exposure and will need specific responses to be implemented or allowed for will be marked as 'Active' in the risk register. Those of lower priority will be marked as 'Non active'.

7.4.5 AGREE RESPONSES TO RISK

The ultimate purpose of identifying and assessing risks is to initiate appropriate responses. These responses fall into two broad categories:

- actions that should be undertaken to prevent, contain or mitigate the impact or occurrence of the risk;
- actions for which a contingency should be allowed, which will only be used should the risk actually occur.

Agreed actions should all be summarized within the risk register.

7.4.6 CONTAINMENT

Containment activities are undertaken whether or not the risk event actually occurs. For example, in an e-commerce programme, there may be a concern that an initial rush to use the new capability may be such as to swamp the computers and cause the service to collapse. An appropriate mitigation action might be to hire and install on a temporary basis additional computer servers to cope with any such a rush. The problem with such an approach is that the costs are incurred whether or not the rush occurs. An alternative approach might be to prevent the risk by requiring users to pre-register and limiting those who do to the capacity of the system.

The containment plan is a plan for containing risk to acceptable levels. It may seek to eliminate the risk entirely. Alternatively, it may not eliminate the risk but manage it in an agreed and understood way.

Containment activities are implemented during the life of the project or programme and must be put in place before the risk might occur.

Sometimes, it may make sense to adjust plans so that the risks occur earlier. For example, where there is uncertainty about whether or not it will be necessary to modify software from a supplier, scheduling for early delivery will allow time to make the modifications without disrupting other project activities. Of course, this may increase planned costs (if only in cash flow charges) but the reduced potential impact may allow the programme to reduce the contingency required to cover possible disruption to the other activities.

One approach to coping with risk is to transfer its impact to another party. A frequent request from public sector organizations is for external contractors to 'share the risk'. Thus, for example, those tendering to supply a new Internet-based service may be required to base their remuneration on the number of citizens that actually use the service.

Another approach is to pass as much of the risk as possible to suppliers or customers. Through clear terms and conditions, it is possible to pay another party to bear part of the risk. Currently this approach is very much in favour with UK public bodies, who seek to put as much as much of the risk associated with building new public facilities such as schools and hospitals onto the external contractor through Private Finance Initiatives and similar contractual arrangements. However, nothing comes free and the cost to the public purse of operating in this way is higher than with traditional procurements. Furthermore, it is rarely possible to remove risk completely this way, as involving a contractor carries risk in itself.

It is important to remember that risk containment tasks may give rise to secondary risks. For example, the hiring of extra computer equipment may create a risk of incompatibility with existing equipment. Where such secondary risks are not covered within the containment plan and any related contingency plan, they should be raised as new risks and processed accordingly.

A single containment plan may apply to a number of risks and there is often a 'many to many' relationship between risk reduction tasks and risks. There may be a containment plan for risks on a specific project or programme or more general containment plans for all programmes in an organization.

7.4.7 CONTINGENCY

In contrast to containment, contingent activities only take place if the event occurs. In the e-commerce programme described above, an initial rush might also overwhelm the staff that pick, pack and despatch products. However, it may be possible to cope with a temporary rush by hiring in temporary staff from a recruitment agency. Since these can normally be brought in at short notice, there is no need to commit to such action 'up front'. Instead, the extra staff need only be hired should the rush actually occur. Such staff will be expensive and budgets must contain a contingency fund to pay for them. However, if an overwhelming rush does not occur, the money will not need to be spent and may be reabsorbed as profit or allocated to some other purpose.

Because only some of the identified risks will actually occur, it is rarely necessary for the contingency fund to be large enough to handle all risks. Instead, it is normal to discount the contingency by the likelihood of occurrence. Thus, if coping with a risk would cost £100 000, but there is only a low probability of it occurring (say less than 20 per cent), contingency fund of only £20 000 would be allowed.

The important point to remember is that the contingency that you include in your programme plan is only an *allowance* to cover possible future risks; it is unlikely that it will be adequate to cover fully the impact of all of the risks should they occur. The best that can be expected is that if every component project within the programme includes adequate allowances, then the aggregate effect over a long time and over all the projects within the programme will effectively be neutral – that is, some component projects will have bad luck and use up relatively large amounts of contingency, but most will not and the total amount of contingency used will thus be equal to or less than the total amount allowed.

The rules for using contingency, and the authority for deciding on its use, will usually be defined within the risk management strategy. Typically, projects may only be able to call on the contingency fund with the approval of the programme manager, while the programme can only use the fund with the authority of the programme board.

Containment and contingency arrangements can be expensive. In some major IT-based initiatives, 20 per cent to 30 per cent of the cost may be consumed in such arrangements. In politically sensitive programmes, which depend upon the continuing goodwill of the government, contingencies can be even higher. Accordingly, it is vital for initial business cases to include them.

Note that, although the examples given above all relate to money, contingency can also refer to time and effort.

If there are many small risks (low likelihood/low impact) and a few big risks (high likelihood/high impact), it may be sensible to manage the small risks in a single containment plan and a single contingency plan. This will enable the programme's management to concentrate on preparing the plans for the big risks.

7.4.8 IMPLEMENT RESPONSES

All prevention, containment or mitigation activities must be adequately completed to have effect. Accordingly, they will need to be included in programme and project plans and their completion monitored in the same way as other programme and project activities.

7.4.9 REVIEW

Throughout the life of the programme, risk exposures will change as circumstances change and existing plans for managing them may become irrelevant or inefficient. New risks may emerge, old risks may disappear and risks may change in terms of likelihood and impact. If properly managed, some of the changes may be advantageous.

Typical sources of change are:

- **Timescales**: The timing may have changed, in particular the start and end dates.
- **Requirements**: The customer requirements may have changed.
- **Terms and conditions and service level agreements**: The detailed terms and conditions or service level agreements for doing the work agreed during programme initiation may have changed the risk.
- **Suppliers**: Suppliers may have 'upgraded' their offerings or may now offer alternatives with better performance and/or price.
- **Non-customer agreements**: Agreements with contractors, and so on, may no longer reflect the final contract, in particular quotations may no longer be valid.
- **Staffing**: Staff available to the programme management team may have changed or be more expensive.

347

- **Knowledge**: Research may have provided a better understand of technical risks.

Because of such changes, it is necessary to review the risk registers at regular intervals and revise them appropriately. The stages in your review of risks are:

1. Review and update the risk register: What changes are needed to the risk assessments and their associated containment plans and contingency plans?
2. Update the programme and project plans: What changes are needed to the project plan to reflect changes to the containment and contingency plans?

Risk management is not necessarily either sequential or compartmented. Different aspects may proceed in parallel and there is constant iteration amongst the various activities. New options for handling risk are always being created. The programme manager should try to anticipate changes so that they can influence their impact, rather than just responding to the changes when they occur.

It is therefore essential to have a short review of risk at many stages of the programme management process. At this occasion, the team should consider what new risks have emerged, asking what risks need no longer cause concern and what existing risks need to be modified to reflect the latest position. Changes to the risk register should reflect these changes and may be audited to maintain records throughout the programme lifecycle.

7.4.10 UPDATE RISK REGISTER

The risk register should be kept up to date throughout the life of the programme. This will provide a consistent set of up-to-date assessments of the various risks and the plans to handle them. This then provides one of the major sources of information against which to monitor the programme and against which to prepare revised plans from time to time.

In major programmes, maintaining the risk register and associated assessments and liaison can be a full-time task, allocated to a risk manager. Such a person may also have control of risk contingency funds. However, identifying risks and drawing them to the attention of the project or programme management teams is the responsibility of all who work within the programme.

After each major review of the risk register, it is usual to present a report to the programme board so that it can reappraise the likely success of the programme.

7.5 CONCLUSION

Cardinal rules for risk management:

- Do no harm. No risk should be greater than the benefit. Don't replace one risk by another greater one.
- Try to make small improvements at each stage. Risk management cannot predict whether or not events will occur. The goal is to improve, constantly and in measured steps, the probability of success or the opportunity for success, whenever feasible.
- Never focus on future intentions, always on current capability. Don't fool yourself into thinking that, because there are intentions to do something, things will work out that way. Risk management is based upon what feasibly can be accomplished not what is hoped to be accomplished.
- Without management commitment there can be no effective risk management. If senior management such as the programme board neither actively supports nor foresees the need for risk management, then there is little point in pretending to do it.

REFERENCES

OGC (2005) *Successful Delivery Toolkit*, available from www.ogc.gov.uk/ soltoolkit.

Vase, D. (1999) *Quantitative Risk Analysis: Guide to Monte Carlo Simulation Modelling*. Chichester: Wiley.

8 Programme assurance and quality

8.1 INTRODUCTION

Establishing an effective regime to determine quality requirements and ensure that they are met is vital to the success of every programme. Without such a regime, it is unlikely that the long-term objectives of the programme will be achieved. Moreover, this regime must be much more comprehensive than that which applies within individual projects. Not only must it ensure that the deliverables of all projects are of adequate quality, but that they can be combined with others to create the necessary capabilities that will deliver the long-term objectives of the programme.

8.2 QUALITY IN A PROGRAMME ENVIRONMENT

There are many definitions of quality, but the one that seems to apply best in a programme environment is:

> that combination of attributes that determine the ability of the programme to meet its objectives.

Some of these attributes can be verified by testing the quality of the various programme outputs, such as the deliverables created by the component projects; other attributes can only be assured by developing outputs in accordance with defined processes or ways of working, while others are so difficult to define that one can only rely on the judgement and professionalism of experienced staff.

This very vagueness and uncertainty makes the management of quality, within a programme environment, of paramount importance. The objective of this management function is to provide assurance that all aspects of the programme are working to achieve results of sufficient quality to achieve the long-term objectives of the programme.

Because so many of the quality attributes of a programme are difficult to define in a manner that allows easy measurement, this frequently requires the use of subjective judgement. It usually requires considerable experience to make such judgements, together with the skills to explain the issues to others and to convince them that the resultant conclusions are valid. Furthermore, the focus of this function is the achievement of long-term objectives, and these objectives may change during the life of a programme to reflect changing corporate priorities. Accordingly, quality management within a programme environment requires a full understanding of these corporate priorities and hence it has a strategic dimension. By contrast, the management of quality within a component project is generally more straight-forward, being focused on ensuring that the project deliverables will meet their agreed acceptance criteria and thus achieve sign-off on-time and within budget.

Thus the management of quality within a programme environment is different to that within a project environment. This difference can be illustrated by Case Study 8.1, which shows how a component project can be a success and deliver near-perfect quality, yet the overall programme can be a dire failure. This episode demonstrates the difference between quality within a project and within a programme. The IT supplier organized his activities as a project and achieved success, in that he successfully delivered the agreed facilities to the specified levels of quality. By contrast, the client did not achieve success because he failed to understand and agree the overall quality needs of the programme. As a result, the programme's long-term objectives could not be met.

CASE STUDY 8.1: EXAMPLE OF PROJECT SUCCESS WITHIN A FAILED PROGRAMME

Some years ago, a large IT supplier was contracted to deliver a mission-critical IT system to an important UK Government agency. because the contract was for a substantial fixed price, the supplier appointed a highly experienced project manager, who implemented state-of-the-art project management methods. Largely as a result of this, 18 months later, the completed system was delivered on time and fully in accordance with the contract and specification that had been agreed at the start. Moreover, the cost of the work, and thus the supplier's profit, was almost exactly what had been anticipated at the start.

All had not been plain sailing. The cost of developing the software turned out to be significantly higher than originally planned, but by delaying the procurement of

---

hardware until the last possible moment, the project manager was able to make savings that almost exactly matched the over-runs on the software. So pleased was the supplier that for several years afterwards the project was referred to as a 'model' and used as an example of good practice within internal training programs.

The customer was less happy. During the development period, the project sponsor had retired. His successor had different ideas and when the new system arrived, working procedures had changed and were no longer consistent with what was delivered. As a result, the new system was abandoned after 6 months of struggle. The supplier was blamed for the failure and a replacement IT system, based on different technology, was procured by the customer from elsewhere.

To reflect these differences between the management of quality within project and programme environments, the term programme assurance is used for the function at programme level, and quality management at project level.

8.3 PROGRAMME ASSURANCE

The objective of the programme assurance function is to implement a programme quality environment that ensures that quality requirements are identified, understood and fulfilled through all parts of the programme and through all programme activities. These activities include those of the programme management function and other 'programme-level' activities, as well as all relevant activities within the component projects.

In practice, it is common for component projects to have their own quality management function. Accordingly, some elements of quality management may be delegated from the 'programme' level to the 'project' level. This is particularly the case where different organizations are undertaking different projects, such as applies within a consortium. In these circumstances, it is unusual for a single project management methodology to be mandated for every project, since many organizations have their own distinct approach to quality and requiring changes to this could create more quality problems than would be resolved through consistency. However, what is important in these circumstances is to do the following:

- Establish a common interface between the component projects and the 'programme level'.
- Ensure that the systems operating within the component projects meet the requirements of the programme, as determined by the programme assurance function.

● Provide the programme assurance function with adequate visibility of what goes on within the component projects. This may require regular quality reporting plus audit arrangements so that the programme assurance function can confirm that what is reported is correct and truly representative of project reality.

The programme assurance function will be under the control of the programme assurance manager, who will ensure that the overall structure of quality management arrangements within a programme are consistent with that displayed in Figure 8.1.

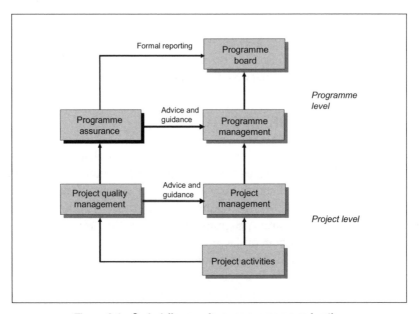

Figure 8.1   Context diagram of programme assurance function

As Figure 8.1 shows:

● Projects should have their own quality management functions, under the control of a project quality manager, responsible for ensuring that all project deliverables meet their quality requirements. This may, of course, also require the projects processes to meet certain standards. For example, designers of buildings will have to ensure that the requirements of the relevant design standards are met. The assumption here is that quality management is a proactive function that adds value to the project through advice and guidance, and is not purely a reactive function that polices conformance.

- The project quality management function will be required to work in accordance with standards and processes laid down by the programme assurance function and will be required to report to this function. Where external contractors or third parties are undertaking the component projects, the nature of these standards, processes and reporting will usually be laid down in the contracts or in schedules that amplify the basic contractual requirements and obligations.
- The programme assurance function will also establish standards, processes and reporting requirements for all activities undertaken at the programme level and will provide appropriate advice and guidance to ensure effective quality with the minimum expenditure of time, money or effort.
- The group with overall responsibility for ensuring that the programme achieves its objectives and delivers the expected business benefits is the programme board, chaired by the programme sponsor. However, this group is not full-time and relies upon the programme assurance function to provide it with the information that it needs. Accordingly, there must be a direct line of reporting between this board and programme assurance, which is independent of the day-to-day management of the programme.

It should be noted that responsibility for ensuring adequate quality within the programme ultimately lies with the programme board and, whilst they may delegate its achievement and measurement, they can never ignore it. For this reason, it is frequently appropriate for the programme assurance manager to be, ex officio, a member of the programme board.

8.4 PROGRAMME QUALITY STRATEGY

The programme's approach to managing and assuring quality will be defined within the programme quality strategy. This document should describe the approach, processes, controls and procedures that will apply to all groups working within the programme. If well written, it will also contribute tremendously to generating a common understanding of processes amongst all parties within the programme and thus to facilitating speedy and effective communication between them.

The quality strategy will be one of a series of documents that describe the programme and its component projects. Typically this strategy will complement the programme delivery strategy that describes the work to be undertaken and identifies the key milestones. In addition, the programme quality strategy will also be complemented by separate project quality plans describing how quality will be achieved within the component projects. In this way, those working within the component projects can use familiar methods and techniques, while still interfacing with and conforming to the requirements of the programme as a whole.

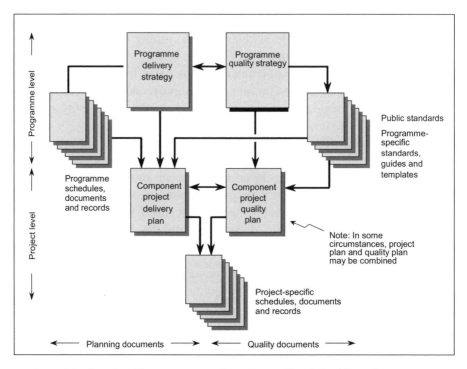

Figure 8.2   Overview of the programme quality strategy and its relationship to other programme and project documentation

A typical relationship between these various documents can be seen in Figure 8.2. An important function of the programme quality strategy will be to identify the other documents and to describe how they all relate to each other. For example, the organization may have committed itself to following the requirements of the ISO9000 series of internationally recognized quality standards. Also the quality plans of the component projects are likely need amplifying with detailed documents, such as test specifications and acceptance test schedules.

Many organizations, such as those in the finance or energy industries, are subject to special regulation by government agencies. Depending on the circumstances, compliance with such regulations can be regarded as an aspect of quality, as can any special health and safety requirements. Alternatively, where these requirements are extensive and highly specialized, it may be necessary to create an additional 'compliance' or 'industry liaison' function within the programme. However, even if this alternative approach is deemed necessary, the quality strategy should clearly explain how such compliance activities interface with other quality activities and how responsibility for their management interfaces with that of programme quality (see Newton, 1998, for guidance on financial compliance).

It is normal for the requirements of the programme quality strategy to take precedence over all other quality plans and documents so that, in the event of any apparent contradiction, the requirements of the strategy will be followed.

8.5 CONTENTS OF PROGRAMME QUALITY STRATEGY

The programme quality strategy must establish the framework within which quality is achieved throughout the whole programme.

First, it must establish the basic quality requirements of the programme. These will typically be based upon what is needed to ensure that the long-term business benefits of the programme are achieved, as discussed in Chapter 5, 'Benefits management'. For example, in a school or hospital being built under a 20-year design/build/operate contract, it will be necessary to ensure that build quality will be sufficient to give 20 years of relatively trouble-free maintenance. This basic requirement can be amplified within the component project quality plans, for example, the build-quality required for building cladding, or the build-quality and quality of components required for uPVC windows.

Second, the strategy should define the approach to verifying that quality requirements have been met. This might include specifying performance standards, workmanship standards or particular methods or techniques of testing. For example, it might lay down that every deliverable must be specified within a 'product definition', as recommended by the PRINCE2 project management methodology (see OGC, 2001). Such definitions describe the quality requirements of each deliverable, the standards to be achieved and the methods by which their completed quality can be ascertained. In some cases, the testing is so critical that the programme assurance function will undertake the tests; in others, responsibility may be delegated to the project quality managers.

Third, where the nature of the work requires it, the strategy may also specify the approaches and methods that must be followed within the component projects. This may go against the principle of allowing the component projects to decide 'how' they meet their quality requirements, but is essential where quality cannot be fully ascertained through final testing. For example, a suite of computer programs may have a near infinite number of paths through it, only a small fraction of which can ever be exercised by any reasonable form of testing. In such a circumstances, the testing can only ever be on a sample basis and it is essential that the software has been developed in a methodical and consistent manner if the results of sample testing are to be taken to apply to the whole suite. The strategy may also need to specify the quality of components and the methods by which they are processed, particularly in complex machines or systems that can only be tested upon completion. Naturally, the strategy would require that such components be checked upon receipt or procured from approved quality assured sources.

Fourth, the strategy should describe the roles and responsibilities for specifying and achieving quality throughout the programme. It is especially important that the programme assurance manager has a clear line of contact and reporting to all within the programme engaged in activities bearing on quality, independent of the management of the component projects. Furthermore, to be effective, project quality managers need to have sufficient knowledge and experience to fulfil their role effectively and may need to have dedicated staff and other resources to handle the workloads. It may be necessary, therefore, for the strategy to specify the qualifications and support that component project quality managers should have.

In mature organizations, programmes and projects will use processes, methods, techniques and tools, based on 'best practice' and learning from previous programmes and projects. Effectively, these become part of the 'corporate culture' of the organization. The strategy should explain how these will be adopted to the particular circumstances of the programme. Typically they will include an explanation of how verification will be undertaken and results reported and of the escalation procedures to be used when the process is out of control.

Some further guidance on programme assurance roles and responsibilities can be found in Section 8.10 'Programme assurance roles and responsibilities'.

Fifth, it is vital that the programme's quality assurance function has full visibility of all aspects of quality throughout the programme. This will be achieved in part by the regular reporting of quality activities from the component project managers to the programme assurance manager, together with the escalation of exception issues and concerns from the 'project level' to the 'programme level'. It is usually also essential that the quality managers of the component projects keep proper records, such as details of tests, and that these are easily available for review by the programme assurance function. Similarly, the strategy should define the nature and scope of reporting that the programme assurance function will provide to the programme board and other important stakeholders.

This may involve, among other things, establishing statistics to demonstrate the conformance to agreed quality standards. It may also involve working with the benefit manager to establish the likelihood of anticipated business benefits being achieved.

Again, the need for independent reporting may conflict with the wish of the programme manager that all external communication should be channelled through them. Spelling out obligations and responsibilities in advance will help to reduce the risk of subsequent tensions

Sixth, there need to be mechanisms for verifying that all the component projects are, in fact, working in accordance with the strategy, that the records being kept are accurate and that adequate levels of quality are being achieved. A key element of this would be the initial review of component project quality plans by the programme assurance manager. This will ensure that, before any work begins, the quality plans and procedures are likely to be adequate to meet the overall quality requirements of the programme. However, ensuring that they are actually being followed will usually require a programme of internal audits, whereby experienced members of the programme assurance function check aspects of the work of the projects. Further guidance on programme auditing can be found below in Section 8.10 'Programme assurance roles and responsibilities'.

Finally, the way by which the strategy can be adjusted, and by which any such adjustments are reflected throughout the component projects, needs to be defined. However thoroughly the strategy has been prepared, at the start it is likely to need changing during the life of the programme and the mechanisms and responsibilities should be clearly defined at the outset.

8.6 RELATIONSHIP OF PROGRAMME QUALITY STRATEGY TO FORMAL CONTRACTS

Just as there can be tensions between the programme manager, who will seek to control all aspects of the programme, and the quality assurance manager, who needs visibility and independent access, there can be tensions between the programme assurance function and the management of the component projects. This can be especially so when the projects are being undertaken by external contractors. For example, such contractors may seek to ensure that all communication with the programme goes exclusively through the project manager or even the commercial manager.

Similarly, the contractors may seek to limit audit rights or restrict access to their project records. To avoid any doubt and to minimize subsequent difficulties, conformance with the programme quality strategy should be specified within the formal contract. Agreeing such a requirements can be difficult, but is essential if the programme assurance function is to have the visibility it needs to achieve long-term quality throughout the programme.

8.7 TESTS, CHECKS OR REVIEWS AND ACCEPTANCE STRATEGY

As indicated in the programme quality strategy, appropriate tests, checks or reviews should be used within the component projects to ensure that all deliverables are:

- **verified**: that is, all critical stages have been checked for correctness of work;
- **validated**: that is, that the correct deliverable has been produced;
- **subjected to formal acceptance by the programme** – indicating that all required activities are complete and that all necessary test records are complete and appropriately filed.

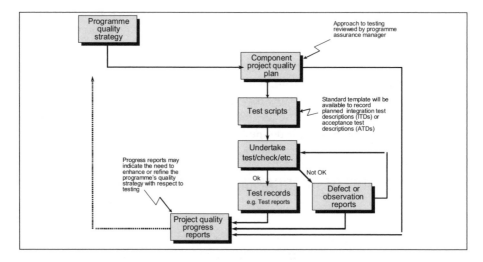

Figure 8.3   Outline relationship between various quality documents and testing activities

The relationship between the principal documents and test/check/review activities is shown in Figure 8.3. All necessary testing, checking or review activities should be planned in advance for each project and each deliverable. These activities should include performance and acceptance tests, as required. The specific aim of individual testing activities will vary according to the deliverable or aspect of work involved. However, their general aim will be to ensure that all aspects of the delivered facility are correct in terms of:

- **Functionality:** All the agreed features and facilities, as defined in the controlling specification are available and operating as specified.
- **Technical adequacy:** Performance will meet the agreed requirements.
- **Consistency with agreed architectures:** It will integrate effectively with other systems or facilities.
- **Robustness:** It will be reliable when introduced into service and will operate without excessive maintenance expenditure.
- **Maintainability and serviceability:** It will be possible to support, maintain and upgrade in the future.
- **Usability:** The target audiences will be able to use the deliverable without constant recourse to customer support, and so on.
- **Documentation:** All necessary supporting material, such as user manuals or operating instructions, are completed, reviewed and under appropriate configuration control.
- **Records**: All test reports, review records, sign-offs, and so on, are available for inspection and adequately filed to provide traceability should it be necessary to follow up a problem at some future date.

The approach to testing to be adopted within each project should be outlined within the programme quality strategy and amplified either within the project quality plans of the component projects or within supporting schedules that are referenced within those plans. One widely used approach is to adopt product-

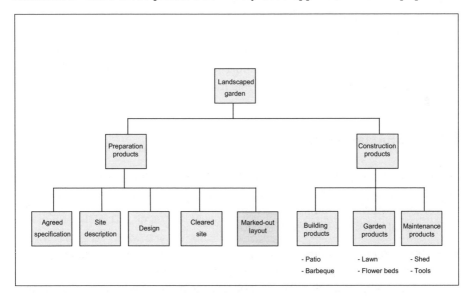

Figure 8.4   Example of the breakdown of specialist components of a landscaped garden project

361

based planning, as recommended by the PRINCE2 methodology. Here, all deliverables or products to be created by the project are identified within a product breakdown structure.

Figure 8.4 shows an example of such a structure. Creating this structure involves breaking the final deliverable of the project (for example, a landscaped garden) into its constituent parts and sub-parts. This helps clarify all necessary work for its creation and provides an easy to understand image of the project and its deliverables.

Typically, completing the project or programme will involve the creation of three categories of products:

- specialist deliverables, those that the programme must create in order to achieve its objectives;
- management deliverables, which are needed to support the successful management of the project;
- quality deliverables, which are needed to ensure that all products produced conform to requirements.

Each of these categories will need to be broken down in the product breakdown structure.

Each product or deliverable is then described within a product definition document, which will include a specification of its quality requirements and of the methods by which the achievement of those requirements can be verified, for example, by tests, checks or reviews.

An example of a product description, for one of the products needed to complete the landscaped garden featured in Figure 8.4, can be seen in Figure 8.5. Such descriptions provide a clear and unambiguous specification of each deliverable and of what will be required to ensure that it will be satisfactory.

8.8 PROGRAMME AUDITS

Programme audit involves examining the activities that make up the programme to confirm that the programme is being managed effectively and is on track to deliver the required benefits and outcomes.

This usually involves two levels of auditing:

- At the 'project level', the focus of audits should be the conformance of the projects to agreed plans and procedures, in order to provide confidence that the component projects will deliver on time, to budget and to agreed standards.
- At the 'programme level', the focus should be on the delivery of business

Program ABC: Project XYZ
Product Description
Product title: Agreed specification
Purpose: Confirm mutual understanding of the client's exact requirements.
Description: Follow standard specification format, using document template number AB47. Must include list of all plants, plus illustrations.
Inputs: Proposal document (final version, as supplied in February). Subsequent client interview notes.
Format or presentation: See description. Ensure full-colour reproduction of plant details.
Responsibility: Chief Designer
Quality Requirements: Must be acceptable to client. Must conform to Royal Landscape Society Guidelines, version 2.
Tests, Checks or Reviews: Internal sign-off by Chief Designer and by Account Manager. Account Manager to gain client sign-off before any work starts.
Special Resources: Prior to sign-off, this document must be reviewed by George Thompson to confirm suitability of proposed plants for a high-acid soil location.

Figure 8.5 Example of a product description showing quality requirements and the specific tests, checks or reviews needed to verify achievement of those requirements

363

benefits, as opposed to whether the minutiae of agreed standards and procedures have been followed. Programme audits are thus more business oriented than traditional quality audits (see Case Study 8.2).

CASE STUDY 8.2: AUDITING INDUSTRY WIDE PROGRAMME

BACKGROUND

Among the most complicated programmes being undertaken today are those resulting from the privatization of formerly nationalized industries. To ensure that state-controlled monopolies are not replaced by privately owned ones, such initiatives frequently involve splitting up the former monoliths into a range of competing organizations. However, these competitors must also cooperate with each other on activities on which the whole industry depends. Achieving such cooperation among commercial rivals is one of the greatest challenges that can face a programme manager.

In the UK, official regulators have been created to 'police' the newly emergent business landscapes. However, while they have considerable powers to intervene in specific circumstances, they must frequently rely on encouragement, particularly when it requires industry participants to assist each other. This was the case with a recent UK deregulation programme.

Here, the introduction of a further element of competition within a former nationalized industry required almost 40 different organizations to cooperate in the adoption of new working practices. While some of the players specialized in particular market niches with only a limited number of customers, others were vast enterprises serving many millions. These latter organizations were totally dependent on complex IT systems to provide speedy and efficient service and to maintain safety critical records. Because of the new ways of working, these IT systems required considerable adjustment and the cut-over from the old systems to the new had to occur simultaneously throughout the industry over a single weekend.

This imposed a deadline on all parties, who had to ensure that IT projects, organizational change projects and staff training projects were all coordinated so as to be completely ready on the appointed date. Furthermore, the success of the whole initiative required all parties to be able to communicate speedily with each other. Accordingly, internal testing and preparation had to be matched with external testing and preparation with all others within the industry.

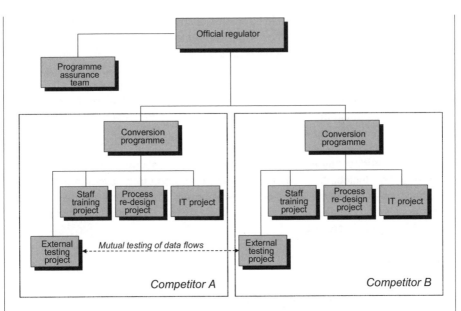

Figure 8.6   Summary of the structure of an industry-wide change initiative

PROGRAMME ORGANIZATION

Ultimate responsibility for ensuring a successful conversion to the new ways of working lay with the official regulator, who had to oversee the whole industry-wide portfolio of programmes and to make the final go/no-go decision once satisfied that all parties were sufficiently ready. To verify that the information provided by industry participants was accurate, an independent programme assurance team was established, staffed by experienced external consultants with IT, business change, auditing and industry knowledge. The overall structure of the initiative was thus in accordance with Figure 8.6.

CUT-OVER READINESS AUDITS

A vital task for the programme assurance team was assessing the industry's readiness to go live on the agreed date. To this end, a programme of 2-day audit visits was arranged with the key players, supplemented by a questionnaire-based survey of the remainder. During the visits, the readiness of each organization was assessed in terms of internal testing, external testing, cut-over plans, contingency arrangements in case of a failure during the cut-over weekend and the readiness of the staff who would have to operate the new procedures.

Standard auditing techniques were used. Prior to the audit, advice had been issued on the type of questions that would be asked and the likely categories of people who would be expected to provide the information. At the start of each audit a 'kick off' meeting was held to confirm the objectives and scope of the audits and to agree a mutually convenient schedule for interviews. In this way the impact of the audits on work plans of interviewees was minimized. At the completion of each audit, the findings were reviewed and any necessary actions agreed so that identified gaps in preparedness could be closed. Subsequently, these findings and actions were confirmed in a written report.

During the audits, key members of each organization's programme team were interviewed, including sponsors, programme managers, programme office managers and quality managers or their equivalents. Supporting evidence, such as test results and detailed cut-over plans, was reviewed to confirm what had been learnt during the interviews.

THE RESULTS

Although all data collected was treated as confidential to the organizations that provided it, summary information was made available to the whole industry as the audit visits progressed. This helped to resolve some of the uncertainties that organizations faced in completing their final plans, as well as encouraging all to complete their preparations. Moreover, certain common problems were quickly identified by the auditors and passed to the regulator, who was able to initiate industry-wide corrective actions early enough for them to be effective by the planned cut-over date.

By combining the results of the audit visits, the results of the questionnaire survey and feedback on the completion of actions agreed during the visits, the programme assurance team was able to provide an comprehensive and accurate picture of readiness across the whole industry. This enabled the regulator to authorize the final 'go ahead', confident that all likely problems could be coped with and that the industry would be able to cut over to the new working methods without any disruption to customer services or safety.

The basic principles to be followed when selecting aspects and projects to be audited, and the approaches and techniques to be used, should be specified within the programme quality strategy or within a separate document referenced within the strategy. Whichever type of document is used, it should cover both types of audit and should also lay out the processes for communicating the results of audits to the component projects and the timetables and other arrangements by which appropriate corrective actions must be completed.

'Project level' audits correspond to traditional quality audits. By contrast, 'programme level' audits require an understanding of the business environment in which the programme is operating and the business priorities of the programme board. It therefore requires a more sophisticated approach than traditional quality audits. Some specific areas of activity that may repay attention by the 'programme level' auditors include:

- the effectiveness of risk management, particularly in relation to the risks to delivery of long-term business benefits;
- the interfaces with other initiatives within the organization, especially where these other initiatives are likely to require implementation resources from within user departments that will also be required by the programme;
- the exploitation and use of lessons learned from other programmes within the organization;
- the engagement with stakeholders, including proactive consideration of their interests in the programme and the impact of the changes on them;
- implementation and contingency arrangements for dealing with the unexpected and ensuring continuity of day-to-day business operations during implementation.

The scale and frequency of such audits will depend upon the criticality and importance of the projects and activities to be audited. It will also depend upon the frequency and extent of any audits from outside the programme: for example by the organization's own quality assurance function, or within individual projects. If done well, audit takes time and resource: moreover, it can be stressful and disruptive to those doing the work. Accordingly, care should be taken to avoid duplication and over-auditing of certain areas, while leaving other areas of the programme untouched. It is much better for a programme to undertake a limited number of well-planned audits that result in real improvements than a large number of repetitive audits that have little positive impact. To maximize the benefits received by the programme from all audit activities, the programme assurance manager should liaise with all organizations to agree a single schedule of audits and to agree for relevant audit results to be shared.

The ultimate objective of auditing is that the programme results in more business benefits being achieved than would have been the case without the audits. Although the prospect of being audited may cause programme and project staff to work with greater care than otherwise, the greatest impact will result from the agreement and implementation of improvement plans in response to the findings of the audits. Accordingly, adequate time and effort should be allocated to following up the audit findings, agreeing improvement plans and then ensuring that these plans are actually implemented. This can be particularly difficult and time-consuming when such plans require external contractors to undertake activities that they would prefer to avoid.

It should be noted that, within a well-run programme, there will also be routine measures of programme performance being generated, for example by the programme office. Programme audits may thus complement existing routine arrangements in indicating the overall health of the programme. Of course, one of the key roles in such circumstances is to confirm that the picture provided by such routine measures is fair and accurate.

8.9 PROGRAMME ASSURANCE AND RISK MANAGEMENT

Inadequate attention to quality, whether of deliverables or processes, will create risks to the achievement of programme objectives. There is thus an interface between the management of programme quality and the management of programme risks. In principle, quality assurance seeks to minimize or manage generic risks, while the programme's risk management function seeks to mitigate or manage specific risks.

It is important that the programme's arrangements and implementation of risk management should be assessed at appropriate points during the programme, and the audit programme can be a means of achieving this. Some critical success factors for the effective management of specific risks are:

- nominated individuals with clearly defined responsibilities to support, own and lead on risk management;
- a pragmatic risk management approach, and the benefits of following it, clearly communicated to all personnel involved with the programme;
- existence of an organizational culture that supports well-thought-through risk taking;
- management of risk fully embedded in management processes and consistently applied;
- management of risk closely linked to achievement of programme objectives and benefit delivery;
- risks actively monitored and regularly reviewed on a constructive 'no-blame' basis.

Additionally, the effectiveness of risk management is subject to audit, with a particular emphasis on ensuring that:

- risks to the programme are identified and managed effectively;
- products and output will be delivered on time, in budget and to an acceptable standard;

368

● when complete and the programme outputs are handed over and are used by the operational parts of the organization, they will perform well enough to realize the benefits required.

8.10 PROGRAMME ASSURANCE ROLES AND RESPONSIBILITIES

It is essential that a clear structure be established for the programme assurance function. This is especially important in large and complex programmes or where external contractors are involved, because the function must have independent access to and visibility of all aspects of the programme and of its component projects.

Figure 8.7 shows a possible structure. The programme assurance manager reports directly to the programme board, alongside the programme manager who is responsible for the day-to-day management of the programme. The programme assurance manager is responsible for creating the programme quality strategy and for ensuring its effective implementation throughout the programme.

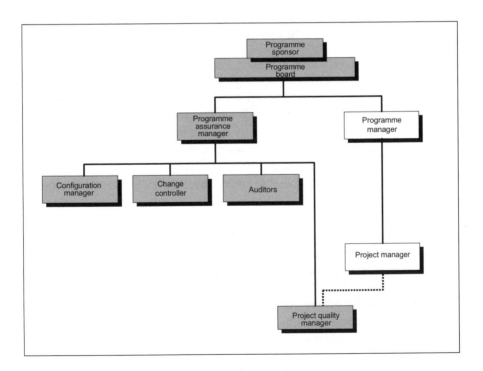

Figure 8.7   Typical quality organization within a large programme

369

Other responsibilities for the programme assurance manager include:

- reviewing and approving the quality plans of component projects;
- assessing the state of quality throughout the programme and reporting this back to the programme board;
- establishing the extent to which the programme is likely to deliver the expected business benefits. This could be in cooperation with the benefits manager (see Section 5.7 'The benefits manager');
- providing guidance to the board on any aspect of quality;
- through leadership and training, creating a quality culture throughout the programme;
- liaising with other internal and external auditing groups (and possibly with contractor quality auditors) to agree a coherent audit schedule that minimizes audit overload and work disruption;
- ensuring (in conjunction with the contract negotiators) that appropriate terms and conditions are specified within any external contracts to ensure that adequate visibility and access is available for all aspects of quality throughout the programme.

Three other managers or teams – the configuration manager, the change controller and the quality auditors – directly assist the programme assurance manager:

- **Configuration manager:** responsible for documenting and implementing the programme's policies on configuration management (as described in Chapter 9, 'Configuration management'). Other responsibilities include ensuring that the configuration register is correctly maintained and assisting the auditors with reviews of the effectiveness of configuration management arrangements throughout the programme.
- **Change controller:** responsible for documenting and implementing the programme's policies on change control[1] (as described in Chapter 12, 'Management of scope and change').
- **Auditors:** those that undertake the audits of component projects and other groups within the programmes. They may work singly or as teams, depending upon the area being audited. The key requirement is that they have the skill and experience to undertake effective audits that will reveal the likelihood or otherwise of business benefits being achieved. They will also need to be able to discuss their findings with the projects and groups that they have audited and gain agreement to appropriate improvement actions.

---

1 Change control should not be confused with organizational change management, which is the responsibility of the change manager and is discussed in Section 5.7.1 'The change manager'.

Because of the special requirements of 'programme level' audits, it is likely that many of the auditors will be senior staff who are loaned for the duration of the audit. Typically such staff will work alongside a full-time quality auditor who is experienced in the procedures and paperwork of auditing.

Another possible approach is to use the various quality managers of the component projects to audit each other. This is difficult to organize but, if it can be achieved, it not only makes the audits intensely practical but also helps to spread a common approach to quality throughout the programme.

In the structure shown in Figure 8.6, the quality managers of the component projects report directly to the programme assurance manager and have only an indirect line of reporting to the component project managers. This not only provides speedy and direct communication on quality matters but also ensures that the project quality managers are truly independent of the projects that they are responsible for. In practice, it may not always be possible to achieve this: for example, where an external contractor is undertaking the project.

The exact roles and responsibilities of the quality managers of the component projects will depend upon the programme quality strategy and on how responsibility for quality is shared between the 'programme level' and the 'project level'. However, they typically include:

- preparation of project quality plans that are consistent with the programme quality strategy and are acceptable to the programme assurance manager;
- establishment and execution of appropriate test plans for all deliverables;
- ensuring that appropriate quality records are maintained to demonstrate completion of all required tests and to confirm the use of specified processes and working methods;
- assisting the programme assurance function with audits and ensuring that all agreed improvement actions resulting from audits are successfully completed;
- providing regular reports and statistics to the programme assurance manager, as required by the programme quality strategy;
- assisting the programme assurance manager to establish a quality culture within their project.

The programme assurance manager may also have a close working relationship with the manager of the programme office and with the technical design authority. The programme office manager is usually responsible for maintaining the programme's files and records and these may include quality, change and configuration records. (Further guidance on the programme office can be found in Chapter 13, 'The programme office'.)

The technical design authority is the person, or group, who is responsible for the design of the facilities that the programme is delivering. Accordingly, the technical design authority is likely to be deeply involved in establishing standards of workmanship, devising test schedules, and assessing the impact of change. From time to time, the authority may assist the programme's audit teams to audit technically complex areas of the programme.

It is not usual for these two functions to report directly to the programme assurance manager.

8.11 QUALITY COSTS

Achieving adequate levels of quality often requires considerable attention to detail. Where operational staff are fully trained and well motivated, this attention to detail may be largely second nature. However, in less ideal circumstances, this may require additional management effort together and/or additional resources. Moreover, the verification that adequate levels of quality have been achieved in the form of tests, checks or reviews may represent a significant part of the programme's effort. Because of this, achieving quality can be seen by some as expensive. However, the costs of not achieving adequate levels of quality can be considerably higher.

CASE STUDY 8.3: QUALITY COSTING AT A BUILDING SOCIETY

STUDY BACKGROUND

In the competitive world of building societies,* much attention is focused on the branches where the society and the public come face to face. But behind the scenes, a vast amount of administration must be undertaken. Even with the aid of sophisticated computer systems, this still involves a large amount of patient, time-consuming and methodical work by administrative staff. Moreover, new types of mortgage have meant a great increase in the complexity of work, while competition generates continuous pressure to reduce costs.

For this reason, a top-10 building society decided to review the quality costs associated with its mortgage administration activities as part of a programme of

* In the UK, building societies provide savings bank and housing mortgage services to the general public. Originally they were mutually owned by their depositors and lenders, but over recent years many have converted themselves into joint stock companies or been taken over by major banks. In the USA, similar services are provided by 'savings and loans' organizations.

---

corporate change. The effectiveness of the department depended almost entirely upon the individuals working within it. The contribution that they made depended in large measure upon their motivation and enthusiasm and upon the IT systems with which they had to work.

The aim of the review was to identify improvements that could be made to systems in order to raise morale and to generate continuous, long-term improvements in efficiency and effectiveness. Furthermore, the review had to 'mesh in' with existing schemes to produce an overall departmental culture committed to self-improvement. This commitment was incorporated into the project title, 'Programme to Improve Departmental Effectiveness' – PRIDE.

KEY FINDINGS

Using the Feigenbaum 'Prevention, Appraisal, Failure' model (see Feigenbaum, 1981), approximately 20 per cent of the total 'back office' costs were identified as being directly related to quality. In addition, seven areas of activity were identified where time or costs could be saved by the introduction of improved systems or more streamlined working methods.

THE RESULTS

Following the review, a series of initiatives were launched to overcome each area of weakness. These ranged from simple ideas, such as issuing all staff with personal organizers, to more complex ones, such as redesigning the screens of the supporting IT systems to provide speedier access to key information.

In their first 12 months, these initiatives not only reduced costs through eliminating wasted effort, but produced significant and measurable improvements in staff satisfaction and morale. For example, in spite of redundancies:

- those expressing satisfaction with annual appraisal had risen by 75 per cent;
- those expressing satisfaction with equipment and resources was up 40 per cent;
- the number of staff feeling that they had made career progress in the last 12 months was 70 per cent higher.

Moreover, departmental effectiveness had clearly improved as a result of the change programme. The percentage of staff in other departments who expressed satisfaction with the service provided to them by the Mortgage Administration department, rose from 75 per cent to 90 per cent – a source of 'pride' to all involved.

Gaining a reasonable understanding of these costs is vital if quality is to be effectively discussed at the 'programme' and 'strategic' level, for without such understanding it is impossible to understand the impact of changing priorities or of adjusting the programme's portfolio of component projects (see Case Study 8.3).

A widely used model for analysing quality costs is that promoted by Feigenbaum (see Feigenbaum, 1981). In this model, costs are divided into three categories:

- **The costs of failure** – what will it cost to rectify things that were not created right first time. Over the life of a major facility this may represent a huge share of the total cost. Even during the development phases, they may be a major part of the effort and thus cost. For example, in the software industry, rectification of code that has failed its tests may take as much time and effort as originally writing it.
- **The costs of appraisal** – what will it cost to assess whether adequate levels of quality have been achieved. This would include the costs of tests, checks and reviews, including the costs of the staff and other resources, such as special equipment, that will be needed as well as the costs of any quality audits. It would also include the costs of specifying and agreeing the tests, checks or reviews that will be needed.
- **The costs of prevention** – the cost of setting up adequate systems to minimize the likelihood of failure. This category includes the costs of establishing actual requirements, of preparing the programme quality strategy and related plans, of educating and training staff to ensure adequate and consistent levels of quality and the costs of monitoring and reporting quality achievement.

Most studies of quality costs show that there is a trade off between the costs of prevention and appraisal and the costs of failure that result from inadequate attention to prevention or appraisal (see Porter and Rayner, 1992). In particular, the more that is spent 'up front' in activities designed to ensure that products are created 'right first time', the less will be spent on correcting the results of failure later on. Furthermore, when a high degree of confidence exists in the initial development processes, the cost of appraisal usually also falls as well, since (for example) it may no longer be necessary to test all occurrences, but merely a representative sample.

Other studies also show that until sufficient attention is given to prevention activities, few have any understanding of the scale of failure costs and their impact. Typically, as spending on prevention activities increases, there is a more than proportional decrease in the failure costs. Because of this, it is sometime asserted that 'quality is free' (see Crosby, 1979).

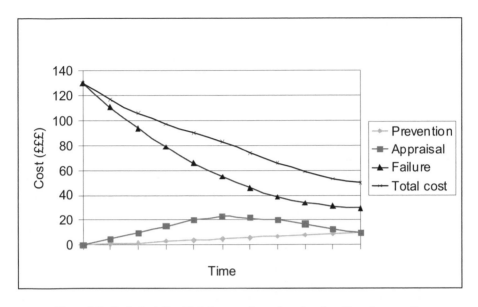

Figure 8.8   Typical relationship between various categories of quality cost as spending on prevention increases

The typical relationship between these various cost categories and the trade offs as prevention spending increases is summarized in Figure 8.8.

By making the costs of quality visible in this way, the programme will be better able to initiate effective discussion of quality issues among those responsible for the governance of the programme. Furthermore, it may be possible to identify areas where cost can be saved without compromising quality.

Conventional financial accounts maintained for projects and programmes are rarely adequate to fully identify quality costs. Furthermore, the conventional accounts, which are based upon actual expenditures and incomes, will always be a prime driver of strategic decision making about the programme, whereas the quality costs will always involve a degree of speculation. Because of this, it is vital to ensure that any estimates of quality costs correlate to the relevant equivalent items within the conventional accounts.

8.12 QUALITY LEADERSHIP

It is human nature, when coping with a crisis or problem, to focus on immediate requirements. Within programmes, this can mean that quality requirements, which by their very nature are focused on the long-term objectives (such as

375

preventing failure in use), take second place to the achievement of time schedules or budgets. Careful planning, the establishment of good working methods and procedures, and effective auditing can do much to overcome this natural human tendency. However, consistent high quality requires a change in attitude among all concerned. Accordingly, quality education at all levels of the programme, aimed at creating a working environment in which compromising on quality is no longer regarded as an option, is perhaps the most important task of the programme assurance manager.

To be effective, such education must be relevant to the programme and those who work within it. Because of this, standard off-the-shelf training courses are rarely of value. Instead, it is valuable to collect statistics on the quality actually achieved within the programme and use these as the starting point for training. Such statistics can be obtained from the regular quality reports of the component projects and from project- and programme-level audits. Collecting such statistics is also necessary to provide the programme board with confidence that the programme will achieve its long-term objectives.

The programme board itself is likely to be one of the groups that benefit the most from such training. Frequently the members of this board will have had no formal training in their roles and responsibilities and may have only a general understanding of how quality is achieved within a programme environment. Moreover, while the role of monitoring quality may be delegated to the programme assurance manager, overall responsibility remains with the programme board.

REFERENCES

Crosby, Phil (1979) *Quality is Free*. New York: Mentor Books.
Feigenbaum, A.V. (1981) *Total Quality Control*. New York: McGraw-Hill.
Newton, Andrew (1998) *The Handbook of Compliance*. London: Financial Times/Pitman.
OGC (2001) *Managing Successful Projects with PRINCE2*. London: The Stationery Office.
Porter, Leslie and Rayner, Paul (1992) 'Quality Costing for Total Quality Management', *International Journal of Production Economics*, 27: 69–91.

9 Configuration management

9.1 INTRODUCTION

Most programmes generate a huge number of individual products, where 'product' means anything that must be produced, including documents and items of software. Some of these will be intended for delivery to the client organization, whilst some will be intermediate products, not intended for delivery but essential steps in the process of creating those deliverables. All these products need to be identified, controlled and protected. Furthermore, their relationship to each other must be similarly identified and controlled. Configuration management is the process that achieves this.

Without configuration management, few modern programmes could succeed. Essential documentation would be lost, making it impossible to demonstrate that what has been delivered conforms to client requirements. Post-delivery maintenance and support would be a nightmare, since there would be no way of knowing the exact make up of deliverables. Controlling design changes would be impossible, because there would be no records of which particular changes had been incorporated into each deliverable. Without a comprehensive set of quality records it would be impossible to demonstrate that all necessary quality checks and reviews have been completed, including those needed to prove that delivered products are safe and legal. In short, configuration management in some form is required for all products created by a programme.

The term configuration management originated in the software industry, where it was used to keep control of the various versions of programs and other files of data that were created during the course of a software development initiative. In such environments it is vital to ensure that all delivered items are compatible with each other throughout their development. However, the same principles and practices can be applied more widely, not just to software but to all the paperwork and other information that might be created by a programme and its component projects. This has been traditional within the engineering and related industries, where control of drawings and identification of design variations has been an essential discipline for nearly 200 years.

A 'configuration' is a combination of things that together make up a recognized unit. In the context of a software development initiative, the delivered unit might be a particular release of the software, consisting of hundreds of files of data, code and configuration information, all of which need to be consistent for the release to operate correctly. In the context of a civil engineering programme, the delivered unit might represent a particular structure, requiring a comprehensive set of drawings, test certificates, operating instructions, and so on.

In most programmes, the management documents themselves are major configuration items. Documents such as the vision statement, the business blueprint, and the programme plan provide essential information that must be distributed to various stakeholders as sets of documents in electronic and/or paper form. As the programme progresses, this information will be refined, updated, amended and extended, and will need to be re-distributed to the relevant stakeholders. The effective management of this information so that it remains up to date and aligned with what is really happening 'on the ground' is vital to the success of most programmes. These sets of documents describe the configuration of the programme.

9.2 ELEMENTS OF CONFIGURATION MANAGEMENT

There are four basic processes involved in configuration management:

- deciding what will be subject to configuration management for the programme and identifying the constituent items;
- identifying when a constituent part of a 'configuration' will be agreed and 'frozen' so that future changes to it are only made with appropriate levels of agreement and approval;
- maintaining records of all current and historical information concerned with each 'configuration';
- reviewing or auditing the system to ensure that there is conformity between the documented 'configuration' and the real configuration that has been delivered to the business.

As described below in Section 9.3, the way in which these processes should be implemented within the programme should be documented within the programme's configuration management plan.

9.2.1 IDENTIFICATION OF CONFIGURATION ITEMS

The first step in establishing effective configuration management for a programme is to identify the different categories of item that will need to be under control. As explained above, such categories will typically include design documents, deliverables and quality records, as well as programme management documents. They will also usually include original specifications, contracts and change control records. Every programme is different and each will have to establish its own requirements.

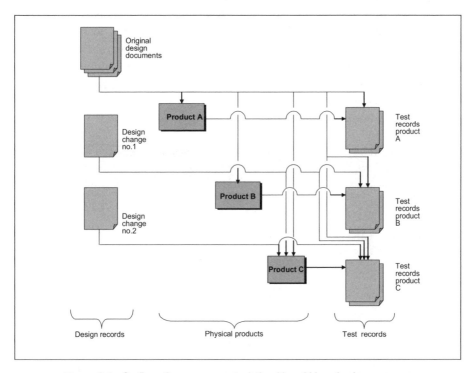

Figure 9.1   Configuration management relationships within a simple programme

Figure 9.1 shows a sample structure for a very simple programme. In this example, the only items that need to be kept under configuration management are the end products themselves plus the design documents and test records. The diagram shows that even with this minimal requirement, the number of potential relationships is considerable once two design changes have occurred. For example, the test records for Product C must demonstrate that all the requirements of the original design, plus each of the changes that affect it, have been correctly incorporated.

379

The individual products that must be subject to configuration management are referred to as 'configuration items' and it is essential to give each such item a unique identifier. This may be complemented by a document number, or a product serial number, to provide a clear and unique identification. It will then be possible to prepare a register or other index listing all configuration items. An example of part of a configuration register is shown in Figure 9.2. This example is based upon that of a programme which involved establishing a network of computer centres to support Internet websites. It was necessary to record the serial number and model number of every piece of computer hardware (including, servers and routers) plus the exact versions of every piece of software and every file of supporting data that was loaded onto the hardware. As new versions of software were created to overcome faults in the original, the details in the configuration register had to be updated. In this way, the exact configuration of each computer centre could be identified at any point in time. Furthermore, this register enabled the relevant delivery records, acceptance certificates (and thus relevant test records) and change notes to be speedily identified.

Config ref.	Location	Description	Batch/ model/ version	Serial no.	Date installed	Delivery/ release note	Change note	Accept cert.	Remarks
1	Brussels Data Centre	XYZ Co 1200 Mhz Pentium III server	G10/4	AZ-675-423	12/10/04	ZX667	–	AN012	
2	Brussels Data Centre	ABC Co 16 Gbyte storage array	16A	897-91-34	12/10/04	AS215	–	AN012	Co mounted in rack 44 with server
3	Brussels Data Centre	MS-Windows® 2000	5.00 Service Pack 4	5999-OEM-0099011-08013	12/10/04	–	–	AN012	
4	etc.	etc.	etc.						

Figure 9.2   Example of a configuration register

Typically every configurational item will have been subject to some form of checking or testing, whether goods receipt checks when material is received from suppliers, factory acceptance tests at the completion of manufacturing, or site acceptance tests upon completion of installation. During such quality assurance activities, the serial numbers or equivalents will be confirmed.

In many large programmes, proprietary software tools are used to maintain the configuration register.

9.2.2 VERSION CONTROL AND THE REPORTING OF CHANGES

Many products are likely to change over time. This is particularly the case with documents that are like to be subject to several cycles of revision, each resulting in a new version. In these circumstances, it is essential to establish clear programme-wide standards for version control. Thus, each new version of a document can be uniquely identified – for example Document 27 – version 1, Document 27 – version 2. In some circumstances, for example in parts of the public sector, at may also be necessary to place each draft under version control so that a complete audit trail of changes can be maintained. Typically such drafts are identified by letters (draft A, draft B, and so on) to distinguish them from final versions which are identified by numbers (Final 1, Final 2, Final 3, and so on). It may also be necessary to keep review comments in case there is any subsequent dispute about who did or did not request a revision.

Figure 9.3 shows the process flow for documents where each draft version must be kept under configuration control. Here the configuration register will be updated each time a new version of the document is created and a copy of the

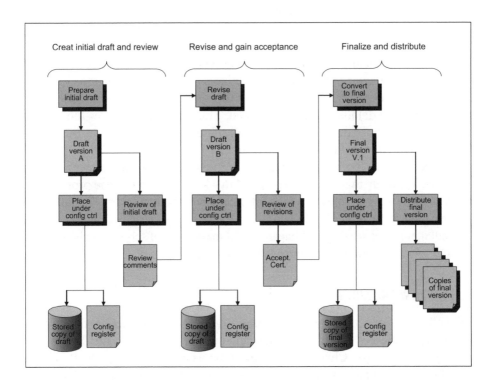

Figure 9.3   Possibile document creation and review process

381

version will be filed so that, if necessary, it will be possible to revert to an earlier version of the document

If a full audit trail of changes is required, as may be the case with drafts of contract documents, then all revisions should be marked on the document, with appropriate markings or 'red lining'. If copies of review comments and acceptance certificates are also kept, it will be possible to completely reconstruct the process of revision in event of some subsequent query.

Deciding on the level of detail for each 'configuration' and its constituent items depends on the nature of the programme and its deliverables. Selecting too low a level of detail may result in additional unnecessary administrative overheads and cause frustration to those creating the deliverables.

9.2.3 MAINTAINING CONFIGURATION RECORDS

It is essential to define in advance at what points in the development cycle different categories of products will come under the control of the configuration management system. In the example shown in Figure 9.3, documents come under control as soon as the first complete draft has been prepared. In other circumstances, it might be decided that this was unnecessary and they would only be placed under such control when they have completed all their review processes and been established as 'Final'. Even so, new versions may need to be prepared, either because experience shows the originals to be inadequate or a change in requirements necessitates a revision, and the configuration register will need to be updated with details of the new version. This will not only allow the current status of each configuration set to be identified, but will also allow its change history and the history of each item to be traced.

To keep effective control of changes, it is essential to start with an agreed baseline. Typically this would correspond to a key milestone in the programme, such as the commissioning of a major item of plant, the handover of a building or similar facility, or the delivery of a new release of software. Scope and change management, as described in Chapter 12, 'Management of scope and change', can then be used to manage all changes to that baseline.

9.2.4 REVIEW AND AUDIT

Like all other aspects of the programme, configuration management activities should be subjected to regular review and audit, as defined in the programme quality strategy (see Chapter 8, 'Programme assurance and quality'). This is usually a particularly valuable exercise since the nature of configuration management makes it prone to error and omission. Yet, unless records are very accurate and complete, the benefits of configuration management will be missed.

An effective review or audit will measure the degree of accuracy and completeness of the records. This can be done by taking a sample from the configuration register and verifying that they correspond exactly to the relevant 'real life' products.

Unfortunately, this is not always easy to undertake, for example, where equipment and software is installed at remote locations. An alternative approach might be to establish some form of continuous review system, for example, by requiring support or maintenance staff to record configuration information every time they visit a remote site. This can then be compared with the information on the configuration register and any discrepancies noted. The audit function can then review these discrepancies to establish the effectiveness and accuracy of that aspect of configuration management.

9.3 CONFIGURATION MANAGEMENT PLAN

Details of how the aims of this process are to be achieved in the work being undertaken must be defined in a configuration management plan, which may either be a stand-alone document, or part of another plan. This should identify:

- the categories of product that are subject to configuration management;
- how configuration items will be uniquely identified;
- information to be recorded for each item;
- procedures, methods and tools to be used, including quality control, system review and audit arrangements;
- roles and responsibilities.

Whether part of a larger programme plan or a document in its own right, the configuration management plan will be subjected to the same degree of control as other programme management documentation. In other words, it is likely to be a configuration item in its own right.

Case Study 9.1 at the end of the chapter contains an example of a configuration management plan developed for a large software development programme. This programme involved a consortium of companies, hence the references to the 'XYZ Consortium'. Within this consortium, a software tool called 'Config-Connect' was used to maintain the configuration register and other configuration management information.

The plan itself is a configuration item and is subject to full document control, the details of which are described in the control information on the title sheet and elsewhere in the document.

9.4 CONFIGURATION MANAGEMENT ROLES AND RESPONSIBILITIES

The overall responsibility for configuration management within a programme inevitably lies with the programme manager, who may well choose to delegate the role. Typically there are three possible routes for such delegation:

- To the project managers: the individual projects create the deliverables and are thus ideally placed to manage the recording of configuration information.
- To the programme office: as described in Chapter 13, 'The programme office', the programme office provides the administrative support to the programme and may well be best placed to maintain configuration management records such as the configuration register.
- To a configuration manager: in a large programme, the work load may be such that a dedicated configuration manager must be appointed to oversee the whole process and ensure that adequate records are maintained.

In practice, most programmes adopt a combination of all three and describe this within the configuration management plan.

9.5 DOCUMENT MANAGEMENT

Traditionally, configuration management was regarded primarily about the control of sets of tangible products and the processes used to control the supporting documentation were regarded as a separate discipline called 'document control'. However, programmes are increasingly about organizational change where the main products take the form of documents. Accordingly, the control of documents, that is, the procedures used to achieve smooth and speedy production of good quality documentation for the programme, is now frequently regarded as an element of configuration management.

Some organizations are now using electronic records management software to control the creation, reviewing, filing, retrieval and version control of documents. In such systems, the rules and procedures covering the management of documents are built into the software, thus ensuring consistency and automatically providing records on current versions, document history and audit trails of amendments.

Examples of document control items can be found in the sample configuration management plan in Case Study 9.1. These control items ensure that readers can be confident that they are dealing with the correct version of this and any related documentation.

384

9.6 ESCROW ARRANGEMENTS

Sometimes it is necessary for copies of products to be held 'in escrow', particularly where the product is intangible and dependent upon the expertise of its creators to be effectively managed or maintained. This is frequently the case with computer software.

Escrow is defined as:

> a written legal engagement to do something, kept in a third person's custody until some condition is fulfilled.

Typically, a customer will require copies of the specifications and/or source code of software that has been delivered by an outside supplier to also be deposited with an independent third party, as protection against any future failure to maintain them (for example, through bankruptcy of the supplier). Under the pre-defined circumstances, the third party will then release the material to the customer, for use either by themselves or by another supplier, to facilitate support and maintenance of the product.

Escrow agreements normally require that records are maintained of the 'current versions' that are installed. This will require the configuration management system to record details of every software release and delivery baselines, and even of individual software patches.

CASE STUDY 9.1: SAMPLE CONFIGURATION MANAGEMENT PROCEDURE

XYZ Consortium

Consortium Configuration Management Procedures

Project number   EC987654

Issue   B

Issue date   14 September

Status   Draft

Document reference   LOG-P006

Security category   None

Distribution   Consortium Information Centre
                        Consortium Document Repository
                        Project Managers of all component
                        projects

Prepared by   A. B. Ceedy, Manoz
                        Goodguy

Reviewed

Approved (Consortium)   ....   Consortium Quality
                                                                               Manager

Authorized (Consortium) ....   Consortium
                                                                               Programme
                                                                               Manager

1.0 INTRODUCTION

1.1 PURPOSE

Control of software items and other deliverables created during the development and the integration processes will be essential to the success of the XYZ Programme. For this reason, a comprehensive set of configuration management processes, supported by the 'Config-Connection' computer system, will be implemented. These processes will be collectively described as the Configuration Management System.

The purpose of this document is to describe these processes. A separate document [1]* will describe the operation of the 'Config-Connection' tool, which will be an integral part of some of these processes.

1.2 SCOPE

The Configuration Management (CM) System will ensure that all critical items are identified and safely stored, that all identified bugs are recorded and corrected, and that different versions of CM items are identified in order to minimize the chance of incorrect versions being used.

CM items will include all software and scripts developed by Consortium Partners, together with all test datasets.

Excluded from the CM System will be any processes required to receive, record or manage items of hardware or of commercial off-the-self software and licences. These categories of items will be controlled by the Help Desk, which uses the 'Super-Help' tool. Help Desk processes are described in the Help Desk procedures document [2].

The CM System will include the recording and handling of Observation Reports (ORs) and will replace the Cortex-based OR system adopted is an interim measure.

1.3 SUMMARY

In principle, software items will be placed under configuration control when they have completed their initial development and been handed over from the development teams (including Partner teams) to the Consortium's integration teams. The key stages through which such items will normally progress are shown in diagrammatic form in the lifecycle diagram that forms Figure 9.4.

As shown in the diagram, all software items will be placed under the control of the CM System, once they are handed over from the relevant development team or from

---

* Numbers in square brackets [ ] are references to documents that are identified in the List of References in Section 1.7.

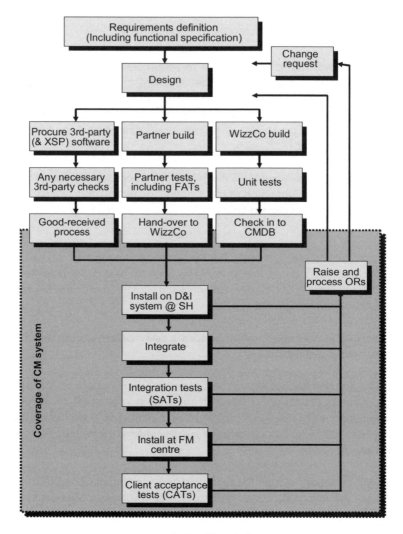

Figure 9.4   Outline lifecycle diagram

a third-party supplier such as WizzCo's Cross-Sector Products Division. Once under the control of this system, any bugs, problems or difficulties discovered with an item at any subsequent stage in the lifecycle will be recorded on ORs.

Details of the individual procedures to be followed for key CM activities can be found in sections 2 to 6, including:

- checking-in of items for integration (see Section 2.0);
- recording of the integration process (see Section 3.0);
- recording of the final acceptance processes (see Section 4.0);
- recording and management of ORs (see Section 5.0);
- production of management information (see Section 6.0).

The CM system will also interface with the Change Control System (see Section 7.0).

1.4 AMENDMENT HISTORY
The revision history of this document is shown in the Table 9.1 below.

Table 9.1   Amendment history

Date	Issue	Status
20 June	A	Initial draft procedure by M. Goodguy
14 Sept	B	Rewritten to conform to processes required by 'Config-Connection' tool.

1.5 STATUS, CHANGE FORECAST AND CONFIGURATION MANAGEMENT
Once approved and authorized, it will be mandatory on all Consortium staff to conform to this document. Variations will only be allowed with the permission of the Consortium Quality Manager.

Any revision to this document will be subject to review and approval and will be made available to all groups through the Consortium's central documentation repository. All revisions will be shown in the Amendment History table.

1.6 ABBREVIATIONS
The abbreviations in Table 9.2 have been used within this document.

Table 9.2   Table of abbreviations

Abbreviation	Explanation
ARD	Application Test Description
CAT	Client Acceptance Test
CM	Configuration Management
CMDB	Configuration Management Database
FAT	Factory Acceptance Test
FM	Facilities Management
ITD	Integration Test Descriptions
OR	Observation Report
SAT	Site Acceptance Test
XYZ	XYZ Limited (the client)

1.7 REFERENCES

The documents listed in Table 9.3 are referenced within the text of this document.

Table 9.3   Table of document references

Ref	Title	Remarks
1	'Config-Connection' User Guide	
2	Help Desk Procedures	
3	Consortium Change Management Procedures	LOG-P009
4	Integration Plan	Created by Chris Cocoa
5	Requirements Specification	Version 1.0
6	Functional Specification	
7	Acceptance Test Strategy	LOG-P014
8	Consortium Change Management Procedures	LOG-P009

Except as noted, all references relate to the latest version of the document.

2.0 CHECKING IN ITEMS FOR INTEGRATION

This process records the handover of CM items from development teams to the integration team. The development teams may be those of WizzCo or of Consortium Partners. The process is shown in diagrammatic form in Figure 9.5. The text below describes the key stages of this process in greater detail.

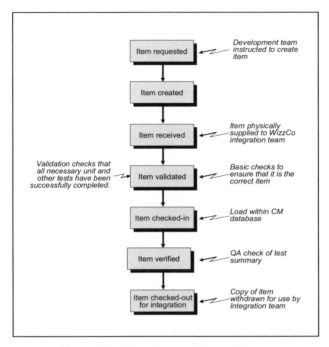

Figure 9.5   Principal stages of the receipt process

2.1 ITEM REQUESTED

The starting point of the process is the agreement that a specific Consortium Partner or WizzCo development team will create a set of deliverables. These deliverables will typically include executable code, compile and run-time scripts and operating instructions.

This agreement may be recorded on Work Package Definition documents, but the exact form will vary, depending upon the circumstances.

2.2 ITEM CREATED

During the Create stage, the item will be built and subjected to comprehensive testing to verify that it meets all the specified requirements. These tests will be recorded in a manner agreed with the Consortium Quality Manager.

2.3 ITEM RECEIVED

When complete and fully tested, the item will be supplied to the WizzCo integration team.

Typically, a collection of items will be supplied together in the form of a 'drop', which may include

- executable code;
- source code;
- compile and runtime scripts;
- operating instructions and user training material.

All deliveries must be accompanied by a Delivery Note identifying exactly what is being delivered and accompanied by a Test Summary.

2.4 ITEM VALIDATED

Before accepting the item, the integration team must check that what they have received is valid – that is, it is the correct item as agreed with the development team. This will involve confirming that all received items match the Delivery Note.

Actions to take if items are missing or incorrect will depend upon the circumstances. If the wrong items have been received, the whole 'drop' should be rejected. However, if some minor items are missing it may be appropriate to accept the drop provided arrangements are put in place to receive the missing items.

Validation will be undertaken by the integration team, who will be best placed to understand what the drop should consist of. Their decisions with regard to any further actions that they have initiated will be recorded on the Delivery Note.

2.5 ITEM CHECKED-IN

The received item should now be passed to the Configuration Manager who will check the item into the Configuration Management Database (CMDB) using the 'Config-Connection' tool.

Guidance on using the 'Config-Connection' tool to check-in items will be found in [1].

Note that several version of the same item may be created within the CMDB, as a result of receiving different software 'drops'. The 'Config-Connection' tool will ensure that these are separately identified.

2.6 ITEM VERIFIED

The Delivery Note and supporting documentation will now be passed to the Consortium Quality Manager who will verify that the testing undertaken by the development team has been adequate.

Actions to take in the event that such testing is deemed to have been inadequate will vary. For example, it may be possible for the integration team to rectify a minor omission, while a major omission may require the whole drop to be rejected.

In evaluating the adequacy of testing, the Consortium Quality Manager will refer to any test plans previously received from the developers.

In the event that testing is deemed to have been inadequate, an OR will be raised to record the problem and manage its rectification. (See Section 5.0 for further guidance on ORs).

The various Test Reports and supporting documentation will be filed for future reference.

3.0 ITEM CHECK-OUT

Once recorded within the CM system, items may be checked out from the CMDB by the Integration Team for integration with other items into a full system 'build'.

Guidance on using the 'Config-Connection' tool to check out items will be found in [1].

3.1 RECORDING THE INTEGRATION PROCESS

This process records the integration of items into a single 'build' of the system. This process will be undertaken in accordance with the Integration Plan [4]. The process is shown in diagrammatic form in Figure 9.6.

The key stages of this process are described below.

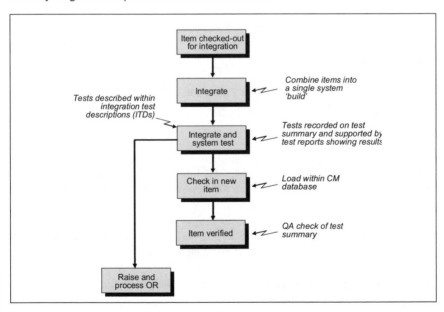

Figure 9.6   The integration process

3.2 CHECK-OUT ITEM

Validated and verified items are checked out from the CMDB, as described in Section 2.7.

3.3 INTEGRATION AND SYSTEM TESTING

In practice, integration of items and the various necessary tests (integration and system test) will be combined. The result will be a 'build' of the system providing a specified set of functions and features. These functions and features will be cross-referenced to XYZ requirements as specified in the Requirements Specification and Functional Specification documents [7] and [6].

The necessary testing will be defined in advance by the integration team in Integration Test Descriptions (ITDs). These will be reviewed for adequacy by the Consortium Quality Manager. The results of tests will be recorded on Test Reports.

Any errors discovered during these tests will be reported on ORs, which are described in greater detail in Section 5.

Note that the Integration and System tests will take the place of tests formally described as Site Acceptance Tests (SATs), since they will confirm the satisfactory operation of the build on the development and integration hardware at Stephenson House.

3.4 CHECK-IN NEW ITEM

When the new build has been completed and adequately tested, it will be passed to the Configuration Manager for checking in to the CMDB as a new item, in the same way as described in Section 2.5.

As part of the checking in process, any data sets used to test the build will also be checked into the CMDB. This will allow them to be used again on further builds or as part of the Acceptance process.

3.5 VERIFY ITEM

The Test Reports of all tests will be passed to the Consortium Quality Manager who will verify that the testing undertaken by the development team has been adequate, in the manner described in Section 2.6.

In the event that some aspect of testing is deemed to have been inadequate, an OR will be raised to record the problem and to manage its rectification.

Note that, in practice, the process of verification is likely to be undertaken in stages throughout the integration phase.

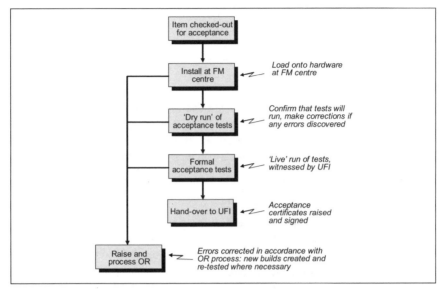

Figure 9.7 **The acceptance process**

The various Test Reports and supporting documentation will be filed for future reference.

4.0 RECORDING THE ACCEPTANCE PROCESS

The Acceptance process will demonstrate to XYZ that the final build of the system meets their requirements. The overall strategy for Acceptance Testing is described within the Acceptance Test Strategy document [7]. The key stages are shown in Figure 9.7. The key stages of this process are described below.

4.1 CHECK-OUT ITEM
The completed and verified build will be checked out from the CMDB, as described in Section 2.7. It may also be necessary to check out test datasets for use during Acceptance Testing.

4.2 INSTALL AT FM CENTRE
The software build will be installed on the target hardware, that is, at SuperComm's Facilities Management Centre in Hounslow.

4.3 DRY RUN CLIENT ACCEPTANCE TESTS
To verify the correct operation of the system on the target hardware, the full set of Client Acceptance Tests will be run. These tests will be defined on Acceptance Test Descriptions (ATDs). Included within the tests will be any needed to verify the system's performance.

ATDs will be designed to test all those aspects of the system that are of interest to XYZ.

Further guidance on Acceptance Tests can be found in the Acceptance Test Strategy document [7].

Any errors discovered during these tests will be reported on ORs, which are described in greater detail in Section 5. Where necessary, new builds will be created, checked into the database and re-tested. The end result of this stage will be a build which will run all the specified tests with no significant errors.

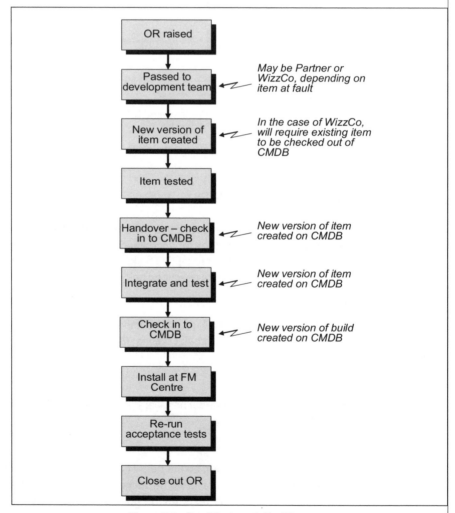

Figure 9.8   Possible stages in the OR process

4.4 RUN 'FORMAL' CLIENT ACCEPTANCE TESTS

This stage involves re-running the tests defined within ATDs in the presence of client appointed witnesses. The organization of these tests is described in outline in the Acceptance Test Strategy document. Detailed timetables for such testing will be agreed with XYZ in advance.

No significant errors should be should discovered during this stage but, if they are, they will be reported on ORs and handled accordingly.

4.5 HANDOVER TO XYZ

When the build has successfully completed its Client Acceptance Tests, certificates to this effect will be issued.

5.0 RECORD AND MANAGE ORS

As described in Sections 2, 3 and 4, ORs will be used to record any errors discovered during the development process and to manage their rectification. The actual stages followed by an OR will depend upon the stage at which it was raised, but the maximum possible set of stages in the process are shown in Illustration Figure 9.8. These stages are described below.

5.1 RAISE OR

The details of all discovered faults will be recorded within an OR.
These details will include:

- the items affected and their version number;
- the Test Description (ITD or ATD) and the test case that found the problem;
- the severity – that is:
  - major ORs relate to problems that stop the testing process and must be corrected before the test can be completed;
  - intermediate ORs relate to problems that are likely to prevent acceptance of the system and thus must be rectified before the completion of the whole process, but which do not prevent the completion of the rest of the individual test sequences;
  - minor ORs relate to problems that will need to be fixed but will not prevent acceptance by XYZ and may thus be fixed after the completion of the acceptance testing process.

5.2 PASS TO DEVELOPMENT TEAM

The OR will be passed to the appropriate team for correction. If the problem is suspected to be caused by a fault in the initial 'drop', it will be passed to the original development team, which could be a Partner.

5.3 NEW VERSION CREATED AND TESTED

The correction of the error will require a new version of the faulty item to be corrected. In the case of WizzCo created items, this will require the existing item to be checked out of the CMDB, as described in Section 2.7. In the case of Partner-created items, it will require that Partner to access their own configuration management system.

As part of this stage, it will be necessary to undertake sufficient tests to verify that the item now operates correctly. It may also be necessary to conduct regression and performance tests to verify that, in correcting the reported problem, no new problems have been created.

5.4 HAND-OVER NEW VERSION

Once satisfactorily completed and tested, the new version of the item must be passed to the Configuration Manager for checking in to the CMDB.

Guidance on using the 'Config-Connection' tool to check out items will be found in [1].

5.5 INTEGRATE AND TEST

The corrected Item may now be checked out of the CMDB, and combined with other items to create a new version of the build. This new build will need to be tested as necessary. As with the item, such re-testing may include regression and performance tests to verify that, in correcting the reported problem, no new problems have been created.

5.6 CHECK IN TO CMDB

Once adequately tested, the new version of the software build will be passed to the Configuration Manager for checking in to the CMDB.

5.7 INSTALL AT FM CENTRE

Once adequately tested, the new version the build can also be taken to the FM Centre for installation, replacing the version previously installed.

5.8 RE-RUN ACCEPTANCE TESTS

The tests that identified the original problem can now be re-run. If the problem has not been resolved, it will be necessary to repeat some or all of the previous steps.

Note that a copy of the previous version will still exist so that, in the event of the new version being a complete disaster, it will be possible to revert to the previous.

5.9 CLOSE OUT OR

Once the reported problem has been satisfactorily resolved, the OR may be closed out.

The OR and the various Test Reports and supporting documentation will be filed for future reference.

Guidance on using the 'Config-Connection' tool to check out items will be found in [1].

6.0 ANSWERING ENQUIRIES AND PRODUCING MANAGEMENT REPORTS

The 'Config-Connection' tool allows a range of management reports to be created upon request, as well as providing answers to ad-hoc enquiries.
Standard reports that will be produced include:

- current status of all items;
- items making up a particular version of a build;
- current status of all ORs.

Examples of ad-hoc enquiries include:

- current status and change history of a particular item;
- current status and history of a particular OR;
- outstanding ORs by organization responsible for their correction;
- list of all outstanding 'major' and 'intermediate' ORs

Guidance on using the Config-connection tool to print out management reports and to answer enquiries will be found in [1].

7.0 INTERFACE TO SCOPE CHANGE CONTROL

Although the Configuration Management system does not handle Scope Change Control, it will interface with the Scope Change Control System. This latter system is described within the Consortium Change Management Procedures [8].

In particular, the fact that a CM item is subject to a Change Note should be recorded within the CMDB. Moreover, all new items or new versions of items created as result of changes, should reference the relevant Change Note(s).

Guidance on using the 'Config-Connection' tool to print out management reports and to answer enquiries will be found in [1].

10 Internal communications

10.1 THE IMPORTANCE OF INTERNAL COMMUNICATION

In large and complex programmes, internal communication within the programme teams can be every bit as important to success as the external communication that takes place with stakeholders.

Yet such internal communication is often neglected. This is often because of an assumption that normal commercial disciplines and management structures will be sufficient to ensure that everything necessary gets done. While this may be valid in a normal business environment, programmes are anything but normal. Their whole purpose is usually to organize some major change to the business, that is, to change what is considered as normal. Furthermore, although they may last for many months or even years, programmes and their component projects are temporary organizations to which staff may have only limited long-term allegiance and commitment.

Moreover, because every programme is a unique, one-off initiative,[1] it will inevitably face some unique issues and challenges that have not had to be resolved before. In these circumstances, the traditional control structures that assume omniscient managers resolving all problems in advance and giving necessary orders to their minions is inappropriate and it is much more necessary to rely on the skill and judgement of individual teams and staff members to overcome the unexpected, only escalating the really serious issues and challenges that are outside their resources to resolve. Because of this, programme staff need a greater understanding

---

1   Of course, while a particular programme may be unique to the business unit experiencing it, the programme may have similarities with programmes undertaken elsewhere or earlier programmes undertaken within the same organization. Thus there may be pools of experienced staff who have already faced and resolved similar issues and challenges elsewhere. This is one reason why organizations engage external consultants with prior experience to play leading roles within their programmes.

of the objectives and background to the programme, of the contribution that their work should make to achieving these objectives, and of how their work fits in with and is depended on by other parts of the programme. Since programmes change, this understanding has to be renewed throughout the life of the programme.

Finally, large programmes almost always involve geographically disbursed teams drawn from different organizations. These teams may have noticeably different technical backgrounds, experiences and cultures. Furthermore, many programmes now have significant international elements. For example, within civil engineering programmes, major components and items of technology may be procured from America or the Far East, while many programmes involving IT now include teams of computer developers and support staff from Eastern Europe or the Indian sub-continent. In these situations, it is not only the 'corporate' cultures that are different, but also the national cultures that they are drawn from. These differences of geography, background and culture create great potential for misunderstanding of even the simplest of instructions.

These factors men that effective internal communication is vital to the success of most programmes and it must be planned, organized and monitored like any other element of programme management.

10.2 A MODEL OF COMMUNICATION

Figure 10.1 below shows a model of communication. In the model, the sender (the

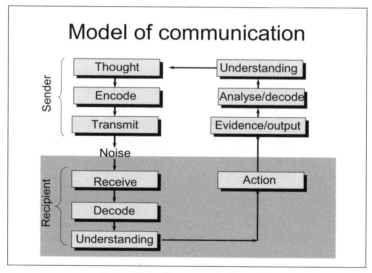

Figure 10.1   The communication cycle

person initiating the communication) needs to convert their thought or idea into a suitable message ('encode'), which can be transmitted over an appropriate medium to the recipient. The recipient will need to receive, decode (read/hear) and understand the message in order for anything useful to happen ('action'). For example, the programme manager might wish to send out a general instruction to the managers of the component projects. In this case, the programme manager would be the sender, while the various project managers would be the recipients, whom the programme manager hopes will receive, understand and act upon the instruction.

In spite of the sender's best efforts, the message may not be received or 'noise' in the system may cause it to be corrupted. This noise might be that sender and recipient have different cultural backgrounds and therefore interpret the messages in different ways. For example, the author once sat in a meeting at a UK Government research establishment called to discuss 'FM' where it took several minutes for all attending to become clear as to what this acronym meant: the radio specialists had assumed it meant 'frequency modulation' while the computer services specialists had assumed it meant 'facilities management'.[2] Fortunately, the face-to-face contact quickly resolved the misunderstanding and those that then realized they had nothing to contribute left the meeting. Had the communication been undertaken solely by e-mail or telephone, the misunderstanding would probably have taken much longer to identify and resolve and considerable time and effort would have been wasted in the meantime. Furthermore, where there is uncertainty or doubt, it is normal for busy human beings to put the communication to one side with the aim of understanding what is required later when more time is available. Thus messages that are not fully understood are unlikely to be acted upon. For this reason, effective communication requires the sender to seek feedback in the form of confirmation that the message has been received and understood and that appropriate actions have been (or will be) completed. In order to reduce the chances of misunderstanding, an important communication tool for many programmes is a basic glossary that can be used by all the different component projects and teams to ensure common understanding of technical terms and acronyms.

Figure 10.1 only shows one-way communication, for example, from a manager to a member of their staff. However, effective communication must be a two-way process and a successful programme manager will put as much emphasis on receiving communications from the various teams and ensuring appropriate

---

2   The web site www.acronymfinder.com lists 47 different interpretations of the acronym FM, including 'Foreign Minister', 'Fault Management' and 'Filosofian Maisteri' (the Finnish equivalent of a master's degree).

responses as they do to sending out instructions to those teams – that is, where the teams or team members are the 'sender' and the programme manager or members of the programme office are the recipients.

Many aspects of programme organization and planning, such as those outlined in Chapter 2 'The programme management process', are designed to ensure that essential instructions and understanding are communicated to those who need them. They include the production of programme and tranche plans. These, in turn, will drive the production of project plans within the component projects and work package definitions (WPDs) describing what those working within the project teams must undertake. These documents are usually complemented by a range of standards, programme guides and templates to help members of the programme complete the work outlined in project plans and WPDs.

10.3 ENSURING RELIABLE FEEDBACK

All programmes will require regular feedback to the centre so that progress can be measured and monitored and so that any problems with dependencies can be anticipated. These will normally follow a standard cycle, such as that shown in Figure 10.2.

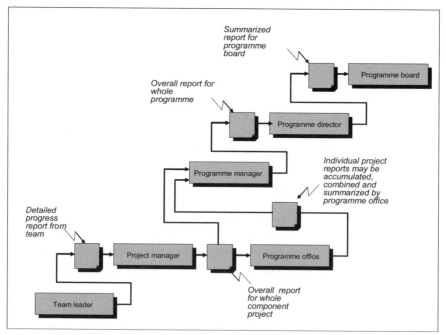

Figure 10.2   A typical programme progress report cycle

Normally templates are provided for each type of report to ensure that the relevant information is included. However, even with the best possible templates, the progress reports may not always present a clear, complete and easy-to-understand picture of what is really happening within the programme. This may because of the normal human wish to delay until the last possible moment the conveyance of bad news, such as that a project is likely to deliver late, since circumstances may yet change – the project may strike lucky and catch up on lost time or requirements may alter, meaning that delay is no longer critical.[3] In the case of subcontractors, this instinct for self-preservation may be combined with a wish to avoid contractual penalties.

Yet without such information, the programme manager cannot fulfil their role of fully understanding what is happening and of taking action to keep the programme on course. One technique to overcome this problem is to ensure that progress reports include full information on the achievement of milestones.

Milestones are agreed key points in the progressive completion of the programme and its component projects. Major milestones should be broken down into minor milestones to give an appropriate granularity of control. For example, a programme that is expected to last 18 months and is to report monthly might chose to have minor milestones within each component project at roughly 2-weekly intervals. In this way, any delays will become apparent within the monthly reporting sequence. At the same time, there will not be so many milestones as to drown the big picture with unnecessary detail.

Milestone trend charts are a simple but effective way of monitoring progress against milestones. They give an 'at a glance' summary of the state of the project or programme that is unambiguous and difficult to fake. Case Study 10.1 presents guidance on these charts, as published by a large IT-based programme operating within the finance sector.

---

3 In many corporate cultures such delay would be in the interests of the programme or project, since any indication of difficulty results in a flurry of demands by senior management for meetings, information and progress reports which consume so much time and effort that the eventual delay is even greater than might otherwise have been the case.

CASE STUDY 10.1: GUIDE TO USING MILESTONE TREND CHARTS

Purpose	Milestone Trend Charts provide an effective tool for obtaining and communicating a clear view of how the project is progressing.
Written by	PRIDE Programme Manager.
Responsibility	PRIDE Project Managers
Requirement	Mandatory on all PRIDE component projects.
Approval process	The choice of milestones to monitor should be agreed with the senior user and with the PRIDE Programme Manager.
Other tasks	Details of all expected milestone completion dates should be supplied to the Project Office.

Background

Every project within the PRIDE Programme must have a plan, which identifies the various activities that are needed to achieve a satisfactory completion. Some of these activities will represent the achievement of key objectives or the delivery of key deliverables. The completion of such activities will mark important 'milestones' for the project.

By monitoring these milestones, rather than the detailed activities themselves, the Project Manager and others can obtain a better idea of how the project is progressing. Milestone trend charts are an easy way to monitor milestones. They show the current status and the past history of a project in one easy-to-understand chart.

The charts show the current expected completion date for each milestone within each project. At every review period (typically each week or each month), the estimated completion dates are reviewed and a new set of points plotted. The two sets of points are then joined by lines to clearly show the trend. Over time, the complete history of the project can be seen. A consistently vertical line shows that everything is going to plan, while a line that slopes to the right indicates slippage.

The great value of the charts is that they makes any slippage clearly obvious – thus encouraging informed discussion leading to effective corrective action.

PRE-REQUISITES

Pre-requisites for effective use of the charts are:

- a comprehensive project plan, based upon a practical work breakdown structure.
- an intelligent selection of milestones to monitor
- regular and effective monitoring of the progress on each set of activities, leading to realistic estimates of when each milestone is likely to be achieved.

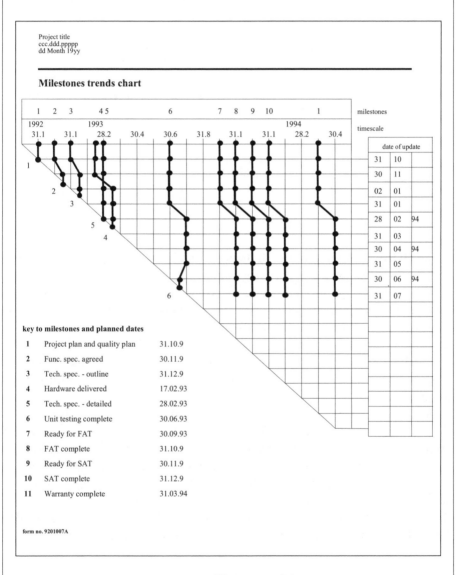

Figure 10.3   Milestones trend chart

EXAMPLE

An example milestone trend chart is included in Figure 10.3. It shows how a chart might appear after 10 monthly periods of monitoring, at which point 6 of the 11 milestones are complete and the remaining five are all running 1 month late.

The horizontal axis shows time forward and the vertical axis shows reporting dates. The dots represent the expected completion dates for each milestone.

At the start of a project, the planned dates for each milestone are marked in the top of the chart. At each subsequent review point, for example, each weekly progress meeting, a new set of dates are marked with dots and then the two sets of dots are joined together with trend lines. If all lines are vertical, then all is progressing to the original plan. However, if there have been changes or delays, the lines will trend to the right.

At any time the chart provides a quick visual display of when milestones are expected to be achieved and over time the chart will provide a complete history of the project.

Not all feedback should wait to the next regular reporting point. Crises and emergencies that are beyond the scope of the individual teams or projects should be escalated to the programme manager as quickly as possible, so that corrective action can be organized. Such crises might include the realization that a product on which another component project is dependent is going to be delivered late or an awareness that a component project might exceed its agreed tolerances (as outlined in Section 3.3 'Project environment'). Roles, responsibilities and procedures for such escalation should be agreed and communicated throughout the programme.

Other feedback should include programme and organizational issues, such as the working conditions in which certain staff have to operate. These would normally be covered within regular reports, but may also need to be reported on an emergency or out of course basis. Typically such issues are recorded within an issues log, which is made available to all so that they may comment. All who raise issues should receive some sort of response, even if the response is not the one that was sought. The fact that a response was sent will confirm to the person that raised the issue that the message has been received and understood.

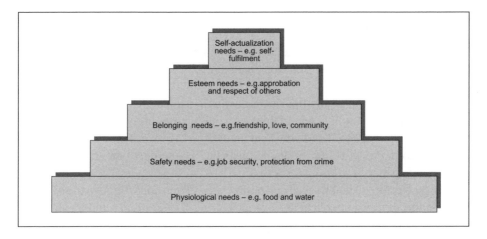

Figure 10.4   Maslow's hierarchy of needs

10.4 COMMUNICATION FOR MOTIVATION

Within a large, complex and long-running programme, communication can play a vital role in maintaining morale and efficiency. As identified by Abraham Maslow and others, human beings tend to want more than basic essentials. Maslow identified a pyramid of needs ranging from the basic physiological needs like food and water required for physical survival through to the need to fulfil potential as human beings, termed self actualization needs. As the circumstances of human beings improve, they take lower-level needs for granted and focus on achieving the higher needs, and if these higher needs cannot satisfied, become they become upset and demoralized. Thus the explorer lost in the desert will focus on finding water to survive (that is, fulfilling the most basic of physiological needs) yet once rescued and returned to London, he will take water for granted but become dissatisfied if he does not gain election to the Council of the Royal Geographical Society in recognition of his achievements (that is, esteem needs). Figure 10.4 summarizes this hierarchy of needs.[4]

Within most programmes there is a similar hierarchy of needs:

● When first joining the programme, those involved require basic instructions to answer the question 'What am I expected to do?' These represent the programme equivalents of physiological needs. They can be met by providing role descriptions, terms of reference or WPDs.

---

4   For a list of books by Maslow see www.maslow.com. For a summary of his hierarchy of needs theory and other theories of motivation see Kakabadse et al. 1987.

- After a while, programme staff are likely to become more concerned about ensuring a degree of security and predicting stability in their work. They will want answers to questions such as 'How long will this role last?' or 'What will I do once I have finished this work package?' These correspond to Maslow's 'safety' needs.
- Many staff will want more than just salary as a result of their employment. They will want to establish friendship with colleagues and build networks of acquaintances that will not only help them to do their work more effectively but will also make working life more pleasant. These correspond to Maslow's 'belonging' needs.
- Most of us like to feel wanted and appreciated. Thus opportunities to shine and gain the approval of colleagues or managers will be sought – that is, Maslow's 'esteem' needs.
- Finally, most of us want to feel at peace with our inner selves through knowing that we are doing a worthwhile job and making the world a better place for our families, our friends and the world at large.

Within a programme, effective, multi-way internal communication is essential if staff are to fulfil needs other than the most basic. For example, for most programme staff, a feeling of job security can only be achieved through seeing the larger picture and gaining a view of how one's immediate role will develop, while the esteem of colleagues can only be achieved if these colleagues are aware of what has been achieved and who has contributed to it. But unless these various needs are met, morale is likely to slip. Except in the direst economic circumstances, these will result in good staff leaving the programme and the demoralized remainder working with less enthusiasm and lower efficiency.

The need for good communication has been identified by many as essential to maintaining an enthusiastic and motivated workforce. Figure 10.5 shows a model of motivation, based upon the theories of Molander (1986). In this model, the drivers to improve the way that people work include the following:

- The basic confidence of those involved in their ability to meet expectations, as would be provided by training, mentoring or previous experience, is the bedrock of motivation.
- Confidence and enthusiasm will be increased if access is provided to suitable tools to assist with the works involved in the programme.
- Feedback on progress, showing how those involved are performing against expectations and demonstrating successes that have been achieved is an essential motivator. Hence communicating early successes is important.
- Understanding the reason for the work provides context for all involved. Thus

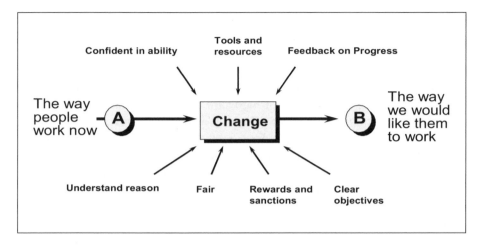

Figure 10.5 Model of motivation

internal communication must ensure that staff know why the activity is needed and how it will contribute to the objectives of the programme.

- The rewards, such as pay, and the basis for additional rewards (for example, bonuses for extra effort) or sanctions for insufficient effort (for example, dismissal from the programme) must be clear and understood.
- The rewards and sanctions should be deemed fair and reasonable.
- Above all, clear objectives are essential, so that all involved know what is expected of them.

Just as with Maslow's theory of needs, best practice with respect to staff motivation requires comprehensive communication throughout the programme and many techniques can be adopted to achieve this in a time- and cost-effective manner. One approach is to use cascade briefing to ensure that key messages are passed down throughout all levels of the programme and that feedback and issues are passed back up. With this technique, a formal briefing note is prepared by the programme manager and circulated to every component project manager; these will then call a briefing and pass the information to their team leaders (adding local material as they do so); the team leaders will then, in turn, convey the briefing material to their teams. During these briefings, team members will notify their leaders of issues and concerns, which are then passed back up the line in the same way as the reporting structure outlined above in Figure 10.2.

Cascade briefings can be supported by other mechanisms, such as programme intranets and regular update messages circulated by e-mail, DVD or newsletter. These can be a good way of circulating good news within the project so as to

411

maintain morale. They can also help to build a team spirit by giving the programme a 'brand' or recognized identity that members can be proud to be associated with, thus helping to satisfy their need to belong. This brand can be reinforced with a well-thought-out slogan or logo, but beware – an inappropriate slogan or logo, or one that is perceived as imposed from above, can actually harm morale. In fact, the best slogans or logos are often those that are acquired by accident. For example, when in World War II, in North Africa, German propagandists called the British 8th Army 'rats'; the British and Australian soldiers adopted the title with pride and became known forever as the 'Desert Rats'.

Newsletters and briefings can also be a good way of publicizing the achievements of individual teams or team members, thus helping to satisfy their need for the esteem of their colleagues. However, all these are about issuing the messages that the sender wants and are sometimes referred to as 'push' techniques. The recipients can only react to them and they have no control over the time, place, or method. Because they have no choice, human peversity will inevitably lead to some team members avoiding such communication through non-attendance at meetings, throwing newsletters in the bin or just sleeping through the briefings. Good practice will also ensure that there is a range of 'pull' techniques available, whereby those who need information can obtain it when they want it.

A good example of a 'pull' mechanism is to create a central repository of programme documentation to which all who need it have access. In the modern world this must almost invariably be an electronic repository, such as would be provided by a programme portal.[5] Through this portal, those with appropriate access privileges can read and retrieve all programme documents, including programme plans so as to see objectives, the plans of other component projects so as to see progress on dependencies, performance data to show how one's own team compares with others in the programme, plus all the various standards, guides, glossaries and directories that may be needed from time to time. The usability of any such portal is greatly increased through careful organization of information, ideally with some form of searchable index.

One reason why there is often reluctance to establish such a repository is unwillingness to make available all information to everybody. For example, business cases may contain financial information that it would be prudent not to make public. Also, the programme manager or programme director may not wish details of unresolved issues and internal debates to be made available outside of the programme. However, a well-structured repository, supported by clearly

---

5 Nowadays, creating such a portal is relatively easy. For example, ProjectPlace will allow a ready-made portal to be rented. Details of ProjectPlace can be found at www.projectplace.co.uk.

defined and well-communicated procedures, standards and/or guidelines about who can access what, can provide a high degree of control while still maximizing the amount of information that programme staff can readily access.

Whatever method is used to distribute important information or to make it available on demand, it must be recognized that staff will leave the programme and new joiners will replace them. Such new joiners will not have the background knowledge of existing staff and are likely to need guidance as to what is available where. Some form of 'Joiners Pack' can provide this. By providing a potted introduction to the programme and identifying what information they will be supplied with or are expected to find for themselves, such packs not only speed up the process of making new joiners fully effective, but also help them to feel welcome within the team, thus contributing to satisfying the new joiner's 'belonging needs' as discussed above.

10.5 ROLES AND RESPONSIBILITIES FOR INTERNAL COMMUNICATION

Overall responsibility for internal communication will normally rest with the programme manager. However, as with stakeholder management, internal communication is a non-trivial exercise and will require time, effort and money to be devoted to it. It is likely to require constant effort throughout the life of the programme, as documents are amended and revised, indexes kept up to date and new initiatives implemented. For this reason, it is common for large programmes to employ full-time or part-time communication managers to ensure that all this gets done. The communication manager might cover external (that is, stakeholder) communication as well as internal communication. Alternatively, it may be that the needs of the programme team are so important and distinct that two separate posts are required.

Whichever approach is adopted, it is vital to ensure that all interested parties, both within and outside the programme, are covered in one way or another. This is not always straightforward because there can be difficulties in establishing exactly who is within the programme as opposed to outside it. For example, it is common for user staff to be involved in specifying requirements, in devising business processes and in acceptance testing end-products and deliverables. Moreover, user staff will usually be involved in some form of training activity. Thus, at some stages such staff will be working within the programme and might even be deemed to be programme resources under the control of the programme manager and/or the manager of a component project, yet at others they are clearly outside the programme and working for the line management. The communication needs of all interested parties, both inside and outside the programme, should be fully

413

analysed, as outlined in Chapter 6 'Stakeholder management' and the internal communications plan should take full account of these needs and of how they might change from time to time during the life of the programme.

The communications manager might well be a member of the programme office and make use of the resources of that office to manage the various communication strands and channels. A key responsibility will be devising and maintaining the internal communication plan. This should be developed in accordance with the same principles as the stakeholder communication plan discussed in Chapter 6. Indeed, in some circumstances it may be practicable to combine the two plans and to implement them together.

A key capability of the communication manager should be the ability to understand the communication needs of the different groups and to create useful, easy-to-understand and easily accessible communication items, using the various channels available to the programme and in accordance with the communication plan.

10.6 THE TYRANNY OF E-MAILS

The ideal means of communication remains face-to-face contact, but the size and complexity of modern programmes mean that the time for such meeting is limited and other methods must be used. Typically all members of programme teams are now linked by e-mail and this tends to be the standard tool for day-to-day communication. Unfortunately, the ease with which vast numbers of e-mails can be generated, frequently with enormous attachments, has not been matched by any increase in the human ability to read, understand and process them. Where staff are working remotely, they may not have easy access to high-speed communication lines and the mere process of downloading multiple e-mails with large attachments can take significant amounts of time. Moreover, because of the pressures of work, many of these that have been time-consumingly transferred may remain unread in in-boxes until they become obsolete and are deleted. But even the process of reviewing the in-box and deleting such unread e-mails takes time. Thus, e-mails are a mixed blessing and their management can represent a significant but unrecorded cost to the programme. Indeed, they illustrate the point made over 200 years ago by Joseph Priestley, the 18th-century discoverer of oxygen:

The more elaborate our means of communication, the less we actually communicate.

Part of the answer is to instil e-mail disciplines within the programme to overcome these problems of 'e-mail overload'. These should include clear guidance on:

- limiting those that need to be 'copied in' to e-mails, so as to reduce the total number arriving in people's in-boxes on a 'just in case' basis;
- using meaningful descriptions in the subject fields to make it easy for the recipient to see the relevance and importance of each e-mail;
- making it explicit in the opening lines of every e-mail as to whether it is 'for information only' or requires specific actions or responses;
- using alternative methods to help people to keep up to date, such as with accessible repositories of progress reports and issues registers (as discussed below) that all team members may access should they wish to be informed;
- balancing e-mail communication with others methods – face-to-face meetings, teleconferences, telephone, intranets, and so on, as defined within the internal communication plan.

Included within the e-mail discipline can be the use of the electronic calendars that most e-mail systems now incorporate. If these diaries are kept up to date, it makes it much easier for others to arrange appropriate meetings and teleconferences, thus encouraging communication by other means.

These disciplines should be laid out in the internal communications plan, or in additional guidance to that plan, as described in Section 10.5 'Roles and responsibilities for internal communications'.

A key role in reducing the urge to e-mail is to ensure that all members of the team know who is responsible for what and how to contact them by alternative means. For example, e-mails are frequently used because telephone directories are not kept up to date. Providing all team members with an up-to-date programme directory, either in-hard copy form or electronically within a central repository, can greatly improve internal communication. Such a directory should list normal land-line phone numbers, mobile phone numbers, office or base location and secretary or message-point phone numbers. Ideally, it should include the job-titles or roles in the programme, so that the user can be sure that the correct person is being contacted.

10.7 MEASURING COMMUNICATION EFFECTIVENESS

Like every other aspect of the programme, the effectiveness of internal communications should be measured and ways of further improving it, whilst minimizing expenditures of time and cost, should constantly be sought.

The analysis and monitoring of reported issues, as outlined above, may provide some guidance on the effectiveness of communication. This may identify particular problems that recur or groups and teams that seem to have disproportionate difficulty. A lack of reported issues from a particular group may also indicate lack of awareness of feedback and issue reporting mechanisms.

The Programme Management Maturity Model (PMMM), as described in Chapter 15, provides a starting point for formal measurement on a programme-wide basis. This tool provides a free and easy to use facility to benchmark the maturity of the key management processes of a programme, including internal communication, against each other and against those of other similar programmes.

More detailed information on the effectiveness of internal communication can be obtained by conducting surveys among programme staff. Case Study 10.2 at the end of this chapter gives examples of the sort of information that may be obtained in this way. The survey used in this study employed a hard-copy questionnaire, handed out during lunchtime in the staff canteen, part of which is shown as Figure 10.7. Electronic survey tools now make the tasks of distributing and analysing even large and complex surveys relatively easy.[6] However, no tool can replace the careful thought that is required to ensure that a survey will be easy to understand and will provide the data, information and understanding that is required.

With large and diverse programmes involving people from many different back-grounds, it may also be worth considering some form of culture analysis, so that the results of different groups to the same survey can be calibrated to allow for different cultural responses to communication and to questions about such communication.

Finally, the audit programme outlined in Chapter 8 'Programme assurance and quality' should cover internal communication together with other aspects of the programme.

With information from issues, surveys and audits, it should be possible for the programme manager to gain a view as to the overall effectiveness of internal communications activities and of any weaknesses. These can then guide improvement efforts so that communication, like every other aspect of the programme, is continuously improved.

10.8 INTERNAL COMMUNICATION AND LEADERSHIP

Good communication is critical to effective leadership. All great leaders, whether politicians, military commanders or captains of industry, have sought to ensure good communication with those they lead. For example, Napoleon was renowned for his chats with officers and non-commissioned officers on the eve of battle and

---

6 A number of such tools are readily available, including Survey Shack, which can be accessed via the Internet at www.surveyshack.com.

the feeling that this engendered, that 'their general' understood them and shared their dangers and was one of them, was a key factor in the French army's ability to conquer most of Europe.

Some fortunate souls have an instinctive capacity for communication and have little need to plan for it or to use the tools and techniques outlined above. However, the rest of us are likely to need some help, particularly when seeking to run a large and complex programme. The internal communication manager can provide part of this help, but they can only facilitate the process. In the end, it will be the views of the programme manager and/or the programme director that the teams will seek, not the views of intermediaries.

Good leaders make a point of meeting as many of the staff they control as possible. Thus good programme managers will seek to hold meetings with all of their teams as frequently as possible, irrespective of how geographically remote the teams are. This not only helps to promote the leader amongst the teams, but also tends to make subsequent communication by less direct means (for example, video conference, telephone or e-mail) easier and more effective.

While meeting with staff, true leaders make a point of listening and noting what is said and then responding to it. The response may not always be positive: the project manager who pleads for more resources may have to be told 'No', but if this is done with an explanation of why it may inspire the project manager to try harder. And great leaders don't wait for direct contact before responding. When Abraham Lincoln, President of the USA during the American Civil War, heard of a widow whose four sons had all been killed in the service of the Union Army, he sent her a personal note. While the note could never bring the young men back, it demonstrated that he understood her grief and genuinely cared about it.

But the written or spoken word is only one way in which messages are communicated. What is known as 'non-verbal' communication can be equally as important. Just as politicians who preach morality to others and are then found to engage themselves in sordid vice lose credibility, the same will apply to the leaders of programmes. Programme managers have to demonstrate by their actions as well as by formal communications that they understand the difficulties that the programme's teams are facing and care about them and will do what they can to alleviate them. A good example of this was noted by the author on a recent train journey between London and Leeds in the UK. A conversation with the Dining Car Steward revealed that the Chief Executive of the railway company had recently complemented the Steward on the quality of the napery in his dining car. When asked why the Chief Executive had visited the car, the Steward explained that there had been difficulties with an item of kitchen equipment and the Chief Executive had wanted to see the problem for himself. Doubtless the story had already been relayed to all the railway's other dining car staff, with clear messages for all: that at any time

417

the Chief Executive could arrive, so make sure your work is up to scratch because he will notice, but more importantly, that he cares about details and responds to reports of difficulties – and all this achieved without a single e-mail or formal meeting!

CASE STUDY 10.2: ABCA INTERNATIONAL COMMUNICATION STRATEGY

INTRODUCTION

The ABC Agency (ABCA) was a relatively new organization, which was undergoing a massive programme of change. It was recognized that achieving this change with the minimum disruption and upset required speedy and effective internal communication.

Various studies had indicated that, although internal communication was improving, it was still inadequate, resulting in duplication of effort. Even though the ABCA had many different 'channels' of communication, these needed to be used effectively and in combination if all necessary messages were to be sent, received, understood and acted upon. This was particularly important for the Corporate Quality Directorate (the Directorate), which has a key role in managing this important programme of organizational change and improvement.

WHAT THE CONSULTANTS PROVIDED

External consultants were asked by the Director of Quality to review ABCA's internal communication situation and to propose a strategy that could be followed by the Directorate to ensure programme success. This strategy would identify the key messages that the Directorate should convey to, and receive from, other parts of ABCA and the most appropriate means for conveying them.

The assignment involved a review of available channels, of the groups to be communicated with and of the 'messages' to be passed. With the information so gained, a series of 'models' were developed to demonstrate the effectiveness of communication. From these an overall approach was devised to the planning, management and measurement of communication.

This review included the analysis of various surveys and measures that already been obtained as well as the application of an ABCA-wide 'Canteen Questionnaire' to provide a baseline against which improvements in internal communication could be measured. This approach was used because the questionnaire could be handed out to a large and representative cross-section of ABCA's staff without any significant distribution costs and could be completed by staff whilst they dined, thus avoiding any claims about disruption to essential work. A part of this questionnaire is shown in Figure 10.6, while Figure 10.7 shows one comparison of the distribution of survey responses against the distribution within the organisation as a whole, showing that the survey achieve a high level of representation.

Please would you help us by answering a few simple questions whilst you dine. When you have finished, leave the questionnaire on the table to be collected.

Please tick appropriate box

1. Do you know of the existence of the ABCA Business Management System (BMS) ?... ... ... Yes ❑ No ❑

    If Yes – Do you make use of it ? ... ... Yes ❑ No ❑

    If Yes – approximately how often ?

    occasionally ... ...   ❑

    less than once a week ... ...   ❑

    between 1 and 5 times a week ... ...   ❑

    more than 5 times a week? ... ...   ❑

2. Do you know of the existence of the <u>electronic</u> version of the Business Management System, which can be accessed via a PC ? ... ... Yes ❑ No ❑

    If Yes – Do you use this version when accessing the Business Management System ?

    never use the electronic version ... ...   ❑

    sometimes use the electronic version and

    sometimes the 'paper' version   ...   ❑

    always use the electronic version... ...   ❑

3. Do you know of the ABCA procedure for initiating improvements to the way that ABCA works? ... ... Yes ❑ No ❑

    If Yes - Have you actually used the procedure to initiate an improvement ? Yes ❑ No ❑

P.T.O.

Figure 10.6   Example of part of ABCA 'Canteen Questionnaire'

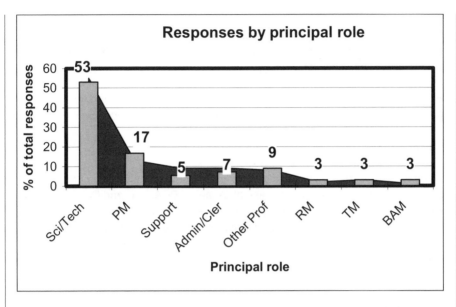

Figure 10.7   Responses to 'Canteen Questionnaire' showing how distribution of survey responses matches distribution of roles within the organization as a whole

The survey was able to pinpoint specific areas where existing communication activities had not been fully successful. Figure 10.8 shows that nearly half did not know of the existence of a particular procedure, while nearly 40 per cent new of it but did not use it. Other analyses pinpointed the groups and teams with least penetration, allowing remedial effort to be focused where it would make the greatest impact.

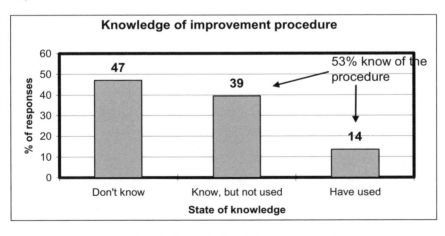

Figure 10.8   Example of analysis: Knowledge of improvement procedure

Following the survey, a series of workshops were then held with the Directorate's staff at which the approach was discussed. Staff were then able to prepare detailed communication plans, which collectively provided a practical, effective and monitorable communication strategy.

Finally a series of pilot communication initiatives were implemented, including the publication of appropriate features within ABCA's corporate newspaper.

THE RESULTS

A key element in the success of the assignment was the involvement of ABCA staff. Interviews and discussions took place at all main ABCA sites and Directorate staff worked with the consultant to analyse problems and identify solutions. The agreed strategy was subsequently implemented and enabled the Directorate to establish common standards and procedures throughout all the ABCA's many groups and teams.

REFERENCES

Kakabadse, A. Ludlow, R. and Vinnicombe, S. (1987) *Working in Organizations.* London: Gower.

Molander, C. (1986) *Management Development – Key Concepts for Managers and Trainers.* Bromley: Chartwell-Brett-Studentlitteratur.

11 Programme accounting and financial control

11.1 THE ROLE OF PROGRAMME ACCOUNTING AND FINANCIAL CONTROL

Programmes of change, in common with all forms of enterprise, require careful financial management. Whether a programme exists in the public or private sector, there will always be an imperative to deliver the benefits at the agreed, or ideally lower, cost. Introducing and maintaining a robust process for programme accounting and financial control cannot guarantee that a programme adheres to its financial constraints; however, the lack of such a process will almost certainly ensure that it does not.

The very nature of change programmes often makes it extremely difficult to estimate their costs and durations during the early planning stages. As a result, initial estimates may need to be revised many times as the true extent of the programme becomes better understood. Effectively managing this uncertainty is the key requirement of a robust and reliable programme accounting and financial control process.

The Holyrood Programme, described in Case Study 11.1, appears to be almost the perfect example of how poor programme financial management led to massive cost overruns. What is clear about the Holyrood Programme is that the new Scottish Parliament Building could never have been delivered for the original £50 million estimated cost. Had the programme team used best practice programme accounting and financial control, a number of the major shortfalls would have been avoided, for example:

- the original estimates would have been 'sense checked' to ensure that there were no major omissions;
- change control would have ensured that all requests for change were costed prior to approval and that updated costs were included in the programme's estimates of the cost to complete;

423

- periodic 'cost to complete' reporting to senior stakeholders would have ensured that escalating, or decreasing, estimates of the costs to complete were communicated.

CASE STUDY 11.1: THE HOLYROOD PROGRAMME

The design and construction of the Scottish Parliament building in Edinburgh, that is, the Holyrood Programme, graphically demonstrated how a programme can be a success on many levels but be blighted by cost overruns. The programme was initiated in 1998 by a decision to create a building for the new Scottish Parliament on the site of a former brewery at Holyrood in Edinburgh and construction work started in 2000.

While critical acclaim for the parliament building has been widespread, the level of concern over the cost overrun from the original estimate of less than £50 million to a final cost in excess of £400 million, led to the establishment of a public enquiry by Lord Fraser of Carmyllie. His report (the Fraser Report, Fraser, 2004) indicated that this extreme overrun had arisen due to a combination of factors, all related to inadequate accounting and financial control:

- The original estimate was completely unrealistic. Major cost elements, such as 4 acres of land at the foot of Edinburgh's Royal Mile, professional fees and value added tax, were all omitted from the original estimates. Lord Fraser commented: 'This unique one-off building could never ever have been built for £50m and I am amazed that for so long the myth has been perpetuated that it could.'
- The size of the building was increased by approximately 50 per cent during the construction period.
- The whole programme was subjected to ongoing delays and disagreements, often resulting from changes to the basic design of the building. Lord Fraser's final report says: 'It is difficult to be precise but something in excess of £150m has been wasted in the cost of prolongation flowing from design delays, over-optimistic programming and uncertain authority.'

The Fraser Report also comments on the degree to which key stakeholders were not kept aware of escalating costs. In his speech presenting the Report, Lord Fraser says: 'It still astonishes me that first Scottish Office Ministers and later the Scottish Parliamentary Corporate Body [SPCB] and Holyrood Progress Group [HPG] were kept so much in the dark over the increases in cost-estimates. It would have seemed to me to be axiomatic that those who are democratically accountable for public expenditure should be kept advised of looming increases. And for year after year they were not.'

It may be that a programme ultimately costs considerably more than originally envisaged. This may not necessarily a bad thing: if the scope has expanded or if new benefits are achieved, all may be well. What is vitally important is that organizations make decisions on whether to continue or desist with a programme in full knowledge of all the financial implications. Although the Members of the Scottish Parliament might have been content to make additional funds available for the Holyrood Programme in light of their changed requirements, due to a lack of proper controls they were never asked and British taxpayers had to fork out nearly £400 million more than they had expected.

Through the mechanism of the business case, programme costs are closely linked with programme benefits and programme team members involved with accounting and financial control are likely to also be required to maintain records of the achievement of benefits. This chapter, however, will focus exclusively on accounting for costs, while the accounting and reporting of benefits is discussed more fully in Chaper 5 'Benefits management'.

Financial control is exercised using similar techniques to those employed to control other aspects of a programme. A financial plan, also referred to as a budget, should be prepared, based upon the programme approach adopted. The actual expenditure should be monitored against the baseline provided by this budget. A programme budget will be the sum of the individual budgets for component projects, except during the earliest period of the programme, that is, during the Start-up stage, when individual project budgets may not yet have been established.

The objective of the programme accounting and financial control process is to provide transparent, auditable financial control of the programme and requires the following steps:

1. Develop, document and agree expenditure plans for the programme, that is, prepare programme budgets.
2. Record all financial transactions incurred by the programme, that is, capture actual financial performance.
3. Identify and report variances from budget to programme management, that is, highlight exceptions.
4. Identify and evaluate opportunities for corrective actions, that is, quantify remedial actions.
5. Review and revise expenditure plans for the programme, that is, begin the cycle again.

Detailed explanation of the steps required to develop, maintain and manage the programme's financial plan are set out below in Section 11.11 'Programme accounting and financial control through the lifecycle'.

The less certain the eventual approach required to achieve a programme's goals, the more often the financial re-planning cycle will need to be undertaken. Also the less likely are original estimates to accurately reflect the ultimate cost of the programme. Financial plans can only be as reliable and accurate as the programme plans and assumptions upon which they are based. Programme sponsors and other members of the programme board will need to be reminded of this critical factor throughout the programme's lifecycle. Programmes often find themselves short of funds when the full scale of the programme becomes apparent and initial estimates, and allocations, frequently prove inadequate.

The financial procedures of most organizations are not designed for the management and control of programmes. Rather, they are designed for the measurement and reporting of profits and losses arising from ongoing business. This creates a number of challenges for the programme's finance team, which will be responsible for programme accounting and financial control, including:

- Organizational accounting and control is focused on periodic (typically annual and monthly) reporting. Programmes, in contrast, extend over several years, with reporting focusing more on products and deliverables.
- An organization's financial reporting is typically based on profit or cost centres and expenditure types, for example salary costs, accommodation, depreciation. An organization's accounting function will therefore typically establish a cost centre for a programme, or, more usefully, one for each component project within the programme, to collate costs incurred. Effective project and programme management requires a more detailed breakdown of expenditure than is typically available at the programme 'cost centre' level, that is, a focus on products and deliverables.

All programmes must operate within the host organization's financial management environment; however, this is unlikely to provide the level of detail required for effective control. It will therefore usually be necessary for the programme to establish its own financial management procedures to supplement those of the host organization. Such procedures must ensure that the programme has at all times a realistic estimate of its likely costs and is therefore is able to provide the host organization with a clear indication of the level of funding that it will be required to provide in the future, that is, the estimated cost to complete (ECC).

11.2 SCOPE OF PROGRAMME ACCOUNTING AND FINANCIAL CONTROL

Programme accounting and financial control is the process that provides senior management with assurance that the programme can be completed within the financial constraints placed upon it. To do this, the costs of the programme will need to be collected and collated in such a way as to provide insight into the financial well-being of the programme.

Costs incurred by a programme can usually be categorized into one of three broad categories, namely:

- **Labour**: Costs incurred in the provision of individuals to undertake work on the programme. Labour costs may be incurred as a recharge of employee costs from their 'home' cost centre within the organization, or as an invoiced charge from a supplier company providing programme team members such as the costs of computer programmers to undertake work on an IT systems project within the programme.
- **Equipment, supplies and services**: Items used to construct programme deliverables or complete programme deliverables, such as a computer software package, or consumable items used by the programme team.
- **Overheads**: Costs allocated to the programme to reflect the use of the host organization's infrastructure and services. These costs are usually based on a pre-agreed formula and include charges for items including accommodation, utilities and shared services, including accounting.

These categories are very broad and accounting records will typically be maintained at a more detailed level, detailing specific types of expenditure within each category.

When considering the cost of a programme, it is vital to focus on the final cost, that is, how much the programme will ultimately cost to deliver the benefits required. At any given time during the lifetime of the programme, the estimate of final cost will comprise three elements:

- **Spent**: Expenditure already made, that is, invoices and salary cost paid to suppliers and programme team members.
- **Committed**: Expenditure for which a contractual commitment to pay has been made. Committed costs include such items as equipment and supplies ordered, where cancellation is prohibited by the terms of the supply contract or notice period payments for programme team members.
- **Planned**: Expenditure that is expected to be required but where no binding commitment has yet been entered into.

As expenditures move through the levels of commitment, from 'planned' to 'committed' and ultimately to 'spent', the opportunity to avoid this expenditure, in the event of a change in the programme plan, will diminish. Programme accounting and financial control must ensure that the level of commitment with the programme is consistent with certainty of how goals will be achieved. It is inappropriate to have a situation where a programme's approach is highly uncertain yet the majority of its costs are either 'spent' or 'committed'. In the event of a change in the programme plan, or some other change in circumstance, a programme team can only exercise influence over 'planned' expenditure, although some 'committed' costs may be deferred subject to the payment of penalties. Therefore it is essential that as well as reactive monitoring of a programme's financial status programme accounting and financial control must be proactive in ensuring that levels of 'committed' and 'spent' cost are consistent with a programme's certainty of outcome.

The key questions to which the programme accounting and financial control function must be able to provide answers are:

- What is the current best estimate of a programme's final cost?
- How certain is this estimate?
- How does this estimate compare with the original (baseline) and most recent estimates?
- What opportunities exist to address adverse variances in these estimates?

If a programme's accounting and financial control process can consistently and accurately answer these questions, it will be well equipped to help the programme achieve its financial goals.

11.3 PROGRAMME VERSUS PROJECT ACCOUNTING AND FINANCIAL CONTROL

The principles of accounting and financial control apply equally to projects and programmes and the four questions posed above are equally relevant for both. The key requirements when establishing a programme accounting and financial control process are that all:

- projects within the programme use common methods to identify, record, classify and report costs;
- projects report in a consistent, complete and timely manner to the programme;
- project financial plans, that is, budgets, are developed and updated in a consistent manner.

In most programmes there are usually relatively few financial transactions relating specifically to the programme level, the majority being accounted for in the individual projects within the programme. Programme level expenses typically involve costs for the programme team and organizational recharges, which may be subsequently charged to the component projects. The role of programme accounting and financial control is primarily to consolidate expenditure information from individual projects to provide a programme level view.

11.4 ROLES AND RESPONSIBILITIES WITHIN THE PROGRAMME FINANCE TEAM

It is possible to have a situation where the programme and the organization are one and the same, for example when planning and staging a major event such as the Olympic Games where an organization is created specifically to deliver the programme. This, however, is not normally the case. In the majority of cases, programmes take place within a 'host organization and are required to comply with established procedures of that host.

Any host organization will have procedures in place to undertake accounting and financial management. Each programme will need to consider its own specific requirements for financial control, while ensuring that its approach can be implemented within the host organization's accounting procedures. No organization is going to change its accounting procedures to accommodate a single programme, no matter how significant. The financial management of a programme will usually require input from three groups, although the roles of two of these, programme and project accounting, may be undertaken by the same individuals.

Figure 11.1 shows the relationship between these three roles.

The three groups involved are:

- **Host organization's finance function**: This group is responsible for all financial management activities of the host organization. Procedures will be in place setting out how the organization must account for the financial transactions of programmes and projects. It is important that the programme manager engages with the finance function as early as possible in the programme lifecycle, to fully understand what information, in what format, is available from the organization's accounting systems. It is also important to consider what information the host organization's finance function will require from the programme.

    During these early discussions, ideally during the Start-up stage,[1] the programme manager and the organization's finance function should agree the

1 See Chapter 2 of this handbook for a description of the various stages in the programme lifecycle.

information that will flow, in both directions, between finance and the programme. It is commonly the case that finance will establish the programme as a 'cost centre', or a number of cost centres, within the accounting system. The programme will then be required to comply with the reporting requirements set upon all cost centres. In preparation for these early discussions, the programme manager must consider whether a single cost centre for the programme, or individual ones for each component project, will best support financial management.

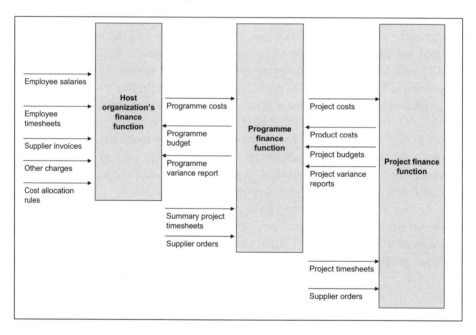

Figure 11.1   Information flows in two directions between programmes and the host accounting function

- **Programme accounting and financial control**: in the case of a very large programme, this role will be undertaken by a specialist programme finance function, while in a smaller programme it will be fulfilled within the programme office (see Chapter 13, 'The programme office'). If a specialist position is to be created, a secondee from the organization's finance function will be a useful addition to the programme team.

During the Programme Execution stage, the programme accounting and financial control function will receive periodic cost information from the organization's finance function. This information is likely to be less detailed than required to manage the programme's finances. The programme's finance function will need to further analyse the organization level information, using additional data collected by the programme, to identify the costs attributable to each project.

The programme's finance function will also be responsible for the collation of project budgets, that is, financial plans, into a programme-level budget, in compliance with organizational budgeting timetables and procedures. Also the preparation and presentation to organizational management of periodic financial performance reports, that is, financial variance reports.

Situated as it is between the organization and the component projects, the programme's finance function must give considerable early thought to its information requirements prior to the commencement of the Programme Execution stage. It is considerably easier to establish procedures to collect relevant information before the programme moves into full operation.

- **Project accounting and financial control**: Detailed financial control will be exercised at the project level; therefore a key role of the project finance function will be to identify and allocate costs within the project, specifically to the individual deliverables or products.

  The project finance function will also be responsible for developing and maintaining project budgets, that is, financial plans as well as preparing periodic budget variance reports setting out achievement against budget.

The programme/project hierarchy will normally be consistent with the host organization's operating structure. The broader organization structure will have divisions, functions and departments established in some hierarchical form. The host organization will also have established levels of authority for the commitment and expenditure of monies with which the programme will be required to comply. During the early stages of the programme it is important to fully understand these rules and agree with the organisation's finance function how they will be applied within the programme. Failure to establish these rules and procedures may result in difficulties and delays during programme execution if expenditures cannot be properly authorized. Delegation of financial authority is normally based on individuals' seniority within the organization and levels of expenditure, that is, the greater the expenditure the more senior a member of staff is required to authorize it. The programme needs to ensure that a number of sufficiently senior people are available to authorize the expected levels of expenditure for the programme. This may well involve members of the programme board acting as authorization for major expenditures. It is important to note that gaining access to very senior staff can often take time; a factor to bear in mind when planning significant expenditures. (See Chapter 3, 'Programme organization and governance' for further information on the programme board.)

11.5 EXERCISING FINANCIAL CONTROL OVER A PROGRAMME

A programme should follow essentially the same process for exercising financial control as that used for any other aspect of the organization, for example, division, profit centre, department. The standard financial control process comprises four steps (see Figure 11.2):

1. Develop and document expenditure plans, that is, prepare programme budgets.
2. Record all financial transactions,that is, capture actual financial performance.
3. Identify and report variances from budget, that is, highlight exceptions.
4. Identify and evaluate corrective actions, that is, quantify and initiate remedies.

After the fourth step, the whole cycle begins again from revise and document expenditure plans.

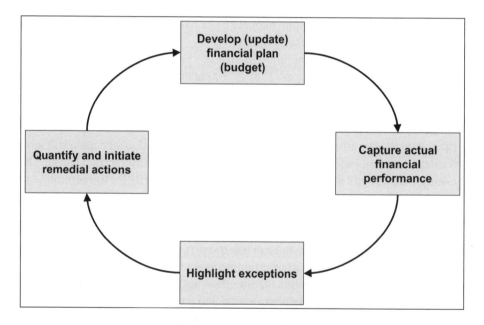

Figure 11.2   Financial control cycle

In this manner, targets are set, progress monitored, variances identified and remedies implemented. It is a classic control process and one that is normally applied consistently across an organization's functions and departments. Programmes typically span long periods of time and measurement of expenditure to date does not always provide a complete picture of financial well-being. To effectively manage the finances of a programme or project, it is necessary to understand progress towards the goal, in addition to time passed since the programme or project commenced. The author has experience of organizations that, finding themselves with a programme that appears to be under-spending, have sought to withdraw funding and redistribute it to other programmes. This was the reverse of the appropriate action required, as the programmes were under-spending due to the late completion of a number of deliverables. A measurement approach that reflects the achievement of programme goals in financial reports is earned value analysis, a more comprehensive discussion of which is included later in this section.

11.6 COLLECTING PROGRAMME COSTS

Costs are incurred whenever the programme team undertakes work to create programme deliverables. As indicated earlier in this chapter, these are usually categorized as labour equipment, supplies and services or overheads.

Each type of input cost will have its own source document that must be analysed and the cost recognized as a programme cost. The capture and initial analysis of data from these documents is usually carried out by the organization's finance function as part of its responsibility to account for all financial transactions. The finance function will allocate programme costs to cost centres and account classification codes as agreed with the programme, ideally during the Establish stage of the programme lifecycle. The finance staff will use the same procedures used for all the organisation's costs and each cost category will have specific documentation that will enable the finance functions of the organization and the programme to fully analyse the cost. These documents typically include:

- wage/salary payment details and timesheets for own employee labour costs
- contractor invoices and timesheets for contractor labour costs
- supplier invoices, employee expense claims, contractor expense claims for equipment, supplies and services costs
- cost transfers and allocation agreements for overhead costs.

Initially the organization's finance function will use these prime documents to identify costs to be charged to the programme or elements within it if lower level, for example, project cost centres have been established. These cost allocations will be made up as follows:

- **Own employee labour**: There are two, common, arrangements under which an organization's own employees are assigned to a project or programme:

- – An employee is transferred from their 'business as usual' (BAU) department to the project or programme, which agrees to be charged their salary and employment costs. In this situation the cost centre for the individual will be temporarily changed within the organization's payroll system and the cost for the individual will be charged to the project/programme's cost centre each accounting period. This mechanism effectively charges the transferred staff to their correct cost centre, but it provides no insight into what work the individual is undertaking. To capture this additional information, the programme will need to establish additional procedures, usually based on a programme timesheet for completion by staff that provides 'task level' activity information.
- – An employee working for a service department of the organization, such as IT Services, is assigned to complete programme tasks. Often service departments will have a timesheet system in place that enables the 'cross charging' of staff time to departments and programmes. In these circumstances the programme under consideration will be allocated a 'job number', which will enable service department staff to charge their time to the programme. In the absence of such a system, alternative charging arrangements will be required. If the service department employee is working full time on the programme, a solution similar to that outlined above may be appropriate; if not, some form of agreed inter-departmental charge will be required. Even in situations where inter-departmental timesheets are present, it may still be the case that these provide insufficient detail and therefore a more detailed programme timesheet may be required. For most programmes, it is safe to assume that a programme-specific timesheet system will be required to support financial management and resource planning, delegation and loan.

- **Contractor labour**: Contract labour, that is, programme team members who are not employees of the host organization, will be charged via an invoice from the supplier. Such an invoice should, as a minimum, provide details of the programme/project cost centre to which it relates. Standard finance function practice is to reject all invoices that do not quote a valid customer purchase order reference and cost centre. As with own staff, however, unless specific arrangements have been made beforehand with the supplier, it is unlikely that sufficient detail will be provided to identify tasks undertaken. A programme-specific timesheet procedure covering own and contract staff will generally be required. Most organizations require contractor timesheets to be completed, authorized and matched against supplier invoice details prior to paying such invoices. This is generally considered good controls practice, as it prevents payments for unauthorized time.

- **Equipment, supplies and services**: These cost are presented via supplier invoices and, to a lesser degree, staff expense claims. Whenever the programme requires equipment, supplies or a service, the organization's finance function will normally require that a purchase order is raised with a properly accredited supplier. Where a supplier is required by the programme that is not currently approved by the organization, authorization will usually need to be obtained before an order can be placed and potential delays in obtaining approval for new suppliers need to be considered when planning the programme.

  A purchase order, as well as a description of the goods or services required, will contain details of the cost centre(s) to which charges should be made. This information will allow the organization's finance function to correctly allocate the costs to the programme or project incurring the expenditure. Programme and project managers should keep details of all purchased items to enable costs to be further allocated to specific deliverables.

  Employee and contractor out-of-pocket expenses can, especially for multi-national programmes incur significant costs. Overall charges for expenses will normally be debited to the programme cost centre(s) from the employee expense system or contract supplier invoices. In both cases, it is likely that additional information, for example a copy of the employee's expense claim form, will be required to support the allocation of costs to deliverables.

- **Overheads – cost transfer and allocation agreements**: It is common for programmes and projects to be allocated a proportion of general overheads in common with other parts of the organization. Overheads will typically fall into one of two categories:

  - Specific overheads: These are re-charges for services and facilities provided by the organization to the programme, for example for office accommodation used by the programme or procurement costs incurred purchasing equipment and services through the organization's procurement function.

    These types of re-charges will normally be made on some rational basis, such as the amount of accommodation or floor space occupied. These re-charges will therefore be similar to external services, differing only in the supplier being the host organization.

    Allocating this category of costs to programme deliverables is usually undertaken by utilizing the basis of charge to the programme to allocate the cost to a deliverable.

  - General overheads: These are non-specific charges to reflect the general overheads of the organization, such as maintaining the senior management team. Some organizations do not charge these types of costs directly to programmes and projects, others do. For those that do, it will usually involve a general, negotiated, charge to cover non-programme-specific cost, such as general management. Here again, some agreed basis will be required to allocate general overheads to deliverables.

Overhead costs will appear on the periodic programme cost centre reports as transfers, initiated by the organization's finance function. During the Define stage of the programme lifecycle, it is important to agree with the organization's finance function the basis and quantum of these charges, in sufficient detail to be able to fully account for all charges and understand any changes during the life of the programme.

By receiving, recording and classifying all the above financial transactions, including those at the programme level, the organization's finance function will identify the costs incurred by the programme each period. This will indicate to both programme and organizational management how much is being spent in each of these categories and how that compares to plans and budgets. However, this input-based categorization of cost is of limited value in programme decision making. Of far greater importance is the cost of outputs. To create this output-focused view of costs, the programme's finance function will need to establish and maintain a deliverables costing process that allocates costs to individual programme products, as illustrated in Figure 11.3.

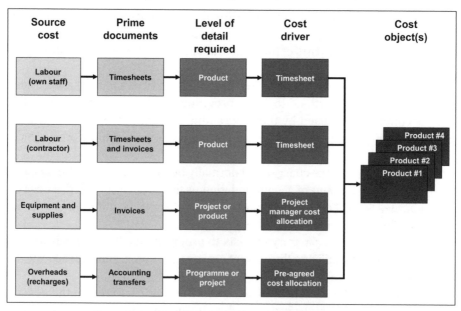

Figure 11.3 Allocation of costs to cost objects, that is, products

11.7 ANALYSING PROGRAMME COSTS

As described in Chapter 5, 'Benefits management', benefits are achieved when programme deliverables are combined to deliver (enhanced) capabilities. A programme of change potentially develops a number of capabilities and achieves a number of benefits for the host organization. An interesting question to ask of any programme is, 'which capabilities deliver the greatest benefits, most cost effectively?' Figure 11.4 illustrates a simplified example where, although the total benefits of the programme outweigh the costs, Capability #3 costs more to deliver than the benefits it achieves. This is vital information for organizations that wish to optimize the use of scarce resources and funds. When managing a programme, the most important costs to understand are the costs of deliverables, that is, products. A programme's main objective is creating 'quality' deliverables, on time and within agreed cost, which are then combined to deliver capabilities, which result in the achievement of benefits. Identifying and measuring the cost of each deliverable will enable the programme to assess the viability of each element within the benefit plan.

Figure 11.4 illustrates how source costs can be allocated and apportioned via cost objects, that is, deliverables, to capabilities, thereby enabling a comparison between the costs and benefits of each element of the programme. Further details regarding the relationships between deliverables, capabilities and benefits can be found in Chapter 5, 'Benefits management'.

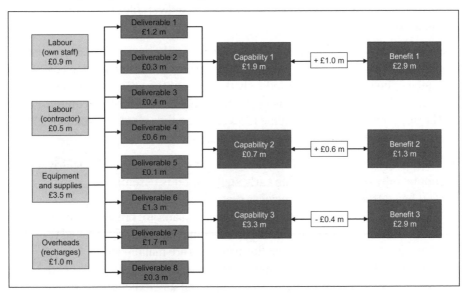

Figure 11.4   Evaluation of costs and benefits

11.7.1 COSTING DELIVERABLES

The principles outlined below are consistent with costing best practice for any organization. The approach is essentially the same: each source cost is traced via 'cost drivers' to its ultimate 'cost object'. In the case of programmes, cost objects correspond to deliverables. It will probably assist the reader at this point to define the terms used to describe the costing process:

- **Source cost**: Costs charged to the programme via the mechanisms described above, that is, salary, equipment and services and overheads.
- **Cost pool**: Aggregation of source costs into common groups for example, all salary and contractor costs may be accumulated into a single labour cost pool if all staff complete a common timesheet.
- **Cost object**: Programme deliverable, that is, products of the programme.
- **Specific cost**: cost incurred specifically for an identifiable cost object, for example, item of equipment purchased to be included in a deliverable.
- **Allocate cost**: Direct linkage of a source cost to a cost object, for example, allocation of the cost of a piece of equipment to the deliverable into which it is incorporated.
- **Cost driver**: Factors that link source cost to cost object, for example, the cost driver that links an individual salary cost to a deliverable is time spent working on each task, that is, timesheet information.
- **Apportion cost**: Assign costs from a cost pool or source cost using a cost driver, for example, assign all labour costs to deliverables based on timesheet analysis.

Figure 11.3 illustrates how these elements link together to produce costs for each cost object. It is important to recognize that the costs allocated to each cost object will need to be recalculated periodically throughout the programme lifecycle and so a repeatable, documented, process to undertake the exercise is required.

The key points in the programme lifecycle when the actual costs of deliverables should be compared against the expected benefits are:

- During the Define stage: Detail concerning source costs and cost drivers will not be fully developed at this early stage, but it is essential to establish costs and benefits as part of the business case.
- During the Establish stage: Here, as detailed plans are prepared and estimates become more reliable, deliverable costs should be regularly updated to ensure that expected surpluses of benefits over costs are maintained.
- During the Manage Programme stage: Output costs will need to be periodically updated to identify the impact of any expenditure variances on specific deliverables and benefits. These updates will incrementally replace

planned costs with actual costs incurred to date, thereby refining the expected cost of producing each deliverable. It is important to monitor the cost of each deliverable, as even while the overall programme may remain on budget, variations between types of expenditure can dramatically impact individual deliverable costs and therefore net benefits achievable.

- During the Close stage: A final calculation of deliverable costs to be compared to original estimates as part of the 'lessons learned' procedures.

As the programme progresses, the data used to identify the likely cost of each deliverable will migrate from being wholly estimates during the Define stage, to being wholly actual at the Programme Close stage.

11.7.2 CALCULATING THE COST OF DELIVERABLES

Calculating the actual costs of deliverables need not be difficult. Below the five steps needed to produce accurate and credible costs for each are outlined:

1. Collect and collate source costs into cost pools.
   All identified costs should be assigned to one or more cost pools. Common cost pools include:
   - labour – all labour costs to be apportioned using timesheet or activity data;
   - labour related services – costs other than labour that are also allocated based on timesheet, or activity data, for example, accommodation rental, office equipment rental;
   - specific costs – which can be directly allocated to deliverables;
   - travel and subsistence – allocated based on travel and subsistence returns;
   - organizational overheads – allocated to deliverables using the cost driver as used to allocate programme charge.
   See section 11.7.1 'Costing deliverables' for more guidance on cost pools.
2. Assemble cost driver data.
   Each cost pool, with the exception of specific costs, requires cost driver information to enable allocation of cost to deliverables. When identifying cost pools, as part of designing a costing approach, it is vitally important to ensure that cost driver information is available for each cost pool: it is no use aggregating all labour costs into a cost pool if no timesheet data is collected. Similarly, if staff and contractors complete different timesheets, processed through different systems, it may be more practical to establish two cost pools, one for each group. A further consideration is that cost driver information must be available on the same timetable as other accounting data. If accounting data is collected on the basis of each calendar month and timesheet data is collected

weekly, there will be reconciliation issues to resolve whenever months do not end on a weekend.

Detailed transaction data is assembled to provide cost drivers for each cost pool. Clearly this can only be accomplished if transaction data has been captured in a manner that enables costs to be allocated properly. For example, timesheets will need to provide analysis of team members' effort analysed directly to the deliverables worked or to the task undertaken. Ensuring that the data required is consistent and available is a key consideration of the design stage of a deliverable costing approach.

3. Allocate specific costs.

Specific costs are those costs with a clear linkage between the item procured and a programme deliverable. For example, if a new call centre is a programme capability and a call handling system a deliverable, then items of computer hardware and software that comprise the system would be clearly identified and directly allocated to the cost of the deliverable.

Specific costs will generally comprise higher value, purchased items, and can be allocated directly using information included in the deliverable definition and purchase order documentation. The period between ordering an item of equipment and its delivery, and hence payment may be very long. It is important to include full details of the item and its intended use in order documentation if confusion due to changes in programme team members, and so on, is to be avoided.

4. Apportion cost pools using cost driver data.

Cost driver data provides a mechanism to assign costs to deliverables. For example, using the breakdown of time provided by timesheet analysis, labour costs can be linked to the deliverables that have consumed the effort. Similarly, expenses such as travel and accommodation can be directly allocated by use of codes applied to individual expense claims.

Where no clear link exists between costs incurred and a deliverable, it will be necessary to establish a mechanism for apportioning these costs. Accommodation costs and charges for office space used by the programme teams cannot be directly allocated to deliverables, unless each one has its own dedicated space. More usually, team members will occupy space and work on a variety of deliverables. Accommodation costs are therefore normally allocated to deliverables in relation to labour cost, effectively as an additional cost of a team member. This is logical and generally will be regarded as equitable. There are no hard and fast rules for how cost allocations should be undertaken; the main requirement is that all stakeholders believe them to be effective and equitable in identifying the cost of deliverables.

Programme Financial Performance Report

Period Ended – 30 June 2005

Programme Number 1

Cost and Benefit Report

Ref: Project Title / Deliverable	Original budget	Latest budget	Spend to date	Committed cost	Planned cost	Completion cost	Completion variance	Benefits assigned Planned	Expected	Benefits return % Planned	Expected
P. 001 Project 1	375,000	400,000	350,000	75,000	50,000	475,000	-75,000	750,000	1,000,000	200%	210.5%
Deliverable 1 – 1	75,000	75,000	50,000	50,000	15,000	115,000	-40,000	150,000	250,000	200%	217.4%
Deliverable 1 – 2	35,000	45,000	45,000			45,000	0	50,000	70,000	143%	155.6%
Deliverable 1 – 3	225,000	255,000	230,000	25,000	35,000	290,000	-35,000	375,000	480,000	167%	165.5%
Deliverable 1 – 4	40,000	25,000	25,000			25,000	0	175,000	200,000	438%	800.0%
P. 002 Project 2	800,000	750,000	275,000	355,000	45,000	675,000	75,000	2,000,000	2,000,000	250%	296.3%
Deliverable 2 –1	500,000	450,000	160,000	205,000	40,000	405,000	45,000	1,200,000	1,200,000	240%	296.3%
Deliverable 2 – 2	200,000	200,000	85,000	100,000	5,000	190,000	10,000	450,000	450,000	225%	236.8%
Deliverable 2 – 3	100,000	100,000	30,000	50,000		80,000	20,000	350,000	350,000	350%	437.5%
P. 003 Project 3	900,000	950,000	175,000	25,000	1,300,000	1,500,000	-550,000	2,500,000	2,000,000	278%	133.3%
Deliverable 3 – 1	500,000	450,000	65,000	25,000	650,000	740,000	-290,000	1,500,000	1,200,000	300%	162.2%
Deliverable 3 – 2	100,000	200,000	45,000		250,000	295,000	-95,000	250,000	200,000	250%	67.8%
Deliverable 3 – 3	100,000	100,000	25,000		175,000	200,000	-100,000	250,000	150,000	250%	75.0%
Deliverable 3 – 4	100,000	100,000	25,000		125,000	150,000	-50,000	250,000	250,000	250%	166.7%
Deliverable 3 – 5	100,000	100,000	15,000		100,000	115,000	-15,000	250,000	200,000	250%	173.9%
P. 004 Project 4	1,250,000	1,250,000	875,000	125,000	200,000	1,200,000	50,000	3,250,000	4,000,000	260%	333.3%
Deliverable 4 – 1	1,000,000	1,000,000	750,000	75,000	135,000	960,000	40,000	2,500,000	3,000,000	250%	312.5%
Deliverable 4 – 2	250,000	250,000	125,000	50,000	65,000	240,000	10,000	750,000	1,000,000	300%	416.7%
P. 005 Project 5	850,000	825,000	350,000	25,000	500,000	875,000	-50,000	1,500,000	1,000,000	176%	114.3%
Deliverable 5 – 1	850,000	825,000	350,000	25,000	500,000	875,000	-50,000	1,500,000	1,000,000	176%	114.3%
Programme total	4,175,000	4,175,000	2,025,000	605,000	2,095,000	4,725,000	-550,000	10,000,000	10,000,000	240%	212%

Figure 11.5   Example periodic cost and benefit report

5. Calculate deliverable costs.

Once all costs have been allocated to deliverables, they can be added together to produce the total cost of each deliverable. The sum of the costs of all deliverables should equal the total of the programme. If this is not the case, then some element of cost has been omitted or duplicated. The programme board should periodically review the projected cost of each deliverable and thereby each capability, in conjunction with projected benefits, to ensure the continuing viability of each business case component.

Figure 11.5 shows an example of a periodic cost and benefit report of the type that may be used to inform stakeholders of the financial 'health' of the programme. As can be seen, the report contains information on both 'input costs', that is, labour, equipment and so on, and 'output costs' that is, deliverables and capabilities.

11.8 CERTAINTY OF COST

As discussed earlier in this chapter the cost estimates of a programme will evolve from estimates, indeed often 'guesstimates' at the outset of the Start-up stage, to actual costs at the Programme Close stage. As illustrated by the Scottish Parliament building example in Case Study 11.1, the difference between the two figures can be dramatic. Even allowing for failure to identify significant cost items such as land, the programme was more than 100 per cent overspent. Remarkably, this is not, according to research, an uncommon level of overspend. As the programme proceeds and cost estimates become more accurate, they often, unfortunately, increase. The latitude allowed to the programme to respond to these potential cost overruns will inevitably be constrained by not only the 'spend to date' but also the level of costs committed to but not yet spent. As explained in section 11.2 'Scope of programme accounting and financial control', there are three sets of cost figures for any element of the programme: spent costs, committed costs and planned costs.

Figure 11.6 illustrates how the level of commitment to expenditure changes through the programme lifecycle. In the early stages, the majority of cost is planned, that is, there is a budget but no commitment or expenditure; by the end everything is spent. In the interim, the programme moves through a process of committing and spending money.

The nature of programmes is that they continue over a long period and are subject to considerable change in the environment in which they operate. It is therefore safe to assume that during a typical multi-year programme, there will be changes in the approach taken and the activities planned to be undertaken. Given

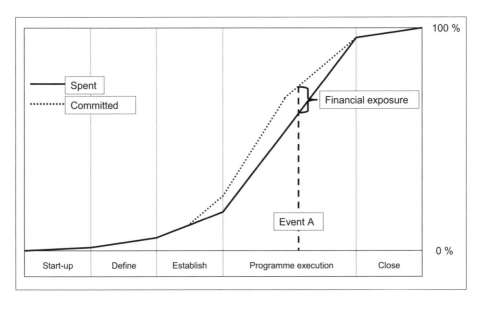

Figure 11.6   Spent, committed and planned costs

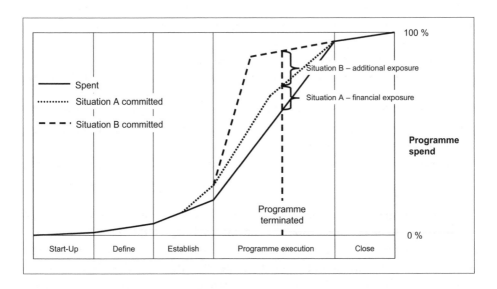

Figure 11.7   Spent, committed and planned costs – additional exposure

this uncertainty and change, it is important not to commit to any more cost than is absolutely necessary.

Figure 11.7 illustrates this point by showing two potential situations arising when a programme is terminated:

- In situation A, committed costs are greater than spent costs, but not significantly so. If the programme were terminated at this point all of the spent cost would be a loss; would be all the current committed, that is, the gap between the Spent and Situation A Committed lines.
- In Situation B, committed costs are running considerably ahead of expenditure. If the programme were terminated at this point all of the spent cost would be lost as would all the current committed, that is, the gap between the spent and Situation A committed lines.

Should a programme need to be terminated, or significant changes need to be made to its approach, the less costs committed in advance the better. However the nature of the programme may dictate that significant expenditures will need to be committed long before the goods or services are received and paid for. An example would be a programme with a significant element of bespoke equipment or construction, such as developing an oil field production environment. Here, much equipment will be 'purpose built' with long lead times and major elements of cost will be totally committed well in advance of payment and ultimate use. While this may be an extreme situation, it is often necessary for the programme to commit some costs in advance. The critical management decision is, 'How far forward is it safe to commit?' This question must always be answered in the context of the specific programme under consideration, but a good general rule is that costs should only be committed as far into the future as the programme has confidence that its planned approach will be undertaken. The multiple tranche approach recommended for use during the Programme Execution stage of the programme lifecycle supports the management of cost commitment by authorizing work packages for a period during which the stakeholders are confident the programme's approach will be maintained.

No one expects a programme to be summarily terminated. However, minimizing exposure to committed cost is an important risk mitigating action for any programme.

Collecting data in a format that enables analysis of spent, committed and planned cost to be achieved requires careful planning. Of the three classes, cost committed is usually the most difficult to ascertain. Planned costs can be derived from the programme budget and actual spend to date is a key element of the information collected by the organization's finance function and further analysed by the programme's finance team. Identifying committed cost is usually more complex as each team member who is authorized to spend on behalf of the programme will need to report all commitments made. In addition, when monies are spent, the appropriate commitment must be reduced to avoid double counting. In practice, the main area of committed cost, certainly by value, will involve purchased goods and services. While there may be some commitment to notice periods for team members, particularly contractors, this can usually be calculated once, for example, 1 month's cost for each individual, and rolled forward throughout the life of the programme. Large commitments for bought in goods and services will need to be logged and reclassified as spent when the expenditure is made.

There are computerized commitment accounting systems available on the market, but these may be appropriate only for very large programmes. A more typical approach is to require copies of all purchase orders to be forwarded to programme's finance team, who will maintain a log of open orders and their value. Maintaining a log of this kind enables a breakdown of the programme's costs to be produced using the relationship:

$$\begin{array}{cccc} \text{Expected cost} - & \text{Actual spend} - & \text{Committed but} = & \text{Planned but} \\ \text{to complete} & \text{to date} & \text{not spent} & \text{not committed} \end{array}$$

Whenever decisions that will significantly change a programme are being considered, it is important to remember that both spent and committed costs are no longer available to be reallocated to other priorities, that is, only the planned costs that are yet to be spent or committed are avoidable costs.

11.9 EARNED VALUE ANALYSIS

Traditional accounting and financial control is based on time periods. An organization's accounts are prepared for financial years; budgets are broken down into months, and reported monthly. The predominant question asked by senior management is: 'Is income and expenditure consistent with what we expected by this date?' If the organization is half way through the year, if it has earned half its planned revenue and spent half its planned expenditure then things are generally considered to be going well. This is somewhat simplistic, but in essence is how organizational budgetary control is structured. However, this approach is inappropriate for programme cost control where success depends on what has been achieved, not the time taken to achieve it. Most programme and project reporting identifies delays and most report cost to date. Very few link these two elements together to quantify and explain the impact of delays, or advances, on the cost performance of the programme. Earned value analysis (EVA) is a technique that makes this linkage.

EVA measures programme and project progress and quantifies the impact of both the time and efficiency of implementation on performance. EVA considers that for a programme or project to be over- or under-spending against its time-based budget, either:

- activities are being undertaken more or less efficiently than planned; and/or;
- activities are being completed sooner or later than originally planned.

These two effects can interact in complex ways to produce counterintuitive information and outcomes. Consider, for example, the two scenarios listed below.

- Scenario A: Activities require far greater resources than estimated (adverse cost variance) and progress on completing activities is much slower than planned (adverse schedule variance); altogether a poor situation, but it is entirely possible that due to lack of progress, cost reporting will indicate that less than budgeted cost has been expended (favourable total expenditure variance).
- Scenario B: Activities require less resource than estimated (favourable cost variance) and progress on completing activities is faster than planned (favourable schedule variance); an excellent situation, except that because work not yet scheduled is being undertaken, the overall cost variance will likely be adverse, even allowing for the favourable cost variance.

Separating out and quantifying these two elements, cost (efficiency) and schedule provides a much clearer understanding of the status of the programme or of its component projects.

A simple example should help to illustrate how EVA achieves this. Consider two programmes, each with a budget of £10 million pounds, each planned to run for 2 years, and each reporting its financial position after 6 months. Programme A has expenditure to date of £2 million versus a budget of £2.5 million, while programme B has expenditure of £3.5 million versus an identical budget. Which programme is doing well, which badly?

Traditional budgetary control and financial reporting would indicate that programme A is ahead of budget by £500 000 while programme B is overspent by £1 million. This would typically lead to programme A being praised and told to 'carry on the good work' while programme B would be admonished to 'cut costs'. The reality of the situation is that without additional information it is impossible to say which programme is performing well or less well. The additional information required relates to the work that each programme has completed. If we knew that programme A had completed only 15 per cent of its work due to delays and staffing problems, while Programme B had completed 45 per cent of its work helped by favourable weather conditions and early availability of key staff, a different opinion would emerge.

This revised assessment is set out in the table in Table 11.1 below.

Table 11.1   Comparison of two sample projects

Programme	Duration	Budget to Date	Work Completed	Earned Value	Spend to Date	Variance
A	24 Months	£2,500 k	15%	£1,500 k	£ 2,000 k	£ 500 k [Adverse]
B	24 Months	£2,500 k	45%	£ 4,500 k	£ 3,500 k	£ 1,000 k [Favourable]

While this example is simplistic, it illustrates the limitations of a purely time-based view of financial progress and shows how EVA can provide a clearer explanation of what is occurring.

EVA has a tradition and background in government and military procurement programmes, especially in the United States. Complex rules defined for use in this often confrontational, 'cost plus' environment has led to a general belief that EVA is complex and bureaucratic to operate. This need not be the case. If the main principles of EVA are applied without the complex rules that have been applied by some government agencies, the technique can provide insightful information concerning the financial and general well-being of a programme and its component projects.

EVA brings quantification to assessments of project, and therefore programme, schedule and cost performance. It does this by establishing a clear scope and detailed breakdown of what needs to be achieved. It then monitors achievement against this baseline in a disciplined manner. Experience from the United States (Fleming and Koppleman, 2000) indicates that reliable indications of performance and out-turn can be derived once a project or deliverable has completed 15–20 per cent of its planned work. The process required to enable EVA is entirely consistent with the one advocated throughout this handbook for the development and management of a robust programme plan.

Figure 11.8 provides an illustration of a programme cost and benefit report containing the key elements of earned value reporting.

A worked example of the use of EVA can be found in Case Study 11.2.

447

Programme Financial Performance Report

Programme Number 1   Period Ended – 30 June 2005

Financial Performance

Ref:	Project title	Original budget	Latest budget	Budget change	Budget to date	Spend to date	Variance to date	Committed cost	Committed + spend cost	Committed + spend %	ECC index
P. 001	Project 1	375,000	400,000	-25,000	400,000	350,000	50,000	75,000	425,000	106%	120%
P. 002	Project 2	800,000	750,000	50,000	250,000	275,000	-25,000	355,000	630,000	84%	84%
P. 003	Project 3	900,000	950,000	-50,000	150,000	175,000	-25,000	25,000	200,000	21%	154%
P. 004	Project 4	1,250,000	1,250,000	0	675,000	875,000	-200,000	125,000	1,000,000	80%	106%
P. 005	Project 5	850,000	825,000	25,000	325,000	350,000	-25,000	25,000	375,000	45%	105%
	Programme total	4,175,000	4,175,000	0	1,800,000	2,025,000	-225,000	605,000	2,630,000	63%	114%

Earned Value Performance

Ref:	Project title	% Work planned	% Work completed	Planned value	Earned value	Variances Schedule	Variances Cost	Performance indices CPI	SPI	ECC From	ECC To
P. 001	Project 1	100.0%	81.3%	400,000	325,000	75,000	-25,000	92.9%	81.3%	430,769	530,178
P. 002	Project 2	33.3%	40.0%	250,000	300,000	-50,000	25,000	109.1%	120.0%	687,500	572,917
P. 003	Project 3	15.8%	13.2%	150,000	125,000	25,000	-50,000	71.4%	83.3%	1,330,000	1,596,000
P. 004	Project 4	54.0%	62.0%	675,000	775,000	-100,000	-100,000	88.6%	114.8%	1,411,290	1,229,188
P. 005	Project 5	39.4%	40.0%	325,000	330,000	-5,000	-20,000	94.3%	101.5%	875,000	861,742
	Programme total	43.1%	81.3%	1,800,000	1,855,000	-55,000	-170,000	91.6%	103.1%	4,734,560	4,790,025

Figure 11.8   Example programme cost and benefit report

CASE STUDY 11.2: EARNED VALUE ANALYSIS EXAMPLE

GENERAL PRINCIPLES

The first step to establishing an EVA regime is to clearly define the programme's scope. EVA texts, such as Fleming and Koppleman (2000) recommend starting by developing a work breakdown structure (WBS) for each component project within the programme as a means of identifying all of the work to be undertaken. Alternatively a product breakdown structure as recommended by the PRINCE2 method provides an alternative approach to defining the scope of the component projects. Whatever approach is used, once the deliverables (or products) have been identified, documented and agreed and the activities required to produce each one identified, resources can be estimated and timings planned. Only with a detailed analysis of the work to be done, the effort and therefore cost to complete it, and a timetable for when each activity will be completed, can an EVA approach be undertaken. In addition, progress reporting, at the activity level, is required, indicating when activities commence, the degree to which they are complete, and their expected completion date. Equipped with this information programme managers can quantify and therefore report, the following:

- **Estimated Cost to Complete (ECC)**: How much the programme is planned to cost to deliver. Derived from the total planned work and the planned cost of work.
- **Planned value (PV)**: The value of work planned to be completed at any point in time. Derived from planned work (to date) and the planned cost of work.
- **Earned value (EV)**: The value of work completed at any point in time. Derived from actual work (completed to date) and the planned cost of work.
- **Actual cost (AC)**: The cost expended and/or committed to date. Derived from the cost collection and analysis processes described earlier.

These four components provide the building blocks that a programme manager can utilize to report progress and cost performance for all projects within the programme.

Figure 11.9 sets out information about an example project with three specific deliverables. A programme would comprise a number of projects but one is sufficient to illustrate the use of EVA.

This project has three deliverables and runs for the duration of 2005 during which time 2100 days of activity are planned to have been undertaken at a final cost of £2.1 million. As at the reporting date, 800 days were planned in total to be completed but only 750 have been. For simplicity of this example, each day's work on the project is assumed to cost £1000. To calculate the EVA variances, two values

449

Project Status Report – 30th June 2005	Project 1			
	Deliverable 1A	Deliverable 1B	Deliverable 1C	Total
Start date	01-Jan-05	01-May-05	01-Jun-05	01-Jan-05
End date	30-Jun-05	30-Nov-05	20-Dec-05	20-Dec-05
Total work (days)	400	750	950	2,100
Planned work – to date (days)	400	250	150	800
Completed work – to date (days)	325	300	125	750
Cost per day	£1,000	£1,000	£1,000	£1,000
Estimate to complete	£400,000	£750,000	£950,000	£2,100,000

Figure 11.9   General information for Project 1

must be calculated, PV and EV, while a third, AC, must be extracted from the financial records of the project. Equipped with this information the programme manager can proceed to calculate EVA cost and schedule variances.

Figure 11.10 shows the calculation of PV and EV for Project 1 together with AC to date.

Project Status Report – 30th June 2005	Project 1			
	Deliverable 1A	Deliverable 1B	Deliverable 1C	Total
Planned value (PV) to date	£400,000	£250,000	£150,000	£800,000
Earned value (EV) to date	£325,000	£300,000	£125,000	£750,000
Actual expenditure (AC) to date	£350,000	£275,000	£175,000	£800,000

Figure 11.10   PV, EV and actual expenditure for Project 1

Overall, Project 1 has spent £800 000, exactly the sum authorized in its time based budget. Without the additional information provided by EVA, the programme manager might decide that all is well and take no action. However, the project has only achieved £750 000 of value.

EV VARIANCES AND WHAT THEY MEAN

As can be seen from the data in Figure 11.10, there are several things going on at once within each deliverable, which is making it difficult to evaluate their performance. More or less costs are being incurred than planned to complete activities, and more or less activities are being completed than was planned. EVA isolates these, potentially confusing effects into two variances:

- **Schedule variance (SV)**: the difference between planned and completed work, that is:

$$SV = PV - EV$$

Project Status Report – 30th June 2005	Project 1			
	Deliverable 1A	Deliverable 1B	Deliverable 1C	Total
Cost variance (CV)	-£25,000	£25,000	-£50,000	-£50,000
Schedule variance (SV)	£75,000	-£50,000	£25,000	£50,000
Total variance (TV)	£50,000	-£25,000	-£25,000	£0

Figure 11.11   SV and CV for Project 1

- **Cost variance (CV)**: the difference between the planned cost to achieve the completed work and the AC, that is:

$$CV = EV - AC$$

The sum of these two variances is the total variance (TV), which is equal to the traditional budget variance. Figure 11.11 shows SV and CV for the example project. As can be seen, a different picture emerges from this EVA. Deliverable 1A, which is well under budget by conventional thinking, is now shown to be both overspending by £25 000 and behind schedule to a value of £75 000, with the schedule effect completely masking the cost overspend. Conversely, deliverable 1B's traditionally measured overspend is actually a function of better than planned progress combined with efficiency improvements. Deliverable 1B may be overspent by traditional measures, but is in fact making excellent progress.

USING EV TO MANAGE PROGRAMME FINANCES

To further illustrate and communicate the status of projects and their component parts, EVA utilizes two Performance Indexes:

- **Cost performance index (CPI)**: the ratio of EV to AC, that is:

$$CPI = EV/AC$$

- **Schedule performance index (SPI)**: the ratio of EV to PV, that is:

$$SPI = EV/PV$$

An aggregate performance index (API) can also be derived by multiplying CPI and SPI. This API provides a single measure of the effectiveness with which the project is converting resources into deliverables relative to the plan. An index value greater than 1 indicates progress ahead of plan, less than 1, behind. Figure 11.12 shows performance indices for the three example project deliverables.

451

Project Status Report – 30th June 2005	Project 1			
	Deliverable 1A	Deliverable 1B	Deliverable 1C	Total
Cost performance index (CPI)	92.9%	109.1%	71.4%	93.8%
Schedule performance index (SPI)	81.3%	120.0%	83.3%	93.8%
Aggregate performance index (API)	75.4%	130.9%	59.5%	87.9%

Figure 11.12   Performance indexes for Project 1

The information in Figure 11.12 indicates that Project 1 is converting resources into deliverables, approximately 88 per cent as effectively as planned. Deliverable 1B is being produced significantly more effectively than planned, while deliverable 1C is consuming nearly twice as much resource as planned.

PREDICTING ECC

If there is one piece of information a programme manager wants and needs more than any other it must be the ultimate, total cost of the programme, that is, the ECC. With such a figure available throughout the life of the programme, many decisions would become much simpler. Sadly, this is never going to happen, at least not with complete certainty. However, by developing a structured and detailed cost plan, updating it regularly as new information becomes available and reporting regularly to all stakeholders, a working approximation can be maintained. One difficulty with this approach is that refreshing cost estimates for a large programme is a time-consuming and expensive procedure. Refreshing full cost estimates can only realistically be undertaken maybe every 3, but more likely every 6 months. How, then, can a programme manager ensure that significant events do not occur between cost updates that may lead to a change in ECC?

EVA provides mechanisms that, while not providing a 100 per cent accurate forecast, can indicate changes in potential ECC:

- Dividing the current baseline ECC, that is, the one against which all performance measures have been calculated, by the CPI provides an indication of the likely cost of the programme, assuming current cost effectiveness is maintained.
- Dividing ECC by the API indicates likely cost assuming overall programme effectiveness is maintained. The use of the API assumes that time delays or gains translate directly into cost increases or savings. This is not always the case and so the API-based ECC is generally regarded as an extreme estimate.

The two estimates are normally used together to create a range of potential ECC. Figure 11.13 shows the ECC range for Project 1

Project Status Report – 30th June 2005	Project 1			
	Deliverable 1A	Deliverable 1B	Deliverable 1C	Total
Estimated cost to complete (CPI)	£430,769	£687,500	£1,330,000	£2,240,000
Estimated cost to complete (API)	£530,178	£572,917	£1,596,000	£2,389,333
Cost to complete (original)	£400,000	£750,000	£950,000	£2,100,000

Figure 11.13   ECC for Project 1

These calculations indicate that Project 1 will probably cost somewhere between £2.25 million and £2.40 million to complete as against the £2.10 million originally budgeted. This may not be sufficiently scientific to extract further funds from the organization immediately, but tracking these values each month and using them to challenge future cost estimate updates will provide a useful indication of cost trends.

11.10 PROGRAMME EVENTS REQUIRING ACCOUNTING AND FINANCIAL CONTROL INFORMATION

In addition to periodic updating and reporting to stakeholders on the financial well-being of the programme, financial management information and expertise will be required to provide 'ad hoc' information to help manage key events in the life of a programme. It is impossible to predict the precise programme events that will occur throughout a programme's lifetime, or the information required to address them. However, if finance data is maintained that identifies major categories of expenditure, levels of cost commitment and the cost of deliverables, the programme will be well equipped to meet these challenges.

Examples of the types of programme events that may occur and the types of financial information that will be required are listed in the sub-sections below.

11.10.1 COST OVER RUNS; PROSPECTIVE OR ACTUAL

When the programme out-turn cost, or ECC, is predicted to exceed its budget, cost data will be used to evaluate options and select the most cost effective manner for costs to be brought back into tolerance. Questions asked in such a review will typically include:

- How extensive is the expected/actual overspend?
- What category(s) of spend is predicted to exceed budget?
- Which deliverables are expected to exceed planned cost?

453

- What level of uncommitted cost is available to redirect or reduce?
- What, if any, underspends exist within the programme that may offset this overspend?
- What impact will this overspend have on the programme business case?
- What is the impact on cost of any corrective actions identified?

11.10.2 SCOPE CHANGES: ASSESSMENT AND EVALUATION

Scope changes almost always impact the budgeted cost of a programme. If the programme is asked to extend its scope, for example by involving more users or rolling out in more countries, the chances are the cost will rise. Likewise, scope reductions should lead to cost reductions. Evaluation of potential changes to scope benefits greatly from the availability of deliverable costs. By utilizing previously calculated costs for each programme deliverable, scope changes can be quickly and effectively evaluated. Where the change in scope involves producing more, or less, of an existing deliverable, for example, when adding an additional country to an international systems roll-out, the calculated cost for the existing deliverable provides an excellent starting point. Adjustments may be required for differences in scale, and so on, but a basis for estimation is provided. In the simplest example, costing the addition of another location may involve taking the cost of each deliverable required, as currently calculated, and adding this to the current budget.

Questions to be addressed when evaluating scope changes include:

- Is the scope change a matter of producing more (or less) of current deliverables, or are entirely new deliverables required?
- How different in scale, if at all, are the change request deliverables from those currently planned?
- How will changes in deliverable scale impact on cost?
- For scope changes that require new deliverables, what information concerning existing deliverables can be used to assist cost estimation?

If costing of programme deliverables has not been undertaken, estimating the cost impacts of change requests is considerably more difficult. For a programme that has a large number of change requests to evaluate because it is operating in a highly uncertain environment, the benefits of a full understanding of deliverable costs can be significant in saved time and programme cost.

Further guidance on managing changes to scope can be found in Chapter 12, 'Management of scope and change'.

11.10.3 ALTERNATIVE METHODS AND APPROACHES TO ACHIEVING OUTCOMES

It is inevitable that, during the lifetime of a programme anticipated methods of developing deliverables and achieving objectives will be subject to change. Over time, circumstances will change and new technologies and techniques may become available, which may lead to a re-evaluation of how activities are best carried out.

The work required would be similar to that required when costing change requests. Indeed method changes can be considered to be a form of change request, and should result in a change/no change evaluation. Evaluating method changes is usually less complex than other forms of change request as there is little or no impact on the benefits delivered by the programme.

11.10.4 NON ACHIEVEMENT OF BENEFITS

If it becomes evident that an expected benefit will either not be delivered or will be diminished, it will be necessary to consider whether this invalidates the programme's business case, making it necessary to terminate or modify work required to achieve it. The important calculation is whether the programme is still capable of delivering a net positive benefit. That is, over the evaluation period (normally specified by organizational policy) do the benefits outweigh the costs of delivery?

If, despite a reduction, the programme's benefits were still deemed to be greater than the costs achieving them, it would be rational to continue with the programme. Alternatively a reduction in the likely benefits might mean that other programmes or projects, currently not being pursued, might make better investments. The original calculation of deliverable costs and the maintenance of best estimate out-turn costs for each deliverable provides key information for the evaluation of the relationship between cost and benefit.

Questions to be addressed when evaluating the likely achievement or not of benefits include:

- Are the expected benefits (still) deemed to be greater than the cost of delivering them?
- If the net benefits are still positive, are they still sufficient to warrant continuing to pursue them?
- What can be done to reduce the cost of acquiring these benefits to return them to a net positive contribution?

11.10.5 CHANGING PRIORITIES

As an organization's priorities change over the lifetime of a programme, its focus and priorities may need to change. Changes to priority will impact the order in which the programme undertakes elements of its work together with the timing and value of benefits realized and costs incurred.

The establishment of detailed cost analysis and deliverable costs and their use in the financial planning and modelling of the programme will enable the programme team to respond to the inevitable requests to evaluate new options and approaches.

Questions to be addressed when evaluating changing priorities include:

- Are the quantity or quality of deliverables to be changed or just their timing?
- Do the proposed changes impact the cost of producing other deliverables, and to what extent?
- What impact on the timing of costs and benefits will a re-prioritization have?
- What impact on programme costs and benefits will a re-prioritization have?

Changing the priorities driving a programme can have profound impacts, effectively changing the whole approach. Effective analysis and decision making requires the programme team to be able to model various scenarios based on detailed understanding of costs and benefits.

11.11 PROGRAMME ACCOUNTING AND FINANCIAL CONTROL THROUGH THE LIFECYCLE

Each stage in the programme lifecycle has differing requirements and priorities. While the tools and techniques discussed in this section have applications throughout, the significance of each changes as the programme proceeds. The following sections describe the key activities required at every stage of the lifecycle and provide guidance on what needs to be achieved during each one. The full lifecycle is described in detail in section Chapter 2, 'The programme management process'.

11.11.1 START-UP STAGE

The purpose of the Start-up stage is to evaluate if the proposed programme is worth pursuing and therefore justifies an initial investment to develop an approach and plan (that is, proceed to Define stage).

Upon completion of the Start-up stage, the organization must decide if resources, time and money are to be committed to a full evaluation of the costs and benefits of the programme. As a result, the Start-up stage should be relatively short and focus on developing a high-level business case for the proposed programme, together with more detailed estimates of the work required to complete the next stage, Define Programme.

The Start-up stage is designed to answer the question: 'Is this programme worth an investment of resources to define it, or should it be discarded now?' Cost information to help answer this question, plus estimates of the cost of undertaking a Define Programme stage will be estimated. To provide this information, a range of accounting and financial control tasks will need to be undertaken, as described in the following sections.

11.11.1.1 Estimate programme costs

It is always a challenge to strike the correct balance between too much and too little detail when attempting to define the broad outline of a prospective programme. Too little detail and a completely unachievable programme may be moved forward to the Define Programme stage, too much and disproportionate cost will be expended before any management scrutiny takes place. The critical point is that estimates from the Start-up stage only commit the organization to fund the next stage (Define) of the programme; errors in detail can be corrected at the next stage. While it is important not to 'over engineer' estimates at this point, it is still necessary to develop cost estimates in a clear and structured manner. The initial cost estimates will form a central element in the justification of the programme and will therefore be subject, quite correctly, to significant scrutiny.

Application of four principles will help ensure that this scrutiny can be faced with confidence:

- Use a small number of broad cost categories: Rather than attempt to quantify each individual cost element that will eventually be incurred by the programme, better at this stage to use a smaller number of broad categories. For example, a programme may eventually involve six grades of software engineer, three levels of project managers, plus numerous other skills, both employees and contractors. Because of the prevailing uncertainty at this stage it is best to establish a small number of cost bands, for example, one average for all software engineers, and use this in early estimates. This approach reduces both the number of cost categories in the initial calculation and does away with the entirely spurious impression of accuracy that a more detailed calculation confers.
- Use estimates based on prior experience or established 'rules of thumb', and

so on. If the organization has experience of implementing elements of the proposed programme, cost information from these prior programmes and projects can be of great assistance. Even if prior experience does not relate to identical situations, good estimates can be extrapolated from past experience. It is also possible to select individual elements of the programme and apply 'benchmark' costs to help build up total programme cost. Benchmark costs often exist in organizations or can be acquired from consultants and other third parties.

These examples are illustrative only but are typical of the knowledge held, often only in individuals' heads, within organizations. These benchmarks and 'rules of thumb' should be fully considered when calculating early estimates of programme cost either to identify prospective costs or to validate estimates built up by other means. Even where the programme team rejects a specific benchmark as inappropriate, the programme board should be comforted that previous experience has been fully considered. In the construction industry, average building costs per square metre are well known and enable initial estimates to be calculated and verified quickly.

- Identify and document all assumptions underpinning values. The cost calculated at this stage will almost certainly be the least accurate estimate that will be made throughout the programme. As estimates of cost change, it is important to ensure that the reasons for change are traceable. No one should be blamed for a misassumption in an early estimate, but when it comes to light it is important to understand how it will impact the overall cost of the programme. In the example quoted earlier from the Scottish Parliament Building, the public enquiry identified that the costs of critical items such as the purchase of land were not included in the original estimate (see Case Study 11.1)

  It is important therefore to document all assumptions made in arriving at initial cost estimates. It is also important that an assumptions log be created at this time and updated every time the programme costs are reviewed and/or revised. An assumption included in the cost estimate of a programme may be that an existing business process and supporting system will be re-used, at relatively little cost. When it later transpires that due to differences in operation procedures, an entirely new process and system are required, the cost implications may be significant. Programme managers need to know these critical assumptions so that as and when they change, or are threatened with change; their impact on the programme business case can be fully evaluated.

- Identify programme and project management costs separately. Project and programme management costs are best estimated as separate elements of the programme cost. This is because these costs relate to the overall scale of the programme and are often substantially 'fixed', that is, they tend not to change except in response to major changes in the programme, such as duration. If, as is often the case, these costs are estimated as a percentage add-on to the programme costs, for example 10 per cent added on to the estimated cost of developing the programme deliverables, there is a risk that future changes in total cost will adversely impact programme management resources. Identifying and estimating these costs separately, even at this early stage is also important in identifying the programme and project management 'overhead', often a contentious and emotive topic.

11.11.1.2 Estimate BAU costs

BAU costs will often be a critical component of the programme's business case. Frequently, the cost of operating the organization, both before and after the changes delivered by the programme, will be a central factor in deciding whether or not to continue with the programme. When estimating these before and after costs, the same principles as those suggested for programme costs should apply that is:

- broad cost categories
- estimates based on prior experience
- clear assumptions.

Members of the programme board and of the organization's senior management will usually need to be involved in these estimates, both to ensure their validity and, more importantly, as the first step in taking responsibility for delivery of the ultimate benefits.

However, it should always be born in mind that many desirable business benefits can never be expressed in monetary terms and beneficial changes to the before and after BAU costs will rarely be the sole justification for a programme. Further guidance on determining the likely benefits of a programme can be found in Chapter 5 'Benefits management'.

11.11.1.3 Report stage costs

Funding to undertake the Start-up stage of a programme will normally be provided from either a specific budget maintained by the organization as a whole or from the budgets of the departments that are most likely to benefit. As there is no programme to fund until the business case and approach developed during this stage has been adopted, programme-specific funds are not usually assigned. Reporting on costs incurred during the stage itself, therefore, will vary depending on the specific arrangements that apply within the host organization. Commonly, a fixed sum will be assigned to the team undertaking the Start-up stage to enable then to complete their work. The programme manager should expect to keep time and expenditure records for the team, most commonly to report to the budget holder providing the funds. The key financial performance objective is to produce the Start-up stage deliverables within the cost budget assigned.

11.11.1.4 Estimate tolerances

It is usual to set cost tolerances within which project and programme estimates are required to fall. Estimating tolerances represents the range of values, usually above and below the estimated costs, within which the ultimate result is expected to fall. The range about the estimate is usually expressed in terms of; 'plus or minus 25 per cent' or less commonly 'plus 25 per cent, minus 10 per cent, the first indicating a possible range of £750 000 to £1 250 000 for a programme with £1 000 000 estimate, the second a range of £900 000 to £1 250 000.

It is clearly the case that the earlier in the programme lifecycle the estimate is made, the less likely it is to exactly predict the eventual cost incurred. For this reason, it is common for the target range of estimating tolerances to be narrowed as the programme progresses through its lifecycle. So, while a tolerance range of plus or minus 25 per cent may be set at the Define Programme stage, plus or minus 10 per cent may be required for estimates undertaken during the Manage Programme stage.

Organizations with experience of managing many, similar, programmes and projects can possibly identify with some certainty that at a given point in the lifecycle costs will be within plus or minus X per cent. Others facing a completely new challenge may have no clear idea of the accuracy of their estimates at any given point. Targets set and management responses to future over-, or under-spends, should reflect the degree of certainty realistically capable of being applied to tolerances at any time. If information is not available to produce a narrow tolerance band, even though one is demanded by organizational policy or senior management decree, the result is likely to be an estimated packed with hidden contingencies. It is in the interest of realistic and traceable estimating to always attempt to produce a 'best endeavours' estimate, reflecting currently available information as well as possible.

11.11.2 DEFINE PROGRAMME STAGE

During this stage, the programme team will refine its approach and develop plans to deliver the required benefits. This will enable the programme board to decide if the programme should proceed to the Establish Programme stage. The Start-up stage should have been relatively short and focused on developing estimates of the work required to complete the Define Programme stage. This stage should in turn address the question: 'What benefits will the programme deliver, how will they be achieved and what will it all cost?' Output from the stage will include an overall programme plan and business case, plus detailed plans for the initial set of component projects to be undertaken.

11.11.2.1 Reassess programme costs

Prior to the Define Programme stage, estimates will only have been made at a high level and broad assumptions are used to produce an acceptable level of accuracy in a relatively short period of time. During the Define Programme stage, these assumptions and estimates will be reassessed to provide a more complete and accurate cost projection. The Define stage plan, prepared during the previous stage, should have provided resources with the skills and experience to undertake the appropriate level of cost estimation, as well as defining the tasks to be undertaken. Updating and enhancing cost estimates during this stage will include the following activities:

- Whereas original estimates were made using benchmarks and other broad estimating approaches, all available information needs to be utilized in the Define stage. The decision to be made at the end of this stage may commit the organization to substantial cost. Now is the time to ensure that cost estimates are as reliable as practical.

  Two areas likely to account for a major proportion of the total programme cost are team members and purchased equipment. Team member costs are a function of the amount of work to be undertaken, that is, the number of days to be worked, while purchased costs reflect suppliers' costs to supply. In the case of organizational change and IT-based programmes, these two areas will often cover in the region of 80 per cent of the total programme cost and should therefore be the focus of activity. Ideally, multiple suppliers should be approached with draft specifications of the products or services required and quotations sought. The lowest cost bidder should not necessarily be assumed as other important decision factors will apply when supplier selection takes place. Also, it is not to be assumed that the supplier whose price is used at this stage will necessarily win the work. The objective at this stage is to create a realistic cost estimate. Estimates of the required amount of work will usually be derived by working with prospective internal and external providers of resources and skills to identify the skills and effort needed to complete the defined tasks.

461

- Having identified in greater detail the resources and skills required to undertake the programme, specific staff grades and cost rates can now be applied to provide a more accurate picture of staff costs. This step can only be properly undertaken when a full understanding of the work to be carried out has been achieved.
- While the members of the programme team assigned to work on the financial estimates are collating additional information from suppliers and others, the wider team will have been refining the programme approach and plan. As these elements come together, a far more complete and robust set of financial cost estimates will emerge. In the light of this, all previous assumptions and estimates should be reviewed and revised to ensure that they reflect how the programme is currently planned to be undertaken.

11.11.2.2 Reassess likely benefits and BAU costs

In addition to upgrading estimates for the cost of delivering the programme, the team will probably also be given the task of reviewing the estimates for the likely benefits to be achieved from the programme, which may require estimated costs of BAU to be upgraded. Exactly what needs to be estimated and calculated will depend upon the specific nature of the changes planned and the benefits anticipated. However, the programme team will typically be required to work closely with the business owners of the affected areas, that is, systems and processes, so as to quantify the impact of the programme on the organization's cost of operation. The steps to be undertaken may include:

- Agree areas, that is, processes and systems, impacted by the programme.
- Describe the current situation and ways of working for the areas identified.
- Establish current cost baseline for affected areas, allowing for future growth and other known changes.
- Calculate projected cost baseline at programme implementation date.
- Describe and document planned programme changes.
- Define and agree cost and resource levels required to operate post programme.
- Calculate post-programme BAU costs, and cost change (from baseline).
- Communicate BAU costs to business process owners and the organization's finance function for inclusion in future business plans and budgets.

The objective of this review is to calculate likely benefits, which may include the changes to BAU costs, in a sufficiently robust manner to support a decision by the programme board on whether or not to proceed with the programme.

11.11.2.3 Agree accounting and financial control procedures

All accounting and financial control processes for the programme must be agreed with the organization's finance function. During the Define stage, reporting timetables and information to be provided, both to and by the programme, should be agreed to ensure that requirements are practical and will not require significant additional investment or ongoing cost to fulfil. If specific, potentially costly, arrangements are required, these should be factored into any programme cost estimates produced. Also at this stage it is important to consider the structure to be used to construct the programme cost budget. Once a significant expenditure is incurred and recorded using one structure, it can be very difficult to change. Therefore, it makes sense to ensure that the correct reporting structure is used from the start. Some common principles should be applied:

- Programmes and projects have a hierarchical relationship that should be reflected in data gathering and reporting, that is, programmes are comprised of projects, which in turn are comprised of work packages.
- A common structure of cost categories and elements, that is, types of expenditure, should be established and used for all constituent projects. Not every project will incur expenditure of every type, that is, some projects may have no purchase equipment while others have significant expenditure, some may use all own staff, others all contractors. Nevertheless a common set of expenditure categories and elements should be defined and included in templates used to estimate individual projects, and sub-projects where appropriate. Adopting this approach, it is possible that the project cost estimation spreadsheet may have a number of blank rows or zeros; however, there are two advantages:
  - Future changes in approach can be reflected in the cost estimate without disrupting the costing spreadsheet. Note: programme and project estimating are mostly undertaken using spreadsheets.
  - Project costs can be consolidated into programme estimates using common templates. This is a largely administrative concern, but the effort required to maintain and consolidate multiple formats of project estimate is significant and wasteful.

  The duration and complexity of a typical change programme means that the detail of plans and costs are likely to change during the lifecycle. Development of a cost structure capable of accommodating future extensions and changes will greatly reduce rework later in the programme.

463

11.11.2.4 Report stage costs

Activities undertaken during Define Programme stage will normally be funded by the allocation of a specific budget agreed as part of the completion of the Start-up stage. The costs for the Define Programme stage will need to be reported to the programme board, plus others concerned with the financial management of the organization. It is not usually necessary to establish as sophisticated a level of cost reporting as will be required during the later stages of the programme; however, some straightforward, periodic reports of expenditure versus plan will be required.

11.11.2.5 Review tolerances

It is common practice to establish estimating tolerance levels for the programme's cost estimates, which are reviewed and progressively narrowed as the programme proceeds through the lifecycle and uncertainty is reduced. What is most important is that the programme team, the organization's finance community and programme board or other members of the senior management agree estimating tolerances prior to commencement of each stage in the programme lifecycle. Applying arbitrary, unduly restrictive tolerances and targets on the programme team at an early stage can have a long-term detrimental effect as over-optimistic assumptions are made and justified to fit within target costs. The problems will only emerge much later when, with the programme well under way the true costs emerge and the shortfall of allocated funds curtails progress. What is required at this stage is the most realistic estimate possible, so that the programme board can make a rational 'go/no-go' decision while sunk costs are at a minimum. Highly restrictive cost guidelines and tolerances tend to encourage 'padding' of estimates and are very unhelpful at this stage.

11.11.3 ESTABLISH PROGRAMME STAGE

The Define Programme stage has concluded with an agreement to proceed with the programme; if any other decision is taken there is no need for the Establish Programme stage. This stage 'establishes' the processes and infrastructure the programme will require to be successful. Any organization needs some degree of management process if it is to operate effectively; the key requirement is to design and implement just enough control to ensure success without incurring a heavy penalty of non-value added work.

11.11.3.1 Refine programme costs

Programme costs will continue to be refined during this stage, with the main focus on the activities included in the initial set of component of projects. As more detailed plans are developed for these projects, the related cost estimates will need to be amended to reflect updated assumptions. If detailed planning of the component projects indicates a significant change in the cost of undertaking the programme, sufficient to potentially breach the agreed estimating tolerances, this should be raised immediately with the programme board. A decision whether to terminate the programme or establish a higher level of funding will be required before further work is undertaken.

BAU costs will not typically be formally reviewed and updated during this stage. If new information becomes available that potentially impacts the programme's business case, this should, of course, be communicated to the programme board.

11.11.3.2 Establish accounting and financial control procedures

Establishing appropriate financial controls and procedures is a key task during the Establish Programme stage. Prior to this stage, agreement will have been reached with the organization's senior management and finance function as to what information is required, when and in what format. During the Establish Programme stage, procedures will be put in place to ensure delivery of the agreed information and undertake all necessary financial control procedures. Some of these procedures will be highly influenced, or even mandated, by the organization, as they will be required to link to existing, well-established, control procedures. Other procedures may be entirely new to the organization, if, for instance, a programme of this scale has not previously been undertaken, and greater flexibility may be possible. It is vital that the organization's finance functions are fully satisfied with all arrangements prior to commencement of reporting. This may also involve approval from an independent internal audit function and even approval from the external auditors in the case of very significant programmes. The organization's finance director or senior financial officer should be able to provide guidance on all of these matters.

In order to undertake the agreed programme accounting and financial control procedures the programme is likely to require skilled resources, probably within the programme office team. Depending on the size of the programme and the sophistication of accounting systems available, resource requirements may vary from a part of an individual's role to a several person dedicated team. It is important to identify the work to be undertaken prior to staffing the programme office team. Appointing a programme accountant prior to fully defining the role

465

may result in a serious mismatch of work to be done and resource to undertake it.

11.11.3.3 Report stage costs

Actual expenditures will accelerate during this stage, as the programme team begins to grow and substantial elements of work are undertaken. While the genuine work of the programme will not have commenced, the effort required to establish infrastructure and facilities can be significant. Now that the organization has committed to the programme, reporting Establish stage costs becomes the starting point for full programme accounting and financial control. To this end, all costs incurred and committed during this stage should be reported using the formats and timetables agreed for the programme.

Estimates are not typically reassessed during this stage and so tolerances will generally remain unchanged from the Define stage.

11.11.4 MANAGE PROGRAMME STAGE

The Manage Programme stage is the heart of the programme. This stage will represent the vast majority of effort, cost and duration consumed by the programme. It is during this stage that programme accounting and financial control is particularly valuable, its objectives being to ensure that:

- up to date estimates are prepared and maintained to reflect current programme plans and assumptions;
- costs actually incurred are as planned – or, if not, appropriate corrective actions are taken;
- the organization is provided with periodic and realistic estimates of the cost to complete the programme;
- the cost impact of change or potential change on the programme is evaluated.

11.11.4.1 Manage Programme costs

As the programme progresses and produces deliverables (products), its understanding of the challenges ahead and how to resolve them should improve. This improved understanding should be reflected in more robust ECC calculations. The critical financial consideration in any programme or project is: 'What will the final bill be?' If a programme is currently over-, or under-spending but the programme team and senior management are confident that the ECC, that is, the total cost of the programme, will be as budgeted, then the original business case is still valid. If, however, the programme is exactly on budget today but cost to complete is expected to exceed plan by 20 per cent, the business case is potentially unachievable. Financial estimating throughout the Manage Programme stage should seek to bring all available information, that is, latest plans, current expenditures and commitments, and so on, together to produce the best possible estimates of the programme's ECC.

Preparation of cost estimates and financial reporting needs to be coordinated with the financial planning activities of the organization. While the programme in question may be very large and spending significant amounts of money, it will only form one part of the organization's undertakings. As such, the programme will need to comply with the financial planning and reporting timetable of the organization. It is vital to fully understand the requirements of this timetable so that programme planning and estimating activities can be integrated into it. It would be unhelpful, to say the least, to be required to produce revised cost estimates in March, June, September and December, if the programme proposes to undertake major plan reviews in January, April, July and October. In this example, moving the plan updates to 1 month later will enable up-to-date plans to be used to revise cost estimates. Programme managers may suggest that the finance function should move its timetable; however this is unlikely to happen as the finance timetable is inevitably linked with a range of other commitments, including the financial accounting calendar. It is usually much simpler for the programme to understand these constraints and work within them. It is highly likely that periodically, maybe quarterly, possibly half-yearly, the programme team will be required to fully re-evaluate the programme cost estimates. This process requires input from the whole programme team, but especially the programme manager and the managers of the component projects. These individuals will need to coordinate the estimates for the various work packages and projects that comprise the programme.

If it is assumed that these revisions will occur half-yearly and that the programme will last 3 years, re-evaluating the cost estimates will be undertaken at least six times. It is therefore worthwhile establishing a process and procedures for the collection and collation of cost estimates across the programme. Such a process should include:

- common templates, possibly based upon spreadsheet pro-formas, for collection of data;
- standard resource/skill group definitions and costs;
- guidelines on estimating and peer review;
- timetable for preparation, review and collation of information.

Defining a process of this type at the commencement of the programme has numerous benefits over time:

- Programme team members become adept at completing the documentation, thus saving valuable time and effort, plus errors are reduced;
- planning and reporting structures can be made consistent, thus supporting review and feedback;
- new members of the programme team can 'pick up' departed colleagues' previous plans and estimates more easily;
- variances between plan versions can be traced down to low levels of detail;
- consistency of planning approach and presentation is ensured.

For the programme manager, it would be disastrous to have each project providing different levels of information in different formats. Establishing common procedures is essential if this classic problem is to be avoided.

11.11.4.2 Monitor estimates of BAU costs and benefits

As the programme proceeds, so a greater understanding of the likely costs to be incurred, benefits accrued and issues influencing them will be achieved. This knowledge and experience should also provide a greater certainty of future BAU costs and how these will be impacted by the programme.

Where changes to BAU costs represent a fundamental part of the programme's business case, for example, the programme's benefits are provided by the achievement of reduced BAU costs, a consistent and repeatable process is required to review and revise costs and benefits throughout the lifetime of the programme. This review should take into account changes to programme costs and benefits, as well as the relationship between them. For example, if costs have doubled, but the estimate of likely benefits has trebled, the business case is still worth pursuing. However, if costs have increased relative to benefits, the business case may no longer be valid.

The validity of the programme's businss case should be reviewed and approved, at regular intervals, by the programme board.

11.11.4.3 Review accounting and financial control procedures

The procedures that were established during the Establish Programme stage should be capable of providing all programme accounting and financial control requirements. It is highly likely, however, that some amendments to the designed procedures will be required sometime during the lifetime of the programme. Periodic reviews of the programme accounting and financial control procedures should be undertaken, as for all programme control procedures. These reviews are typically undertaken at the end of tranches or upon completion of a planning and reporting cycle. Where shortcomings and/or a need to change procedures are identified, corrective actions should be coordinated with amendments and improvements to other control procedures such as those for change control, risks and issues.

Lessons learned from changes and improvements identified should always be fed into the programme's lessons learned report to assist future programmes and projects.

11.11.4.4 Report stage costs

Reporting stage costs is clearly a significant element of programme accounting and financial control during this stage. As previously stated, such reporting should be linked to the organization's financial reporting timetable and will usually require different information at different times, that is:

- Monthly: The organization's financial reporting timetable will typically be based around a monthly cycle. Reporting will involve the programme finance team undertaking the following activities:
  - Collect and collate financial information: Financial data will, as previously discussed, be fed to the programme from the various financial systems and processes of the organization. The task of the programme finance team is to validate this information, to ensure all assigned costs do relate to the programme and to collect any additional information that may add context and relevance.
  - Monitor financial performance: Once the costs incurred and committed to date have been collated, they are compared with planned expenditure to highlight variances. Variances are differences between planned and actual expenditure. Variances can be positive, expenditure less than plan, or negative, expenditure greater than plan and can be caused by an almost limitless number of events.
  - Undertake variance analysis: Understanding why variances have occurred is important for three reasons:
    - to identify inefficient or ineffective working that can then be rectified; or
    - to identify efficient or effective working that can then be replicated; or
    - to identify where estimates have been unrealistic and need to be amended.

  In any of these cases, the learning that arises from identifying the root cause of the variance assists in improving future estimates and plans.

Positive variances are often not investigated, or if so not as thoroughly as negative ones. While this is understandable, overspends are of greater concern, but underspend variances should always be fully investigated. They can often unearth areas where estimates are too conservative, more efficient working methods have been identified, or both. This knowledge may then be transferable to other areas of the programme and lead to further gains.

- Report programme financial performance to senior management: The programme will report financial performance using the formats established during the Establish stage, following the finance timetable. It is highly likely that the programme will be required to provide this information to both the organization's finance function and its own programme executive and board. Every attempt should therefore be made to gain agreement to utilize the same information and formats for both audiences.

- Quarterly/half yearly/annual: In addition to the monthly reporting cycle other information will be required on a less regular basis. Depending on organisational requirements, as discussed above, re-estimating programme 'cost to complete' and reviewing the business case may be undertaken quarterly, half yearly or even only annually. In the author's experience half yearly is most common but circumstances may dictate a more, or less, frequent review and refresh.

- Ad hoc: As well as scheduled activities there is always a need for 'ad hoc' assessments and evaluations in response to programme events. Common reasons to create such assessments include:
  - evaluate impact of change requests;
  - evaluate alternative approaches and methods;
  - adjust for changing business priorities;
  - evaluate the possible non achievement of expected benefits;
  - assess the impact of cost over-runs, prospective or actual.

11.11.4.5 Re-estimate tolerances

As the programme progresses and greater knowledge and understanding is gained, so estimating tolerances should be reduced. Re-estimating during this stage will normally utilize narrower tolerance bands than previously. Tolerance bands may also vary within the Manage Programme stage. For example, the estimates for the initial component projects may be subject to tighter limits than later projects, reflecting the greater certainty of estimates for these earlier projects.

11.11.5 CLOSE PROGRAMME STAGE

When the programme has completed all its planned activities and the business has received the capabilities it needs to achieve the planned benefit, it is time to pack up and close the programme. If the programme's finance function has been effective, all of this will have been achieved, if not within the original budget, within a level of investment that the organization has agreed and authorized. It is undoubtedly true for programmes and projects that often, even where they have been exceptionally well run, closure is poorly handled. Team members are often speedily re-assigned to other programmes and no time is available to properly tie up all the loose ends.

This is a particular problem with respect to programme accounting and financial control. As explained in Chapter 5, 'Benefits management', the realization of benefits is usually achieved by those using the new systems and facilities, not those who created them. As a result, the benefits can be realized only after a period of use. Thus the benefit management process may need to continue long after the programme has been closed. However, the programme records, especially those describing the BAU situation at the start of the programme, are essential to successful benefit management. Accordingly, ownership of all such records must transfer to those who will continue the benefit management process, such as a strategic planning group or the organization's finance function.

Furthermore, all financial records are required to be maintained for a period of, typically, 7 years for the purposes of audit and inspection. If the programme has maintained financial records, these need to be placed in safe storage against the possibility of being required in the future.

11.11.5.1 Close down accounting and financial control procedures

As part of dismantling the programme's accounting procedures, it is important to undertake a lessons learned review. This will help to identify future opportunities to improve the programme's accounting and financial control activities and should involve a wide spectrum of stakeholders including:

- the organization's finance function
- project and programme managers
- programme board members and senior managers; particularly those taking responsibility for benefits
- members of the programme finance team.

Key lessons learned should be added to the wider programme learning and also circulated within the organization's finance community for future reference.

471

In addition to identifying the lessons learnt, a major activity during the Close Programme stage is to hand over programme accounting records to the organization's finance function for safe keeping. As previously stated, these records need to be retained by the organization and time should be set aside to both physically hand over the records and explain to members of the finance function exactly what is being transferred, how it is organized, and so on.

Stage costs for closure should be reported using the procedures maintained throughout the programme. It is likely that the final few periods may be reported by the host organization's finance function if the programme finance team has disbanded before all expenditures have been accounted for.

There are no estimates to apply tolerances to at this stage in the programme, only actual costs. It is always interesting to reflect on the relationship between the original estimates and the final costs. An example such as the Scottish Parliament Building outlined in Case Study 11.1 highlights that these two figures are often total strangers.

Once the programme has been closed down there should be little left for the programme's finance team to do, other than transfer of all financial information to the organization's finance function.

11.12 ACCOUNTING FOR PROGRAMME COSTS

Accounting for programme and project costs is generally less complex than accounting for a whole organization. A central concept in accountancy is that, for any time period, costs and revenues are to be matched. This leads to accounting mechanisms such as stock holding, capitalization of expenditure and depreciation to reflect when resources are consumed rather than when they are acquired. Programme and project cost records are normally maintained on an expenditure basis, that is, costs are recognized by the programme when they are committed and incurred. As a result, an organization's finance function will often make adjustments via its accounting systems and records to reflect programme costs consistently with all other expenditures.

A sample programme scenario may help to illustrate this point. Assume a programme's purpose is to build, equip and initiate a new call centre to handle customer queries. The programme's major deliverables are:

1. a new building, to house the call centre
2. fitting out of the building
3. a new computer and communications infrastructure, to handle voice, text and on-line queries

4. new working processes and procedures
5. recruitment of staff
6. training of staff
7. testing of all systems and procedures
8. transfer of customer records from existing systems
9. handover of working systems or facilities to operational management.

Most organizations, especially in the private sector, would capitalize a significant proportion of the cost of this programme and depreciate (amortise) it over the expected lifetime of the facility. Items (1), (2), (3) and (7) are prime candidates for capitalization, while most of the other categories may also comply, to some degree, depending upon the specific make up of the expenditure. As far as the programme is concerned, providing records have been maintained that allow the cost of items (1) through (9) to be quantified, this information can be handed over to finance for processing into the organization's accounts. Programme managers are not normally required to make, or even fully understand, the details of these types of accounting adjustment. For any programme, the organization's finance function will be able to explain fully the policies and procedures that apply for capitalization of expenditure. The programme manager's key responsibility will be to ensure that sufficiently detailed transaction records are maintained to enable these accounting adjustments to be made and audited. Costs not capitalized will normally be charged as operating costs of the organization in the financial period in which they are incurred. In the case of a large programme where relatively little is capitalized this may have a significant impact on the organization's financial performance for that period. Extremely significant programmes, such as a post-merger integration programme, will often be reported separately in an organization's published accounts to highlight their impact on financial performance.

11.13 CONCLUSION

Financial management is a fundamentally important part of programme management, with cost overruns often the most visible manifestation of a troubled programme or project. There is clearly no magic solution to achieve effective financial management within a programme, but by adhering to the key principles outlined above major shocks can be avoided. If those responsible for programme success address each of the items on the checklist in Figure 11.14, they will have significantly improved their chances of remaining in control of their programme's finances.

1. Specify and confirm the programme's scope, by developing deliverable (product) breakdowns.

2. Develop cost estimates at the deliverable (product) level and aggregate to project and ultimately to programme level.

3. Create project and programme management deliverables for items such as programme support office and project/programme management and estimate their costs as for other deliverables.

4. Develop and agree benefits breakdown structure linking benefits through capabilities to deliverables (see Chapter 5 'Benefits Management').

5. Define cost benefit valuation for each delivered capability by linking benefits derived and cost of deliverables.

6. Baseline initial cost benefit evaluation, once approved by the programme board.

7. Design and implement cost and other transaction data gathering and reporting procedures.

8. Periodically collect, collate, monitor and report programme costs and benefit achievement.

9. Periodically review and revise cost and benefit estimates.

Figure 11.14   Checklist of key programme accounting and financial control activities

Many programme and project managers are somewhat overawed, even intimidated, by the financial management aspects of their programmes or projects. This is often because, like all professions, accounting and finance have their own language and techniques of which programme and project managers often have little or no training or experience. As a result, the whole topic can be very confusing for the uninitiated. For this reason, it is very important for programme and project managers to work closely with their colleagues in finance to make sure that the correct skills and experience are brought to bear. For large programmes it will often prove valuable to have someone from finance join the programme team, even on a part-time basis, to provide expert advice and guidance.

REFERENCES AND FURTHER READING

Fleming Quentin W. and Koppleman, Joel M. (2000) *Earned Value Project Management.* Newtown Square, PA: Project Management Institute.

Fraser of Carmyllie, Lord (2004) 'Holyrood Enquiry: Final Report.' Available: www.holyroodinquiry.org/final_report/report.htm.

For an introduction to project and programme accounting see:

Chapman, John (2005) *Project and Programme Accounting: A Practical Guide for Professional Service Organisations and IT.* Hook: Project Manager Today Publication.

12 Management of scope and change

12.1 INTRODUCTION

Change is like death and taxes, it affects us all and is particularly significant for programmes that, by their nature, must operate over a long period of time. Almost all programmes are subject to substantial change of objectives or scope at least once during their lives and many are subject to almost constant change. Yet unless these changes are properly handled, they will destroy the programme. Indeed, inadequate management of scope and change is one of the principal causes of cost and time over-run and of eventual failure for both programmes and for their component projects.

The sources of these changes are many and various. Frequently the stakeholders of a programme alter their priorities over time. This may be because business strategies have changed, because the commercial environment within which the business operates has changed, or it may be because, through working on the programme, the programme director and the programme board have a greater understanding of the benefits and costs and potential for enhanced functionality, resulting in revisions to the business case. Alternatively, those involved in the programme or its component projects may uncover misunderstandings or errors in the original objectives, specifications or estimates, resulting in a need to adjust the scope or content or costings of the programme. Figure 12.1 summarizes the different sources of change.

Without adequate management, these changes will occur in an unstructured manner, resulting in uncoordinated or haphazard modifications being made to the scope of the programme or to its basic architecture. The impact of these changes in terms of the work content and therefore timing and cost may be very significant, particularly if there is no equivalent change to budget or time estimates or expectation of business benefits. Without control, such changes may cause the objectives of the programme and the stakeholders' expectations of what it will

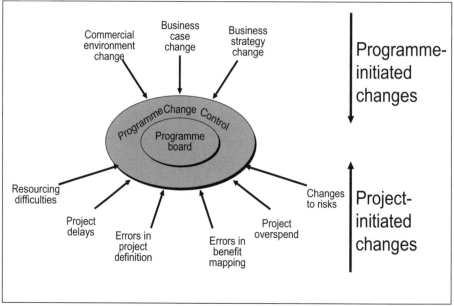

Figure 12.1   Sources of changes to scope

deliver to grow without the necessary increase in budgets or resources, a near fatal condition often referred to as 'scope creep'.

In addition, many changes will require adjustments to work plans and excessive amounts of change can completely destabilize a programme. Without adequate management procedures, even well-meant proposals for beneficial change can have an unsettling effect by soaking up resource in investigating impacts and by creating uncertainty among programme staff and programme stakeholders.

Yet a dogged resistance to change can be just as bad, resulting in the delivery of systems and facilities that are no longer appropriate to the needs of the organization. What is required is a management process by which ideas for change may be defined, considered, decided upon and communicated as a part of a rational management process.

Changes may expand or contract the scope of the programme. Usually it is the business or those who will use the programme's outputs that seek to expand scope, while it is the contractor or those undertaking the work that seek to reduce it. Either way, effecting any such change is likely to have an impact on many other aspects of the programme, including products that have been completed or planned. For example, expansions of scope in one part without any equivalent reduction of scope elsewhere may add to the likely benefits, but will almost certainly also increase the workload and thus the costs and duration of the programme. Management of scope and change ensures that the programme recognizes when changes are required and then initiates a predefined process that ultimately provides appropriate information to the programme board, enabling a rational decision to be made on whether or not to implement the requested change.

12.2 PROGRAMME CHANGE VERSUS PROJECT CHANGE

Many of the issues associated with the management of scope and change are the same within programmes as within project. In both cases, there needs to be a rational process to ensure that the advantages likely to result from implementing the change will outweigh the drawbacks such as additional costs.

However, controlling the scope of a programme is a more complex task, as the relationship between the advantages and the drawbacks is much more complex and less clear-cut. Whereas projects are expected to deliver defined products, to a specified level of quality within an agreed time and budget programmes are intended to deliver business benefits, often associated with organizational change. Thus, evaluating whether the provision of an additional business feature makes it worth delaying the delivery of another can be far from simple. For this reason, managing the scope of a programme requires a strategic insight and an understanding of the programme's objectives and expected business benefits, as well as an agreed process. Furthermore, a change to aspects of one of the programme's component projects may dictate consequential changes to those of other projects, resulting in a need to adjust agreed project plans and to coordinate the changes across the programme.

As shown in Figure 12.1, changes may be initiated at the programme level and passed downwards to the component projects, or initiated within one or more component projects and escalated upwards. An example of the former would be where a take-over or merger leads to a change in corporate strategy or priorities, requiring a change to the programme and its component projects: an example of the latter would be where a project discovers some unexpected difficulty, such as encountering difficult ground conditions or polluted land that requires unplanned or remedial action.

In summary, within a programme, change can impact any or all of the following:

- resource requirements
- budgets
- quality standards and inspection requirements
- timescales by when new capabilities and facilities must be available

- the risk profile
- the governance of the work including processes, procedures and roles
- the portfolio of projects that make it up, their priorities and their inter-dependencies.

Above all, programmes are designed to deliver business benefits and all changes in scope have the potential to change these expected benefits. Managing change to scope at the programme level is thus fundamentally about managing change to expected business benefits and judging whether these changes are worth the associated cost, time and effort.

12.3 SCOPE MANAGEMENT WITHIN THE CIVIL ENGINEERING INDUSTRY

In some industries, custom and practice dictate standard approaches to the handling and management of changes. For example, in the civil engineering and construction industries in the UK, there is normally a contractually defined procedure for managing change requests. Work on buildings and engineering structures is often undertaken under an adversarial form of contract between a client and an external contractor. In essence, the client, supported by a technical team, defines in great detail the structure to be built and the contractor offers to supply that structure for a fixed price.

It is often the case that requirements for change emerge during the construction period. These are referred to as architect's instructions or change orders. These fall into three main categories:

- Change may be due to changes in client requirements, such as a hospital requiring space for a new piece of equipment or a new tenant demanding changes to a shopping centre design after the contract has been signed. The client, supported by the technical team of architects and engineers, will propose such changes and the impact of these will be negotiated between the client and the contractor.
- The contractor may request a change order having found a situation that they could not reasonably have foreseen. For example, extremely unusual weather, unexpected ground conditions or the discovery of an archaeological site may be the cause of a request from the contractor for a change order.
- The contractor may request a change order or architect's instruction to clarify some detail in the documentation defining the scope of what has to be delivered.

480

In all three cases, the contractor will typically aim to maximize the impact of these changes (and thus the additional income that will result), explaining how they will cause delay and extra expense. Indeed, sometimes whole teams of quantity surveyors or claims engineers are employed to develop the opportunities provided by change requests.

In an attempt to reduce these claims and the consequential costs of change, the client and technical teams will try to define the structure precisely and formalize a contract that defines as many aspects of the project as possible, including the process for issuing change requests. Despite such efforts an industrial sub-sector exists of expert witnesses and legal advisors whose sole occupation is to debate, argue, arbitrate and settle disputes arising from these claims.

12.4 SCOPE MANAGEMENT WITHIN A PROGRAMME ENVIRONMENT

In most programme management environments, the relationship between the 'client' and 'contractor' is often very different to the clear-cut but adversarial relationship prevalent in civil engineering undertakings. This is especially the case with programmes of organizational change, where the two parties are departments or groups within the same organization, such as the internal IT department and a business division such as accounts. There may a memorandum of agreement (MoA) or a service level agreement (SLA), but often no formal agreement exists to cover the work and the relationship. Not surprisingly in these circumstances, there is often no agreed process for managing change to the scope of the work.

In addition, partly due to the non-tangible nature of the work, it may not be feasible to define the deliverables in the degree of detail normal on a construction project. There may also be no (or only a weak) definition of the scope of work and no (or a vague) definition of the processes for managing the project and managing changes to the scope of the work. Therefore changes are treated in an informal manner and little rigour is applied to understanding their implications. This can cause damage to the programme and large increases in the risk of failure.

Frequently, changes to the scope are not reflected in any consequential change in timescale or budget. Also, the emphasis on the operation of the system is overlooked as new and potentially irrelevant functionality is added. Sometimes a consequence of some minor change is to reduce the value of important functionality elsewhere in the system.

To make sure of success, it is vitally important to ensure that everyone on the programme understands the expected benefits of the programme, so that any request for change can be evaluated in terms of the effect it is likely to have on those benefits. A useful technique here is to create strategy maps so that the relationship between the expected business benefits and features or capabilities created by the programme can easily be understood. (These maps are discussed in Chapter 5, 'Benefits management').

12.5 KEY ELEMENTS OF SCOPE MANAGEMENT

An agreed definition of the anticipated scope of work and of the intended benefits is a prerequisite to effective management of change and thus to programme success. Without such a definition, it will be impossible to understand the impact of any requested changes. Furthermore, without a firm and agreed baseline to start with, it may not even be possible to agree what the change is about or its extent. Yet, as described in the previous section, defining such a baseline can be remarkably difficult. Moreover, many programmes start with what is believed at the time to be a clear and comprehensive definition of scope, only to find it completely inadequate once subjected to the stresses of change.

This can be a major problem with externally managed programmes where the contractor and the customer believe that they have agreed everything, only to find that every change exposes a difference of understanding that may lead to argument, dispute and even litigation. Seeking to reduce the risk of dispute by negotiating a voluminous contract can actually make matters worse by creating a second definition of what is required. Because contractual negotiations are usually heavily influenced by legal and procurement staff, the emphasis can be very different from that of the original proposal, creating a source of serious disappointment and misunderstanding. It is vital, therefore, to ensure that the formal contract not only meets the requirements of legal and procurement specialists, but also conforms to the contractor's proposal and to the customer's business requirements.

Generally, the longer a programme has been running, the more difficult and costly it will be to integrate changes. For example, it is clearly much easier to make a change at the programme definition stage, when all that has to be reworked are the paper-based specifications, than it is to make a change once new deliverables are being subjected to final testing, when the whole product must be re-manufactured. Accordingly, it pays to involve all potential stakeholders in the early stages of a programme, as described in Chapter 6, 'Stakeholder management'.

12.6 ROLES AND RESPONSIBILITIES

While any person or group involved in some way with the programme should be in a position to request a change, the responsibility for deciding whether or not to implement a change should always rest with the programme board. As explained in Chapter 3, 'Programme organisation and governance', the programme board is responsible for the overall success of the programme, for ensuring that it delivers the expected business benefits and that the investment of time and money in creating those benefits is worthwhile. Of course, the board may delegate the powers to review and even to decide on changes to a smaller group of technically competent people – often referred to as a change advisory board (CAB). However, such a group will only be acting on behalf of the programme board and it is good practice for all the CAB's decisions to be subject to ratification by the programme board.

Frequently the important decision with respect to requests for change is not whether to implement or not, but how to implement. In particular, the results of a requested change might be deemed beneficial in the long term, but potentially disruptive in the short term. In such circumstances, it is common for new phases to be added to programme, in which new projects are undertaken to implement such long-term changes.

Not every change request needs to be handled at the programme level. Where the component projects are given a degree of tolerance, they may make their own decisions about whether or not to accept small changes. Only requests for change that would cause a component project to exceed its tolerance limits, which would require a new project to be initiated, or which would impact more than one component project, need to be referred to the programme level for consideration.

Frequently, a change controller or scope change manager will be appointed to ensure the smooth running of the scope change process. They will be responsible for documenting and implementing the programme's policies on change control.[1] The change controller/scope change manager will be responsible for documenting and implementing the programme's policies on controlling all changes. Other typical responsibilities include:

- Maintain a register of all requested and agreed changes.
- Arrange for impact of requested changes to be speedily assessed and reported.
- Convene and chair the change control sub-committee of the programme

---

1   Change control should not be confused with organizational change management, which is the responsibility of the organizational change manager and is discussed in Section 5.7.1 'The organizational change manager'.

board, which is responsible for approving or refusing requests for change. This sub-committee is sometimes referred to as the CAB.

- Communicate decisions on changes to all those involved, including ensuring that any separate recording and invoicing of work associated with changes is correctly undertaken.
- Ensure that work plans are adequately revised when major changes are agreed.
- Ensure that all changes are correctly completed and tested.
- Oversee the emergency change procedures and ensure that procedures are not misused and that all such changes are correctly completed and appropriate paperwork maintained.

It will be vital for the change controller/scope change manager to interface with the configuration manager to ensure that all agreed changes are reflected within the relevant configuration management records. (See Chapter 9, 'Configuration management' for guidance.)

12.7 A PROGRAMME CHANGE REQUEST PROCESS IN DETAIL

The procedures roles and responsibilities can be laid down within the programme quality strategy or within a separate document that is referenced by that strategy. (See Chapter 8, 'Programme assurance and quality' for guidance on the programme quality strategy .)

Because of the programme assurance function's involvement in specifying standards throughout the programme, this function is frequently also made responsible for change control. Change control is the process of managing and controlling the changes to programme and project deliverables, documents and other tangible products. It is thus closely related to configuration management. (See also Chapter 9, 'Configuration management'.)

Typically, programme-wide change management process involves nine key activities:

1. **Initiation**: Changes may be requested by any party involved within the programme. All requests for change should be formally recorded as a change control request.
2. **Change review**: The change control request is reviewed, initially to ensure that it is relevant to the programme and then to prioritize it. Typically, changes are prioritized as normal or emergency. Emergency changes are those that are so urgent that they must follow a short-cut process. The circumstances in which this process may be followed should be clearly defined.

3. **Impact assessment**: Normal changes must be assessed for their likely impact on the programme in terms of cost, timescales, performance, and so on. Although providing benefits to those making the request, changes will involve time, cost and disruption to the agreed work plans of others. It is vital before making a decision that these negative impacts are fully understood. This is especially important if external contractors are involved, since most changes will involve extra costs.

The focus of assessing impacts on a programme will be different from assessing them on a project. In the latter, if the change means the project will take longer or cost more, this is often a good reason for rejecting the change. In a programme, it is necessary to consider the extra dimension of benefits. For example, if an unexpected opportunity arose part way through the programme that increased its cost by £1 million and extended its duration by 2 months, the project view might be that it is a bad idea. However, if that change increased the value of tangible benefits from £5 million to £10 million and shortened the payback by 50 per cent with no increase in risk, from the programme point of view the change might be very acceptable.

Impact assessment should be fully comprehensive. As well as the likely effect on costs and timescales, it should assess the impact on the business benefits that the programme will make possible (including the time schedule by when they can be realized). The assessment should consider any consequential effects that 'knock on' from one project to another in terms of time and cost, as well as of benefits. It should also consider any changes to risk profiles or quality assessment requirements.

Reviewing the impact of change is not a trivial activity. Unless time, cost and resource has been allowed for the work within original estimates, reviewing changes can disrupt the mainstream activities and thus create serious stress for the affected projects and for the programme as a whole. Where requests for change are frequent, it may be necessary to create a special group to undertake this work. This group should include appropriate designers and 'system architects' to ensure that changes do not compromise the integrity of originally proposed designs. It should also include business analysts and/or benefit managers to ensure that the impact on anticipated business benefits is understood.

4. **Approval**: Once assessed, it will be possible for the programme to make a decision on whether the benefits of the change outweigh the likely costs in terms of money and disruption.

It is important when considering changes to maintain the 'big picture', namely the overall purpose and objectives of the programme. This perspective can easily be lost when considering the detailed costs and schedules within a

485

large programme. In general, additional complexity makes it more difficult to achieve objectives and all changes tend to add to complexity.

5. **Plan change**: Once approved, work can begin on planning how the change will be implemented. Major changes may require existing programme and project plans to be revised. Minor changes may merely require an adjustment to the work plans of a single project. Once approved, all work on the change will normally be separately recorded for costing and/or invoicing purposes.

6. **Build and test**: Once the plans for changes have been accepted, the technical staff within the project(s) can undertake the necessary changes – for example, create the new deliverable or amend an existing one.

7. **Implement**: Once satisfactorily tested, the change will be ready for implementation. This may involve installing on the 'live' environment.

8. **Acceptance**: Any necessary reviews or acceptance tests at 'programme level' must be completed and formally approved by the change initiator. These might involve actual users in assessing the usability of the new facilities.

9. **Complete change paperwork**: Finally, the necessary paperwork should be completed, including the accumulation of costs. It may also be necessary to update configuration management records.

Case Study 12.1 provides an example of a change control procedure, as applied to a large IT programme involving a consortium of companies. This case study also shows a sample change control request form.

CASE STUDY 12.1: SAMPLE SCOPE CHANGE PROCEDURE

ABC Programme

Scope Change Procedure

Project number	EC98764
Issue	1.1
Issue date	17 August
Status	Draft C1
Document reference	CON-P009
Security category	None
Distribution	Consortium Website Consortium Document Repository
Prepared by	A.B. Ceedy — Prime Contractor Scope Change Controller
Reviewed	P.R. Ess, Programme Manager R.S. Teeyuvee, Tech Design Authority
Approved (Prime Contractor)	.... Prime Contractor Quality Manager
Authorized (Prime Contractor)	.... Prime Contractor Project Manager
Agreed (Partners)	....
Agreed (Client)	....

1.0 INTRODUCTION

1.1 PURPOSE
The purpose of this document is to ensure that all requests for change to matters covered within the ABC contract or within Partner sub-contracts are captured, assessed, authorized and implemented in a manner that minimizes impact to the ABC Programme while providing the necessary flexibility in approach that ABC, Prime Contractor and our Partners require.

This document, and the supporting template (ABC-CCN) will help all members of the Consortium, and ABC to initiate, process and manage changes in a manner that is easy to understand and consistent throughout the Programme.

1.2 SCOPE
The procedures described in this document will apply to all members of the Consortium and to ABC when requesting changes to the contract, sub-contracts or engineering changes (that is changes to items of work that have already been undertaken). Such changes could include:

- scope or contents of the contract – including schedules and annexes;
- requirements definition documents;
- items of software;
- programme procedures;
- hardware infrastructure;
- user manuals and other deliverable documentation.

Unless otherwise stated, the procedures will apply through all phases of the Programme, including the Support Phase.

The procedures will apply to all types of contractual change:

- those affecting only the contract between Prime Contractor and ABC;
- those affecting only the sub-contracts between Prime Contractor and one or more Partners;
- those affecting the contract between Prime Contractor and ABC and which also require 'back-to-back' changes involving Partner(s).

1.3 SUMMARY
This document describes how to request a change and obtain a decision from an authorized representative using a Contract Change Request (CCR). A copy of the necessary form can be found within Appendix A of this document and as the ABC-CCN template available on the Consortium web site. The URLs are:

http://public.PrimeContractor.com/~ABC/Log&ABC&Part/Cons_Docs/Templates/index.htm

or

https://public.PrimeContractor.com/~ABC/Log&ABC&Part/Cons_Docs/Templates/index.htm

Following the procedures described in this document will ensure that all changes to scope are:

- fully investigated – so that any changes to estimated costs or completion dates are known in advance;
- agreed with ABC and/or Partners and formally approved so all changes in cost, milestone dates or deliverable items are expected and can be traced;
- tested and accepted, to minimize the risk of new faults being introduced into the system;
- managed and controlled so that the implementation of changes does not upset existing operations;
- recorded so that all costs, including the assessment of impact and the preparation of proposals and estimates, are captured.

The procedures described in this document are consistent with the requirements for change control outlined within the draft ABC contract.

1.4 AMENDMENT HISTORY
The revision history of this document is shown in the Table 12.1, below.

Table 12.1   Amendment history

Date	Issue	Status
27 June	A	Internally reviewed for basic scope and concepts.
16 July	A.2	Revised and simplified.
19 July	A.3	Approved and authorised by Prime Contractor Project Manager. Presented to John Snooks of ABC on 21 July . Deemed to be agreed by ABC on 4 August.
9 Aug	1.0	Converted to Microsoft Windows format. Issued to Consortium partners.

1.5 STATUS, CHANGE FORECAST AND CONFIGURATION MANAGEMENT

This document will become definitive when it is signed on the control sheet to indicate that it is approved by the Quality Manager, authorized by the Prime Contractor Project Manager and agreed by ABC and Partners.

Copies of this document will be made available to ABC and to all Partners through the Consortium website. All groups involved with the ABC Programme will be expected to follow the procedures that it describes.

It is expected that these procedures will be subjected to revision. All such revisions will be subjected to review, authorization and client agreement and will be made available to all groups through the Programme's central documentation repository. All revisions will be shown in the Amendment History table.

A summary of the current status of all Change Requests will be kept on the project website.

1.6 RESPONSIBILITIES

Responsibility for managing changes has been allocated to the Prime Contractor Scope Change Controller (PCSCC).

The procedures require a Change Advisory Board (CAB) to approve and prioritize changes. Initially the Board will consist of:

- the PCSCC, the Prime Contractor Project Manager and the ABC Programme Manager for changes involving the ABC contract; and
- the PCSCC, the Prime Contractor Project Manager and the Partner Project Manager for changes involving a Partner sub-contract.

Any changes that they are unable to agree upon will be escalated to Prime Contractor's Government Division Director and to ABC's Director of IT and/or to the relevant Partner Director. Should agreement not be possible at this level then the contract or sub-contract disputes procedure may be invoked.

1.7 ABBREVIATIONS

The following abbreviations have been used within this document.

Table 12.2   Table of abbreviations

Abbreviation	Explanation
ABC	ABC Limited – the client
CAB	Change Advisory Board
CCR	Change Control Request
CCN	Change Control Note
IT	Information Technology
PCSCC	Prime Contractor Change Manager
RFC	Request for Change
URL	Uniform Resource Locator

1.8 REFERENCES

An example of the form to use for CCRs/CCNs is enclosed as Appendix A.

Related processes, such as those for configuration management, are described within the Programme's Quality Plan – Reference CON-P001.

2.0 NORMAL CHANGE MANAGEMENT PROCEDURES

The normal procedures for initiating, processing and implementing changes (as opposed to any necessary emergency procedures) are shown in diagram form in Figures 12.2 and 12.3.

As a working guideline, subject to the quality of information received from the change originator, minor changes should be processed to approval status (that is, ready for presentation to ABC or Partner) within 5 days of receipt by the PCSCC, significant changes within 10 days of receipt, and major changes as soon as feasible with respect to the level of impact assessment that may be required. Note that, as explained in Section 2.3, the time required for impact assessments themselves may need to be agreed with ABC.

The sections below describe each of the stages in the diagram.

2.1 INITIATE CHANGES

Changes will normally result from discussions between Prime Contractor and ABC, but may be initiated by any party involved within the Programme, including Partners. All requests for change should be recorded either electronically or manually on a CCR form.

491

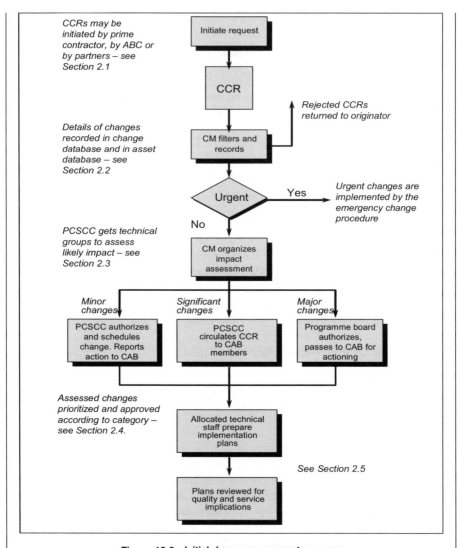

CCRs may be initiated by prime contractor, by ABC or by partners – see Section 2.1

Initiate request

CCR

Rejected CCRs returned to originator

Details of changes recorded in change database and in asset database – see Section 2.2

CM filters and records

Urgent — **Yes** → *Urgent changes are implemented by the emergency change procedure*

No

PCSCC gets technical groups to assess likely impact – see Section 2.3

CM organizes impact assessment

Minor changes

PCSCC authorizes and schedules change. Reports action to CAB

Significant changes

PCSCC circulates CCR to CAB members

Major changes

Programme board authorizes, passes to CAB for actioning

Assessed changes prioritized and approved according to category – see Section 2.4.

Allocated technical staff prepare implementation plans

See Section 2.5

Plans reviewed for quality and service implications

Figure 12.2   Initial change management processes

Electronic transmission of Change Requests is preferred for efficiency. The receipt of electronic versions by e-mail will be taken as an effective 'signature' of the e-mail content. As described in Section 1.3, the CCR form can be obtained from the Consortium website. Also, a sample copy of the form is attached to this document.

The basic details of the change should be recorded on Part 1 of the form. If necessary, additional material should be attached. In all cases, the form should be sent to the PCSCC for recording and processing.

If the change is being requested by a Prime Contractor member of staff it must be signed by the Prime Contractor Project Manager: if it is being requested by a Partner, it must be signed by the Project Manager for that Partner: If it is being requested by ABC, it must be signed by the ABC Programme Manager or another authorized ABC signatory. Only requests so signed will be accepted by the PCSCC.

2.2 SCOPE CHANGE MANAGER REVIEW

The PCSCC will conduct a preliminary review of the CCR to confirm that it is relevant to the Programme and that it contains the necessary information and that it is appropriately signed. If it is, they will record the CCR in the Change Register and allocate a Change Request Number (CRN). If it is not, they will return the CCR to the originator with the reason(s) for rejection.

The PSCC will also decide whether the Request is so critical that it must be processed according to the Emergency Change procedure. If it is, it will be handled in the manner described in Section 3 of this document. If it is a normal CCR, the PCSCC will pass the details to an appropriate person for impact assessment.

The PCSCC will record their actions on the master copy of the form and will ensure that this form is suitably filed. The master copy can then be used to monitor the progress of the change throughout its lifecycle.

2.3 IMPACT ASSESSMENT

Impact assessment is the evaluation of impact of the change in terms of:

- time required to undertake the investigation
- time to implement the change
- overall resources required
- changes in system performance and security
- effect of the above on service levels
- effect of the above on estimated costs to ABC
- effect of the above on achieving any of the Consortium's milestones
- effect on expected benefits.

In a simple case, the PCSCC may be able to complete the assessment themselves. However, in many cases, the assessment will require the time and skill of one or more other members of the team.

Where implementing the CCR will require a 'back-to-back' change with a Partner (that is, a consequential change agreed between the Prime Contractor and the Partner that exactly mirrors the change agreed between the client and the Prime Contractor), the assessment process will include raising, negotiating and agreeing 'in principle' a Change with a Partner. Such changes have to be agreed in principle, since will be conditional on ABC agreeing to the Change.

493

All time spent on assessments, whether by Prime Contractor or Partner staff, must be recorded and identified on time-sheets and progress reports. If the time required for assessment is likely to exceed 2 hours, the PCSCC should gain formal clearance from the ABC Programme Manager so that time so spent may subsequently be charged back to ABC.

When the full impact is understood, the assessor should complete and sign Part 3 of the CCR form. If the change is assessed to be a major change, or if requested so to do by ABC or by the PCSCC, the assessor should prepare a full proposal.

2.4 APPROVAL

The assessor may recommend that the change be rejected. More usually, they will propose an impact category. The possible categories are:

- Minor: Does not require expenditure for a currently agreed work package to increase by more than 10 per cent. Does not change any milestone.
- Significant: increases one or more work package by more than 10 per cent but, less than £100 000, or changes an intermediate milestone but does not involve change to a major milestone – that is, does not change one of the agreed major deliveries such as the 'Launch system on 3/4/00' (milestone 12).
- Major:
  - increases total cost by £100 000 or more; or:
  - changes a contractual milestone, or
  - adds new requirements not included within the existing contract; or
  - has a significant effect on expected benefits.

ABC changes that will affect a Partner sub-contract will require 'back-to-back' Change Requests to be agreed in principle with the Partner as part of the assessment process.

The process for approval will depend upon the assessed category of impact.

- Minor changes require approval by the Prime Contractor Project Manager and the ABC Programme Manager and/or Partner Project Manager.
- Significant changes should be prioritized and approved by the CAB.
- Major Prime Contractor/ABC Changes should be referred to ABC's Director of IT for consideration, while major Partner/Prime Contractor changes should be referred to the relevant Partner Director. If acceptable to them, such changes should then be passed to the CAB for prioritization and formal approval.

A Prime Contractor Quotation Management Summary will be required for major changes AND for any others where the total cost is equal to or greater than £100 000. This Summary will be subject formal review by the Prime Contractor.

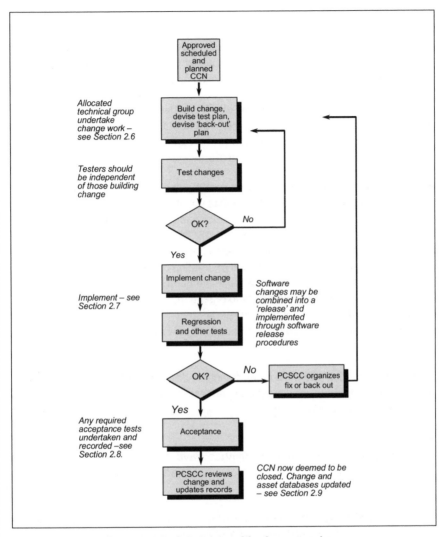

Allocated technical group undertake change work – see Section 2.6

Testers should be independent of those building change

Implement – see Section 2.7

Software changes may be combined into a 'release' and implemented through software release procedures

Any required acceptance tests undertaken and recorded –see Section 2.8.

CCN now deemed to be closed. Change and asset databases updated – see Section 2.9

Figure 12.3   Latest stages of the change procedure

2.5 PLAN CHANGE

Once approved, the CCR becomes a Change Control Note (CCN) and is allocated a CCN Number. Signatures recording such approval will be recorded on a CCN Cover Sheet, a copy of which can be found in the Appendix.

Where 'back-to-back' changes are required to cover Partner activities, these will also need to be approved and signed off.

495

Once approved, CCNs for engineering changes will be passed to appropriate staff to plan the implementation. The scale of such planning will depend upon the size and scope of the change. Minor changes may merely require a time-slot to be allocated into someone's work plan, while major changes may have the characteristics of a small project and require complex plans.

The proposed plans should be summarized within Part 1 of the CCN and this section should be countersigned by the Prime Contractor Quality Manager to confirm that the quality aspects of plans are adequate. Among the items that the Quality Manager will be particularly interested in are:

- the plans for testing the completeness of the change, including any regression tests needed to verify that the change has not affected any existing capability and volumetric tests to verify that system performance will not be affected;
- the plans for acceptance to ensure that ABC or Prime Contractor will be able to accept the change once it is fully implemented;
- back-out arrangements to provide full restoration of normal service in the event of the change not working properly when implemented within the live system;
- configuration control arrangements to ensure that the configuration management and/or asset databases are correctly updated;
- where 'back-to-back' changes are need for Partner activities, Partners' plans are adequate.

Some changes, such as simple amendments to documentation, may not need to go through all the possible implementation stages. However, the plans should identify all the stages that are necessary.

2.6 BUILD AND TEST

Once the plans for engineering changes have been accepted, the allocated technical staff can undertake the necessary changes – for example, build the amended software.

Once built, the changed item must be reviewed or tested. Whenever possible, this should be undertaken by staff independent of those who built the change. The type and extent of testing will be defined within the plans and will depend upon the nature of the change. In some cases, it may be necessary to undertake volumetric and regression testing.

A key element of testing will be the formal acceptance by ABC (Prime Contractor/ABC changes) or Prime Contractor (Partner/Prime Contractor changes).

2.7 IMPLEMENT

Once satisfactorily tested, the engineering change will be ready for implementation. This may involve installing on the live system.

After installation, changed items will normally need further testing to verify that they operate correctly in the live environment and that they have not affected some unchanged aspect of the system. Should a significant problem be discovered, the change must be 'backed out' and the system restored to its pre-change condition.

2.8 ACCEPTANCE

Any necessary reviews or acceptance tests must be completed and formally approved by the change initiator. Records of all such reviews and tests should be recorded and filed and summarized in Section 2 of the CCN form.

2.9 COMPLETE CHANGE

Finally the PCSCC should complete Section 3 of the CCN. This will confirm the correct accumulation of costs. The PCSCC should also verify the update of Configuration Management and other databases.

3.0 EMERGENCY CHANGE PROCEDURES

Emergency changes are those where the normal procedures would take too long. Typically, this procedure will only be used for engineering changes to correct 'Category 1' faults in live systems. Part 1 of the CCR form contains a field for recording the reference of the relevant Observation Report or Defect Note.

Initiators may mark their CCRs as 'emergency'. The PCSCC will confirm this if they deem such a classification as appropriate and will decide the necessary actions in consultation with the Prime Contractor Project Manager.
Once actions are agreed, the PCSCC will organize the speedy build and implementation of a suitable work-around to correct the problem. Subsequently, the Change Manager can initiate a permanent change.

The PCSCC should ensure that the amount of change going through the emergency procedure is minimized, since tests and quality controls are limited.

ABC	ABC Consortium **Change Control Request**	Consortium Logo

Initiator's Reference:	Change Request No: CCR

Part 1 - To be completed by the initiator:	Initiating Change	
Name:	Organization:	Location:
Title:	Telephone No.:	Fax No.:
Project:	Associated Observation Report or Defect Report. (if any):	

Type of Change – ENGINEERING/CONTRACT
(* Delete as appropriate)

Brief description of the requested change (attach marked up/revised text, Defect Note, non-conformity record or other supporting information as appropriate):

List configuration items requiring change - title, reference number, version number (Engineering Change only):

Justification for change:

NORMAL/EMERGENCY PROCEDURE REQUESTED *
* Delete as appropriate

Is further information attached Y/N* (* Delete as appropriate)	Authorized: Project Manager (if not Initiator)	
Signed (Initiator):		Date:

Please send this form to the Prime Contractor Change Manager

Part 2 - Change Manager Decision	Initiate Assessment	
REJECT/NORMAL/EMERGENCY* (* Delete as appropriate)	Passed to (Name of employee) Date Passed	Organization

498

ABC

ABC Consortium
Change Control Request

Consortium Logo

Part 3 – To be completed by appointed Impact Assessor:	Assessment of Impact:
Date received:	Change Request Number:

Analysis (continue on a separate sheet if necessary):

Likely impact on time and milestones

Likely impact on estimated costs – professional £

- M & E £

Likely impact on performance or service levels

Recommendation: ACCEPT/REJECT*
(*Delete as appropriate)

Change category **Minor** Impact Only	**Significant** More than minor impact	**Major** Impact

(*Delete as appropriate)
Other documents required YES/NO
(List as appropriate)

Partner Change Required YES/NO   **Number of Partner CCR**

Signed (Assessor):	Date:

Part 4 – To be completed by CAB:	
Decision: APPROVED/REJECTED (*Delete as appropriate)	**Review/Meeting Ref** (if necessary):
Reason for approval/rejection:	
Date change to be implemented by:	
Date CCR signed off (Signatures on Signature Sheet):	**ABC CCN Number** **Partner CCN Number** (if appropriate)

ABC

ABC Consortium
Change Control Request

Consortium Logo

Part 1 – To be completed by the Change Implementor/Builder:	CCN No.:

Implementation Plan (list changed items by title, reference number and new version number):

Backout Plan required YES/NO	If Back-out Plan is required, attach plans
Test Plan required YES/NO	If Test Plan is required, attach plans

Signed (Implementor):	Date:
Signed (Quality Manager):	Date:

Part 2 – To be completed by Tester/Acceptor	Tests Change

Tests Successful   YES/NO
(*Delete as appropriate)

If tests failed, briefly state findings:
(attach test records or reference Defect Report)

Signed (Tester)	Date
Signed (Acceptance):	Date:
Signed (Other)	Date

ABC

ABC Consortium

Change Control Request

Consortium Logo

Part 3 – To be completed by the Change Manager	CCN No.:
Change implemented: YES/NO (*Delete as appropriate)	If change isn't implemented and working effectively, briefly describe actions taken: (e.g. change fixed, backout plans implemented etc.)

Configuration Items Changed

Item	Old version	New version

Results/benefits obtained

Total Costs
Impact Assessment – £   Implementation – £

Signed (Prime Contractor Change Manager):	Date:

501

13 The programme office

13.1 WHAT IS A PROGRAMME OFFICE?

To consider this question we need first to examine the environment in which programme management exists, and to then consider how it needs support. This book is about programme management. This chapter concentrates on the support that a programme office can provide. However, given that programmes depend on information and understanding about matters outside their boundary, this chapter also considers the interfaces to these areas external to the programme. Figure 13.1 describes the total environment and suggests where programmes might need help.

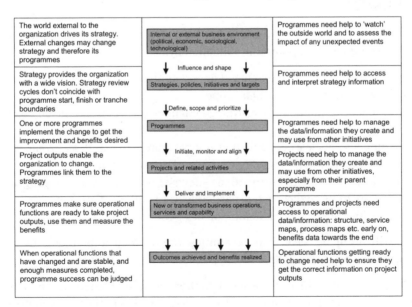

The world external to the organization drives its strategy. External changes may change strategy and therefore its programmes	Internal or external business environment (political, economic, sociological, technological)	Programmes need help to 'watch' the outside world and to assess the impact of any unexpected events
	↓ Influence and shape ↓	
Strategy provides the organization with a wide vision. Strategy review cycles don't coincide with programme start, finish or tranche boundaries	Strategies, policies, initiatives and targets	Programmes need help to access and interpret strategy information
	↓ Define, scope and prioritize ↓	
One or more programmes implement the change to get the improvement and benefits desired	Programmes	Programmes need help to manage the data/information they create and may use from other initiatives
	↓ Initiate, monitor and align ↓	
Project outputs enable the organization to change. Programmes link them to the strategy	Projects and related activities	Projects need help to manage the data/information they create and may use from other initiatives, especially from their parent programme
	↓ Deliver and implement ↓	
Programmes make sure operational functions are ready to take project outputs, use them and measure the benefits	New or transformed business operations, services and capability	Programmes and projects need access to operational data/information: structure, service maps, process maps etc. early on, benefits data towards the end
	↓ ↓ ↓ ↓	
When operational functions that have changed and are stable, and enough measures completed, programme success can be judged	Outcomes achieved and benefits realized	Operational functions getting ready to change need help to ensure they get the correct information on project outputs

Figure 13.1 Programme management environment

503

In the parts of this chapter that follow, consideration is given to:

1. the needs of the programme itself;
2. the need (if any) for information from, and feedback to the strategy group;
3. instructions from programmes to their projects and feedback from them;
4. information needs between the programme (and its projects) and relevant operational functions.

A programme office is a collection of functions that provides services to programmes. While these functions must be operated by physical entities, this does not mean they must all be located in the same physical area:

- Programme and project offices can be combined or separate.
- Global organizations might need multiple offices in different locations.
- Some service can be provided from outside of the programme office, for example, part time help from programme/project managers.

The appropriateness of different structures is considered later in this chapter.

13.2 HOW A PROGRAMME OFFICE CAN HELP

13.2.1 STRATEGY

Many programmes exist to implement part of the organization's strategy. A programme office can support this obligation by:

- helping the programme teams get access to the correct versions of strategic information, as relevant to their scope;
- informing programmes when strategy changes (or when significant change is pending);
- directing lessons learned and other information to the strategy group, so they can understand whether strategic initiatives are successful;
- when strategic initiatives are not as successful as expected, the programme office can help analyse why, particularly to differentiate between a poor strategy idea and bad implementation of a good strategic idea.

There will often be several programmes required to implement the whole strategy. The programme office can help maintain the full picture:

- The programme office can assess whether the sum of outcomes and benefits from all programmes will satisfy the strategic vision of the future state of the organization.

- The programme office can help spot where some programmes may be in danger of implementing change not required by the strategy.
- The programme office can make sure programmes are aware of each other's strategic contribution to avoid conflict, make teams aware of cross-programme dependencies and to promote synergistic approaches through cross-programme collaboration.

The programme office can help with strategic implementation in a variety of different roles:

- Be responsible for managing the implementation of the strategy, via an overarching strategic programme or similar.
- Support the team that is responsible for managing the implementation of the strategy, via an overarching strategic programme or similar.

Figure 13.2 shows how strategy can link to programmes via a strategic plan.

The UK Office of Government Commerce (OGC) promote the first role above but via a Centre of Excellence (COE).[1] The concept of a COE, while promoted by the UK Government, is equally important to the private sector. Excellence in the execution of programmes leads to operational improvements, important in both the private and public sectors. This is further explored later in this chapter when the alternative structures of a programme office are explained.

13.2.2 PROGRAMME

Programmes need to be managed with three different perspectives in mind, as explained below. Help for the programme, from the programme office, needs to reflect these perspectives.

1. The programme itself:
    - Expertise on programme management method, processes and standards that are used within the organization.
    - Audit/assurance to ensure compliance with the programme management method, organization standards, regulatory standards or legislation.

---

1 **COE Information Pack v3.1** (© Crown copyright OGC April 2004, www.ogc.gov.uk/embedded_object.asp?docid=1004430):
'Perhaps the most significant aspect of a COE that differentiates it from a programme or project support office is the relationship it has with the department's Management Board. A COE should provide the Management Board with strategic oversight of the department's portfolio of programmes and projects. This "helicopter view" will bring visibility to the interrelationships and interdependencies across the portfolio and support the Management Board in its judgements and decision-making on strategic priorities and commitments.'

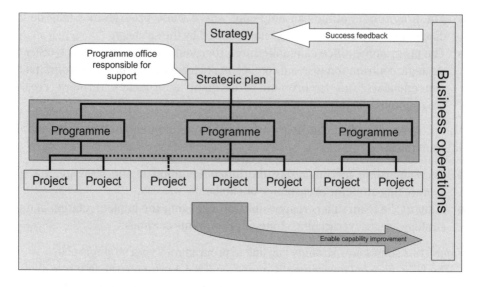

Figure 13.2   Showing how programmes relate to strategy and projects

- Custodians of programme information, to include master/baseline copies of documentation, configuration management, version and change control.
- Provision and analysis of programme information via reporting or other methods.
- Advice to the programme director or programme manager to support their decision making.
- Coaching and mentoring of any of the programme team.
- Assistance with related techniques: investment appraisal, prioritization, non-financial benefits measurement methods, and others. This may sometimes be provided via an alliance between the programme office and other functions such as finance.
2. The world external to the programme; the organization and its strategies, policies, standards, and so on:
   - Events external to, but relevant to, a programme often occur in an area too large to be practically monitored by the programme team. The programme office can coordinate 'watchers' who spot external events and together with programme office staff analyse how these might impact programmes.
   - The analysis of such external information often requires expertise that is not available from members of the programme team. The programme office can maintain relationships with experts inside and outside the organization, to act as a clearing house for demand for such expertise.

506

- A programme may need to exchange information/data with other business systems, for example finance. The programme office is often best placed to design, establish and maintain these interfaces for the benefit of all programmes. The programme office may need to be further supported by technical staff, such as IT.
3. Inwards to the projects in the programme:
   - A huge volume of information/data will flow between a programme and its projects. The programme office is often best placed to design, establish and maintain the interfaces between programmes and projects for the benefit of all programmes. The programme office may need to be further supported by technical staff such as IT.
   - Most of the work in a programme is carried out in its projects. The standard of project management is therefore critical to the success of the programme. The programme office can help ensure that projects are aware of, and adhere to, standards of management required by the programmes. This can be carried out by the project part of the programme office, or through the relationship between the programme office and separate project offices. This also applies where projects are run by an external organization through outsourcing or other contractual arrangements.

13.2.3 INFORMATION

Programmes create and consume large volumes of information. Each piece of information has a lifecycle, for example, draft, reviewed, approved, updated, archived. Documents in a programme rarely exist in isolation, they relate to others in that they derive information from them or are combined with them. When programme teams need to use information they need to ensure that they gain access to the correct versions, and that they get the complete set of information. The programme office can help as custodians of the repository and via configuration management (see also Chapter 9, 'Configuration management'). Figure 13.3 shows a typical set of programme documentation.

13.2.4 RESOURCES

Programmes and their projects require resources sometimes on a full-time basis and sometimes part-time. These resources can be people, where the requirement will be for specific skills, or physical where the requirement will be for specific functions (for example, testing facilities).

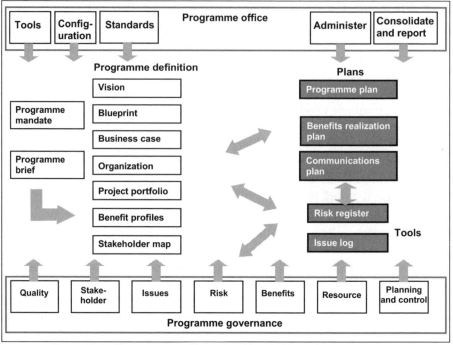

Figure 13.3 The programme office can provide valuable services to programmes

A programme office can assist with resource management as follows:

- Maintains a database of resources, their skills/attributes, location, availability, contact details and managerial responsibility for the resource.
- By identifying commitments on other programmes/projects and/or on business as usual (BAU) activities that will impact the ability of a programme to deliver.
- Maintains relationships with external organizations who can supply resources: contract agencies for staff, organizations who rent plant and equipment, agencies who rent/let building space.
- In some organizations, the programme office actually has responsibility for managing the allocation of resources on programmes and projects. Where resources are employed on more than one programme (or project) and BAU activities at the same time, some form of matrix management must be employed.

13.3 PROGRAMME OFFICE STRUCTURES

While programme offices must consist of physical entities, people, facilities, tools and equipment, they do not need to exist as one single functional unit. Programme offices can be:

- a single function, more applicable to smaller enterprises;
- separate functions for programmes and projects, often due to some of the reasons below, for example, a programme office at a regional head office, with a project office in each local business unit;
- Separate functions in different geographic regions, where it is important the programme office fully understands the local culture, legislation and business practice
- separate functions aligned to the organization structure; this is common among large global organizations.

Where there are separate function units, the structure must be carefully designed to ensure good communication between each unit (see Figure 13.4). The corporate programme office must ensure effective dissemination of corporate information to the regions, and monitor activity in the regions to ensure compliance with corporate requirements. Regional programme offices must likewise ensure regional information is disseminated to business unit project

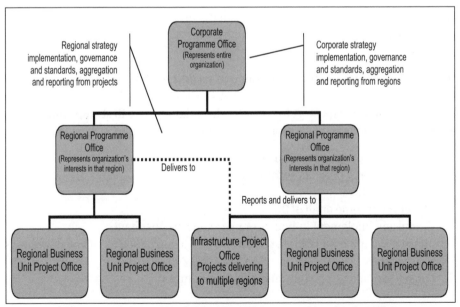

Figure 13.4   Communication between multiple programme and project offices

offices, and monitor activity in the business units to ensure compliance with corporate and regional requirements.

13.4 DESIGNING AND BUILDING A PROGRAMME OFFICE

13.4.1 VISION, OBJECTIVES, SCOPE AND CONSTRAINTS

As already noted earlier in this chapter a programme office can exist in many different formats. Before jumping to any conclusions about what the design of the programme office will look like, its purpose must be clearly defined. Treat the whole exercise as a programme: start by producing a brief that clearly states the vision, the objectives of the services the programme office will provide. Chapter 2 'The programme management process' explains how to run a programme.

13.4.2 BLUEPRINT (DESIRED FUTURE STATE), OUTCOMES AND THE APPROACH

The initial brief will need to be broken down into more detail, so you have clarity and agreement on the nature of the components of the desired programme office. This will typically need to cover:

1. processes
2. capabilities
3. staff
4. facilities
5. tools.

The desired outcomes should be stated as targets, in 'SMART'[2] terms wherever possible.

Only now should you start to consider the solution. The first step should be to examine the options. The checklist below lists some examples of what to consider:

1. one physical programme and project office;
2. programme and projects separated;
3. the virtual office;
4. outsourcing some or all of the services required;
5. design and implement in-house, or use external consultants;
6. phasing the implementation, so you don't try to introduce too many new things too quickly;
7. consideration of geography and differing cultures.

---

2 SMART – Specific, Measurable, Actionable, Realistic, Timely.

13.4.3 DESIGN AND PLAN

Take into account the following physical aspects:

1. processes
2. information flows
3. information systems
4. organization and people
   a. roles and responsibilities
   b. profiles
   c. skills and knowledge.

The following are the cultural (soft) aspects to consider:

1. working with the programme board;
2. working with the programme director;
3. working with the programme manager;
4. working with the project managers;
5. working with the other internal managers;
6. working with the programme and project teams;
7. working with the external organization;
8. use of a programme office as a training ground for programme and project managers;
9. conflicts between other duties where some staff are allocated to the programme office part-time.

Consider potential implementation issues. Implementing a programme office can be an equally major challenge. Careful consideration should be given to introducing the changes in phases (programme tranches). Give consideration to the following when designing the implementation plans:

1. The current state of the organization:
   - current processes and tools for managing programmes and projects;
   - how consistently they are used;
   - the success rate of programmes and projects, lessons that can be learned;
   - attitudes to programme and project management, from inside the programme and project teams, and from outside them, especially those who receive the project outputs;
   - the overall organization attitude to processes and control.
2. If many of the organization's processes are not clearly defined, control methods for the organization tend to be ad hoc and there is a belief among managers that this stuff just adds bureaucracy. These and other similar symptoms of poor organization maturity suggest the implementation should be on many tranches over a longer period of time.

3. Are there other parts of the organization that have already achieved a successful programme office implementation? Is that part of the organization well respected? If yes, consider getting them to help your implementation. This help can be both with physical aspectss (such as tools) and soft or cultural aspects (helping you to persuade the doubters that this is worthwhile).

13.4.4 MANAGING THE IMPLEMENTATION

The work described above, and the full process for managing a programme as described in Chapter 2, will help you prepare for a successful implementation of the new programme office. At this point, you should have an agreed outline design, plans, costs and agreed business case, and clearly defined benefits.

The implementation therefore follows those plans.

13.5 PREPARING THE PROGRAMME OFFICE FOR NEW PROGRAMMES

13.5.1 LOOKING AHEAD

As new programmes start the programme office may be required to provide support with:

1. Getting access to information, strategy, lessons learned from other programmes, and other material, as the programme produces its definition (see Chapter 2. 'The programme management process').
2. Defining a programme also includes work to design the governance arrangements. Part of this will include the design and specification of the programme infrastructure. The programme office can help here with its knowledge of programme management infrastructures, and that it might actually be involved later to set up that infrastructure.
3. The programme must establish an adequate infrastructure before the first tranche is started (see Chapter 2). Otherwise the programme risks getting out of control very quickly. A programme office is often commissioned to do this work.
4. During the life of the programme, the programme office will usually be required to provide services to support the programme.

Like any other part of an organization, the programme office has to operate with limited finite resources. It therefore needs to look ahead to manage its own activities, to ensure the demands on it from programmes do not exceed its capacity. Where the programme office is virtual and or some of its staff are part time, it needs to assess this capacity by also looking at the workloads of resources in other parts of the organization.

There are several areas the programme office should monitor to help it advise on and prepare for new programmes. These are described below.

13.5.2 WATCHING THE STRATEGY

Strategy normally changes on a regular cycle, typically each year to coincide with the financial year end. Sometimes it changes abnormally to react to severe unexpected changes. Any change in strategy may have a consequential impact on programmes and they in turn may need to change. The current strategic programme may need to be extended, as the new strategy now looks 1 year further ahead.

From this, the programme office can make a high-level assessment of the likely demands on its services. If this is likely to greatly exceed its capacity, it should advise the strategy group that this is a risk to the implementation of the strategy via the strategic programme.

13.5.3 MONITORING THE STRATEGIC PROGRAMME

Programmes differ from projects in that they operate in a much more uncertain environment. Projects tend to have definite start and finish points, with the aim of delivering a predetermined output, giving them relatively clear development paths from initiation to delivery. Programmes, on the other hand, typically have a more strategic vision of the desired end-goal, but no clearly defined path to get there. Programmes are able to deal with the uncertainty surrounding the achievement of the vision, whereas projects work best where the outputs can be well defined (OGC, 2003). Programmes that implement strategy will therefore change as they adjust to these uncertainties while still striving for success and the benefits required. This means the demands on the programme office are also like to change, both in terms of the volume and type of support required and the timing of that activity.

The programme office, as a critical resource for these programmes, will need to advise on its ability to provide the inputs required, so the programmes remain realistic.

13.5.4 MONITORING INDIVIDUAL PROGRAMMES

As explained above, the role of the programme office differs during the life of a programme:

1. Defining the programme:
   a. providing access to information the programme needs to prepare its definition and plans;
   b. helping to design the infrastructure to support the programme;
   c. advising on techniques such as risk analysis and planning.
2. When the Define stage ends and before the first tranche:
   a. helping to establish the infrastructure and ensure the programme team and programme office staff are ready to start the management and governance activities.
3. During management and governance:
   a. running some or all of the infrastructure;
   b. administering programme information;
   c. reporting;
   d. managing the communications systems;
   e. and more as may be described in the programme definition.
4. Closing the programme:
   a. providing information to help with the end of programme reviews;
   b. decommissioning the infrastructure.

The nature and scale of the service required of the programme office and the programme plan give the programme office valuable information in order to manage its own activities.

13.6 TOOLS FOR THE PROGRAMME OFFICE

A programme office will often be expert in the use of tools that aid both programme and project management. In any programme there will be large volumes of data/information flowing between the programme and its projects. Tools for programme management that cannot interface with those projects are probably of limited assistance.

13.6.1 PROJECT MANAGEMENT TOOLS

Project management software is about modelling the project: you can model how to put the roof on, how to test the software, when to deliver the printing press. Modelling helps people to see a little way into the future and therefore it helps people make decisions that affect the project. It is the people, and the decisions they make, that affect the project, not the tools.

13.6.2 PROGRAMME MANAGEMENT TOOLS

In an organization where all work in programmes and projects is planned, and resources are allocated and assigned to do work, people find out what they are supposed to be doing this week by reference to their computer.

The software knows what is going on in other parts of the organization and each person is kept in touch with plans, changes to projects, assignments and many other things that are added to the system by other people. Each person finds out what they should be doing by looking at their part of the plan, and can report back what they have actually done, thereby affecting other people's plans.

The software is no longer an external model of the project; it plays a central role in modelling and in communicating information across the organization. People do not wander about picking up projects at random and progressing them a little. They put the programme management tool at centre stage and tell each other what's going on through the system.

The interaction between people, their work and the purpose of the programmes should be understood and reflected in all plans and documents. Very few organizations have achieved this level of maturity, however.

13.6.3 DO YOU NEED SOFTWARE TOOLS?

You might need software tools to support your programme management techniques for the following:

- It is easier to encourage and enforce standards through a software system. It is simpler to ensure that everyone uses the same milestones on their plans and that every plan shows the design work being signed off by the main board before manufacturing begins. It is easier to get people to plan in a consistent and predictable way with a systematic approach. A software system will underpin this.
- It should be easy to extract from the mass of data the information each manager needs. Each manager's requirements will be different: project managers want details of their projects, departmental managers want to know what is going on within their teams, programme managers want an overview of all projects, individual resources want to see what they are supposed to be doing. This kind of manipulation of data is what computers are good at doing.
- There is going to be a lot of information. You might easily have 3000 or 4000 tasks in a plan mixed in with resources, calendars, costs and baselines. It all gets a bit voluminous – not complex, but overwhelming. Computers, especially big computers, are good at dealing with large volumes of structured data.

515

13.6.4 A WORD OF CAUTION

Effective programme management requires a number of component parts to work well, in their own right and through interaction with each other. These parts are:

1. process (the steps, methods, and techniques used to plan and manage)
2. people (with appropriate skills and experience)
3. information
4. systems/technology.

Most failings in programme and project management are caused by process and people, and can often be evidenced through the poor information available. Only rarely is technology the root cause of such problems. However, many organizations that are experiencing programme and project management difficulties rush out and buy the latest and best software system, expecting it to be some sort of 'silver bullet' that will magically fix their problems.

If you have deficiencies in your programme or project management, thoroughly investigate the process used and the capabilities of the people. Fix any problems here, before any consideration is given to new software.

13.6.5 TYPES OF SOFTWARE TOOLS

13.6.5.1 Consolidation model

The consolidation model approach has been available for some time (see Figure 13.5).

In this approach, each component team plan their own work using a popular

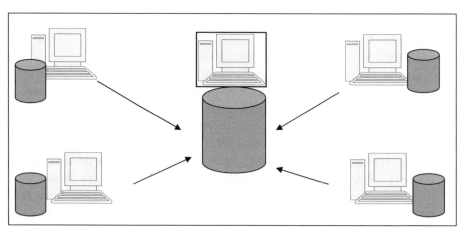

Figure 13.5 Consolidation model

software tool. Periodically, these plans are transmitted to a central location – such as the programme office – where they are poured into a great big pot and consolidated into a meaningful programme plan.

Reports are then generated from the consolidated plan and distributed. This transmission is done electronically with e-mail or other message-based systems.

- **Advantage**: Simple for the remote planners, relatively cheap software, allows use of popular desktop tools.
- **Disadvantages**: Difficult to achieve consistency. If tasks and resources don't have exactly the same name or code, this leads to chaos and confusion. Also tends to be unreliable as the underlying process requires everyone to update their plans on the same timetable. Therefore, it requires a team of consolidators to resolve the chaos, which is slow and time-consuming. Then finally the output has to be interpreted, giving scope for miscommunication.

13.6.5.2 Centralized planning model

In the centralized planning model, all teams access a central database where all activity and resource information is held. Everyone accesses this database using the same software (see Figure 13.6). This tends to require heavyweight, multi-user software.

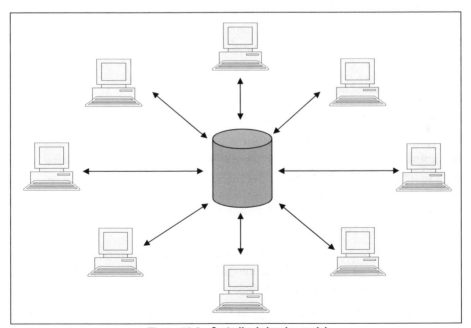

Figure 13.6   Centralized planning model

517

- **Advantages**: The data is always fully consolidated and as up-to-date as the latest input. Teams can produce their own reports. It is easy to create logical links between team plans and the model can handle programme-wide resources and the sharing of common resources between teams.
- **Disadvantages**: Expensive software and communication. Software tends to be powerful but as user-friendly as a cornered rat!

13.6.5.3 Person to person model

The person-to-person model is a very common approach. Each team plans its own activities and sends relevant information to those who need to know by e-mail; for example, every Tuesday an e-mail sent giving the status of each work package in terms of end-date, issues, and so on.

- **Advantages**: Cheap and easy (uses the existing e-mail network). Flexible – each team can use its own tools.
- **Disadvantages**: Tends to be uncontrolled and anarchic. Creates yet another flood of e-mails, which need to be retrieved, studied and interpreted in order to work out what is happening. It can be very difficult to identify resource conflicts, to govern, to establish accuracy or the value of the information being received. Furthermore, the ease of use of these tools tends to promote 'I will send to everyone to be sure' syndrome, thus greatly reducing the effectiveness of communications (see also Chapter 6 'Stakeholder management', and Chapter 10, 'Internal communications'.

13.6.5.4 Web publishing systems

Typical functions of web publishing systems are:

- reports published to a central website;
- timesheets are browser based, but not all such systems support planning;
- a webmaster maintains site;
- browser access to information;
- possible to examine reports and deduce impact;
- cross-project reports.

Here everyone maintains their own plans, but publishes reports to a central website (Internet or intranet). Thus, for each team, the website will show a Gantt chart, resource usage diagrams, cashflow curves, and so on.

- **Advantages**: Uses simple desktop tools that now have a web publishing capability. Rapid dissemination/easy access to reports.

- **Disadvantages**: Reports can vary widely and have to be interpreted. It can be very difficult to identify resource conflicts and inter-linkages. It is also often difficult to govern or to establish accuracy or value of information being received.

13.6.5.5 Direct update model

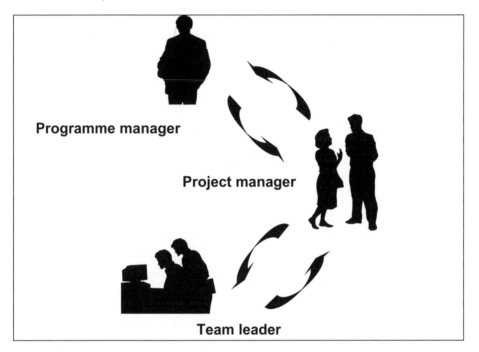

Figure 13.7   Direct update model

The direct update model is the latest approach and likely to be the way forward. Each team maintains its own plans, but connections are built in so that the update of a subordinate plan automatically updates the other plans that it affects. There are two types of connection:

- delegation of work packages from senior management down to projects and teams (as many levels as needed);
- loan of resources from pools to projects.

- **Advantages**: Immediate and direct update of all affected plans. No accidental overloading of resources. These systems have an auditable distribution of work. Each team has control over its own plans, but others have complete visibility. Activity descriptions can be in the local spoken languages of component teams – Spanish, Italian, English, and so on.

● **Disadvantages**: All must use the same tool. Relies on a relatively high level of programme organization and maturity.

13.6.6 PROGRAMME OFFICE TOOLS

These are software tools designed specifically for the programme and project office. Inevitably they often include functionality found in other programme and project management tools. Typically they provide facilities for:

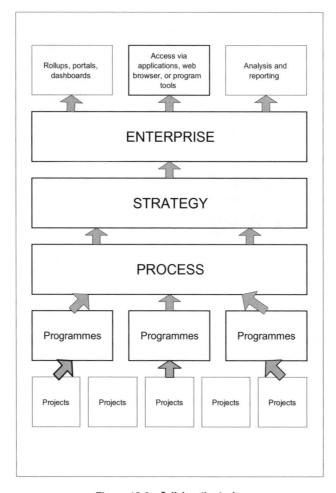

Figure 13.8   Collaboration tools

- risk and issues
- request for information
- personal expenses
- change control
- financial control
- benefits
- capacity planning

13.6.6.1 Collaboration tools

Programme teams have always needed to share information. This is difficult when the members are located in different geographical regions. Collaboration software tools are now quite sophisticated in that they don't just store and share documents and data, they help manage it (workflow and version control), control access to it (authority and relevance), and they can analyse and transform it to provide easier-to-digest business intelligence (see Figure 13.8).

Programmes have a workspace that can be structured so documents are organized for easy access.

Typical functions are:

- document storage
- version control
- chat rooms
- forums
- discussion threads
- contact lists
- resource/equipment tracking.

- **Advantages**: Easy to store, access and share programme information and data, wherever you are; often all you need is a PC with an Internet browser and a broadband connection (or equivalent).
- **Disadvantages**: If not carefully controlled, they become cluttered with too many documents; users cannot find the correct versions, are misled by what they read, and become disillusioned. While they are excellent for sharing information around the world, there are times when only a face to face meeting is really effective (see Case Study 13.1).

CASE STUDY 13.1: EXAMPLE OF POOR IMPLEMENTATION OF A PROGRAMME TOOL

A major global organization with hundreds of business units introduced a collaboration system in just one of these business units. Senior programme and project staff were trained and given controlled access to workspaces for their programmes and projects. All were encouraged to use the new tools and to share important information.

For the first week or two all went well. But after about 6 weeks, there were over 16 000 documents. The tool helped you find lots of documents and data, but it became very hard to get the information and knowledge you really needed.

Because programmes and projects seemed to work well locally, they assumed the processes used were good and well established, and the capabilities of the staff were good enough to manage complex structured information. In reality, while projects ended successfully, there were lots of deficiencies that were not visible as much information was stored on local PCs, in the project manager's desk, and so on. Problems resulting from this were often resolved by working harder and longer days. The use of this tool exposed the weakness in the processes used to manage programmes and projects, resulting in poorly structured and configured information.

The moral is that these tools are not 'magic'. They require more organization, processes and active responsibility than their manual counterparts to control them. However, if you put this structure and control in place, they then work much better than their manual equivalents.

13.7 PROGRAMME OFFICE INTERFACES

Programmes often cut across operational functions and thus have numerous potential interfaces:

- In a change management environment, interfaces are the operational areas of the organization that are being changed.
- For operational management, BAU activities that may or may not be changed by the programme but which supply or need programme information:
  - financial controls
  - resource ownership (matrix environment)
  - technical, IT and manufacturing services.

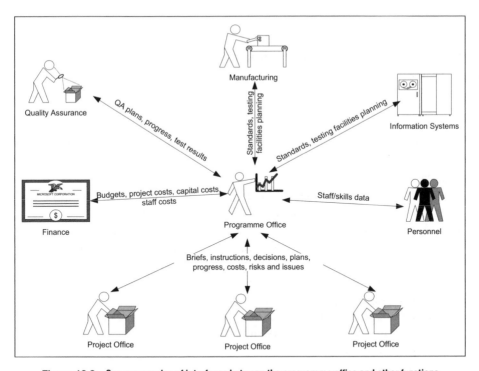

Figure 13.9   Some examples of interfaces between the programme office and other functions

13.8 PROGRAMME OFFICE ROLES AND RESPONSIBILITIES

13.8.1 OVERVIEW OF THE ROLE OF THE PROGRAMME OFFICE FUNCTION

The programme office may support a single programme, or it may support a number of programmes. The scope of roles for the programme office will vary depending on the size and capabilities of the organization. For example, with appropriate expertise, the programme office may be a 'centre of excellence' for all programmes and projects within the organization, providing specialist expertise and facilitation across the programme and its projects.

The programme office can provide some aspects of assurance for the programme. However, it is important to have an independent assurance function in addition to any internal assurance function.

The core function of the programme office is to provide an information hub for the programme (see Figure 13.9). This will typically involve the following:

● Tracking and reporting:

- tracking measurements;
- reporting progress on progress.
- Information management (websites are useful tools for providing these facilities):
  - holding master copies of all programme information;
  - generating all necessary quality management documentation
  - maintaining, controlling and updating programme documentation;
  - establishing and maintaining the index to an electronic library of programme information.
- Financial accounting:
  - assisting the programme manager with budget control for the programme;
  - maintaining status reports on all projects in the programme.
- Risk and issue tracking:
  - analysing interfaces and critical dependencies between projects and recommending appropriate actions to the programme manager;
  - maintaining the list of stakeholders and their interests.
- Quality control:
  - establishing consistent practices and standards adhering to the programme governance arrangements, including:
    - project planning;
    - reporting;
    - change control;
    - analysing risks and maintaining and updating the risk log for the programme.
- Change control:
  - registering changes for subsequent investigation and resolution;
  - monitoring items identified as requiring action;
  - prompting timely actions;
  - reporting on whether required actions have been carried out.

The programme office may be sufficiently resourced to provide additional expertise across the programme, for example:

- providing a strategic overview of all programmes and interdependencies, and reporting upward to senior management;
- providing consultancy-style support to project delivery teams at initiation and throughout the lifecycle of the programme; ensuring a common approach is adopted and sharing good practice;
- carrying out health checks and advising on solutions during the lifetime of the programme and individual projects; for example, facilitating workshops involving project teams, stakeholders and members of the programme team.

13.8.2 PROGRAMME OFFICE SKILL SETS

Programme office skill sets are as follows:

- Planning:
  - programme and project planning techniques;
  - use of software tools for scheduling and resource management;
  - use of software tools for reporting, analysis and communication of plans;
  - process and tools to capture actual progress, such as via time-sheets.
- Risk and issues:
  - techniques for risk and issue analysis;
  - procedures to manage risks and issues;
  - administration of the associated action plans.
- Financial staff:
  - cost estimating;
  - cost tracking and analysis such as via earned value;
  - an understanding of financial methods used for the depreciation and amortization of programme and project costs; for example to appreciate why the depreciation charges for fixed assets procured by a programme might be allocated to the programme costs, rather than the acquisition cost.
- Programme librarian:
  - manage programme- and project-oriented filing systems, both physical and electronic;
  - configuration management (see Chapter 9);
  - maintain knowledge about how to access relevant information outside the programme office; other systems in the organization, Internet resources, for example.
  - keeping reference material up to date.
- Change control function:
  - techniques for assessing requests for change;
  - procedures to manage requests for change;
  - administration of the associated action plans .
- Administrator:
  - general office duties;
  - arranging travel;
  - booking facilities for programme and project teams.

The following will interact with the programme office:

- programme board
- programme director
- programme manager

- project manager
- project team leaders
- external groups.
  - stakeholders
  - groups external to the organization, for example contractors.

REFERENCES

OGC (2003) *Managing Successful Programmes: Delivering Business in the Multi-project Environments*. Second edition. London: The Stationery Office.

14 Programme knowledge management

14.1 INTRODUCTION

The objective of a knowledge management process is to capture and share knowledge, while through monitoring and review, ensuring that it is a worthwhile and valuable asset. In the case of programme knowledge, that is, the knowledge the organization has or can obtain that will improve a programme's likelihood of success, this knowledge includes:

- knowledge of the organization, that is, context
- knowledge of how to achieve the business change objectives of the programme, that is, best practice
- knowledge of how to manage the programme itself, that is, programme and project lessons learned.

Programme knowledge management procedures have a strong tendency, if they exist at all, to focus exclusively on the third item, programme and project lessons learned. This represents a missed opportunity as careful consideration of all the knowledge required by the programme can result in significant savings in time, cost and frustration.

Effective knowledge management improves the organization's ability to respond quickly and with greater insight to the issues and challenges that arise during the life of the programme. This will, in turn, lead to the identification of more creative and effective solutions to these problems.

Knowledge captured must be specific and appropriate to the requirements of the programme, and should access the expertise and experience of the programme team and the wider organization. During the Closure stage, most programmes will undertake specific steps to ensure that programme knowledge is captured and make it available for subsequent use in the organization. While this final review is important and valuable, it is insufficient and, of course, too late. An

527

ongoing process of collecting, collating and distributing knowledge also needs to be in place to ensure that existing information is fully utilized.

Each programme needs to develop an effective knowledge management process, one that will identify, quantify, plan and manage knowledge of value to the programme. Knowledge management activities will begin during the Define stage, be developed during the Establish stage and continue throughout the programme's life.

Potential knowledge requirements will be initially be identified during the Define stage and a knowledge management process defined during the Establish stage. By the time the Establish stage is complete, a knowledge management plan will have been developed that defines the knowledge to be captured, its estimated cost, and how its transfer and sharing will be achieved. Activities for achieving knowledge sharing will be incorporated into the integrated programme plan to ensure they are resourced, scheduled and controlled.

An effective knowledge management process addresses the capture and transfer of knowledge from both within the programme and outside. Knowledge takes many forms, but three types of knowledge are of potential value to a programme, and need to be considered:

- **Organizational context**: Knowledge concerning how the organization operates, for example, organization structure, financial information, roles and responsibilities.
- **Best practice**: Knowledge concerning how the best organizations undertake similar processes and procedures, for example, benchmarks, best practice approaches and tools.
- **Programme and project lessons learned**: Knowledge related to managing this and previous programmes, for example, communications, leadership, programme management tools.

Before considering in more detail what needs to be done to implement a programme knowledge management process, it is worth reflecting upon why managing knowledge is important:

- knowledge capture creates an enterprise that remembers what it knows;
- people require knowledge to make change happen;
- knowledge encourages the cross-fertilization and cross-contribution of ideas;
- lack of knowledge breeds uncertainty and anxiety, which in turn interferes with focus and productivity.

A knowledge management process needs to provide a clear approach to collection, communication, and use of knowledge by the programme team.

Even when knowledge management is considered by a programme manager or team members, there is often a very narrow definition of knowledge applied. Therefore the programme may only consider technical information relative to the programme deliverables as knowledge. In truth, there is a very wide range of knowledge that can benefit the programme, including:

- **Technical**: Scientific and/or technical information, often directly applicable to programme deliverables.
- **Metrics**: Statistics, trends, financial information, performance measures, historic data.
- **Procedural**: Procedures, standards, specifications, regulations.
- **Functional**: Best practice, lessons learned.
- **Managerial**: Business plans, budget information, issues and trend analysis.
- **Organizational**: Strategic plans, systems maps, knowledge maps, competitive analysis.
- **Relational**: Internal/external relationships and experience, customer information, supplier information.
- **Programme**: Tools, techniques, skills.

There are no hard and fast rules, but any or all of the above knowledge may be of value to the programme. Only by considering each category, in the context of the programme's objectives, can a programme manager be certain of identifying knowledge that may be of value.

14.2 A KNOWLEDGE MANAGEMENT PROCESS

In its simplest form, a knowledge management process comprises seven steps:

1. Identify knowledge that is likely to be valuable to the programme.
2. Quantify currently available knowledge.
3. Establish goals, approaches and procedures for knowledge management.
4. Capture knowledge.
5. Categorize and store knowledge.
6. Communicate and share knowledge.
7. Monitor and review the knowledge capture process and amend as required.

Organizational needs and programme information are inputs to the process while the outcomes are programme lessons learned, business solutions and good practices that are shared within the programme and with the wider organization. A process is illustrated in Figure 14.1, which provides a framework for an effective knowledge management process.

529

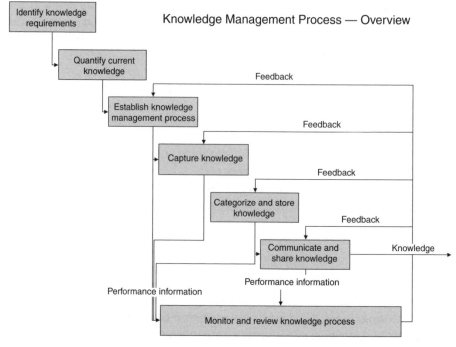

Figure 14.1   Knowledge management process model

14.3 KNOWLEDGE MANAGEMENT ROLES AND RESPONSIBILITIES

For knowledge management to be effective, it is necessary for it to be the responsibility of one or more people within the programme. The allocation of full- or part-time resources will vary depending on the size and complexity of the programme and the level of knowledge to be managed.

The key roles in a knowledge management process are:

- **Knowledge sponsor**: A senior member of management and the programme board who will be responsible for overall direction of the knowledge management process. This person should be senior enough to have budget authority to allocate resources, and credibility to obtain buy-in from other leaders in the organization. The knowledge sponsor needs to understand and support the importance of knowledge management and assure its results are leveraged to improve the business.
- **Subject matter experts (SMEs)**: Contributors, from within the organization or outside, who are recognized as authorities on a given subject. Like 'expert

witnesses' it is important that all stakeholders recognize the SME as someone who possesses the necessary experience and knowledge to input to the programme.

- **Programme knowledge lead**: Design, develop, implement and maintain processes, tools and policies to capture, store and share internal and external information with all relevant individuals and teams.
- **Programme manager:** Ultimately responsible for:
  - securing senior management commitment to knowledge management;
  - defining the knowledge management process;
  - defining the roles and responsibilities for the process;
  - determining and securing the necessary resources;
  - managing the knowledge management process.

  These responsibilities may be carried out by the programme team or delegated to a knowledge management team if the scale of the task is sufficient.

- **Programme team members**: Must:
  - understand the importance of knowledge and knowledge management to the success of the programme;
  - understand the knowledge management process for the programme; and
  - abide by that process and contribute to its effectiveness.
- **Other stakeholders**: When developing a knowledge management process, it is necessary to consider all individuals or groups outside the programme who may need to take part in the process. For example, this may include the enterprise's senior management, human resources (HR) function and representatives from major stakeholder groups including unions and employee representatives.

14.4 KNOWLEDGE MANAGEMENT THROUGH THE PROGRAMME LIFECYCLE

Knowledge management requires a clear set of objectives, fully aligned with the programme's objectives.

The plan to implement knowledge management must be based upon a clear understanding of the requirements for knowledge within the programme, key knowledge management activities and measures of success. These measures must be integrated into the overall programme measures of success to ensure visibility.

It is also important to identify the useful knowledge that exists within the programme team in addition to that within the wider organization. This knowledge may include programme experience, best practices and organizational context. Within each of these areas, there may be valuable information available, some of which is not generally considered to be knowledge.

The knowledge management process continues throughout the programme lifecycle with different priorities at each stage, as follows:

14.4.1 DEFINE STAGE

During the Define stage the objectives for knowledge management are focused on understanding the programme's potential requirement for knowledge. This involves identifying what knowledge would be valuable to the programme and therefore enhance its likelihood of success.

Given that, during this stage, there is no firm commitment to undertake the programme, significant resources should not be expended acquiring or organizing specific knowledge. The objective of this stage is to present to the programme executive the programme's requirement for knowledge and a plan to obtain and provide that knowledge throughout the life of the programme.

14.4.1.1 Identify knowledge that is likely to be valuable to the programme

During the Define stage it is important to consider what information (knowledge) may be of value during the programme and how it can be assembled. The danger here is of defining knowledge too narrowly, considering only programme-related knowledge. Information concerning the context of the programme has the potential to be even more valuable. Consider for example a programme to implement an Enterprise Resource Planning (ERP) system across a manufacturing company. There would be great value in having knowledge concerning:

- organizational context – for example, the business processes and organization structure of the company today;
- best practice – for example, how world class manufacturing companies have implemented ERP systems to greatest benefit;
- programme and project lessons learned – for example, how have the most effective ERP implementations been organized and run.

While it may seem difficult to think of all the knowledge that might be of value during a major programme, some significant elements can be identified and efforts put in place to obtain the knowledge required. The deliverable from this step is a 'wish list' of knowledge.

14.4.1.2 Quantify currently available knowledge

Having created an initial wish list the next question to address is: 'How much of this information is available today?' A comparison between the wish list and current knowledge assets will highlight any significant shortfalls. In addition to assessing the knowledge currently available it is also important at this stage to evaluate the organization's processes for accumulating and disseminating knowledge. If there are sophisticated procedures for capturing internal and external knowledge, the programme can, and should, use these to its advantage. If there are no such procedures in the organization, the programme will need to develop the data-gathering and sharing processes it will need.

14.4.1.3 Establish goals, approaches and procedures for knowledge management

Any process or procedure requires clear goals and objectives if it is to be effective. Examples of goals for a programme knowledge management process include:

- Programme goals for knowledge capture/sharing:
  - The programme will identify and use relevant knowledge existing in the organization.
  - Knowledge sharing 'events' (for example, meetings and other forums) will be held on a regular basis and will include all appropriate programme members.
  - 'Lessons learned sessions' will be held, at the end of each phase of the programme, to collect working practices to improve the ways of working.
  - The programme will have a common repository to store all relevant/appropriate information.
- Programme goals for wider knowledge sharing
  - The programme will share all relevant knowledge within the organization.
  - The programme will utilize all appropriate organizational knowledge management processes and information sources.
  - The programme will collect, collate and utilize knowledge from appropriate external sources.
- Team member goals:
  - Programme team members will be evaluated on their knowledge management contribution to the programme.
  - Programme team members will be trained in the use of the programme knowledge repository as well as processes, procedures and policies in relation to knowledge management.
  - Programme team members will be trained in the use of appropriate organizational information systems and repositories.

533

- Each programme team member will be responsible for documenting lessons learned on an ongoing basis.
- Appropriate programme members will be involved in relevant meetings, discussion forums, and so on, to share and learn.
- Programme team members will ensure programme knowledge is made available to the wider organization.

Individual team member goals should be confirmed when the programme team is assembled (Establish Stage) but the broad objectives need to be identified concurrently with the wider programme objectives.

At this stage in the development of a programme knowledge management process, a programme manager should have three important pieces of information:

- a list of information and knowledge that will be valuable to the programme;
- a corresponding list of information and knowledge that is currently available, together with an assessment of the organization's capability to keep this information up to date;
- established goals and objectives for the knowledge management process.

Knowledge Required	Value to the Programme	Potential Source	Potential Cost of Acquisition	Recommendation
Organizational process maps and procedures	Very high	Quality management function	Minimal	Obtain – link with quality management intranet
Best practice process templates and benchmarks	Medium	Baldrige Business Best Practices*	High	Do not obtain – poor fit with requirement considering cost
Best practice process templates and benchmarks	Medium	Industry benchmarking forum	Fairly low	Obtain – better fit with requirement than Baldrige Business Best Practices at lower cost
Programme office set-up and organization	High	Gantthead.com online repository	Fairly low	Do not obtain – lower cost option available
Programme office set-up and organization	High	*Gower Handbook of Programme Management*	Very low	Obtain – excellent value for money

* Baldrige Best Practices is a web-based consultancy service that provides best practice definitions and benchmarks. See www.bestprocess.com.

Figure 14.2   Example knowledge acquisition plan

This information should now be collated to form the beginnings of a knowledge accquisition plan (see Figure 14.2).

The next step is to determine where any information and knowledge not currently available can be obtained. Two primary sources need to be considered:

- **Created by the programme:** For example, capturing lessons learned as the programme progresses. Most project and programme management methods discuss lessons learnt and stress the importance of learning reviews at key points in the lifecycle. These events, either at the end of an individual Project or at some other key stage in the programme, are a valuable mechanism to capture the experience of the 'front line troops' before it is lost. The requirement for these learning events should be defined at this stage. Precise guidelines as to when and how they should be undertaken will be developed during the Establish stage.
- **Obtained from sources external to the programme:** For example, obtained from a best practice website or purchased from a research organization such as Gartner or Forrester. An area of knowledge management that usually attracts less attention and consideration is sources external to the programme. There are a myriad of external sources that can provide knowledge to a programme, these include, arranged in, roughly, order of cost of acquisition:
  a. academic and other public domain sources – free of charge
  b. the organization's own 'SMEs' – usually free of charge
  c. books and periodicals – inexpensive
  d. specialist web portals, for example, Gantthead.com, or The Balanced Scorecard Institute – fairly inexpensive
  e. research organizations, for example, Gartner, Forrester – fairly expensive
  f. management consultants – expensive
  g. experts and 'gurus' – very expensive.

This is just a sample of the potential sources of information and knowledge that can be valuable to a programme. Like all other decisions, a cost–benefit calculation needs to be done and the most cost-effective solutions adopted. Paying $10 000 for a technology expert who can save the programme weeks of work and move benefits delivery forward may be the bargain on the year. Spending $39.99 on a book that is of no relevance is a waste of time (to read it) and money. Therefore the need for knowledge must be clearly identified to avoid acquiring the wrong knowledge, and the value of each element on that knowledge needs to be assessed, so you know what it is worth.

It is worth mentioning the Internet at this stage. The Internet has changed the world of knowledge and particularly 'free' knowledge – just ask any student doing their homework. The Internet and all its associated technologies provide huge opportunities for knowledge management and these should be considered and explored. However, knowledge on the web is generally unstructured and the biggest problem with any 'Google' search is the mass of material that comes back. In some instances it will be more cost-effective to pay for targeted knowledge than to rely on 'free stuff'.

14.4.1.4 Measures of success

Having established the objectives related to knowledge management, one way to ensure that knowledge management activities are completed is to incorporate knowledge management measures of success into the programme's overall measures. This means that if the planned knowledge management activities are not successfully carried out, the programme will not be deemed a complete success. The same principle should be applied to programme team member's personal performance targets and addressed during regular performance appraisals.

When the programme board and executive consider the proposal to initiate the programme at the end of the Define stage, there should be a clear statement of what knowledge will be required, how it will be obtained and what it will cost, as part of the overall programme definition.

14.4.2 ESTABLISH STAGE

The Establish stage is where procedures and processes are put into place to manage the programme. For knowledge management, the agreed processes to acquire, store and distribute the knowledge and information required by the programme are set up during this stage.

14.4.2.1 Establish knowledge management processes

When establishing knowledge management, there are four 'enablers' that support an effective process:

- **People and culture**: Creating the appropriate values and behaviours that support knowledge management.
- **Structure**: Defining roles and responsibilities that make people accountable for knowledge management.
- **Process and policies**: Establishing methods and procedures to ensure knowledge management is achieved consistently.
- **Technology**: Using tools that enable knowledge capture and sharing.

When determining the approach for capturing and sharing knowledge, the application of each enabler should be considered. For example, consider the technology enabler in the context of the requirement for local versus global knowledge sharing. If sharing knowledge is considered to be best achieved 'face to face' and the dispersion of the team is 'global', then videoconferencing might provide a solution. However, if the team is located together, in person meetings would be the best solution, with technical enablers such as electronic white boards and videos being most appropriate. Each element needs to be considered to arrive at a practical and cost-effective solution. In developing an approach to knowledge management, it is useful to identify the critical features of each of the enablers listed above for each type of knowledge under consideration; see Figure 14.3 for an example.

	People and Culture	Structure	Processes	Technology
Organizational context	Willingness of the organization to share information with programme	Senior organizational information owners on programme board	Programme team included on distribution of organizational knowledge sharing	Programme team provided with access to organizational information and knowledge systems
Industry/sector best practice	Openness of the programme team and wider organization to ideas from outside	Organizational SMEs attached to programme team External experts co-opted to programme team	External knowledge watch Subscription to external knowledge sources	Links to 'on-line' knowledge sources and repositories
Programme/ project knowledge	Willingness to learn from and share with others Incentives to share knowledge	Programme team and governance structured to encourage knowledge sharing	Post-project learning reviews Programme milestone learning reviews	Programme knowledge repository

Figure 14.3 Knowledge management approach

A full exploration of each enabler for each type of knowledge will provide a good indication of what needs to be in place to encourage and support effective knowledge management throughout the lifetime of the programme.

14.4.2.2 Categorize knowledge

Captured knowledge is of limited use without an effective categorization scheme that identifies the structure for organizing and accessing knowledge/information. Therefore a categorization scheme is vital for effective knowledge management. In addition to enabling information to be stored in logical, organized groupings, it should allow users to access and use information more effectively.

When evaluating and/or developing a categorization scheme, the following factors need to be taken into account:

537

- Categories of knowledge that the programme team is likely to be searching for; for example, one categorization that will almost certainly need to be considered is knowledge type, that is, organizational context, best practice and programme and project lessons learned.
- What the nature of the information is and the people who will be using the process and systems.
- The categorization scheme should be flexible to allow for additions or changes as the information collection grows, and have the following characteristics:
  - logical, clear and internally consistent, using basic concepts;
  - using a common language understood by the programme team;
  - providing multiple access points (for example, subject, author).

This handbook itself provides an example of a knowledge categorization structure for programme management. The lifecycle, that is, Start-up, Define, Establish, Execute and Closure provide one dimension while the various procedures required, for example, benefits or governance, provide another. Filing an element of knowledge under benefits during the Establish stage would both identify exactly where it could be used to best advantage and make it accessible to an enquiry solely focused on benefits.

14.4.3 EXECUTE STAGE

The Execute stage is where the programme is delivered. It is here that the processes and procedures designed and established in earlier stages are operated to support the programme in achieving its objectives.

For knowledge management, this involves constantly identifying, obtaining, storing and disseminating information and knowledge throughout the lifetime of the programme.

14.4.3.1 Storage and distribution of knowledge

Technology support for the storage and distribution of knowledge has never been so extensive or so inexpensive. Most organizations of any size have an intranet or some similar tool that can be adapted for knowledge sharing. The vast majority of employees in large organizations are now very familiar with the Internet and the conventions and standards it has brought to knowledge sharing.

The most challenging aspect to knowledge storage is, as discussed above, establishing a categorization and organizing structure that will allow information to be retrieved by users. In truth even this requirement is being reduced as many Internet sites now include free text search facilities that allow users to find documents even when not deposited where expected. It is wise, however, to adopt a system of categorization, as unstructured searches often return far more 'chaff than wheat'.

The technology of information storage is a massive topic that probably warrants its own handbook. What is important for the success of knowledge management within a programme is the identification of:

- the type and volume of information that the knowledge management system will be required to handle;
- the nature of enquires most likely to be made of the information;
- the technical platforms and skills of the seekers of knowledge.

Armed with this information, a constructive discussion can be undertaken with the organization's IT function to design and build the necessary repositories, queries and reports.

14.4.3.2 Communicate and share knowledge

The transfer of skills and knowledge is the defining element of a knowledge management process. Knowledge transfer is a two-way effort – the owner of the knowledge must want to share and the receiver must want to learn.

To transfer knowledge and skills effectively it is important to consider:

- where specifically (internally and externally) and how the knowledge is going to be applied;
- when (in the programme life-cycle) the knowledge is needed;
- what time, money and people resources are availability to share, capture and transfer knowledge;
- what capabilities/skills/aptitude/limitations are present in the organization.

It is important to manage expectations and understand the barriers to, fears of, and desires for, knowledge management that exist, including:

- not having enough time;
- no incentive to share and learn, often characterized as 'not invented here';
- not aware of what to share with whom, how, when, and so on;
- not understanding applicability and not being aware of the bigger picture;
- cultural and language differences;
- not using appropriate media.

In determining the approach to be taken for knowledge sharing, it is also important to consider:

- What skills and knowledge does each individual bring with them to the programme and what do they require to do their job effectively?

- Where do the skills and knowledge required by each individual to carry out their work and achieve their personal development goals reside (think of people as well as other sources, for example, training and relevant databases)?
- What media can best be used to transfer that knowledge?

14.4.3.3 Build awareness

All programme members need to be aware of the concepts and principles of knowledge management and be trained on the various processes, tools and techniques adopted.

Training needs to be provided to ensure competence for programme team members in:

- processes, procedures and policies in relation to knowledge management;
- tools and techniques used to facilitate knowledge management;
- how to use the common knowledge repository.

14.4.3.4 Monitor and review the knowledge capture process and amend as required

The arrangements for monitoring the achievement of knowledge targets and reviewing plans needs to be incorporated into the programme plan. Monitoring arrangements should include:

- success criteria against which knowledge management will be evaluated;
- monitoring methods for capturing and sharing;
- frequency and timescale monitoring;
- reporting procedures;
- communications mechanisms for disseminating lessons learned.

Throughout the programme lifecycle, the knowledge management process should monitor the knowledge accumulated and disseminated, the actions taken, and the effect of those actions, to determine whether it is achieving its objectives. All effectiveness measures need to have been defined during the Define stage and incorporated into the programme plan.

Where actions are not completed or prove to be less effective than anticipated, it will be necessary to determine the cause of the shortfall. Actions to address the shortfall must then be planned and incorporated into the programme plan through the normal planning process. Approved actions become part of the programme plan in the same way as any other remedial action or task.

Recommendations to improve knowledge management will also need to be assessed. This may require changes to planned activities and/or new activities.

540

These new or amended activities will also need to be subject to the standard change procedures and, if accepted, incorporated into the programme plan.

14.4.4 CLOSURE STAGE

The Closure stage of any project or programme always presents a challenge. Typically, the team has finished its assigned tasks, the deliverables have been accepted by the organization and everyone is keen to get on to the next challenge. It is often the case that because of a rushed and unstructured closure potentially valuable knowledge, accumulated at great cost and effort, is lost.

Two contributory reasons are:

- Many projects and programmes do not have a formally planned Closure stage; they simply drift away.
- Many organizations have no obvious home for this new knowledge. This is particularly true of programme and project knowledge, where the organization has no established function responsible for programme and project management.

Throughout this handbook the authors have stressed their belief in the importance of the Closure stage of the programme lifecycle as a mechanism to ensure that a programme is properly closed down and all resources and knowledge are handed back to the organization in an orderly manner. Knowledge management fits specifically into this category.

When planning the knowledge management process for a programme, the final question to address is: 'What will the programme do with the accumulated knowledge when it disbands?'

Some elements of the knowledge collected by the programme will be common to the organization and therefore already held elsewhere, for example, financial data. The balance, however, needs to be found a home where it will be at least held safely, or better still, developed and used.

It is likely that programme knowledge will end up in several 'homes' as there is normally not a single part of the organization that covers all of the programme's scope. Typically the systems knowledge passes to the IT function, the people knowledge to HR, and so on. This is probably the best solution in most cases, but in today's world of intranets and data warehouses, more innovative solutions may be possible.

If during the lifecycle of a programme the team has established the following, then it will have done a pretty good job of knowledge management:

1. What knowledge would be valuable to the programme.

2. What knowledge was already available, and therefore what more was needed.
3. Where and how to get hold of the missing knowledge and keep it all up to date.
4. How to store and circulate the knowledge collected to help the programme succeed.
5. The knowledge management changes needed as the needs of the programme change.
6. Where and how to hand the accumulated knowledge back to the organization at the end of the programme.

14.5 WIDER KNOWLEDGE SHARING

Throughout the programme, and particularly during the Closure stage, it is important to consider sharing knowledge with the wider organization. Programme knowledge may appear only to be relevant to the programme team; however, it may be that this knowledge, such as best practice and lessons learned, could be of considerable value elsewhere in the organization.

There may not be formal procedures for cross-organizational sharing of knowledge. If there are then clearly these should be used to the full. If not, there are other ways the programme's experience can be shared with a wider audience. Examples include:

- Articles and features in organizational newsletters and publications: Many organizations have regular newsletters, both traditional and, increasingly, online. Editors of these publications are always pleased to receive interesting 'copy'.
- Presentations to 'Interest Groups': Some organizations have various interest groups in place who come together periodically to share information. A common example would be an annual sales conference or meeting of the finance community. Identifying an element of the programme's learning of particular interest can provide an interesting presentation topic for one of these sessions.
- Presentations to management teams: Offers to present learning and programme findings to organizational management teams will often be well received, again providing that the topics selected are relevant and of some practical value.

It is necessary to be proactive in knowledge sharing. It is unlikely that the world will beat a path to your door to find out what you know. Some individuals will seek out knowledge, either because they have open minds and a willingness to share or because they are in a 'tight spot'. Aside from the enthusiastic and the desperate, however, you will need to seek out the majority of your colleagues and sell them the knowledge your programme has amassed. Why would you bother? There are several reasons why it is worth making the effort, and this author speaks here from direct personal experience, including:

- It is important that the knowledge so painstakingly accumulated is shared. If only one other project or function benefited from it, the savings could still be substantial.
- Programme team members can and should benefit from recognition that they have accumulated and assimilated new knowledge. There is no harm in being well known as an expert in some field or other.
- Whenever knowledge is shared it grows. As members of the programme team share their learning so their colleagues provide feedback and their own similar experiences and so the total organization's knowledge grows, to the benefit of all.

14.6 CONTINUOUS IMPROVEMENT

As for any aspect of a programme the knowledge management process should develop and evolve throughout the lifecycle. This chapter has attempted to provide guidance to assist the programme manager establish a practical knowledge management process and thereby increase the programme's chances of being successful. It would be something of a miracle if any process established at the beginning of a long programme were to be totally appropriate throughout its lifecycle. The key then is continuous vigilance and a focus on the programme and knowledge management objectives that were set at the outset. If the knowledge management process is not delivering useful new information, skills and insights to the project and programme teams, it will be necessary to review and, if required, revise, the process.

14.7 CONCLUSION

The management of knowledge is an important aspect of programme management and requires formal processes and procedures, as with all other aspects of a programme. The level of knowledge management resource and expertise required for a given programme will depend on factors such as size, complexity, degree of innovation, and the availability of applicable, existing knowledge.

Defining and implementing a knowledge management process requires skill and experience in the following areas:

- knowledge classification
- knowledge capture and sharing
- knowledge repositories
- best practices concepts
- lessons learned concepts
- re-use concepts
- workshop facilitation
- communications development.

The infrastructure and tools necessary for knowledge management can vary widely. They are, in part, influenced by the programme's size, complexity, geographic diversity, and the enterprise's culture and expectations. For example, one organization's way of working may dictate that programme updates are delivered electronically to all staff while another may expect updates to take the form of face-to-face meetings. Such factors must be considered when determining knowledge management requirements.

Most programmes will at least need to consider tools such as word processing, database packages and particularly intranet and web-based environments to maintain knowledge information and records. Programmes will also need to consider more mundane facilities such as those required for meetings, workshops, and pilots of new processes and systems.

The purpose of this chapter has been to set out the steps to be taken to implement knowledge management into a change programme. Figure 14.4 sets out where each of these steps fits within the programme management lifecycle described in Chapter 2.

Knowledge management is a topic not covered in the majority of programme management texts and approaches. *Managing Successful Programmes* (OGC, 2003), for example, makes no reference to knowledge management. Therefore, many would not regard it as a required discipline for a successful programme. On the other hand, a number of recent legislative changes, including Sarbanes–Oxley, Basel II and International Accounting Standards,[1] have led to far-reaching

---

1 The Sarbanes–Oxley Act (2002) compelled all United States registered companies to make an annual public attestation to the completeness and effectiveness of their regimes of financial control. Basel II (International Convergence of Capital Measurement and Capital Standards: A Revised Framework) defines new regulations to be adopted by the world's largest economies, for the calculation of capital to be held by banks and similar financial institutions. International Accounting Standards provide common approaches to corporate accounting throughout the world. All three legislative and regulatory changes are far reaching and highly complex.

Start-up	Define	Establish	Execute	Close
Knowledge management not normally considered during initial assessment	Define expected knowledge requirements	Design and establish knowledge management processes	Execute knowledge management processes	Undertake end of programme knowledge management events and activities
	Identify existing knowledge assets	Assign and agree individual knowledge management goals to team members	Monitor knowledge management processes	Assess overall knowledge management effectiveness and report to management
	Assess effectiveness of current knowledge management processes	Develop and agree knowledge management categorization	Assess effectiveness of knowledge management and amend approach as required	Transfer accumulated knowledge to the organization
	Establish programme knowledge management goals	Develop knowledge management tools and systems	Evaluate knowledge management achievements of team members	Close down knowledge management processes
	Define measures of knowledge management success			

Figure 14.4   Knowledge management quick reference

programmes that have been highly dependent on knowledge management. The identification, interpretation and dissemination of knowledge are key components of success in this type of programme, as it can be for many others. Conventional programme management thinking does not require, or encourage, consideration of knowledge management. This section has been included because the authors believe that knowledge management can contribute to programme success.

REFERENCES

OGC (2003) *Managing Successful Programmes: Delivering Business Change in Multi-Projeect Environments*. Second edition. London: The Stationery Office.

545

Part III

Programme Management Maturity

15 Measuring programme management maturity

15.1 INTRODUCTION TO PROGRAMME MATURITY

Many organizations have a desire to improve their ability to deliver change through efficient and effective programmes. This requires the ability to establish and operate mature management processes within their programmes. A key first step in attempting to improve processes within programmes is to understand their current levels of maturity.

This should not be done on the basis of a single measure. Every organization will have achieved certain levels of maturity in each of the key areas of programme management and every organization will have requirements and ambitions to improve in some of those areas. The existing levels of maturity and the relative priority for improving in each of the key areas will vary from organization to organization.

It is useful to consider an organization's current levels of maturity and potential for improvement in maturity levels in each of the key areas of programme management. This chapter is designed to help in achieving these objectives. It has two main sub-sections:

- Section 15.2 identifies the ten 10 key processes within programme management and outlines the Programme Management Maturity Model (PMMM), a benchmarking tool that may be used to compare programme against programme, organization against organization or organization against the average of a large number of organizations that have previously used the model.
- Section 15.3 explains how, once the organization understands its own maturity, the Programme Management Improvement Process (PMIP) may be used to select, prioritize, plan and implement improvements in each of the key areas.

The PMMM requires a questionnaire to be completed and returned to the authors. A copy of this may be obtained from the website of ProgM, the joint programme management special interest group of the British Computer Society and the Association for Project Management. Its website is located at www.e-programme.com.

Consultancies and similar business improvement organizations are free to benefit from delivering services utilizing the PMMM and PMIP. However, these models are the copyright of the respective author teams and this should be acknowledged in any resource based upon their use. Figure 15.1 contains a copy of the PMMM's copyright notice, which explains the basis on which the model may be used.

> The Programme Management Maturity Model is copyright. It was authored by Geoff Reiss (Chairman of the Program Management Group plc) and by Paul Rayner (Managing Consultant for LogicaCMG UK Limited). Its development was encouraged by ProgM – the joint programme management special interest group of the British Computer Society and the Association for Project Management.
>
> As a service to the programme management community, ProgM will maintain a database of all relevant Model data that has been sent to it and will make appropriate summaries of this data available from time to time. This database and its contents are copyright and are the property of ProgM. All information submitted to ProgM for inclusion in this database will be treated in confidence and will not be individually identified and will not be supplied to third parties or used in any way other than to enhance the database without the explicit permission of the submitter.
>
> Neither the authors nor ProgM make any claim as to the suitability of the Model for any particular purpose and would advise users to seek professional advice before undertaking any actions as a result of using the Model. Furthermore, the Model is still in the process of development and therefore subject to change.
>
> Use of this Model is free and no charge should be made for its use. Organizations are free to offer and charge for investigative and consultancy services using the Model, but no charge may be made for the Model itself. Any use of the Model or a derivative of it or of the ProgM database or any data obtained from it must acknowledge the copyright(s) described above.

Figure 15.1 Copyright notice of the PMMM

15.2 USING THE PROGRAMME MANAGEMENT MATURITY MODEL

15.2.1 INTRODUCTION

The ultimate measure of success for any programme must be the achievement of expected business benefits. Sometimes it may be possible to structure a programme so as to deliver a constant stream of benefits from early on, so that success (and thus the adequacy of its management processes) is quickly visible. Unfortunately, such situations are likely to be rare and a major act of faith is required to invest millions in the hope of achieving business benefits in the distant future. In such circumstances, there is a need for some interim indication of whether a programme is being managed appropriately and thus likely to deliver all of its potential.

One approach to achieving such an indication is to audit the processes used against best practice, such as that described within this handbook. This is frequently undertaken by internal quality assurance departments, and is the basis for obtaining certification against the ISO9000 series of quality management standards. When properly conducted by experienced auditors, this approach can be tremendously valuable. Further information on auditing can be found in Chapter 8, 'Programme assurance and quality'.

Auditors who are experienced at reviewing programmes, however, are not always available. Moreover, audits frequently tend to focus on the details of compliance against standards rather than the overall effectiveness of management. To overcome these problems, two of the authors of this handbook have devised an alternative approach, using the PMMM.

15.2.2 PROGRAMME MATURITY

This approach recognizes that one rarely achieves immediate perfection in any human activity. Usually, improvements are achieved gradually and that progress is often uneven. Moreover, different organizations have different corporate cultures. As a result, those responsible for managing programmes have to commence from different starting points, depending on the maturity and sophistication of the cultures within which their programmes operate. In effect, programmes, like many other aspects of life, have to learn to walk before they can start to run. On this basis, programmes can be classified according to increasing stages of maturity.

The stage where there is virtually no development of programme-level functions and processes is referred to as 'innocence'. As these functions and processes become more developed, the programme will pass through five stages of maturity:

551

1. The simplest types of programme are primarily a collection of projects or work streams with few 'programme-level' functions and little coordination. This 'initial' stage is often found where projects are combined into programmes merely to facilitate budgetary control.
2. As programmes become more mature, plans are developed to coordinate the component projects, although such 'programme-level' plans are rarely fully implemented and in practice there is little effective coordination between projects/work streams. This is the 'repeatable' stage.
3. Further development of programme management results in the achievement of a basic level of coordination between projects/work-streams and of control at 'programme' level, that is, the 'defined' stage.
4. Maximizing the efficiency of a programme requires a high degree of coordination between projects/work streams and of programme-level control, with all necessary programme-level tools and resources available. Such programmes are referred to as 'managed';
5. The highest stage is reached where programmes are 'optimized', meaning that programme managers have all the visibility and control that is required and are proactively leading the programme, in line with the organization's corporate strategy.

All programmes are unique and each programme manager will have their own set of priorities and available skills. Accordingly, it is normal to find that some elements of a programme are well developed while others are less so. The PMMM recognizes this by allowing for maturity to vary across each of the key processes that are the core of programme management.

Implicit in this approach is the idea that process maturity is beneficial to programme success. Evidence to support this is provided by a survey of programme management undertaken by KPMG, the global accounting firm.[1] This survey focused on the programme office, which is normally responsible for establishing, maintaining and 'policing' the management processes on which the PMMM is based. Using the input of 134 organizations from around the world, this survey showed that where the programme office and its processes are mature, the likelihood of programme success increased. For example, the report states that '96% of those who deemed their programme office to be mature reported successful delivery of all the component projects within their programmes'. This success rate was reduced to 76 per cent where the programme office was merely 'grown up' and to only 53 per cent where the programme office was immature.

---

1 '2002 Programme Management Survey', summary and details available from www.kpmg.co.uk.

An explanation of the role and function of the programme office can be found in Chapter 13 'The programme office'.

15.2.3 THE PMMM

The PMMM incorporates the concepts described above in the form of a questionnaire. Each stage of maturity for each of the 10 key programme management processes is summarized by a question. A programme can then be rated on the basis of the answers to the questions. An example of part of the questionnaire is shown below in Figure 15.2.

Please answer the following questions about **quality management and auditing** within the programme. Please tick one box for each question.

Ref	Question	None	Partly	Fully
		Tick one box per question		
6.1	The quality requirements of all deliverables are defined and agreed.	☐	☐	☐
6.2	Component projects/work streams have defined and agreed plans for verifying and validating the quality of all their deliverables.	☐	☐	☐
6.3	The projects/streams' quality plans are effectively implemented and the programme has a defined and agreed plan for confirming the quality of all deliverables.	☐	☐	☐
6.4	Effective audit arrangements are in place to verify the conformance of all parts of the programme to agreed plans, processes and quality requirements.	☐	☐	☐
6.5	The quality performance of all parts of the programme is measured, monitored, reported and used as a basis for initiating on-going improvements in programme performance.	☐	☐	☐

Figure 15.2   Example of part of the questionnaire for the PMMM

Using a computer spreadsheet and a graphics tool, the ratings can be converted into a visual profile of the programme, showing which processes are well developed and which less so. At the current time, ProgM provides a free service to generate such profiles. The quid pro quo is that the ratings data can be anonymously added to the database of programmes that the organization maintains. Since the PMMM's initial creation, ProgM has analysed a large number of different programmes of all types from around the world and the results have been incorporated into the database. This database can now provide a benchmark against which any programmes can be compared.

15.2.3.1 A typical profile

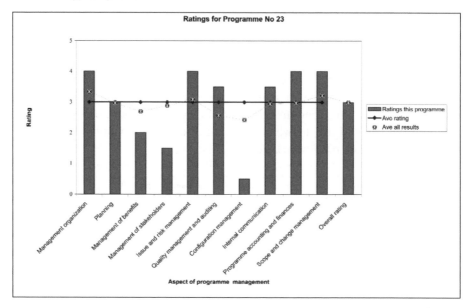

Figure 15.3   Example of programme profile from the PMMM

Figure 15.3 shows a typical programme profile, as produced by the PMMM. Within Figure 15.3:

- The 10 solidly filled vertical bars show how the programme rates in terms of the 10 key aspects of programme management. These are rated on a scale of 0 to 5, where 0 indicates that the element is totally ignored and 5 indicates a comprehensive and fully effective implementation. In this example, the ratings vary from a healthy 4 (for elements such 'Management organization') down to 0.5 (for 'Configuration management').
- The horizontal line shows the average rating for all elements of this programme; in this example the average is almost exactly 3 (which implies a reasonable overall level of maturity for the programme).
- The diagonally shaded bar at the right shows the rating given for the programme as a whole. In this example, a rating of 3 has been given, which is almost exactly the same as the average for the individual elements, suggesting that those completing the questionnaire have a realistic view of the programme's maturity.
- Finally, the points marked as asterisks (*) show the average ratings for each element from the programmes in the database. This allows the programme to be benchmarked with its peers. For example, the average rating for the

'Management organization' element of this programme is higher than the average in the database, indicating that here the programme manager is doing relatively well. By contrast, the ratings for 'Stakeholder management' and 'Configuration management' are below the averages in the database, suggesting that these are potential areas of weakness that should be reviewed.

The PMMM assumes that component projects have their own organizational structures and management disciplines, which are separate to those used at the programme level. This assumption makes the PMMM consistent with project management methodologies such as PRINCE2.

The questionnaire used to collect data for the PMMM can be completed within about 20 minutes and is accompanied by comprehensive instructions to ensure consistency. It is freely available on the ProgM website as described in Section 15.1, 'Introduction to programme maturity'.

15.2.3.2 Internal benchmarking

By using the PMMM on different programmes and on the same programme at different times, the profiles can demonstrate where there is scope for improvement and how programmes have changed over time.

Figure 15.4 shows the differences between two groups of programmes within the same financial organization. The well-established programmes (A) had been running for many months and had developed relatively mature processes. By contrast, the newer programmes (B) had only just been initiated and their processes were largely inchoate, with major gaps for processes such as quality management.

Figure 15.5 shows the profiles for a programme within another financial organization before and after a 'rescue mission'. In this profile, the PMMM ratings for May are shown in white and the ratings for the same programme for 3 months later are shown in grey. The profile shows the improvements achieved by a few months' intensive effort in applying the best practice described within this handbook.

The database does suggest that there are differences between the approaches taken by different industries. For example, as Figure 15.6 shows, programmes that are largely based on IT have the same overall average scores as non-IT based programmes, yet a review of the profiles shows that IT-based programmes typically score below average on 'Benefit management' and 'Stakeholder management', while scoring above average on 'Risk and issue management' and on the 'Management of scope and change'.

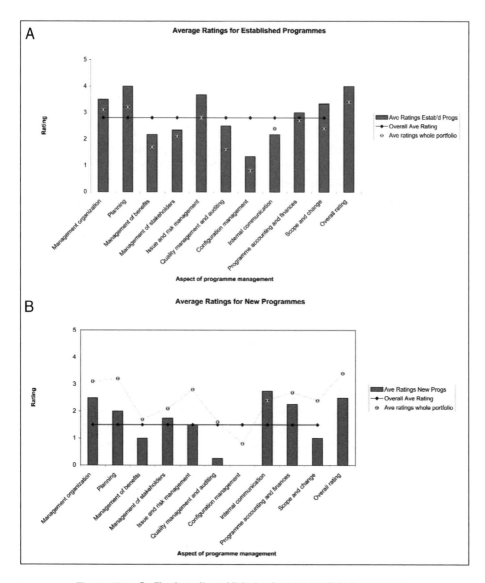

Figure 15.4   Profiles for well-established and newly established programmes

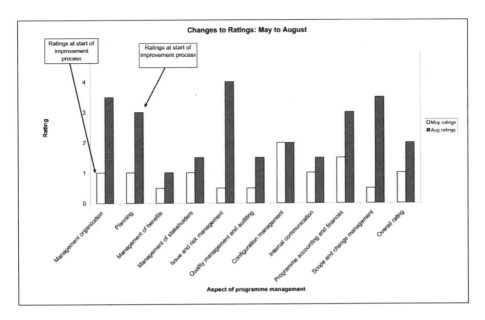

Figure 15.5   'Before' and 'after' profiles

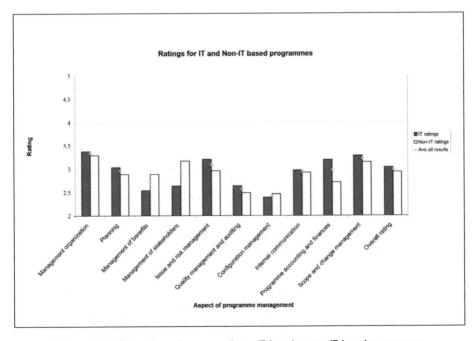

Figure 15.6   Comparison of average ratings – IT-based vs. non-IT-based programmes

557

Similarly, with the data currently available, the public sector programmes within the database show a different average profile to private sector programmes, as shown by Figure 15.7.

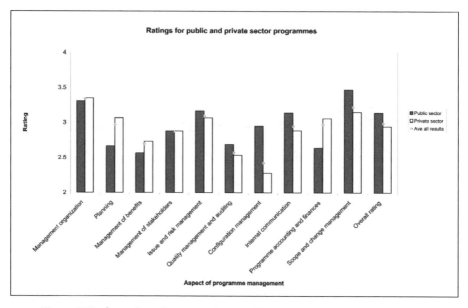

Figure 15.7   Comparison of average ratings – public sector vs. private sector programmes

15.3 CONCLUSIONS

The PMMM and its resultant profiles have been tested on major programmes within a range of industry sectors, from all continents, and has been shown to help all types of organization to achieve their programme objectives. In particular, it:

- demonstrates the extent to which a programme is structured and managed in accordance with recognized best practice;
- shows where within an individual programme there is the most scope for improving its management;
- provides a measure of how programme management is improving over time;
- enables organizations new to programme management to measure their uptake of appropriate processes and procedures.

The PMMM has also shown that it provides an effective way of describing programmes and thus of understanding their strengths and weaknesses. Its graphic profiles are easy to understand and thus facilitate the agreement of improvement actions. It is being used within several major British private-sector organizations as a basis for benchmarking between programmes. Its use can help to give confidence that the investment of time, money and effort into the programme will eventually deliver the business benefits that are expected.

16 Improving programme management maturity

Once a programme's maturity has been established through use of the PMMM, the organization may wish to improve its own maturity and therefore its ability to deliver benefits. The PIMP will help to identify potential improvements in each of the 10 aspects of programme management used by both the PMMM and the PMIP.

This chapter outlines steps that an organization may consider when improving its own maturity in programme management. Each of the tables below is laid out in the same manner. On the vertical axis are the six levels of maturity:

- Innocence
- Initial
- Repeatable
- Defined
- Managed
- Optimized

For each level of maturity and for each aspect of programme management there are three columns as follows:

- **Summary**: A summary of the typical organization at this level of maturity in the selected aspect of programme management
- **Characteristics**: A more detailed outline of the typical organization at this level of maturity in the selected aspect of programme management
- **Corrective Actions**: The steps the organization may take to increase their level of maturity by one level in this aspect of programme management.

There are therefore 10 tables each with six rows and the three columns above, as follows:

- Improving programme organization and governance

- Improving programme planning and control
- Improving benefits management
- Improving stakeholder management
- Improving risk and issue management
- Improving programme assurance and quality
- Improving configuration management
- Improving internal communications
- Improving programme accounting
- Improving management scope and change.

These tables should help an organization in two ways:

- to plan improvements in programme maturity;
- to establish the objectives of change projects designed to improve programme maturity.

REFERENCES

OGC (2003) *Managing Successful Programmes: Delivering Business Change in Multi-project Environments*. Second edition. London: The Stationery Office.

16.1 IMPROVING PROGRAMME ORGANIZATION AND GOVERNANCE

For further guidance on the corrective actions listed in the table below, consult Chapter 3, 'Programme organization and governance'.

Level	Summary	Characteristics	Corrective actions
Innocence	No formal programme team, roles not defined, no clear decision-making framework	While programme teams are formed (or form themselves) they are not designed and there is no evidence that the best people available were chosen. While team members may have role titles, there are no job descriptions. It is unclear who has what authority. They 'make up' the programme lifecycle[1] as they go, perhaps based on bits of formal methods. There is little consistency of method from one programme to another. There is also little consistency of organization or method within the component projects that make up the programme. The lack of a decision making and control framework for the programme means that senior members of the programme team are often confused about its true state. They manage by 'gut feel' which they may	1. Make sure every programme has a team created according to a rational process of design, identifying the key posts that need to be filled and with all key members having clearly defined roles and responsibilities. 2. Decision control points must be applied at least at the end of defining the programme (the Define stage) see Chapter 2 'The Programme management process') and at each tranche (see Section 2.1.4 'The programme lifecycle is not a linear process') boundary. 3. Basic procedures will be established for communications, reporting and decision making.

---

1 Lifecycle – the route or roadmap describing the steps and actions to be followed to get to the end of the programme, please also see Chapter 2. 'The programme management process'.

Level	Summary	Characteristics	Corrective actions
		sometimes refer to as 'experience'. The 'doers' on the programme are confused about how they need to report progress or problems, and may often carry out work, or commit to work, well beyond their authority.	4. Establish the basics of a programme management method[2] for all programmes and, similarly, establish a project management method for all projects inside programmes. This must cover the essentials: planning, monitoring, reporting, benefits identification and tracking, key decision making at least at tranche boundaries.
Initial	Programmes have teams designed at an early stage in their lifecycle. They follow basic but consistent procedures for communication, reporting and decision making. Each person working on the programme understands their roles and responsibilities. The roles and responsibilities of component project managers are defined and agreed.	While there are basic procedures and decision-making rules, which are carried out by programme team members who have defined roles and responsibilities, the primitive nature of these means that programmes still tend to spend a lot of time 'fire fighting' unexpected problems. Too much information/data will be incomplete or out of date. Such information will often not be well suited to the needs of the recipients. So while decision making is attempted as per the prescribed procedures, it is not very effective.	5. Make sure all programmes implement and enforce basic procedures to share their learning experiences (good and bad) as they get to grips with these methods.
Repeatable	All programmes and component projects follow a documented standard method	While the programme now follows a defined and agreed approach to organization, decision making and reporting, the summary nature	6. Establish a complete method filling the gaps with adequate detail. Determine where the method needs

2   For example a method like *Managing Successful Programmes* (OGC, 2003), which provide the process, techniques, documentations, frameworks, roles and responsibilities for programme management.

Level	Summary	Characteristics	Corrective actions
	though this is basic and not complete. Programmes and component projects openly share their experiences with each other and attempt to improve their governance effectiveness.	of this means they still too often rely upon their 'experience' to manage some of the detail. Much of the management effort is still reactionary and so 'fire fighting' unexpected problems is still commonplace. Communications, reporting and decision making usually happen at the right time, but information/data is still often out of date and or incomplete. So while decision making is more timely, unfortunately it is still not as effective as it could be. This manifests itself in yet more problems and aggravates the fire fighting mentioned above. While there is good evidence of programme teams trying to learn from each other, this is not managed. Consequently improvement is sporadic, and more down the sheer energy of some team members, than the 'appliance of science'.	to be supplemented with techniques, for example, risk analysis. 7. Recognize that there is much to learn. Prepare and execute a plan for the development of key staff who will work on programmes. This must enable each person to attain the competencies required for them to successfully contribute to the management of programmes. This is much more than training and you should reflect this in this plan, in that it should allow time for staff to learn, be supported during this period, and set realistic expectations. For example, it takes years for most people to become fully competent programme managers.
Defined	A full standard programme management method is documented and being used by most programmes. However, they still have much to learn to use it effectively.	While programmes now follow a standard method, they are not yet adept enough to properly configure it to their own specific needs. Some therefore often find they are doing too much paperwork and complain of unnecessary bureaucracy. A complete set of programme management	8. Appoint a mentor to help key members of the programme team to learn how to appropriately and effectively use the methods and tools now in place. 9. If a complete set of programme management tools are not yet in

Level	Summary	Characteristics	Corrective actions
		and related techniques have been defined but the teams are not yet experienced enough to use them effectively. This shows in two ways, first the outputs from the use of these techniques are flawed, sometimes leading to bad decisions, and second, some team members still ignore the techniques. Because of inconsistency the quality of data and information is poor.	place, this must be addressed now. These must be able to fully support programmes and their projects for at least the following: • communications • planning; time, resource and cost • reporting and analysis of actual progress • document management • risk and issues management. Implementation of these tools must include adequate training for all users, followed by an allowance thereafter for on the job learning, until the desired proficiency has been achieved. 10. The programme office must now be established to take responsibility for many of the above actions, and then to actively support all programmes and their projects.
Managed	Programme teams are actively supported by mentors and a programme office, to help them use the approved methods, and to	The organization now manages all its programmes (and their projects) using standard methods fully supported by good tools and experts (the programme office and mentors).	11. Programme teams will have learnt how to be more self-sufficient in the 'manage' part of the programme and this will be releasing time for the mentors and the programme office

Level	Summary	Characteristics	Corrective actions
	use the programme management tools effectively. Teams attempt to scale and configure the method to suit the characteristics of their own programme. Information/data is usually up to date and complete. The relationship between the programme and the rest of the 'client' organization, including other relevant programmes and initiatives, is defined and agreed. The programme office is actively engaged in all programmes and provides an overarching view of all programmes to inform the most senior management (e.g. board of directors in the private sector).	Programmes have up to date and substantially complete information/data both to instruct and to support decision making. Communications also actively use this good information by following an agreed communications plan, and this can be seen to be positively influencing stakeholders. All members of the programme, and those inside each component project, understand the purpose of the work they are doing, especially the links with the overall vision and the benefits each project will enable (see Section 5.2, 'Programmes, projects and benefits'). They are clear about their roles and responsibilities, and are well informed about the tasks allocated to them. You can see these people are more confident about their work. However, most people seem to still concentrate on doing just enough right to avoid the big problems. There are few programmes that can demonstrate effective optimization of their solutions, resource utilization, project selection and benefit realization. This might be further compromised if at the most senior management level, prioritizing and choosing	to move on to this next set of improvements. 12. The mentors and the programme office need to become more actively engaged with each programme in the early part of the lifecycle, especially when 'defining the programme'. They must help the teams to improve the way they discover and evaluate the options, and then show them how to objectively choose the best mix of solutions, being the best balance between cost, benefits and risk. 13. The organization's most senior management must now establish procedures and methods to put new initiatives into priority order to get the best return from the resources invested. The senior management should communicate clearly their strategies and policies, ensuring that new programmes clearly demonstrate a strong mapping to

Level	Summary	Characteristics	Corrective actions
		the best initiatives to start is still informal. The effect of this is to reduce the morale of some programme teams that are striving hard to improve.	the stated strategic imperatives, objectives and policies. 14. Get formal reporting from each programme at key decision points, or in exceptional circumstances. They will expect these reports to demonstrate the programmes are optimized effectively
Optimized	All programmes have well designed teams, follow standard methods scaled and configured appropriately, all supported by adequate tools which provide complete, up-to-date relevant information. Everyone is fully aware of their roles and responsibilities and clearly demonstrate this through their actions and behaviours. They spend sufficient time preparing the programme to find the best solutions, thus providing the best return form the resources available.	Senior management make 'optimized' choices by prioritizing new initiatives against their strategies and policies. They provide clear and comprehensive briefs to start new programmes. They demand that the programme teams not only demonstrate they are in control but also show tangible evidence they are making the most of the resources made available to them. Senior management accept that some initiatives will be 'strategic bets', and may fail through market or other external factors, rather than programme management ineptitude. They support this culture, first via the initial brief, by making such factors clear and, second by stopping programmes where the market response or external factors prove to be not favourable. They do this without	15. Having reached this optimized state, the organization, especially its most senior management, must now make sure the programme teams do not revert back to bad practice. Senior management must encourage continued improvement and establish a method to report and measure this improvement on a regular basis.

Level	Summary	Characteristics	Corrective actions
	This optimization continues throughout the programme as the teams continuously prove their solutions are working and if needed improve them to further increase the benefits.	any blame on the programme, providing the programme has produced this proof and evidence as quickly and cheaply as possible. Programme teams spend sufficient time in their preparatory activities, especially defining the programme. They do not rush to get on with it, nor do they prematurely jump to solutions. They do this because they have seen this approach work well in other programmes. Time is spent assessing how the standard method, and the supporting tools, can be appropriately applied to the specific need of each programme. The output from this work is a clear set of configuration instructions, which enables effective frameworks to be established to manage and govern the rest of the programme. These instructions also specify how the supporting tools need to be prepared. The team makes sure all of this is in place and working before they start any projects or other work in the first tranche. Senior members in the programme team (programme director, programme manager, business changes manager(s)) realize that programmes often have to be managed where	

Level	Summary	Characteristics	Corrective actions
		there is uncertainty and no clearly defined path to the success the organization desires. They recognize that this sometimes comes from the need to prove strategic bets. They plan the programme to get early proofs, so where success is not possible due to unfavourable market or external circumstances, the programme can be stopped with minimal expenditure. Programmes actively share their lessons learned, and most will try to learning from other programmes, to help them prepare and manage their programmes to get the best cost–benefit ratio. When the programme is first prepared and planned, they will not accept that this is the best solution they can find. Throughout the life of the programme the teams will be constantly seeking to improve the solutions, to increase the benefits. At the end of the programme, teams will no longer rush off to their next assignment, because they and senior management realize the value of what can be learned from a review and analysis of what has been achieved. They have also learned that by carrying out this review and analysis work	

Level	Summary	Characteristics	Corrective actions
		throughout the programme (e.g. at the end of each tranche), the work at the end when closing the programme no longer needs to be so daunting.	

16.2 IMPROVING PROGRAMME PLANNING AND CONTROL

For further guidance on the corrective actions listed in the table below, consult Chapter 4, 'Programme planning and control'.

Level	Summary	Characteristics	Corrective actions
Innocence	Little planning is undertaken. Some high-level bar charts and resource estimates may exist. Progress reporting is informal and infrequent.	Some project managers within the organization will use a mixed selection of graphics and project management tools to draw bar charts. These will have few if any logical links and few if any resource allocations. There will be no standard formula for planning nor organizational standards. Plans will be normally out of date and there will be no standard process for updating the plan through an update cycle. Senior managers will be presented with a variety of plans drawn in different ways and be unable to see an overview of projects in any valuable form. Plan ownership and the responsibility for planning is unclear. There will be little respect for planning throughout the organization. There may be a timesheet system but it will be unconnected with the planning activity.	1. Agree on a standard format for plans. 2. Establish a plan update cycle on a regular basis. 3. Produce summary plans for senior management covering all projects in a consistent manner. 4. Establish responsibility for planning.

Level	Summary	Characteristics	Corrective actions
Initial	Majority of individual projects and workstreams are planned in terms of activities, milestones and deliverables. Progress reporting varies in completeness and accuracy.	The organization will use a desktop project management tool to draw simple barcharts without any supporting precedence or activity diagrams. These will have some logical links. There may be some broad resource estimates of resource types. A project plan will form part of the process to initiate a project, but will not be always delivered. Project plans will be generally out of date and unrepresentative of the state of the project or its future. Periodically plans are summarized into a tabular overview of all projects. There will be no organizational planning standards. Plans are owned by the project managers. The relationships between project managers and the resources they plan to use will be unclear. There may be a timesheet system but it will be unconnected with the planning activity.	5. Ensure that all projects have a plan and that all plans meet organizational standards. 6. Encourage everyone to adhere to the standard plan update cycle. 7. Ensure project managers own their project plans. 8. Implement a timesheet system that may not be linked to planning but is capable of being so linked. 9. Assign responsibility for cross-project interactions to a programme office role.
Repeatable	The programme is planned —i.e. projects have project plans. Relationships between projects are understood and inter-project dependencies	The organization will use a desktop project management tool to draw barcharts. These will have logical links, but few if any resource allocations. Most projects will have a plan at the time of initiation. The tools used and style	10. Ensure that all projects have a project plan prior to start. 11. Ensure that all projects have an up-to-date plan throughout their lifecycles and use the management

Level	Summary	Characteristics	Corrective actions
	are identified and agreed. Progress reporting uses commonly accepted approaches.	of these plans may vary widely. The plans are generally reasonably up to date and may be compared with the original baseline created when the project was given the go-ahead. Resource planning is in general terms and of limited practical value. Inter-project dependencies are shown on each project plan, but there is no mechanism to warn if these are at risk other than through manual checks. These individual barcharts are collected periodically and summarized manually into a programme plan for reporting purposes by programme support office staff. Manual checks report inter-project links at risk. Organization-wide resource planning will be intermittent and not well respected. There will be some simple organizational planning standards published by the programme support office but few projects will adhere to them. Plans are owned by the project managers, programme managers and team managers. Team members are not consulted and feel excluded from the planning process.	reporting system to report on exceptions. 12. Ensure that the programme support office is collecting up-to-date plans on a regular basis and reporting on cross-project interactions of both a logical and resource conflict nature. 13. Use management reporting to report on project progress and status as well as compliance with planning and control standards. 14. Ensure all project managers have planning knowledge and/or the ability to call for help from the programme support office to maintain plans in a compliant manner. 15. Encourage team leaders to plan their own work across many projects.

Level	Summary	Characteristics	Corrective actions
Defined	Common planning, control and reporting procedures are defined and documented, including resource allocation.	There will be a timesheet system, but it will be unconnected with the planning activity. Each project manager in the organization will use a copy of the standardized desktop project management tool to draw barcharts. These will have logical links and resource allocations. The plans will normally be reasonably up to date and may be compared with the original baseline. Inter-project dependencies are shown on each project plan. Some resource planning is carried out, but the responsibility and authority for prioritizing work across the organization is not clear. There is a regular consolidation process to draw the plans together to evaluate problems connected with programme-wide resource shortfalls and at-risk inter-project dependencies. Also the plans are summarized regularly into a programme plan for reporting purposes. This work is carried out by a programme support office team. There will be organizational planning standards; the programme support office will play a supporting role in maintaining	16. Establish clear responsibilities for planning and control at all levels, including programme, project and team levels. 17. Establish a process for agreeing and managing inter-project links. 18. Ensure that the programme support office is able to collect all plans electronically, generate management reports and recognize and report on cross-project interdependencies. 19. Establish project and programme planning standards and encourage all team members to use these. 20. Encourage all team leaders to plan the workload of their team members. 21. Implement a timesheet system linked to planning.

Level	Summary	Characteristics	Corrective actions
		users to see their personal targets and to these standards but not all projects will adhere to them.	
		Plans are owned by the project managers, programme managers and team managers. Team members feel little sense of involvement with the plans.	
		There will be a timesheet system but it will be unconnected with the planning activity.	
Managed	Effective systems are in place to monitor progress of projects and their interdependencies. Planning is an ongoing process in response to new and changed circumstances. Programme control procedures are proactive and support achievement of programme goals.	An enterprise-wide programme planning system is in place, but not all staff are trained in its use. Planning is carried out on most projects and some non-project work, but not always to a specific corporate standard. Some projects not approved through the system are progressed. The distribution of work (programme to project, project to phase, project to functional team, project or functional team to individual) is agreed and audited in some but not all cases. Most resources are planned individually but there are methods by which the system is circumvented and this overrides true project prioritization. Resources are frequently planned to be overloaded. An integrated timesheet system allows all	22. Agree procedures for assigning individuals to work in project teams and for the delegation of work from projects to specialist teams, from programmes to project and project to phase managers if appropriate. 23. Establish a culture where all work is planned including projects, non-project and non-work activities. 24. Minimize the amount of work that is done outside of the planning and control system and implement systems to make such connivance obvious. 25. Encourage users to inspect their personal target and report back regularly and completely through

Level	Summary	Characteristics	Corrective actions
		feed back their achievements and their predictions of work remaining and this feeds into the planning process. Timesheets are not always submitted regularly and plans drift out of date as a result. The programme support office will play a supporting role in maintaining these standards and most projects will adhere to them. The programme support office will have installed systems so that overview plans and reports are automatically generated. This will include a RAG status report for all projects.[3] Plans are owned by the project managers, programme managers and team managers. Team members feel a limited sense of involvement with the plans.	their timesheets. Ensure that timesheets are routed to the correct manager or managers. 26. Encourage senior management to expect regular simple reports on the status of all projects including progress, budgets and adherence to governance standards. 27. Make the planning and control system central to the ethos of the organization. 28. Ensure everyone is adequately trained in the use of the tools, methods and processes in use.
Optimized	Regular and effective mechanisms are in place to assess the effectiveness of programme planning and control, report this	The authority to instruct individuals is totally clear. Resource planning accurately predicts the organization's capability and the loaning of resources from team to team is clearly understood. Resources are not accidentally	The organization has established a process of ensuring that the organization itself, its existing staff and future members of the staff understand their processes and continue to examine

3 A RAG status report highlights the problems by scoring points in various categories, including R = red = severe warning; A = amber = warning; G = green = no warning.

Level	Summary	Characteristics	Corrective actions
	information to senior management and develop improved processes as required.	overloaded. Team members understand the organization's priorities. Plans are rarely more than 7 days out of date and higher level plans are automatically updated from lower level plans. An automatic system warns of planning and work being done contrary to the standards and on projects that are not currently 'live'. An integrated timesheet system allows all users to see their workload and feed back their achievements and their predictions of work remaining and this feeds into the planning process. 90% of timesheets are submitted and approved on time. The programme support office will play a central role in maintaining planning standards and all projects will adhere to them. This will be a part of a corporate governance standard such as PRINCE2. The programme support office will have installed systems so that overview plans and reports are automatically generated. Also exception reporting is automatically generated. There is wide respect for planning and a sense of shared ownership of plans that spreads across the whole team.	them in an endeavour to continually improve through learning and knowledge management.

16.3 IMPROVING BENEFITS MANAGEMENT

For further guidance on the corrective actions listed in the table below, consult Chapter 5, 'Benefits management'.

Level	Summary	Characteristics	Corrective actions
Innocence	No formal processes exist for the identification, implementation and subsequent realization of business benefits.	The programme manager and project managers do not understand the concepts of benefits management, or how they relate to the delivery of the programme or each component project in the programme. The business case for each programme has only a vague reference to the expected benefits. Project and programme teams do not focus on benefit delivery.	1. Identify the reasons why each programme has been put in place. List out the expected benefits, the timescale for the delivery of each, and which projects they relate to. 2. It is likely that some projects in a programme, and potentially some programmes are no longer relevant and may need to be stopped.
Initial	There is some benefits identification. A broad consensus exists that the programme will deliver business benefit, but it is not fully quantified.	The programme manager and project managers believe that their work will deliver benefit to the organization. There are generalist statements such as 'the systems will be improved', but these are not supported by any form of measure. There is no tracking of the actual benefits.	3. Identify the main business benefits that the programmes expect to deliver. Behind this look at each of the component projects and list out what their deliverables are. For each deliverable, gives its connection to an expected benefit, the dependencies required, and the changes within the organization that will result.

Level	Summary	Characteristics	Corrective actions
Repeatable	There is a consensus in the organization of what is benefits management. A framework exists for identifying the types of benefits that a programme expects to accrue.	Programmes are set up with benefit delivery in mind. There is agreement among stakeholders that change is required to improve the processes in the organization. However, programme managers and project managers follow their own standard, with loose linkage back to the strategy of the organization as a whole.	4. Start to bring together different example benefit cases and identify a common standard. 5. Reconcile programmes back to business strategy. For each benefit ensure that this can be quantified in terms of its classification, expected time-scale for delivery and which stakeholder(s) will receive the benefit.
Defined	There are defined processes for the definition and measurement of benefits.	Some programme and project managers understand that a focus on benefit management is a key requirement. However, the level of knowledge and understanding of benefit management techniques is inconsistent and, in some areas, weak. There are unquantified definitions of benefits, especially of non-financial benefits.	6. Provide training on benefits management. Appoint benefit managers with specific responsibility for identified benefits, especially non-financial benefits.
Managed	The benefits identification process starts before the programme, but this only loosely linked to the organization's strategy From identification of the idea through to delivery of	The organization starts with a benefits identification phase. Stakeholders are included in this work. A list of benefits and non-benefits, their classification, the stakeholders who will gain from the benefit and their expected timescales for delivery are agreed.	7. At this level there needs to be feedback into the programme office of the lessons learned in benefits management. 8. Programme managers and project managers need to meet to look at how the process can be optimized.

Level	Summary	Characteristics	Corrective actions
	the change there is complete lifecycle benefits management.	Each project has a business case that includes a benefits case. Programmes and projects are selected and prioritized on the basis of these business cases. The business case is continually updated as the project progresses and these changes affect programme viability or prioritization. On project completion, the programme office is advised of the outcome of the project in relation to the benefits case. Each benefit has an owner with responsibility for maintaining focus on that benefit. The programme office tracks benefits that are delivered after the project is completed.	9. Establish a process for linking benefits to the organization's strategy and for selecting and prioritizing programmes based on these business cases. 10. Establish a process for establishing and modifying baselines for benefits and for monitoring actual delivery of benefits against the baseline.
Optimized	There is effective benefits management from the definition of the organization's strategy, through programmes to project delivery. Changes to the organization's strategy can be quickly reflected in changes to programme definition. Lessons learned about	With all processes in place and working effectively, supported by objective evidence that they are working as well as possible, all those involved in the programme should have a high degree of confidence in its success and trust in those responsible for its direction and management. The programme team, including project managers, meet regularly to look at the benefits management lifecycle. It is recognized that changes happen. To meet	

Level	Summary	Characteristics	Corrective actions
	benefits management are fed back into the programme and project lifecycle.	this, the lifecycle is updated regularly. There is confidence in the organization that programmes that are run will deliver the benefits expected. The maturity of the business understands that some programmes are strategic, which will not have a benefits case. However for the others, both those in the programme and its stakeholders recognize that its purpose is to deliver business benefit.	

16.4 IMPROVING STAKEHOLDER MANAGEMENT

For further guidance on the corrective actions listed in the table below, consult Chapter 6, 'Stakeholder management'.

Level	Summary	Characteristics	Corrective actions
Innocence	Programme and project stakeholders are not formally identified. The role and responsibilities of the programme sponsor is not recognized.	This situation reflects 'innocence' in that the importance of proactively managing programme and project stakeholders is not recognized or accepted. As a result, no list of programme stakeholders and their individual characteristics will have been created. No processes or procedures to manage programme stakeholders will exist nor will their value be recognized. At this level of maturity the specific and critical role(s) of the programme sponsor(s) will not have been identified or established. When asked to identify the programme sponsor(s), programme managers will often answer, 'The board' or 'the management team' without being able to ascribe responsibility to a specific individual(s).	1. Recognize the importance of proactive programme-level stakeholder management. Before any specific actions can be taken to manage stakeholders, it is necessary that both the programme team and the organization recognizes the vital importance of stakeholder management in project and programme success. 2. Identify key stakeholders for the programme and its component projects. Once the value of stakeholder management to programme success has been acknowledged, the first step towards establishing a stakeholder management process is to identify key stakeholders, together with details of their relationship with the programme. Key stakeholders will typically be those who are either

Level	Summary	Characteristics	Corrective actions
			significantly impacted by the programme or capable of having significant impact upon it. 3. Identify and engage programme sponsor(s). Every programme (or project) should have a sponsor(s) who fully accepts responsibility for ensuring that the programme achieves its business objectives. If no sponsor has been appointed this should be done as a crucial first step. Note that Sponsors may be identified under other names, such as programme director or senior responsible owner. (For further guidance on this see Chapter 3.)
Initial	Some stakeholders identified for some projects. Sponsor informally committed to programme.	At this level, the value of stakeholder management is accepted, but only key stakeholders will have been identified as having a sufficient impact on the programme to warrant specific programme management attention. It is also possible that stakeholders will only	4. Identify *all* project and programme stakeholders. All stakeholders should be identified and their relationship with the programme evaluated. Once this exercise has been completed, it will be possible to assess the interventions required for

Level	Summary	Characteristics	Corrective actions
		be identified for certain 'critical' projects within the programme. The risk inherent in this level of maturity is that unidentified stakeholders may adversely impact the programme at some point in the future. The general characteristic of this level of maturity is that only some, not all, of the programme stakeholders will have been identified and assessed. Also, while a sponsor may have been appointed, they will not be playing a sufficiently proactive role in the programme to ensure success. Sponsors will often be informally committed to the programme but presume that the programme manager will be able to achieve success without significant input from themselves.	each class of stakeholder. 5. Analyse stakeholders and identify interventions required to achieve required levels of stakeholder engagement. Establish action plans to close gaps between current and target levels of engagement for each stakeholder group. 6. Engage project and programme sponsors. Sponsors' roles should be formally agreed and documented in the programme definition document or equivalent. Sponsors' roles and responsibilities for delivering programme benefits should also be included in the individuals' goals and objectives.
Repeatable	Stakeholders identified for all projects and the programme, stakeholders' roles in/impact on the programme evaluated. Stakeholder interventions identified.	At this level, all stakeholders have been identified and evaluated as to their importance to the programme and a series of actions identified to optimize stakeholder commitment. In addition a programme sponsor will have been formally appointed.	7. Define a standard approach to stakeholder management. A process for the ongoing management of stakeholders needs to be defined and implemented. This process will enable programme managers to continuously monitor

585

Level	Summary	Characteristics	Corrective actions
	Sponsor formally committed to programme.	What will be absent are processes and procedures to continuously identify new stakeholders and stakeholder management activities required to ensure that engagement is continuously improved and maintained. The risks at this level are that new stakeholders will not be identified as they emerge throughout the programme lifecycle and that changes in levels of commitment will not result in amended interventions. Sponsors will be formally committed to the programme at this level, but they may not proactively intervene to ensure programme success.	the state of stakeholder opinion within the programme. The process will also set out how interventions to improve stakeholder interaction with and support of the programme should be initiated and progressed. 8. Document process as a stakeholder management strategy and agree its adoption with key programme stakeholders. As for any programme process, that for stakeholder management should also be approved for adoption by the programme sponsor and programme board. 9. Define communication plan. Good, two-way communication will be a key to successful stakeholder management. Once the overall strategy has been agreed, it should be possible to produce a detailed plan of what will be communicated, to whom, for what purpose, when it will be communicated and how it will be communicated. (See Chapter 10 for further guidance on communication plans.)

Level	Summary	Characteristics	Corrective actions
			10. Develop sponsors. Initiate 'coaching' of programme sponsor(s) to ensure that they are fully aware of emerging issues and their role in assisting resolution. This is a somewhat informal process involving frequent dialogue with sponsors to maintain a high level of ongoing involvement.
Defined	Stakeholder management processes for the programme, and its component projects, have been defined, documented and agreed. Sponsors recognize their role and responsibilities and proactively intervene to ensure success.	This level is characterized by stakeholder management processes and strategy having been defined and documented, but not universally implemented. To move on from this level to the next it is necessary to implement the strategy across all aspects of the programme.	11. Implement agreed stakeholder management strategy. Implement the agreed strategy and ensure adoption by all component projects. 12. Measure effectiveness of stakeholder management. Add reporting on levels of stakeholder commitment and opinions to periodic reporting. For example programme steering committee reports. 13. Periodically review levels of stakeholder commitment and initiate/amend actions as required. The effectiveness of the programme's management of

Level	Summary	Characteristics	Corrective actions
			stakeholders should be regularly reviewed by the programme board, as part of its overall review and governance of the programme.
			14. Maintain sponsor engagement through ongoing dialogue with the programme sponsor(s) to ensure involvement.
Managed	Stakeholder commitment and their impact upon the programme is periodically reviewed following which corrective actions and interventions are made/amended as required. Sponsors are fully engaged and provide direct input to issue resolution as required	The stakeholder management process and strategy is implemented. However, it is more effective in some areas than others. The relative support, or lack thereof, of each stakeholder will be periodically assessed and interventions and corrective actions initiated or amended as and when required. Corrective actions will be managed to completion within the programme planning and progress management procedures. Programme sponsors will provide full support with appropriate interventions as required.	15. Use Sponsor(s) and/or programme board to overcome difficulties. Where stakeholders are less supportive than they might be, the influence and support of the sponsor(s) or programme board can be brought to bear – in line with the agreed stakeholder management strategy.
			16. Share stakeholder management best practices with other programmes. Initiate communications between programmes and projects to share best practice stakeholder management. Find out how other programmes overcome problems with tricky stakeholders.

Level	Summary	Characteristics	Corrective action
			17. Also, seek to gain the 'political' support of other programmes and initiatives.
Optimized	Regular and effective mechanisms are in place to assess the effectiveness of stakeholder management, report this information to senior management and develop improved processes as required.	The optimized stakeholder management process will: ● Identify all programme stakeholders. ● Evaluate stakeholders for impact on or by the programme. ● Identify interventions required to achieve desired levels of stakeholder commitment and support. ● Proactively manage stakeholders to improve overall commitment and support. ● Ensure effective two-way communication with all stakeholders. ● Report regularly to programme board or equivalent on the relative levels of support for the programme. ● Seek continuous improvement to the stakeholder management process. ● Share best practice with other programmes.	Stakeholder management is about people. The programme manager should never relax and should always keep close to the key stakeholders, understand their concerns and adjust the stakeholder management strategy and detailed communication plans as circumstances change.

16.5 IMPROVING RISK AND ISSUE MANAGEMENT

For further guidance on the corrective actions listed in the table below, consult Chapter 7, 'Management of risks and issues'.

Level	Summary	Characteristics	Corrective actions
Innocence	No formal processes exist for the management of issues or risks, either at the 'programme' level or at the 'project level.	All good programme and project managers will seek to resolve issues and anticipate risks, but there are no consistent processes and some will do it better than others. No risk or issue registers exist, or if they do, they are they are out of date and their status is unknown, so they are not used in any meaningful way. There are no processes for reporting on issues and risks. In all probability, there is no agreement on exactly what constitutes a risk and what an issue. When significant issues arise, much time and effort is spent in agreeing how to deal with them, to the detriment of other aspects of project and programme management. Unforeseen risks cause even greater disruption and, as a result, create a climate of managerial instability, in which plans are constantly being changed. Furthermore, this instability makes it difficult	1. Establish agreement on what constitutes an issue and what a risk. 2. Require project managers to identify and record all significant risks and issues with registers, as recommended by good project management practice (e.g. PRINCE2). 3. Ensure that all project managers regularly review their registers and take effective action to resolve issues and to eliminate, mitigate or contain the risks within their span of control.

Level	Summary	Characteristics	Corrective actions
		to accurately forecast likely completion dates, cost out-turns or benefit delivery, which, in turn, tends to create mistrust between 'project-level' and 'programme-level' management. It also creates distrust between those involved in programme governance (see Chapter 3) and the programme's executive management.	4. Define and agree a programme-wide process for regularly reviewing issues and risks and for escalating to the programme manager those that are outside the power of the individual project managers to resolve.
Initial	Processes exists for projects, but there are no programme-level processes for collating, evaluating or managing issues or risks. Project processes may be inconsistent with each other.	Project managers identify issues and risks and record them in a sensible way, such as in a formal issue or risk register. They use their skill and experience to resolve those that it is within their power to do so. However, because there is no formal process for escalating risks to a higher level, major risks and issues, which are outside the scope of the individual project to resolve, are not addressed. Furthermore, risks that are common to several projects are addressed in an ad-hoc way within each project, duplicating effort and sometimes leading to conflict between projects. Major risks and issues that need to be resolved at the 'programme' or even at the 'strategic' level remain unaddressed, thus	5. Ensure that escalated issues and risks are properly recorded in 'programme-level' issue and risk registers and are subject to regular review at the programme level. The programme manager may decide that some of these issues and risks do not warrant escalation and may refer them back down to the project manager, but will initiate

Level	Summary	Characteristics	Corrective actions
		continuing the managerial instability characteristic of the 'Innocence' level.	appropriate action to resolve all those that have to be dealt with at the 'programme' level.
			6. Ensure that the review communicates to individual project managers any agreed actions to resolve issues and risks common to several projects.
			7. Establish appropriate contingency arrangements, whereby, in agreed circumstances, the programme manager can divert resources and funding from successful component projects to those that are experiencing difficulties. Alternatively, the programme manager can approve delivery delays as a response to specifically identified risks.
			8. Allocate responsibility to the programme office to verify that risk registers are kept up to date and that appropriate actions are taken. (See Chapter 13 'The programme office', for guidance on programme offices.)

Level	Summary	Characteristics	Corrective actions
Repeatable	Basic processes exist at the 'programme' level for the collating and evaluating of programme-critical issues and risks. Processes also exist for escalating the relevant issues and risks to the 'programme' level from the component projects.	A common set of processes exists across the whole programme to manage and report on issues and risks and, wherever possible, actions are taken within the programme to resolve issues and to eliminate, contain or mitigate risks. Common approaches are adopted to resolving issues and risks that are common to several component projects. Where possible, resources or funding is diverted from successful projects to those that are facing unexpected difficulties. Essentially, risks and issues within the programme are managed and controlled. However, there is a gap between the programme and the organizational strategy, which restricts the programme's ability to deal with major strategic issues and risks. This may be because those charged with overall governance of the programme (e.g. the programme board) ignore their responsibilities with respect to strategic issues and risks, or because they fail to communicate their views to the programme manager. As a result, strategic instability, confusion and distrust is likely to continue.	9. No programme can thrive unless it has effective governance arrangements, such as a coherent and committed programme board, (as described in Section 3.6, 'Programme governance'). 10. With such arrangements in place, define and agree a process for regularly reporting strategic risks and issues to the 'strategic' level.

593

Level	Summary	Characteristics	Corrective actions
Defined	Effective processes exist for escalating relevant issues and risks from the programme to the strategic direction of the organization.	Although strategic issues and risks are reported to the strategic level, they are not always responded to effectively. This causes difficulties for the programme and frustration to those with responsibility for managing it. This may be because of incompleteness or inadequacy of the strategy that the programme is seeking to implement, it may be because internal politics prevents the governance arrangements from working effectively, or it may be because those involved in programme governance are not clear on their roles and responsibilities. It may also be because business circumstances have changed and the programme is no longer perceived by some to be necessary. As a result, business units may have lost (or never had) real confidence in the programme to deliver worthwhile benefits and feel that the money would be better spent elsewhere. Finally, it may be because internal political debates and issues have not been adequately addressed.	11. Provide guidance or training for all those involved in programme governance, so that they fully appreciate their role in the whole issue and risk management process. This could include the programme board and/or the organization's main board of directors/senior management team. 12. Ensure that the programme manager has regular face-to-face meetings with the board or its equivalent to review and agree actions on strategic issues and risks. 13. Review the business justification for the programme, to confirm that it still makes sense and the programme is (or will) deliver worthwhile business benefits after allowing for the risks that have been identified. 14. Seek agreement on contingency arrangements for the programme, such as agreeing a degree of 'tolerance' around costs, to give the programme manager a contingency

Level	Summary	Characteristics	Corrective actions
			which they may apply to mange risks and issues.
Managed	Effective systems are in place at all levels to identify, monitor, report on, collate and actively manage all issues and risks. Risk management includes actions to eliminate, mitigate or contain risks and the control of contingency arrangements in the event that risks actually occur.	While formal processes to manage issues and risks are agreed and in place at all levels, it is not clear that these are as effective or as efficient as could be. While the number of unpleasant surprises affecting the programme should be reducing, there are complaints that procedures are unnecessarily clumsy and onerous and should therefore be simplified or that problems still occur and that procedures should therefore be made more rigorous.	15. Arrange for issue and risk management processes to be audited, with a view to identifying any gaps or duplications. (See Chapter 8, 'Programme assurance and quality' for guidance on auditing.) 16. Hold workshops with the various groups involved in issue and risk management to capture their views on how the management of issues and risks could be improved. 17. Using the output from the audits and workshops, make improvements to the issue and risk management processes throughout the programme.
Optimized	The effectiveness of issue and risk management arrangements are regularly monitored and reviewed and reported back to	With all processes in place and working effectively, supported by objective evidence that they are working as well as possible, all those involved in the programme should have a high degree of confidence in its	

Level	Summary	Characteristics	Corrective actions
	senior management. Where necessary, issue and risk management processes are improved.	success and trust in those responsible for its direction and management. This does not mean that further issues will not appear or that new risks will not threaten the programme, but it does mean that there should be warnings and time to notify those involved and for them then to respond.	

16.6 IMPROVING PROGRAMME ASSURANCE AND QUALITY

For further guidance on the corrective actions listed in the table below, consult Chapter 8, 'Programme assurance and quality'.

Level	Summary	Characteristics	Corrective actions
Innocence	No formal processes exist for the management of quality at either the 'programme' level or within the component projects.	Most staff working on programmes and projects will naturally strive to do their best and produce reasonable quality deliverables within the time available. However, without common processes and management commitment, the results are likely to be inconsistent and unpredictable. At this level of quality process development, there are no common procedures for establishing the levels of quality required, or even what the user's actual requirements are. With no common processes for ensuring the achievement of quality, much depends upon the experience and attitude of the staff involved, which is likely to result in some individuals spending effort and resource on unnecessary refinements – i.e. 'gold plating'. At the same time, without clear and agreed objectives for quality, more tangible criteria of success, such as on-time delivery, usually take precedence. This may result in	1. Establish agreement on the quality objectives of the programme. 2. Ensure that these are prioritized so that staff have guidance when there is a need to make trade-offs, e.g. performance versus long-term reliability. 3. Ensure that all quality requirements are understood in this way, including (where appropriate) performance, reliability, maintainability, usability, legal and regulatory compliance, health and safety. 4. Cascade these objectives down to the individual projects that compose the programme. 5. In turn, ensure that the quality requirements for each product or deliverable created within each component project are identified and documented.

Level	Summary	Characteristics	Corrective actions
		skimping on key elements of deliverables, resulting in subsequent unreliability and difficulty in operation. With quality determined by the random application of individual experience and perception of programme priorities, gold-plating can exist side-by-side with inadequate product quality, resulting in expensive deliverables that fail to deliver long-term satisfaction. Because there are no agreed requirements nor any agreed standards for measuring the quality levels that are actually achieved, there is little effective communication of quality issues within the programme or with users. The likely result of this will be almost certain disappointment among users when products are finally delivered.	6. Ensure that detailed information is captured in the programme from its projects, to verify that the quality process is being followed and that products are not being delivered in an unacceptable state.
Initial	The quality requirements of all deliverables are defined and agreed.	Quality requirements are generally understood, but there is no common understanding on how to achieve them or on the amount of time, money or effort that should be spent. Depending on time and cost pressures, some projects may be spending	7. Embed procedures to ensure that success criteria is agreed with the 'users/customers', and that this is developed into testing plans approved by the users/customers.

Level	Summary	Characteristics	Corrective actions
		excessively on unimportant aspects, while others are skimping in order to achieve time and cost targets. The users are not fully aware of exactly what they are going to receive in terms of quality and are likely to have excessive expectations that are likely to be disappointed when the final capabilities are delivered. Users' own responsibilities for providing input and for assessing results (e.g. acceptance testing) are not defined and thus are likely to cause difficulty when products are made available for testing and acceptance. Because quality is not taken seriously enough, project plans are inadequate with respect to quality. Thus, nobody can be certain that any necessary tests, checks or reviews can be completed without delaying delivery. As a result, meeting quality requirements is often sacrificed to delivering products on time.	8. Establish mechanisms for users[4] to review and agree the quality requirements of key deliverables and their roles and responsibilities in undertaking the necessary tests, checks or reviews. 9. Ensure that the resource requirements both within the projects and among users are fully understood. Verify that key resources, such as critical pieces of equipment or expert staff, will be available on the scheduled dates. 10. Ensure that the necessary tests, checks and reviews are included or allowed for within component project plans. 11. Ensure that quality activity is managed, particularly agreeing corrective actions with users when testing fails.

---

4 'Users' here means representatives of those who will use the resultant facility. In many cases these will represent the external 'client' organization and such tests will form part of the process of formal acceptance. In other cases these will represent the internal business units for which the facility is being developed. In either cases 'users' can represent those who literally will use the facility (e.g. clerical staff) and those responsible for their management. In some circumstances it might include strategic-level staff, such corporate lawyers or main board directors.

Level	Summary	Characteristics	Corrective actions
Repeatable	Component projects/work-streams have defined and agreed plans for verifying and validating the quality of all their deliverables.	While quality requirements are understood at all levels and effective action is taken at the 'project' level to ensure that they are met, few mechanisms exist to verify that what is being reported by component projects up to the 'programme' level and beyond is truly representative of the real situation.	12. Document the programme's approach to the achievement of quality within a programme quality strategy, (as outlined in Section 8.4, 'Programme quality stratgey'). 13. Arrange for staff to be involved in tests, checks or reviews to have appropriate training or supervision, so that these activities can be undertaken efficiently and effectively. This applies to both programme and user staff. 14. Establish common, programme-wide approaches to recording the results of tests, checks and reviews and of reporting the results from the project level to the programme level and from the programme level to the strategic or organization level so that an overall view of the achievement of quality within the programme can be obtained.
Defined	The quality plans of component projects are effectively implemented	Component projects have plans in place and appropriate tests, checks or reviews are undertaken. Common approaches are	15. Appoint an independent auditing function for the programme to undertake audits of key component

Level	Summary	Characteristics	Corrective actions
	and the programme has a defined and agreed plan for confirming the quality of all deliverables.	adopted throughout the programme and quality achievement is reported upwards to the 'programme' level. However, there is no independent conformation that what is being reported is fully representative of the true situation.	projects and of critical aspects of the programme. (See Section 8.8, 'Programme audit' for further guidance.) 16. Establish an audit schedule, prioritized according to the importance and difficulty of the project or programme aspect. 17. Make sure the 'schedule' mechanism can react to unpredictable events that might trigger the need for an 'unscheduled' health check audit if the programme gets into difficulties. 18. Liaise with other internal and external organizations that might wish to undertake audits of the programme so as to avoid duplication of audits with the resultant risk of 'audit fatigue'. 19. Establish a standard approach by which the results of audits may be summarized for all those involved in programme governance, so that they fully appreciate the state of quality achievement throughout the programme.

Level	Summary	Characteristics	Corrective actions
Managed	Effective audit arrangements are in place to verify the conformance of all parts of the programme to agreed plans, processes and quality requirements.	The costs of quality, both to achieve it and the consequences of not achieving it, are not understood. There is no understanding, other than in a general way, of the trade-offs between quality and other project and programme attributes, such as time or cost. Although quality issues can be escalated, overall governance arrangements are insufficient for strategic decision making that would involve a trade-off between the achievement of quality and the achievement of other programme and project attributes. In particular, the costs of achieving adequate quality, and of not achieving it, are not fully understood.	20. Arrange for the results of audits to be complemented by other metrics and diagnostic tools, such as the PMMM (see Section 15.2, 'Using the Programme Management Maturity Model'). 21. Using audits and metrics, establish the overall costs of quality (see Section 8.12 'Quality costs'). 22. Ensure that the results of quality activities, plus quality costs and other quality metrics, are summarized for those engaged in programme governance and that these regularly review these summaries and initiate appropriate corrective action as necessary. 23. Review all reported failures (whether the result of tests, checks or reviews conducted during the execution of the programme and during any subsequent warranty or guarantee period) to ascertain if there are any patterns of failure. If there are, investigate the 'root causes' and implement appropriate

Level	Summary	Characteristics	Corrective actions
			corrective action, such as revising processes, improving staff training, adding additional tests, checks or reviews, etc.
			24. Review the quality activities (procedures and tests, checks or reviews) to eliminate unnecessary or superfluous ones. Also, review the effectiveness of remaining procedures and test, check or review approaches to ensure that they are effective in terms of the benefits achieved and the time, money and effort expended. Simplify, streamline or eliminate where appropriate.
Optimized	The quality performance of all parts of the programme is measured, monitored, reported and used as a basis for initiating ongoing improvements in programme performance.	With all processes in place and working effectively, supported by objective evidence that they are working as well as possible, plus a full understanding of the costs of quality and how they relate to each other, all those involved should be confident that the programme will meet its quality objectives without any unnecessary expenditure of time, money or effort.	25. Although quality management processes may now be deemed to be fully mature and operating at the highest level, it is possible to use the information provided by the quality management system and the audits to imrpove other aspects of the programme.

Level	Summary	Characteristics	Corrective actions
			• Ensure that quality continues to be given adequate attention at all levels, including at the 'strategic' and 'programme' levels.
			• Review the quality objectives in the light of changing circumstances and priorities and adjust the detailed quality requirements of programme deliverables as necessary.
			• Continue to educate and train at all levels, both to ensure that those new to the programme understand what is required, and to remind the others of what they might have forgotten.
			• Review quality activities to continuously improve all programme and project activities.
			• Ensure the knowledge gained from audits and metrics is used to improve the programme management process and quality activities/techniques, so that quality management becomes more and more cost effective.

Level	Summary	Characteristics	Corrective actions
			The measurement of this 'cost effectiveness' over time, must demonstrate continuous improvement, and should be an inclusive part of the quality management system for programmes and projects.

16.7 IMPROVING CONFIGURATION MANAGEMENT

For further guidance on the corrective actions listed in the table below, consult Chapter 9, 'Configuration management'.

Level	Summary	Characteristics	Corrective actions
Innocence	No formal processes exist for the management of configurations or the control of individual items or products.	There are no formal or agreed processes in place for configuration management or for the control of items, products or systems. Individual team members may have instituted their systems, but these vary in effectiveness and only cover the specific items on which they work. Furthermore, there are no registers of items or, if they do exist, they are out of date and their status is unknown. Because of this, time is frequently wasted as a result of misunderstanding product status, for example, by working on older versions of products. The lack of adequate records or identification also means that it is not possible, without a great deal of effort, to trace delivered items back to the relevant test or inspection records. Without consistent records of the versions of components in delivered systems, much time and effort is spent whenever the system is amended or updated. Frequently such amendments or updates prove incompatible, resulting in failures in service.	1. Investigate the different categories of items that must come under configuration control. 2. Require project managers to identify all products and to record their status in a configuration register as they are developed, checked and delivered.

Level	Summary	Characteristics	Corrective actions
Initial	Items to be subjected to configuration management have been defined and agreed, although the processes within component projects may be inconsistent with each other.	All items produced within the component projects are now recorded and there is visibility of what is delivered. However, there may be differences in the way that component projects maintain their records and it is still not possible to link together all the items that make up a configuration of the delivered systems.	3. Establish consistent programme-wide procedures to record what is actually delivered – including individual component items, serial numbers, versions – through the development and implementation of a configuration management plan. 4. The configuration management plan should define when a constituent part of a 'configuration' will be agreed and 'frozen' so that future changes to it are only made with appropriate levels of agreement and approval. It should also establish standard processes throughout the programme for the maintenance of all records concerning current and historical information related to each 'configuration'. 5. Make sure the plan covers all relevant products, including programme management documents and software items.

Level	Summary	Characteristics	Corrective actions
Repeatable control over configuration items.	Adequate plans exist for establishing and maintaining configuration items.	A common set of processes now exists across the whole programme to manage configuration items. However, implementation may not be as rigorous as required and there is no data to indicate the accuracy of configuration registers or other records.	6. Allocate and make clear responsibilities for operating configuration management processes. 7. Ensure that configuration registers are visible at the programme level. If necessary, arrange for copies of registers to be provided to the to the programme support office on a regular basis. 8. If necessary, provide training or education to programme and project staff on the importance of maintaining configuration records.
Defined	Configuration plans are effectively implemented and are providing comprehensive information on the status and relationships of all configuration items.	There is now a programme-wide view of how the configuration management system is actually working with data available to show where it is effective and where it is not.	9. Establish a process of reviewing or auditing the configuration records within each component project to ensure that there is conformity between the documented configurations and the real configurations that have been delivered. 10. Undertake any necessary actions to rectify any weaknesses identified by the reviews or audits – e.g. extra

Level	Summary	Characteristics	Corrective actions
			resources, closer supervision, reallocation of roles
Managed	Audits or similar review activities are undertaken to confirm the accuracy of configuration management information and effective action is taken to resolve any discrepancies.	Configuration management is implemented throughout the programme but, inevitably, there are areas where the implementation is not as effective as in others. However, it is not easy, without in-depth process audits, to identify which these areas are prior to any such inadequacies causing difficulties.	11. Link configuration management review to other programme processes, such as post-installation servicing in order to gain an ongoing view of the accuracy of configuration management records. Allocate responsibility, e.g. to the programme support office, for collating such data. 12. Ensure that configuration management is also linked to the change control process and to any processes for the re-release or update of delivered systems. 13. Identify areas of persistent inadequacy in configuration management, either within aspects of the processes (e.g. test recording, delivery recording) or within individual projects.

Level	Summary	Characteristics	Corrective actions
Optimized	Configuration management activities are integrated with other programme processes so that all change to configuration items can be traced back to the originating event and forward to the programme's products and deliveries.	A comprehensive system is in place, which all involved understand and operate correctly, which provides meaningful management data and is subject to continuous review/audit and improvement. The system is fully integrated with other relevant systems and provides comprehensive audit trails for all delivered systems.	At this level of maturity problems caused by inadequate or missing records will largely have been eliminated, but the programme should not be complacent and should seek continually to maintain and improve its configuration management processes.

16.8 IMPROVING INTERNAL COMMUNICATIONS

For further guidance on the corrective actions listed in the table below, consult Chapter 10, 'Internal communications'.

Level	Summary	Characteristics	Corrective actions
Innocence	No organized or planned internal communication.	Most staff working on projects will naturally strive to find out what they are supposed to do and to notify colleagues when they have done it. However, without planned and organized internal communications, they are likely to misunderstand what is required and fail to pass information to those that need it. Instead, news and ideas are passed around informally by the 'grapevine', and often incorrectly. Unconfirmed rumours abound. Moreover, the lack of effective communication gives everyone a feeling of being kept in the dark, resulting in the demoralization of many programme and project staff.	1. Define what needs to be done by each project and team in the form of work package definitions so that everyone has a basic idea of what is expected of them. 2. If this has not already been done, produce an overall programme plan describing the objectives of the programme and identifying the various projects. Ensure that this plan identifies key roles and responsibilities. 3. Establish regular reporting structures so that the programme manager and their staff can be kept up-to-date on progress. Provide templates to give guidance on what is to be included within such reports. 4. Establish an issues register and mechanisms by which all programme members can raise issues or concerns about the

Level	Summary	Characteristics	Corrective actions
			programme or their part of it. Part of this mechanism must be arrangements for all such issues to be reviewed and responded to reasonably quickly. (See also Chapter 7, 'Management of risks and issues'.) 5. Establish escalation processes whereby urgent issues and problems outside the span of control of the managers of the component projects can be communicated quickly to the programme manager and, if necessary, to the programme director or the programme board.
Initial	Limited formal communication occurs, mostly in the form of instructions being passed down from the programme manager to component projects and teams about what needs to be done.	Basic managerial information is communicated, but it tends to be largely about the issues of concern to the programme manager. It is largely formal and in a large and complex programme feedback may be insufficiently detailed or precise to give the programme manager a clear idea of what is really going on throughout the programme. The needs of for knowledge and communication of different groups within	6. Establish a system of milestones and sub-milestones and ensure progress against them is reported at regular intervals. This will ensure that progress can be effectively monitored. 7. Use milestone trend charts to make progress easily visible. 8. Conduct an analysis of internal groups to identify what their

Level	Summary	Characteristics	Corrective actions
		the programme are not fully understood and there is no coherent plan for ensuring that all teams and groups within the programme are adequately communicated with. Other than the overall responsibility of the programme manager, responsibilities for ensuring adequate communication and for managing it are unclear. In all probability, inadequate time or budget is allocated to internal communication.	communications needs are and to identify the best ways of fulfilling them. 9. On the basis of the analysis, prepare an internal communications plan (either as a stand-alone plan or as part of an overall communications plan involving external stakeholders as well as internal team members, as described in Chapter 6, 'Stakeholder management'). 10. Appoint an Internal communications manager, or equivalent, with the necessary resources and budget, to help the programme manager to organize all the necessary regular communication, as identified in the communications plan.
Repeatable	Basic communication occurs in a reasonably regular and predictable fashion, but many team members are still in the dark about how their work contributes to overall success.	Regular two-way communication now takes place between the programme's management team and the project managers. There is an understanding of the communication needs of all groups and there are plans, people and budgets to see that these needs are met. Notwithstanding the above, many within the	11. If appropriate to do so, establish a system of briefings, such as cascade briefings to ensure that messages are communicated throughout the programme. These can be linked into regular reports to ensure that feedback gets back to the

Level	Summary	Characteristics	Corrective actions
		programme do not have a clear view of where they fit into the overall picture or of how their work contributes to the achievement of the programme's objectives. The main focus should now turn to the effective implementing of the communications plan, using tools and techniques that ensure that all have access to the information that they need.	programme manager. If necessary, provide formal training to the managers of the component projects and their team leaders to ensure that briefings are effective and successful. 12. Establish a programme repository where all programme plans, guides, and other documentation can be accessed by team members. Ensure appropriate access control arrangements to prevent sensitive information falling into inappropriate hands, but generally make it easy for those within the programme who need information to get at it. 13. Allocate responsibility for keeping the repository up to date, e.g. to the programme office.
Defined	Good communications exist within the programme, but there is still scope for improvement so as to maintain team morale and	Effective communication on key concepts and issues now exists throughout the programme, yet there are still places and groups that are not as motivated as they could be. Moreover, internal communication activities are not as	14. Irrespective of the distance, time and costs involved, seek for the programme manager and other key members of the programme's management to meet as many as

Level	Summary	Characteristics	Corrective actions
	to improve the efficiency and effectiveness of communications processes.	efficient or as effective as they could be. Because of the effort or time involved, those working on the programme don't always avail themselves of the communications facilities that exist. Even where good communications exist, there may still be uncertainties over the meaning of messages due to cultural or other differences amongst the programme's component projects and teams.	possible of the programme's staff on a face-to-face basis. If this is not practical, seek regular video conferences to complement regular reporting. 15. Consider reducing the burden of keeping in touch by establishing common e-mail disciplines throughout the programme, thus reducing the number of unnecessary e-mails and allowing programme members to focus on the ones that matter. 16. Consider producing a programme glossary of acronyms and terms and make its use is mandatory to reduce the scope for misunderstanding between component projects and their teams. 17. Consider publishing and maintaining an internal programme directory with current telephone numbers and e-mail addresses, to make it easier for team members to contact each other. 18. Depending upon the analysis of

Level	Summary	Characteristics	Corrective actions
			needs (see above) establish news-letters, or similar, to broadcast the achievements of programme team members and to build team spirit.
			19. Consider giving the programme an identity or personality, through some form of logo or slogan.
			20. Help new joiners to the programme to quickly 'get up to speed' by producing a new joiners pack that provides the background information that they need to become effective, including details of internal communications arrangements and where to find information.
			21. Seek to measure the effectiveness of internal communications, e.g. by undertaking surveys.
			22. On the basis of these surveys, refine the internal communications plan so as to improve effectiveness.
			23. Use internal audit arrangements to establish the effectiveness of internal communications and identify any groups that are left out.
Managed	Good, effective and comprehensive communications are believed to exist throughout the programme, but there are no measures or benchmarks to demonstrate that they are as good as they could be.	Although internal communication now appears to be effective throughout the programme, there are no independent measures of the effectiveness or efficiency of the process. Because of this, it is difficult to make a business case for any further investment in internal communication.	

Level	Summary	Characteristics	Corrective actions
Optimized	The efficiency and effectiveness of internal communications between all parts of the programme is measured, monitored, reported and used as a basis for initiating ongoing improvements in programme performance.	With all processes in place and working effectively, supported by objective evidence that they are working as well as possible, all those involved should be confident that the programme will meet its objectives without any unnecessary expenditure of time, money or effort. However, circumstances change and internal communications, like every other aspect of programme management, will need to be kept constantly under review to ensure that they continue to be both effective and efficient.	24. Use feedback from audits and surveys, from face-to-face meetings, and from the issues log to keep the communications plan up-to-date and to make internal communications ever more effective.

16.9 IMPROVING PROGRAMME ACCOUNTING

For further guidance on the corrective actions listed in the table below, consult Chapter 11, 'Programme accounting and financial control'.

Level	Summary	Characteristics	Corrective actions
Innocence	Programme accounting and financial control processes are either completely lacking or applied without any consistency.	What programme budget setting occurs, it is only undertaken at a highly superficial level, e.g. only a total expenditure budget for the programme is set, with no detailed breakdown. Where undertaken, recording of programme expenditure is performed by the organization's finance function, independent of the programme team. No analysis of project or lower level costs is undertaken.	1. A programme-level cost estimate and budget, derived from individual project estimates is a minimum requirement for any programme. Development of such an estimate should be seen as a first, essential task. 2. The programme management team should take responsibility for identifying and recording cost and expenditure information concerning the programme. The team should work with the organization's finance function to ensure cost and expenditure date is available.
Initial	Processes are ad hoc and often chaotic. The organization does not provide a consistent financial reporting environment. Success depends on the	The accounting and financial control processes vary according to the experience and preferences of individual project managers. Component projects within the programme have different levels of detail for time and expenditure recording and cost	3. A common set of processes for the development and presentation of detailed project-level budgets should be designed and implemented throughout the programme.

Level	Summary	Characteristics	Corrective actions
	competence and heroics of the people engaged in the programme.	reporting, making cost comparison between component projects very difficult. The programme management team (probably through the programme office) undertake cost and expenditure recording and reporting for the programme as a whole.	4. Consistent levels of recording, analysis and reporting of time and cost information should be established throughout the programme, consistent with the budget breakdowns established in action 3 above. These procedures should be implemented in all the projects making up the programme to ensure that costs are effectively analysed and reported at project level.
			5. A standard timetable for the analysis and reporting of project and programme cost information should be implemented. This should be consistent with that of the organization's finance function to allow any necessary cross-checking between the programme and the organization's cost records.
			6. In accordance with the standard timetable, each project manager should cross-check the costs recorded for their project against those recorded in the organization's

Level	Summary	Characteristics	Corrective actions
			financial records, and should arrange adjustments to correct any discrepancies within the organization's records.
Repeatable	Accounting and financial control activities are somewhat repeatable. The organization may use some basic procedures to track cost and schedule.	Common levels of reporting are in place for cost estimates/budgets, time and cost expenditure for all projects within the programme. Information is escalated up from the project level to the programme level. Cross-checking of project and programme cost against estimates and reporting of variances may occur for some parts of the programme.	7. The programme manager should report costs and variances against estimates to the programme board. Where separate boards also exist for component projects, similar cost and variance reporting should be undertaken by the project managers. 8. Project managers should break down the estimates and record or calculate the costs incurred for each deliverable to be produced by the component projects.
Defined	Accounting and financial control processes are well established and understood.	Specific levels of estimating, budgeting, time and expenditure recording plus cost reporting are established for all projects within the programme, providing details to the level of individual project deliverables. Timetables and methods for undertaking all accounting and financial control processes	9. Establish targets in terms of time and quality (accuracy, completeness etc.) for undertaking all the programme's accounting and financial control processes, within the programme and for all the component projects.

Level	Summary	Characteristics	Corrective actions
		have been established and implemented throughout the programme. Reconciliation of project and programme cost records to the organization's accounting records is routinely undertaken. Procedures for calculating the estimated costs to complete (ECC) of individual project deliverables are defined and implemented. Cost and schedule variances for the programme are calculated and regularly reported to the programme board.	10. Implement procedures to monitor the targets set in action 9 above. 11. Educate and inform programme and project teams in the use of financial information for decision making and problem identification. 12. Use the programme's accounting and financial control information, such as ECC and cost variances, to proactively manage the programme and its component projects. 13. The programme board should use the records of programme and project costs and variances to periodically review and re-assess the programme's business case.
Managed	The programme manager and their team effectively control all aspects of the programme's costs and finances.	Performance targets are established for the entire programme's accounting and financial control processes. Compliance with these standards is monitored by the programme manager and, where appropriate, reported to the programme board. The programme's financial performance variances are proactively managed and remediation action undertaken where appropriate.	14. Establish reviews of all the programme's accounting and financial control processes to: • identify shortcomings in process performance; • identify potential improvement actions; • assess the likely costs and benefits of potential improvement actions

Level	Summary	Characteristics	Corrective actions
			and select most effective; • implement improvement actions. 15. Where risk or priority is low, the frequency of monitoring or reporting should be relaxed to allow programme and project staff to focus efforts on the more critical elements to the programme.
		The reported costs of the programme are used to monitor, assess and amend the programme's business case, as required. Costs are estimated and variances are calculated, down to the level of individual deliverables, and corrective actions initiated where necessary to control costs.	
Optimized	Programme continually reviews and improves its accounting and financial information and this is used to manage the programme effectively.	The performance and effectiveness of the entire programme's accounting and financial control processes are regularly reviewed and improvements identified where required. Levels of detail and periodicity of reporting may be varied between projects and/or deliverables to reflect relative risks and priorities.	16. The lessons learned from within this programme, including any rules of thumb or estimation techniques, should be communicated to other programmes to help them to improve their accounting and financial control.

16.10 IMPROVING MANAGEMENT OF SCOPE AND CHANGE

For further guidance on the corrective actions listed in the table below, consult Chapter 12, 'Management of scope and change'.

Level	Summary	Characteristics	Corrective actions
Innocence	No clear, comprehensive and unambiguous definition exists of the scope of the programme. No agreed processes exist for managing change.	Definitions exist of the scope of the programme and its business objectives, but they are incomplete or imprecise. The full scope may be defined within various documents, which do not all coincide. In an externally managed programme, the emphasis of the contractor's proposal and the formal contract may be different. In this uncertainty, different stakeholder groups have different views of the full scope and of the programme's priorities and objectives. As a result of the above, there is no firm and agreed 'baseline' on which to base requests for change.	1. Establish a single, coherent and internally consistent document or set of documents that define what the programme is expected to achieve. This may be a high-level document that binds together existing specifications, contracts and definitions and resolves inconsistencies between them. 2. Ensure consistency between the objectives of the programme (i.e. business benefits) and the defined scope. 3. Ensure that all key stakeholders understand this definition and agree to it. Gaining such agreement would normally be the responsibility of the programme director or the sponsor.

Level	Summary	Characteristics	Corrective actions
Initial	A clear baseline of the scope and contents for the whole programme is defined and agreed, but as yet this programme scope has not been broken down in any meaningful fashion into component projects. No process for managing change exists.	Without a clear breakdown into component projects, it is difficult to be certain which parts will be affected by any particular change in scope. This makes assessing the total impact of a requested change virtually impossible. Changes are made, but the implications are not understood.	4. Break down programme into component projects, with each project having a clear and defined set of deliverables. 5. Link benefits to individual projects and to specific project deliverables to confirm that all project deliverables are required and that they will deliver all the expected business benefits. (See the discussion on benefit models in Section 5.6.) 6. This approach also makes it possible subsequently to assess the impact of any requested change on the business benefits that will eventually be delivered.
Repeatable	The division of the programme's scope and contents into component projects/work-streams has been defined and agreed but no consistent mechanisms are in place to ensure that all changes to the programme's scope are fully recorded.	Although there is a clear and comprehensive initial baseline for the scope of the programme, processes used to manage changes to that scope are ad hoc and inconsistent. Different projects use different approaches and there is no guarantee that all changes are notified to the programme, nor that agreed changes are matched by appropriate changes to budgets and time scales.	7. Ensure all changes are recorded. Define, document and implement a change control process, such as that shown in Chapter 12. 8. Ensure application throughout programme in the operation, roles and responsibilities of the change control process. Provide appropriate training and guidance

Level	Summary	Characteristics	Corrective actions
		As a result, it is difficult to be certain of the revised cost of the whole programme or of the time schedules when the various facilities and capabilities of the programme will be delivered.	to the managers of all component projects. 9. Ensure that all requests for change at any level are notified to the programme management team and recorded. 10. Ensure that the programme office maintains an accurate, complete and up-to-date register of all agreed changes, so that the current state with respect to changes of scope of the whole programme and of all its component projects can be seen. 11. Make sure that the programme board understands its role in authorizing and controlling changes. If appropriate, create a sub-committee of the board (e.g. change advisory board) to oversee the change control process and to authorize individual changes.
Defined	Consistent mechanisms are in place to ensure that all changes to the programme's scope are recorded, although	Changes are recorded and it is now possible to be confident of what is within and without the scope of the programme. However, impact assessment is inconsistent and there	12. Ensure all changes fully assessed for impact before approval. 13. Establish a specialist group or sub-committee to assess the impact of

625

Level	Summary	Characteristics	Corrective actions
	impacts are not always fully assessed.	is no certainty that changes to scope are fully matched by appropriate changes to cost or timescales. Frequently, it is assumed that because the change is relatively small, its impact can be absorbed within the tolerance allowed to component projects. This may be the case with an individual change but the collective effect is to blow the tolerance and create unconstrained 'scope creep'. The impact of a change within one project on other component projects not always assessed.	all changes. This assessment should include impact on cost, budget and delivery of benefits for all affected projects. 14. Ensure that all assessment covers impact on all projects, and that appropriate changes are made to time schedules and budgets of any projects with 'knock on' impact. 15. Where the impact of any one change or a collection of minor changes is such as to exceed the time or cost tolerance of projects, ensure that this is considered by the programme board (or a change sub-committee) and appropriate action taken. If no additional budget or time can be provided, ensure equivalent changes are made to the scope elsewhere to compensate.
Managed	Consistent mechanisms are in place to ensure that all changes to the programme's scope are fully assessed for impact and formally authorized prior to implementation.	While formal processes to manage all changes to scope are agreed and in place at all levels, it is not clear that these are as effective or as efficient as could be and that the impact of all changes (especially those agreed early in the programme before	16. Ensure that assessment of change impact fully covers the impact on business benefits. Where necessary, ensure that the business case and other benefits documents (such as the benefits strategy – see

Level	Summary	Characteristics	Corrective actions
		adequate procedures were in place) have been fully allowed for. There are complaints that procedures are unnecessarily clumsy and onerous and should therefore be simplified. At the same time, uncertainties about exact scope still occur and there are claims that change control procedures should therefore be made more rigorous. While the impact of requested changes is now fully investigated and reported through to those that requested the change, the likely impact on other business units is not always fully reported through to those units or to the main board.	Section 5.8.1) are updated when change requests are agreed. 17. Also make sure that the impact assessments also consider risk and that risk registers are fully and appropriately updated when change requests are agreed. 18. Ensure notification to the main board or to the boards of other programmes wherever a change to this could impact overall corporate strategy or the success of other programmes. 19. Arrange for change management processes to be audited by the programme assurance team to confirm full and effective implementation (see Section 16.6). Make any necessary improvements or corrections as recommended by the audit. 20. Review the tolerances for component projects in the light of agreed changes and, where appropriate, revise them.

627

Level	Summary	Characteristics	Corrective actions
Optimized	The assessment of changes includes evaluating the impact on the programme's expected business benefits and programme budgets. An understood process for managing change is established and followed on all programmes. Lessons are learned about managing change from programmes and fed back through the programme office.	With all processes in place and working effectively, supported by objective evidence that they are working as well as possible, all those involved in the programme should have a high degree of confidence in its success and trust in those responsible for its direction and management. This does not mean that further issues will not appear or that new risks will threaten the programme, but it does mean that there should be warnings and time to notify those involved and then for them to respond.	21. The programme board should review the revised programme scope and check it against the current business case for the programme and/or against any revised corporate strategy to ensure that the programme continues to provide the best possible value for money to the organization. 22. Secure in the knowledge that the agreed scope of the whole programme and of its component projects is fully understood, the programme board can seek ways in which the programme can further contribute to the achievement of overall corporate strategy. 23. Fully confident that it has control over the programme's scope and the business benefits that will result, the programme board can identify the key lessons learned and pass them on to other programmes that have yet to reach the same condition.

Appendices

A Glossary

The following glossary of terms includes terms introduced within this guide and others that are relevant to programme management. It is based on *Managing Successful Programmes* (OGC, 2003).

Audit	A formal process of investigation to verify that some activity is being or has been undertaken in accordance with agreed standards or plans.
Balanced scorecard	A management tool to convert an organization's vision and strategy into a comprehensive set of performance and action measures that provide the basis for a strategic management and measurement system.
Baseline	A snapshot of a position or situation that is recorded. Although the position may be updated later on, the baseline remains unchanged and available as a reminder of the original state and as a comparison against the current position.
Beneficial impact	The impact a programme has, or is expected to have, on a specific key performance indicator.
Benefit	A desired or actual outcome from a programme, such as increased market share, reduced production costs.
Benefit breakdown structure (BBS)	In a BBS benefits are grouped into 'packages' representing the lowest level unit of benefits for estimation, tracking and realization purposes.

Benefit dependency table	See *benefits matrix*.
Benefit owner	Person who must ensure the programme's outputs are used as effectively as possible and that the resulting change is measured to determine what benefits are realized.
Benefit profile	The complete description of information about a benefit, including metrics.
Benefit realization plan/schedule	A complete view of all the benefit profiles in the form of a schedule to show the relationship between a programme's outputs, the consequential changes as defined in the blueprint and benefits.
Benefit workshop	A working session held prior to the start of a programme with the aim of fully understanding and defining the expected benefits.
Benefits classification	A method of grouping benefits into like kinds, these groups being selected for the convenience of the organization.
Benefits estate	Plans describing in a properly structured way that is to be measured to ensure realization of benefits.
Benefits management	The activity of identifying, planning, optimizing, measuring, and tracking the expected benefits from business change to ensure that they are achieved by the business as a whole.
Benefits manager	Optional role to assist the business change manager with data gathering and other roles relating to benefits delivery and monitoring.
Benefits matrix/ benefits dependency table	A table-based benefits description to define and develop a full benefits profile – attributes, supporting outcomes and initiatives (enablers, impacts, business changes, technical changes, people changes, business processes).
Benefits model	A diagrammatic representation of benefit relationships and benefit components.
Blueprint or business architecture blueprint	A model showing the difference between the current state of an organization and the required future state highlighting people, processes, information and technology capabilities.

Business case	A document aggregating the specific programme information on overall costs, the anticipated benefits, the timeframe, and the risk profile of the programme.
Business case management	How the programme's rationale, objectives, benefits and risks will be balanced against the financial investment, and how this balance will be maintained, adjusted and assessed during the lifetime of the programme.
Business change manager	The person responsible for managing all the changes to the business required by the programme, so that the changes are achieved with minimal disruption to existing services and the benefits are maximized.
Business dashboard	A mechanism for presenting data about a business for day-to-day monitoring.
Business environment	Context in which a programme of change is managed.
Business Excellence Model	Framework for organizational self-assessment (see also *EFQM*).
Business objective	An objective or goal that an organization has expressed as part of its overall strategy.
Business user	The individual or role responsible for a part of an organization that will receive a new capability from a programme, improve some facet of that part of the organization and therefore deliver one or more benefits.
Centre of excellence	A centre of excellence is a focal point for supporting the department's individual programmes and projects, and for driving the implementation of improvements (extracted from OGC, 2003 – see also *programme office*).
Change management	(1) The task of managing change; (2) An area of professional practice; (3) A body of knowledge.
Communications plan	A plan of the communications activities during the programme, which is a key tool in managing stakeholders and maintaining focus among a programme team.
Delegation	The process by which some work (for example, a project, programme, work package or task) is requested by one part of an organization and carried out by another.

Dependency network	A representation of all the inputs and outputs from the projects, treating each project as a 'black box' and showing how the outputs of some projects are inputs to dependent projects.
Dis-benefit	A planned or unplanned negative impact of a change.
Earned value management	A management technique that relates, over time, the planned value of work to the actual value of work and the actual cost of achieving that work. This technique is often mandated in certain defence contracts.
Economic profit	The difference between business revenue and total opportunity cost. This is the revenue received by a business over and above the minimum needed to produce a good.
EFQM	European Federation for Quality Management. This organization promotes the Business Excellence Model as a tool for business improvement. This model is now the recommended standard for comparative benchmarking within UK public-sector organizations (see also *Business Excellence Model*).
Environment	Context in which a programme of change is managed.
Environmental scanning	Identification of risks (internal and external) beyond the scope of the immediate programme of change.
Gap analysis	Comparison of the future expected organizational state with the current state.
Governance	A framework for the programme that defines the strategies for managing quality, stakeholders, issues, risks, benefits, resources, planning and control.
Hard (tangible) benefit	Benefits that are directly quantifiable, for example, 'reduction in operating costs of £xm per annum'.
Heath check	A process of reviewing a programme or project during its lifecycle.
Investors in People (IIP)	A standard dealing with training and development in organizations. The standard is a good-practice benchmark indicating a minimum level of behaviours and actions.

IRR
The abbreviation for the internal rate of return, which is the discount rate that produces a zero net present value (NPV) from a one or more predicted cash flows.

Issue resolution strategy
Description of how issues will be handled and resolved.

Issues log
The log of all issues raised during the programme.

Key performance indicator (KPI)
A mechanism for quantifying organizational targets and measuring progress towards their achievement.

Lagging measures
Measurement of the benefit metrics after the change programme is completed.

Leading measures
Identification of the delivery progress of those products required for each benefit in order to track whether the change programme is on target to deliver the benefits.

Lessons learned report (LLR)
Information on the lessons learned during a change project or programme (things that went well and things that went badly) that can be usefully applied to other projects and programmes. This is normally a part of the post-implementation review.

Matrix management
The management of programmes and projects across a group of functional specialist groups. See also *delegation* and *resource loan*.

Methodology
A series of processes, procedures and role definitions providing consistent governance for programmes, projects or both.

Net present value (NPV)
NPV is the value of an investment's future net cash flow minus the initial investment.

OGC
Office of Government Commerce, publishers of PRINCE2 and *Managing Successful Programmes* (2003) and other publications.

Organization
How the programme will be managed throughout its lifecycle, the roles and responsibilities of individuals involved in the programme, and personnel management or HR arrangements.

Organizational capability	The combination of people (their skills and experience), processes and supporting tools/infrastructure used by an organization to deliver and adapt successfully to change.
Organizational capacity	An organization's ability to accommodate change while remaining productive. Key indicators are capability, resilience, demand, legacy, impact and readiness.
Outcome	The resulting effect on the organization and/or business environment from delivery of the programme. See also *business benefit*.
Post-implementation review (PIR)	A review of a programme after implementation of changes to review achievements and gain experience that might be used in future programmes. See also *lessons learned report*.
PPSO	See programme office.
PRINCE2	Projects in Controlled Environments is a structured method for effective project management published by OGC. See also *OGC*.
Programme	A portfolio of projects and benefits designed to deliver change of strategic importance to an organization.
Programme assurance	A function that provides independent advice and guidance to the programme board that the information they are receiving is valid and fully representative of the true state of the programme.
Programme brief	An outline description of the programme's objectives, desired benefits, risks, costs and timeframe.
Programme director	The role with ultimate responsibility and accountability for the programme (also referred to as senior responsible owner or programme executive).
Programme management	The coordinated management of a portfolio of projects (involving activities and work streams) that deliver change to achieve outcomes and benefits that are of strategic importance.
Programme management centre of excellence	See *centre of excellence*.

Programme Management Maturity Model (PMMM)	The PMMM provides a mechanism through which an organization or a group within an organization can: ● evaluate itself in programme management terms; ● compare its own maturity with other organizations on a fair basis; ● compare its own maturity with benchmarks from similar organizations; ● understand its strengths and weaknesses; ● develop a plan to improve its ability to deliver successful programmes.
Programme manager	The role responsible for the setting up, running and coordination of the programme. Also provides the overall 'healthcheck' that the programme is on track to deliver the required benefits and outcomes.
Programme mandate	The trigger for the programme from senior management who are, or may be, sponsoring the programme.
Programme office	A programme office may have a wide range of roles, including administrative support, collecting and collating data across programmes, multi-programme and multi-project report generation, ownership of methods and providing a centre of excellence for the programme, its governance and its delivery objectives. It is also known as a programme support office, PPSO or programme/project support office.
Programme plan	A key control document for the programme providing the basis for tracking the impact of each component project on the programme's overall goals, benefits, risks and costs.
Programme support office	See *programme office*.
Project deliverable	An item that a project has to create as part of the requirements. It may be part of the final outcome or an intermediate element on which one or more subsequent deliverables are dependent. (May also be referred to as a product.)
Project portfolio	A list of all the activities (projects and workstreams) that will be required to deliver the required 'future state'.

637

Quality management strategy	How the programme will achieve the required levels of quality in the way the programme is set up, managed and run, and how the programme's deliverables will be managed in order to maintain accurate information on all aspects of the programme.
Resource loan	A process by which one or more resources are transferred temporarily between teams.
Risk management strategy	How the programme will establish and maintain an effective risk management regime on the programme.
Risk register or risk log	A log of the identified risks to a programme of change (and the related projects) providing complete management information about the risks and their status at any one time.
Return on capital employed (ROCE)	A measure of the returns that a company is realizing from its capital. Calculated as profit before interest and tax divided by the difference between total assets and current liabilities, that is; the efficiency with which capital is being used to generate revenue.
Return on investment (ROI)	A measure of a programme's profitability. ROI measures how effectively the programme uses capital to generate financial benefit; the higher the ROI, the better.
Rate of return on investment (RRI)	The ratio of the additional annual income or profit generated by an investment to the cost of the investment.
Scenario-based planning	Management tool to provide greater clarity on the likely impact from uncertainties.
Shareholder value	The value that a shareholder is able to obtain from their investment in a company.
Soft (intangible) benefit	Benefits that are difficult to quantify, for example, improvements in public perception. See also *benefit* and *hard (tangible) benefits*.
Sponsoring group	Senior-level sponsorship of the programme providing the investment decision and top-level endorsement of the rationale and objectives for the programme.
Stakeholder	An individual, group or organization with an interest in or influence over the programme.

Stakeholder management strategy	How the programme will identify and analyse the stakeholders and how ongoing communications will be achieved between the programme and all its stakeholders.
Stakeholder map	A matrix showing stakeholders and their particular interests in the programme.
Strategic alignment	A high-level customer-driven method for developing strategy.
Strategic planning	A disciplined effort to produce fundamental decisions and actions that shape and guide what an organization is, what it does, and why it does it, with a focus on the future.
Tranche	A group of projects structured around distinct step changes in capability and benefit delivery.
Transition	A passing or change from one place, state, condition, and so on, to another.
Vision statement	An outward-facing description of the new capabilities resulting from programme delivery.

REFERENCES

OGC (2003) *Managing Successful Programmes*. Second edition. London: The Stationery Office.

B Sources of additional information

The three parts of this appendix are included to provide links to further information on the topic of programme management:

- Professional development
- Publications
- Internet sites.

The fact that most of the sources of information in this section are UK based reflects the UK base of the authors and the lead the UK has in this topic at the time of writing.

B.1 PROFESSIONAL DEVELOPMENT

THE OFFICE OF GOVERNMENT COMMERCE

The Office of Government Commerce (OGC) offers a wide range of useful resources for programme managers. This includes the central: Managing Successful Programmes (MSP) as well as PRINCE2 and the Management of Risk (MoR).

- Website: www.ogc.gov.uk/

THE APM GROUP

The APM Group is an independent commercial organization that specializes in accreditation. Since the launch of PRINCE2 in 1996, the group has, on behalf of OGC, and in partnership with it, developed and managed the accreditation of PRINCE2, MSP and the MoR.

The APM Group website is informative about MSP – what it is, who owns the method, which qualifications are available and who you can contact for training courses.

● Website: www.apmgroup.co.uk

PROGRAMME AND PROJECT SUPPORT OFFICE CERTIFICATION (PPSO)

PPSO certificates are available at foundation and advanced levels.

Entrants to the advanced level must hold the foundation certificate and while there are no prerequisites for entry to the foundation exam, candidates are strongly advised to book onto accredited training courses.

Experienced project support personnel who do not wish to take accredited training may choose to take the foundation exam directly. In addition, if they can demonstrate 2 years' relevant experience, they may apply as a direct entrant to the advanced exam.

The accredited course at foundation level is a minimum of 24 hours' training. The multiple-choice exam is 45 minutes long.

The course at advanced level is a minimum of 32 hours' training. This is followed by an oral exam.

● Website: www.bcs.org.uk/iseb

UK PROJECT MANAGEMENT DEGREES COURSES AND EDUCATIONAL ESTABLISHMENTS

Project Management BSc (Hons)

Project Management for Construction
University of Brighton
Tel: +44 1273 600 900.

Construction Project Management
University of Central Lancashire
Tel: +44 1772 892 400
Fax: +44 1772 892 935.

Quantity Surveying with Project Management
NE Wales Institute of HE P/as Coch
Tel: +44 1978 290 666.

MSc Degrees in Project Management

MSc in Project Management
University of Aberdeen Department of Engineering
Tel: +44 1224 272 559.

MSc in Project Management
Cranfield School of Management
Tel: +44 1234 751 122.

The Cranfield College of Project and Programme Management offer two annual courses: The Postgraduate Diploma in Programme Management and the Master's Degree in Project and Programme Management.

MSc in Project Management
GEC Management College at Dunchurch
Tel: +44 1788 810 656.

MSc in Project Management
The Engineering Construction Industry Training Board (ECITB)
Tel: +44 1923 400 998.

MBA IMSc in Project Management
Henley Management College
Tel: +44 1491 571 454.

MSc in Engineering Project Management
Lancaster University Professional Development Unit
Tel: +44 1524 593 418.

MSc in Project Management
Leeds Metropolitan University
Tel: +44 113 283 1726.

The Leeds Metropolitan University offers a 3-year undergraduate course leading to a bachelor degree in pure project and programme management. Other universities and centres for further education offer project management first degrees but most are focused on the construction industry.

MSc in Project Management
University of Portsmouth Accounting & Management Science
Tel: +44 23 9284 4602.

643

MSc various
UMIST
Tel: +44 161 236 3311

GEC Management College at Dunchurch
Tel: +44 1788 810 656.

Cranfield School of Management
Tel: 01234 751 122

AD-HOC PROGRAMME MANAGEMENT TRAINING

The National Computer Centre (NCC)

The NCC offers a 1-day workshop entitled 'Programme Management Master Class' at their Manchester headquarters.

- Website: www.ncc.co.uk/events

A number of commercial organizations offer training courses and workshops in programme management and a few have been included here. Inclusion does not indicate any approval or accreditation of the specific organization. The rate of expansion in programme management training and changes in commercial offerings does mean that intended students must make their own decisions.

Xansa plc

- 'Introduction to Programme Management'
- 'Managing Successful Programmes'
- 'Programme & Project Support Office Advanced'
- 'Programme & Project Support Office Foundation'.

- Website: www.xansa.com/training/topics/programmemanagement/

ESI

- 'Requirements Management: A Key to Project Success'
- 'Rapid Assessment and Recovery of Struggling Projects'
- 'Aligning Project Management with Corporate Strategy'
- 'Programme Management'
- 'Managing Complex Projects'.

- Website: www.esi-uk.com

The Projects Group

- Programme Management Overview
- Website: www.tpgacademy.com/MainsiteFrameset.asp

Courses from The Aim Academy

- 'Effective Programme Management'
- 'Benefits Management Techniques'
- 'Programme Health Check Workshop'

- Website: www.learnprojectmanagement.com

Eurim – the European Information Society Group

- 'Modernising Government and Programme Management'
- 'The Critical Success Factor'
- 'Programme Management Workshop'
- Tel: +32 9 210 98 22
- Website: www.eurim.org/briefings/BR33final.htm

Unicom

- Website: www.unicom.co.uk
- Tel: +44 1895 256484

Hawksmere (various courses)

- Website: www.hawksmere.co.uk
- Tel: +44 1207 824 8257

Publishing Training Centre

- Publishing Programme Management (a 4-day residential workshop in Oxfordshire)
- Website: www.train4publishing.co.uk/content/guideto/editorial/manage.htm

B.2 PROGRAMME MANAGEMENT PUBLICATIONS

Title: *Managing Successful Programmes: Delivering Business Change in Multi-project Environments.* 2nd Edition
Author: OGC
Date: 2003
Publisher: The Stationery Office
ISBN: 0113309171

Managing Successful Programmes has been published in two editions – the first in 1999 and the second in 2003. It describes the framework and strategies of programme management: the OGC's approach to managing change and delivering business benefits from a set of related projects. It talks about programmes becoming increasingly important as a management tool for integrating complex activities into a cohesive unit of focused effort and the delivery of benefit.

The drivers for change may be internal, such as improving the quality of products, or external, such as new government policy.

It contains 116 printed pages and is available as a softbound book or CD-ROM through:

- www.tso.co.uk/programme_management.html
- www.theprojectshop.co.uk/index.html

Title: *Programme Management Demystified: Managing Multiple Projects Successfully*
Author: Geoff Reiss
Date: 1996
Publisher: Chapman Hall
ISBN: 0419213503

Each project has its own restraints of time, cost and resources and must also be seen in terms of its effect on other projects and resources. If programme management takes place in the normal three-dimensional world, then project management takes place in a flat two-dimensional world. An early introduction to the topic.

Title: *One Project Too Many*
Author: Geoff Reiss and Geof Leigh
Date: 2005
Publisher: Project Management Publications
ISBN: 19003911120

This is an educational novel. In addition to the story, the book contains all the information created and used by the team as they struggle to get one important project off the ground and introduce a programme management regime in their organization. Available through:

- www.pmtoday.co.uk/books.asp
- www.gowerpub.com

  Title: *50 Checklists for Project and Programme Managers*
  Author: Rudy Kor, Gert Wijnen
  Date: 1999
  Publisher: Gower
  ISBN: 0566082780

This book provides practical, hands-on advice to follow a natural progression through each stage of a project or programme. The book ensures each aspect of the work is covered systematically and effectively. As well as the 50 checklists, there are more general tips.

  Title: *An Introduction to Programme Management*
  Author: CCTA
  Date: 1999
  Publisher: CCTA
  ISBN: 0113306113

This early book from the CCTA (now the OGC) provides an introduction to programme management and explains how it differs from project management. Guidance is given on when to use programme management on key activities and responsibilities involved. The benefits of programme management are explained.

  Title: *Project Workout A Toolkit for Reaping the Rewards from All Your Business Projects* 3rd Edition
  Author: Robert Buttrick
  Date: 2005
  Publisher: Pearson
  ISBN: 0273681818

This third edition has been received with good reviews. As its title implies, the book contains 'workouts' with exercises, problem posers and techniques to help the reader put the book into practice. It focuses on business change projects.

Title: *Managing Risk for Projects and Programmes*
Author: John Bartlett
Date: 2002
Publisher: Project Manager Today Publications
ISBN: 1900391104

This book attempts to address the generally poor attention given to risk in projects and programmes. It aims to provide the reader with a sufficient understanding of the subject in order to practice consistently good risk management. It also shows why risk management should be the premier focus for managers, over and above the other project management elements. It is not a book about the history of risk or the science of probability. It is rather a book that gives a practical view of risk management for any type of project or programme.

Title: *Managing Programmes of Business Change*
Author: John Bartlett
Date: 2002
Publisher: Project Manager Today Publications
ISBN: 1900391082

The latest, third edition, of this indispensable handbook is now available with new chapters on benefits management and soft systems thinking.

The enlarged and updated the text remains one of the few practical books on programme management. John Bartlett says: 'there is an acute lack of proven techniques to tackle large programmes of business change – a fact all too often highlighted in well publicised programme failures. Programme management must develop into a much more sophisticated discipline in order to tackle the complexities of this accelerating change.'

This book's structured approach for managing business change, complements existing programme methodologies.

The author's own practical experience, both in business and IT, and in project and programme management, is clearly evident. The book is based on concepts from various methods which he has honed in practice, including the structured method published by OGC.

Title: *The PPSO Handbook, vol. 1: Foundation*
Author: David E. Marsh
Date: 2004
Publisher: Project Manager Today Publications
ISBN: 1900391058

Title: *The PPSO Handbook, vol. 2: Advanced*
Author: David E. Marsh
Date: 2004
Publisher: Project Manager Today Publications
ISBN 1900391066

Title: *Managing Cross-functional Projects*
Author: Dick Billows
Date: 2000
Publisher: The Project Management Institute
ISBN 1900391074
Available through:
● http://www.4pm.com/

B.3 INTERNET SITES PROVIDING INFORMATION ON PROGRAMME MANAGEMENT

www.e-programme.com

ProgM (the Programme Management Special Interest Group of the Association for Project Management and the British Computer Society)

www.groups.yahoo.com/group/IDSIG_Potential_Members

International Development Special Interest Group (IDSIG), which is for people who sponsor, execute, participate in or are directly or indirectly affected by projects funded by such organizations as the World Bank, Asian Development Bank, UN Projects Office, World Health Organization, OXFAM, Red Cross, or other non-governmental organizations. The IDSIG has a discussion group and notice board available on their website.

www.pm-group.co.uk

The Program Management Group.

www.ogc.gsi.gov.uk

Office of Government Commerce.

www.apm.org.uk

The Association for Project Management (APM). Address:

150 West Wycombe Road,
High Wycombe,
Buckinghamshire, HP12 3AE
Tel: +44 1494 440090 Fax: +44 1494 528937
Email: secretariat@apm-uk.demon.co.uk

www.apmgroup.co.uk

The APM Group Ltd (APMG), which administers training for PRINCE2, MSP and The MOR. Address:

7–8 Queens Square
High Wycombe
Bucks HP11 2BP, UK
Tel: +44 1494 452450 Fax: +44 1494 459559

www.inst-mgt.org.uk

The Institute of Management: Address:

Management House
Cottingham Road
CORBY
Northants
NN17 1TT, UK
Tel: +44 1536 204 222 Fax: +44 1536 406 810

www.managers.org.uk/institute/home_3.asp?category=3&id=4

Chartered Management Institute.

www.planningplanet.com/index.asp

The Useful Planning Planet.

www.hqbcs.org.uk

British Computer Society. Proms-G is the project management special interest group of the British Computer Society.

www.bcs.org.uk/iseb

The Information Systems Examination Board (ISEB). Contact: Claire O'Neill, ISEB Exams Officer. Address:

ISEB, The British Computer Society
1 Sanford Street
Swindon SN1 1HJ, UK
Tel: +44 1793 417480 Fax: +44 1793 480270
Email: iseb@hq.bcs.org.uk

www.pmi.org

The Project Management Institute (PMI). Contact for the UK Chapter of PMI: Mr Guy Lee. Address:

PMInst (UK) Ltd
160 Rayleigh Road
Hutton
Essex, CM13 1PN, UK
Tel: +44 1277 224287

http://pmi-issig.org/AboutUs.asp

The Project Management Institute Information Systems Special Interest Group. PMI-ISSIG's mission is to become the professional information systems project management organization of choice by providing the greatest value to current and prospective worldwide members through the delivery of quality and unique services and products in a cost-effective manner.

www.som.cranfield.ac.uk/som/mscppm

Cranfield College of Project and Programme Management.

www.lgc.co.uk/service.asp?intElement=2569

LGC is under contract to both the UK government and the European Union to manage programmes that provide advice, training and educational opportunities to the chemicals, life sciences and biomaterials sectors.

www.ogc.gov.uk/sdtoolkit/reference/deliverylifecycle/impplans/prog_mgmt.html

Headings relating to programme management at the UK government site include:

- What is a programme?
- What is programme management?
- Why use programme management?
- Critical success factors for programmes
- Programme Management organisation
- The processes of programme management
- Further information.

www.lgc.co.uk/casestudy.asp

Case studies relating to programme management available this LGC site include:

- Quid Thematic Network for Enforcement Practitioners
- DTI Building up Biomaterials Programme
- LGC Biomaterials Partnership®
- Government Chemist Programme
- Valid Analytical Measurement (VAM) Programme
- Department of Health – NEAT programme
- EU Devices Materials Networks
- DTI – LINK Programme.

www.ipmacourse.dk/articles/g/programme.pdf

Covers topic such as programme management and project portfolio management: new competences of project-oriented companies.

http://www.pmforum.org

Provides instant access to worldwide project management information.

www.psoforum.com

The Project & Programme Support Office Forum.

www.pmi-pmosig.org

The PMI® Program Management Office Specific Interest Group (PMOSIG) is a knowledge-based component of the Project Management Institute (PMI) with membership representing 49 countries, 171 chapters, nearly 1200 postal codes, the top vertical markets and more than 400 leading companies and government entities around the world.

www.cio.com/archive/010102/project.html

How to kill an enterprise project.

www.eitforum.com

The Portfolio Management Forum contains a number of relevant papers including for example:

- 'Closing the Gap: Using Benchmarking to Drive Process Improvement'
- 'Strategy Mapping: How to Transform Your Strategy into Decisive Results'
- 'Using Metrics and Benchmarks to Assess and Compare Performance'.

LGC is under contract to both UK government and the European Union to manage programmes that provide advice, training and educational opportunities to the chemicals, life sciences and biomaterials sectors.

http://www.mapnp.org/library/prog_mng/prog_mng.htm

Program Planning and Management, written by Carter McNamara, MBA, PhD. Applies to non profit-making and for-profits organizations.

C   A worked example

BACKGROUND

Tony Chatter is the Director of Personal Communications.

The division recognized a number of training requirements required as a part of the division's contribution to the wider BPR programme in hand throughout the organization as a whole.

They have established a team of the most senior managers, who have proposed a strategy to improve the organization's abilities in the long term as well as meeting the relatively short-term training needs. This personal development programme is expected to improve the capabilities of all staff through personal development plans and an in-house training facility.

Currently they do not have adequate processes and facilities to produce development plans for staff or to enable staff to achieve their personal development goals.

This programme has already started. You receive a memo and strategy documents as your initial input. The memo and extracts from the strategy are on the following pages.

MEMO

From: Tony Chatter   To: Jo Soap

Jo,

As you have probably heard Albert has left the organization and been elected to parliament. This was totally unexpected and I now have a problem finding someone to fill the role of continuing with the good work he was doing.

He had been given the task of preparing a programme definition for the Personal Development Initiative. He had made a start on this and while I do not know a lot about the detail I can summarize the idea as follows.

We carry out a wide range of training workshops for our staff covering management topics such as project management, programme management, safety, team building, as well as technical topics connected to our specialized work including the retraining of copper engineers to work on phone boxes.

At the current time, most of the training is contracted out to third parties by the HR department so training courses are delivered by external training providers supplying lecturers, course content and materials, hotels for space and catering, hire companies for computers and other training equipment.

The increase in training demand from the BPR programme, plus the constant rise in travelling and accommodation costs on training trips has created a view that this has become a very expensive operation.

In addition, we do not know what benefit we are getting from all this training and whether we are meeting the needs of the staff. This latter point will become even more important as we start to focus on performance improvement measures for staff.

The organization is considering creating a training department with its own lecturers, building, IT installations, audio-visual equipment and kitchen. We have discussed this with some other divisions and they have indicated that they too share the same problems and would use our facilities if we offered them. We have also noted that some external organizations (such as our subcontractors) also do not have adequate training facilities.

I know this is very brief but I hope you will be able to prepare a proper programme definition from the enclosed part-completed document

---

handed to me by Albert before he left for Westminster, and get it ready for the Senior Responsible Owner.

I have attached the vision statement that started the whole process going. Albert has developed this further; please ensure his version is understood and accepted.

Tony Chatter
Director, Personal Communications Division

VISION STATEMENT: PERSONAL COMMUNICATIONS DIVISION TRAINING PROGRAMME

Our current training arrangements require us to hire external facilities for every training event. The strategy group have compared this with other divisions and similar operations who have their own purpose-built training facilities. If we develop a similar purpose-built training centre and supporting facilities, we can expect our training cost per head to reduce by 25 per cent, and to be able to increase the opportunities for training from 15 days per year per head to 20 days.

Organizational policy will require us to demonstrate performance improvements, including the performance of members of staff. These improved facilities and processes will enable us to establish a clearer understanding of training needs for each member of staff, to provide appropriate training when needed, and to demonstrate staff performance improvements.

Some other divisions also lack adequate training facilities. A preliminary survey by the strategy group indicates they will be willing to use our facilities. This is expected to contribute 25 per cent to its operating costs.

There are three business imperatives:

Business imperatives	Priority
Staff performance improvement must be demonstrated to satisfy new corporate policy	High
Training costs must reduce by at least 25% per capita	High
Train a number of engineers to support PhoneBox operations	High

657

PROGRAMME DEFINITION: PERSONAL DEVELOPMENT INITIATIVE

PURPOSE OF DOCUMENT

The definition work has produced more detail and a better insight into the programme proposed. A programme is a major undertaking and often requires significant investment. It is important that those who will approve the programmes and the investment can be convinced that there is a sound basis for proceeding. This document will demonstrate that sound basis because it:

- allows the reader to trace its origins back to the strategy, which was effectively the organization's original instruction;
- provides a breakdown of the who, what, why, how and when, against which senior management can use their judgment objectively;
- demonstrates that the programme teams will be given explicit and clear direction from the outset, thus increasing the likelihood of success.

VISION STATEMENT

[The vision statement must state the problem/opportunity and, via the initiative the benefit expected.]

The overall objective of the organization is to be the most successful worldwide telecommunications group through the provision of world-call telecommunication products and services. In particular, the organization has made a clear statement on customer commitment based on value for money and excellent performance backed by guarantee.

To make a contribution to these objectives the Business Processes Reorganization (BPR) programme will have to find ways to increase performance in many individual processes within the business. The programme will also provide a measurement and coordination system to demonstrate the improvements delivered.

Now that the BPR programme is underway it has become clear that Telekom BV does not have adequate means to develop its staff, so they will be able to effectively operate the new and improved processes, that will be the outcome from this programme. A separate initiative (this programme) will address this problem. The strategy group have compared Telekom BV with other telcos who have their own purpose-built training facilities. If we develop a similar purpose-built training centre and supporting facilities, we can expect our training cost per head to reduce by 25 per cent, and to be able to increase the opportunities for training from 15 days per year per head per annum to 20 days.

Many other organizations in the region also lack adequate training facilities. A preliminary survey by the strategy group indicates they will be willing to use our facilities. This is expected to contribute 25 per cent to its operating costs.

BUSINESS OBJECTIVES

Business imperatives (strategic objectives)	Priority
50% decrease in staff numbers and unit costs	High
Provide a service level where a new telephone installation is delivered within one day	High
Provide a service level where all faults will be cleared within one day	High

Business imperatives (this programme's objectives)	
Staff performance improvements must satisfy the requirements of the BPR programme	High
Training costs must reduce by at least 25% per capita	High

BLUEPRINT

[This section describes what the organization's entities will look like in the future. The future state can be a desire or a prediction (if it is outside the organization's control). At this stage no assessment has been made of changes needed due to the interdependencies between processes and other entities. This 'impact' is described in the next section below.]

BUSINESS MODELS OF FUNCTIONS, PROCESSES AND OPERATIONS, INCLUDING OPERATIONAL COSTS AND PERFORMANCE LEVELS, OF THE REQUIRED FUTURE 'STATE'

[Operations are those parts of an organization that focus on carefully managing the processes to produce and distribute products and services. Major, overall activities often include product creation, development, production and distribution.

Functions are the activities carried out to manage and control the operations. These include planning/scheduling, control, quality, maintenance, procurement, inventory/stock, manufacturing, distribution.

Processes are a predefined linked set of steps that provide the roadmap and control to ensure activities are conducted efficiently and effectively. A process often crosses several operational units and includes many functional activities.]

659

BUSINESS PROCESSES: PERSONAL COMMUNICATIONS DIRECTORATE: PERSONAL DEVELOPMENT INITIATIVE

Process name	Description of future process	How will it differ from today
Define personal development needs	Assess, define, and agree each individual's personal development needs.	More structured approach, via agreed process, will ensure each individual's needs are based on an objective assessment and there is agreement between that person and their manager. This will provide input to 'Create personal development plan'.
Create personal development plan	A plan for every member of staff stating how their development needs will be met. Updated each year.	Today it is an informal ad hoc process, and impossible to assess the total training requirements. A common process for all departments will ensure all staff and their managers agree on a training plan, and that the overall requirements can be assessed. It will enable central training managers to be sure adequate training facilities are available.
Monitor personal development	By interviews and other techniques we will monitor the benefit gained from each workshop. By twice yearly staff appraisals we will assess how the performance of each	No formal monitoring of personal development is currently held.

Process name	Description of future process	How will it differ from today
	individual member of staff has improved.	
Offer training workshops	Develop and otherwise acquire training workshops in a variety of topics to meet the demands defined.	Today this is derived from training workshops available on the open market.
Deliver training workshops	We will provide appropriate facilities and capabilities to meet most of the needs of our training requirement.	Currently each individual selects and attends workshops through their own volition.
Manage training facilities	Assess all individual development plans, to make sure the training parts are appropriate, and the total requirement for training facilities is realistic (within physical and financial capacity). Book and reserve facilities for internal training and to external organizations, where there is surplus capacity.	Management of own facilities, with a known capacity, will ensure that the training parts in development plans for all staff are realistic, whereas today we are dependent on external facilities, the availability of which is less predictable and more expensive.

OPERATION AND FUNCTIONS (OTHERWISE KNOWN AS CAPABILITY GROUPS)

[Here we have considered those functions/capabilities that are relevant to this programme. Capabilities will sometimes be delivered (at least in part) by information or manufacturing systems.

Future target should include performance and cost information where applicable.]

661

HR – training

Function/capability	Current	Future target
Deliver training	Internal ability to deliver training is very limited. This is assumed to be one important factor that inhibits the effectiveness of training. 90% of training is delivered by external organizations. 15 days per year per head per annum.	90% internal, only highly specialized training, infrequently required, to be delivered by external organizations. Training cost per head to reduce by 25%. 20 days per year per head per annum.
Manage training	Limited to booking external courses from ad hoc demand from managers.	Organize staff appraisal and personal development bi-annual activities. Develop realistic organization-wide training plans. Organize individual training events and workshops to meet the needs of the personal development plans. Manage and maintain the new training facilities.

Support Services – IT

Function/capability	Current	Future target
HR support systems	None	Extend HR system to support: • Staff appraisals • Staff development plans • Training needs analysis • Managing training facilities • Managing training events

Operations – management

Function/capability	Current	Future target
Manage personal development of staff	Informal and ad hoc, but effective for each individual member of staff.	Build on current good practice and demonstrate incremental improvements year on year. Total training needs are realistic and within capacity to deliver. Personal development plans are documented, and results assessed in appraisal, so performance improvements can be measured objectively.
Personal development	Informal and ad hoc, but effective for each individual member of staff. Variations often due to different motivations across individuals. Some are very keen to agree their development plans with their manager, others don't bother unless chased.	All staff to be appraised using the same methods and at the same intervals. All staff to update their personal development plans and agree with their manager twice a year. All staff to attend requisite training. All staff to report their performance improvements against objective measures agreed in their plan.

Operations – engineers

Function/capability	Current	Future target
Personal development	Informal and ad hoc, but effective for each individual member of staff.	All staff to be appraised using the same methods and at the same intervals.

Function/capability	Current	Future target
	Variations often due to different motivations across individuals. Some are very keen to agree their development plans with their manager, others don't bother unless chased.	All staff to update their personal development plans and agree with their manager twice a year. All staff to attend requisite training. All staff to report their performance improvements against objective measures agreed in their plan.

[The 'Impact and Change's parts of the following sections show additional changes required due to the interdependencies between operations, processes, and functions, and other entities.]

Operations outputs – products and services

[Describes any existing products and services that will be affected by the programme, and any new products and services that will be required.]

Function or service	Description of current products	Future target
Training workshops	Buy 90% of them in from external training organizations.	Will develop training workshops for 90% of our needs and sell extra capacity to other divisions.
Specialized training workshops	Buy 100% of them in from external training organizations.	No change.

Operations outputs – products and services: impact and changes

[The changes here should be regarded as additional to the products and services table above.]

Function or service	How will these be affected by, or affect process changes?	By how much or less volumes?
Training workshops	Offer training workshops	Marketing materials will be needed to promote them to other divisions.
Specialized training workshops	Manage training facilities	This process must include steps to book courses and facilities from third-party training organizations for specialized training

Operations delivery logistics – channels to market

[Describes any existing channels that will be affected by the programme, and any new channels that will be required. If you make available a product or a service to another organization, even if it is free, you must have at least one channel to promote and 'sell'.]

Channels to market	Description of current channels	Description and targets for future channels
Professional publications	None	This is one option for a new way to sell extra training capacity, at least one of these channels will need to be set up.
Internet	None	This is one option for a new way to sell extra training capacity, at least one of these channels will need to be set up.
Via a third party	None	This is one option for a new way to sell extra training capacity, at least one of these channels will need to be set up.

Operations delivery logistics – channels to market: impact and changes

[The changes here should be regarded as additional to the channels to market table above.]

Channels to market	How will these be affected by, or affect process changes?	By how much more or less volume?
Offer training workshops	Can't offer to other Divisions without at least one channel.	Don't exist today, will need to create.

ORGANIzATION STRUCTURE

[Staffing levels, roles and skill requirements necessary to support the future business operations. Any necessary changes to organizational culture, style, or existing structures and personnel may also be included.

As all staff in this programme are affected by the programme they are therefore stakeholders, and have been included in the table below. For clarification, staff are marked with an asterisk.]

Stakeholder groups

Internal and external stakeholders who are dependent on the future success of the organization and who will be affected by the changes to its architecture.

[This is your prediction of the changes to stakeholders' roles and numbers.]

Stakeholder groups	Role	How much will it grow/ shrink?
Management*	Assess and plan the development of all members of staff. Monitor the improvements in the organization's effectiveness through performance improvements of the staff.	None

Stakeholder groups	Role	How much will it grow/shrink?
All staff*	Consider their own needs and take part in personal development.	None
HR*	To help individuals to monitor their own needs and to identify areas of weakness at both a personal and organizational level.	+1 in 1st year. Staff to manage improved personal development and training processes.
Third-party training provider	These will be replaced in all but the most specialist areas.	–90%
Training staff*	A training team will be built to provide the training requirements.	+6
Catering staff*	The catering team will expand to provide catering in the training facility.	+2

* = staff

Stakeholder groups – impact and changes required

[The changes here should be regarded as additional to the stakeholder group table above.]

Stakeholder groups	How will these be affected by, or affect process changes?	By how much?
Management	Define personal development needs. Create personal development plan.	Need training on new process. Need training on new process.

667

Stakeholder groups	How will these be affected by, or affect process changes?	By how much?
	Monitor personal development.	Need training on new process.
All staff	Define personal development needs.	Need training on new process.
	Create personal development plan.	Need training on new process.
	Monitor personal development.	Need training on new process.
HR	Managing and supporting all new processes.	+10% over 3 years
	Define personal development needs.	Design new process and training on it for other staff.
	Create personal development plan.	Design new process and training on it for other staff.
	Monitor personal development.	Design new process and training on it for other staff.
	Offer training workshops.	Design new process and training on it for other staff.
	Deliver training workshops.	Design new process.
	Manage training facilities.	Design new process.
Third-party training provider	Offer training workshops.	Possible new role, selling our training workshops to other divisions.
Training staff	A training team will be built to provide the training requirements.	+12
	Deliver training workshops.	Learn new process and training workshop.
	Manage training facilities.	Learn new process and be trained on the parts for which they are responsible.

Stakeholder groups	How will these be affected by, or affect process changes?	By how much?
Catering staff	The catering team will expand to provide catering in the training facility.	+2
	Manage training facilities.	Learn new process and be trained on the parts for which they are responsible.

Figure C1 shows the current staff structure.

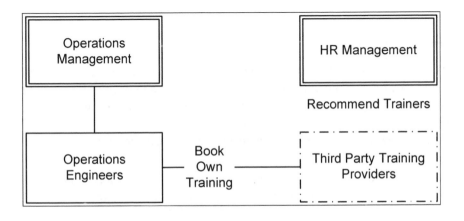

Figure C1   Current staff structure

Figure C2 shows the target staff structure.

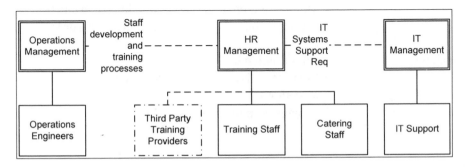

Figure C2   Target staff structure

Culture

HR's role will change significantly. They will expand to directly manage most of the training, and will own the supplier relationship with third-party training providers. They will also enforce the new staff development and training processes. For this to be successful they will need to extend their relationship with Operations Management.

TECHNOLOGY, IT SYSTEMS, TOOLS, EQUIPMENT, BUILDINGS AND ACCOMMODATION

[Required for the future business operations together with details of reuse of existing infrastructure or implementation of new infrastructure to support the 'future state'.]

Information systems

[The changes here show the impact on current systems to support the future processes as described in the business process table above. Information systems are not just IT systems, they could for example be staff records on a manual card index.

If appropriate you would have a table for manufacturing systems.]

Information system name	*How will these be affected by, or affect process changes?*	*By how much more or less throughput?*
HR	Define personal development needs.	New, but could link to current staff records.
	Create personal development plan.	New, but could link to current staff records.
	Monitor personal development.	New, but could link to current staff records.
Training	Offer training workshops.	New system.
	Deliver training workshops.	New system.
	Manage training facilities.	New system.

Operational locations

[Describes any existing locations that will be affected by the programme, and any new locations that will be required.]

Locations	Description of current locations	Future locations required
Training centre	Hotels and other similar centres, hired on an 'as needed' basis.	Own training facilities as near to Headquarters as possible.

Operational locations – impact and changes

[The changes here should be regarded as additional to the operations locations table above.]

Locations	How will these be affected by, or affect process changes?	How much more/less capacity needed?
Training centre	Deliver training workshops.	Will need 12 training and breakout rooms, 2 personal rest areas, and a catering area.
	Manage training facilities. Will need to ensure this takes into account the capacity limits of the new facility.	

DATA AND INFORMATION REQUIRED FOR THE FUTURE BUSINESS OPERATIONS

[Together with details of how existing data and information will be changed or redeveloped to provide the necessary requirements for the 'future state'.]

Information	Requirements
Staff	Develop: 1. competency records 2. appraisal records 3. development goals and plans.

Information	Requirements
Training	Develop: 1. training course information 2. training schedules 3. course booking records.
Catering	Develop: 1. stock records 2. catering schedules.

BUSINESS CASE

[This section contains a financial justification for the programme by demonstrating that there is a good return on the investment required. It is supplemented by non-financial benefits.]

BENEFITS SUMMARY

This summarizes the benefits the programme is expected to achieve. It may be given to the programme as part of the brief. Work in the Definition stage will validate the realism of these targets. See 'Benefits profiles' and 'Business case' below.

Description of benefit	Target	When required	Depends on	Conflicts
1. Reduction in currently growing cost of training	Stabilize total costs at current levels – 0% increase by 2004. Decrease cost per person per day by 25%.	Mid 2004	Training facility operation and new processes to manage it.	None

Description of benefit	Target	When required	Depends on	Conflicts
2. Reduction in growing accommodation and travelling costs for training	Stabilize at current levels – 0% increase by 2004.	Mid 2004	Training facility operation and new processes to manage it.	None
3. Income from delivery of training workshops to selected, adjacent organizations	+£200,000 by 2005.	First sales 2004	Training facility operation and new processes to manage it. Developing capacity to offer a wider range of workshops. Developing the capacity to offer and sell workshops.	Our needs to be met first
4. Better qualified and more appropriately trained staff	First performance improvement results. Increase training days per person per annum from 15 to 20.	End 2004	New personal development processes, staff getting the training they need in their plan, which in part depends on new training facilities being available.	None
5. Reduced staff turnover	–10%	2005	Training facilities meeting the personal development needs of the staff. Personal development plan for staff contribute to better job satisfaction.	None

Financial Appraisal

All financial values are in £s

Assumptions

New building cost	1,500,000	
Running cost per year	500,000	incl new staff
Number of staff to be trained	200	p.a.
Current cost per head per day	400	
Days training per year	15	current 20 planned
Specialist training outsourced	10,000	p.a.
Sales of workshops	200,000	100 days, 10 per course, @ £2.00

Current	1	2	3	4	5
Staff training		−1,200,000	−1,200,000	−1,200,000	−1,200,000

Proposed					
Building and staff	−1,500,000	−500,000	−500,000	−500,000	−500,000
Specialist		−10,000	−10,000	−10,000	−10,000
Training sales		200,000	200,000	200,000	200,000
Sub total		−310,000	−310,000	−310,000	−310,000
Benefit	−1,500,000	890,000	890,000	890,000	890,000

Proposed–Current

Time Period	1	2	3	4	5	Totals (no time value)
Programme costs	(1,500,000)	0	0	0	0	**(1,500,000)**
Benefits	–	890,000	890,000	890,000	890,000	**3,560,000**
Net benefits	(1,500,000)	890,000	890,000	890,000	890,000	**2,060,000**

Time Period	1	1+r	(1+r)^2	(1+r)^3	(1+4)^4	
5%	1.000	1.050	1.103	1.158	1.216	
10%	1.000	1.100	1.210	1.331	1.464	

Present values of net benefits (NPV)

5%	(1,500,000)	847,619	807,256	768,815	732,205	**1,655,896**
10%	(1,500,000)	809,091	735,537	668,670	607,882	**1,321,180**

Pay back NPV at 5%

Figure C3   Financial appraisal

Risk and Issues Summary

Risk	Prevention	Mitigation /contingency
There is risk that we may not be able to attract and retain suitable staff to provide the wide range of educational and training needs.	Start recruitment early. Contact existing freelance trainers. Research training marketplace.	Be prepared to use contract staff if can't recruit.
We may not be able to locate suitable premises or land on which to build suitable premises.	Wide research. Consider new build and existing. Consider part of existing.	Explore lease options to be used as last resort.
We may be able to attract delegates from appropriate local organizations.	Use expert services of established training organization to sell sources for us. Early contact with possible customers. Help them to define their needs.	
We may find it difficult to keep abreast of developing trends in both training delivery and technical matters.	Do not overload training team. Devote time to continuing development of training team.	

Assumptions:
1. Discount rate will be approximately 5%.
2. Funds and resources will be available when required.
3. Land or buildings can be procured in the timeframe required.
4. There will be no significant changes to the parent BPR programme.

675

PROGRAMME ORGANIZATION STRUCTURE

Figure C4 shows the programme organization structure.

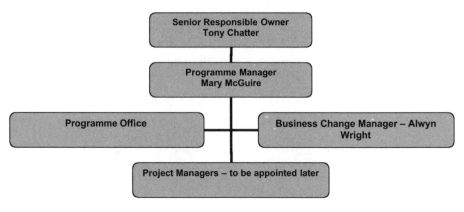

Figure C4 Programme organization

Note: Standard MSP roles and responsibilities apply.

PROJECT PORTFOLIO

Project	Principal outputs
New training building project	1. Land 2. New training building, including catering facilities. IT facilities part of the IT project.
IT project	3. IT infrastructure 4. IT software systems configured to support the new processes (part of training project) 5. Support arrangements.
Training project	6. New processes (see Figure C5) 7. Training and catering staff employed and trained 8. HR and operational staff trained in the new processes as applicable.

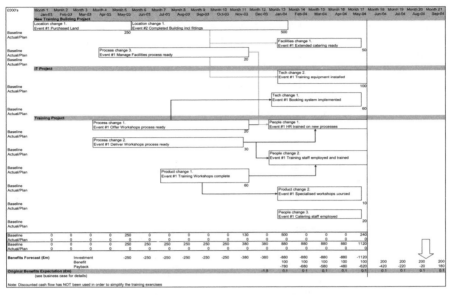

Figure C5   Project portfolio showing dependencies

BENEFITS PROFILES

[These tables show what will need to be measured and the estimated net benefits expected. The programme will need to define how these measurements will be made, develop processes and methods for the measuring, and get agreement from the operational part of the organization concerned. This must be done before the improvements are put into operational use.]

Description of benefit	Target	When required	Dependencies	Conflicts
1. Reduction in currently growing cost of training	Stabilize total costs at current levels – 0% increase by 2004. Decrease cost per person per day by 25% thereafter whilst increasing training days per person per annum from 15 to 20.	Mid 2004	Training facility operational and new processes to manage it.	None

677

KPIs in operations affected	Changes to processes	Projects related	Owner
Training cost per person per training day.	Offer training workshops. Deliver training workshops. Manage training facilities.	Building, IT, training	HR Director

Values £000s	2003–Year 1				2004–Year 2				2005–Year 3			
	Q1	Q2	Q3	Q4	Q1	Q2	Q3	Q4	Q1	Q2	Q3	Q4
Measure and record training costs including third-party purchases, accommodation and travel costs through the evaluation period as cost per person per training day	**Current values**											
	400	400	400	400	400	400	400	400	400	400	400	400
	Planned values											
							77.5	77.5	77.5	77.5	77.5	77.5
	Net benefit											
							222.5	222.5	222.5	222.5	222.5	222.5

Current £1,200,000 for 200 staff at 15 days per annum – $1,200,000/(200 \times 15) = 400$
Planned £310,000 net cost per annum for training for 200 staff at 20 days per annum – $310,000/(200 \times 20) = 77.5$
Net Benefit 200 staff at 20 days per annum @ £890,000 – $890,000/(200 \times 20) = 222.5$
Note: Because measure is cost per person per day and number of days per person per annum changes from 15 to 20 *you cannot* get the net benefits as Current – Planned.

Description of benefit	Target	When required	Dependencies	Conflicts
2. Reduction in growing accommodation and travelling costs for training	Stabilize at current levels – 0% increase by 2004. Reduce by 90% thereafter.	Mid 2004	Training facility operational and new processes to manage it.	None

KPIs in operations affected	Changes to processes	Projects related	Owner
To current KPI	No current process	Building, IT, Training	HR Director

Values £000s	2003–Year 1				2004–Year 2				2005–Year 3			
	Q1	Q2	Q3	Q4	Q1	Q2	Q3	Q4	Q1	Q2	Q3	Q4
Measure and record training accommodation costs through the evaluation period **Current values**	150	150	150	150	150	150	150	150	150	150	150	150
Planned values							15	15	15	15	15	15
Net benefit							135	135	135	135	135	135

Description of benefit	Target	When required	Dependencies	Conflicts
3. Income from delivery of training workshops to selected, adjacent organizations	+£200,000 p.a. by 2005	First sales 2004	Training facility operational and new processes to manage it. Developing capacity to offer and sell a wider range of workshops.	Our needs to be met first.

KPIs in operations affected	Changes to processes and operations	Projects related	Owner
No current KPI	No current process	Building, IT, Training	HR Director

679

Values £000s	2003–Year 1				2004–Year 2				2005–Year 3			
	Q1	Q2	Q3	Q4	Q1	Q2	Q3	Q4	Q1	Q2	Q3	Q4
Measure and record training income monthly for 18 months after projects handed over	**Current values**											
	0	0	0	0	0	0	0	0	0	0	0	0
	Planned values											
							50	50	50	50	50	50
	Net benefit											
							50	50	50	50	50	50

Description of benefit	Target	When required	Dependencies	Conflicts
4. Better qualified and more appropriately trained staff	First performance improvement results by end 2004. Increase training days per person per annum from 15 to 20	End 2004	New personal development processes, staff getting the training they need in their plan, which in part depends on new training facilities being available.	None

KPIs in operations affected	Changes to processes and operations	Projects related	Owner
None current	No current processes	Building, IT, Training	HR Director

Values out of 10	2003–Year 1				2004–Year 2				2005–Year 3			
	Q1	Q2	Q3	Q4	Q1	Q2	Q3	Q4	Q1	Q2	Q3	Q4
Survey and record views of the staff on their ability to perform their current functions, expected future functions and the appropriateness of personal development opportunities on offer	**Current values**											
	Planned values											
	Net benefit											

Description of benefit	Target	When required	Dependencies	Conflicts
5. Reduced staff turnover	–10% of current rate	2005	Training facilities meeting the personal development needs of the staff. Personal development plan for staff contribute to better job satisfaction.	None

KPIs in operations affected	Changes to processes and operations	Projects related	Owner
Attrition rates	None	Building, IT, Training	HR Director

681

Values – % leaves per annum	2003–Year 1				2004–Year 2				2005–Year 3			
	Q1	Q2	Q3	Q4	Q1	Q2	Q3	Q4	Q1	Q2	Q3	Q4
Number of leaves per annum as % of total staff	**Current Values**											
	15	15	15	15	18	18	18	18	20	20	20	20
	Planned Values											
									13	13	13	13
	Net Benefit											
									7	7	7	7

STAKEHOLDER MAP

Names	Interests (+)/Concerns (▽)							
	Own develop-ment and training	New job	Develop-ment of their/ all staff	Manag-ing the changes	Personal impact of the changes	Could act as sales channel	Loss of income	Learn new processes
Management	+		+	▽				
All Staff	+				▽			
HR	+		+	▽				
Training staff		+						▽
Third party						+	▽	
Training providers								
Catering staff		+						▽

PROGRAMME PLANS: PERSONAL DEVELOPMENT INITIATIVE

PURPOSE OF DOCUMENT

1. The definition work has produced more detail and a better insight into the programme proposed. A programme is a major undertaking and often requires significant investment. It is important that those who will manage and contribute to the programme understand what activities need to be carried out and the schedule that needs to be achieved. If the plans are not met, the programme will almost certainly not be a success.
2. It also provides a baseline reference point against which actual progress can be measured to determine whether progress is on track.
3. Finally, it provides a basis for communicating to and explaining the programme to stakeholders.

PROGRAMME AND BENEFITS REALISATION PLANS

Approach

Training facilities: Preferably these should be purpose built on land acquired by us, as this will provide a building and facilities which best fit our requirements. If this is not possible then consider purchasing and modifying an existing building. Leasing should only be considered as a last resort, as this is expected to be less cost effective in the long term.

Process design: External experts will be appointed to assist with the design of new processes and the improvement of existing processes, as we have limited internal expertise.

Training staff and workshops: Staff will be recruited who are experienced trainers for the telecommunications industry. They will present the workshops themselves, so they need to be recruited in advance of when the first new courses will be held.

IT systems: Preference will be given to extending the existing HR system with standard modules. If this is not possible, consideration should be given to a separate but standard system that can be integrated into the current system. Bespoke systems will only be considered as a last resort.

683

Programme plan and benefit forecast

Figure C6 shows the programme plan and benefit forecast.

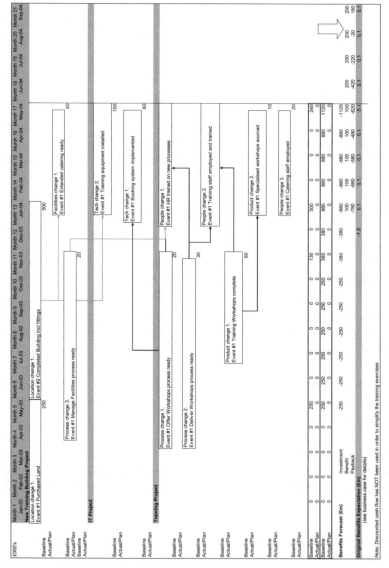

Figure C6 Programme plan and benefit forecast

Resource Plan

Figure C7 shows the resource plan.

Staff	Month 1	Month 2	Month 3	Month 4	Month 5	Month 6	Month 7	Month 8	Month 9	Month 10	Month 11	Month 12	Month 13	Month 14	Month 15	Month 16	Month 17	Month 18	Month 19	Month 20	Month 21	Month 22	Month 23	Month 24
New Training Building Project																								
Project Manager	0.05	0.05	0.05	0.05	0.05	0.25	0.25	0.25	0.25	0.25	0.25	0.25	0.25											
Business Analyst																								
Systems Designer																								
Facilities Manager	0.1	0.1	0.1	0.1	0.1	0.1	0.25	0.25	0.25	0.25	0.25	0.25	0.25											
Process Designer				0.25	0.25	0.25	0.25	0.25	0.25	0.25	0.25													
UAT											1													
HR Manager																								
Systems Developers																								
IT Project																								
Project Manager													0.3	0.3	0.3	0.3	0.3							
Business Analyst													0.8											
Systems Designer														1										
Facilities Manager																								
Process Designer																	3							
UAT																								
HR Manager																								
Systems Developers															2	2	2							
Training Project																								
Project Manager				0.5	0.5	0.5	0.5	0.5	0.5	0.5	0.5	0.5	0.5	0.5	0.5	0.5	0.5							
Business Analyst																								
Systems Designer																								
Facilities Manager																								
Process Designer					1	1	1	1	1	1	1	1	1	1	1	1	1							
UAT											4													
HR Manager					0.1	0.1	0.1	0.1	0.1	0.1	0.1	0.1	0.1	0.1	0.1	0.1	0.1							
Systems Developers																								
Programme #1																								
SRO	0.1	0.1	0.1	0.1	0.1	0.1	0.1	0.1	0.1	0.1	0.1	0.1	0.1	0.1	0.1	0.2	0.2	0.2	0.05	0.05	0.05	0.05	0.05	0.05
Programmer Manager	1	1	1	1	1	1	1	1	1	1	1	1	1	1	1	1	1	1	0.25	0.25	0.25	0.25	0.25	0.25
PPSO	0.1	0.1	0.1	0.1	0.1	0.1	0.1	0.1	0.1	0.1	0.1	0.1	0.1	0.1	0.1	0.1	0.1	0.1	0.1	0.1	0.1	0.1	0.1	0.1
BCMs	1	0.2	0.2	0.2	0.2	0.2	0.2	0.2	0.2	0.2	0.2	0.2	0.2	0.2	0.2	1	1	1	0.1	0.1	0.1	0.1	0.1	0.1

Figure C7   Resource plan

685

Milestone plan

End Dates

Project #1 New Training Building:

Locate and purchase either suitable land or building	May 2003
Modify or build training facilities, including catering	Jan 2004
Extended catering ready	May 2004

Project #2 IT:

Install IT and audio-visual equipment	May 2004
Booking system implemented	May 2004

Project #3 Training:

Offer workshops process	Nov 2003
Deliver workshops process	Nov 2003
HR trained on new processes	May 2004
Training staff recruited and trained	May 2004
Catering staff employed	May 2004
Create training workshops	Nov 2003
Specialized workshops sourced	May 2004
Open training facilities	May 2004

Programme evaluation period:

Starts	June 2004
First staff appraisals, personal development plans	June 2004
Second staff appraisals, measure performance improvement	Jan 2005
Mid-point assessment	Sept 2004
Ends	Jan 2005

TOLERANCES

[The programme manager must report an exception to the senior responsible owner as soon as it is detected that the programme (or its current tranche) cannot be completed inside the tolerances stated.]

- ± 10% of the approved programme budget, and approved tranche budgets
- +5% of the approved milestones.

COMMUNICATIONS STRATEGY AND PLAN

[Some of this is derived from the stakeholder analysis above and some is to support the good management of the programme.]

What	Who	How	To	When	Why
Programme definition	Programme manager	Team briefing workshops	Programme team project teams as appointed	When approved	Explain what the programme is about
Programme overview	Senior responsible owner (SRO) and manager	Presentation	All managers and staff affected	At start and as each change is due to be implemented	Explain what it is all about and why. How it affects them. How they will be supported.
Highlight reports	Programme manager	E-mail, discuss at monthly meetings	SRO	Monthly	Report progress
End tranche and end programme reports	Programme manager	E-mail, present and discuss at review meetings	SRO	As they occur	Report achievements, get approval to continue
Progress bulletins	Programme manager	Intranet and notice boards	ALL	Milestones to announce good news	Keep staff informed and motivated
Exception reporting	Programme manager	Direct contact with SRO, e-mail report, then meeting to discuss	SRO	*Immediately*, if programme has or is predicted to go out of tolerance	Don't expect to deliver agreed benefits, need to reconsider if programme is viable/ desirable

687

GOVERNANCE ARRANGEMENTS : PERSONAL DEVELOPMENT INITIATIVE

PURPOSE OF DOCUMENT

'Governance' means the functions, processes and procedures that define how the programme is set up, managed and controlled.

Programmes involve a substantial amount of change for individuals, staff, operations, support services and the business environment in which the organization(s) is operating. Governance arrangements need to be established to provide a framework for this upheaval and transformation. Programme governance provides the 'backdrop' for all activities of managing the programme and achieving the programme's outcomes.

- This document describes the agreed governance arrangements and will be used as a point of reference throughout the programme. It will be used as a guide to establish and implement the governance arrangements for the programme.

BENEFITS MANAGEMENT STRATEGY

Benefits have been identified and estimated, owners assigned and measurement methods and values agreed. These are described in the benefits profiles.

Benefits forecasts will be updated throughout the programme based on actual progress to date and any revision to plans. This will be reported at each monthly progress meeting, and at each tranche end. If at any time the programme manager assesses that benefit forecasts will be outside agreed tolerances, this will immediately be reported to the SRO as an exception.

At each end of tranche, the Programme Manager will organize a review of benefits as above, and will also look for new (or increased) benefits/disbenefits.

The programme manager will ensure that any benefit measurement tools required are included in the brief(s) to one or more projects in the programme.

BENEFITS MODEL

[The benefits model is shown in Figure C8.

Figure C8 has been extended to show the events that will allow each benefit to start (Figure C9), and a flow diagram showing the events arranged in logical and chronological order (Figure C10). From this, a benefits curve can be produced (Figure C11) to check if the total benefits over time meet the requirements.]

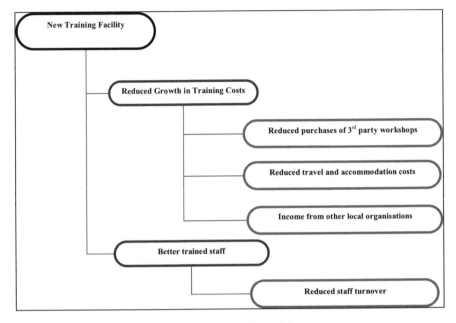

Figure C8 Benefits model

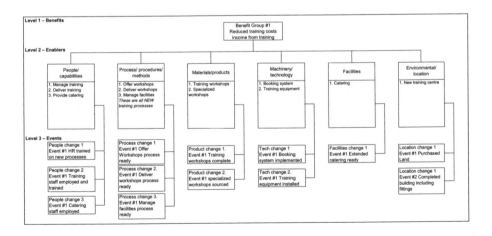

Figure C9 Benefits breakdown events

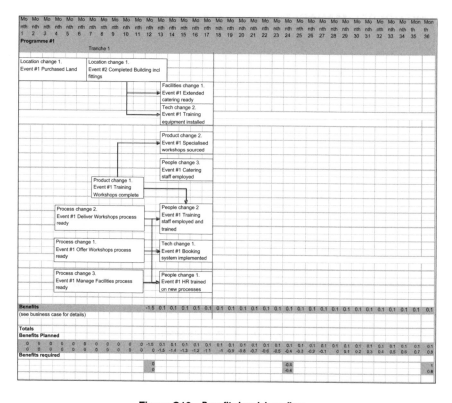

Figure C10   Benefits breakdown flow

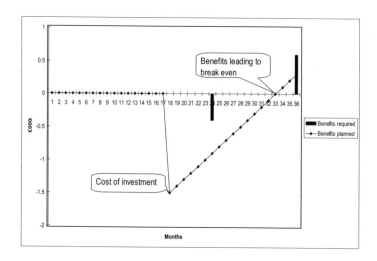

Figure C11   Benefits curve

STAKEHOLDER MANAGEMENT STRATEGY

[If you find the organization has a culture which is more resistant to change than you expected you may need to develop something more elaborate here.

The stakeholder map and stakeholder strategy have been combined into one table.]

Names	Interests/concerns (+/–)	Strategy/actions
Management	+ their own development and training + development of their staff – managing the changes	Thorough briefing at the beginning of the programme. Regular communications throughout the programme. Face-to-face meetings on difficult issues as soon as they arise.
All staff	+ their own development and training – personal impact of the changes	Thorough briefing at the beginning of the programme, and each project, where they are personally affected. Regular communications throughout the programme. Face-to-face meetings on difficult issues as soon as they arise.
HR	+ their own development and training + development of all staff – managing the changes	Thorough briefing at the beginning of the programme, and each project, where they are personally affected. Regular communications throughout the programme. Face-to-face meetings on difficult issues as soon as they arise. Support from specialists to help them manage their projects and design their new/improved processes.

Names	Interests/concerns (+/–)	Strategy/actions
Training staff	+ new job – learn new processes	Thorough induction as they are appointed. Adequate training on their parts of the new processes.
Third-party training providers	+ could act as sales channel – loss of income	Explanation at the beginning of the programme and projects, clarify impact on them. Communication throughout as impact on them gets closer.
Catering staff	+ new job – learn new processes	Thorough induction as they are appointed. Adequate training on their parts of the new processes.

ISSUE RESOLUTION STRATEGY

There are three types:

1. Programme issue
   - any failure in the programme, actual or suspected;
   - a concern about any part of the programme;
   - a question to clarify a misunderstanding;
   - a problem with any part of the management of the programme.

After inspection these issues may become 'requests for change' or 'off specification'.

2. Request for change
   - to the scope;
   - to the definition of a product;
   - to a product that is complete and has been accepted.

3. Off specification
   - where a product fails to meet its agreed specification.

ISSUE RESOLUTION PROCESS

1. Log the issue, as a programme issue.
2. Analyse the issues and decide on the course of action (programme manager) or if necessary agree the recommendations to the SRO. The latter action is needed if the course of action will take the programme out of tolerance:
   a. a misunderstanding, explain to the originator;
   b. treat as a request for change;
   c. treat as an off specification;
   d. more evaluation needed.
3. Request for change evaluation:
   a. cost to carry out the change, affect on the programme budget;
   b. effort to carry out the change, affect on the plan schedule;
   c. consequential affect on dependent products;
   d. priority.
4. Request for change recommendations after evaluation:
   a. implement the change, request or approve an exception plan, which may then change the budget and schedule;
   b. do the change in a later project;
   c. ask for more information;
   d. reject.
5. Off specification evaluation:
   a. does/does not involve change to a product;
   b. can/cannot be done in the agreed cost/time tolerances;
   c. impact of the fault.
6. Off specification recommendations after evaluation:
   a. correct the fault;
   b. make the correction in a later project;
   c. ask for more information;
   d. accept the fault.
7. All decisions must be recorded and actions monitored.

RISK AND ISSUE REPORTING

1. Monthly – a summary showing new, closed and outstanding, with highlights on any significant new risks or issues, and unacceptable progress on agreed actions.
2. Monthly – from projects to programme manager, information as above.
3. Immediately – if any new risk of issue is predicted to take the programme outside the agreed tolerances, or if the impact is greater than just this programme.

RISK MANAGEMENT STRATEGY

1. Identify the risks.
2. Analyse the risks.
3. Plan to manage the risk.

Risk analysis must be conducted continuously throughout the programme. Risk associated with the management of the programme should be reviewed when there is a significant change to the:

1. programme team structure
2. roles of any member of the programme
3. new members joining the programme
4. programme management method
5. programme management processes/lifecycle
6. stakeholders
7. scope
8. there is an unexpected event external to the programme which might have a detrimental effect on it.

Risk associated with the products the programme/project will deliver should be reviewed at the following points:

1. before authority is sought to startup a programme or start project initiation;
2. before authority is sought to start the programme (at the end of the Define stage);
3. before authority is sought to end a tranche and start the next tranche;
4. before authority is sought to close the programme;
5. when there is a request to change; the scope of the programme, the products, any constraints or deadlines.

QUALITY MANAGEMENT STRATEGY

Quality acceptance criteria will be produced for all products to be delivered by the programme and its projects, and for those to be used internally by the programme and its projects.

When ready, each product will be inspected against those criteria. The results will be discussed at a quality review and any remedial actions agreed.

No products will be handed over for operational use until they have been approved by quality assurance.

Products that are intended for internal use by the programme and its projects will not be used until approved by quality assurance.

RESOURCE MANAGEMENT STRATEGY

The programme manager and project managers will be assigned full-time, though project managers may manage more than one project.

All other staff will be assigned part-time, and schedules will therefore need to account for their business as usual (BAU) commitments. Plans have been agreed with operational managers. They will be informed monthly about any plan changes and the impact on assignments to their staff. Four weeks before staff are due to take up their programme/project assignment, the programme manager will remind operational managers. Operational managers will again be reminded 2 weeks before assignments start. If there are any severe conflicts between operational duties and programme/project assignments, operational managers must notify the programme manager immediately. Operational managers will be notified 2 weeks before staff are due to be released from their programme/project assignments.

Similar arrangements will be negotiated with third-party suppliers, and will be part of the contractual procedures.

Index